Activities

for
Junior High School
and
Middle School Mathematics

Volume 2

Activities

for
Junior High School
and
Middle School Mathematics

Volume 2

Readings from the *Arithmetic Teacher, Mathematics Teacher, Mathematics Teaching in the Middle School*, and *Teaching Children Mathematics*

Compiled by

Kenneth E. Easterday
Auburn University, Auburn, Alabama

F. Morgan Simpson
Auburn University at Montgomery, Montgomery, Alabama

Tommy Smith
University of Alabama at Birmingham, Birmingham, Alabama

NATIONAL COUNCIL OF TEACHERS OF MATHEMATICS
Reston, Virginia

Library of Congress Cataloging-in-Publication Data:

Main entry under title:
Activities for junior high school and middle school
  mathematics.
  Bibliography: p.
    1. Mathematics—Study and teaching. 2. Teaching
—Aids and devices. I. Easterday, Kenneth E.
II. Henry, Loren L. III. Simpson, F. Morgan.
IV. Arithmetic teacher. V. Mathematics teacher.
QA 16.A27   510′.7′12   81-14024
ISBN 0-87353-189-2   AACR2
ISBN 0-87353-465-4 (vol. 2)

Printed in the United States of America

Contents

5. Number and Number Relationships

6. Number Systems and Number Theory

7. Computation and Estimation

Introduction

ONGOING research and the results of teacher practice in middle school and junior high school classrooms continue to provide strong support for the use of activities. Using activities builds on the theories of Bruner and Lesh; Behr, however, has pointed out the necessity of a clear relationship between the activities and mathematical concepts. Activities are one means of connecting both the various strands of mathematics with one another and mathematics with other disciplines. The use of activities addresses the needs of more holistic and diverse learners and motivates all learners.

This book is a sequel to the 1981 *Activities for Junior High School and Middle School Mathematics.* For that book we selected articles published before 1980 in the *Mathematics Teacher* and the *Arithmetic Teacher.* For this volume we have selected articles published from 1980 to July, 1997 in the *Arithmetic Teacher (AT), Teaching Children Mathematics (TCM), Mathematics Teaching in the Middle School (MTMS),* and *Mathematics Teacher (MT).* Because some of our readers may not be as familiar with one journal as with another, we have included articles from the Ideas section of the *Arithmetic Teacher,* the Investigations section in *Teaching Children Mathematics,* and the Activities section of the *Mathematics Teacher.*

This volume has been organized around the strands of middle school mathematics as presented in the *Curriculum and Evaluation Standards.* Our goal was to select the most appropriate articles for each strand. A special section on assessment was included and attention was given to issues such as diversity.

We hope that these articles will be a meaningful and useful resource for you.

1

Mathematics as Problem Solving

PROBLEM solving should be the central focus of school mathematics. This position has been affirmed by the NCTM in documents such as *An Agenda for Action* (NCTM, 1980) and by the placement of problem solving as the first standard for each section of the *Curriculum and Evaluation Standards* (NCTM, 1989). NCTM journals have devoted much attention to this topic in various issues. The activities identified in this chapter provide examples of problem-solving tasks and investigations appropriate for middle grades students.

In his article, Stonewater gives the Mangoes Problem and the Sailors and Coconut Problem as examples of problems that help students practice strategies such as *guess and check, draw a picture,* and *work backwards.* The problems also lend themselves to instructional strategies such as cooperative group problem solving. Finally, the article includes examples of students' solutions and suggests examples of extension problems.

Lancaster gives students a chance to be a "Mathematics Investigator" in applying problem-solving strategies to a real-world problem related to carpets. The problem lends itself to using tables, graphs, and technology in a search for solutions. Overall, the problem depicts a realistic situation in which a person would really use mathematics.

Teachers often use nontraditional problems to encourage students to develop problem-solving skills that go beyond those of typical classroom exercises or word problems. In "Don't Give Up!", Kraus presents three problems that require in-depth reasoning, deduction, and persistence on the part of students. Such problems help to develop in students a disposition to become problem solvers.

Ewbank uses *cryptarithms* to develop problem-solving skills and to reinforce basic number concepts such as the additive identity property. Inventing and solving cryptarithms such as SEND + MORE = MONEY, can be used to gain students' interest and promote critical thinking. Students enjoy solving puzzles, and their motivation to persist at problem solving is increased.

The last two articles of this chapter link problem solving with discrete mathematics topics. Zaslavsky describes problems in network theory as opportunities for students to look for patterns, to see real-world applications, and to provide multicultural experiences. Examples given from African culture employ network problems. Freidler's examples use graphs to solve scheduling problems. An advantage of using such problems from discrete mathematics is that they often have few prerequisite mathematical skills. Other advantages include the attraction such problems have for students and the relevance of such problems to the real world.

JERRY K. STONEWATER

The "Mangoes Problem"

WHEN I BEGIN A FRIDAY MATH CLASS WITH SOMETHING OTHER THAN PROBLEM solving and my students remind me that Fridays are reserved for problem solving, I know I've done the right thing. When students ask for additional copies of the problems because their parents also enjoy doing them, I know I've done the right thing. When I lose track of math time and dismiss my math class late—and only then reluctantly— I'm *sure* I've done the right thing.

—BARB URELL
Fifth-grade teacher and member,
Ohio Problem Solving Consortium

LOOK at the mangoes problem in figure 1 and work on a solution before reading the rest of this article. Pay particular attention to how you go about solving the problem. Look for alternative solution strategies if you get stuck.

The mangoes problem is a favorite of teachers involved in the Ohio Problem Solving Consortium, a collection of teachers throughout the state who are interested in enhancing the problem-solving abilities of their students.[1] Because the problem is solvable by at least four different strategies accessible to middle school students—*guess and check, draw a picture, work backward,* and *use a variable*—it is an excellent example for demonstrating the power and richness of mathematics when multiple solution strategies can be employed in problem solving. This problem can also be used for a variety of instructional purposes, including assessment, where the focus might be on assessing students' ability to use a variety of strategies, or as a task for a cooperative-problem-solving group, where the goal is to use as many different strategies as possible in solving the problem.

This article outlines each of the four solution methods for the mangoes problem, discusses how middle school students approached the problem, suggests two interesting generalizations of the problem, and gives an example of a related problem ("Sailors and Coconuts," fig. 3) that can be used as an extension to explore further the four strategies discussed.

To see how middle school students worked in cooperative groups to solve the mangoes problem, we observed the classes of two Consortium-member teachers. In our initial conversation with Barb Urell, a fifth-grade teacher, we were concerned that the problem might be too difficult for her students, both because it involved fractions

---

[1] The Ohio Problem Solving Consortium was funded through the Eisenhower Program by the Ohio Board of Regents, grant number 8-19, *The Ohio Problem Solving Consortium*, 1988.

Jerry Stonewater *teaches at Miami University, Oxford, OH 45056. He has directed the Ohio Problem Solving Consortium.*

Students work together on the mangoes problem

ACTIVITIES FOR JUNIOR HIGH SCHOOL AND MIDDLE SCHOOL MATHEMATICS

and because she had only recently introduced the working-backward strategy to the class. In Karen Fitch's eighth-grade class, we expected many of the students to try the use-a-variable strategy and approach the problem algebraically, since the class was a first-year-algebra class. To our surprise, the fifth graders had little difficulty with fractions and were able to try working backward; and *no one* in the eighth-grade class tried an algebraic approach without prompting. The class had been studying algebra for only about five weeks, so these students may not have been ready to translate a word problem into an algebraic expression.

Guess and check: The guess-and-check strategy starts with an original guess for how many mangoes were in the bowl prior to the King's entry into the kitchen. Students then use the structure of the problem to see if their initial guess works to solve the problem correctly. If their initial guess fails to work, they make another, it is hoped "better," guess and check to see if it works. They continue this process until they make a correct guess. Some students may make wild and unreasonable guesses, so teachers should point out how to make "reasonable" first guesses and discuss the importance of making a table to collect and organize the data.

We observed many students who seemed comfortable using the guess-and-check strategy. Often, someone in the group would quickly observe that an initial guess had to be divisible by 6 so that the King could take one-sixth of the mangoes. For example, Bill, a fifth grader, guessed that 24 mangoes were in the bowl originally. When

checking his guess, however, he found that it resulted in 4, not 3, mangoes at the end. Since this outcome was too many mangoes, Bill revised his initial guess downward to 18, the next-smallest multiple of 6. This number, he found, worked.

We saw a similar guess-and-check approach with a group of four eighth-grade boys. They also decided that the initial guess should be divisible by 6, so their initial guess was 12, leaving them with 2 mangoes at the end. They then reguessed 18 correctly.

Not all groups noted the relevance of the initial guess's being a multiple of 6. In the eighth-grade class, Phil's group tried 12 for an initial guess, then 14, suggesting that they were not aware of the relevance of divisibility by 6. For their guess of 14 they got off track and did the following computation on a calculator: $14/1 - 1/2 - 1/3 - 1/4 - 1/5 - 1/6$. Note that the order of this error is in the work-backward direction. Perhaps group members were trying to combine, inappropriately, the two methods. Later in the class period we noticed that they had returned to guess and check and solved the problem correctly.

We did see one eighth-grade group make unreasonable guesses of 1000, then 100, then 30, and finally 20, 19, then 18. This group did not seem to use any heuristic that could have guided their guesses except that when their final answer was too big, they knew that their next guess should be "smaller."

Draw a picture: The easiest solution method to this problem is surprising in its simplicity. Start by drawing a rectangle to represent all mangoes in the original pile

The "Mangoes Problem"

One night the King couldn't sleep, so he went down into the Royal kitchen, where he found a bowl full of mangoes. Being hungry, he took 1/6 of the mangoes.

Later that same night, the Queen was hungry and couldn't sleep. She, too, found the mangoes and took 1/5 of what the King had left.

Still later, the first Prince awoke, went to the kitchen, and ate 1/4 of the remaining mangoes.

Even later, his brother, the second Prince, ate 1/3 of what was then left. Finally, the third Prince ate 1/2 of what was left, leaving only three mangoes for the servants.

How many mangoes were originally in the bowl?

Fig. 1

Mangoes Solution: Draw a picture or diagram

Entire rectangle represents original number of mangoes

King removes 1/6 of mangoes

Queen removes 1/5 of remainder

First Prince removes 1/4 of remainder

Second Prince removes 1/3 of remainder

Third Prince removes 1/2 of remainder

3 mangoes left

Fig. 2

prior to the removal of any of them. Since the King took one-sixth of this pile, divide the rectangle into six equal strips and "remove" one strip (see fig. 2). Notice that five strips remain, from which the Queen removed one-fifth, so this one-fifth is also represented by one of the original strips. Continuing, when the first Prince removes one-fourth of what is left, the one-fourth is represented by one of the strips. Similarly, the one-third, one-half, and 3 remaining mangoes are each represented by a strip. In the final analysis, since the 3 mangoes equal one strip and originally six strips were involved, the number of original mangoes must have been $6 \times 3 = 18$. The draw-a-picture strategy presents a nice concrete, visual representation of the problem.

The draw-a-picture strategy led to some of our most interesting observations. All the draw-a-picture approaches we observed were in the fifth-grade group, although it is certainly possible that some eighth graders either thought about this approach or tried it without our noticing it. In the fifth-grade class, Julie and Robin first drew six circles and shaded one to represent the one-sixth the King took. They then explained that the Queen ate one-fifth of what was left, so they had shaded one of the remaining five circles. They continued this process until they had shaded the last of the original six circles drawn. Then they explained that since the last circle represented three mangoes, the solution must be $3 + 3 + 3 + 3 + 3 + 3$, writing each 3 above one of the circles they had shaded. Interestingly, the girls drew the circles and shaded them left to right, but they added the 3s and wrote them above the circles from right to left, reversing their direction. Also noteworthy is the way they generalized their six-circle model so that each circle stood for 3 mangoes.

Two other fifth-grade groups drew a picture but divided a pie into six wedges. Sally's group shaded one wedge, noted five remaining wedges, and shaded one of them. She continued until she had shaded five of the six wedges. Finally, thinking about the sixth wedge, she said, "That's three." The entire group then got involved in a discussion about how to obtain the

That's 3

final answer. They rejected, in order, the following approaches: 3 + 5 (3 mangoes for the sixth wedge plus five wedges), and 3 times 5; then they agreed on 3 times 6 for 18. The final group we observed approached the problem in a similar manner but was also unsure how to compute the total once they knew that the last wedge represented 3 mangoes. They never went beyond adding 3 mangoes and 6 wedges.

Work backward: Working backward is not always easy for middle school students, nor is it easy for adults. The strategy requires three steps: start at the end of the problem—the 3 remaining mangoes; reverse each of the steps in the problem, being careful to determine the amount at this step; and work the problem from end to beginning by performing the inverse operation at each step.

Applying these steps to the mangoes problem results in the following:

1. At the end 3 mangoes are left, representing one-half of the pile that the third Prince took. Thus, the third Prince had 6 mangoes before removing his half.

2. To determine how many the second Prince had before removing his third, we must realize that the 6 mangoes left after removal represent *two*-thirds of the pile from which he took his third. Thus, 6 is two-thirds of the number in the pile, or $6 \times 3/2 = 9$, the number in the pile before removal.

3. By continuing backward in this manner, 9 mangoes represent *three*-fourths of the pile before the first Prince took his, so $9 \times 4/3 = 12$ mangoes were in the pile the first Prince used.

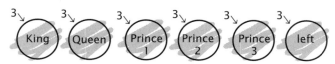

ACTIVITIES FOR JUNIOR HIGH SCHOOL AND MIDDLE SCHOOL MATHEMATICS

4. Similarly, the Queen's pile was 12 × 5/4, or 15, and the King's must have been 15 × 6/5, or 18, the answer to the problem.

We first observed Holly, a fifth grader, trying to work backward. She persisted with this strategy for most of the forty-five minutes we were in the classroom and eventually obtained the correct answer. First she started with the 3 remaining mangoes and quickly reversed to the previous step, where she said that 6 mangoes must have been left at that point: "You must have something to take half away to get three." But then she was stuck for a long time, finding it difficult to reverse the "one-third." Eventually it appeared that she accomplished this reversal to obtain 9, but she may have arrived at that number using a guess-and-check substrategy.

A second group of fifth-grade students mixed a work-backward strategy with the strategy of looking for a pattern. The group worked backward from 3 to 6 to 9 and then observed the pattern of "add 3 each time while working backward" to obtain 18. Another group of fifth graders combined three strategies: work backward, draw a picture, and look for a pattern. Their picture was 3, then 6, then 9 "circles" to represent mangoes. They also observed that they were adding 3 mangoes each time in the work-backward solution.

The most brilliant application of working backward came from Sam, who reversed the entire problem, applied all the correct work-backward operations, and obtained the correct solution in less than three minutes! In moving backward from the 6 to the 9 mangoes, he argued as follows: "Six represents two-thirds of something, so one-third must be three. So to get three-thirds, you must add the six (for two-thirds) to three (for one-third) and you have nine mangoes." Then, going the next-backward step, he said, "Nine needs one-fourth" (his words, meaning that since nine is three-fourths of the previous amount, it "needs" another fourth of this amount added to it), "so nine is three-fourths; divide by three (i.e., 9/3) and add this to nine, obtaining twelve." He continued quickly in this way to the final, correct solution.

In the eighth-grade classroom we observed a group combine working backward with the guess-and-check approach. They started at 3, then had a discussion of what operation they were performing to get 6: "We multiplied by one-half; no, we divided by one-half. No, we multiplied by two and that is six." To get the next-previous step in working backward, they started with guess and check: first they tried 8, but 1/3 × 8 did not result in 6; next they tried 9, and that number worked. Finally, Tim saw the pattern of add 3 each time, so they also used the pattern strategy to obtain the correct answer.

Use a variable: Setting up an algebraic equation to solve this problem can be formidable for middle school students, yet some might try this approach, especially if they are learning some algebra. Let x be the number of mangoes in the bowl before any are removed.

1. Since the King removed $(1/6)x$, then $x - (1/6)x$ mangoes are left after his removal. Thus, $(5/6)x$ mangoes are left.

2. The Queen removed one-fifth of $(5/6)x$, so $(5/6)x - (1/5)(5/6)x$, or $(4/6)x$, mangoes are left after her removal.

3. The first Prince removed one-fourth of $(4/6)x$ mangoes, so $(4/6)x - (1/4)(4/6)x$, or $(3/6)x$, mangoes are left after the first Prince's removal.

4. The second Prince removed one-third of $(3/6)x$, so $(3/6)x - (1/3)(3/6)x$, or $(2/6)x$, mangoes are left.

5. Finally, the third Prince removed one-half of $(2/6)x$, leaving 3 mangoes, so $(2/6)x - (1/2)(2/6)x = 1/6x = 3$. Solving $1/6x = 3$ results in $x = 18$.

Extension problems: To challenge students to make generalizations and recognize patterns in mathematics, the mangoes problem can be extended. Teachers can use these extensions to generate many variations of the root problem for their own classroom instruction.

Extension 1: Suppose ten people take the "remaining" mangoes, just like in the original problem, that is, the first person takes one-tenth of the mangoes in the bowl, the second takes one-ninth of the remaining mangoes, the third takes one-eighth of the remaining ones, and so on, until only three are left. How many were in the original bowl?

Extension 2: Work a number of mango-like problems starting with ten people, then nine people, then maybe only seven people.

Sailors and Coconuts

Three sailors were marooned on a deserted island that was also inhabited by a band of monkeys. The sailors worked all day to collect coconuts but were too tired that night to count them. They agreed to divide them equally the next morning.

During the night, one sailor woke up and decided to get his share. He found that he could make three equal piles, with one coconut left over, which he threw to the monkeys. Thereupon, he had his own share and left the remainder in a single pile.

Later that night, the second sailor awoke and, likewise, decided to get his share of coconuts. He also was able to make three equal piles, with one coconut left over, which he threw to the monkeys.

Somewhat later, the third sailor awoke and did exactly the same thing with the remaining coconuts.

In the morning, all three sailors noticed that the pile was considerably smaller, but each thought that he knew why and said nothing. When they then divided the remaining coconuts equally, each sailor received seven and one was left over, which they threw to the monkeys.

How many coconuts were in the original pile?

Fig. 3

Figure out how many mangoes were originally involved in each problem. Then make a generalization that would enable you to tell how many mangoes were in the original bowl if three were left and you knew how many people removed mangoes.

Other working-backward problems: Two additional entertaining work-backward problems are challenging to middle school students and can incorporate multiple problem-solving strategies. Each is a version of the sailors-and-coconuts problem in figure 3. If you tried to solve this problem, you should get 79 coconuts for an answer. Try doing the problem by working backward, but combine this strategy with drawing a picture while working backward. For a variation of the problem, instead of telling students that each sailor received seven coconuts and one was left for the monkeys, tell them that each sailor received an equal number of coconuts at the end and one was left over for the monkeys. This generalized problem requires the students to make various guesses for

how many coconuts each sailor received at the end. Thus, the original working-backward strategy must be combined with a guess-and-check approach. Students quickly can eliminate certain guesses because resulting numbers are not divisible by 3 (for dividing among the three sailors). Teachers are encouraged to try this variation to see what their students can do.

Conclusion

Middle school students really can engage in fairly sophisticated mathematical problem-solving behavior and can use numerous problem-solving strategies to reach a successful conclusion. We saw students accurately implement the tactics of guess and check, work backward, draw a picture, and look for a pattern. More important, we saw students switch between strategies when one failed them. Other students were able to use a general overall strategy to solve the problem but incorporate substrategies within this overall strategy as needed. Such

mathematical behavior should be encouraged and fostered whenever possible.

The mangoes problem, its extensions, and the sailors-and-coconuts problem all offer an excellent way for middle school teachers to continue addressing the problem-solving goals in the NCTM's *Curriculum and Evaluation Standards* (1989). These problems certainly address multistep problem solving and present situations that have multiple representations. Whether these problems are used in a cooperative setting or with individual students, they confront the student with a situation in which the richness of mathematical problem solving and the variety of solution methods can be experienced and enjoyed.

Reference

National Council of Teachers of Mathematics. *Curriculum and Evaluation Standards for School Mathematics.* Reston, Va.: National Council of Teachers of Mathematics, 1989.

RON LANCASTER

Mathematics Investigator

Shaking Out Rug Prices

*(A similar advertisement appeared in the *New York Times:* to protect the original vendor, the name has been changed.)

THE Carpet Baggers, which carries various Persian carpets, is both advertising its product while trying to educate consumers about the competition's pricing scheme. Use the information in this advertisement to answer the following questions. *Cost* refers to what a store pays to buy a carpet from the manufacturer, which is the same as the *wholesale* cost. The *retail* price refers to the amount the customer has to pay. Assume that the wholesale cost is the same for products from both The Carpet Baggers and all its competitors.

Prepared by Ron Lancaster, St. Mildred's Lightbourn School, Oakville, ON L6J 2L1.

Questions

1. Suppose that the wholesale cost of a Persian carpet is $1000. What would be the retail price of this carpet at The Carpet Baggers? What would it be at one of its competitors? How much would you save by buying at The Carpet Baggers?

2. What are two ways to calculate (cost × 3) – 40% to find the competitor's retail price? Which of these two ways did you use in problem 1? Which way benefits the customer the most? How do you know?

3. Complete the following chart. Use what you learned from problem 1 to compute the competitor's retail price in the best way for the customer.

What pattern do you see relating the wholesale costs and the corresponding savings? How could this pattern help you extend the table?

4. To better visualize the pattern of savings, graph the money saved at The Carpet Baggers versus the wholesale cost. Put the wholesale cost of the carpet on the horizontal axis and the amount saved on the vertical axis. Graph all the points from the foregoing chart—the first point is (500, 250) and the last is (6000, 3000). What do you notice about the seven points you graphed?

5. Draw the line that includes all seven points on your graph. How does any point on that line, chosen at random, show the relationship between the wholesale cost of a carpet and how much you saved when buying that

Wholesale Cost of Carpet	The Carpet Baggers' Price	Competitor's Price	Savings When Bought at The Carpet Baggers
$500	$650		
1000		$1800	
1500			$750
2000			
2500			
4000			
			3000

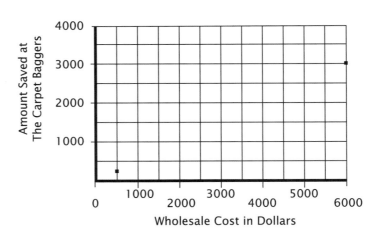

carpet at The Carpet Baggers? Choose some wholesale costs, such as $2300 or $4400, and show how the corresponding points of the graph help you estimate the savings for each wholesale cost.

6. A customer took a month to decide to buy a new carpet from The Carpet Baggers. During that month, the wholesale cost went up by $500. Use either the graph or the table you developed to find how much more money she saved by buying later. Was she wise to wait?

Algebraic thinking

7. Let *C* represent the wholesale cost of the carpet. Develop expressions for each of the following:

   a) The retail price *A* of the carpet at The Carpet Baggers

   b) The retail price *B* of the carpet at a competitor

   c) The amount saved *S* by buying at The Carpet Baggers

8. If you have access to a TI-81 graphing calculator, use your answers to problem 7 to complete the following program. What does this program do?

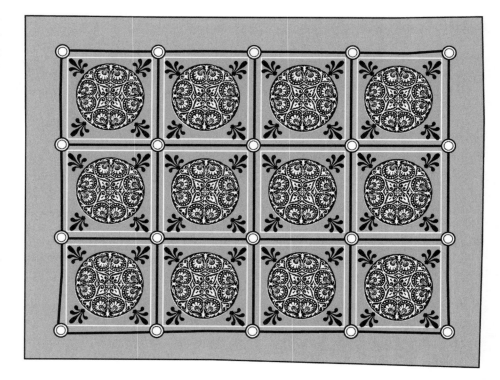

Prgm: CARPET
:ClrHome
:Disp "WHAT IS THE COST"
:INPUT C
:ClrHome
 → A
    → B
    → S
:Disp "THE CARPET BAGGERS"
:Disp A
:Disp "COMPETITOR"
:Disp B
:Disp "AMOUNT SAVED"
:Disp S

Input different values for the wholesale cost of a carpet to test the program.

9. Estimate the area of one of the small squares on the 9-foot-by-12-foot carpet shown. Estimate the area of one of the circles on this carpet.

10. The carpet shown is 9 feet by 12 feet and costs $9900 at The Carpet Baggers. Find the cost per square foot of this carpet. What might a similar 6-foot-by-8-foot carpet cost? A 13-foot-by-17.5-foot carpet?

11. Create a problem of your own that involves this carpet and ask a friend to solve it.

W I L L I A M   H .   K R A U S

Don't Give Up!

THE importance of persistence in problem solving was made clear to me last year as I taught a new course in problem solving. In particular, three problems that I had seen many times before took on new meaning as I was forced to analyze them from the point of view of a teacher.

The Water-Jug Problem

How can you carry exactly four gallons of water from a river if only a three-gallon jug and a five-gallon jug are available?

This well-known problem has a simple set of conditions. Despite its apparent simplicity, students often have difficulty solving it. Figure 1 illustrates one solution to this problem.

Step 1: You have the choice of filling either jug. Figure 1 shows that the five-gallon jug is filled.

Step 2: Dumping the five-gallon jug would be senseless because you would be back to the beginning. Filling the three-gallon jug would be senseless because in the next step you would have to dump one of the jugs and you would be right back to step 1 (with one jug filled and one empty). Thus the only sensible try is to dump the five-gallon jug into the three-gallon jug, leaving two gallons of water in the five-gallon jug.

Step 3: Dumping the two gallons would be senseless because you would be back at step 1 (with one jug filled and one empty). Filling the five-gallon jug would be senseless because in the next step you would have to dump one of the jugs and you would be back to step 1. Thus the only sensible step is to dump the contents of the three-gallon jug.

William Kraus *teaches at Wittenberg University, Springfield, OH 45501. His interests include problem solving and instructional games. He has written over twenty commercial instructional games.*

Similarly, in each of the remaining steps only one move is sensible.

Step 4: Transfer the two gallons of water to the three-gallon jug.

Step 5: Fill the five-gallon jug.

Step 6: Transfer one gallon of water to fill the three-gallon jug, leaving four gallons in the five-gallon jug.

Step 7: Dump the contents of the three-gallon jug. You now have four gallons of water, and the problem is solved.

Like most readers, I had solved this problem and problems similar to it many times before. However, this time I noticed two things: (1) Only one move is sensible at each step (except the first); all other moves immediately and obviously backtrack to a previous step: (2) The choice made in the first step does not matter; a similar solution exists if you start by filling the three-gallon jug. Thus if you understand the conditions of the problem, the most important thing you must do to solve it is *not to quit*. This observation holds for any solvable water-jug problem involving two jugs.

The Missionaries and Cannibals Problem

Three missionaries and three cannibals wish to cross a river, using only a boat that can hold only two people. Unfortunately, if at any time the cannibals outnumber the missionaries, then those missionaries will be eaten. How can the crossing be safely made?

Most people find this very well known problem difficult to solve. However, an analysis of the solution in figure 2 shows that this problem is similar to the water-jug problem in that if you understand the conditions of the problem, then the key to solving the problem is persistence.

Step 1: Having one person row across and then back is senseless. Sending two missionaries across results in the demise of

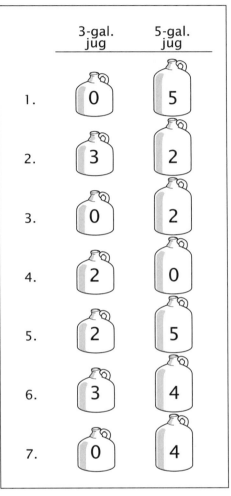

Fig. 1. Water-jug solution

the remaining missionary. Thus two first moves are possible: Two cannibals can cross, or as shown in figure 2, one missionary and one cannibal can cross.

Step 2: One person must return, and it cannot be the cannibal.

Step 3: Sending one person across is nonproductive. Sending two missionaries or one missionary and one cannibal results in a meal for two of the cannibals. Thus only one move is possible: the two cannibals must cross. The resulting position

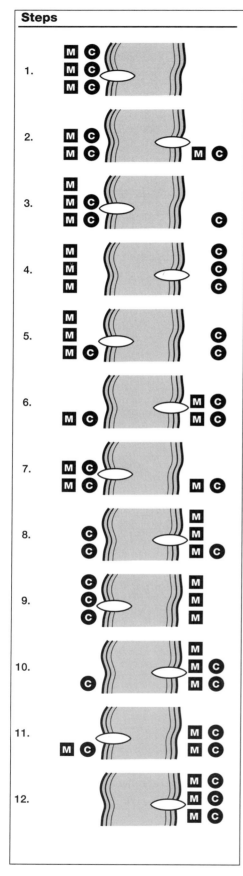

Fig. 2. Missionaries-and-cannibals solution

would also have been reached if the two cannibals had crossed the river in step 1.

Step 4: One cannibal must return.

Step 5: Again only one move is possible: two missionaries must cross.

Step 6: Sending back the two missionaries who just arrived is senseless. Sending back one missionary or one or two cannibals is fatal. Thus only one move is possible: a missionary and a cannibal must return.

This step in the problem is critical. Many would-be solvers notice that the resulting position looks a lot like the position reached after step 1 and they give up. In fact, the position is not the same, because the boat is not on the same side of the river. As the reader can verify, in each of the remaining steps, except step 10, only one move is sensible. In step 10, sending back either a missionary or a cannibal for the remaining cannibal works. Thus the problem solves itself as long as the solver does not give up. What makes this problem a challenge is not that the steps in solving the problem are difficult but that the solver is severely tempted to give up hope.

The Census-Taker Problem

During the recent census, a man told the census taker that he had three children. When asked their ages, he replied, "The product of their ages is 72. The sum of their ages is the same as my house number." The census taker ran to the door and looked at the house number. "I still can't tell," she complained.* The man replied, "Oh, that's right. I forgot to tell you that the oldest one likes chocolate pudding."† The census taker promptly wrote down the ages of the three children. How old are they? (Krulik and Rudnick 1980, p. 97)

This problem deserves to become a classic. I have given the problem to many of my classes of preservice elementary education students and to many groups of in-service teachers, but only a few of them have solved it. The problem hits the solver with a double whammy. At the spot in the problem marked with an asterisk, the reaction of many solvers is, "But we don't know what the house number is!" At the spot marked with a dagger, the reaction of many solvers is, "What does chocolate pudding have to

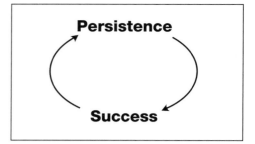

Fig. 3. Persistence-success cycle

do with the problem? There is no way I'll be able to solve this problem." And then most people give up.

Once again persistence pays off, although unlike in the two earlier examples, it will not guarantee a solution. The key is to do something. The easy tack to take is to list the possible ages using the first condition. Twelve combinations of three numbers have a product of 72. Simply listing these combinations helps most solvers see the significance of the house number, and then the significance of the statement regarding chocolate pudding. Most solvers do not list all the combinations because they are convinced that doing so will be fruitless.

Conclusion

Many of my students believe that they cannot solve problems like the three discussed here. This belief becomes a self-fulfilling prophecy—the reason that they are unable to solve these problems is that they believe they cannot. Such students need to be encouraged to persist, and they need to develop repertoires of heuristics to try when they are not sure what to do.

Problems like these can be useful tools in developing persistence in problem solvers. Students can be shown that they cannot *not* solve them as long as they do not give up. As students work individually on such problems, perhaps the most important thing a teacher can do is supply words of encouragement: "You're on the right track. Keep going." "What can you do?" (reply) "Good. Try it." "You can do it. Keep going."

With problems like those discussed in this article, such words of encouragement are frequently all that is needed for students to find a solution. Thus students begin to develop a sense that their efforts make a difference and that they do not need "clues" from the teacher to solve problems.

Persistence often leads to success. Repeated success builds confidence that leads to greater persistence. We need to get students started in the persistence-success cycle.

On more complex problems, words of encouragement may not be enough. Students may need suggestions about *what* to try. "Write down what you know and what you don't know in the problem." "Can you organize the information you know? Can you make a list or a chart?" "Can you draw a picture or a diagram?" "Can you solve part of the problem?"

Over time a class can develop a list of "things to try when you are not sure what to do," gradually building a repertoire of heuristics. Students can refer to this list when they get stuck, thus relying more on themselves and less on the teacher. The teacher's role becomes nurturing the development of the problem-solving skills—setting up problem-solving opportunities and encouraging students as they struggle to find solutions.

Reference

Krulik, Stephen, and Jesse A. Rudnick. *Problem Solving: A Handbook for Teachers.* Boston: Allyn & Bacon, 1980.

WILLIAM A. EWBANK

Cryptarithms: Math Made Me Daft, Momma

MOST readers of this journal have encountered

$$
\begin{array}{r}
\text{(I)} \quad S\,E\,N\,D \\
+\ M\,O\,R\,E \\
\hline
M\,O\,N\,E\,Y
\end{array}
$$

and similar arithmetical puzzles, where the challenge is to find the digit represented by each letter. Like mazes, these arithmetical puzzles are easy to start but not so easy to conquer! These puzzles are called cryptarithms and have been staple fare for puzzlists for a long time. In addition to the famous plea for cash, the NCTM 1982 calendar of problems contained these specimens (NCTM 1982):

$$
\begin{array}{r}
\text{(II)} \quad T\,H\,R\,E\,E \\
+\ F\,O\,U\,R \\
\hline
S\,E\,V\,E\,N
\end{array}
$$

$$
\begin{array}{r}
\text{(III)} \quad O\,N\,E \\
+\ O\,N\,E \\
\hline
T\,W\,O
\end{array}
$$

$$
\begin{array}{r}
\text{(IV)} \quad S\,A\,V\,E \\
+\ M\,O\,R\,E \\
\hline
M\,O\,N\,E\,Y
\end{array}
$$

$$
\begin{array}{r}
\text{(V)} \quad S\,E\,N\,D \\
M\,O\,R\,E \\
+\ G\,O\,L\,D \\
\hline
M\,O\,N\,E\,Y
\end{array}
$$

$$
\begin{array}{r}
\text{(VI)} \quad F\,O\,R\,T\,Y \\
T\,E\,N \\
+\ T\,E\,N \\
\hline
S\,I\,X\,T\,Y
\end{array}
$$

$$
\begin{array}{r}
\text{(VII)} \quad A\,A\,A \\
B\,B\,B \\
+\ C\,C\,C \\
\hline
F\,G\,H\,I
\end{array}
$$

(VIII) $(HE)^2 = SHE$

(IX) $SEND \div A = GIFT$

By William A. Ewbank, *Taylor University, Upland, IN 46989*

The purpose of this article is to take this usually esoteric pursuit and show that it can be enjoyable for the average student in middle school and above.

Middle school mathematics often consists of exposure to more and more mathematics, much of it outside the context of problem solving. Inventing and solving of cryptarithms, however, involve the basic mathematics learned in primary school in a problem-solving mode. The goal is very easy to understand; reaching it involves logic, basic understanding of place value, and clear thinking.

Solving and inventing cryptarithms are both valuable experiences. Examine puzzles II through VII. Which would you tackle first? Most people would choose puzzle III because it is the shortest and has a lot of repetition of letters. In other words, it is the simplest. The fewer the letters, and the more often they are repeated, the easier the puzzle will be to solve. We could adopt a classification scheme as follows: a puzzle will be assigned a ratio a/b, where b is the total letters used and a is the number of *different* letters used. To illustrate, we have classified the cryptarithm used for the title of this article, which appeared in a French book (Bouvior 1981):

$$
\begin{array}{r}
M\,A\,T\,H \\
M\,A\,D\,E \\
M\,E \\
+\ D\,A\,F\,T \\
\hline
M\,O\,M\,M\,A
\end{array}
$$

Total letters used: 19
Different letters used: A, D, E, F, H, M, O, T; total: 8

$a = 8,$ $b = 19,$ ratio = 8/19

This is a fairly complicated example. The aim in devising puzzles for beginners should be to keep b fairly small and a small in relation to b. On this basis,

$$
\begin{array}{r}
O\,N\,E \\
+\ O\,N\,E \\
\hline
,T\,W\,O
\end{array}
$$

scores fairly well at 5/9. Eight out of nineteen is a low ratio. It is desirable, but very difficult, to achieve a ratio less than one-half. The value of a must be ten or less, because each letter must stand for a *unique* digit.

The invention of a good cryptarithm starts with the task of devising suitable catchphrases or aphorisms. Other versions involving an alphabetical pattern (such as puzzle VII) are possible but not so appealing. Meaningless jumbles of letters should not be used. No skill is involved in assigning letters in a random fashion.

We now give some simple examples, including some seemingly valid puzzles that prove to be impossible. We use Ø for zero to avoid confusion with the letter O, and we number columns 1, 2, ... , from the right. The value of a/b is given to the right of the puzzle.

$$
\begin{array}{r}
1. \quad D\,O \\
+\ G\,O \\
\hline
N\,O\,W
\end{array} \quad \frac{5}{7}
$$

A good starter for beginners

$$
\begin{array}{r}
1.a. \quad G\,O \\
+\ O\,N \\
\hline
R\,O\,N
\end{array} \quad \frac{4}{7}
$$

Impossible. In column 1, O + N = N gives O = Ø. This means (column 2) that G + Ø = has no solution for G.

$$
\begin{array}{r}
1.b. \quad I \\
A\,M \\
+\ A \\
\hline
M\,A\,N
\end{array} \quad \frac{4}{7}
$$

Impossible. The A in the second number (column 2) reappears in the answer sum, and therefore no 1 is carried to column 3. Therefore M cannot be assigned 1, its only possible value.

ACTIVITIES FOR JUNIOR HIGH SCHOOL AND MIDDLE SCHOOL MATHEMATICS

2.
```
      D O
  +   G O    4
  -------
      O N    6
```

The value of O can be seen to be neither Ø, 1, nor 2 because in column 2, D + G = O, and two different numbers cannot total Ø, 1, or 2 (unless one is Ø). Apart from this restriction, many solutions are possible.

3.
```
      B O W
  +   W O W    5
  ---------
      D O G    9
```

Several solutions. At first sight it seems that O must be Ø, but another possibility is

4.
```
      T W O
  +   T W O    6
  ---------
    F O U R   10
```

A good example for those getting a taste for these puzzles. F must be 1, and R must be even.

5.
```
      F E
      F I
  +   F O    6
  -------
    F U M    9
```

Impossible. F must be 1 (column 3), and therefore F + F + F (column 2) could not exceed 9 and carry 1 to column 3.

6.
```
      F O U R
  +   O N E    8
  ---------
    F I V E   11
```

Several solutions. R can be found quickly.

7.
```
      F O U R
  +   F I V E    8
  -----------
      N I N E   12
```

At least 16 solutions

8.
```
      W O O F
  +   W O O F    6
  -----------
    D O G G Y   13
```

Good—a nice catchphrase, and a low ratio, caused by much repetition of letters

9.
```
      M O O
  +   M O O    4
  ---------
      C O W    9
```

Another rare example of a good catchphrase with a ratio less than one-half; attractively simple

10.
```
      S A N T A
  +   C L A U S   10
  -----------
    S N O R E S   16
```

Here's a more complex puzzle, which proves to be impossible for these reasons: A = Ø and S = 1 are starters. In column 3, N + A = R or N + A = R + 10 or N + A + 1 = R or N + A + 1 = R + 10. Since A = Ø, R ≠ Ø. Also N ≠ R. So N + 1 = R or N + 1 = R + 10. Since N = R + 9 is true only if R = Ø, then N + 1 = R and nothing carries from column 3 to column 4. So in column 4, A + L = O or A + L = O + 10. A = Ø, which means that L = O or 1Ø, which is impossible. Therefore no solution exists.

The popular format for cryptarithms is the addition problem, and no rules are imposed except for the basic one that each letter has to represent a unique digit. More examples follow. The name of the sophomore elementary education major who created each puzzle is given beneath the puzzle. Some departure from the usual format is seen.

11.
```
      H I
  +   F I    6
  -------
    B U Y    7
```
(Teresa Nevil)

12.
```
      A L L
  +   T H E    7
  ---------
    W A Y      9
```
(Sherry Smith)

13.
```
      E A T
  +   E A T    6
  ---------
    G A I N   10
```
(Jeff Beck)

14.
```
      T V
  +   I S    7
  -------
    B A D    7
```
(Julie Mervau)

15.
```
      H O T
  +   D O G    8
  ---------
    B U N      9
```
(Lisa Cheek)

16.
```
      J O H N
  +   N Y B E    9
  -----------
    G O O D     12
```
(Jen Aldridge)

17.
```
      G O D
  +   I S L    8
  ---------
    O V E      9
```
(Jen Aldridge)

Subtraction problems are possible, and they allow the catchphrase to end with a word smaller than the rest. An example is this:

18.
```
      L O V E
  -   O V E R    6
  -----------
      A L L     11
```

Generally the leftmost digit is not allowed to be Ø. But one author devised this:

19.
```
      . F E
      . F I
  +   . F O    6
  -------
    F . U M    9
```

See puzzle 5. F must be Ø. Several solutions can be found.

Sometimes anagrams can be used, and these rate highly because of their low ratio (Wayne 1978):

20.
```
      M A D E
  +   M E A D    4
  -----------
    E D A M     12
```

21.
```
      L I V E
  +  V I L E    4
  ---------
    E V I L    12
```

And some authors make bold to venture into other bases (Trigg 1972):

22. AM + PM = DAY   5/7 (base six)

Multiplications can appear either in equation form (23) (Trigg 1973) or as algorithms (24) (Wayne 1978):

23.   (I) (AM) (NOT) = BLUE   10/10

Two solutions

24.
```
        H E
    x   I S
    -------
      B I G
    F O R         10
    -------
    T R I G       14
```

Of course long multiplications and divisions are much harder, both to devise and to solve. Here is a long division (Wayne 1977):

```
          I S
      ---------
  M Y) J U G
      N O          9
      -----
      M U G        15
      M U G
```

Not all students in the class will be able to devise cryptarithms, but all can try; and all can solve the puzzles, providing that frustration is not caused by starting with puzzles that are too difficult. Being able to devise puzzles with unique solutions sets apart the experienced puzzlist from the beginner. But within your class, it does not matter if several solutions are possible. Multiple solutions make the puzzle easier to solve and are good for morale. The best puzzles have unique solutions, however.

In solving cryptarithms, students should be encouraged to be methodical and to write down their reasoning. A useful start would be to list the letters alphabetically and to write any comments and findings opposite them. For example:

```
  M A T H        A =
  M A D E         D =
      M E         E =
+   D A F T       F =
M O M M A         H =
                  M = 1
                  O =
                  T =
```

Then rewriting the cryptarithm in skeleton form, inserting known and key digits, may be useful.

```
    1 A . .
    1 A . .
        1 .
+    . A . .
  1 . 1 1 A
```

We can now see from column 3 that A + A + A = 1 or A + A + A = 11; or A + A + A = 21 or A + A + A + 1 = 1 or 11 or 21 (if 1 is carried from column 2); or A + A + A + 2 = 1 or 11 or 21 (if 2 is carried from column 2); 2, 4, 5, 6, 7, 8, or 9 do not satisfy any of these equations, leaving the options of Ø or 3 or 7 for A.

Cryptarithms have a very high potential for developing concentration and for fostering higher cognitive levels of thought. Many students of average and below-average achievement can devise suitable puzzles for their classmates and perhaps surprise themselves, especially if their more mathematically inclined friends have a struggle to solve their puzzles. We would all like the report they take home to be

MATH MADE ME GLAD, MOMMA!

Solutions

I.
```
    9567
+   1085
   10652
```

II.
```
   26811
+   4708
   31519
```

III.
```
     231
+    231
     462     and others
```

IV.
```
    9486           9376
+   1076        +  1086
   10562   or     10462
```

V.
```
    6054           7894
    1720           1038
+   9734        +  2054
   17508   and    10986
```

VI.
```
   29786
     850
+    850
   31486
```

VII.
```
     888
     777
+    444     and
    2109     others
```

VIII. $25^2 = 625$

IX. $7852 \div 4 = 1963$

1.
```
      76
+     86
     162     and others
```

2.
```
      13
+     23
      36     and others
```

3.
```
     196
+    696
     892     and others
```

4.
```
     765
+    765
    1530
```

6.
```
    1230
+    259
    1489
```

7.
```
    1960
+   1572
    3532     and others
```

8,
```
    8776
+   8776
   17552
```

9.
```
     199
+    199
     398     and others
```

11.
```
      85
+     35
     120
```

12.
```
     122
+    394     (# 10 on worksheet 2)
     516
```

13.
```
     627
+    627
    1254
```

14.
```
      72
+     84
     156     and others
```
(#13 on worksheet 2)

15.
```
     625           543
+    123        +  246
     748   and     789
```
(#11 on worksheet 2)

16.
```
    3824
+   4061
    7885
```

17.
```
     263
+    415
     678
```

18.
```
    8723
-   7235
     488
```

19.
```
     .03
     .04
+    .09
    0.16     and others
```

20.
```
    1692
+   1269
    2961
```

21.
```
    8019
+   1089
    9108     (# 12 on worksheet 2)
```

22. 34 + 54 = 132 (base six)

23. (1) (26) (345) = 8970
and
(2) (14) (307) = 8596

24.
```
      78
×     52
     156
     390
    4056
```

25.
```
        59
  14)826
       70
      126
      126
```

References

Austin, Joe Dan. "Creating Cryptarithms with a Computer." *School Science and Mathematics* 87 (April 1987) :308–11.

Bouvior, Alain. *La Mystification Mathematique.* Paris: Hermann, 1981.

National Council of Teachers of Mathematics. *A Year of Mathematics* (Calendar for 1982–83). Reston, Va.: The Council, 1982.

Trigg, Charles W. (1972) In Kuenzi, N. J., and Bob Prielipp, *Cryptarithms and Other Mathematical Pastimes,* p. 6. Indiana, Pa.: School Science and Mathematics Association, 1979.

————. (1973) in Kuenzi, N. J., and Bob Prielipp, *Cryptarithms and Other Mathematical Pastimes,* p. 6. Indiana, Penn.: School Science and Mathematics Association, 1979.

Wayne, Alan. (1977) In Kuenzi, N. J., and Bob Prielipp, *Cryptarithms and Other Mathematical Pastimes,* p. 8. Indiana, Penn.: School Science and Mathematics Association, 1979.

————. (1978) In Kuenzi, N. J., and Bob Prielipp, *Cryptarithms and Other Mathematical Pastimes,* pp. 8, 9. Indiana, Penn.: School Science and Mathematics Association, 1979.

Bibliography

Andree, Josephine, and Richard V. Andree. *Cryptarithms.* Washington, D.C.: Mu Alpha Theta, 1978.

CRYPTARITHMS
SHEET 1

A popular form of number puzzle is the cryptarithm, like this:

$$\begin{array}{r} D\,O \\ +\ G\,O \\ \hline N\,O\,W \end{array}$$

In this kind of puzzle, each time a letter is used it stands for the same digit. Each letter must stand for a unique digit. A good idea is to write out the letters in the puzzle in alphabetical order and to enter on this list anything you can. Here is a start:

1.

$$\begin{array}{r} D\,O \\ +\ G\,O \\ \hline \text{N}\,O\,W \end{array}$$

D =
G =
N = 1
O =
W = even

To break the code, you hunt for clues. As soon as you find what a letter stands for, fill in the problem and the list. Do you see why N must be 1? Do you see why W must be even? After this you may have to use "trial and error."

How many of these can you solve? (One of them is impossible.)

2.

$$\begin{array}{r} D\,O \\ +\ G\,O \\ \hline O\,N \end{array}$$

D =
G =
N =
O =

3.

$$\begin{array}{r} B\,O\,W \\ +\ W\,O\,W \\ \hline D\,O\,G \end{array}$$

B =
D =
G =
O =
W =

4.

$$\begin{array}{r} T\,W\,O \\ +T\,W\,O \\ \hline F\,O\,U\,R \end{array}$$

F =
O =
R =
T =
U =
W =

5.

$$\begin{array}{r} F\,E \\ F\,I \\ +\ F\,O \\ \hline F\,U\,M \end{array}$$

E =
F =
I =
M =
O =
U =

6.

$$\begin{array}{r} F\,O\,U\,R \\ +\ O\,N\,E \\ \hline F\,I\,V\,E \end{array}$$

E =
F =
I =
N =
O =
R =
U =
V =

CRYPTARITHMS
SHEET 2

7.

```
  F O U R
+ F I V E
  N I N E
```

E =
F =
I =
N =
O =
R =
U =
V =

8.

```
  W O O F
+ W O O F
D O G G Y
```

D =
F =
G =
O =
W =
Y =

9.

```
  M O O
+ M O O
  C O W
```

C =
M =
O =
W =

10.

```
  A L L
+ T H E
  W A Y
```

A =
E =
H =
L =
T =
W =
Y =

11.

```
  H O T
+ D O G
  B U N
```

B =
D =
G =
H =
N =
O =
T =
U =

12.

```
  L I V E
+ V I L E
  E V I L
```

E =
I =
L =
V =

13.

```
  T V
+ I S
B A D
```

A =
B =
D =
I =
S =
T =
V =

Now that you know how cryptarithms work, you could invent your own! It is much easier to choose a suitable catchphrase first, then match numbers to the letters. Any short phrase that makes some kind of sense would do, so long as it has not more than *ten different* letters (preferably fewer). Keep the phrase brief, and include some repetition of letters. Otherwise it may be too difficult to solve!

CLAUDIA ZASLAVSKY

Networks— New York Subways, a Piece of String, and African Traditions

CHILDREN now growing up in our rapidly advancing technological society must be prepared to cope with problems that will arise not only in this century but also in the twenty-first century. Yet we ourselves do not know what kind of society today's children will face in the future. The best we as mathematics educators can do is to encourage children to deal with new situations, to be unafraid of challenges, and to learn to think.

One topic that can help us to achieve these goals is network theory. The advantages and positive outcomes of activities based on this topic are numerous:

1. Opportunities for real problem solving, encouraging children to look for patterns and to arrive at generalizations based on their own explorations and analyses.

2. Familiarity with applications of mathematics in the real world. Sophisticated applications of network theory (or graph theory, to use the mathematicians' terminology) including planning pipelines for oil and water transmission, designing printed circuits, laying out telecommunications systems, even collecting the garbage efficiently (figs. 1, 2). Mathematicians have developed new

theories in the course of working on such applications.

3. Integration of mathematics with social studies, art, and literature as children study examples of networks in other societies, and learn to appreciate the common elements in diverse cultures.

Fig. 1. Network of streets, Long Island, New York

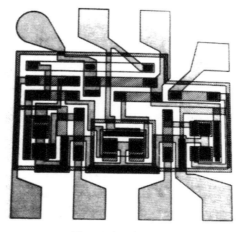

Fig. 2. Printed circuit

PHOTOS BY SAM ZASLAVSKY

4. No necessity for previously acquired skills or computational ability to carry out these activities.

5. Accommodation to individual differences in style and pace of learning among the students in a class. Since the activities are open-ended, each child can go as far as he or she is capable.

6. Discussion and cooperation among students as they compare their methods and results.

7. Positive attitudes toward mathematics. Most children are both fascinated and challenged by such activities.

In this article I shall offer applications of network theory in our own and in other cultures, discuss several methods of analysis, and suggest further activities suitable for various grade levels.

Network Problems

The bridges of Königsberg

A network consists of a set of points and the line segments connecting these points. In this article I shall deal only with traceable networks, those that can be drawn without lifting the pencil from the paper or going over a line segment more than once. Probably you have created many such networks as you doodled with a pencil or idly traced patterns in the sand at the beach. When I was in fifth grade, I spent many hours drawing the pattern in figure 3, trying to convince myself that points A and B were the only possible starting points. The Swiss mathematician Leonhard Euler was the first to develop a theory of networks. In 1736 he solved the famous

Claudia Zaslavsky *was formerly a mathematics teacher in the New York State public schools. She is now an educational consultant, author, and leader of workshops for teachers on cultural application of mathematics She is the author of several books, most recently one for children,* Count on Your Fingers African Style.

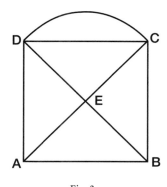

Fig. 3

problem of the Seven Bridges of Königsberg by proving that it was impossible to cross each bridge exactly once and return to the starting point. With this solution Euler initiated the field of mathematics known as topology. He regarded his work as merely a contribution to recreational mathematics. Today one can earn a doctor of philosophy degree in some small aspect of this vast field.

Subways of New York

We can update the Königsberg bridge problem. The map of New York City in figure 4 shows the subway connections from Manhattan to the boroughs of the Bronx, Queens, and Brooklyn. Is it possible to start on the island of Manhattan, use each subway line exactly once to travel to and from the other boroughs, and complete the trip in Manhattan?

Euler's analysis began with a diagram called a network. He reduced each separate region to a point called a vertex, and each bridge became a line, or arc, connecting two vertices (fig. 5). The task is to trace the figure, starting at a vertex and returning to that point, without taking the pencil off the paper or going over a line more than once. One may go through a vertex as many times as necessary.

By a similar analysis (fig. 6), it is clear that a subway trip that starts in Manhattan must end in Queens.

A network that can be traced in one sweep is called *traceable* (or *traversable* or *universal*). What kinds of networks are traceable? Is it possible to determine whether or not a network is traceable without actually trying to trace it? Here is a clue: A traceable network must have a starting point and a finishing point, which may be at the same vertex or at two distinct vertices. Knowing this, however, other ques-

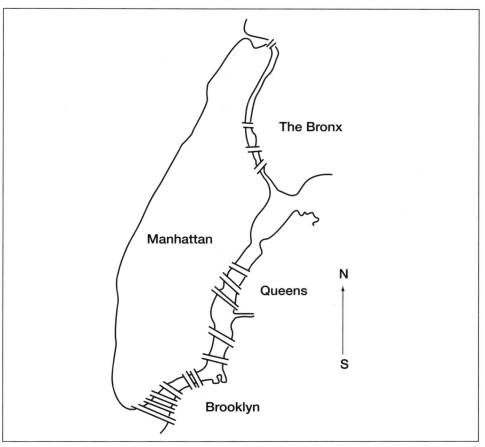

Fig. 4. New York subways

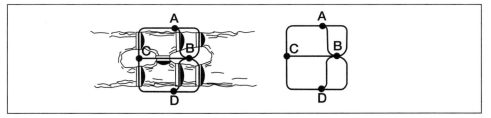

Fig. 5. Euler's analysis of the problem of the Königsberg bridges

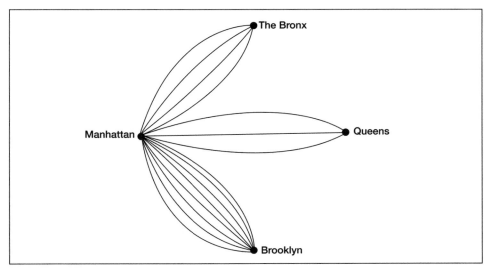

Fig. 6. Diagram of New York subways

tions arise: If the two points are distinct, can the starting point and the finishing point be interchanged? Can the starting point be chosen at random?

Have your students draw several simple examples of networks of their own and discuss their conclusions. Hirsch (1975) has provided some excellent reproducible activities based on network theory.

A Piece of String

One method of analysis is to look at existing networks, as we have just done, to determine whether they are traceable. A different approach is to make networks that we know are traceable and examine their properties. A length of string for each student is the only material required.

Tie a knot at one end of the string. Mentally label that end *S* (start) and the other end *F* (finish). Of course the two letters can be interchanged. Certainly the path from *S* to *F* is traceable, no matter how the string is arranged, provided segments do not overlap.

Now consider the possible cases (see fig. 7):

1. On the simplest path, the string does not cross itself. The path can be open (fig. 7a) or closed (fig. 7b) where points *S* and *F* merge into one point.

2. Introduce a vertex, *A,* as in figure 7c. The path enters vertex *A* and then exits from vertex *A*.

3. Loop the string at one or more points between *S* and *F,* as in figures 7d and 7e. A highway cloverleaf (fig. 8) intersection is a good example of such looping. Every path that enters *A* also exits from *A*.

4. The path can go through point *S* and/or point *F* more than once (figs. 7f, 7g, 7h, and 7i).

We can classify the paths as either *merged*, where points *S* and *F* merge into one point, or *separated*, where *S* and *F* are separate and distinct. Merged paths are illustrated in figures 7b, 7d, 7f, and 7g. In the other examples in figure 7, the paths are separated.

Look again at the merged paths. It does not matter at which point we start and finish. For example, one can draw the figure eight,

starting at any point on the path.

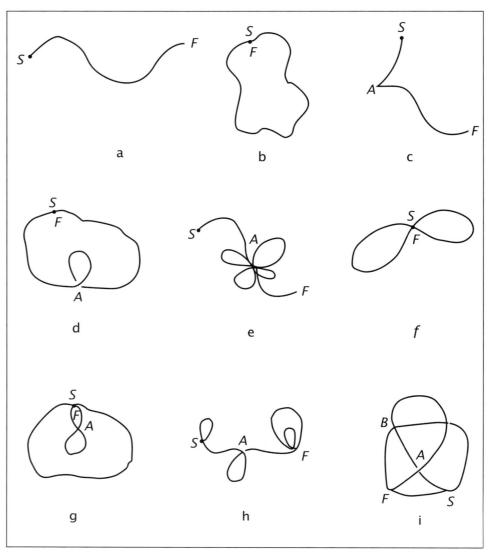

Fig. 7

Fig. 8. Network of highways, George Washington Bridge vicinity, New York City

Examine the points marked *A* and *B* in all the examples in figure 7. At each point the path enters and then exits. In every case an even number of line segments (2, 4, 6, …) meet at point *A* or point *B*. As long as the number of line segments (or arcs, or edges) meeting at a point is even, traceability is not affected.

The crucial test comes when we examine what happens at *S* and *F* in those networks where *S* and *F* are two distinct points. There we see an odd number of arcs (1, 3, 5, …) meeting at *S* and at *F*. In each path exactly two points—namely, *S* and *F*—have an odd number of arcs meeting at those vertices.

The *degree* of a vertex is the number of arcs meeting at that vertex. Every vertex is of either odd or even degree. We have observed traceable networks that have two vertices of odd degree. Can the string be arranged so that there is exactly one vertex of odd degree? Can a traceable path have more than two vertices of odd degree?

We can conclude from our observations that there are two types of traceable networks:

(1) Networks in which all vertices have even degree. The starting point can be anywhere.

(2) Networks in which exactly two vertices, the starting and the finishing points, have odd degree. All other vertices have even degree.

In African culture

Experiences with networks can enrich the teaching of social studies, literature, and art. They need not be confined to the mathematics period. The activities described here are authentic aspects of African culture. Each student will require the following materials:

Copies of the networks shown in figures 9, 10, 11, and 12
Several sheets of centimeter grid paper
Pencils and colored markers

First Chokwe network

Before the time of formal schooling, radio, or television, children in Africa, as well as in other parts of the world, learned the ways of their people from their parents and grandparents. The children would gather around the fire in the evening and

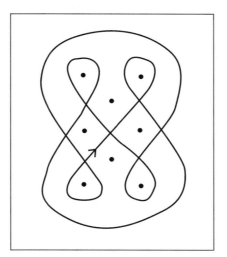

Fig. 9. Chokwe network

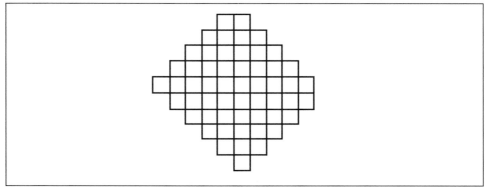

Fig. 10. Chokwe network

Fig. 11

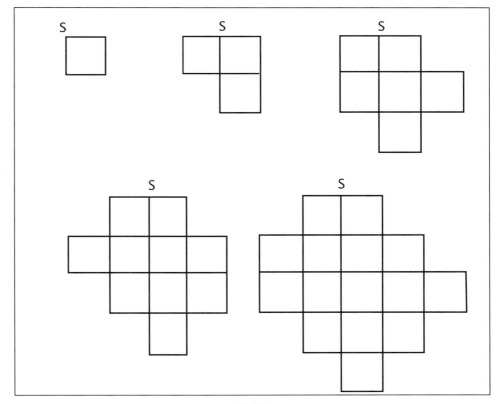

Fig 12

listen to stories about their ancestors, about animals, and about everyday life.

The Chokwe people, who inhabit adjoining regions of Zaire, Angola, and Zambia, have a long tradition of drawing network patterns in the sand to illustrate their stories. The network in figure 9 poses a riddle. Can you guess what it is? Here are some hints: It sends messages, dancers love it, and the top and bottom are both covered with skins. (Answer: a two-headed drum)

Activity for students. Trace the network in figure 9 without taking your pencil off the paper or going over a line more than once. Next, copy the network on another sheet of paper, but first make the pattern of dots to serve as a guide in drawing the design.

Second Chokwe network

The network in figure 10 illustrates the Chokwe people's myth about the beginning of the world. The story tells why the Sun and the Moon always reappear, but Man (and Woman) eventually must die. (Young children enjoy dramatizing the story.)

HOW THE WORLD BEGAN

Once upon a time the Sun went to pay his respects to the god Kalunga. He walked and walked until he found the path that led to Kalunga. When he arrived, God gave him a rooster and said, "See me in the morning before you leave."

In the morning the rooster crowed and woke the Sun. Then the Sun went back to see God, who said, "I heard the rooster crow, the one I gave you for supper. You may keep him, but you must return every morning." That is why the Sun goes around the earth and appears every morning.

The Moon also went to visit Kalunga. He, too, received a rooster, and it woke him the next morning. When he returned with the rooster under his arm, God said, "I see that you did not eat the rooster I gave you yesterday for your supper. That is good. You must come back to see me every twenty-eight days." That is why we see the full moon every twenty-eight days.

Then Man went to see Kalunga and was given a rooster. But Man was very hungry after his long trip. He ate part of the chicken for supper. The next morning the Sun was already high in the sky when Man awoke. He quickly ate the rest of the rooster and hurried to see God. Kalunga said to him with a smile, "Where is the rooster I gave you yesterday? I did not hear him crow this morning."

Man was afraid. "I was very hungry and I ate him," he said.

Then God said, "That is all right, but listen. You know that the Sun and the Moon have been to see me. Each of them received a rooster, just as you did, but they did not kill theirs. That is why they will never die. But you killed yours, and so you must die as he did. And, at your death, you will come back to see me."

And so it is. Haven't the Sun and the Moon always appeared, just as in the days of our great grandparents? But men and women do not live forever.

Activities for students. Start at the arrow and trace the path to the god Kalunga in one sweep of the pencil. The simplest path is to follow each line as far as possible before turning. How many other paths can your students discover? A further challenge is to trace the figure without *crossing* any line. The 6-by-6 square array of dots serves as a guide when the pattern is copied on a sheet of graph paper.

Create a work of art by drawing the "path to Kalunga" on colored oaktag and then gluing yam over the pencil lines. Of course, only one continuous length of yarn is required.

Bakuba networks

Along the Kasai River, in Zaire, live the Bakuba, known widely for the beautiful and intricate patterns in their weaving and woodcarving. The ethnologist, Emil Torday, who wrote about the lives of these people early in the twentieth century, tells of coming on a group of children drawing in the sand (fig. 11). They asked him to draw the design without lifting his finger. He could not do it, and great was the children's joy when the white man failed to accomplish the task.

The Bakuba children were imitating the weaving patterns of their elders, the patterns in raffia cloth and the fishing nets drying on the banks of the river. From the everyday tasks of the village, these children themselves had devised a game so sophisticated as to baffle the learned European anthropologist. What better way to learn mathematics!

Activities for students. The task given to Torday is not impossible, but it may be difficult. A good technique for solving a problem like this is to try some easier problems of the same kind on graph paper, and then build up to the tough one (fig. 12). Are the vertices odd or even? How many odd vertices are there? Can your students continue the growth pattern until they reach the network described by Torday, which has ten small squares in the longest row and column?

The following are suggestions for further activities with African networks:

1. Create attractive designs by filling in the small squares of the Bakuba design with various colors.

2. Draw a Bakuba network so large that it fills almost an entire sheet of graph paper.

3. Analyze the growth pattern of the Bakuba networks as they become successively larger. Count the number of small squares in each column (or row) and then in the entire figure. Surprisingly, the sums of the squares in each figure are the triangular numbers—1, 3, 6, 10, 15, ... Since the triangular numbers are the sums of the consecutive counting numbers: 1, 1 + 2, 1 + 2 + 3, …, the result may not be so surprising after all.

See Zaslavsky (1973 (a) and (c), 1975, 1979) for additional suggestions about activities based on African culture.

Additional network activities

There are many other examples of networks and the application of the ideas of networks. For example, children could be asked to classify the printed letters of the alphabet according to the number of separate paths needed to form each letter. Try this with cursive writing, too. You might also try it with other alphabets in some classes.

You could have children analyze road and street maps, and pose problems based on these maps. For example, what path leads to the most efficient garbage collection in your neighborhood? (See Jacobson 1974.) Look for network patterns in fabrics and artifacts, as in figures 13 and 14.

Learn the game of Sprouts. (See Hirsch 1976.) Refer to the many suggestions in Jacobs (1970).

Conclusion

The National Council of Teachers of Mathematics (1980, pp. 2, 3) recommends that "the development of problem-solving ability should direct the efforts of mathematics educators through the next decade.... Fundamental to the development of problem-solving ability is an open mind, an attitude of curiosity and exploration, the willingness to probe, to try, to make intelligent guesses." Applications of network theory fulfill these objectives admirably.

The activities that have been described in this article can be adapted to various grade levels, from lower elementary through secondary. I have found that students consider network games so much fun that they refuse to believe they are doing "real" mathematics. Yet they are engaged in problem-solving activities on a high level.

Network theory is an integral part of the curriculum in England and other European countries. Isn't it time that we introduce our children to this vital topic?

References

Hirsch, Christian R. (a) "Games, Graphs, and Generalizations." *Arithmetic Teacher* 23 (December 1976): 608–10.

———. (b) "Graphs and Games." *Mathematics Teacher* 68 (February 1975): 125–28.

Jacobs, Harold R. *Mathematics, a Human Endeavor.* San Francisco: Freeman, 1970.

Jacobson, Herbert R. "Ecology, Rapid Transit, and Graph Theory." *Arithmetic Teacher* 21 (April 1974): 291-93.

National Council of Teachers of Mathematics. *An Agenda for Action.* Reston, Va.: The Council, 1980.

Zaslavsky, Claudia. (a) *Africa Counts: Number and Pattern in African Culture.* Boston: Prindle, Weber & Schmidt, 1973. Paperback: Westport, Conn.: Lawrence Hill, 1979.

Fig. 13. Carved calabash, "wise man's knot" pattern, Nigeria

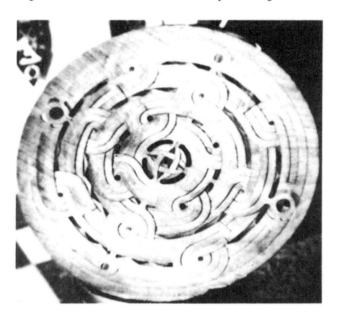

Fig. 14. Wooden tray, Surinam

———. (b) "African Network Patterns." *Mathematics Teaching* 73 (December 1975): 12–13.

———. (c) "Mathematics in the Study of African Culture." *Arithmetic Teacher* 20 (November 1973): 532–35.

———. (d) "Symmetry Along with Other Mathematical Concepts and Applications in African Life." In *Applications in School Mathematics,* pp. 82–97, 1979 Yearbook of the National Council of Teachers of Mathematics. Reston, Va.: The Council, 1979.

LOUIS M. FRIEDLER

Problem Solving with Discrete Mathematics

THE NCTM's *Curriculum and Evaluation Standards for School Mathematics* (1989) calls for an emphasis on problem solving at all levels and recommends introducing discrete mathematics topics. In fact, the first standard for grades K–4 states that "the study of mathematics should emphasize problem solving ..." (p. 23). The section on high school standards recommends that discrete mathematics topics be included because so much current "information processing requires the use of discrete (discontinuous) mathematics" (p. 176). Is this material appropriate for elementary school? The 1991 NCTM Yearbook (Kenney 1991) contains articles concerning this material at all levels. Although Graham (1991) makes several excellent suggestions for specific discrete topics for elementary students, most authors refer to the same two or three problems on Euler paths. (See Kaczmar [1992].) So the questions remain. How can elementary school teachers implement these ideas? What are other sources for appropriate problems? What methods of presentation will work? How do we use a problem-solving approach with this material?

I come to these questions with a perspective different from that of the typical elementary school teacher. I am a research mathematician and college mathematics teacher and had never thought about elementary school mathematics until my daughter entered school. This background as a mathematician affects both the topics I choose and my method of presentation. I have recently been working with groups of children at Swarthmore-Rutledge (S-R)

Louis Friedler *teaches at Beaver College, Glenside, PA 19038. He is interested in teaching and mathematics-curriculum development at all levels, elementary through college.*

Elementary School for two and one-half years. During the 1992–93 school year, eighteen fifth graders came to school forty-five minutes early once every other week to pursue mathematics.

My objectives in working with the children have been to use discrete-mathematics topics to explore problem solving, to introduce the students to mathematics that they will find stimulating and that is related to current "real" mathematics, to give them challenging problems yet let them feel successful, to have them explain their reasoning, and to encourage group interaction. In Pólya's (1945, 1966) paradigm for problem solving, students are given difficult problems and told to look first at simple or special cases. When I work with elementary school students, we start with simple examples. That is, we first consider challenging problems and then break them down into smaller parts. For example, in the class-1 problems that follow, most students attempting problem 7 would find it

extremely difficult without first doing problems 1–6. Once students discover the patterns in problems 1–5 and have solved problem 6, they can successfully solve item 7. It is relatively unimportant whether students learn discrete mathematics in elementary school; it is important that they understand that mathematics is more than arithmetic and that they know how to, and wish to, attack new problems.

To begin, I ask students to work in groups of four to five. Although that number was originally determined by the configuration of the room, I have found that it works well, and this finding is supported by other authors (see, e.g., Slavin [1988, 12]). When asked a question, I am more likely to ask another question than to answer it. It is difficult to avoid helping, but students will turn to each other to work out answers if allowed. Our classroom is noisy; students argue with one another about solutions. When students explain their reasoning, they frequently suggest ideas different from

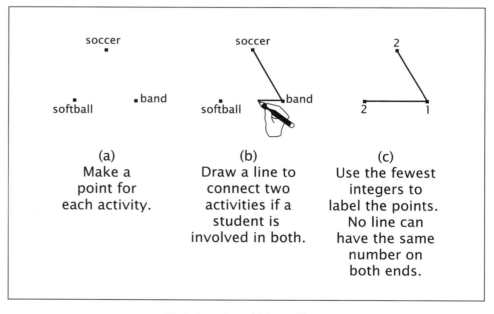

(a)
Make a point for each activity.

(b)
Draw a line to connect two activities if a student is involved in both.

(c)
Use the fewest integers to label the points. No line can have the same number on both ends.

Fig. 1. A graph model for problem 1

what I had in mind. They are encouraged to believe that more than one correct way may be possible to solve a problem. The real-life context for each problem appeals to the students.

The students who regularly attend the mathematics group are motivated and bright. Yet I have successfully tested the class-2 problems and several similar problems with a more heterogeneous group. Students respond to the excitement of mathematics. The following describes two typical classes, which might vary in length from thirty to fifty minutes.

Class 1:
Scheduling Graphs

Problem 1: The S-R Elementary School needs to schedule soccer, band, and softball so that no child will have two activities occurring at the same time. Vanessa attends both band and softball, Daniel attends both soccer and band, and no other student attends more than one activity. What is the smallest number of class periods we need so that we can schedule all the activities with no conflicts?

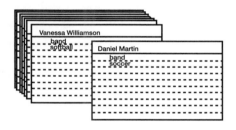

Students will quickly realize that the answer is two: put band in one period and softball and soccer in a second period. Viewing a graph model for this problem will make future problems easier. We have a point, or vertex, for each activity (see fig. 1a), and we draw a line, or edge, between points if a student is in both activities. (See fig. 1b.) We label each point with a positive integer so that if two points have an edge between them, they have different labels. The problem of finding the smallest number of periods is the same as the problem of finding the smallest possible number of different labels. We could label each point with a different integer and thus use three periods, but figure 1c shows that it can be done with only two integers. Since one

number alone would lead to conflicts, two is the smallest number.

Problem 2: We have the same situation as in problem 1 except that the activities are Girl Scouts, band, clarinet lessons, soccer, gymnastics, and softball. Zak attends band and soccer; Jillian has soccer and gymnastics; Pat signs up for soccer, band, and clarinet lessons; Kathy has gymnastics and soccer; Zoe takes softball and gymnastics; and Sorelle attends Girl Scouts, band, and clarinet lessons. If no other child attends more than one activity, what is the smallest number of class periods necessary so that we avoid conflicts?

Using the same ideas as in problem 1, we draw a graph model, label the vertices, and find that the answer is three. (See fig. 2.) Note that even though students start at different points and label points differently in the process, they should all arrive at the same conclusion. If students have trouble with this problem, I encourage them to try problems 3–5 first and then return to this one.

Instructions for problems 3–6

For each of the problems that follow, pretend that each point represents an activity and that an edge between two points implies that a child is in both activities. What is the smallest numbers of periods necessary to avoid conflicts?

Problem 3: (See fig. 3.) Do you see a pattern of graphs? What is the next graph in this sequence? Do you see a pattern to the smallest numbers of periods? What is the pattern? How many periods would be necessary if we had a similar graph with 10 points?

The children will eventually see this pattern emerge: 3-2-3-2-.... Some of my students expressed this pattern as "Three when there is an odd number of points, two when there is an even number." With

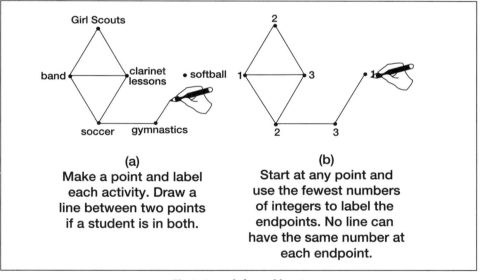

(a)
Make a point and label each activity. Draw a line between two points if a student is in both.

(b)
Start at any point and use the fewest numbers of integers to label the endpoints. No line can have the same number at each endpoint.

Fig. 2. A graph for problem 2

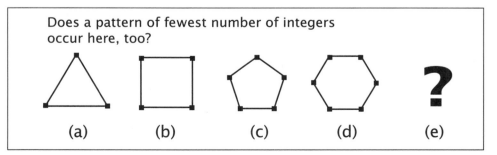

Does a pattern of fewest number of integers occur here, too?

(a)   (b)   (c)   (d)   (e)

Fig. 3. A pattern of graphs for problem 3

ten vertices, only two periods are needed. If children have trouble seeing the pattern, I might ask them to find the number of periods necessary if we had seven or eight vertices.

Problem 4: (See fig. 4.) Do you see a pattern of graphs? If so, what is the next graph in this sequence? Do you see a pattern to the smallest numbers of periods? What is the pattern? How many periods would be necessary if we had a similar graph with 10 points?

The pattern for the smallest integers is 2-3-4-5-.... When each vertex is connected to every other vertex, the smallest numbers of periods possible is the same as the number of vertices. Students quickly see this pattern and are able to guess how it continues.

Problem 5: (See fig. 5.) Do you see patterns in the graphs and in the number of periods? If so, what are they?

The pattern of smallest integers is 3-4-3-4-.... Notice the relationship between this problem and problem 3.

Problem 6: (See fig. 6.) Find the smallest numbers of integers necessary to label each of these graphs.

This problem does not present a pattern of graphs but rather gives students a chance to use the patterns they developed in previous problems to solve more difficult problems. The answers for these graphs are (a), 2; (b), 3; and (c), 3.

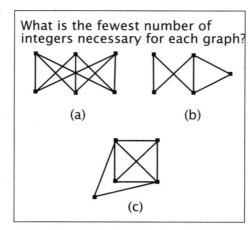

What is the fewest number of integers necessary for each graph?

(a)   (b)

(c)

Fig. 6. Three different types of graphs that are not intended to form a pattern

Problem 7: What is the fewest number of periods necessary to schedule soccer, swimming, band, Boy Scouts, baseball, and computer club? Alec attends Boy Scouts and band; Adrian has Boy Scouts and baseball; Noa takes band, soccer, and computer club; Dinah attends soccer, swimming, and band. Emily has swimming and computer club; and Matt takes baseball and swimming. No other student attends more than one activity.

Students will discover from problem 4 that if every point is connected to every other point, then we need the same number of class periods as we have points. That discovery makes problem 7 accessible, since a subgraph of that problem fits this description. (See fig. 7.) The answer is 4.

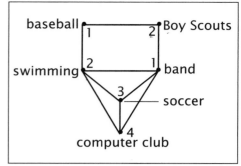

Fig. 7. A graph for problem 7

Concluding remarks for class 1

Although the process of labeling graphs or, equivalently, finding the smallest number of class periods necessary to avoid conflict, is relatively easy in the foregoing problems, no known efficient algorithm can do it. (See Garey and Johnson [1979] for an explanation of what qualifies as an "efficient" algorithm.) In so doing, children are working problems related to unknown, current mathematics.

Class 2: Tournaments

In the first type, or single-elimination tournament, winners continue to play until they lose, which is best explained by the following problem.

Problem 8: Noa, Sorelle, Ian, and Zak are trying to decide who is the best Tetris player. Tetris is a challenging computer game. They pair up and play a game. The winners play each other and the losers stop. How many total games are played?

After the students determine that the answer is three, we draw a chart to help with future problems. (See fig. 8.) Each horizontal line represents a game to be played.

Problem 9: Eight children, instead of four, are in a single-elimination Tetris tournament. Again, children are paired and the winners play on while the losers stop. Play continues until one child wins. Draw a picture and determine how many total games are played.

Since eight students are playing, four initial pairs are possible. The chart should have four lines in the first column, then two, then one to total seven games. (See fig. 9.)

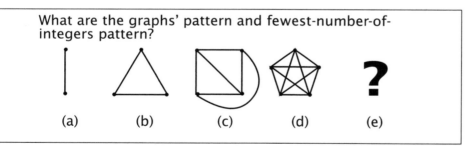

What are the graphs' pattern and fewest-number-of-integers pattern?

(a)   (b)   (c)   (d)   (e)

Fig. 4

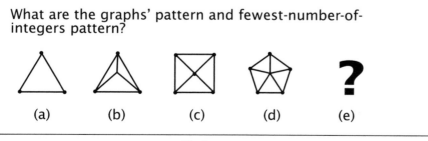

What are the graphs' pattern and fewest-number-of-integers pattern?

(a)   (b)   (c)   (d)   (e)

Fig. 5

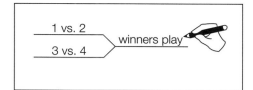

Fig. 8. A chart for a single-elimination tournament with four players

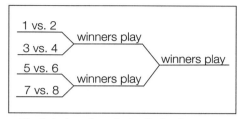

Fig. 9. A chart for a single-elimination tournament with eight players

Problem 10: What is the number of games necessary to find the winner in a single-elimination Tetris tournament with sixteen children? With thirty-two children?

Problem 11: The NCAA (Men's) Basketball Tournament has sixty-four teams and is single elimination. How many games are played? What pattern have you found? Why does it work? (Hints available.) What if ten teams played and some teams had "byes," that is, did not play on some rounds. Would your method still work?

The children will soon see the pattern: the number of games is one less than the number of players. One explanation for the reason it works, as several students discovered, is that the same number of games are played as the number of losers to games because every team except the eventual winner loses exactly one game. Some of the small groups needed a hint, such as "How many games were lost?" to understand the reason the pattern works.

In the second type of tournament, called a round-robin, each team plays every other team exactly one time. The winner is the team that wins the most games. However, in a round-robin tournament, more than one winner is possible, since more than one team may win the most games. We also consider a second question: Can we make a list in which each team beats the team directly below it? In this list, the team at the top is not necessarily the winner. It is not always possible to make an ordered list of winners in a round-robin tournament.

Problem 12: Three classes had a soccer tournament. Mrs. MacLaughlin's (*M*) class beat Mrs. Jones's (*J*) class, Mrs. MacLaughlin's beat Mr. Shaffer's (*S*), and Mrs. Jones's beat Mr. Shaffer's. Draw three points to represent the three teams and label them *M*, *J*, and *S*. Draw an arrow from one point to another if the first team beat the second. Next to each point list the number of games won by that team. Who won this tournament?

Can you list the teams in an order so that each team beats the team just below it and loses to the team just above it?

(See fig. 10.) *M* won the tournament by winning more games. Since *M* beat the other teams, it must be at the top of the list. Since *S* lost to both teams, it must be at the bottom of the list. The solution in figure 10 is the only possible list that satisfies the conditions. After giving students sufficient time to work on problem 12, show them the solution so that they can continue with the next problems.

Problem 13: Mrs. Howe's (*H*) class joined the tournament. Her team beat Mrs. MacLaughlin's and Mr. Shaffer's teams but lost to Mrs. Jones's team. Add a point and arrows for Mrs. Howe's team to the picture you made for problem 12. Label the new point *H*. Now who won the tournament?

Can you add Mrs. Howe's team to the list you made from problem 12? If so, please add. It is not necessary that a team in the list beats all the teams below it or loses to all the teams above it. More than one list is possible. Can you find two different lists?

(See fig. 11.) Three teams tie for the tournament title with two wins each. Notice that two listings are possible of the teams that solve the second part of the problem. Students may at first have trouble with the idea that the list is not "transitive," that is, it is not necessary that a team beats all the teams below it in the list. The two lists correspond to two different methods of thinking about the problem. We might attack the problem by going down the list we found in problem 12 from the top and inserting the new team (*H*) above the first team it beat (*M*). We might also start at the bottom, go up until we find the first team that beat *H*

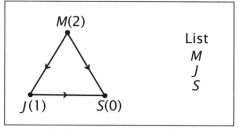

Fig 10. A diagram for a round-robin tournament with three teams and an ordered list of teams

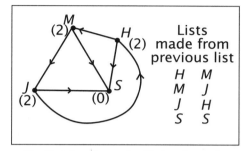

Fig. 11. A fourth team is added to the previous round-robin tournament

(*J*), and then insert *H* between *J* and *S*. Although *M* is above *H* in the second solution, it is not true that *M* beat *H*; this outcome is not required in the problem. The next two problems use the same method of solution as shown in problem 13.

Problem 14: Add a fifth team to the tournament. You decide which teams it beat and which ones beat it. Can you decide who won the tournament?

Add this new team to the list you had in problem 13. Explain your method.

Notice again that the team with the most wins is not necessarily the team at the top of the list.

Problem 15: Say we had a tournament with eleven teams and each team has already played every other team. We have already made a list in which every team beat the team just below it and lost to the team just above it. If another team entered the tournament and played every other team, explain how you would add this new team to the list.

When I used this problem with a heterogeneous class, the first child who understood the method of solving the problem was later described to me as "weak in math computation" by the teacher. The student was thrilled to be successful with these problems.

The problem of making the list described in the foregoing is called *finding a*

Hamiltonian path through the tournament. Hamiltonian paths were developed by the Irish mathematician Sir William Hamilton (1805–1865) to solve a puzzle he invented. The idea outlined in problem 15 is really a standard inductive proof—an idea that in a more abstract setting can appear quite difficult. We conclude with a problem that one class found to be the most challenging but also the most fun.

Problem 16: If we have three players in a round-robin tournament, then only two results are possible: either each player wins exactly one game or one player wins two, a second player wins one, and the third player wins none. (See fig. 12.) We can write these two possible tournaments as 1-1-1 and 2-1-0. Any other tournament is the same as one of these two—it just has different players in different positions in the triangles. The problem is to discover how many different tournaments are possible if we have four players. Again we count two tournaments as the same if they are the same except for the labels. Hint: Start by drawing a square.

See figure 13 for the four possible tournaments. With some classes it may be necessary to show the children that 3-1-1-1 is one of the answers so that they can find the others. Several children observed that the total number of games played is six. One said, "You could just distribute the six in any way." But then she realized that not all possibilities worked. "It couldn't be 3-3-0-0 because then two points would not be connected." She quickly found the four possible tournaments.

Suggestions and Final Comments

Many sources are available for other problems in discrete mathematics; one of the most accessible is Ore and Wilson (1990), and my favorites are Rosen (1992) and Tucker (1984). Problems from these books can be adapted to the foregoing approach. Some other sources for appropriate but not necessarily discrete problems are Smullyan (1978), Gardiner (1988), and Gardner (1978). Fellows (1993) has written about discrete mathematics in the elementary school from the perspective of a research computer scientist. He makes many excellent suggestions.

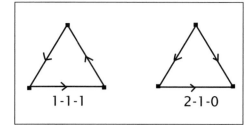

Fig. 12. The two possible results of three people in a round-robin tournament

I have come to truly love working with elementary school students because of the excitement they demonstrate about learning. One day I asked the children if we should stop or work more problems. They all yelled that they wanted to work more problems. My calculus students rarely show such enthusiasm. It is my hope that students exposed to exciting problems in mathematics in elementary school will maintain that enthusiasm.

Bibliography

Fellows, Michael R. "Computer Science and Mathematics in the Elementary Schools." In *CBMS Issues in Mathematics Education: Mathematicians and Education Reform 1990–1991*, vol. 3, edited by Naomi D. Fisher, Harvey B. Keynes, and Philip D. Wagreich, 143–63. Washington, D.C.: Mathematical Association of America, 1991.

Garey, Michael R., and David S. Johnson. *Computers and Intractability.* New York: W. H. Freeman & Co., 1979.

Graham, Claire Zalewski. "Strengthening a K–8 Mathematics Program with Discrete Mathematics." In *Discrete Mathematics across the Curriculum, K–12,* 1991 Yearbook of the National Council of Teachers of Mathematics, 18–29. Reston, Va.: The Council, 1991.

Gardiner, A. *Mathematical Puzzling.* Oxford: Oxford University Press, 1988.

Gardner, Martin. *Aha! Insight.* New York: Scientific American and W. H. Freeman & Co., 1978.

Kaczmar, P. "Graph Theory." Paper presented at the P.C.T.M. Conference, Valley Forge, Pennsylvania, March 1992.

Kenney, Margaret J., ed. *Discrete Mathematics across the Curriculum, K–12.* 1991 Yearbook of the National Council of Teachers of Mathematics, 18–29. Reston, Va.: The Council, 1991.

Martin, George E. *Polyominoes.* Washington, D.C.: Mathematical Association of America, 1991.

National Council of Teachers of Mathematics. *Curriculum and Evaluation Standards for School Mathematics.* Reston, Va.: The Council, 1989.

Ore, Oystein, and Robin J. Wilson. *Graphs and Their Uses.* Washington, D.C.: Mathematical Association of America, 1990.

Pólya, George. *How to Solve It.* Princeton, N.J.: Princeton University Press, 1945.

———. *Let Us Teach Guessing.* Washington, D.C.: Mathematical Association of America, 1966. Videotape.

Rosen, Kenneth H. *Discrete Mathematics and Its Applications.* 2d ed. New York: McGraw Hill, 1992.

Slavin, Robert E. *Student Team Learning: An Overview and Practical Guide.* 2d ed. Washington, D.C.: National Education Association, 1988.

Smullyan, Raymond. *What Is the Name of This Book?* New York: Simon & Schuster, 1978.

Tucker, Alan. *Applied Combinatorics.* 2d ed. New York: John Wiley & Sons, 1984.

The author would like to thank Celeste MacLaughlin and Elma Jones for their help and encouragement in coordinating his work with the Swarthmore-Rutledge Elementary School children and also Diane Anderson and Richard Polis for their helpful suggestions in the preparation of this article.

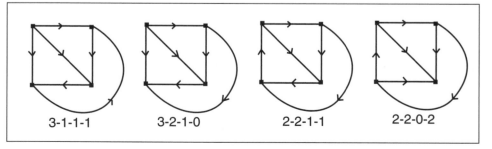

Fig. 13. The four possible results of four people in a round-robin tournament

2

Mathematics as Communication

THE belief that we learn and refine our learning through the act of writing has long been accepted. Although the nature of mathematics may be debated, mathematics is communicated through the use of symbols and terminology unique to the field. Mathematical concepts are learned through the use of examples and nonexamples expressed in oral and written formats.

Larry Buschman's article, "Communicating in the Language of Mathematics," provides a wide variety of activities. The activities include what he identified as mathematical communication structures, which were unique in the review literature.

Margaret McIntosh offers a partial list of "500 Writing Formats" and an e-mail address where one can complete the list. The article includes specific sample abbreviated writing tasks.

Journal writing was recommended by a number of authors. One excellent example is "Journal Writing: An Insight into Students' Understanding."

Class newspapers were another commonly referenced activity. "Mathematics News Gazette" and "Math Time Herald" are good examples of class newspapers at different levels.

"Mathematics and Poetry: Problem Solving in Context" uses a unique approach and gives an excellent reference list.

LARRY BUSCHMAN

Communicating in the Language of Mathematics

AS THE classroom mathematics curriculum expands to encompass the entire range of skills included in the NCTM's *Curriculum and Evaluation Standards for School Mathematics* (1989), the process by which a student arrives at the answer to a problem becomes as important as the answer itself. Answers alone often fail to reveal the nature of a student's thinking, the strategies used in the problem-solving process, or the level of understanding. Additionally, the *Standards* document includes the expectation that students will be able to "relate their everyday language to mathematical language and symbols" (NCTM 1989, 26).

Using oral or written communication as a tool with which students can reflect their understanding of mathematics helps them make connections and personalize mathematical concepts. When students communicate mathematical information, they remember it, understand it, and use it to uncover and find even more information (Perkins 1992).

Teachers need to know how to help students grow into accomplished communicators of mathematics who can describe their thinking processes clearly. Teachers must help students make their thinking visible to others by encouraging them to talk and write about the process they use to solve problems.

The author's past efforts to encourage students to discuss and explain their problem-solving process have focused on (1) journal writing, (2) student-authored story problems, (3) the mathematician's chair, (4) cooperative-learning activities, and (5)

Larry Buschman *teaches a blended first-, second-, and third-grade classroom at Jefferson Elementary School, Jefferson, OR 97352. He is exploring the use of portfolios and rubrics to assess students' communication skills and mathematical understandings.*

parent newsletters. However, two articles in the May 1992 issue of *Educational Leadership*—"Creating Tests Worth Taking" by Grant Wiggins and "Evaluating Problem Solving in Mathematics" by Walter Szetela and Cynthia Nicol—present more ideas to add to the existing student-communication activities occurring in a second-grade classroom. The goal of embedding speaking and writing into the daily mathematical activities of students is being met through the following activities.

Mathematics Journal

Ask students to keep a mathematics journal, which not only can constitute a major part of the daily curriculum but, when added to a student's portfolio, can furnish an ongoing record of the student's mathematical growth.

In our classroom, students begin each day by recording statistical data related to the date, weather, and various problem-solving activities (fig. 1): (1) day, date, number of school days attended in the current school year, and number of school days remaining; (2) at least five number sentences that equal the date; (3) the weather report—temperature, precipitation, wind speed, wind direction, and cloud type; (4) predictions for the next day's weather and the color, size, and shape of the next day's calendar piece; (5)

answers to various measurement activities, such as the time shown on a Judy clock, the amount of money in a container, the weight of an object or group of objects, or an estimation of the quantity, weight, or length of an object using a standard for comparison; and (6) the solution to an open-ended mathematics problem.

At the end of each day, students use their journals to reflect on the day's mathematics activities. Students are asked to think about how they would answer such questions as "How did you help another person?" and "What did you learn that you did not know before?"

Student-Authored Story Problems

Ask students to create original story problems for someone else—a classmate, a teacher, a student in another classroom, or a family member—to solve.

The directions to the student include the following:

- Write a story problem using your imagination or the information in a picture, newspaper advertisement, poster, or short story.
- Have other people solve your problem.
- After seeing the solutions to your problem, lead a class discussion about your problem and the solutions.

Mathematician's Chair

Ask students to sit in a chair that has been designated the "mathematician's chair" and to share original problems that they have authored or solutions to a problem written by someone else.

A mathematician's chair is very similar to an author's chair, except that students share with their classmates mathematics problems and solutions rather than stories or books. Expect students, while in the math-

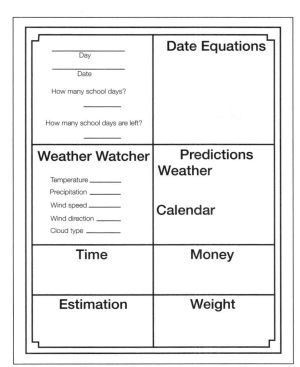 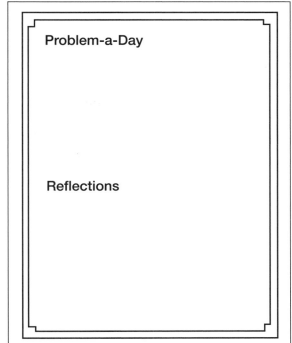

Fig. 1. Mathematics journal

ematician's chair, to use effective speaking skills and to communicate their thoughts clearly and completely. Also, expect classmates to use effective listening skills and to give the author useful and usable feedback:

- What did you like about the problem?
- Do you agree or disagree with the solution?
- How could the author improve the problem or solution?
- How could the author change the problem to create a new problem or change the solution to arrive at a new way to solve the problem?

Cooperative Learning

Have students engage in cooperative problem solving by asking them to describe the process that they will use to solve a problem, to work collaboratively on the problem, and to reflect on the effectiveness of the group and the contributions of individual members.

Talking with peers in cooperative-learning groups is especially important for young children. Students become comfortable with new words when they are free to experiment with language in a nonthreatening environment. To communicate their thinking to others more effectively, students must have frequent opportunities to

hear and speak mathematics with peers, teachers, and parents.

Family Newsletter

Ask students to write weekly or monthly "Family Newsletters."

Give the following directions to the students:

- Pretend you are a reporter for a newspaper. Write a story about something that occurred in mathematics class since the last "Family Newsletter." Use your journal and portfolio to help write the story.
- Ask at least two other students to listen to the story so that they can offer ideas for improvement.

Mathematics Communication Structures

"Mathematics communication structures" were created to add variety to students' communication tasks. Each structure listed subsequently was designed to give students a framework that supports and enhances the process of mathematical communication.

Structure 1

Present a problem and the answer arrived at by an imaginary person. Have the student

write a letter to this person, explaining agreement or disagreement with the answer.

- Directions to the student: (1) Write a letter to the person who solved this problem. (2) Explain why you agree or disagree with the answer.
- Sample problem: Which number does not belong? Kristina thinks the answer is 6.

$$\begin{array}{c|c} 6 & 12 \\ \hline 10 & 13 \end{array}$$

Structure 2

Present an already solved problem with a significant error. Have the student comment on the error by reacting to a series of questions about the solution.

- Directions to the student: (1) Read the problem and look at how this person solved the problem. (2) Answer each question that follows the problem.
- Sample problem: Chris and Bob have to be home by 9:00 P.M. It is now 7:00 P.M. How many hours may they play before they have to go home? Travis solved the problem this way.

$$\begin{array}{r} 9 \\ + 7 \\ \hline 16 \end{array} \quad \text{I say 16 hours.}$$

Explain whether Travis's reasoning was correct or incorrect.

Structure 3

Present a problem with all the facts and conditions, but have students write a different question for the problem. Have the students solve the new problem and tell why their new question made the problem more or less difficult to solve.

- Directions to the student: (1) Solve the problem as stated. (2) Write a different question but do not change any other part of the problem situation. (3) Solve the new problem and explain why this problem was easier or harder to solve than the original.

- Sample problem: This shape is made by stacking cubes on top of one another. How many cubes are in the bottom layer?

Structure 4

Present a problem and a partial solution. Have the students complete the solution.

- Directions to the student: (1) Finish the solution to this problem. (2) Describe another way to solve the problem.

- Sample problem: List all the ways that you could score 18 points by throwing two darts. Here is Aaron's partial solution:

One dart hit the 3 and the other dart hit the 15.

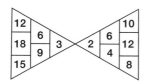

Structure 5

Present a problem with facts unrelated to the question. Have the students identify these facts and rewrite the problem, leaving out any irrelevant information.

- Directions to the student: (1) Which facts are not needed to solve the problem? (2) Rewrite the problem, leaving out any unneeded information. (3) Solve the problem.

- Sample problem: Farmer Brown has 10 cows and 23 horses. Farmer Smith has 16 cows and 17 horses. If Farmer Brown and Farmer Smith put all their cows in the same barn, how many cows would be in the barn? (Written by Melissa Santoyo, Jefferson Elementary School)

Structure 6

Present a problem and have the students explain how to solve the problem using only words. Have the students construct and solve a similar problem.

- Directions to the student: (1) Using only words, tell how you would solve this problem. (2) Write a similar problem and describe all the ways that the two problems are alike and different. (3) Solve the problem you wrote.

- Sample problem: Jill threw three darts at the target shown. What is the largest score she could make?

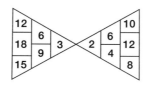

Structure 7

After the students have solved a problem, have them write a new problem with a different context, preserving the original problem structure.

- Directions to the student: (1) Solve the problem. (2) Tell how you solved the problem. (3) Write a new problem that can be solved in the same way. Give your problem to another person and check the solution.

- Sample problem: Tim and Bill are going camping for three days. The guidebook says that four campers need six liters of water for each day. How much water do you think that Tim and Bill should take on their camping trip? Explain your answer.

Structure 8

Present a problem without numerals. Have the students estimate the missing numbers, research appropriate numerals, and solve the problem. The problem should be based on a real-world situation—the missing information should be available to the student by gathering these data.

- Directions to the student: (1) Estimate the answer. (2) Complete the problem using the data you have gathered. (3) Solve the problem and tell how you found the answer.

- Sample problem: Mr. Buschman drives ____ miles to work each day. How many miles does he drive to work during October?

Structure 9

Present the students with a graph or table and have them write a story that represents the data on the graph or table.

- Directions to the student: Write a story about the data in this graph or table.

- Sample problem: Ben's shadow at the same time each day

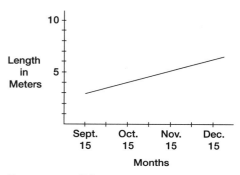

Structure 10

Present the students with trends or sample data. Ask them to make predictions to complete the table and write a story that includes the data in the table.

- Directions to the student: (1) Look carefully at the data. (2) Make predictions using the data and fill in the missing information in the table. (3) Explain why you think your predictions are accurate. (4) Write a story that includes the data in the table.

- Sample problem: Rainfall amounts measured in inches

	Portland	Jefferson	Baker	Astoria
Jan.	6.4	5.9	4.3	10.6
Feb.	6.8	6.2		11.3
Mar.		4.4	1.7	
Apr.	3.4	3.1	0.5	
May				7.5
June	1.0		0.0	4.3

Structure 11

Present the student with a real classroom problem that requires a group of students to share actual objects in the classroom or on the playground. Have the student develop and test a plan for sharing the objects.

- Directions to the student: (1) Make a plan for sharing the objects in the problem. (2) Test your plan to see how it works. (3) Have another student tell why he or she thinks your plan is fair or unfair. (4) Write your teacher a letter in which you describe your plan and tell how well your plan worked.
- Sample problem: You have ten students in your group, but your group has only two bags of pattern blocks. You will get to use the pattern blocks for twenty minutes each day this week. Only one student can use a bag of pattern blocks at a time. Develop a plan for how your group can share the two bags of pattern blocks.

Structure 12

Ask the students to write and publish an original story problem in the form of a "letter problem" (fig. 2). Once completed, letter problems are placed in classrooms through-out the school for other students to solve. Solutions are mailed to the problem's author through the in-school mail-delivery system.

- Directions to the student authoring a letter problem: (1) Write five original story problems. Meet with two other students and use consensus building to choose the best problem. (2) Edit and publish your problem. (3) Place several copies of your problem in chosen classrooms. (4) Read all solutions and reply to each person, telling why you agree or disagree with the solution.
- Directions to the student solving a letter problem: (1) Take one letter problem from the display. Solve the problem, write in detail how you found the answer, and tell why you think your answer is both correct and complete. (2) Mail your solution to the author of the problem through the in-school mail-delivery system. You will receive a reply in a few days.

Structure 13

Present the students with a very open-ended problem and have them request the information needed to solve the problem.

- Directions to the student: (1) Request any information you need to answer the question. (2) When you think you have enough information, solve the problem. (3) If you find that you need more information, request help from your teacher.
- Sample problem: How much will it cost for the second-grade field trip? When introducing this type of problem to students, begin with a whole-class activity using oral requests and responses, which are recorded and displayed on the overhead projector. As students become comfortable with making requests, ask them to work problems individually or in small groups and to make their requests in writing. By varying the type of information given to students, teachers can control the level of difficulty of the problem. For example, if a student asked, "How much does the bus for the field trip cost?" one of the following replies could be given: $150.00; each bus costs $75.00; each bus costs $55.00 for the driver and $20.00 for gasoline; or each bus costs $8.35 an hour for the driver and $0.05 a mile for the gasoline.

Fig. 2. Letter problem

Structure 14

Ask the students to revise a fairy tale or folk tale to include numerical information. This new version of the tale can then be used as a source for generating story problems.

- Directions to the student: (1) Pick a favorite fairy tale or folk tale. Read the tale you have chosen to an adult. (2) Rewrite the tale by adding numerical information. (3) Write five story questions that someone else could answer using the added information.

- Sample tale: "The Five Bears" by Andrea Kachel, grade 2, Jefferson Elementary School

Once upon a time there were five bears. The Papa bear was the oldest. He was 39 years old. Next came the Mama bear. She was 35 years old. Next came their son, Andrew. He was 18 years old. Next came Andrea. She was 9 years old. Last came Jessica. She was 3 years old and a real brat. Every day Mama bear would leave for work at 7:00 in the morning and she would get home at 5:00 in the afternoon. The children left for school at 8:00 in the morning and came home on the hot, noisy, bumpy bus at 3:30. Papa bear took baby Jessica to the day care at 9:00 in the morning on his way to work in the honey factory.

Conclusion

Students need time to observe, to work together, and to construct an understanding of the language of mathematics and to make it their own. Personal knowledge becomes useful and usable in social situations when combined with the knowledge of others. Thoughts, ideas, and the meanings of words are focused and clarified when individuals engage in conversation.

As soon as students use words, they make their understanding of mathematics more precise and more general at the same time. Only by using words in many situations and contexts do students come to understand the full meaning of each word. When students write or talk about mathematics problems, they test, expand, and extend their understanding of mathematics. When students write or speak, they do not use language just to express their thoughts; they use the process of communicating with others to engage in a conversation with their own mind.

References

National Council of Teachers of Mathematics. *Curriculum and Evaluation Standards for School Mathematics.* Reston, Va.: The Council, 1989.

Perkins, David. *Smart Schools: From Training Memories to Educating Minds.* New York: The Free Press, 1992.

Szetela, Walter, and Cynthia Nicol. "Evaluating Problem Solving in Mathematics." *Educational Leadership* 49 (May 1992): 42–45.

Wiggins, Grant. "Creating Tests Worth Taking." *Educational Leadership* 49 (May 1992): 26–33.

Bibliography

Andrini, Beth, and Spencer Kagan. *Cooperative Learning and Mathematics.* San Juan Capistrano, Calif.: Resources for Teachers, 1989.

Cambourne, Brian. *The Whole Story: Natural Learning and the Acquisition of Literacy in the Classroom.* New York: Ashton Scholastic, 1988.

Goodman, Ken. *What's Whole in Whole Language?* Portsmouth, N.H.: Heinemann Educational Books, 1986.

Johnson, Terry, and Daphne Louis. *Bringing It All Together: A Program for Literacy.* Portsmouth, N.H.: Heinemann Educational Books, 1990.

Routman, Regie. *Invitations: Changing as Teachers and Learners K–12.* Portsmouth, N.H.: Heinemann Educational Books, 1991

MARGARET E. McINTOSH

500+ Writing Formats

AS MATHEMATICS teachers, we realize that we need to have our students write as one of the ways of "learning to communicate mathematically," as recommended by NCTM's *Curriculum and Evaluation Standards for School Mathematics* (1989). The *Standards* document expands on this idea (p. 6) by stating,

> The development of a student's power to use mathematics involves learning the signs, symbols, and terms of mathematics. This is best accomplished in problem situations in which students have an opportunity to read, write, and discuss ideas in which the use of the language of mathematics becomes natural. As students communicate their ideas, they learn to clarify, refine, and consolidate their thinking.

The suggestions presented in this article offer a multitude of opportunities for students to communicate their ideas in writing, using the language of mathematics.

These writing ideas were generated when I began looking at Tchudi and Huerta's (1983) list of approximately 100 discourse forms for content writing, with the intent of applying these discourse forms to writing in the mathematics classroom. As I compiled the list, I started adding to it and eventually generated over 500 different writing formats. Since then, neither I nor any of the teachers with whom I have shared this list has ever again felt at a loss when trying to develop writing tasks for our students. Even the most talented and prolific writer or

Margaret McIntosh, *mcintosh@pogonip.scs.unr.edu, teaches at the University of Nevada, Reno, NV 89557-0029. She is interested in investigating reading and writing strategies that help students learn in mathematics.*

lesson-plan maker will be unable to run through all these format suggestions!

The following bulleted list is selected from a compilation of over 500 writing formats, a sample of which is shown in figure 1. For a complete list, send a self-addressed, stamped envelope to the author or contact her by e-mail at the address given here. A sample abbreviated writing task is included for each prompt in the following list, and three of the prompts show the full writing assignment that was given, along with a sample student response to each.

- **Abridgment:** Write an abridgment to solving a linear equation.
- **Address:** Provide the address of the vertex angle in an isosceles triangle.
- **Advice column:** Write an advice column for fellow mathematics students.
- **Alternative to counting sheep (for insomniacs):** Count prime numbers.
- **Analogy:** Write an analogy that describes the relationship between factoring and multiplying binomials.
- **Anecdote:** Write an anecdote about pi (π).
- **Anthem:** What would be the words to the "Mathematics Anthem"?
- **Assumption:** Write three mathematical assumptions in complete sentences.
- **Bedtime story:** Write a story about a line, beginning with "Once upon a time there was a line …" and telling how it grows and has a relationship with, or becomes, a circle, angle, triangle, ray, line segment, or the like.
- **Biographical sketch:** Write a biographical sketch of any female mathematician currently living.

- **Boast:** Boast about everything you know about a topic in mathematics.
- **Calendar quip:** Make up a mathematical quip to be used for each month on a calendar.
- **Code:** Write a secret code to your boyfriend or girlfriend using mathematical symbols, numbers, or equations.
- **Commercial:** You are the producer of a television commercial. You have $20 000 to spend. Devise your budget and justify it to the client.
- **Complaint:** Write a letter to a member of Congress complaining about the customary system of measurement and wondering when the United States will be going metric.
- **Consequence:** What is the consequence for answering an integer problem with the wrong sign?
- **Diet:** Look at the diet-meal outline and calorie counter you have been given. As a dietitian, plan meals limited to a certain caloric amount and write out your recommendations for your patient.
- **Elogium:** Pi (π) has died. The elogium should reflect its status and position in the world.
- **Epilogue:** Write the epilogue of your mathematics career.
- **Epitome:** Describe the epitome of a mathematician.
- **Explanation:** Write an explanation of why you need to know the Pythagorean theorem.
- **Fable:** Read a fable and write a word problem based on the story in the fable. (See **fig. 2.**)
- **Family tree:** Make a "family tree" of mathematics-related topics, skills, numbers, and so on.

abbreviation	anything written in	birth announcement	cinquain
ABCs of something	runic characters	blessing	cipher
abecedarian	aphorism	boast	clue
abridgment	apologue	book	code
absolution	apology	book jacket	collection notice
abstract	appeal	book review	college-application
acceptance speech	application	bookplate	letter
accolade	article	brochure	comic strip
account of . . .	ascription	bulletin	commemoration
acknowledgment	assembly directions	bumper sticker	commendation
acronym	assertion	calendar	concatenation
adaptation	assignment	calendar quip	confession
address	assumption	calorie chart	confutation
address book	astrological prediction	campaign speech	congratulatory note
advertisement	autobiography	cantata	conjecture
advice column	award	captain's log	consequence
agenda	axiom	caption	contest rules
agreement	baby book	cartoon	contract
aha!	baccalaureate address	case study	conundrum
allegory	ballad	catalog description	conversation
alternative to counting	ballot	censure	convocation
sheep (for insomniacs)	banner for display	character sketch	correspondence
amendment	beauty tip	charter	(series of)
analogy	bedtime story	checkbook register	counterfeit document
anecdote	beginning	cheer	couplet
annotation	belief	children's book	covenant
announcement	bill of lading	choral reading	cover letter
anthem	bill of sale	chorus	creed
anthology	billboard	chronicle	critique
anything boustrophedonic	biographical sketch	church bulletin	
	biography		

Fig. 1. A few of the 500+ writing formats

Read several of the fables that I have brought to class. Then, choose one to use as a basis for a word problem. Your word problem will include the information from the fable, so it will be much longer than typical word problems (but more like real-life word problems). You will give this problem to someone else in the class who will solve it. Be sure you have included all the information that someone will need to solve the problem.

The hare ran 60 mph ⎤ the race is 60
The tortoise ran 20 mph ⎦ miles long

The Hare + the tortoise raced, starting at the same place following the same path, ~~the hare ran~~ which was 60 miles to the finish. The hare ran at the speed of 60 mph, + the tortoise ran 20 mph for the whole race. The hare got cocky and sat down for a nap + slept for 3 hrs. Who won?

Fig. 2. Fable-writing task and a student's response

- **Filibuster:** Filibuster a math fact. Write out your ideas first.
- **Folderol:** Identify some folderol in the current chapter. Explain why it should be removed from our textbook.
- **Folktale:** Turn a word problem into a folktale, or vice versa.
- **Habit:** Describe how to improve your mathematics test scores by improving your study habits.
- **Hagiography:** Create a patron saint of mathematics. Explain why you chose her or him.
- **Hyperbole:** Write a story problem involving hyperbole about a geometric shape.
- **Index:** Index your own mathematics notes.
- **Insult:** Use mathematical terminology to write an insult—appropriate to the meaning of the term, of course.
- **Interview:** Write questions for an interview that you will conduct with someone in the workforce about how mathematics is used in her or his job.
- **Justification:** Write a justification for each mistake you made on the last mathematics test.
- **Lampoon:** Write a lampoon of your mathematics teacher.
- **Letters of credence:** Solicit letters of credence from mathematicians advocating or defending the use of calculators in the classroom and on standardized tests.
- **Lie:** Write four correct statements or four correct equations about mathematics and one lie. Give to someone else to choose the false one and write why it is false, or a lie.
- **List:** List steps in solving problems.
- **List of items for sale at an auction:** Write a list of items to be auctioned off and include their prices. Buy $75 worth of items. What did you buy? Why?
- **Memory:** Make up a mnemonic to memorize the quadratic formula.
- **Myth:** What are your misconceptions about mathematics, class, or me?

ACTIVITIES FOR JUNIOR HIGH AND MIDDLE SCHOOL MATHEMATICS

- **Palindrome:** Make up your own mathematics term that is a palindrome. Give it a definition.
- **Pedigree:** Explain how numbers can be used when figuring out a pedigree.
- **Poster:** Make a poster to relate an equation of a line to snow skiing, showing positive and negative slope.
- **Prescription:** Write a prescription for being a good mathematics student.
- **Probability:** What is the probability that a basketball player with a 40 percent shooting average will make two shots in a one-and-one situation? Explain how you arrived at your answer.
- **Quip:** Write a quip to help you remember a mathematical formula.
- **Rondeau:** Write a mathematics rondeau that will help you on your next test. (I promise to include it in the test!)
- **Rules of etiquette:** Make up a rule of mathematical etiquette (e.g., check your work when you are finished).
- **Sale notice:** Design a sale notice in which the percent of discount is used in two different ways.
- **Self-description:** Describe yourself geometrically.

- **Sermon:** Write a sermon preaching the value of knowing your multiplication tables.
- **Speech:** Write a speech you would make to next year's mathematics students. (See **fig. 3.**)
- **Spelling bee:** Create a spelling list of names of occupations that use mathematics.
- **Supervisor's report:** Write a supervisor's report on your employee, a cashier, telling him or her why it is important to improve mathematics skills.
- **Survival guide:** Write a survival guide for this class. It *will* be passed along to the next class, so make it useful!
- **Syllogism:** Write an illogical syllogism and explain why it cannot happen.
- **Tall tale:** Write a tall tale explaining how natural numbers become radical.
- **Trivia:** Use a recent *Guinness Book of World Records* and find what you think to be the most trivial statistic; explain your reasoning.

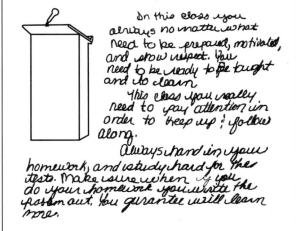

If I could give a speech to students coming into your algebra class next year, here is what I would say in my speech....

Think hard about this because you might actually get to give it!

Fig. 3. Speech-writing task and a student's response

- **True-false statements:** Given a mathematics equation, determine whether the statement is true or false and explain why.
- **T-shirt:** Create a T-shirt that shows something you have learned in mathematics. (See **fig. 4.**)

Design a T-shirt that advertises something you have learned in mathematics this summer. Your T-shirt may have both graphics and words. Take time to sketch and write out your ideas before you design your final product. (We may actually produce some of the really good ideas on real T-shirts, if the class wants to!)

(a) Front of shirt

(1000 doors are in a row, numbered 1, 2, 3 – 1000.

1000 people go down the line of doors.

– 1st person opens all the doors.

– 2nd person goes to every 2nd door and closes them.

– 3rd person goes to every 3rd door and if the door is open, the person closes it and if it is closed, then the person opens the door

– 4th person goes to every 4th door and repeats #3

– 5th person goes to every fifth door and repeats #3

– 1000th person goes to the 1000th door and opens it if closed and closes if open.

Question: How many doors are open? How many doors are closed?

Only doors that are perfect squares will be open. For example, in the number sequence 1, 2, 3, 4, 5, 6, 7, 8, 9, 10, only doors 1, 4, & 9 are open. This is true because 1, 4, and 9 are perfect squares. So you can find out which doors are going to be open if you just multiply the number by its self.

The next open doors will be 16 (4×4), 25 (5×5), 36 (6×6), 49 (7×7), etc.

Since door 956 is not a perfect square, the door is closed.

(b) Back of shirt

Fig. 4. T-shirt–designing task and a student's design

- **Wanted poster:** Write word problems in the form of "Wanted—Dead or Alive"— a variable that solves the following . . . .
- **Wise saying:** Collect as many sayings that contain numbers as you can, for example, "six of one, half-a-dozen of another."
- **Wish:** I wish this problem would . . . .
- **Written apology for maladroitness:** Write an apology for doing a problem incorrectly or making a dumb mistake.
- **Yarn:** Rewrite one of your homework word problems as a yarn.
- **Yearbook inscription:** Write out the yearbook description that you would put in a person's yearbook, basing it on his or her personality in mathematics class.
- **Yellow pages:** List the types of mathematics necessary for the businesses listed in the yellow pages.

The more than 500 formats, a few of which are shown in figure 1, lend themselves to writing tasks of every length— from bumper stickers to encyclopedia entries to plays to treatises. I find that this variety keeps the writing fresh. A number of ways can be used to present these tasks to students.

1. Print all the writing formats on cards that students can go through whenever they need a fresh suggestion.
2. Print all the writing formats on posters and hang them around the room for inspiration—yours and the students'.
3. Keep a notebook of the writing formats, and of former students' creations based on the writing formats, where current students can access them.

4. Keep the writing formats for yourself to use when creating new lesson plans.
5. Present the writing formats to students with the challenge that they see what new ideas they can add to the list, since 500 or so can seem limiting!

Creating Your Own Writing Tasks for Mathematics

The way other teachers and I have worked with the list of over 500 writing ideas—and the way that you can, too—is to focus on an objective that we have in mathematics, such as, "Students will be able to use the correct mathematical language to describe various types of triangles." Then we look over the list of over 500 writing formats with an eye to finding one or more that will allow us to create a writing assignment that requires students to practice or demonstrate their acquisition of the objectives. For example, in looking over the list, I think that "acceptance speech" is the format I want to use to go along with the previously mentioned objective about triangles. The writing task I create for students is as follows:

Write an acceptance speech made by any type of triangle. In this speech, have the winning triangle note all his/her/its unique qualities and have him/her/it recognize the special qualities of all the other types of triangles.

For students to complete this task, they have to know all the characteristics of each different kind of triangle. In addition, they have a chance to *think about* and *write* the mathematical language in a creative way. These assignments are a wonderful way to involve students who may be less involved with some of the other learning tasks in mathematics. As a side benefit, these writings are fun to read and grade!

I encourage you to generate your own writing assignments that allow students to think about mathematics as they communicate through writing. Send your favorites to *Mathematics Teaching in the Middle School* for consideration for "The Thinking of Students" section. We will appreciate seeing what you and your students have done!

References

National Council of Teachers of Mathematics. *Curriculum and Evaluation Standards for School Mathematics.* Reston, Va.: The Council, 1989.

Tchudi, Stephen N., and Margie C. Huerta. *Teaching Writing in the Content Areas: Middle School/ Junior High.* Washington, D.C.: National Education Association, 1983. C

KAREN S. NORWOOD AND GLENDA CARTER

Journal Writing:
An Insight into Students' Understanding

DURING the first ten minutes of our fifth-grade mathematics class, students are busily writing in their journals. We use journal writing to focus students on a review or to assess their ideas about a topic before its introduction. We have also used this activity to assess how well students understand a topic in progress. We find that journal writing often brings to light thoughts and understandings that typical classroom interactions or tests do not elucidate. An example of this type of journal writing is illustrated in figure 1. As is evident from the product of the writing task, this student can do a multiplication problem algorithmically but lacks a conceptual understanding of the operation. This student's lack of understanding can be further explored by other journal writings or by a direct interview to find out where the student has gotten off track. Journal writing enables us to recognize that this student needs remediation.

Because we have experienced some roadblocks in incorporating journal writing into the classroom, we would like to offer the following suggestions:

1. Since students are often more resistant to new processes and procedures once the school year has started, we recommend introducing journal writing at the beginning of the school year. Let students know that journal writing is an expected activity for mathematics class that can give them a greater understanding of mathematics and give the teacher a better understanding of

A fifth-grade student is communicating her understanding of the day's lesson to her teacher.

their knowledge of mathematics. Explain the reasons for asking them to write.

2. Prepare a special booklet journal in which students can take pride and over which they can have ownership.

Suggest that they submit drawings for the cover of the journal. Duplicate the cover on colored paper, fold the cover, and insert plain white pages. A sample cover, such as the one in figure 2, serves to illustrate to the students that this product is special and is to be used only for their thoughts about mathematics.

3. Decide how long to allow students to write; set an egg timer to go off when time has expired.

4. Since students tend to write more if they are instructed to address their comments to a friend or family member, have them write to someone specific.

5. Clearly explain your expectations to your students, and give them details concerning how their writing will be evaluated.

6. Introduce journal writing by using exercises that are affective in nature (see fig. 3). For instance, students are able to respond more easily to a question such as "How did taking the math test make

Karen Norwood *teaches at North Carolina State University, Raleigh, NC 27695. She has written supplementary materials for alternative assessment for several textbook companies.* Glenda Carter *is the Associate Director of the Center for Research in Mathematics and Science Education at the same university. Her research focuses on alternative assessment.*

Fig. 1. Student's journal writing on multiplication

MY MATH JOURNAL

BY:

Fig. 2. Sample journal cover

you feel?" than to a cognitive question such as "Explain how to subtract 1/5 from 1/2."

7. Respond to the students' writings on a frequent basis. Let the students know that what they write is indeed being read. Reading five journals a night is a realistic goal. The wealth of information that can be gained from the journal is worth the time it takes to read and respond to students.

8. Don't give up. Be patient. Students who are unaccustomed to writing in mathematics class may become frustrated. It will take time for students to understand their teacher's expectations for them.

9. Join the students in writing. Address the topic from a teacher's point of view. Share your writings with your students.

10. Exhibit, with students' permission, those writings that most closely illustrate desirable characteristics, such as clear, concise explanations and creative word problems.

Like most worthwhile endeavors, helping students produce journal writing that will affect their understanding of mathematics and illustrate their feelings and knowledge of mathematics will require time and patience. It will also require practice on the students' part. The following prompts might help students start their journal writing. The topics in parentheses can be changed to reflect curriculum content in a given classroom.

1. Write a "mathematics autobiography." Describe your earliest experiences in mathematics both in and outside of school.

2. Explain in your own words the meaning of (area, perimeter, ratio).

3. Explain what is most important to understand about (adding fractions with unlike denominators; multiplying decimals).

4. Describe any places you became stuck when solving a problem, and tell what you did to get unstuck.

5. What I like most (or least) about mathematics is

_____

_____

_____

6. Write a letter to a student who will be taking this class next year, giving some advice about this class.

7. Something I'd really like to know about mathematics is

_____

_____

_____

8. The most important thing I learned about mathematics this week is

_____

_____

_____

Sometimes teachers may wish to have

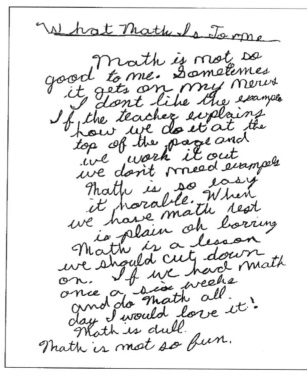

Fig. 3. Students' feelings about mathematics

ACTIVITIES FOR JUNIOR HIGH AND MIDDLE SCHOOL MATHEMATICS

students do expository writing. The following examples are the types of questions to which students can be asked to respond in their journals.

1. Write a story problem that can be solved by using $12 \times 7 = 84$.
2. Find a graph in a newspaper or magazine. Write a paragraph about what the graph represents and why the graph is drawn the way it is.
3. Please draw a picture, a diagram, or a model to illustrate ($1/3 \times 1/2$; the difference between area and perimeter).
4. Your best friend was absent from school today. Write a letter to him or her to explain what you learned in mathematics class.
5. Explain to your cousin how multiplication is like addition. You may use pictures or graphs.
6. Explain to your cousin how division is like subtraction. You may use pictures or graphs.
7. Explain to your sister or brother in fourth grade how to add 1/2 and 1/3. Be specific. You may use pictures or graphs.
8. How do you use fractions in your life?
9. How are fractions and decimals alike? Different?

The NCTM's *Curriculum and Evaluation Standards for School Mathematics* (1989) calls for teaching students to communicate mathematically. Journal writing in the mathematics classroom offers students that opportunity. It enables students to use the skills of reading, listening, viewing, and questioning to interpret and evaluate mathematical ideas. Journal writing can also be designed to allow students to explore connections within mathematics and between mathematics and other subjects. When journal writing occurs regularly, students learn to value the opportunity to reflect on their new learning and relate their new learning to what they already know.

A better understanding of students' thinking in mathematics is needed if mathematics education is to be improved. Research has indicated that many traditional tests are not giving a clear enough picture of students' conceptual development in mathematics to assess their progress or misunderstandings. Journal writing is a simple, inexpensive tool for alternatively evaluating students' progress.

Bibliography

McIntosh, Margaret E. "No Time for Writing in Your Class?" *Mathematics Teacher* 84 (September 1991):423-33.

National Council of Teachers of Mathematics. *Curriculum and Evaluation Standards for School Mathematics.* Reston, Va.: The Council, 1989.

Stenmark, Jean. *Alternative Assessments in Mathematics.* Berkeley, Calif.: University of California, 1989.

Math News Gazette

Student Activity Goals

- Students will communicate about mathematics using a class newspaper.
- Students will work on problems and share the results in a special section of the newspaper.
- Students will report how school personnel, parents, and community leaders use mathematics in their everyday lives and careers.
- Students will use their measurement skills to format the newspaper.
- Students will read about, and report on, books with mathematical themes or content.
- Students will write a critique of mathematics software for a section of the newspaper.
- Students will learn to value the uses of mathematics in everyday life.

Planning for Instruction

If the *Math News Gazette* is to work in a classroom, the project needs to be carefully planned. The tips that follow are designed to work with the format and headlines shown on the student sheet, but teachers are encouraged to have students develop their own headlines and column headings. This activity can be a class project or used for small-group work for several issues.

For a column titled "A Day in the Math Life of My Family," we suggest that students consider a theme, such as Math in the Home, Math at My Mom's Job, or Math on the Way to School. If a child chooses Math in the Home, then such things as meal portions, grocery shopping, bus fares, allowances, or television viewing times might be considered.

The "Interviews" section might feature interviews with other teachers in the school, the principal, the lunchroom director, or leaders in the community. Students could develop a series of questions that could be used with several different people, then compare the responses from those people about how they use mathematics in their everyday lives and in their careers. This pursuit might lead to interesting answers to the question "When are we ever going to use this?"

"Making Cents" might include actual shopping exercises or advertisements with comparison shopping questions. It might also include articles that discuss penny shortages or related problems, such as taking a handful of pennies and graphing the set of mint dates. Students might dig into fictional pieces to include some mathematics about why a penny shortage exists.

For "My House Is Shaping Up," various articles might include a piece on stairs and why they are *x* inches high, how to design a house without stairs for a disabled person, or what shapes one might want to use in a house with small children or visually challenged people.

"What Counts?" "Pattern Mania," and "Check It Out" can be columns with non-routine problems presented for the students to solve. Students could be encouraged to submit their solutions for publication in future editions. "Math by the Month" in this journal may present ideas for these columns.

"The Day the Numbers Disappeared" might contain interviews with people concerning what they would miss if numbers disappeared. Students might write stories about a world where numbers did not exist and how people coped with that problem. Students could conjecture about the way different occupations might be affected if no numbers existed and how those jobs would be changed.

"Who's Who in Math" could feature an outstanding student or adult who works with mathematics, or the teacher could use historical mathematics figures. This article could showcase students with special talents in mathematics.

To prepare for "Book Reviews," the teacher might collect titles mentioned in "Links to Literature" or in the "Reviewing and Viewing" section for student use.

Parents could be involved with interviews and discuss how they use mathematics both at home and at work. They could help with the layout and display of the newspaper. If they work in the newspaper business, they could discuss how a newspaper is written, printed, and distributed.

Math Times Herald

Student Activity Goals

- Students will communicate mathematics ideas using a class newspaper.
- Students will interview school personnel, parents, and community leaders about the ways they use mathematics at home and at work.
- Students will use measurement skills or desktop publishing software to determine layouts for the newspaper.
- Students will gather information on the costs of advertising in the newspaper and graph the results of their data collection.
- Students will read and report on books with mathematical topics and content.
- Students will research mathematical topics and write articles for the newspaper.

Planning for Instruction

If the *Math Times Herald* is to be a successful class project, careful planning is essential. Teachers may want to assign different research and writing teams to each issue if more than one is to be published during the year. The suggestions that follow are designed to work with the format and headlines on the student page, but teachers are encouraged to have students develop their own headlines and column headings. This activity can be a class project, or several small groups can be responsible for writing separate issues. Students can generate their own topics for articles and research that showcase their expertise and interests.

The column titled "Daily Newsworthy Mathematics" might include subsections with weather statistics, school sports statistics, or results of surveys or data gathered by the class. "Break the Math Code" might contain number-pattern problems, cryptograms, or articles on the development of Morse code or Braille with examples for students to decode. An issue of *Student Math Notes* (May 1989) contained an article called "Ciphers," which is good background information for this section.

"Math Mystery Uncovered" might include the teacher's collecting mathematics headlines from tabloids and letting students write related stories. An example would be "*Math Times Herald* writers have 24 heads and 48 legs." Of course, the writers are the class of students. "Dollar Daze" could include an estimation of the school budget and how it translates to x allowances, n loaves of bread, or y pizzas. It might include a survey on the average allowance of the class and ways to ask for a higher allowance. This section could compare exchange rates of foreign currency.

"A Meaningful Moment in Math" could feature an adult or student. Spotlighting a local event or person gives special significance to communications. A special column might feature how to price the newspaper and why. "Numbers Disappear!" might be a series of interviews with parents, teachers, administrators, or community leaders and the effect that living without numbers might have on them. Students could write fantasy stories about civilizations without numbers and how peoples' lives are affected.

Teachers should be encouraged to emphasize the coordination of writing and the use of figures and graphs. The four styles of writing—persuasive, informative, literary, and expressive—can also be emphasized.

Parents could be involved in helping students explore the use of desktop-publishing software to develop the newspaper and could help coauthor several of the columns. Adults who work in the newspaper business could speak to the class about writing and publishing a newspaper, including selling advertisements to cover costs.

Math Times Herald

February, Vol. 1

A Day in the Math Life of My Family

It all started when the alarm went off and I looked to see what time it was....

Interviews

My mom is a police officer, and I interviewed her to find out how she uses math in her job. This is what I found out....

A Meaningful Moment in Math

Sir Edmund Hillary and Tenzing Norgay were the first individuals to climb Mount Everest. At a critical moment, they had to calculate how much oxygen they had and how much they would use in their climb to the top....

Math Mystery Uncovered

Did you ever wonder what they used to measure tall objects or long distances hundreds of years ago? Here's what I found out....

Dollar Daze

Imagine that all A's are worth $0.01, all B's are worth $0.02, all C's are worth $0.03, etc. Find a word that is worth exactly $1.00.

Book Reviews

Watch how Milo makes his way through the numbers in *The Phantom Tollbooth*....

Break the Math Code

3, 5, 7, 11, 13, ____, ____

2, 6, 10, 14, 18, ____, ____

45, 38, 31, _____, ____

Daily Newsworthy Mathematics

Our class decided to take a survey to find out what kind of math was used most by fourth, fifth, and sixth graders. Do you use addition, mental math, estimation, ...?

BULLETIN
Numbers Disappear!

Numbers have totally disappeared. Here's what life is like without numbers....

FRANCES R. CURCIO, MYRA ZARNOWSKI, AND SUSAN VIGLIAROLO

Mathematics and Poetry:
Problem Solving in Context

ALTHOUGH many elementary school teachers routinely share poetry with their students to foster an appreciation of language and literature, poetry can also promote the learning of mathematics. Many poems—through rhythm, rhyme, story, and interesting word choices—evoke situations that engage children and can serve as a basis for mathematical problem solving.

Some ideas and activities designed to integrate poetry into the third-grade mathematics curriculum are presented in this article. The discussion demonstrates how a humorous poem sparked a great deal of lively talk about mathematics and involve third graders in estimating, devising and comparing problem-solving strategies, creating their own mathematical poems, and posing original problems based on their poems. Other poems have similar potential for strengthening students' interest and involvement in mathematics. Suggestions for selecting poetry to complement the mathematics curriculum are included, along with an annotated list of poems, called a "poemography," which is arranged by mathematics content.

Although these activities were implemented in a third-grade class, many of the ideas could be adapted for younger as well as older children on the basis of their interests and abilities. This approach begins with using poetry to generate ideas about mathematics. After sharing problem-solving strategies, children create their own poems using mathematical ideas. Children return to the mathematics as they share their original poems and pose and solve problems related to their friends' writing.

From Poetry to Mathematics

To begin, the classroom teacher read "Smart," "The Googies Are Coming," "Band-Aids," and "Overdues" by Shel Silverstein (1974, 1981). The poems were already familiar to many of the children, since they had been made available during sustained silent-reading time. Before making connections with mathematics, the teacher read the poems aloud to the children, enjoying the language, the sounds, and the thoughts expressed in the poems. She then posed the following question: "What do these poems have in common?" The children responded enthusiastically, noting that all the poems had numbers in them, all rhymed, and all were written by the same author.

To pursue the mathematics objectives for the class of estimating and solving problems with large numbers, the teacher decided to focus on Silverstein's poem "Overdues" (see fig. l). Since the poem deals with a potentially large, but unspecified, amount of money owed as a library fine for an outlandishly overdue book, it set the stage for problem solving in a meaningful yet humorous context.

After several children volunteered to read "Overdues" aloud, the class read the poem together. Since the poem ends with a question, the teacher asked the class, "Well, what should he do?" Suggestions included keeping the book or returning it, which prompted the opportunity for discussing the responsibilities related to borrowing library books. The children described what they would do. Jackie responded, "Pay the fine and be broke." When the teacher inquired why she would be broke, Jackie said, "Because I'd have to pay a lot of money for forty-two years." This reason led naturally to key aspects of the lesson: *estimating* the fine for the overdue book, *formulating* and *solving* a problem related to the situation, *comparing* estimates and computed amounts, and *extending* the problem

Estimating

The teacher probed, "How much does an overdue book cost for one day at your

Frances Curcio *and* Myra Zarnowski *are associate professors in elementary education at Queens College of the City University of New York, Flushing, NY 11367. Curcio is interested in the language of mathematics and communicating in the mathematics classroom. Zarnowski is interested in using literature in content-area studies. Susan Vigliarolo, an advocate of whole language and interdisciplinary, thematic instruction, was teaching third grade at Public School 146Q, Howard Beach, NY 11414, at the time this article was written.*

Edited by Diane Thiessen. *University of Northern Iowa, Cedar Falls, IA 50614-0506.*

MATHEMATICS AS COMMUNICATION

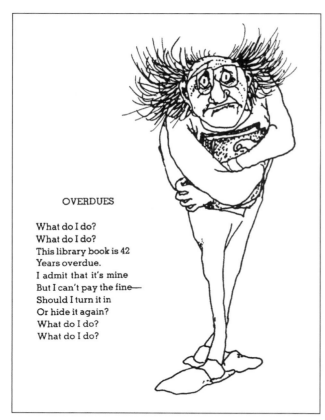

library?" Eric said that his library charges $0.10 a day. Although other children had suggested various amounts, the class decided to use Eric's rate. The teacher then asked the children, "How much money do you think the character in the poem owes for the overdue book?"

As the children offered estimates of $4.20, $50, $1000, $1001, $600, and $400, the teacher recorded them on chart paper, which remained visible during the next phase of the activity.

Formulating and Solving

Vinnie phrased the problem as follows: "How much does he have to pay for the library book that costs $0.10 a day for 42 years?" The children agreed with his phrasing and set to work, using a variety of strategies to solve the problem. Calculators expedited the computation.

Eric began by finding out the number of days in one year and multiplying by 42 years to find the total number of days the book was overdue. He entered 365×42 into the calculator and noted that the book was 15 330 days overdue. Then he multi-

plied 15 330 days by $0.10 a day and found that the character in the poem owed the library $1 533.

Jackie decided to estimate 30 days in a month, multiply by the number of months in a year, and multiply by the number of years to get the number of days that the book was overdue. Her calculation yielded about 15 120 days. When she multiplied 15 120 days by $0.10 a day, she found that the character owed about $1 512.

Shazim began with 7 days in a week. He multiplied by $0.10 a day and found that the rate for each week was $0.70. He estimated that a month has 4 weeks and multiplied 4 by $0.70 to get the amount owed in one month, $2.80. He then multiplied $2.80 a month by 12 months in a year, or $33.60. Multiplying $33.60 a year by 42 years yielded $1 411.20.

Stephanie started with 12 months in a year and multiplied by 42 years to determine the number of months the book was overdue. Then using Jackie's estimate of 30 days in a month, she found the

monthly overdue rate to be $3. She multiplied 504 months by $3 a month and found that the character owed $1 512.

Comparing

As the children shared their strategies, they realized that different strategies yielded different solutions. They questioned each other to make sure that the different strategies made sense. For example, Chris asked Shazim why he did not use 52 weeks in a year. Shazim said that he estimated that each month has about 4 weeks and he based his calculation on this estimate. Using his calculator, Chris found that $0.70 a week times 52 weeks a year yields $36.40 a year. The total amount owed after 42 years would be $1 528.80, much closer to the amounts calculated by Eric, Jackie, and Stephanie. See figure 2.

When the children compared their original estimates with the actual calculations, everyone agreed that the estimate of $1001 was the closest. By revising their initial estimates, the children had the opportunity to evaluate and refine their thinking beyond mere guessing.

Extending

Once the problem was solved and strategies were shared, children were prepared to talk about ways to change the problem.

Child	Strategy	Solution
Eric	365 days × 42 years = 15 330 days 15 330 days × $0.10 a day	= $1 533
Jackie	30 days in a month × 12 months in a year × 42 years = 15 120 days 15 120 days × $0.10 a day	= 1 512
Shazim	7 days in a week × $0.10 a day × 4 weeks in a month × 12 months in a year = $33.60 year $33.60 a year × 42 years	= $1 411.20
Stephanie	12 months in a year × 42 years × 30 days in a month = 15 120 days 15 120 days × $0.10 a day	= $1 512
Chris	7 days in a week × $0.10 a day × 52 weeks in a year = $36.40 a year $36.40 a year × 42 years	= $1 528.80

Fig. 2. Problem-solving strategies used by third graders for compute the amount of an overdue fine at $0.10 a day for forty-two years

They were asked to consider a situation in which a librarian gives the character in the poem a choice. He could either pay $0.10 a day for 42 years, that is, pay about $1533, or he could pay the amount arrived at by doubling $0.01 for 30 days. The children were asked to estimate the cost of doubling $0.01 each day for 30 days and to recommend an option for the character in the poem. Additionally, they were asked to explain their reasoning.

Before computing, the children gave the following estimates: $0.40; $10; $30; $20; $1000; $16; $100. After making the problem simpler by comparing $0.10 a day for 5 days, that is, $0.50, with doubling $0.01 cent for 5 days, that is $0.16, Jackie suggested the 30-day option. Most of the children in the class were convinced by her example. Rafael thought that the 42-year option was better because it would be easier to compute.

The children worked in pairs to double $0.01 for 30 days. Jackie and Chris constructed a table, systematically listing the 30 days and the doubled amount from the preceding day (see fig. 3). When they got to the tenth day, Jackie remarked, "Oh, no! It's better to pay $1 512. " On the tenth day, doubling $0.01 yielded $5.12, whereas paying $0.10 a day yielded only $1.00. Chris used a calculator to check Jackie's doubles. They agreed that on the thirtieth day, the character would owe over $5 million! They decided to advise the character in the poem to pay $0.10 a day for 42 years. The children were excited by, and amazed at, the power of doubling.

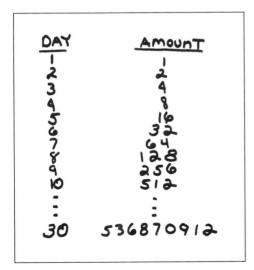

Fig. 3. An excerpt of Jackie and Chris's table of doubles

From Mathematics to Poetry

After reading Silverstein's humorous poems and solving mathematics problems related to "Overdues," the children were ready to create their own mathematical poems. Eric and Dina decided to write poems about money (see fig. 4).

... and Back Again

Once the children wrote their own poems using mathematics and poetic language, they challenged each other to pose and solve the problems embedded in their writing. After reading Eric's poem, Allison said that Eric did not have any money left because he probably bought something for $22. She indicated that after Eric's mom and dad gave him a total of $11, he put it with the $11 that he had already, yielding $22. She made up the following word problem: "If Eric wants to buy a doll for $24, how much more money does he need?" She answered her own question—$2.

When challenged to think of something else Eric might be interested in buying, Allison posed another problem: "If Eric wants to buy a Nintendo game for $100, how much more money does he need?" Using paper and pencil, she proceeded to solve her own problem: $100 − $22 = $78.

Selecting Poetry to Complement the Mathematics Curriculum

When poetry is combined with mathematics instruction, emotion and feeling are evoked. Poetry sparks wonder, surprise, and insight. It appeals to children's sense of humor and their delight in language. At the same time, poetry helps children find depth and personal meaning within the subject matter.

When selecting poems to share with children, it is best to start with poetry the children enjoy most. National studies of children's poetry preferences (Fisher and Natarella 1982; Terry 1974) have found that the poems children like most have rhyme

Mother gave me ten dollars
My father gave me one
I had eleven dollars
But now I have none

by Eric

"Funny Money" by Dina

Soon my picture
Will be on the
MONEY!
My friend thinks that's funny
What's funny
About it
They will have a
New bill
It will
Be $101
That's the one with
My picture on it
Then let's see them laugh.

Fig. 4. Examples of poems written by third graders

and rhythm, tell a story, and deal with everyday experiences. Fortunately, many of these well-liked poems also afford a context for discussing mathematics. The poems listed in the poemography are excellent starting points for primary school investigations.

Teachers interested in helping children write poetry about mathematics topics or other curriculum areas will find Donald Graves's book *Explore Poetry* (1992) to be a practical source of ideas. In the section specifically devoted to mathematics and poetry, Graves remarks that "numbers are always more than numbers" (p. 163), meaning that within the study of mathematics are intriguing stories of people, events, and ideas. Graves demonstrates how to access these stories through writing and sharing poetry. Graves's ideas appear right on target, and their potential is just being realized.

As the connections between mathematics and literature continue to be explored, more of the artificial boundaries that exist between them will be removed. In the process, both subjects will be better understood.

Poemography

Combinations

"Bleezer's Ice Cream" by Jack Prelutsky (1984, 49)

"Eighteen Flavors" by Shel Silverstein (1974, 116)

"The Ice Cream Fountain Mountain" by Eve Merriam (1989, 20-21)

The twenty-eight, eighteen, and thirty-one ice-cream flavors, respectively, that are illustrated in these poems offer a rich context for posing combination problems related to making double- and triple-scoop ice-cream cones with different flavors.

Fractions

"The Will" by Ian Serraillier (in Rosen [1985, 232-33])

The attempt to partition an inheritance of seventeen horses among three sons explores divisibility and fractions as three sons try to fulfill the terms of a will in which the eldest son gets one-half, the middle son gets one-third, and the youngest son gets one-ninth of the seventeen horses.

Money

"Smart" by Shel Silverstein (1974, 35)

As a "smart" child exchanges money by ignoring the value of coins and thinking that the more coins he receives, the more money he has, problems related to the value of the coins and the amount of money lost through the exchanges can be posed, discussed, and solved.

Ratio and Proportion

"One Inch Tall" by Shel Silverstein (1974,55)

A discussion of ratio and proportion can be initiated as a character who is one inch tall encounters some challenging situations.

Word Problems: Join, Separate, and Compare

"Baloney Belly Billy" by Jack Prelutsky (1984, 134)

As the character charges different amounts of money to eat nonedible items, "join," "separate," and "compare" problems can be formulated and solved.

"Band-Aids" by Shel Silverstein (1974, 140)

"Join," "separate," and "compare" problems can be formulated and solved as the character describes the number of Band-Aids located on different body parts.

"The Googies Are Coming" by Shel Silverstein (1974, 50)

The different amounts of money offered by the Googies for children with certain characteristics can be the basis for formulating "join," "separate," and "compare" problems.

"How Much Is a Gross?" by John Ciardi (1985, 28)

Kangaroos in tennis shoes provide a context for computing the number of items in a gross.

"Hungry Mungry" by Shel Silverstein (1974, 160-61)

"Join," "separate," and "compare" problems can be formulated and solved on the basis of the different portions of food and nonedible items consumed by the hungry character.

Bibliography

Ciardi, John. Doodle Soup. Boston, Mass.: Houghton Mifflin Co., 1985.

Fisher, Carol J., and Margaret A. Natarella. "Young Children's Preferences in Poetry: A National Survey of First, Second and Third Graders." *Research in the Teaching of English* 16 (December 1982): 339–54.

Graves, Donald H. *Explore Poetry*. Portsmouth, N.H.: Heinemann Educational Books, 1992.

Merriam, Eve. *A Poem for a Pickle*. New York: Morrow Junior Books, 1989.

Prelutsky, Jack. *The New Kid on the Block*. New York: Greenwillow Books, 1984.

Silverstein, Shel. *A Light in the Attic*. New York: HarperCollins Publishers, 1981.

———. *Where the Sidewalk Ends*. New York: HarperCollins Publishers, 1974.

Rosen, Michael, ed. *The Kingfisher Book of Children's Poetry*. New York: Kingfisher Books, 1985.

Terry, Ann. *Children's Poetry Preferences: A National Survey of Upper Elementary Grades*. 1974. Reprint, Urbana, Ill.: National Council of Teachers of English, 1984.

Wilner, Isabel, ed. *The Poetry Troupe*. New York: Charles Scribner's Sons, 1977.

The authors gratefully acknowledge Emily Rykert, a Queens College graduate intern at Public School 146Q for her assistance during the 1993–94 academic year. Her position was a component of the Cognitively Guided Instruction Primary Preservice Teacher Education Project funded by the National Science Foundation through the University of Wisconsin—Madison to City University of New York—Queens College.

3

Mathematics as Reasoning

MATHEMATICS is not the memorization of tricks and rules. Many students, however, have this distorted view of mathematics. Mathematics is a way of thinking, a way of solving problems, and a way of reasoning. Classroom activities should encourage and expect students to use their powers of reasoning, not their abilities to remember a set of rules.

Michele Warman describes several activities that improve students analytical reasoning skills. Read "Fun with Logical Reasoning," and try its suggestions with your students.

"Students as Researchers: An Inclined-Plane Activity" by Thomas G. Edwards presents an experiment in which students collect data, make conjectures, test ideas, and take measurements. The teacher becomes a facilitator of learning in this interesting experiment.

Additional investigations are described. The first one involves the SkyDome, home of the Toronto Blue Jays baseball team ("The Sky(Dome) Is the Limit"). Next, "Sort Of" describes an activity where students examine collections of objects from different perspectives and identify similarities and differences. Finally, "What's in a Name" presents a class activity using the letters from the students' first names.

MICHELE WARMAN

Fun with Logical Reasoning

THE ability to see patterns and relationships is essential for academic success. Students must be able to sort the barrage of material they are exposed to into manageable sequences they can deal with. Patterns can be mathematical as well as verbal, visual as well as written. Organizing information, evaluating it, and recognizing its interrelationships will help students deal with a future world that promises to be significantly more complex than our world today.

In my capacity as student mentor to a group of gifted elementary school children, I designed a project that consisted of a variety of learning activities intended to stimulate the development of analytical reasoning skills. The objectives of the project were as follows:

1. To help students learn to solve problems by seeing patterns and relationships.
2. To help students learn effective ways of solving problems by drawing correct inferences through inductive and deductive reasoning.
3. To encourage students to read critically in order to improve their thinking skills.
4. To help students learn to express themselves clearly by the proper, use of quantifiers in language.
5. To help students learn to recognize the major components—the premises and the conclusion—of a good argument or word problem.

6. To help students learn, through common sense and example, the importance of determining the truth value of a premise and the validity of an argument.
7. To help students use the technique of set theory to solve problems.
8. To help students make use of diagrams and charts as aids to problem solving.
9. To help students construct their own logic problems.

The exercises and suggestions that follow are a sampling from the course that was developed. I believe the material can be adapted to meet the needs of children of varying ages and ability levels.

Relationships

The exercises in this category were designed to help students see patterns, find relationships, and make "connections."

Figure sequences

The children were shown a sequence of geometric figures and asked to select from a set of four possible answers the next figure in the sequence (fig. 1). In each case, children were given an opportunity to discuss the answers and to argue for or against a particular answer if there was any question about which answer was right.

Figure analogies

In these exercises the children were expected to identify the relationship between two figures and then select from a set of four possibilities a figure that had the same relationship to a given third figure (see fig. 2).

Number sequences

The children were asked to complete sequences of numbers. The following two examples are typical.

Michele Warman *was a high school mentor in the Interage Program for Critical Thinking in the Great Neck School District on Long Island, New York. She designed and implemented projects in logic, probability, and electrical circuitry for gifted elementary school children. After graduating from high school, she entered Princeton University.*

What number comes next in the sequence?

(1) 1, 3, 5, 7, _____

(2) 2, 4, 8, 16, _____

What number belongs in the blank space of the sequence?

(3) 2, 4, _____, 8, 10

(4) 16, 12, 8, _____, 0

Number analogies (open ended)

The following number analogies were deliberately designed to allow for more than one correct solution. This encouraged students to search for all possible relationships and to justify different answers to the analogies. Thus for the first example, students may see the relationship as $3 \times 3 = 9$, so $4 \times 3 = 12$; as well as $3 + 6 = 9$, so $4 + 6 = 10$.

(1) 3 is related to 9 as 4 is related to
_____.

(2) 1 is related to 2 as 2 is related to
_____.

(3) 6 is related to 9 as 12 is related to
_____.

(4) 5 is related to 10 as 10 is related to
_____.

(5) 6 is related to 3 as 7 is related to
_____.

Number analogies (forced choice)

In contrast to the preceding exercises, the following analogies required students to select the relationship on the basis of the available answers.

(1) Which number (10, 12, 16, or 18) completed the analogy?

2 is related to 6 as 4 is related to _____.

(2) Which number (11, 12, 13, or 14) completes the analogy?

4 is related to 9 as 8 is related to _____.

"Think" Problems

The exercises in this category, consisting of riddles, puzzles, and word problems, were designed to have students solve simple problems and analyze the reasoning they used to reach their solutions. Four examples follow.

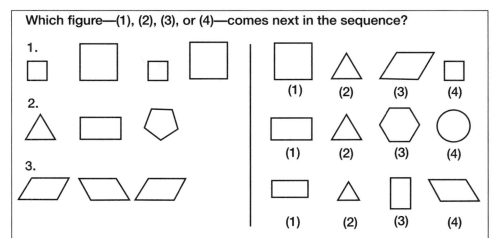

Which figure—(1), (2), (3), or (4)—comes next in the sequence?

Fig. 1

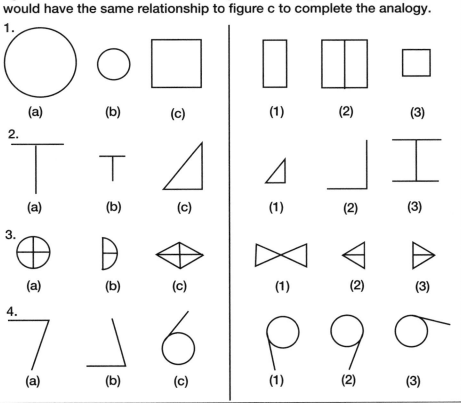

In each of the following examples, examine the relationship between figures a and b, then decide which figure on the right—(1), (2), or (3)—would have the same relationship to figure c to complete the analogy.

Fig. 2

(1) When does 7 plus 6 equal 1?

Answer: When you are looking at a clock.

Surprisingly, the students had very little difficulty with this problem. They reasoned that if they added the two numbers, the result would just increase to 13; but if they arranged the numbers in a cycle, rather than in a number line, they could obtain the correct answer. The clock then became obvious to them.

(2) A drawer contains red and green socks. You want a pair of matched socks. If you reach into the drawer without looking at the socks, what is the least number of socks you would have to take out to be certain of a matched pair?

Answer: Three

The students reasoned that if they took out only two socks, they might get a matched pair, but they might also get one red sock and one green sock. If they took out three socks, however, they would be certain to have a matched pair.

(3) How long would it take for a train one mile long to pass through a tunnel one mile long if the train was moving at the rate of one mile per minute?

Answer: Two minutes

The students reasoned that in one minute the train would be completely within the tunnel, while by the end of the second minute, the train would have exited.

(4) What part of your body are you unable to touch with both hands?

Answer: Your elbow.

This turned out to be a real "hands-on" experience as students tried to find the answer by the most direct means.

Critical Reading

A third group of problems was designed to help students practice critical reading: listing the facts, working directly from what is given, and determining exactly what the question asks. Three examples of this type are included here.

First example

Is the following reasoning correct?

Our soccer team won the championship. Since I am on the team, it follows that I played very well.

Answer: The reasoning is incorrect.

Because the soccer team won the championship does not necessarily mean you played well. You could have played terribly and the team might still have won.

Second example

Take three apples from four. How many do you have?

Answer: Three.

The key to this problem was reading the question carefully. Some students answered this problem incorrectly because they glanced at the question and assumed it said, "How many apples are left?" The question, however, just asks how many you have

after taking the three apples as directed. What was relevant was only how many apples were taken, not from how many apples they were chosen.

Third example

Given: Amy is shorter than Don and Susan. Amy is taller than Thelma, Karen, and Matthew. Michele is shorter than Thelma. Herbert is taller than any of them.

Problem: Find who is taller in each of these pairs.

(a) Matthew or Herbert

(b) Thelma or Michele

(c) Thelma or Susan

(d) Matthew or Don

Answers:

(a) Herbert. The last sentence says that Herbert is taller than any of them.

(b) Thelma. The third sentence says that Michele is shorter than Thelma.

(c) Susan. Since Amy is shorter than Susan (first sentence) and taller than Thelma (second sentence), then Susan must be taller than Thelma.

(d) From the first sentence we deduce that Don is taller than Amy. The second sentence says Amy is taller than Matthew. Therefore, Don must be taller than Matthew.

Drawing a simple picture (fig. 3) might be helpful in solving this reading problem.

Additional brief problems similar to the preceding ones could be used to stimulate students to—

- read for information,
- categorize information,
- ask pertinent questions to help search for an answer,
- think critically,
- use logical reasoning to find the answer.

Using Quantifiers

The following activity was designed to help students become sensitive to the proper use of quantifiers (*all, some, many, most*). Students were asked to determine the truth value (truth or falsity) of each statement and to describe the reasoning they had used to make their determination.

Decide whether the following statements are true or false.

(a) All boys like to play baseball.
                                        True or False?
(Remember, one must find only one boy who doesn't like to play baseball to disprove this statement.)

(b) Everyone likes chocolate ice cream better than vanilla.
                                        True or False?

(c) All kids like chewing gum.
                                        True or False?

(d) Mathematics is interesting.
                                        True or False?

(e) Some books are long.
                                        True or False?

(f) Some dogs meow.
                                        True or False?

(g) All kids like watermelon.
                                        True or False?

(h) Some kids laugh all the time.
                                        True or False?

(i) Most dogs bark.
                                        True or False?

| Don | Susan | Amy | Thelma | Karen | Matthew | Michele | Herbert |

Fig. 3

(j) All dogs bark.

                    True or False?

(k) Many plants need water.

                    True or False?

A good follow-up exercise is to have the students write their own statements and indicate their truth values.

Basic Logical Arguments

Once the youngsters have acquired an understanding of determining the truth value of a statement, the study of an *argument* can be undertaken. The method used was to write several examples of arguments on the chalkboard and to examine their forms. Through these experiences students were helped to see that an argument consists of a series of statements offered as reasons for another statement. The reasons are called the *premises* of the argument and the statement for which the reasons are offered is called the *conclusion* of the argument.

Examples:

(1) *Premise.* Jill is either a boy or a girl.
Premise. Jill is not a boy.
Conclusion. Jill is a girl.

(2) *Premise.* If our teacher is not absent, we will have a spelling test.
Premise. Our teacher is not absent.
Conclusion. We will have a spelling test.

The terms *valid* and *invalid* were introduced. An argument is *valid* if the conclusion is derived from the premises. After examining the preceding two arguments, the students determined that the conclusions did follow from the premises. Consequently, the arguments were valid. The students saw immediately that in the following argument the conclusion did not follow from the premises; that is, that the argument was invalid.

(3) *Premise.* If Mrs. Smith is not absent, we will have a spelling test.
Premise. Mrs. Smith is absent.
Conclusion. Therefore, we will have a spelling test.

After the students can determine the validity of an argument, they can be introduced to the question of whether the conclusion is true or false. A conclusion is true if the premises are true and the argument is

valid. In the following exercises, the students were asked to examine the arguments and determine whether

(a) the argument is valid; that is, the conclusion is derived from the premises; and

(b) the conclusion is true; that is, the premises are true.

Examples:

(1) *Premise.* All baseball players are short.
Premise. John is a baseball player.
Conclusion. Therefore, John is short.

The argument is valid because the conclusion follows from the premises. The first premise, however, is false.

Consequently, the conclusion cannot be true even though the argument is valid.

(2) *Premise.* No student wins at tennis who does not enjoy practicing.
Premise. No student wins at tennis who does not practice well.
Conclusion. Every student who enjoys practicing wins at tennis.

The argument is not valid because the conclusion does not follow from the premises. The first premise says that in order to win, you must enjoy practicing. Furthermore, both premises are false. Consequently, the argument is not valid and the conclusion is not true.

(3) *Premise.* Click-Clack chewing gum made Chris Evert a tennis star.
Premise. You want to be a tennis star.
Conclusion. Therefore, you too should chew Click-Clack chewing gum.

The explanation is left to the reader. An example like this can also lead to an analysis of familiar advertisements.

Venn Diagrams

A simplified Venn diagram can help solve many word problems. The circles or closed curves can be drawn on the chalkboard. Transparency sheets of different colors can be used, or the students can hold hands and form human circles. For example:

Premise. All dogs are mammals.
Premise. Beagles are a type of dog.
Conclusion. Therefore, beagles are mammals.

The construction of the diagram might be as follows:

(1) Let us represent the set of all mammals with a large circle. All different kinds of mammals (skunks, cats, mice, and so on) are inside the large circle.

(2) Now we will represent a kind of mammal, dogs, by a smaller circle within the large circle (fig. 4).

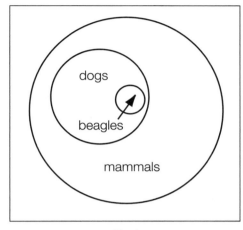

Fig. 4

(3) Beagles are a type of dog. Therefore, if we were to represent beagles by a small circle, we would have to put it inside the circle containing all dogs.

Now we can clearly see that the conclusion that beagles are mammals is based on a valid argument; the circle containing beagles is completely within the large circle of mammals.

Student Problems

The culminating activity of this project was to have the students write their own word problems. The examples included here are some done by fourth graders.

"The Builders"

Given
1. David, John, and Gary are builders.
2. If David builds on block one, Gary builds on block three.
3. Gary and John never build on the same block.

Problem
Who can build on the same block?

Answer
David and John can build on the same block.

"Corey's Snacks"

Given

1. This morning Corey will go to school at 8:00 a.m. At 7:00 a.m. there are ten fruits in the bowl.
2. The bowl contains apples, pears, oranges, and plums.
3. Corey took an apple yesterday and an orange two days ago.
4. Corey never takes the same fruit in two consecutive days.
5. Corey never follows an apple with a pear.
6. Corey waits at least five days between having oranges.

Problem

What fruit is Corey going to take today?

Answer

A plum.

"Chocolate Yesterday, Vanilla Today"

This last word problem, a more difficult type, was solved by a fifth grader using the chart method.

Given

When Amy, Billy, and Cindy eat out, each one orders either chocolate or vanilla ice cream.

1. If Amy orders chocolate, Billy orders vanilla.

2. Either Amy or Cindy order chocolate, but not both.

3. Billy and Cindy do not both order vanilla.

Problem

Who could have ordered chocolate yesterday, vanilla today?

Answer

The key here is to determine whose ice cream orders remain the same. One student simply made a list.

	Yesterday
Amy	vanilla
Billy	chocolate
Cindy	chocolate

	Today
Amy	vanilla
Billy	vanilla
Cindy	chocolate

Conclusion

The exercises that have been described offer a sampling of tools and methods for helping students improve their analytical reasoning skills—their ability to organize information, to think critically, to draw inferences, and to solve problems. When this project was used with a group of gifted eight-year-olds, it generated and maintained an enthusiastic response from the group. The students were eager to share their analyses with each other, and this created an atmosphere in which they felt free to "think out loud." This enlivened and enriched the sessions.

The students perceived that they needed to use reasoning skills to identify the patterns and relationships in the figure and number sequences and analogies. Solving word problems, puzzles, and riddles required students to use critical-thinking skills, including identifying relevant information and making inferences based on inductive and deductive reasoning.

The students became aware of the need to use words more precisely as they uncovered faulty generalizations when quantifiers were used carelessly. They readily shared with one another their analyses, interpretations, and explanations as they sought to determine the validity and truth values of the logical arguments. Charts and diagrams were seen by the children as helpful means for proving their answers.

Just how well some students had progressed was demonstrated when they proceeded to create original problems.

THOMAS G. EDWARDS

Students as Researchers: An Inclined-Plane Activity

A NUMBER of years ago in Geneva Switzerland, Barbel Inhelder and Jean Piaget (1958) conducted a series of experiments to study the development of logical thinking in young children. One of those experiments involved rolling balls of different masses down inclines of varying heights. The object was to see if young children could make appropriate inferences regarding the relationship among the variables in the problem.

This article suggests a means by which a similar experiment might be used as a learning activity in middle school mathematics or science classrooms. This activity is a direct connection between middle school mathematics and science topics. In addition, it presents an interesting context within which students "explore, conjecture, and reason logically" (NCTM 1989, 5). In short, it is a good opportunity for students to exercise their mathematical power.

Consider the following situation:

A ball rolls down an incline. If the mass of the ball and the length and height of the incline are changed, which of these variables has an effect on the time it takes the ball to reach the bottom of the incline?

Certainly, if a teacher were to begin class by (*a*) rolling a ball down an incline; (*b*) suggesting variations in the mass of the ball, the length of the incline, and the height of the incline; and (*c*) questioning the effect of each variation on the time, a problem situation that is loaded with opportunities for student exploration would result. If the students were then

encouraged to conduct those experiments, a good deal of active learning would occur. However, the activity can become even richer.

Learning to listen to students is an area currently generating much interest. In fact, this philosophy might be one of the most powerful classroom venues implied by constructivist theories of learning (Confrey 1990). When teachers take the time to listen to what students have to say, the idea of negotiating shared meanings with them can become a natural extension of classroom activity (see, e.g., Cobb, Wood, and Yackel [1990]). Such a process of negotiation is also what Kamii has in mind when she suggests that teachers of young children exchange points of view with the children and encourage them to think on their own (Kamii 1985). In this way, classroom discourse becomes an interactive process in which ideas are exchanged rather than imposed.

These ideas are exactly the sort of interactions between teacher and students that are implied by the statement "The teacher of mathematics should orchestrate discourse by listening carefully to students' ideas" (NCTM 1991, 35). By fostering mathematical discourse through such a negotiation process, the inclined-plane activity can be enhanced.

The Class Activity

Suppose that instead of beginning class as outlined previously, the teacher were to proceed in a more ambiguous manner. Suppose the teacher begins by rolling a ball down an incline but then asks, "What could we measure here?" Students will generate a list of items to measure that includes all the usual variables of interest.

At this point, the negotiation process must begin, for the student-generated list will contain far too many variables, many

of which are not easily measured. To shorten this list, the teacher might ask, "Which of these things could we measure without too much difficulty?" Once the list has been shortened, an appropriate extension is to ask, "How could we go about measuring these things?" The discussion of measuring techniques that follows is often lively and may present further opportunities for negotiation between teacher and students.

For example, the author discussed the operation of a stopwatch with sixth-grade students and then asked for a volunteer to operate the stopwatch as students measured the time required for a demonstration ball to roll down an incline. Having obtained a measure of the time, using the same timer, the same ball, and the same incline, students repeated the experiment. As might be expected, a different measure of the time was generated.

"'What can we do about this? Which one of these times should we use?" students asked. Students suggested conducting a third experiment, which invariably produced yet a third value for the time.

"Now we are really stuck! What do you think we ought to do now?" Before long, one student suggested finding the average. What a nice way to practice finding averages, in context and for a purpose.

The central feature in this process of negotiation with students is listening to, and building on, their ideas. Doing so clearly shows students that their ideas are valued, and this validation, in turn, contributes to their willingness to become involved in classroom discourse.

The stage is set for a rich activity. Suppose that the teacher and students have agreed on the following list of variables:

- The time it takes the ball to reach the bottom of the incline

- The mass (weight is also appropriate here) of the ball

Thomas Edwards *teaches at Wayne State University, Detroit, MI 48202. He is interested in children's learning of mathematics in urban settings and the use of technology in school mathematics.*

- The length of the incline
- The height of the incline

Suppose also that a method for measuring each variable has also been discussed and that for each the class has agreed to use three different values that can be directly controlled, that is, three different masses, three different lengths, and three different heights. Next the students can be encouraged to collect all the data. This process is greatly facilitated by organizing the class in small cooperative groups of three or four students.

Figure 1 depicts setting up an incline to vary the height while holding the mass and length constant. Students might simply stack textbooks to produce various heights. What is more important is not the precision of the measures of the heights, lengths, and masses but that at least three distinct values exist for each of them.

Often sixth-grade students do not realize that three different masses, lengths, and heights mean that twenty-seven separate repetitions of the experiment are needed. Many believe that three experiments are enough. Frequently the data are collected in a haphazard manner. But at this point, it is important that they proceed to collect *some* data so that they begin to understand the experiment.

Allow students to collect data in whatever manner they prefer for about fifteen to twenty minutes. Then the teacher should intervene. One possible intervention is to suggest organizing the data into tables. By asking students to focus on the quantities that they are varying, the teacher can negotiate a three-by-three two-way table of length against height. Then if the teacher asks for which of the masses this table will be used, students may suggest a separate table for each of the three masses. If not, the teacher should assign the first table to one of the masses and ask what might be done for the second mass. Figure 2 illustrates such a set of three two-way tables. Students should then be able to visualize the extent of the experiment because these tables contain twenty-seven empty cells.

At this point, the data must be collected, which can usually be accomplished in one or two additional class periods. Notice that, as yet, the teacher has not imposed a question on this situation. If teachers listen to students and give them time to think of appropriate responses, the questions will often be supplied by students. One possible approach is to assign for homework only one question, but a question whose difficulty the teacher plays up: "Imagine that your three tables are completely filled with data. All twenty-seven cells are filled in. Can you think of a question that you could use your tables to answer?"

When sixth graders were so queried, they returned with interesting questions that were appropriate to this problem situation.

For example, one student wondered whether the texture of the surface would affect the time. Another student suggested that patterns might appear in the data, and she gave two examples. The students posed more questions than could possibly be answered, but some of them were tackled. Once again, a negotiation process in which the teacher listens to students and asks them to clarify or elaborate on their own and each other's ideas will allow students to consolidate their thinking and draw viable inferences.

For example, figure 3 shows the three-by-three tables completed using hypothetical data. Students should be asked to look for patterns in the data for a specified length for each of the masses. Repeating this process for each of the three lengths should allow students to conjecture that time and height are inversely related: as the height increases, the time for each given length for each of the masses decreases. Likewise, it is not difficult to elicit a relationship between length and time by looking at rows rather than at columns. Students do have difficulty with the question of a possible relationship between mass and time. The structure of the tables requires looking at the same cell entry across all three tables to make an inference about such a relationship. Figure 4 highlights one such set of entries, 0.96, 0.92, and 0.96, respectively. Then, the fact that no such relationship is apparent is somewhat counterintuitive and difficult for some middle school students to accept. It is difficult, but not impossible. To quote one sixth grader, "We need to look to see if they [the corresponding cell entries] are the same *or almost the same*. If they are, then we can say

Height (cm)	Length (cm) 50	75	100
10			
20			
30			

Mass 1

Height (cm)	Length (cm) 50	75	100
10			
20			
30			

Mass 2

Height (cm)	Length (cm) 50	75	100
10			
20			
30			

Mass 3

Fig. 2. A two-way table for balls with three different masses

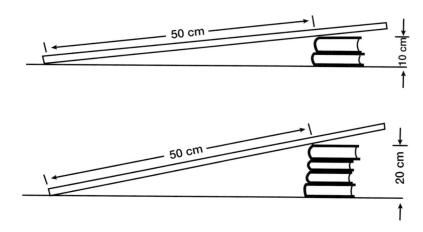

Fig. 1. Setting up an experiment to vary only the height of the incline

Height (cm)	Length (cm)		
	50	75	100
10	0.98	1.40	1.82
20	0.61	0.96	1.29
30	0.10	0.64	1.06

Mass 1

Height (cm)	Length (cm)		
	50	75	100
10	1.03	1.58	1.82
20	0.60	0.92	1.22
30	0.41	0.66	1.04

Mass 2

Height (cm)	Length (cm)		
	50	75	100
10	0.93	1.62	1.67
20	0.57	0.96	1.19
30	0.39	0.63	1.07

Mass 3

Fig. 3. Hypothetical data presented in a two-way table for each mass

that the weight doesn't matter" [emphasis added].

Important Features of the Class Activity

The foregoing activity, which spanned five, forty-two-minute class periods, contains some significant and worthwhile mathematical tasks. Students were directly involved in collecting data by measuring length, height, weight, and time, sometimes using nonstandard units. Collecting reliable measures of time required students to compute arithmetic means, or averages. The students were allowed to use calculators to compute the averages, which lead to issues of number sense and rounding. Since these mathematical tasks were conducted in context and for a definite purpose, they were much more meaningful to the students.

If the mathematical content inherent in these tasks was the only benefit to be gained from using such an activity in a middle school classroom, it is well worth the week-long investment in instructional time. However, other more significant benefits are imbedded in this activity. The foundation of the *Curriculum and Evaluation Standards for School Mathematics* (NCTM 1989) is formed by the first four standards in each grade-level section: "Mathematics as Problem Solving," "Mathematics as Communication," "Mathematics as Reasoning," and "Mathematical Connections." Each of these

four unifying standards plays a major role in the inclined-plane activity.

The mathematical content was introduced and developed in response to a problem situation. Throughout the negotiation process, students' thinking, both oral and written, was elicited, which helped students to develop their ability to communicate mathematically. The communication standard was also addressed when the data collection and tabulation were accomplished in small cooperative groups. The data analysis at the end of the activity involved mathematical reasoning, but, as the students encountered and solved various problems during the data-collection and measurement activities, they also used mathematical reasoning. A good example is contained in the students' discussion concerning the timing issue. Finally, this activity connected mathematics with the physical sciences, and it forged connections among the mathematical concepts and procedures that were actually used to complete the activity.

Even more important, the inclined-plane activity gives the teacher an opportunity to foster mathematics discourse in the classroom. In listening to, and building on, students' ideas, the teacher encourages them to think about the mathematics they are using. Students' thinking about the process of solving a problem is one of the strengths of using small groups in problem-solving activities (Suydam 1987). Hermine Sinclair has

noted that "procedural skills become 'meaningful' not when linked to figurative images …, but to coherent patterns of reasoning" (1990, 28). The best way to ensure that such thinking and reasoning occur is to encourage students to engage in the mathematical discourse of the classroom. To do so, teachers must listen to students.

Conclusion

The NCTM *Standards* documents (1989, 1991) envision a role for the teacher as more of a facilitator of learning than a transmitter of knowledge. This focus requires teachers to think carefully about ways to become facilitators of learning. The negotiation of shared meanings with students is one way, but real negotiation requires that teachers learn to listen to students, which enhances mathematical discourse in the classroom. The foregoing inclined-plane activity presents a number of such opportunities in a context that is at the same time fruitful, rewarding, and entertaining.

References

Cobb, Paul, Terry Wood, and Erna Yackel. "Classrooms as Learning Environments for Teachers and Researchers." In *Journal for Research in Mathematics Education Monograph Series No. 4: Constructivist Views on the Teaching and Learning of Mathematics.* Reston, Va.: National Council of Teachers of Mathematics, 1990.

Height (cm)	Length (cm)		
	50	75	100
10	0.98	1.40	1.82
20	0.61	**0.96**	1.29
30	0.10	0.64	1.06

Mass 1:14g

Height (cm)	Length (cm)		
	50	75	100
10	1.03	1.58	1.82
20	0.60	**0.92**	1.22
30	0.41	0.66	1.04

Mass 2:28g

Height (cm)	Length (cm)		
	50	75	100
10	0.93	1.62	1.67
20	0.57	**0.96**	1.19
30	0.39	0.63	1.07

Mass 3:57g

Fig. 4. Highlighting the time for each of the balls on an incline of the same length and height

Confrey, Jere. "What Constructivism Implies for Teaching." *Journal for Research in Mathematics Education Monograph Series No. 4: Constructivist Views on the Teaching and Learning of Mathematics.* Reston, Va.: National Council of Teachers of Mathematics, 1990.

Inhelder, Barbel, and Jean Piaget. *The Growth of Logical Thinking from Childhood to Adolescence.* New York: Basic Books, 1958.

Kamii, Constance. *Young Children Reinvent Arithmetic: Implications of Piaget's Theory.* New York: Teachers College Press, 1985.

National Council of Teachers of Mathematics. *Curriculum and Evaluation Standards for School Mathematics.* Reston, Va.: The Council, 1989.

———. *Professional Standards for Teaching Mathematics.* Reston, Va.: The Council, 1991.

Sinclair, Hermine. "Learning: The Interactive Recreation of Knowledge." In *Transforming Children's Mathematics Education: International Perspectives,* edited by Leslie P. Steffe and Terry Wood, 19–29. Hillsdale, N.J.: Lawrence Erlbaum Associates, 1990.

Suydam, Marilyn N. "Indications from Research on Problem Solving." In *Teaching and Learning: A Problem Solving Focus,* edited by Frances R Curcio, 99–114. Reston, Va.: National Council of Teachers of Mathematics, 1987.

The Sky(Dome) Is the Limit

Student Activity Goals

Students will—

- determine which numbers seem reasonable in describing a given situation, thereby enhancing number sense;
- use logical reasoning to eliminate possibilities;
- identify an appropriate measurement unit for a given situation; and
- estimate length and time measurements.

Materials

The materials needed are—

- a copy of the reproducible page for each pair of students, and
- scissors for each pair of students.

Planning for Instruction

Teachers might want to consult reference material on famous buildings, such as Paolo Donati's book *Amazing Buildings* (Richmond Hill: Scholastic Canada, 1993). Such books can show photographs and drawings of the interiors and structural characteristics of many famous buildings. In particular, *Amazing Buildings* features a wealth of numerical data used by architects and designers to describe the SkyDome, home of the Toronto Blue Jays baseball team. The investigation, however, can be completed without such references.

Structuring the Investigation

1. Engage the students in a discussion of what measurements or numbers might be used when describing a major-league-baseball park. Invite students to identify diverse data, from the distance between home plate and the left-field wall to the number of hot dogs sold during a "typical" game. Discuss the ways in which these numbers might be useful and to whom.

2. Give each pair of students a copy of the reproducible page, which includes numbers and measures associated with the SkyDome from *Amazing Buildings,* and a pair of scissors.

3. Ask students to cut the bottom sections from the reproducible page and set them aside for a moment. Next, have students cut out the boxes containing numbers and measures at the top and place them beside the description that the students believe is appropriate. Remind them that each number or measurement is used only once. Note that the purpose here is not to test students' knowledge of the answers but to engage students in a discussion about the reasonableness of numbers and their units. Students should use logical reasoning to conclude, for example, that only two descriptions require the use of "time," and since the artificial grass, known as Astroturf, contains several miles of zippers, students can conjecture that it must take ten to twelve hours' to zip the turf and only twenty minutes to close the roof.

4. Students should complete questions 1 and 2. Use an overhead transparency of the reproducible page to lead a discussion in which students recommend the placement of numbers and measurements in the missing squares and compare their answers with the questions. (The answers, as reported in *Amazing Buildings,* are these: Top row—height of the SkyDome is 412 feet, total number of seats is 50 000, number of employees is 2 300, number of light bulbs in field lights is 9 000, length of electrical cable is 120 miles, time needed to close the roof is 20 minutes. Bottom row—height of the Jumbotron screen is 33 feet, number of first-level seats is 23 000, length of the zippers on the Astroturf is 8 miles, time needed to zip the Astroturf is 10 to 12 hours, weight of the roof is 11 000 tons,

and number of private sky boxes is 161.)

5. Ask the students to list several pieces of data that might be included if they were to create a similar scrambled activity about their school building. Write them on the chalkboard. They may include such data as the number of teachers, the cost of a hot lunch, and the distance from the swings on the playground to the front door of the school. Ask each pair of students to create a scrambled list with data related to the school. Students in each team should (a) determine the data that could be used, (b) investigate ways to collect the data, and (c) create the activity using the blank boxes from a student's reproducible page. An effective scramble must contain matches that are neither obvious (e.g., only one description contains "time") nor ambiguous (e.g., several answers are too close to distinguish). Although the page contains ten boxes each for descriptions and numerical data, the total number of boxes will depend on the needs of the class.

6. Once a scramble has been created, each pair should exchange papers with another team and complete the activities. After all the pairs have solved another team's scrambles, discuss the reasoning skills necessary to make an effective scramble and what made some of the questions better than others.

Concluding Remarks

By relating descriptive data about places of interest to the measurements associated with those data, this investigation focuses on an important aspect of enhancing number sense—the notion of reasonable numbers. In addition, students learn about the vast amount of information that is used in planning, constructing, and operating buildings and the role of mathematics in collecting and analyzing the data.

The Sky(Dome) Is the Limit

Cut out the boxes containing numbers and measurements describing the Toronto SkyDome and place them on the appropriate squares containing descriptions.

Height of the SkyDome	Total number of seats	Number of employees	Number of light bulbs in field lights	Length of electrical cable	Time needed to close the roof
Height of the Jumbotron screen	Number of first-level seats	Length of zippers on the Astroturf	Time needed to zip the Astroturf	Weight of the roof	Number of private sky boxes
9 000	20 minutes	8 miles	50 000	120 miles (193 km)	11 000 tons
412 feet	2 300	23 000	161	10 to 12 hours	33 feet

1. How did the units appearing next to the numbers help in making your choices? _____

_____

2. Which items were easiest to determine first and why? _____

_____

Use the boxes below to create your own scramble. Ten of the boxes shoule contain numbers and measurements about the buillding. The others should contain the descriptions.

Sort Of

Student Activity Goals

Students will—

- describe attributes that determine uniqueness,
- identify similarities and differences among items or objects,
- examine collections of objects from different perspectives,
- use elementary number theory to formulate conjectures, and
- recognize that a question may have several acceptable answers.

Planning for Instruction

Classifying and sorting are processes that people use daily. The cafeteria staff needs to consider the four basic food groups when planning meals. Laundry is often sorted by color. Baseball cards are often sorted by team or by duplicates. Ask students how they would sort a deck of playing cards, say, five times, using a different rule each time. Encourage them to consider different ways of sorting things on the basis of invented "rules."

Create four cards, or overhead transparencies, as shown here.

Display all four cards at once and begin by focusing students' attention on the circle card. Ask, "How is this shape different?" Students might note, for example, that the circle is the only shape that "rolls" or is the only one without "line segments."

Continue this discussion with each card until each shape has been uniquely described. Point out that items are often grouped or sorted according to similarities and differences.

Create four more cards or transparencies as shown. Have the students examine them. Explain that they will sort these cards in more than one way.

| FISH | WHALE |
| HUMAN BEING | CHICKEN |

Arrange these cards into two groups by putting the "human being" card and the "chicken" card in one group and the "fish" card and the "whale" card in the other. Show the students this arrangement and, in small groups, ask them to describe a "rule" to explain the sorting method. For example, a group might explain that the "human being" card and "chicken" card are together, because they both have two feet or because they both live on land. They may state that the whale and fish are together because they are both fish, which would be an incorrect rationale for grouping them because the whale is a mammal. One correct rationale would be that both fish and whales live in the water. A variety of answers are acceptable; the key is to have the students debate their reasons in small groups and offer a rational explanation for the arrangement.

Have students demonstrate other possible groupings of these four cards. Discuss their rules and whether they have different rules for the same grouping. Encourage grouping into one, three, and four groups, as well as into two groups.

Extend the idea of sorting in different ways to the numbers found on the pictures of horses on the activity page. Have pairs of students cut out the horses and put them into two corrals so that (1) at least one number is in each corral, (2) all numbers are used once, and (3) a word or phrase describes the "corral rule."

Have pairs share the rationale for their grouping of the horses. Challenge them to corral the horses differently. Encourage unusual groupings based on numerical properties such as these:

5, 16, 21
The sum of the digits is odd.

8, 17, 28, 33
The sum of the digits is even.

21, 33
Divisible by 3

5, 8, 16, 17, 28
Not divisible by 3

8, 16
A power of 2

5, 17, 21, 28, 33
Not a power of 2

If the foregoing directions are followed, students will find a large number of different groupings of the seven numbers—we have seen a class find sixty-three such groupings. Certainly discussing them all is not feasible, but be sure to consider how each number is unique and could be placed in a corral by itself; for example, 16 is the only perfect square listed.

Give students prearranged groups of numbers and ask them to describe a "rule" used to form those groups. For example, 16 and 21 might be corralled because they are each 1 more than a multiple of 5. See if students can discover this rule or some other rule to group 16 and 21.

Call students for lunch or recess according to an unannounced "rule," such as all students wearing blue. Have them determine the rule used or another rule that yields that same grouping. Let them develop a rule to divide the class into a given number of distinct groups.

Connect this investigation to the notions of conjunction and disjunction. For example, ask students to stand if they are eleven years old *and* wearing shoelaces. Compare this group with one formed by asking students who are eleven years old *or* wearing shoelaces to stand. Draw a Venn diagram to illustrate unique and overlapping subgroups. Differences between the disjunctive *or* as used in mathematics and English can be discussed.

To make another language-arts connection, ask students to sort books they have read into groups based on various characteristics. Have them consider many ways to categorizing the books, such as by subject, plot, or setting.

Students need to experience situations that encourage an open mind and a different perspective. This exposure serves to increase both confidence and comfort level in dealing with perceived ambiguity and multiple solutions to problems they face. This investigation is designed to help students see, communicate, and respect alternative points of view.

What's in a Name?

Student Activity Goals

Students will—

- use tables to collect data and solve problems,
- formulate conjectures,
- explore range and compute averages, and
- construct and analyze bar graphs.

Materials

The materials needed are—

- squares cut from the activity page for each letter of the first name of each student,
- a large container,
- a copy of the reproducible page for each student, and
- a teacher's overhead transparency of the reproducible page.

Planning for Instruction

Ask the students how many of them have ever played "hangman" or have watched *Wheel of Fortune* on television. As contestants choose letters to complete the puzzles, on what information do they base their letter choices? The more familiar the contestant is with words in the English language, the greater success is possible. When solving problems, the more information that is gathered, the more potential solutions can be found. The focus of this investigation is on making conjectures and determining probabilities through experimenting with the letters in the first names of students.

Possible Discussion Questions

1. Organize the class into pairs. Have each student write the letters of his or her first name in the squares at the top of the activity page, one letter to a square.

Have each student cut out the squares and place them in a single large class container.

2. Have students predict and record how many three-, four-, and five-letter words can be made from five letters chosen from the container. Share these predictions and discuss the reasoning.

3. Pass the container around and ask each pair of students randomly to remove five letters and place them on their desks. Then ask each pair to record all the three-, four-, and five-letter words that they can form from their letters.

4. Collect the class data using the following table.

Student Pairs

	1	2	3	...
No. of three-letter words				
No. of four-letter words				
No. of five-letter words				

5. Have students construct bar graphs that display the number of three-, four-, and five-letter words formed by each pair by using the grid on the activity page. Discuss the results as a class by asking such questions as What trends did you see? What was the average number of three-, four-, and five-letter words formed by each group? Were some groups more or less able to form words than others? Why?

6. Ask students how many of each letter were in the container in the first place and how they might determine an efficient method of collecting these data.

7. With collected data, have students construct on the activity page bar graphs that depict the frequency of occurrence of each letter in first names in the class. A "concrete" bar graph can be made using the actual letter cutouts from this

activity.

8. Ask the class such questions as, Which letter occurred most frequently? Least frequently? What were the three most common and the three least common consonants and vowels? Did this result agree with your intuition about the frequency with which these letters occur?

9. Inform the class that studies of the frequency of occurrence of the letters of the alphabet in the dictionary have shown that the most commonly occurring consonants in order are T, N, R, H, S, D, and L. The least common consonants are Z, Q, and X, with K, J, and V occurring slightly more often. The letter E is the most common vowel, followed by A and O, with U being the least common. How does this information compare with the data collected? Why might the data be different?

Possible Extension

Have students identify letter usage in the newspaper. Have them choose one paragraph from a local newspaper and tally the frequency with which each letter of the alphabet occurs within that paragraph. By tallying total-class data, a comparison and conjecture can be made about the occurrences of letters in the English language reported in step 9. Another extension involves the students' identifying the nouns, verbs, and other parts of speech from the list of three-, four-, and five-letter words that were formed in this investigation. Challenge the students working in groups to create sentences using these words.

What's in a Name?

[ ] [ ] [ ] [ ] [ ] [ ] [ ] [ ] [ ] [ ]

Write a letter of your first name in each square and cut out the squares with scissors.

Predictions

How many three-letter words do you predict you will be able to form? _____

How many four-letter words do you predict you will be able to form? _____

How many five-letter words do you predict you will be able to form? _____

Data Collection

List all three-letter words that you and your partner could form: _____ _____

_____ _____ _____ _____ How many altogether? _____

List all four-letter words that you and your partner could form: _____ _____

_____ _____ _____ _____ How many altogether? _____

List all five-letter words that you and your partner could form:_____ _____

_____ _____ _____ _____ How many altogether? _____

Graphs

Draw a bar graph to show how many words could be formed by each group containing three, four, and five letters.

Three-Letter-Word Graph

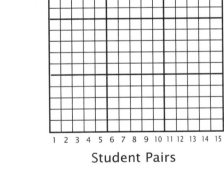

1 2 3 4 5 6 7 8 9 10 11 12 13 14 15

Student Pairs

Four-Letter-Word Graph

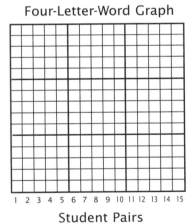

1 2 3 4 5 6 7 8 9 10 11 12 13 14 15

Student Pairs

Five-Letter-Word Graph

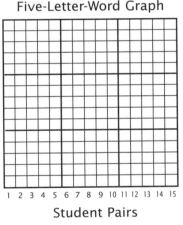

1 2 3 4 5 6 7 8 9 10 11 12 13 14 15

Student Pairs

Draw a bar graph showing the frequency of occurrence of each letter in the first names of students in your class.

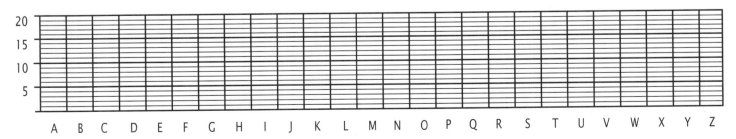

20
15
10
5

A B C D E F G H I J K L M N O P Q R S T U V W X Y Z

4

Mathematical Connections

THERE were a plethora of excellent articles available for this strand and many excellent ones are not included. The selected articles represent a broad range of those available.

"We Had a Math Day" shows how mathematical topics can be incorporated into various subject areas not only for the middle grades but also for the primary grades. Subject areas include language arts, mathematics, science, social studies, music, art, and physical education. This article, one of a number relating to the same concept, is one that the compilers have found very useful.

One of the suggestions in the preceding article is inviting resource people to meet with students. "Students Can Discover the Occupational Link with Mathematics" presents suggestions for meeting this goal. One occupation that would be sure to attract students' attention—astronauts— is represented by "Now and Then: The Long Distance Doctor."

Some articles, such as by "Flower Beds and Landscape Consultants: Making Connections in Middle School Mathematics," incorporated occupations with subject areas. This outstanding article shows how to develop algebraic concepts using geometric concepts and the charting and graphing capabilities of spreadsheets. "Doing Research Together" uses the environment to incorporate mathematics, science, English, and geography. This project could be a year-long activity. The connection between history and mathematics is apparent in "The Civil War and the *Standards*". "Our Diets May Be Killing Us," for nutrition, and "The Case of Video Viewing, Reading, and Writing in Mathematics Class: Solving the Mystery," for problem solving through language arts, are two excellent examples of relating mathematics to other disciplines and current issues before students today. The use of newspapers and other print media to help treat mathematics as current events is provided in "Mathematics as Current Events". "The 12.7 Centimeter Hot Dog Corporation" addresses the business world. An excellent computer program, "Survival Skills," uses a similar strategy.

CAROLYN BOYSAW MASON

We Had a Math Day

WHAT can be done to help students realize that mathematics can be used in all subjects, and that it is an integral part of daily living? Math Day— a day devoted to teaching mathematics in all subject areas—is one way to help accomplish this two-fold goal.

In an effort to help our boys and girls become more fully aware of the usefulness of mathematics and to show its relationship to daily living, "Math Day" was held at Norwood Elementary School. On that day, mathematics was incorporated into the teaching of all subjects. As a result, students were provided a multiplicity of experiences relating mathematics to other subject-matter areas.

To publicize this special day, attractive signs were posted throughout the corridors of the school and special bulletin boards and posters were displayed in the classrooms. The following are some of the captions used:

WE USE MATH EVERY DAY

MATH PAYS

MATH COUNTS

MATH IS BASIC

MATH SWINGS WITH SCIENCE

EXPERIENCING MATH THROUGH ART

METRIC NEWS

MATH NEWS

MATH IN OUR COMMUNITY

MATH IN OUR SCHOOL

MATH AROUND THE COUNTRY

MATH IS HISTORY

GRAPHS ARE IN

Carolyn Boysaw Mason *is currently principal of Spaulding Elementary School in Birmingham, Alabama. At the time this article was written, she was assistant principal in charge of curriculum and instruction at Norwood Elementary School in the Birmingham City Schools.*

Classroom Applications of Mathematical Ideas

Some of the different ways in which mathematical concepts were incorporated into the various subject-matter areas and on different grade levels are listed in the paragraphs that follow.

Primary Grades

Reading

Students solved story problems geared to individual instructional levels. They were guided through the fundamental stages of reading the problem, thinking about it, and solving it.

Second graders read and interpreted graphs displayed on posters and in individual folders.

Children in a third-grade class created their own story problems using phrases such as *fewer than, greater than, total, less, has how many,* and so on.

Students categorized mathematics words. For example:

geometric shapes
    square
    triangle
    polygon
money
    penny
    quarter
    dollar
fractions
    half
    third
    fourth

Simple recipes were made available to students prior to Math Day. One group chose to make "no bake" cookies. After reading the recipe, they had to measure the ingredients using teaspoons, cups, and pints.

Many teachers read to their classes, using books from Crowell's Young Math Books such as *How Did Numbers Begin* and *Zero Is Not Nothing* by Mindel and Harry Sitomer, *Bigger and Smaller* by Robert Froman, and *Fractions Are Parts of Things* by J. Richard Dennis. Book selections were based on students' interests or relationship to the area studied. Low- and high-order questions were asked by the teachers to stimulate class discussions.

Spelling

Words selected from previous mathematics lessons were used for spelling.

Number words through *fifty*
Ordinal names through *tenth*
Words relating to money
Words relating to time and to the calendar
Words for shapes
Metric measurement terms
Words relating to the four basic operations
Words indicating position in space
Words relating to life skills—*birthday, address, phone number*
Words associated with mathematical symbols—

Symbol	Word
=	equal
+	plus
>	greater than
<	less than
–	minus

Emphasis was placed on word meaning as well as structural and phonetic analysis.

Language

Students composed sentences using selected words from the spelling vocabulary. Emphasis was placed on language mechanics and expression.

Mathematical sentences were translated into verbal sentences. For example:

$$20 - 5 = 15$$
Twenty minus five equals fifteen.

A third-grade class took a walking tour in the neighborhood of the school and made a list of the ways in which numbers are used.

For creative writing, students selected one of the following titles and wrote stories or paragraphs to go with their titles.

NUMBERS CAN BE TRICKY

MATH IS IMPORTANT

MATH CAN KEEP YOU HEALTHY

I AM GOOD IN MATH

A VISIT TO THE LAND OF NUMBERS

A VERY IMPORTANT DATE

I LIKE MATH

SPENDING FIVE DOLLARS

MY UNLUCKY NUMBER

BIG SURPRISES IN LITTLE BOXES

Handwriting

Students were given guided practice in—

- correctly forming numerals, 0 through 9,
- writing the date in various forms (birthdates, addresses, zip codes, and phone numbers),
- writing famous birthdates and holidays,
- writing a series of numerals coming before and after specified numbers,
- writing the value of various groups of coins.

Mathematics

Teachers created a mock grocery store at one end of the hall. Students had been earning points for good work and behavior. On Math Day they traded points for play money, which was used to purchase items from the store. They were able to keep the items if they were successful in making the correct change. Parents supervised the grocery store.

First-grade students used hand clocks to show and tell time (hour and half hour) at designated periods during the day.

"Math bees" (similar to the spelling bee) were held for grades two and three in the small auditorium and gymnasium respectively. Many parents attended these events. The winners were awarded badges.

After using scales to find their weights, students compared their weights with those of classmates.

In one group of students, each was given $25.00 to spend for toys. The children used store ads to make their purchases, which were itemized on paper. Each student had to spend the exact sum of money given.

Social studies

Students used maps to compute distances between various places. Several classes constructed graphs illustrating the kinds of transportation that they used for traveling to school.

Science

Temperatures for specified times during the day were recorded on graphs and students compared changes in the temperatures. One second-grade class recorded on a bar graph the number of birds seen at designated times eating from a bird feeder outside the classroom window. The bird feeder had been made by the students.

Music

Students sang and dramatized number songs, such as "Three Blind Mice," "Ten Little Indians," "This Old Man," and so on.

Physical education

Students compared the number of hops and skips done by team members, counted by twos while skipping, and counted by fives the number of full swings (front, back, and front again) while swinging.

Art

Students made pictures with various geometric shapes.

Intermediate and upper grades

Reading

Students read biographies of great mathematicians and made oral reports to the class.

Students in grades seven and eight did research on the following topics:

THE BEGINNING OF METRICS
WHO WAS CELCIUS?
THE FIRST COMPUTER
BUILDING THE PYRAMIDS
THE MAKING OF THE FIRST CALENDAR
THE WORLD'S GREATEST MATHEMATICIAN

Word problems based on real-life situations were provided. After reading each problem, students had to write the operation(s) needed to solve the problem. For example:

Ruthie is taking dancing lessons at $4.25 per lesson. How many lessons will she get for $34.00? <u>Divide</u>

Students matched the prefixes of metric units of measurement with the meanings.

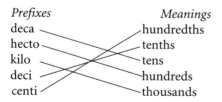

Prefixes		*Meanings*
deca		hundredths
hecto		tenths
kilo		tens
deci		hundreds
centi		thousands

After reading big amounts of money written verbally, students wrote the numerical value. For example:

Twenty million, seventy-five thousand, six hundred three dollars = $20 075 603.00

Students used words with multiple meanings in sentences to emphasize the words' mathematical meanings. For example: check, balance, change.

Students read many books relating to mathematics, such as *The Wonderful World of Mathematics* by Lancelot Hogben; *Man the Measurer* by Roy A. Gallant; *The Story of Numbers* by Patricia Lauber; *Graphs* by Dyno Lowenstein; and *Maps, Tracks, and the Bridges of Königsberg* by Michael Holt.

Sixth-grade students analyzed likenesses and differences in line graphs, bar graphs, pie graphs, and pictographs.

Spelling

The spelling vocabulary was based on previous mathematics lessons.

Words relating to fractions and decimals
Words relating to shapes
Words relating to measurement
Words relating to temperature
Words relating to metric measurement

Students made fractions to show the makeup of the words in terms of vowels and consonants. For example:

degrees   3/7 vowels, 4/7 consonants

Students composed sentences using the mathematics vocabulary to show an understanding of the mathematical meanings. Original word problems were created using catalogs and magazines for data.

For creative writing, each student wrote a story or paragraph(s), after making a selection from the following titles:

MATH INTRIGUES ME
WHAT IS A NUMBER?
HOW TO BECOME A GOOD MATH STUDENT
LIVING LIKE A MILLIONAIRE
WHY I WANT TO BECOME A MATHEMATICIAN
A WORLD WITHOUT NUMBER
MATH IS IMPORTANT
MATH IS EASY
WHY I LIKE (DON'T LIKE) MATH
IF THERE WERE NO CIRCLES

Handwriting

Students made shopping lists showing the various prices for the listing items, using catalogs and magazines for reference.

Mathematics

Students in the various grades were involved in a multiplicity of meaningful activities such as computing hourly wages and overtime pay, calculating interests on savings accounts, balancing checkbooks, using ads from newspapers to "shop for groceries," making cash-register receipts showing the sales tax and total, comparing the prices of the same items from different stores, and converting customary measures to the metric values.

Social studies

Students used the scales on maps and globes to find the distances in miles between specified locations; compared the population density of the United States in certain time periods using pictographs, line graphs, bar graphs, and charts; and constructed graphs depicting the population of various cities throughout the United States.

Science

Science classes were engaged in such activities as calculating the boiling point of water at various altitudes, constructing graphs that showed the noon temperature for five days during the previous week, and using the Fahrenheit and Celsius scales to compare the boiling and freezing points of water.

Music

Students worked on the following projects:

(1) Illustrating musical measure as a mathematical set (fig. 1).
(2) Identifying musical sequence as it related to form, an idea synonymous in principle to arithmetical progression (fig. 2).
(3) Relating the writing of music to fractions. For example:

6/8 time = six beats to a measure with the eighth note receiving one beat

Fig. 1

Fig. 2

Band

Students used musical notation to represent numbers and composed "mathematical sentences" for classmates to solve (fig. 3).

Physical education

Students played games of landing the basketball in the net. Then they made ratios and fractions to indicate the numbers of successful and unsuccessful throws. In other activities, students recorded and averaged the weights of their classmates and computed the average scores of the previous year's volley ball and basketball games.

Art

Students drew pictures using parallel lines and perpendicular lines. Other activities included folding paper to make geometric shapes and building designs using circles.

Extending the Idea

Other activities could also be a part of Math Day. The following are possibilities:

(1) Invite resource persons to speak to the students, relating ways in which mathematics is used in their professions.

(2) Have upper-grade students search for cliches and quotations involving words related to mathematics and then relate the meaning for each one. For example:

If at *first* you don't succeed, try again.
A stitch in time saves *nine*.
A *penny* saved is a *penny* earned.
Three is a crowd.

(3) Arrange for media coverage for Math Day.

(4) Instead of a "Math Day," a "Math Week" could be celebrated. During a "Math Week," mathematics fairs and tournaments could be included in the program.

Summary

Math Day, on which mathematics was emphasized in all subjects, was developed because of the need at our school to provide experiences for students in such a way as to help them (1) see that mathematics is not an isolated subject comprised only of computational skills and (2) develop a positive attitude toward mathematics.

The idea was introduced at an in-service meeting. The rationale and guidelines for the day were presented to the faculty, who accepted the plans with much enthusiasm and made suggestions for greater effectiveness.

The students knew about this special day in advance and eagerly anticipated its arrival. The day itself was filled with many valuable learning experiences, which were geared to the needs, interests, and abilities of our students.

Informal discussions and surveys conducted on the day following Math Day indicated that students could provide more positive responses on the usefulness of mathematics to daily living and the importance of mathematics in various subjects than they could in the previous weeks.

No specific study has been done on the direct effect of Math Day at Norwood School, but the faculty seems to have a greater interest in providing stimulating experiences with mathematics for the students.

♩ = 1 beat

♪ = $\frac{1}{2}$ beat

𝅗𝅥 = 2 beats

𝅝 = 4 beats

𝅗𝅥 + 𝅗𝅥 = _____

𝅗𝅥 + 𝅝 = _____

𝅗𝅥 + 𝅗𝅥 − 𝅗𝅥 = _____

Answers: 2, 6, 3

Fig. 3

J. S. WEATHERS

Students Can Discover the Occupational Link with Mathematics

S *cene:* Mathematics class

Student: Mr. Barkley, what good is all this stuff? I'm never going to have to factor anything!

Mr. Barkley: That's a good question, Rob, but how do you know you won't use it?

Student: I just know. I'll never need this junk!

Mr. Barkley: What type of work are you interested in doing after you graduate?

Student: I don't know … architecture … or maybe trucking.

Mr. Barkley: Architects need advanced mathematics, at least as far as calculus, to compute stresses and foundation supports. To understand calculus, you have to master algebra. Truckers need accounting or engineering if they ever want to go beyond driving.

Student: (to himself) Uh huh, sure. Just get me behind the wheel, and I'm gone!

Alternate scene: Mathematics class

Student: Mr. Barkley, what good is all this stuff? I'm never going to have to factor anything!

Mr. Barkley: That's a good question, Rob, and I'm glad you brought it up. Different people in this class will have different needs for algebra, and rather than try to give a specific answer just for one person, I think it best that I show all of you how to answer that question for yourselves as individuals.

Student: What do you mean?

Mr. Barkley: I have a project in mind for the class.

J. S. Weathers *is a retired high school mathematics teacher and guidance counselor. He now works in the electric motor industry at GMR Inc., 2206 Westbrook Street, Greensboro, NC 27407.*

All Students: (to themselves) Uh, oh! Thanks a lot, Rob!

If you find the scenario of the alternate scene to be more comforting and useful than that of the original scene, the following project may be just right for you and your students.

Objectives

This activity is intended to achieve the following objectives:

1. To positively influence student *attitudes* toward mathematics by showing mathematics to be directly useful to them and to their futures

2. To build a file of information relating occupations to mathematics

3. To increase communication, understanding, and appreciation between students and their parents, extended families, and adult acquaintances

Some possible sources of information are people who hold jobs in careers that appeal to students' imaginations.

Teacher's Materials

The following items are used for this activity:

1. Timetable
2. Initial letter to contact person
3. Partial list of occupations
4. Blind letter to personnel officer
5. Interview agreement
6. Follow-up letter
7. Thank-you letter
8. Sources of contacts

Each student receives a copy of items 1–7.

Procedure

Most students work better when they know what is expected and when, so a timetable is a good place to start (table 1). This table can be altered to suit various situations, but ample time should be allowed for each step and the activity should get off the mark quickly. The teacher begins by discussing the "initial letter" with the class (fig. 1). The letter explains the reason for the project from the students' standpoint and should be covered thoroughly. The students spend the next two weeks deciding which occupations most interest them, using the "partial list" as a guide (fig. 2). The teacher should emphasize that an individually meaningful selection is more important than the "right" or "best" choice. A youngster's fantasy serves almost as well as the heart's deepest wish.

By the end of two weeks, all students should have chosen and signed up for an occupation. Post a class copy of the list on a bulletin board. As many as two students in each class may select the same job classification.

The next step presents some difficulty: finding someone to contact in the selected

Table 1
Timetable 1989–90

Elapsed Time	Deadline Date	Activity
0 weeks	_____	Presentation of initial letter
2 weeks	_____	Signup for occupation
2–9 weeks	_____	Record name of contact person
11 weeks	_____	Turn in letters or permission slips
15 weeks	_____	Turn in replies or follow-up letters
19 weeks	_____	Decision time for some students—second follow-up, phone call, new start, or no credit

```
                                                    Your Street Address
                                                    City, State ZIP Code
                                                    Date
Name of Contact Person
Company Name
Street Address
City, State ZIP Code
Dear Mr. (Ms., Mrs.) Last Name:
    I am a first-year algebra student at XYZ High School in Your City, Your State, and I like
the idea of _____(occupation selected for study) as a career.
    My mathematics class is writing people in interesting occupations to ask them about
the use of mathematics in their jobs and about the mathematics background required for
their work. This information will be presented to the whole class, and your reply will
enable me to earn extra credit.
    If you can find the time, would you please answer these two questions and return your
reply to me? I have included a self-addressed, stamped envelope, but  my teacher
requires all replies to be on your company letterhead.

A.  How much mathematics did you have to take to become a _____
    (occupation selected for study)?
B.  Ignoring requirements for school, how much mathematics do you actually need in
    your job?

    Thank you very much for your help and time.

                                                    Sincerely,
                                                    (Your Signature)
                                                    Your Name, Typed
```

Fig. 1. Initial letter

Occupation	Student Initials	Name of Contact Person	Occupation	Student Initials	Name of Contact Person
Accountant	—	_____	Medical laboratory technician	—	_____
Actuary	—	_____	Medical records technician	—	_____
Advertiser	—	_____	Minister, priest, or cleric	—	_____
Agriculturalist	—	_____	Musician	—	_____
Airplane pilot	—	_____	Nurse, LPN	—	_____
Architect	—	_____	Nurse, RN	—	_____
Auto-body repairer	—	_____	Occupational safety and health specialist	—	_____
Bank officer	—	_____	Optician	—	_____
Bank teller	—	_____	Optometrist	—	_____
Biochemist	—	_____	Personnel specialist	—	_____
Chef	—	_____	Pharmacist	—	_____
City manager	—	_____	Physical or occupational therapist	—	_____
Claims representative	—	_____	Physician (specify)	—	_____
Computer programmer	—	_____		—	_____
Computer technician	—	_____		—	_____
Construction inspector	—	_____	Physicist	—	_____
Construction worker	—	_____	Plumber	—	_____
Counselor	—	_____	Police officer	—	_____
Dental assistant	—	_____	Politician	—	_____
Dentist	—	_____	Psychologist	—	_____
Designer	—	_____	Public relations specialist	—	_____
Dietician	—	_____	Purchasing agent	—	_____
Economist	—	_____	Real estate agent	—	_____
Electrician	—	_____	Retailer or marketer	—	_____
Emergency medical technician	—	_____	Sales person	—	_____
Engineer (specify)	—	_____	Secretary	—	_____
FBI agent	—	_____	Social worker	—	_____
Flight attendant	—	_____	Statistician	—	_____
Forester	—	_____	Teacher, K–12	—	_____
Foreign service diplomat	—	_____	Travel agent	—	_____
Geologist or geophysicist	—	_____	Underwriter	—	_____
Insurance agent	—	_____	Urban or regional planner	—	_____
Journalist or news reporter	—	_____	Veterinarian	—	_____
Landscaper	—	_____	Other occupations (specify)	—	_____
Lawyer	—	_____		—	_____
Marketing researcher	—	_____		—	_____

Fig 2. Partial list of occupations

occupation. Ideally, each student would obtain information from a parent who actually works in the chosen field, since such a discussion offers an opportunity for closer parent-child understanding. After all, how many youngsters fully appreciate what their parents do for a living? Naturally, with changing times, advancing technologies, and fluid employment opportunities, this ideal situation is not the norm. A second good choice of contact is a relative; a third, an adult acquaintance.

Many students, especially those in rural areas, will ultimately rely on total strangers for their information. How do they find these contacts? The suggestion of a telephone book from a large city initially raises a few skeptical eyebrows even though this is a reasonable source, albeit something of a blind one. Company names and addresses are given (without ZIP codes) but not the names of specific contact persons in the company. However, most businesses of any size have an employee or department to handle personnel matters, and a blind letter (fig. 3) or phone call to that anonymous person can yield the name your student needs. Many school, county, and city libraries own out-of-town telephone books, and class members may have relatives or friends in larger towns who would be glad to donate an outdated telephone listing. Since postage to any place in the United States is 25¢ and ZIP code information costs nothing, it makes little difference if the student writes to someone across the city or across the country.

Another source of contacts, but not free unless available in your library, is a list of members of the Chamber of Commerce in the city of your choice. These publications often list companies alphabetically as well as by type and include the names of contact persons. I used one from Raleigh, North Carolina, that lists over 2000 member companies and costs only $14.70 including shipping, handling, and sales tax. Chambers of Commerce are delighted to receive inquiries by interested people.

A third suggestion also comes from the telephone system. Bell South offers business directories titled Regional Industrial Pages for $30. Mine covers all of North and South Carolina and contains thousands of categorized business addresses with ZIP codes and telephone numbers, as well as dozens of Chambers of Commerce in the two states.

Fig. 3. Blind letter

Teachers should note that using these sources to find names of contacts might require class time, but students do not need to find the "perfect" source, only one involved in the appropriate job. If a student chooses an occupation so bizarre that he or she cannot find a readily available contact, a more common one should be selected for purposes of the project, but the young person should be encouraged to pursue the original choice for extra credit. Ask students to enter the names of their contacts on the class sign-up sheet as soon as possible. Publicly filling in the blanks beside their initials will encourage procrastinators to start the project.

As to grading, I suggest either letting the entire project be extra credit on a +5, 0, –5 basis if negative credit is allowed in your school system or averaging a 100, nothing, or a O into the student's fourth-quarter grade with a weight of about 5 percent for 0's and 20 percent for 100's. The student receives high credit for effort producing eventual results, no credit for provable effort with no results, and negative credit for no effort.

The rest of the project is easy, especially for those with patience. Using the initial letter as a guide, students compose their letters, type them if possible, and prepare a self-addressed, stamped return envelope. Both should be folded, inserted, sealed into a stamped envelope properly addressed to the contact person, and turned in to the teacher as a unit by the due date. Those students using parents, relatives, or adult acquaintances as sources of information through personal interview rather than by letter should turn in a signed agreement (fig. 4) at the same time. This requirement assures the teacher that all students have appropriate sources of information. The teacher has the responsibility of determining which students have submitted neither letters nor agreements.

By the appointed date, all students must hand in either their replies or a properly addressed, stamped follow-up letter (fig. 5).

Follow-up letters should be accompanied by a copy of the original letter.

What do the students do if they receive no answer to either letter? Some students will inevitably be disappointed. Not everyone is as interested in students as teachers are. Possible avenues of action for students are (1) a second follow-up, (2) a quick telephone call to the slow contact, (3) another attempt with a new contact or a different occupation (hence the need to begin early), or (4) resignation to failure and to receiving no credit.

All contacts should receive a "thank you" letter in return for their information and effort (fig. 6). Remember that we all need a stroke of appreciation.

Results

Rather than consume class time with formal presentations of the replies, I recommend that the presentations be low key. Simply have one student read a reply to the class each day until all have been read. Replies can be read as soon as received. Small doses of information over a month or two make a better impression than one massive assault that blurs and is soon forgotten. Use the first or last three minutes of class time each day. Teachers may have reservations about the value of reading the replies to the class. Our real-life trucker, for example, wrote the following:

> Concerning the necessity of math in transportation, … a knowledge of general math would be required to be a driver. However, for further advancement it would be beneficial to have more than general. Certain categories of transportation require a great deal of math; such as accounting, analysis, engineering, etc. The more math one has the better the chance of advancement.

An answer like that impresses a class full of students because the reply comes directly and personally from someone deeply involved in the occupation who *knows* about what he says.

Fig. 4. Interview agreement

BIBLIOGRAPHY

Sanders, Hal. "When Are We Ever Gonna Have to Use This?" *Mathematics Teacher* 73 (January 1980): 7–16.

```
                                                    Your Street Address
                                                    City, State ZIP Code
                                                    Date
Name of Contact Person
Company Name
Street Address
City, State ZIP Code

Dear Mr. (Ms., Mrs.) Last Name:

    I know you must be very busy right now, but I hope you can find time to answer my
letter about the requirements for mathematics in _____
(occupation selected for study). Unfortunately, if I do not hear from you, I will have to
find someone else to query or lose my chance at extra credit. I hope you understand.

    Thank you for your help and time.

                                                    Sincerely,
                                                    (Your Signature)
                                                    Your Name, Typed

    P.S. I have enclosed a copy of the original letter in case yours has been misplaced.
```

Fig. 5. Follow-up letter

```
                                                    Your Street Address
                                                    City, State ZIP Code
                                                    Date
Name of Contact Person
Company Name
Street Address
City, State ZIP Code

Dear Mr. (Ms., Mrs.) Last Name:

    Thank you so much for your reply to my project question about requirements for
mathematics in (occupation selected for study). The information was exactly what I
needed.

    Good luck in your work!

                                                    Best regards,
                                                    (Your Signature)
                                                    Your Name, Typed
```

Fig. 6. Thank you letter

BETSY K. BENNETT

Now & Then

The Long-Distance Doctor

BERNARD A. Harris, Jr., MD, the first African American astronaut to walk in space, is an engineer, physician, medical research scientist, and pioneer space doctor. He defines "space doctor" as a physician of the future who will know how to keep people healthy while they are living on a space station, how to treat space-related illnesses and injuries, and what measures to take so that a long-term stay at a space station will not cause health problems when the workers return to earth. He describes his own work as learning all that he can from human experience in space and spacelike conditions so that physicians can be well-prepared, competent space doctors when the first space station is built in the immediate future.

Dr. Harris uses a lot of mathematics in all his work, particularly in developing mathematical models of the adaptation of the human body to a variety of conditions. He uses data from those people who have spent time on space missions and from his own experience on space shuttles and during his walk in space in February 1995. However, a factual account of what has happened to a small number of people is not enough information for a practicing space doctor. Therefore, Dr. Harris studies the information carefully to identify patterns, trends, and formulas that will help him predict what is likely to happen to more people who are in space for longer periods of time. He uses information from the simulations of space conditions created by engineers, and he suggests ways that the simulations could provide more data to help him. He knows that the greatly reduced gravity in space means that mus-

cles perform less work, bones do not have to be as strong, and fluids are distributed more evenly throughout the body. The data from similar effects in patients who are required to stay in bed for some time contribute to his knowledge of the changes in the body under these conditions. As Dr. Harris develops exercises and other measures to benefit inactive patients here on earth, he is learning more about ways to employ similar techniques to help people maintain their strength and muscle tone in an environment of microgravity.

Bernard Harris is doing what he has always wanted to do. He is helping people, and he is an astronaut. He is working at the frontiers of both medical knowledge and human ventures into space.

Born in Temple, Texas, Bernard moved

with his family to Greasewood, Arizona, when he was seven, and soon thereafter to Tohachi, New Mexico, where his mother was a teacher for the Bureau of Indian Affairs. He avidly watched *Star Trek* and other space travel programs on one of the two television channels then available in his town, but he spent far more of his time exploring the hills near his home with his friends. They played a number of roles in their games, building forts and drawing up plans and doing the construction according to their own careful specifications. He studied all the mathematics and science he could in school and participated in rocket and science clubs. He liked music as a listener, but even more so as an active participant in the concert and marching bands. At various times he played the trumpet, tuba, trombone, and saxophone. He played the saxophone with a musical group called Purple Haze in the summers and during his college years at the University of Houston. One of his mother's favorite pictures is of Bernard in seventh grade, then four-feet-eleven-inches tall, nowhere near his current six-foot-three-inch frame, nearly lost in the tuba he played.

When Bernard was fifteen, his family moved to San Antonio, Texas. He continued his mathematics, science, and music study at Sam Houston High School; carefully followed the television coverage of the *Apollo* lunar missions; and met the new family physician, an African American doctor, who influenced and helped him. From early on, his path appears to have been leading directly to his work as a doctor and as an astronaut with the National Aeronautics and Space Administration (NASA). In 1978 he completed his under-

---

Betsy Bennett *teaches at Saint Albans School in Washington, DC 20016. She coaches mathematics teams and the JETS engineering team and has been active in both the NCTM and the Mathematical Association of America (MAA) for a number of years.*

graduate work with a degree in biology from the University of Houston. After finishing his doctorate of medicine at Texas Tech University School of medicine in 1982, he began a three-year residency in internal medicine at the Mayo Clinic. His work with a former flight surgeon and his research in calcium metabolism led to a National Research Council Fellowship at the NASA Ames Research Center in Moffett Field, California, and in 1987, to training as a flight surgeon at the Aerospace School of Medicine at Brooks Air Force Base in San Antonio. When he joined the medical science division at NASA, his duties included investigating space adaptation and managing the Exercise Countermeasures Project, the study of exercises designed to prevent the weakening of muscles and bones during extended space flight.

In January 1990, Bernard was selected as an astronaut candidate by NASA, after meeting the education, experience, and health and fitness requirements of this program of specialized training. The survival training included making parachute jumps into various environments; and engineering classes included studying orbital mechanics, spaceship schematics, and wiring diagrams. Each astronaut on a mission must know how to perform the tasks that might be required of any astronaut on that mission. Bernard officially became an astronaut in July 1991 and was qualified as a mission specialist on space-shuttle-flight crews.

Assigned to STS-55, Spacelab D-2, Bernard spent a year and a half, most of that time in Germany, preparing the research in physical and life sciences that he would conduct on this German-sponsored mission aboard the space shuttle *Columbia* from 26 April to 6 May 1993. During that flight, he logged over 239 hours and 4 641 833 miles in space. Less than two years later on 5 February 1995, he was aboard the space shuttle *Discovery* as the STS-63 payload commander and mission specialist, directing life-science experiments and examining astronauts to help determine what is normal for the human body in space. This voyage was the third for the "spacehab," a term for the smaller, more portable spacelab research unit that is part, but not all, of the work of the space mission. In addition to the twenty-three experiments in progress on board, the shuttle staged a rendezvous with the Russian Mir Space Station and two of *Discovery*'s astronauts, Bernard Harris and Michael Foale, walked in space. Their test of the improvements in the new space suits showed that although the suits protected them quite

effectively from the up to 200 degrees Fahrenheit extremes of heat, the temperature inside the suits dropped to 20 degrees Fahrenheit when the temperature in the coldest attitude fell to −165°F. They were not in immediate danger of frostbite or hypothermia, but it was difficult to keep their hands and fingers flexible enough for other tasks, such as deploying and retrieving the massive Spartan 204 astronomy research satellite, weighing 2800 pounds when not in the zero gravity of space.

Bernard and his wife, Sandra Fay Lewis, and their daughter, Brooke Alexandria, live in Houston, Texas. He holds several faculty appointments, including that of associate professor of internal medicine at the University of Texas medical branch, assistant professor of internal medicine at Baylor College of Medicine, and adjunct Professor at the University of Texas School of Public Health. Through his work at Baylor, he sees patients a few hours each week at the South Texas Primary Care Clinic in San Antonio. His many special honors include a Who's Who Among Rising Young Americans citation in 1992, and NASA donated his space suit to the Edward H. White II Museum at Brooks Air Force Base in San Antonio, Texas. Bernard is a licensed private pilot and tries to find time to pursue his interests in music, scuba diving, running, and sailing.

To Be an Astronaut

For those who would like to follow in Bernard's footsteps in space, NASA has a few prerequisites (NASA History Office 1994).

Applicants for the astronaut corps must meet the following minimum requirements before submitting an application:

- Both mission specialists and pilots must be United States citizens and have a bachelor's degree in engineering, biological science, physical science, or mathematics from an accredited institution. An advanced degree is preferred.
- Mission-specialist candidates must also have three years of related professional experience; a postgraduate degree may be substituted for part or all of that requirement.
- Pilots need at least 1000 hours of pilot-in-command experience in jet aircraft and preferably some flight-test experience.

- Mission-specialist candidates must have uncorrected vision of 20/100 or better, have a blood-pressure reading of no more than 140/90 in a sitting position, and must be between five feet and six feet four inches.
- Pilot candidates must have vision that is 20/50 or better uncorrected, which is correctable to 20/20 in each eye, and must be between five feet four inches and six feet four inches.

NASA offers a wide variety of educational publications and audiovisual materials of special interest to teachers of science and mathematics. NASA Spacelink, an electronic information system, can be accessed by computer through direct-dial modem or the Internet. For more information, contact Education Programs Office, Mail Code CL 01, NASA Marshall Space Flight Center, Huntsville, AL 35812-0001; (205) 544-6360.

Owing to the relatively brief history of the space-shuttle program, a historical feature was not included with this "Now & Then."

Bibliography

Lyndon B. Johnson Space Center. Biographical data on Bernard A. Harris Jr. MD, 12 December 1944.

NASA History Office. Biographical Data, Lyndon B. Johnson Space Center. Houston, Tex.: NASA History Office, 1994.

Phelps, J. Alfred. *They Had a Dream: The Story of African-American Astronauts.* Novato, Calif.: Presidio Press, 1994.

The student activities accompanying this article were developed by Vince O'Connor, mathematics curriculum specialist for the Milwaukee Public Schools, Milwaukee, Wisconsin. O'Connor also served as editor for the middle grades material in NCTM's joint project with NASA called Mission Mathematics: Linking Aerospace and the NCTM Standards. For more information, contact Department I, 1906 Association Drive, Reston, VA 20191-1593.

Answers to the Mission Specialist Activity Sheet

(next page)

1. Student responses will vary. Some possible responses are 10 days, 10 breakfasts, 280 mathematics classes, and about 160 movies.

2. Answers will vary. Some examples of responses are about 1400 trips across the United States, about 167 times around the earth, or about 9 roundtrips to the moon.

3. Approximate calculations: 8 000 miles + 250 miles + 250 miles = 8 500 miles (diameter of the orbit), $\pi D = 3.14 \times 8\,500$ miles ≈ 26 690 miles per orbit, and 4 164 183 miles ÷ 26 690 miles per orbit ≈ 156 orbits.

4. (*a*) Approximate calculations: 4 164 183 miles ÷ 240 hours ≈ 17 350 miles per hour.

   (*b*) Approximate calculations: 240 hours ÷ 156 orbits ≈ 1.53 hours per orbit. He would fly over about 90 minutes later.

5. (*a*) Student graphs will vary. One sample is shown using degrees Fahrenheit:

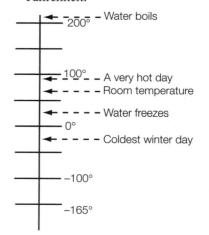

   (*b*) Answers will vary. One line of reasoning: it probably kept the temperature under 100°F. If not, the article would have mentioned the: hot conditions. Since 100°F is just about body temperature, a high temperature less than that would not be a problem.

Mission Specialist Activity Sheet

NAME_____

Understanding the Magnitude of Living in Space

While the astronauts are in the shuttle, circling the globe, life goes on here on earth. What is it *really* like to be up there and to live and work in a weightless environment? The article gives several facts about Bernard's space flight. Sometimes pure numbers do not allow us to get the full impact of the vastness of space or the routine work of a space mission. Let us use those facts to get a better idea about what life is like on a space-shuttle mission.

1. *Time:* Bernard flew on the STS-55 from 26 April to 6 May 1993. The article describes how long the STS-55 was in space. Find other ways to describe the length of the mission, using other units of measure. For example, how many "breakfasts" did the crew eat in space? How many mathematics classes could they have had? How many movies could they have watched?

2. *Distance traveled:* The article states that Bernard logged 4 164 183 miles in space on that mission. How far is that distance in relative terms? Find some interesting ways to help a friend understand that distance. For example, how many times could an astronaut circle the earth in that number of miles?

3. *Orbits:* Some people think that the shuttle's orbit goes halfway to the moon. Actually, the typical orbit is closer to 250 miles above the earth. The circumference of a circle is πD, where D is the diameter of the circle. Assume that the diameter of the earth is 8000 miles. Use these facts to figure out how many orbits Bernard made on the STS-55.

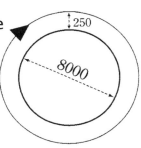

4. *Speed:* We usually talk about speed as miles per hour (mph).

   (*a*) Figure out how fast Bernard was traveling on the STS-55, using miles per hour.

   (*b*) Think about the trip in "minutes per orbit" or how long it took the crew to circle the earth. Suppose that Bernard was flying over your city right now. How long before he would pass over again?

5. *Temperature extremes:* The article mentions how the astronauts tested an improved space suit, which protects them from the extreme temperatures in space.

   (*a*) Make a graph that will help a person understand how hot and how cold the outside temperatures were on the STS-55. Be sure to include some good reference points, such as room temperature, a cold soft drink, and so on.

   (*b*) The article mentioned the low temperature experienced inside the space suit but did not mention the high temperature. How high do you think the temperature rose inside the space suit? Tell why you think that your estimate is a good one.

JIM HERSBERGER AND BILL FREDERICK

Flower Beds and Landscape Consultants:
Making Connections in Middle School Mathematics

FOR several years, the following problem has been presented in algebra and calculus classes, elementary education classes, and in-service sessions on problem solving:

A farmer wants to enclose a pasture using an existing fence and ninety-six meters of fence stored in a shed. What is the largest rectangular pasture that can be made if the farmer uses the existing fence as one side of the rectangle?

This version of the problem has worked very well in various classroom contexts. It has allowed problem solving through systematic trial and error to be tied to graphical solutions of quadratic equations, to algebraic solutions of quadratic equations, and to optimization problems in calculus. In short, the many ways in which the problem can be solved have allowed students to establish connections among concepts, contexts, and procedures.

Using this problem with middle school students requires several modifications designed to reduce the number of whole-number possibilities. Students are placed in groups of three and are given rulers, graph paper, and, depending on the students, calculators. The following problem is handed to each group:

You have been hired by Mr. and Mrs.

Jim Hersberger *and* Bill Frederick *teach at Indiana University–Purdue University Fort Wayne, Fort Wayne, IN 46805. Hersberger has been working in classrooms with middle-grades students and teachers for fifteen years. Frederick has recently completed with twenty-nine middle grades teachers a year-long project that focused on developing algebraic skills using spreadsheets and on constructing appropriate geometric understanding using geometric-conjecturing software.*

Green as landscape consultants. They have twenty-four feet of landscape timber and want to know how best to make a flower garden along the side of their home. Mrs. Green believes that the flower garden should be a rectangle. Mr. Green believes that the foundation of the house should be one side of the rectangle and that all twenty-four feet of timber should be used. They would like you to describe the possibilities to them, with scale drawings, and to furnish a written recommendation specifying what they should do and why.

Having students evaluate mathematical representations and their own thinking is a necessary component of any program designed to encourage higher-level thinking and mathematical reasoning. This version of the problem encourages such evaluation and is preferable to the earlier version for several other reasons. First, the students have a direct stake in the problem; they are the ones with the responsibility, not some mythical farmer. Second, the smaller number of possibilities makes it easy to use graph paper to draw all the possible flower gardens with whole number dimensions. This process helps introduce or reinforce geometric concepts and images in an applied setting. Third, the students are not told what criteria to use in their selection; they must instead reach agreement among themselves about how to evaluate the different possibilities. Fourth, the students must write up their recommendation in a coherent fashion, which establishes yet another context for creating meaning and forming connections.

When this activity is used in this form, interesting discussions always take place. Students invariably ask for further information:

- Do the dimensions have to be whole numbers? (The teacher should affirm that assumption if asked and indicate that alternatives will be considered for a follow-up activity.)
- What are the dimensions of the house?
- How much room do the Greens have in their yard?
- What is the shape of their yard?
- Does the yard have a swing set?
- Are trees present?
- Do the Greens have children?
- Does the yard have fences?

The response to students' questions can vary. Typically, the teacher responds only to the group asking the question, which allows considerable flexibility in answering. For example, one group might be told that the neighbor's yard is eight feet away, and another group, that the neighbor's yard is twelve feet away. This technique later makes it easy for students to see how different beginning conditions affect the final decision. As a matter of classroom management, the teacher can adopt the rule that if three different groups ask the same question, and everyone is expected to work from the same response, the whole class will participate in a discussion to build consensus. This discussion can start as soon as the question is asked for the third time.

Several strategies can be adopted to ensure that the groups do not rely on the teacher and that as much as possible, everyone in the group is fully involved. Some examples of responses by the teacher include refusing to answer at all, usually with a lighthearted comment, such as, "You appear to have mistaken me for a member of your group"; making sure that everyone in the group knows what the question is before responding, usually by moving away and coming back in a few moments to give the group more time for discussion; and having a group member other than the student who requests the teacher's assistance ask the question.

The teacher always makes some suggestions during the groups' consultation time. Not surprisingly, these suggestions should be designed to ensure that during their investigations, the groups consider whether some choices allow more flowers to be planted. However, whether this issue is part of a group's decision process or recommendation is entirely up to its members.

When all groups are finished, they present their findings to the class. During this time, the seeds for more connections are being planted as students see alternative solutions and choices or have their choices and solutions corroborated by other groups. After the presentations, the possibilities for making connections are exploited by extending the investigation.

Some samples of student-generated recommendations offer vivid examples of the amount of involvement in this activity. For examples of students' drawings, see figures 1 and 2.

- We would recommend the rectangle with measurements 4 × 16 × 4 and area of 64 feet It is not the largest, but you still get a good-sized area. It also covers more of the side of your house, so it will give the appearance of a larger landscaped area. There is also room to go 2 plants deep, and it won't eat up a great deal of yard space.

- The 6 × 12 × 6 will give you the most area (72 square feet), and the 1 × 22 × 1

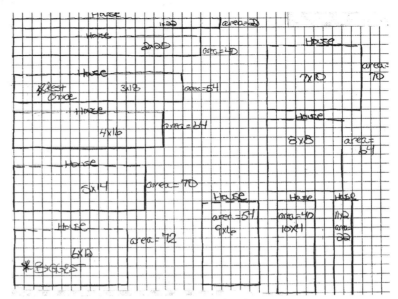

Fig. 1. A group's drawing

and the 11 × 2 × 11 will both give you the least (22 square feet). We think the best one is the 5 × 14 × 5, which gives you 70 square feet, which is almost the largest and doesn't take as much space out of the yard as the largest.

- I would recommend the 2 × 20 × 2 rectangle because it would cover much of the length of the house. Even though it has almost the smallest area, a lot of flowers can be put in a 40-square-foot area, and it will look more full when they start to grow and spread out.

- We prefer the 2 × 20 × 2 garden; it provides easier access to plants without stepping in dirt.

- We would select the 4 × 16 × 4. You would be able to spread flowers and bushes out along the length of the home, and this would be much easier to mow around than some of the others. If this was centered on the length of the home it would look nice. Roots grow down and out through the soil. Although this isn't the largest amount of area, you could still plant a lot. Plus, in most cases people living in a subdivision have neighbors close to them on either side. If you are located in a subdivision with neighbors next door, you won't want your

landscape timber taking up a majority of your yard; this just wouldn't look right.

At this point, and not before, students are asked if a largest area exists and when that area will occur. If a group has created a bar graph of dimensions and areas, that group's work is looked at again by the teacher and then by all the groups. If no group has created a bar graph, the teacher explicitly makes the connection to earlier investigations in which they have used bar graphs and suggests ways in which such

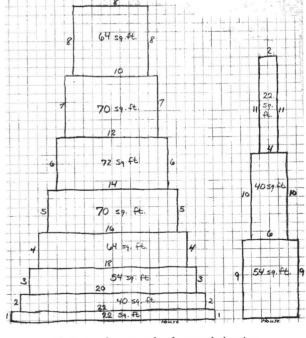

Fig. 2. Another example of a group's drawing

graphs could be applied to this problem. The students are asked to conjecture about what dimensions will lead to the largest area if the amount of timber on hand is different from what they have considered and to justify their response. At this stage, many groups cannot formulate a conjecture.

The method of extending the activity depends on how much technology is available. One easy way is for each group to start with a different amount of timber—typically 12, 16, 18, 20, 28, 30, 32, and 36 feet—and consider the possibilities for the problem again. The resultant bar graphs and tables from each group amply verify "correct" conjectures, supply data for groups who were unable to formulate conjectures earlier, and reinforce the idea that tables and bar graphs are useful tools for displaying information and making decisions.

Most groups decide that they should make the side not touching the wall of the house twice as long as the sides touching the wall but are unable to describe how to find these dimensions except through trial and error. Usually at least one group adds to the statement by suggesting that the total amount of timber should be divided by 4 to determine the desired 2:1 ratio. If several totals that are not divisible by 4, such as 18 and 30, have been included, the class must come to terms with that issue. Groups that have made the "divide by 4" insight will proceed on the assumption that non-whole-number dimensions are allowed. Other groups tend to say, "That would be biggest, but isn't allowed" and then opt for one of the two adjoining possibilities.

One of the most powerful tools for helping students make connections and conjectures is the spreadsheet. Spreadsheets may be used in many ways: as tools to solve problems at advanced levels and with elementary students (Parker and Widmer 1992; Verderber 1992); as tools for creating modern art (Carter 1992); and as tools for helping students formalize or systematize problem-solving strategies (Sgroi 1992). The intent of this extension of the activity is to have students use spreadsheets as tools to investigate their conjectures and to help them make meaningful algebraic connections among variables, graphs, and functions.

In classes where spreadsheets are available, this problem is typically presented after the students have had considerable experi-

ence in using spreadsheets to solve problems systematically. Students generalize their computational understanding of how to do specific arithmetic in a problem to create the formulas that can be used in spreadsheets. Students are asked to explain how to do the arithmetic to find a desired result many times in the process of constructing spreadsheets. The teacher does not tell them how to create the spreadsheets but asks and answers questions to help the students construct the spreadsheets.

Figure 3 shows a completed spreadsheet for the twenty-four-feet-of-timber version. The teacher works with the students to create the spreadsheets, using formulas, copying, and pasting. For example, this spreadsheet was created by filling cell A2 with the number 1. Cell A3 was then filled with the formula (= A2 + 1), which was then filled down to cells A4 through A12. In a similar fashion, cell B2 was filled with the formula (= 24 - 2 * A2), and cell C4, with (= A2 * B2). All formulas were then filled down in the appropriate columns.

Students develop spreadsheets through class discussion augmented by a demonstration computer, preferably with projection capabilities, but the development is perhaps much more effective when students work in pairs in a networked environment. The more students create on their own, with modeling by the teacher and explicit encouragement to look for connections, the more connections they will make.

Finally, in one more attempt to set the stage for more connections to algebraic constructs, the spreadsheet's charting and graphing capabilities are employed (fig. 4).

This visual connection to the problem, along with the precision of the spreadsheet, allows students to experience the graphical nature of the situation in ways that are unlikely to occur from the students' more imprecise, hand-drawn graphs. In addition, it allows students to see how the problems are connected graphically when different amounts of timber yield the same-shaped bar graph every time (see figs. 5 and 6).

The activity and extensions described in this article allow students to develop mathematical concepts connected to area and perimeter in a rich, real-life setting.

They learn to use such mathematical tools as tables, graphs, diagrams, and spreadsheets to explore the problem, see relationships, and make and test their conjectures about those relationships. They think mathematically and begin to think algebraically.

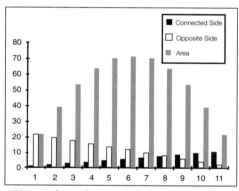

Fig. 4. A flower-bed graph for 24 feet of timber

	A	B	C
1	Connected Side	Opposite Side	Area
2	1	30	30
3	2	28	56
4	3	26	78
5	4	24	96
6	5	22	110
7	6	20	120
8	7	18	126
9	8	16	128
10	9	14	126
11	10	12	120
12	11	10	110
13	12	8	96
14	13	6	78
15	14	4	56
16	15	2	30

Fig. 5. A flower-bed spreadsheet for 32 feet of timber

	A	B	C
1	Connected Side	Opposite Side	Area
2	1	22	22
3	2	20	40
4	3	18	54
5	4	16	64
6	5	14	70
7	6	12	72
8	7	10	70
9	8	8	64
10	9	6	54
11	10	4	40
12	11	2	22

Fig. 3. Flower-bed spreadsheet for 24 feet of lumber

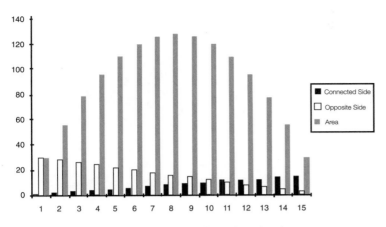

Fig. 6. A flower-bed graph for 32 feet of timber

References

Carter, Claudia J. "Using Technology in Graphing." *Mathematics Teacher* 85 (February 1992):118–21.

Parker, Janet, and Connie Carroll Widmer. 'Teaching Mathematics with Technology: Computation and Estimation." *Arithmetic Teacher* 40 (September 1992): 48–51.

Sgroi, Richard J. "Systematizing Trial and Error Using Spreadsheets." *Arithmetic Teacher* 39 (March 1992): 8–12.

Verderber, Nadine L. "Tin Cans Revisited." *Mathematics Teacher* 85 (May 1992): 346–49.

Whitin, David J. "One Point of View: The Dangers of Implementing the Standards; or, When Bad Things Happen to Good Ideas." *Arithmetic Teacher* 40 (September 1992): 8–9.

KEVIN KINNEAVY

The Pond:
Doing Research Together

NTERDISCIPLINARY approaches to teaching all subjects are central to the middle school concept. Such approaches can be especially useful for teaching mathematics, a subject that has traditionally been the bane of many students' existence. The NCTM recognizes the importance of interdisciplinary instruction in its *Curriculum and Evaluation Standards for School Mathematics* (1989, 84).

Kevin Kinneavy *teaches at Central Middle School, Columbia Heights, MN55421; kevink@metro2.kl2.mn.us. He enjoys teaching mathematics through the use of hands-on, real-world applications; interdisciplinary approaches; and technology in the classroom.*

Photographs by Kevin Kinneavy; all rights reserved.

Unfortunately, many obstacles impede the development of good interdisciplinary units. First, many teachers have difficulty finding appropriate topics that will interest and motivate students. Second, structuring units in ways that adequately address curricular concerns in several major subject areas simultaneously may be daunting. Third, insufficient time for teachers to meet and coordinate lesson plans complicates the preparation of creative interdisciplinary units. Finally, the scheduling constraints within the greater school environment can also hamper the execution of major interdisciplinary units.

With a little support, however, middle school teachers can overcome these difficulties and develop appropriate, creative, and interesting interdisciplinary units for their students. This article describes one such unit designed by myself and the three other teachers on my middle school team: Nancy Gingras, Sylvia Jamros, and Bill LaRose, who teach English, science, and geography, respectively. Working collaboratively as a team, we were able to develop this unit more fully than if any one of us had attempted it on our own. By sharing ideas, we were able to incorporate many key curricular components from each subject area. Working as a team also helped balance the individual work load, as we shared preparation and teaching duties. We also found helpful the accessibility of other people with whom to discuss details and work out daily problems over the course of the project.

Support and Development of the Project

We developed our "Pond Project" as a result of our involvement in 5C5E*, an eighteen-month program that included a summer institute and academic-year workshops. Project 5C5E gave us external support for our project by helping us communicate with other teachers working on similar projects so that we could share ideas and solve the inevitable problems that arose. It also gave us large uninterrupted blocks of time to work together as a team exclusively on this unit. Additionally, 5C5E maintained a resource center with a wide variety of materials to help us develop and execute our unit. Teachers interested in implementing similar projects can find full descriptions and discussion of most of the water-quality tests and other related activities in Mitchell and Stapp (1991), Jacobson (1991 a-c), and Laffond et al. (1992).

The team's involvement in 5C5E also required the support of our school administration, who granted us the professional-leave days to attend workshops. The administration also helped us a great deal by encouraging the development of interdisciplinary projects. Besides our daily individual preparation period, we had a daily team-planning period to work together on such units. Additionally, we were permitted to be creative in the use of our team time and had the latitude to structure the schedule for our team classes as we desired. Many hours were spent during our team-planning period, our preparation periods, and after school discussing, planning, preparing, and reworking the unit. We were fortunate to have the time and flexibility to develop the pond project. Although the time available to us would seem luxurious by many schools' standards, it was necessary to invest that time to develop the project adequately.

*5C5E, the Five College Education in the Earth's Environment, Ecology, and Energy Project, is a research project for K–12 public school teachers funded by the National Science Foundation, grant number TPE 9150262, through the Five College/Public School Partnership in Amherst, Massachusetts. The views expressed in this article do not necessarily reflect those of any of the aforementioned organizations.

Objectives and Goals for the Teachers and Students

The unit we developed was based on the study of a pond and stream located on our school grounds. The overall goals of our unit included presenting all students with interesting and meaningful educational experiences, highlighting connections and relationships among disciplines, making connections between the classroom and the real world, promoting group cohesion and interdependence, and fostering environmental sensitivity. Additionally, this project satisfied my desire to teach mathematics through real applications and hands-on approaches. The initial problem for the students was to find out as much as they could about our pond and determine whether it was ecologically healthy. The students were given various activities to complete in each of their classes to help them collect and later analyze information about the pond. As a result of their research, the students developed a fairly sophisticated understanding of the physical, chemical, and biological characteristics of the pond.

Each teacher was responsible for several interdependent aspects of the study. The eighty students on the team were divided into four heterogeneous classes with each class subdivided into laboratory groups of two to five students. To facilitate daily set-up, collection of data, and clean-up, the students were allotted up to quadruple periods during some of their team classes. Although most of the pond project activities were conducted during an eight-day cycle in autumn and again in spring, a considerable amount of overlap was allowed for preparation and consolidation before and after each cycle in all the team classes.

Fusing Science, Mathematics, English, and Geography

In their science classes, students collected data for water-quality analysis. They took water samples from ten specific sites around the pond and the inlet and outlet streams. Air- and water-temperature measurements were taken at each site, and a series of chemical tests was conducted to measure levels of dissolved oxygen, carbon dioxide, iron, phosphates, nitrates, sulfates, chlorides, pH, and water hardness. Although each student did not collect data for every test at each site, the data collected by the team as a whole furnished ample

data for analysis. Additionally, students studied the plants and animals that live in and around the pond and considered how different test values affect the pond's inhabitants.

Prior to beginning the pond project, in their mathematics classes students familiarized themselves with the metric system through a series of estimation and measurement exercises to facilitate the subsequent collection of data. Once the project formally began, students collected depth-measurement and flow data on the inlet and outlet streams (fig. 1). This pursuit allowed students to study the velocity and volume of water flowing through the pond and observe the effect on the water-quality tests and consequent effect on the pond life.

From the depth measurements taken, students were able to make scale drawings of the cross sections of the inlet and outlet streams and calculate the cross-sectional areas (fig. 2).

Measurements of the water velocity through the cross section were made using toy pinwheels. The pinwheels were calibrated so that the volume of water flowing through the pond could be calculated. The volumes calculated by each student were then compared with those calculated by the rest of the class, and the data were analyzed (fig. 3).

Students also made computations to convert the water-quality test results recorded in science class into usable data for analysis, that is, the number of drops used in a test multiplied by some factor equals mg/L. The final test results were consolidated on data charts for the entire team, and students later put those data on computer spreadsheets. Using Lotus 1-2-3, students constructed tables and graphs for a final analysis of the pond's water quality. Figure 4 shows the table and graph for Dissolved Oxygen Averages; a similar one was constructed for percentage of saturation. Figure 5 shows a report on dissolved oxygen produced by two students.

In their English classes, students began by writing poems to develop sensitivity and a vocabulary for talking and writing about the pond. They worked on computers to write their assignments and were introduced to spreadsheets, which facilitated analysis of the scientific data from the water-quality experiments. Students also wrote a team newspaper, for which they were the reporters and editors. This activity required that they clearly articulate what they were learning. In the spring, the students also produced a video news broadcast to report on events at the pond.

In their geography classes, students worked primarily on mapping the pond area. They measured the length of their strides and practiced pacing to estimate

distances. Students learned to use a magnetic compass in conjunction with pacing to record approximate bearings and distances around the pond. They used homemade astrolabes to measure angles of elevation and depression, and calculated differences in elevation using basic trigonometric relationships. After collecting sufficient data, the students drew topographical maps and built three-dimensional scale models (fig. 6) of the pond area. Some students also used the Internet to communicate with students in other schools whose teachers were working on similar projects in conjunction with 5C5E.

In addition to the formal parts of the pond project, each teacher used various aspects of the project as starting points for other lessons. This overlap gave the students a sense of continuity throughout the school year. For example, the cross-sectional inlet- and outlet-stream drawings became a springboard into concepts of area and volume in mathematics class. Students spent time in science classes studying fossils and then looked in the mud around the pond for imprints that could become fossilized over time. In geography, students charted sunrise and sunset data and studied the weather and its effects on the water

Fig. 1. Students collected data on the inlet and outlet streams

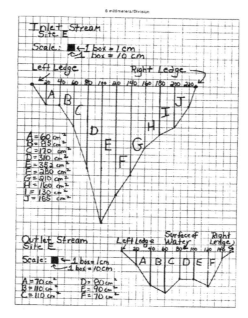

Fig. 2. Cross-sectional areas were calculated and drawn

Flow Measurement Class Data Sheet
Week 1

Date: 10/13/93   Name: Amber
                  Class/Color: Yellow

Inlet Volume Data:

SITE	A	B	C	D	E	F	G	X	Y	Z
VOLUME (cm³)	1035	4	240	57		491				
VOLUME (cm³)	1291					901				
VOLUME (cm³)	1199									

Mean Volume (cm³) = 963   Median Volume (cm³) = 1035

Outlet Volume Data: 4, 57, 491, 801, 1035, 1199, 1291, 2412

SITE	A	B	C	D	E	F	G	X	Y	Z
VOLUME (cm³)	1169	59	904	322		520				
VOLUME (cm³)	1379					705				
VOLUME (cm³)	945									

Mean Volume (cm³) = 750.38   Median Volume (cm³) = 904
59, 322, 520, 705, 904, 945, 1169, 1379

Compare the inlet and outlet volumes and explain the results (what are your conclusions?)

The inlet has less going in the pond then the outlet. I think the reason is because when it rains, most of the water goes into the pond, not the inlet stream. That means most of the water would be going out because the water in the pond has no other place to go.

Fig. 3. Volume data were also included for the inlet and outlet

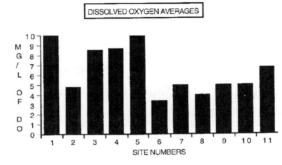

DISSOLVED OXYGEN AVERAGES

CARALEE MANLEY   AMANDA MCLEAN
YELLOW
6/3/94

DATE	1	2	3	4	5	6	7	8	9	10	11 aug.
10/12	6.0	5.0			10.0		5.0				6.5
10/13	7.0		9.0	5.0		0.0					4.7
10/14	11.0	4.0	5.0		5.0		5.0				6.0
10/15				4.0	5.0						4.5
10/19				6.0				4.0	6.5		5.5
10/20				7.0	0.4						3.7
10/21	9.5		10.0								9.8
10/22		6.0	2.0			3.0					3.7
5/10	6.0	6.0		5.0	27.0			7.0			10.2
5/11	13.0		10.0	13.0							12.0
5/16	6.0		21.5	3.0					11.0	10.4
5/17	30.0			22.0					4.0	5.0	15.2
5/18	6.9	4.0	5.0	17.0	17.0	3.5		1.1		7.0	7.7
5/19		4.0		4.0	17.0	6.0			6.0		7.8
5/20				12.0	6.0	4.5	6.0				7.1
5/25	10.0	5.0	6.0	6.0	2.0		3.0		5.5	4.0	5.2
Avg.	10.0	4.9	8.6	8.7	9.9	3.4	5.0	4.0	5.0	5.0	6.8	7.4

Fig. 4. Lotus 1-2-3 printout for dissolved oxygen averages for two students. A similar spreadsheet and graph were produced for percentage of saturation.

and pond life. In English, the pond project formed the basis for a wide variety of potential reading and writing topics. Throughout the year, the pond became a consistent element of the students' learning experience in all their core-subject classes.

At the conclusion of the spring portion of the pond project, the entire team spent a day on a field study at a nearby river. Parents came along as chaperones, and they were impressed with the students' knowledge and ability to explain and complete the tests. The data collected at the river were compared with the data collected at the pond, and conclusions were drawn about the quality of the river water.

Students were also required to create a presentation analyzing and interpreting their data and the implications of those data. Students worked in pairs and chose topics relating to specific aspects of the pond study on the basis of test data, environmental issues, and physical attributes. The presentations included a poster-type display with appropriate charts, tables, graphs, and drawings; an oral explanation; a written report; and their pond notebook containing all data, calculations, and relevant information in a neat, well-organized form. These presentations gave students a sense of closure and offered them the opportunity to demonstrate their newfound knowledge about the pond and its ecology. Since the presentation topics were fairly narrow, each pair was able to research their topic in depth and come up with new and interesting information to share with the team. Although the students were not thrilled at the prospect of preparing yet another presentation so late in the school year, in the end, most students seemed to enjoy both giving and watching the presentations.

Pitfalls and Successes

Projects such as this require that all students be responsible for working cooperatively, completing assignments, staying on

DISSOLVED OXYGEN

Dissolved oxygen or DO is oxygen that has dissolved into the water so that water animals can breathe. It gets into the water by the surrounding air which diffuses into the water.

HOW DOES IT INFECT POND INHABITANTS?

When the water is holding all the dissolved oxygen it can hold at the given temperature, it is said to be 100% saturated with oxygen. If the saturation percent is higher than 125% it could be very dangerous to fish. If it's between 80% and 124% the water is just right. 60% to 79% is a little low but okay. Anything below 60% is not good. When it's below 60% there are probably too many bacteria and other organisms using up the oxygen.

TEST RESULTS

The results of the tests were all fairly close in range except for maybe one or two that were a little high. But that could have been because they were at different sites. Some of the sites could have been in the shade. The saturation results were mostly good. Some of them were below 60%, but the rest of them made sense. The results varied from a little below average to a little above. Some of the reasons for the variation could be because some of the sites were in total sun with not a lot of moving water and other sites were where there was a lot of moving water. (Moving water exposes itself to more air, bringing more air down into the water.)

There were minor differences between the fall and the spring. The fall was slightly lower because it was cooler in the fall and there was not a lot of rain. This spring there has been a lot of rain and has made the pond water higher and faster moving.

There was a of of differences in the different sites. I think the reason was because a lot of the sites were right out in the open sun and only a few were over in the woods in the shade. I think the reason why dissolved oxygen amounts are different in the shade and the sun because water tends to have bigger currents in shady areas.

The day had a big effect on the dissolved oxygen levels because on the days that it rained there is more DO than when the weather is warm. The rain makes the water higher and fast moving. Making it so that it gets more oxygen that dissolves into the water. On sunnier days the water is calm and unmoving making it harder to collect from the air.

GRAPHS

I chose the graphs I did because (which were the graphs of the averages of the drops and the averages of the saturation percentage) they would give me the overall look at the tests. It gave me the basic idea of what sites had more DO and the sites that had less. It also told me what sites had high percentage rates and the ones which were poor.

WHAT COULD HAVE BEEN DONE TO COLLECT BETTER DATA?

The only thing I can think of is if everybody had filled in all there [sic] data. Some of the places on the spreadsheet show that there were a lot of empty spaces. It might have given us a better idea of the dissolved oxygen rates. Another thing would have been to make sure that you did your test carefully and that you did it twice. If one of your test results was very different than your other one it would have been a good idea to do it over again and see which one was off. Our Mahar Pond Project was a great success and I think it should be continued.

Fig. 5 One student's prepared overview of test results and future work

---

task, and generally behaving themselves in an unstructured environment. We found that most students responded well to these responsibilities and welcomed the break from the regular classroom routine. Of course, a few students had difficulties with the individual responsibility. Some had trouble staying focused for extended periods of time and wound up getting into trouble by swimming, splashing, running into the woods, or damaging equipment. Some also had trouble organizing the vast quantities of information. However, many of these problems were reduced during the second year by our giving a little more structure and direction at the beginning of the project, the need for which we had been unable to anticipate our first year. Although we were not completely successful with all students, most became very excited about the pond project. Over the course of the year, many students kept asking when they would get to go out and work on the pond project again.

Equipment and Supplies

Much of the equipment we used—metersticks, stopwatches, clipboards, compasses, miscellaneous laboratory equipment, computers, calculators, video cameras, and the like—is readily available in most schools. The remainder may require loans, donations, or purchases. The chemical test kits required a modest expenditure, but we were able to keep costs down by borrowing a number of test kits from the high school science department and from 5C5E. Other supplies, such as stakes, rope, clothespins, and plastic bottles, were purchased or donated by parents. We also discovered that students needed specific forms on which to record their data, so we created quite a number of worksheets of various types to allow for accurate and complete recording of the data.

Fig. 6. A three-dimensional scale model of the pond was part of the assignment.

Conclusion: Benefits of Interdisciplinary Work

Although putting together a disciplinary unit of this nature requires a great deal of initial planning, preparation, and coordination, the payoff for the students and teachers alike is tremendous.

The pond project provided many occasions for students to practice open-ended problem solving, mathematical reasoning, estimation, and measurement. It required that they communicate their mathematical ideas to others in both written and verbal form. Students had to develop number sense and assess the reasonableness of their results. They worked with the concepts of length, area, volume, measurement of angles, trigonometry, scale drawing, and conversion factors in an applied context. They explored patterns and relationships in the data. They used geometry for mapping and their analysis of the flow, and they used statistics for analysis, interpretation, and presentation of their data. All these aspects of students' mathematical development are cited for increased emphasis in the NCTM's *Curriculum and Evaluation Standards for School Mathematics* (1989, 70–72) and go well beyond the traditional emphasis on computation in the mathematics curriculum.

Furthermore, this project allowed students to explore and achieve to the limits of their own abilities and did not constrain them to the specific material presented in a textbook. Through the study of the pond, the students became actively involved in their own learning and were able to make connections among mathematical ideas. Additionally, by pursuing this project in an interdisciplinary form and applying mathematical ideas to the real world in a concrete way, students came to realize that mathematics does not exist in a vacuum. Mathematics became an important and necessary part of the students' English, science, and geography classes. And each of these, in turn, became an integral part of their mathematics classes.

References

Jacobson, Cliff. *Water, Water Everywhere: Student Reading Unit (Basic Text).* Loveland, Colo.: The Hach Co., 1991a.

———. *Water, Water Everywhere: Teacher's Guide and Experiments.* Loveland, Colo.: The Hach Co., 1991b.

———. *Water, Water Everywhere: Water Quality Factors Reference Unit.* Loveland, Colo.: The Hach Co., l991c.

Laffond, Wanita Sioui, Michelle Lee, Peg McDaniel, Lenore Paul, Norman Price, and Paul Smith. *Mapping the School Grounds.* Amherst, Mass.: The Five College/Public School Partnership, 1992. Available from the Five College/Public School Partnership, P.O. Box 740, Amherst, MA 01004.

Mitchell, Mark K., and William B. Stapp. *Field Manual for Water Quality Monitoring: An Environmental Education Program for Schools.* Dexter, Mich.: Thomson-Shore Printers, 1991. Available from William B. Stapp, 2050 Delaware Avenue, Ann Arbor, MI 48103.

National Council of Teachers of Mathematics. *Curriculum and Evaluation Standards for School Mathematics* Reston, Va.: The Council, 1989.

TRENT M. DOYLE

The Civil War and the *Standards:*
Some Mathematical Activities

The cold passed reluctantly from the earth, and the retiring fogs revealed an army stretched out on the hills, resting. As the landscape changed from brown to green, the army awakened, and began to tremble with eagerness at the noise of rumors.

—*Stephen Crane*

WHEN I lived in Virginia several years ago, I developed a keen interest in Civil War history. The abundance of battlefield parks, museums, and cemeteries located throughout the state generated and sustained my interest to learn more.

Trent Doyle *is a former middle school mathematics teacher currently working as an air-quality scientist with Enserch Environmental Corporation, 143 Union Boulevard, Suite 1010, Lakewood, CO 80228-1824. He aspires to return to teaching at the secondary level.*

A study of the Civil War is frequently included in the middle school social studies curriculum. Reading Stephen Crane's *The Red Badge of Courage* (1990) couples social studies and literature content as a reader is immediately carried on a vicarious journey that personalizes the real dilemmas of a nation undergoing a civil war. An interdisciplinary unit on the Civil War presented classes with a mathematical context.

Many students find middle school mathematics to be "irrelevant, dull, and routine" (NCTM 1989, 65), and I anticipated that coupling topics emphasized by the *Curriculum and Evaluation Standards* (NCTM 1989) with those of the Civil War would stimulate the interest of my students in a manner analogous to the way Crane's story can spark a discussion in a social studies class.

The *Curriculum Standards* advises that "all mathematics should be studied in contexts that give the ideas and concepts meaning" and that students should be given opportunities "to observe the interaction of mathematics with other school subjects" (NCTM 1989, 67, 84). The following three activities may prove useful for others in a similar setting.

Activity 1—Measurement, Ratios, and Proportions

Historical background

The Union's naval blockade of the Confederacy played a key role in disrupting the flow of sorely needed supplies into the South and hindered its trading efforts with foreign markets. The North began its blockade with sixty-nine ships, of which half were sailing vessels. Two hundred

These "soldiers" are participating in the reenactment honoring the 125th anniversary of the battle of Antietam.

steam vessels soon supplemented this effort. In 1861, one in ten Confederate blockade runners was caught. In 1862, the Union began to capture one of every eight ships; in 1863, one of four; and by 1864, one of every two. From 1861 to 1865, approximately 1650 ships served as blockade runners for the South.

Exercises

Ask students to examine the importance of the Union's naval blockade and discuss its impact on the Confederate's war effort. The following mathematical exercises can aid in this analysis.

1. Ask students to determine the amount of Confederate coastline that Union ships had to encircle. This task, given without further elaboration, can challenge students' problem-solving skills, which require defining, clarifying, and planning. Students need some experience in dealing with vague or ill-defined problems. The students or groups that suggest simply looking up the necessary coastline data in an atlas or an almanac should be complemented for their forethought. To assess the viability of such a solution, ask all students to work through the following activity.

Working individually or in pairs, and using string, ask students to measure the Confederate coastline on enlarged maps, detailed enough to show harbors and other ports. Do not forget to include a portion of the Mississippi River as part of the South's perimeter. Using the map's scale, a proportion can be solved that yields the total distance blockaded. The following example assumes a map's scale of 1 inch equals 40 miles. The distance measured is 100 inches, so the actual distance is 4000 miles.

$$\frac{1 \text{ inch}}{40 \text{ miles}} = \frac{100 \text{ inches}}{\text{actual distance}}$$

2. Students can use this result combined with a knowledge of the number of ships at the Union's disposal to calculate the length of coastline for which each vessel was responsible. For our example, the ratio of 200 ships to 4000 miles simplifies to show that each blockade runner was responsible for 20 miles of coastline. An observant individual might point out that not all the coastal waters were navigable and that the blockade runners typically departed from, and returned to, certain ports. Ask students to consider these and other constraints in

their calculations. For example, a student might modify the calculation to incorporate a notion that a steam vessel could cover more territory on a regular basis than a sailing vessel. Another student might suggest that a source of fuel was needed for the steam vessel. Therefore, these ships needed to be located in certain areas. The possibilities for expanding the problem constraints are endless, and they give students practice solving real-world problems.

3. To further analyze the Union's blockading efforts, students can convert into percents the given ratios of blockade runners caught. Again, proportions can be used. In 1861:

$$\frac{1}{10} = \frac{P}{100}$$

Therefore, 10 percent of the blockade runners were caught. Using the foregoing data, an extension activity might center on the following question: By the end of 1864, how many blockade runners for the South were still in operation? Assume the Confederacy had all 1650 ships at the start of the war. A series of proportions could be used to solve this problem. Note how students handle the decimal results. For example, what does 0.5 of a ship mean? In 1861:

$$\frac{1}{10} = \frac{P}{1650}$$

The solution shows that 165 were caught and 1485 remained. In 1862:

$$\frac{1}{8} = \frac{P}{1485}$$

A total of 185 were caught and 1300 remained. In 1863:

$$\frac{1}{4} = \frac{P}{1300}$$

That year, 325 were caught and 975 remained. In 1864:

$$\frac{1}{2} = \frac{P}{975}$$

A total of 487 were caught and 488 remained. To summarize the exercises, ask students the following questions:

- Does a relationship exist between the blockade runners' success and the overall Confederate war effort?

- What is the nature of this relationship?
- What are some reasons for the observed trend in Union effectiveness?

Students' responses have included the following: "The Union improved their ships. As the war drug on, the Confederacy was forced to use their poorer ships"; "As supplies became scarce in the South, the blockade runners took even greater risks. This resulted in an increased rate of capture"; and "As the North gained tighter control of the Southern ports from both land and sea, there were more opportunities to locate and capture the South's vessels."

Activity 2—Percents and Graphing

Historical background

Well over 600 000 Americans died in the Civil War, making it the bloodiest war in our nation's history. The Union had 4 600 000 males available for service; the Confederacy had 1 100 000. Although exact numbers are difficult to obtain, over the war's duration the Union army employed more than 2 500 000 men and lost over 360 000, whereas the Confederates had approximately 1 000 000 men and lost nearly 260 000. More soldiers succumbed to disease than to battle wounds. After examining the admittedly poor medical records for forty-eight of the war's battles, historian Thomas Livermore found that 112 out of every 1 000 Union soldiers and 150 out of every 1 000 Confederate soldiers in battle were wounded.

Exercises

The casualty figures associated with the war's battles certainly tell part of this conflict's grave story. Students can obtain further insight by presenting and analyzing these data. The numerical details of specific battles are located in many texts, which furnish information on battle location, dates, commanders, numbers engaged, and losses for each side. Davis (1982) gives an excellent source of data on the representation and role of individuals from numerous countries and ethnic groups. Many useful, inquiry-provoking activities can be created. The following sample exercises refer to table 1.

1. After giving students a listing or table, such as table 1, ask them to determine other ways to present the data, such as bar

Table 1
Casualties of Major Civil War Battles

Battle	Date	Numbers Engaged North	Numbers Engaged South	Total Losses North	Total Losses South
First Battle of Bull Run	July 1861	30 000	32 000	2 896	1 982
Seven Days	June 1862	91 169	95 481	14 849	20 614
Second Battle of Bull Run	August 1862	62 000	48 527	14 754	8 397
Antietam	September 1862	75 316	40 000	12 410	13 724
Fredericksburg	December 1862	106 007	72 497	12 653	5 309
Chancellorsville	May 1863	118 000	59 500	17 278	12 821
Gettysburg	July 1863	83 289	75 054	23 049	28 063
Chickamauga	September 1863	58 222	66 326	16 170	18 454
The Wilderness	May 1864	101 895	61 025	17 766	11 400
Spotsylvania	May 1864	83 000	50 000	18 399	9 000
Cold Harbor	June 1864	108 000	59 000	7 000	1 500
Petersburg	April 1865	63 299	18 576	4 140	2 500

Note: Total losses denote those soldiers killed, wounded, missing, or captured.

charts, line graphs, pie charts, stem-and-leaf plots, or box-and-whisker plots. A computer with appropriate software packages can be a useful tool of interest to many students. Will some methods, such as converting each side's losses into fractions or percents, make the data more revealing than others? Do the raw numbers alone tell a battle's or the war's whole story? What other information, such as date, location, and strategic importance, might be considered? This activity presents an excellent opportunity for students to contribute information learned in their social studies or history classes.

2. Ask students to pick out a dozen major battles that span the war's five years. For each battle they could calculate the percent of casualties for each side. The following example uses rounded numbers from table 1 and focuses on the First Battle of Bull Run (referred to as First Manassas by the South):

Union: $\dfrac{2\,900 \text{ lost}}{30\,000 \text{ fought}} = \dfrac{P}{100}$

The solution shows that approximately 10 percent of the Northern soldiers were casualties.

Confederate: $\dfrac{2\,000}{32\,000} = \dfrac{P}{100}$

Approximately 6 percent of the Southern soldiers were casualties.

3. Students can then choose a method for graphically presenting their calculations. See figure 1 as an example that was computer generated. Some of my students selected pictographs to present their results. Variations might include analyses based on the battlefield results for specific commanders, months, geographic locations, and distances from supply centers. A time analysis of important battles over the course of the war would also make an interesting study. Students might be asked to investigate these questions:

- During what year was the fighting the most deadly? During which month? In what region?
- When does the war appear to turn in the Union's favor? Why?
- What battle was the worst in terms of

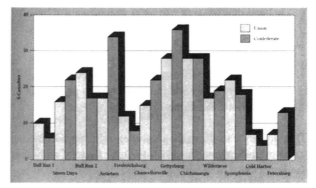

Fig. 1. Percent of casualties for twelve major Civil War battles

casualties and wounded for the Confederacy? The Union? Why?
- What was the probability of a Union soldier's being wounded in battle? A Confederate soldier?

The experience can be enriched if students are prompted to generate research questions, such as the foregoing, on their own.

Activity 3—Statistics and Data Analysis

Historical background

The Union enjoyed vast advantages over the Confederacy in terms of available resources, production capabilities, and manpower. Table 2, adapted from *The Civil War Day by Day* (Long 1971), details some of these advantages.

Exercises

1. Ask students to examine table 2 and to compare the individual line items. Students may use ratios, percents, and graphing techniques to support their comparisons. This activity can be extended to underscore the important contribution made by women and African Americans to each side's war effort. Nearly 3 000 northern women served as army nurses, and approximately 400 women

Table 2

Union and Confederate Resources at the Start of the Civil War

Resource	Union	Confederacy
Total population	22 300 000	9 100 000*
Bank deposits	$207 000 000	$47 000 000
Value of goods manufactured	$1 730 000 000	$156 000 000
Railroad miles	22 000	9 000
Shipping tonnage	4 600 000	290 000
Value of textiles produced	$181 000 000	$10 000 000
Value of firearms	$2 290 000	$73 000
Iron produced (tons)	951000	37 000
Coal produced (tons)	13 680 000	650 000
Corn and wheat (bushels)	698 000 000	314 000 000
Draft animals	5 800 000	2 900 000

*Forty percent of the population of the South were slaves in 1861. Adapted from Long (1971).

actually fought in disguise for both sides. A total of 200 000 African Americans fought for the Union. In addition, since each side sorely needed factory workers to produce war goods, the availability of women and freedmen in the North heightened the Union's advantage in terms of total resources. Ask students to relate these differences to actual battlefield results. Ask them to hypothesize their relative importance individually and compositely. What evidence supports students' rankings?

2. The Civil War truly was a "boys' war." One source broke down the Union army in terms of age:

- 2 million were under twenty-one;
- 1 million were under eighteen;
- 800 000 were not yet seventeen;
- 200 000 were under sixteen;
- 100 000 had not reached fifteen,
- 300 were under thirteen;
- 25 were under ten; and
- 700 000 were older than twenty-one.

These figures can be used in a more advanced discussion of the relationships among mean, median, and mode. The students can work in small groups to calculate these three descriptive statistics from the given data.

3. I asked my classes, "Who won the 'war of numbers'?" Again, such a vague question forced students to pause and formulate a more precisely defined problem on the basis of certain assumptions before embarking on a mere mechanized problem-solving approach. Instead of simply guessing what the teacher wanted, they proposed their own solutions based on their understanding of what was important and relevant to their question. Some of my students presented solutions based on raw casualty figures. Others incorporated percents and performed relative comparisons. Ample opportunity should be given for discussion of problem assumptions along with methods of calculation. I found this entire process especially worthwhile, as it can mirror the type of scenarios students will find outside the classroom.

Extension activity

Students can be given the following information and then asked to trace empirically the effects of slavery on the war efforts of the Union and the Confederacy.

In 1800, over one-half of the nation's 5 million people lived in the South. By 1850, only one-third lived there. Also, by 1860 one of every seven Americans, or about 4 million, were slaves, of which 75 percent lived in the deep South. During the war, approximately 200 000 African Americans served in the Union army, thus constituting about 10 percent of the total northern manpower.

This activity can illustrate to students the importance of using numerical-analysis skills to study history, as well as the importance of using mathematics to communicate and understand concepts. Students can fill in the numerical gaps in the foregoing text and use information presented in their social studies classes or researched in the library to construct mini-research papers that document the impact of slavery on each side. Students should be asked to use facts and figures to support their conjectures.

Summary

The NCTM'S *Curriculum and Evaluation Standards* (1989) recommends that middle school mathematics pay increased attention to "connecting mathematics to other subjects" (NCTM 1989, 70). In the preceding examples, I have attempted to capitalize on my own personal interest in Civil War history by presenting students with important mathematical concepts in an atypical context. Obviously, the Civil War will not immediately capture the interest of all students. Nevertheless, this topic can cause some students "to tremble with eagerness" (Crane 1990, 1). In summary, the "integration of mathematics into contexts that give its symbols and processes practical meaning is an overarching goal of all the standards" (NCTM 1989, 84).

I hope that some of these ideas may prove useful for reawakening the middle school mathematics classroom.

References

Crane, Stephen. *The Red Badge of Courage.* New York: Vintage Books, 1990.

Davis, Burke. *The Civil War—Strange and Fascinating Facts.* New York: Fairfax Press, 1982.

Long, E. B. *The Civil War Day by Day.* New York: Doubleday, 1971.

National Council of Teachers of Mathematics. *Curriculum and Evaluation Standards for School Mathematics.* Reston, Va.: The Council, 1989.

BRENDA K. J. SHANNON

Our Diets May Be Killing Us

A PUSH seems to be on for more real-world applications in the mathematics curriculum at all grade levels. Recommendations from such sources as the NCTM's *Curriculum and Evaluation Standards for School Mathematics* (1989) and the National Research Council's *Everybody Counts* (1989) advocate making mathematics more than just a subject taught one class period of each school day. The time has come to bring mathematics out of the classroom and show the students that the knowledge and skills from mathematics can be beneficial in their everyday lives. But how do we, as educators, actually accomplish this goal?

The author teaches sixth- and seventh-grade mathematics at a middle school and struggles with the same question. The traditional textbook-lecture format minimizes the usability of mathematics and leaves many students wondering why they need the skills taught. The gap between the mathematics in the students' textbooks and the mathematics being used in daily life has been bridged with the Food-Choice Unit described in this article.

The Food-Choice Unit

For one week, the students delve into issues of healthy eating and how their choices today can affect their lives in the future. Specifically, the focus is on the link between heart attacks, the United States's number-one killer, and a diet high in fat.

The following activities are a part of the Food-Choice Unit.

Activity 1: Circle graphs: To begin the unit students are asked to divide a circle into the components they believe make up their

Brenda Shannon *teaches at Osage Upper Elementary School, Lake Ozark, MO 65049. She strives to make mathematics meaningful and entertaining for her students.*

typical food choices. Two examples are shown in figures 1a and 1b. This activity is a good way of identifying what information the students already possess.

Activity 2: Dietary content: As a group the class works toward understanding that foods are made up of proteins, carbohydrates, and fats. All these components are essential to a healthful diet. Currently, approximately 40 percent of the calories in a typical American diet come from fat. Calculations show that if this amount was reduced to 25 percent, about 9000 lives would be saved annually (Bellerson 1991). A diet high in fat not only contributes to cardiovascular disease, particularly heart attacks and strokes, but is also linked to certain cancers, including colorectal, breast, and prostate cancers (Netzer 1987). The graph in figure 2 illustrates what is considered to be the current American diet; the graph in figure 3 illustrates the recommendations from the Senate Select Committee on Nutrition and Human Needs (Brody 1982).

Activity 3: Understanding heart attacks: At this point, the students brainstorm causes of heart attacks. Misconceptions abound

concerning people's lifestyle choices and heart attacks. Although heart attacks were once thought to be a natural part of the degenerative process, current findings show that at least 90 percent of premature strokes and heart attacks are preventable (Piscatella 1987). Lifestyle choices today will help determine a person's susceptibility to heart disease tomorrow. The most serious weakness in the design of the cardiovascular system is the size of the coronary arteries, which are very small, about the size of a piece of cooked spaghetti. As years go by, they begin to get clogged by a layer of fatty deposits. It is important that students understand that although some contributing factors to heart disease are not preventable—for instance, heredity—other factors are part of their chosen lifestyle—for example, high-fat diet, smoking, lack of exercise, and the like.

But why should our students be concerned? Is it not the *adult* population that is dying from heart disease? Yes. But dying is the final sentence of a lifetime of habits—habits that start early. Autopsies of young children who died in automobile accidents in Los Angeles and Cincinnati showed arterial blockages greater than 50 percent in

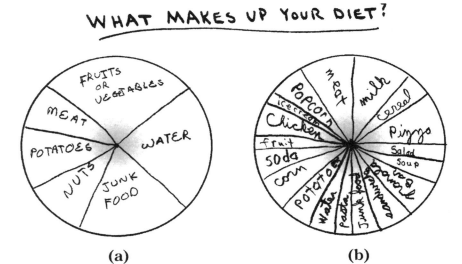

WHAT MAKES UP YOUR DIET?

(a) **(b)**

Fig. 1. Circle graphs that students believe display their dietary content

ACTIVITIES FOR JUNIOR HIGH SCHOOL AND MIDDLE SCHOOL MATHEMATICS

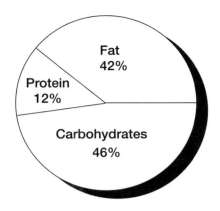

Fig.2. The current American diet (Brody 1982)

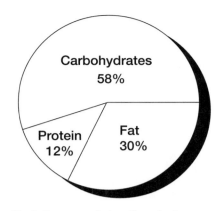

Fig. 3. Recommendations from the Senate Select Committee on Nutrition and Human Needs (Brody 1982)

Item	Percent of Fat
1. 2% milk	38%
2. Light microwave popcorn	30%
3. Fruit Loops cereal	8%
4. Peanut butter	80%
5. Potato (raw)	0%
6. Butterfinger candy bar	40%
7. Planters Peanuts	80%
8. Sour-cream-and-onion potato chips	57%
9. Orange	0%
10. Cheese-and-peanut-butter crackers	40%

Fig. 5. Ten popular foods and their fat content

Restaurant "X"		
	Menu Item	
	HAMBURGER	CHEESEBURGER
Serving Size	102g	116g
Calories	255	305
Protein (G)	12	15
lCarbohydrates (G)	30	30
Fat (G)	9	13
Monounsaturated fat (G)	5	7
Polyunsaturated fat (G)	1	1
Saturated fat (MG)	3	5
Cholesterol (MG)	37	50
Sodium (MG)	490	725

Fig. 6 Nutritional information per serving of typical restaurant foods

children as young as seven years old. A study of grade school children in Michigan found that 98 percent showed at least one major risk factor for heart disease. Twenty-eight percent had high blood pressure; 42 percent had abnormally high levels of cholesterol in the blood. More than half had a combination of three or more risk factors (Piscatella 1987). Even though parents buy the foods brought into the home, many children are permitted a voice in what they choose to eat. Arteriosclerosis—hardening of the arteries—does not begin a few months before a fatal heart attack—it begins at birth. A few preventive steps today may go a long way in improving the health of our students in the future.

Additional statistics, such as those in figure 4, can be presented at this juncture to help bring the message home. The ensuing activities are sure to initiate a rich class discussion.

Activity 4: Reducing dietary fat: Once students understand the basic makeup of foods, the class can begin talking about ways to reduce the amount of fat in their diets. A stick of butter illustrates a food that is 100 percent fat. Students are unaware of many "hidden" fats, for example, an ice-cream sandwich contains 71 percent fat; peanut butter has about 80 percent fat. At this point, the students are eager to know the percent of fat in various foods. Begin with a "guessing game" in which ten food items or their empty containers are lined up on the chalk tray. A sample array is listed in figure 5. In groups, the students should estimate the percent of fat contained in each item. Next discuss students' estimations compared with the actual fat content of each food item.

Although people cannot change heredity, they can choose what they eat, and choosing a diet low in fat is one of the most significant preventive steps available in protecting the heart (Cooper 1988). One homemade cookie with six grams of fat will not condemn anyone to a fatal heart attack; a daily diet of high-fat foods might be doing just that.

Activity 5: Fat content of restaurant foods: Next the class gathers nutritional information from various restaurants and displays it in a chart so that students can view the fat content of foods they enjoy eating. Figure 6 presents an example of typical findings. After noting the kinds of information the chart supplies, students decide that they

A) If six fully loaded 747s were to crash on one day, the headlines would shout about the 2 200 killed. Yet that is the number lost every day—365 days a year—to heart attacks.

B) American heart-attack deaths in one year equal the American deaths in 10 Vietnam wars.

C) Over half of all Americans (51%) die from cardiovascular disease. This statistic means that the total deaths in any given year from all other causes—cancer, automobile accidents, leukemia, airplane tragedies—are still fewer than the deaths from heart and blood-vessel disease

D) Your chance of contracting AIDS: 1 in 1 000 000
Your chance of being murdered: 1 in 10 000
Your chance of dying in an automobile accident: 1 in 5 000
Your chance of dying of heart or blood-vessel disease: 1 in 2

Fig. 4 Additional statistics (adapted from Piscatella 1987)

need to compute the percent of fat. They arrive at the conclusion that they need to know the number of grams of fat and total number of calories for the computation. The percent of total calories that comes from fat is the quantity referred to in the claim that no more than 30 percent of the total diet should come from fat. A large paper clip can represent the weight of one gram. One gram of fat, regardless of the source, contains nine calories. Multiplying the grams of fat in a food by 9 gives the number of calories that come from fat. If students are familiar with proportions, then finding the percent of fat in an item can be expressed as follows:

$$\frac{\text{calories from fat}}{\text{total calories}} = \frac{\text{percent of fat}}{100}$$

Another way to analyze the situation mathematically would be as follows:

one gram of fat = 9 calories

grams of fat × 9 = calories from fat

(calories from fat ÷ total calories) × 100 = percent of fat

For example, restaurant "X" (fig. 6), serves a cheeseburger that has thirteen grams of fat. The total number of calories in a cheeseburger is 305. The proportion would look like this:

$$\frac{13 \times 9}{305} = \frac{\text{percent of fat}}{100}$$

A cheeseburger from restaurant 'X' contains approximately 38 percent fat.

Activity 6: Calculating percent of fat: A handout like that in figure 7 allows the flexibility of students' choosing which restaurant they want to survey as well as presents a wide assortment of foods. The students can discuss their results in groups, or the handouts can be used to make a bulletin board advertising various restaurants.

Activity 7: Guessing game: After students have explored the percent of fat in various foods, once again the class plays a "guessing game." The handout in figure 8 requires the students to estimate the percent of fat in each food before they work the problems. Then they subtract their estimates from the actual answers and record that number to the side. After adding the column of numbers, the students compare their estimation skills with those of their classmates. They are usually pleased that their estimation skills have improved since the previous guessing game.

Extension Activities

The possibilities beyond this point are endless. Teachers will find that students, once they are familiar with the concepts presented, will begin "teaching" other members of their families and will naturally expand the ideas presented. The following are a few extension activities for this unit.

1. Write a paper describing the week's activities. Address these questions: *(a) What* issues were covered? *(b) What* is the importance of a low-fat diet? and *(c) How* will what you have learned affect you now and in the future? Some sample papers are shown in figures 9a and 9b.

2. Four students team up and choose a local restaurant. They obtain the information needed to find the percent of fat in various foods, that is, the calories and grams of fat in each item. They are then asked to present this information to the class in the form of a poster, written handout, graph, dramatization, menu, or the like.

3. At the end of the week, students bring to class snacks that contain less than 30 percent fat. This activity is always one of the students' favorites and is a good

---

NOTICE—OUR DIETS MAY BE HAZARDOUS TO OUR HEALTH

Name of Restaurant: _____

Choose food items for lunch and dinner.
Figure the percent of fat in each item.

(Grams of Fat × 9 ÷ Total Calories) × 100 = % of Fat

Example: Piece of cherry pie (13.6 grams of fat / 260 calories total)

13.6 × 9 = 122.4

122.4 ÷ 260 ≅ .471

.471 × 100 ≅ 47

47% fat

	LUNCH			DINNER	
Item	Calories/ Grams of Fat	% of Fat	Item	Calories/ Grams of Fat	% of Fat
1			1		
2			2		
3			3		
4			4		
5			5		

Fig. 7. Handout for calculating fat content of restaurant foods

ACTIVITIES FOR JUNIOR HIGH SCHOOL AND MIDDLE SCHOOL MATHEMATICS

Food		Serving Size	Grams of Fat	Total Calories	Your Estimate	% of Fat
1	Kiwi fruit	1 med.	0.5	46		
2	Salt-and-vinegar potato chips	1 oz.	10	150		
3	Quaker Crunchy Bran cereal	1 oz.	1	90		
4	Ekrich bologna	1 slice	8	90		
5	Homemade white frosting	av. serv.	6	165		
6	Garlic-and-herb dressing	1 Tbsp	8	72		
7	Swanson Hungry Man turkey pot pie	16 oz.	36	650		
8	Del Monte corn	1/2 cup	1	90		
9	Cinnamon-and-oat-bran breakfast bar	1	4	110		
10	Cashew nuts	1 oz.	14	167		
11	Bon bon	5	11	165		
12	Yoplait banana yogurt	6 oz.	4	180		
13	Del Monte vanilla pudding cup	5 oz.	5	180		
14	Kraft cholesterol-free mayonnaise	1Tbsp.	10	90		
15	Sausage links	1	8	96		
16	Mini ravioli	7 oz.	5	180		
17	Plain doughnut	1	11	200		
18	Blueberry muffin	1	3	110		

Fig. 8 Handout for estimating then calculating fat content of sample foods

This week we learned about the effects our diet has on our lives. We talked about how you can watch how much fat you eat and if you eat to much how you cut back by watching your diet more closely.

One of the reasons, I think, for doing this unit this week was so we could all be better aware of what might happen if you don't watch our diets. The thing that was the interesting to me this week was that the chances of having a heart-attack are 1 in 2 and your chances of getting aids were 1 in 1,000,000.

I think the effect of this unit on me was good. I understand now why my mother always gets products low in fat. Also before now I thought calories were something you didn't want much of, but now I know that calories mean energy. It almost scares me to think about the autopsy of that seven-year old and how clogged his arteries already were. From now on I think I'm going to think about what I eat before I eat it.

(a)

This week we have been talking about foods and their fats, carbohydrates, and how much protein is in them.

In this week I have also learned many interesting facts such as, in the United States 51% of all Americans will die from a heart-attack. The next topic I learned is that if I eat a healthy-diet you will more likely die from something else rather than a heart-attack and how to figure fats.

The most fun or interesting activity I had this week was probably when there were foods on the chalk board's stand and we had to try to pick the closest percentage of fat for the object.

The activities this week will probably influence me in many different ways. One of the ways it will will probably make me eat healthier foods and to be aware of heart-attacks. Another will probably be what foods I should eat.

(b)

Fig. 9. Samples of students' papers summarizing the unit

exercise in getting them involved in their food choices at home. They are encouraged to share recipes for low-fat homemade snacks.

4. In groups, students look for evidence of ways in which the food industry is striving for more healthful products, for instance, a greater variety of low-fat foods, more salad bars available in restaurants, and so on. They can then write a survey asking the general public if any additional improvements are desired. The information can be graphed and presented, along with a persuasive paper, to a source that is most likely to benefit from the information, for example, a local restaurant or supermarket.

5. Students keep a log of the foods they consume for one day or perhaps for one week. They then figure the overall percent of fats, carbohydrates, and protein and use a circle graph to display the results.

6. Misleading advertisements are sought and addressed. Students are surprised to learn that an item advertised as "98 percent fat-free" does not necessarily contain 2 percent fat. How can the producer advertise the content falsely? The percent of fat is determined by weight, not by total calories, which is very misleading to the public, who may not be aware of such advertising schemes.

7. Various cultures can be studied to determine how dietary habits and lifestyle affect the rate of disease. For example, the rate of heart attacks and some cancers associated with a high-fat diet is very low among Japanese natives, who typically eat a diet consisting of 15 percent fat, 15 percent protein, and 70 percent carbohydrates. Yet when Japanese men and women emigrate to the United States and assimilate American eating habits, they begin to experience the same health problems that Americans have.

8. Students can research and report on diseases and conditions that seem to be linked to a high fat diet, among them diabetes, strokes, obesity, some forms of cancer, and high blood pressure (Bellerson 1991).

9. A local dietitian can be invited to talk to the class. Students should generate questions in advance of the visit.

This unit has become a very successful project, and the concepts taught are talked about long after the unit has ended. When the students proudly bring their lunches by my classroom in the morning to show their healthful food choices for the day, I believe that mathematics has played a role in their lives outside the classroom.

References

Bellerson, Karen J. *The Complete and Up-to-Date Fat Book.* Garden City Park, N.Y.: Avery Publishing Group, 1991.

Brody, Jane E. *Jane Brody's Nutrition Book.* New York: Bantam Books, 1982.

Cooper, Kenneth, M.D. *Controlling Cholesterol.* New York: Bantam Books, 1988.

National Council of Teachers of Mathematics. *Curriculum and Evaluation Standards for School Mathematics.* Reston, Va.: The Council, 1989.

National Research Council. *Everybody Counts: A Report to the Nation on the Future of Mathematics Education.* Washington, D.C.: National Academy Press, 1989.

Netzer, Corinne T. *The Fat Counter and the 22-Gram Solution.* New York: Dell Publishing Co., 1987.

Piscatella, Joseph C. *Choices for a Healthy Heart.* New York: Workman Publishing Co., 1987.

FRANCES R. CURCIO AND J. LEWIS MCNEECE

The Case of Video Viewing, Reading, and Writing in Mathematics Class:
Solving the Mystery

THE element of mystery can be a naturally intriguing component of a mathematics lesson for middle school students. Mystery stories capture students' interest and attention and contribute to developing critical-reading skills (Crouse and Bassett 1975; Curcio 1982; Scalzitti 1982). When presenting mystery stories within the context of a mathematics lesson, students often ask, "What does this have to do with mathematics?" Significant connections can be made between solving a mystery and solving a mathematics problem that supply a rationale for incorporating mystery stories in the mathematics class. In particular, similarities in the questions a problem solver asks when confronting a problem (Pólya 1973) and the questions a detective asks in solving a mystery can be found in figure 1. After solving short mystery stories, students will see the connection between solving a mystery and solving a mathematics problem.

During the last several years we have collaborated on a project to illustrate how mathematics is connected to various aspects of the human experience in ways that are relevant to middle school students.

Frances Curcio *teaches at Queens College of the City University of New York, Flushing, NY 11367. She is interested in the language of mathematics and communicating in the mathematics classroom.* J. Lewis McNeece *teaches seventh-grade mathematics at Louis Armstrong Middle School, East Elmhurst, NY 11369. He is interested in interdisciplinary approaches to teaching mathematics with an emphasis on problem solving.*

In so doing, we have integrated The Challenge of the Unknown videotape series (Maddux 1986) and *Square One TV* (1987) into the mathematics curriculum at the Louis Armstrong Middle School, East Elmhurst, New York (Curcio, McNeece, and Rosen 1988). We have designed a problem-solving seminar for heterogeneous groups of seventh graders that incorporates the use of technology, cooperative learning, and reading and writing in the mathematics class. This article describes one of the units on analyzing and writing mystery stories. The process that occurs over the course of several weeks includes viewing videos, reading, and writing.

Video Viewing

Before viewing one of the seven twenty-minute videotapes from The Challenge of the Unknown titled "Information: What Do I Know?" students are asked to discuss such questions as "What sources of information do you use during a typical day? What do you learn from them? How do you use the information? Where do you look for the information you need?" (Maddux 1986, 42). Following the discussion, students engage in activities that require them to analyze various word problems containing insufficient and superfluous information and to rewrite textbook story problems so that some stories have insufficient information and others have superfluous information (Curcio and McNeece 1990).

After students work in cooperative groups, their ideas are reported to the class for further comments and discussion. When students have exhausted ideas, they view videoclips of "Information: What Do I Know?" One of the clips appropriate for the mystery-story unit is a comedy segment titled "The Lineup." While participating in a lineup at a police precinct located next door to a theater, an aspiring actor, played by Bill Irwin, thinks he is auditioning for a part in a play at the 42nd Street Theater. Inaccessible important information (the blocked police precinct sign) and inattention to various clues (most accused criminals do not behave like entertainers) led him to believe he was participating in an audition rather than a lineup. Although no "numbers" link this situation to mathematics, students recognize the need to pay attention to details so that they do not misread or misinterpret a situation. Analyzing the facts and interpreting a situation are essential components of successful problem solving.

Following the tape, we present students with a "How Observant Are You?" exercise in which they are given only one minute to study a photograph of five men standing in a lineup. Then, recalling their observations, they must answer a series of questions. Some of the questions ask, "Which man is the tallest?" "How many are wearing hats?" "How many have their arms folded?" (Maddux 1986, 50). The students are also asked to sketch the scene. As groups compare their responses and sketches, the students realize that some have produced accurate verbal descriptions, whereas others have made accurate sketches. They recognize the need to be observant and attentive to the facts. Looking for similarities and differences among the elements in the photograph contributes to developing pattern-recognition skills. These skills can be invaluable when attempting to solve mathematics problems.

Mathnet episodes on *Square One TV* are also excellent vehicles for making connections between solving mystery stories and solving mathematics problems. In particular, we have used "The Case of the Missing Baseball" to develop the skills of critical viewing and listening. Such episodes capture students' interest and generate excitement as they predict what will happen in subsequent segments of the episode. We supply students with a "Mathnet Casebook" (Children's Television Workshop 1987, 7–9) in which they keep their notes as the case unfolds. Students work in small groups to discuss the actions taken by the Mathnet detectives, George Frankly and Kate Monday. They identify the tools and techniques used in each of the episodes (e.g., drawing a diagram, making a table or graph, using objects, or acting it out), they write their hypotheses based on the facts (e.g., "I think the baseball rolled into Mrs. McGregor's house"), they identify actions taken by the Mathnet helpers (e.g., identifying the problem, reviewing the facts, gathering information, making an estimate), and they record the results of the investigation (e.g., "Once the Mathnetters found Mrs. McGregor's house, they were able to find the baseball").

Viewing the *Mathnet* episodes and using the "Mathnet Casebook" prepares students for the next two phases of the unit—reading mystery stories and writing their own mysteries.

Reading

Following the discussion of the Mathnet case, we make available to students a selection of short mystery stories from Crouse and Bassett (1975), Ripley (1949), and Sobol (1967, 1975). Before reading the stories, students review an activity sheet that states the aim, some guidelines, and some questions to answer (see fig. 2). They analyze and solve the mysteries in their cooperative groups. Students are also given mystery stories written by students in previous classes (see examples in fig. 3). They are usually amazed at what other seventh graders have written, which motivates them to attempt to write their own stories.

Mathematical Problem Solver	Detective
1. Understand the problem What is the unknown? What is the given? What is the condition?	1. Understand the case What are you looking for? What is the given?
2. Devise a plan Do you know a related problem? Can you simplify the problem?	2. Investigate the case Have you solved a similar case? What are the facts?
3. Carry out the plan What information is important? What information is not important? What pieces of information fit together logically? Which information is consistent with the information given?	3. Analyze the facts/data What information is important? What information is not important? Which pieces of information do not seem to fit together logically? Which data are inconsistent with the information given?
4. Look back. Examine the solution obtained. Does it make sense? Is it reasonable? Is it what you expected'	4. Reexamine the facts Do the facts support the solution?
(Pólya 1973, xvi-xvii)	(Adapted from Crouse and Bassett 1975, 598)

Fig. 1. Similarities between questions asked by a mathematical problem solver and questions asked by a detective solving a mystery

Writing

After being involved in the previous video-viewing and reading activities, students are prepared and eager to write their own mysteries. The students proceed in stages on the basis of the ideas in Fennell and Ammon (1985), Ford (1990), and Connolly and Vilardi (1989). The stages are brainstorming, prewriting, writing, conferencing, revising and editing, publishing, and sharing.

Brainstorming can occur in a small-group or large-group setting. We ask students to think of topics suitable for a mystery story. Many of their ideas reflect the violence they experience in their neighborhoods and on television—robberies, murders, and suicides. At times, these topics may become too sensitive. Depending on their level of maturity, we have students discuss the situations and examine their ideas from a victim's point of view. Also, depending on the class, teachers may want to limit the topics that may be used for a mystery story. If limits are imposed, the selections that are presented to students during the video-viewing and reading phases of the unit should be chosen carefully.

After a brainstorming session, students *prewrite*. They select a possible topic and explore ways to create a story about the topic.

Working individually, students are assigned to write a first draft for homework, which is due in several days. They are encouraged to use a computer and word-processing software. If they do not have their own equipment, computer facilities are available in the school's library.

Students exchange the first draft of their stories with group members. At this *conferencing* stage, students critically and constructively analyze each other's work. Their peers help them identify the unintended ambiguities of their stories. Using the advice from teachers and peers, students work individually to *revise* and *edit* their work. During the writing and revising stages, the language arts teachers co-plan assignments that support these activities.

After a final peer review of the stories, the students prepare their work for *publication*. Some students print their stories from a word processor whereas others submit their handwritten work. The culminating activity is the preparation of a class book, which is a collection of the students' work. Depending on the students' decisions, illustrations and an answer key may be included. The students take pride in their work and *share* their stories with other students in the school. Examples of students' stories are shown in figure 3.

ACTIVITIES FOR JUNIOR HIGH SCHOOL AND MIDDLE SCHOOL MATHEMATICS

Mystery Story Unit

Aim: 1. To practice our logic and critical-reading abilities
2. To improve our problem-solving abilities

We will be reading and solving a few mysteries. As you read each story carefully—

1. Note the important details,
2. Make *inferences*, and,
3. Draw *conclusions* and *solve* the mystery.

For each story, answer the following questions:

1. What is given?
2. For what are you looking?
3. Have you ever solved a similar case?
4. What are the facts?
5. What information is important and what information is *not* important?
6. What pieces of information do not seem to fit together logically?
7. Which data are *inconsistent* with the information given?
8. Do the facts support your solution?

Fig 2. Sample activity sheet to accompany mystery stories
(Adapted from Crouse and Bassett 1975)

Final Comments

The activities described in this article are just a few that we have designed to help students realize that mathematics is not limited to "number crunching." Engaging students in the analysis and creation of mystery stories builds a foundation for creative problem-solving experiences. Problem solving requires that students be able to analyze information by recognizing patterns; by analyzing the facts; and by distinguishing among necessary, inconsistent, and superfluous information. The analysis and creation of detective stories combine "reading, critical thinking, and the collection and organization of data" (Fennell and Ammon 1985, 24). Students become attentive to details, inconsistencies, and logical connections between and among information. As students develop these skills, they are having lots of fun!

References

Children's Television Workshop. *Square One Television: Teacher's Guide.* New York: Author, 1987.

Connolly, Paul, and Teresa Vilardi, eds. *Writing to Learn Mathematics and Science.* New York: Teachers College Press, 1989.

Crouse, Richard, and Denise Bassett. "Detective Stories: An Aid for Mathematics and Reading." *Mathematics Teacher* 68 (November 1975): 598–600.

Curcio, Frances R. "The Case of Reading in the Mathematics Class: Solving the Mystery." *Summation* 27 (January 1982): 8–9.

Curcio, Frances R., and J. Lewis McNeece. *Teacher Support Materials to Accompany The Challenge of the Unknown.* Unpublished manuscript, 1990.

Curcio, Frances R., J. Lewis McNeece, and Jamie Rosen. "What's the Problem? A Model for Curriculum Innovation in Mathematics." *Connections* 14 (Spring 1988): 8–10.

Fennell, Francis (Skip), and Richard Ammon. "Writing Techniques for Problem Solvers." *Arithmetic Teacher* 33 (September 1985): 24–25.

Ford, Margaret I. "The Writing Process: A Strategy for Problem Solvers." *Arithmetic Teacher* 38 (November 1990): 35–38.

Maddux, Hilary C., ed. *The Challenge of the Unknown: Teaching Guide.* New York: W. W. Norton & Co., 1986.

Pólya, George. *How to Solve It.* 2d ed. Princeton, N.J.: Princeton University Press, 1973.

Ripley, Austin. *Minute Mysteries.* New York: Harper & Row, 1949.

Scalzitti, Joyce. "Wanted Dead or Alive: Problem-Solving Skills." In *Mathematics for the Middle Grades, 5–9,* 1982 Yearbook of the National Council of Teachers of Mathematics, edited by Linda Silvey and James R. Smart, 182–87. Reston, Va.: The Council, 1982.

Sobol, Donald J. *Two-Minute Mysteries.* New York: Scholastic Books, 1967.

———. *Still More Two-Minute Mysteries.* New York: Scholastic Books, 1975.

The Challenge of the Unknown videotape series and teacher's guide are available from Karol Video, P.O. Box 7600, Wilkes-Barre, PA 18733; please request copies on school letterhead. *Square One TV* no longer airs.

"The Case of the Tumbled Tower"
by Amy S.

Dwayne got up at 6:00 and was watching the sun rise out from his bedroom window. After the sun came up he started working on his toothpick tower in his room. The tower was very fragile. While he was working on his tower his little brother came into the room bugging him. Dwayne's brother wanted to be more like Dwayne and he wanted to build something out of toothpicks, too. He was very jealous of Dwayne.

In the afternoon, Dwayne went out to buy candy at the candy store and he left his little brother home (even though he was supposed to be baby sitting). On his way out of the house, he heard on the radio that there was going to be a slight western wind coming. He then left the house forgetting that he left his bedroom window open. When he saw that he had left the window open, he thought that the wind had blown the tower over. But then he remembered something and said that his little brother must have knocked over

Hints: if Dwayne could watch the sunrise, his window faces east. A west wind would not blow into his room.

"The Case of the Dead Professor"
by Tim R.

Detective "No Clue" had just arrived at the scene of the crime. Professor "Badly Bald" had been at the lab working after hours. He had been working on an experiment to cure baldness. He seemed to have electrocuted himself and ended up blowing the fuses for the whole building. Later on that night another professor, Professor "I Didn't Do It," had also come in to finish an experiment he had been working on.

He said, I came to work late at the lab. I took the private elevator up to the lab when I found Professor "Badly Bald" dead with his head in something that looked like a toaster oven." Then after a pause he said, "I wish I could tell you more, but that's all I know."

Then, all of a sudden Detective "No Clue" said, "I think you can tell us more down at headquarters."

Detective "No Clue" said, "Professor, I hereby arrest you on the charges of murder." Why did Detective "No Clue" say that Professor "I Didn't Do It," did it?

Hints: The inconsistency in the account given by Professor "I Didn't Do It" was that he took the elevator to the laboratory but this route was not possible if Professor "Badly Bald" blew a fuse.

Fig. 3. Examples of seventh grader's mysteries

MARY F. KLEIN

Mathematics as Current Events

THE *Curriculum and Evaluation Standards for School Mathematics* (NCTM 1989) lists "learning to value mathematics" as one goal for students. The intent of this goal is "to focus attention on the need for student awareness of the interaction between mathematics and the historical situations from which it has developed and the impact that interaction has on our culture and our lives." One way to reach this goal is to study the history of mathematics; another way is to study current events and see mathematics in the making.

This article shares some news stories and their sources and describes ways the stories can be used in the classroom. I reserve one bulletin board in my classroom for articles on current events in mathematics. This bulletin board promotes class discussions

---

Mary Klein *teaches at Urbana Middle School, Urbana, IL 61801. She has taught junior and senior high school mathematics, created a mathematics laboratory, coached mathematics teams, and developed computer-assisted instruction. She collects easily explained mathematics applications.*

focusing not only on new ideas and uses of mathematics but also on the people involved with mathematics. My goal is not only to teach mathematics concepts but to convince students that mathematics is being created and used today by a variety of people.

Students are astounded to learn that mathematics knowledge continues to expand and that approximately 200 000 new mathematics theorems are published each year (Davis and Hersh 1981), some of them considered newsworthy. News publications are interested in theorems that are historically interesting or have important applications. Aside from theorems, other newsworthy developments posted here include the discovery of a new largest known prime, the worldwide demand for people competent in mathematics, government pressure not to publish certain mathematical research, and new or important mathematics applications.

My main sources of information are the *New York Times*, *Science News*, and some professional journals. The mathematics articles in newspapers are written not in the "theorem-proof-theorem" format of a

journal but as news stories. Usually an article summarizes the mathematics and discusses the practical implications or the historical factors that make this finding newsworthy. Frequently, it also describes the reaction of colleagues to the information.

For example, in 1988 a mathematician at Tokyo Metropolitan University proposed a proof of Fermat's last theorem using the techniques of a relatively new branch of mathematics called *arithmetical algebraic geometry*. An article in *Science News* described how the suggested proof built on the work of mathematicians at Princeton University, Harvard University, and the Steklov Institute in Moscow (Peterson 1988). In my algebra classes we described the theorem, its history, worked some problems, and watched the newspapers and television as excitement changed to disappointment. The proof remained elusive. We did learn that the time is ripe for a proof, since Fermat's last theorem has been tied to several other conjectures. Proving any one of them would amount to proving the Fermat theorem.

These articles illustrate the scrutiny mathematicians give a proof. The proof

itself was described this way: "Though highly technical, his argument fills fewer than a dozen manuscript pages—short for such a significant mathematical proof." Don B. Zagier, a mathematician at the Max Planck Institute, said, "There are many nice ideas, but it's very subtle, and there could easily be a mistake. It'll certainly take days, if not weeks, until the proof's completely checked." The article ends by stating that it's a time for both caution and excitement" (Peterson 1988).

Articles about theorems usually prompt a discussion of the review process in publishing, the reasons mathematicians publish, and the possible rewards of promotions, pay raises, and glory. In my enriched geometry class, simulating the review process generated a number of interesting student-proposed theorems. (A pleased parent recounted how his son and the son's friends talked about theorems as he drove them to a party.)

Some of my favorite articles are now incorporated into the "Why is it useful?" phase of my lessons. Imagine the effect on my students when I introduce factoring by revealing that during the Reagan administration, the United States government wanted research involving prime numbers and factoring to be kept secret. Students gain new respect for the topic when they learn that banks, industry, and the govern-

ment encode data using a system that requires the factoring of enormous numbers to break the code. I have a great news story announcing that a 155-digit number had been factored into three large primes that were 7-, 49-, and 99-digits long (Kolata 1990, A12). The article gave an overview of the basic idea behind the encoding system and speculated that the new factoring method was a "mixed blessing; an advance that could imperil secrets." Another article described how the factoring was accomplished using approximately 1000 computers located around the world.

News articles reinforce the idea that mathematics is a useful subject with a variety of applications. From news articles we have learned that knot theory is tied to DNA studies in molecular biology and to problems in theoretical physics. Polynomial expressions are used to describe and distinguish knots. The search for a new largest known prime number is fueled not only by curiosity but also by a quest for a way to sell computers. Successfully crunching large numbers indicates that the computer and software are adept in handling long calculations. Mathematics, physics, and computer simulation are being used to create safer and more exciting water slides containing parabolic hills designed to allow the rider to attain momentary weightlessness. An

Australian investment group parlayed its knowledge of probability to win millions in the Virginia lottery. This material is great when a student asks, "Does anyone actually use this math?"

I have used two letters to the editor from the *New York Times* to clarify the idea of irrational numbers and to emphasize the need for precise language. For several years mathematicians from the United States and Japan have been competing to produce the longer decimal expansion of pi. In 1989 Gregory V. Chudnovsky and David V. Chudnovsky at Columbia University in New York City developed a new algorithm producing 1 011 196 691 digits of pi. Shortly afterward a letter appeared in the *New York Times* that was a tongue-in-cheek argument against channeling federal research funds into "big-science" projects at the expense of worthwhile small projects. It suggested a bold project for mathematics: to sequence the entire decimal expansion of pi. We would then be able to stay ahead of Japan (Chernoff 1990, D16). Two weeks later a second letter was published, anxious to correct the errors of the first letter. It explained that pi has been proved to be irrational so it is not merely a very large number (such as the number of atoms in the universe), but a logically endless number" (Abel 1990, A20). Can a number between two and three be considered large?

By the way, the quest for more digits of pi is fueled by such questions as whether the sequence of digits is random and whether faster algorithms can be developed.

Equally useful are articles that describe the demand for people competent in mathematics. It is good for students to know not only that mathematics is useful but that people who know mathematics can earn a nice living. One of my favorite articles laments the fact that the chief actuary of the Social Security Administration was poorly paid compared to his counterparts in industry. He made only about $100 000 that year.

More information on salaries and related topics can be found each November in the Notices of the *Notices of the American Mathematical Society.* In 1991, the median nine-month salary for new doctorates of mathematics entering teaching was $33 000 for men and $33 200 for women. For those entering business and industry the median twelve-month starting salary was $52 000 for men and $48 000 for women, with the maximum that year being $83 000.

Students can earn extra credit by finding a good article on current events in mathematics and producing an oral or written synopsis. Also, such news stories generate questions that make good research projects for students. For example, students are often curious about how factoring is used in encoding and decoding messages. Occasionally, I have assigned a short research paper and asked students to choose their topic from a list of suggestions. My article collection is indispensable when supplying a bibliography for the project.

Collecting these articles doesn't take much time, since a quick scan of the newspaper headlines reveals the useful information. The articles are short, easily read, and easily understood. The mathematics explanations are sketchy, but the title of the journal containing the original research and dates of related stories are often included in the article for the reader wanting more information.

Finding articles to share is worth the investment of time. The reading is enjoyable, I am much more knowledgeable about current ideas in mathematics, and it is fun to surprise students with interesting facts and stories. But most important, this project reveals that mathematics is quite a vital, humane subject. No longer is it just abstractions. The articles show mathematicians interacting with scientists and others on a global scale. They are effective arguments that mathematics shapes our lives in many often unexpected ways.

References

Abel, Ruben. "Fears of a Pi Gap Are, Well, Irrational." *New York Times,* 18 July 1990.

Chernoff, Paul R. "Don't Let Japan Open a Pi Gap with U.S." *New York Times,* 1 July 1990.

Davis, Philip J., and Ruben Hersh. *The Mathematical Experience.* Boston: Houghton Mifflin Co., 1981.

Kolata, Gina. "Giant Leap in Math: 155 Divided to 0." *New York Times,* 20 June 1990.

National Council of Teachers of Mathematics. *Curriculum and Evaluation Standards for School Mathematics.* Reston, Va.: The Council, 1989.

Peterson, Ivars. "Fermat's Last Theorem: A Promising Approach." *Science News* 133 (March 1988): 180–81.

Bibliography

American Mathematical Society and Mathematical Association of America, AMS-MAA Data Committee. "1991 Annual AMS-MAA Survey." *Notices of the American Mathematical Society* 38 (November 1991): 1086–1122.

Broad, William J. "Physics and Computers Create a Science of Aquatic Thrills." New York Times, 7 August 1990, C1.

"Computing a Prime Champion." *Science News* 136 (September 1989): 191.

"Group Invests $5 Million to Corner Lottery Market." *New York Times,* 25 February 1992, A1.

Kolata, Gina. "Progress on Fermat's Famous Math Problem." *Science* 235 (March 1987): 1572–73.

Peterson, Ivars. "A Billion Digits of Pi." *Science News* 136 (September 1989): 166.

———. "Closing In on Fermat's Last Theorem." *Science News* 131 (June 1987): 397.

———. "Doubts about Fermat Solution." *Science News* 133 (April 1988): 230.

———. "The Electronic Grapevine." *Science News* 138 (August 1990): 90–91.

———. "Millions of Digits of Pi." *Science News* 129 (February 1986): 91.

———. "Pi Wars: Dueling Supercomputers." *Science News* 131 (February 1987): 118.

———. "Unknotting a Tangled Tale." *Science News* 133 (May 1988): 328–30.

HOPE MARTIN

The 12.7 cm Hot Dog Corporation

A CORPORATION was formed in the United States fourteen years ago that does not appear on the New York Stock Exchange or any other. It is alive and well and prospering at Northwood Junior High School in Highland Park, Illinois. The "12.7 cm Hot Dog Corporation" is owned and operated by a group of about forty-five eighth graders, who make all the executive decisions concerning the sale of hot dogs, chips, soda pop, and popcorn at home boys' and girls' basketball games and wrestling meets. I started the corporation to bring "real life" into the classroom and encourage students to use their mathematics skills to make the decisions necessary to run a successful business.

At the beginning of each school year, an announcement is made that shares of stock in the 12.7 cm Hot Dog Corporation are on sale for $3.00 a share. Any interested eighth grader can purchase one share of stock. The sale of stock takes about two weeks. The 12.7 cm Hot Dog Corporation has become a "legend," and great interest is expressed on the part of the students. It is not unusual for in excess of 50 percent of the eighth graders to become shareholders. When the sale of stock is completed, a meeting of the members of the corporation is held to assess the amount of capital available to fund the corporation. Since the treasury contains no money prior to the sale of stock, the financial status of the corporation is dependent on the number of members, or shareholders. A treasurer is elected to keep a record of the stockholders, keep the ledger that contains the expenses and receipts, maintain a list of the "wholesale

Hope Martin *teaches eighth-grade mathematics in Highland Park, IL 60035. In addition, she teaches graduate workshops through St. Xavier College and the National College of Education in "Real Life Mathematics" and "Art and Math. "*

prices," and keep track of the "work records" of the shareholders. I conduct the meetings and oversee the project; I also supervise at each of the sales.

Members of the corporation are assigned to find the "wholesale prices" of each of the items to be sold, and a date is set for them to report back to the corporate members, usually about a week hence.

Students learn many things besides mathematical skills.

When the members have all the prices, they decide on the percentage of profit they wish to make and set the "retail price" of each of the items. Since each member owns only one share of stock, every shareholder has an equal vote at the meetings. Once the final votes have been taken, arrangements are made to purchase, deliver, and store the supplies.

A committee is formed to publicize when the hot-dog sales will begin. Students' efforts have varied from dramatic closed-circuit-TV ads to posters in the school hallways.

Before each event, a sign-up sheet is posted on which members of the corporation volunteer for setup (preparing for the sale), fifteen-minute work shifts (three members to a shift), and cleanup. Six shifts are needed for each event. Each member is expected to shoulder his or her burden of the work load. In addition to the mathematical skills of percentage, profit, and loss, the members learn the responsibility that each participant has to the group. A member who cannot work a shift must find a replacement so that the shift will be covered. The students take this responsibility very seriously, and it is rare that a shift does not have the proper coverage. Corporation members keep track of the shifts and automatically cover for a person who has failed to appear for a shift. The students have handled these problems very nicely.

Each sale has a cashier who is responsible for collecting the money from the customers and giving the correct change. After the sale, the cashier leaves a cash reserve in the money box; the remainder is counted and a deposit slip made out for the bank (the school office).

When the selling season is concluded at the end of February, the members vote on what they would like to buy for the school with the profits. They understand that the school has provided them with the facilities to run their business with no overhead expenses and that the profits will be used to purchase something for the school. Over the years, they have voted to purchase classroom sets of calculators, a metric lab for the media center, programmable calculators for use by the special education department, sports equipment to be used at the lunch hours, and games and puzzles for the mathematics classrooms. At this time they vote on what they want to do with their initial investment of $3.00 each. They can elect to have it returned to them, although they never have. Junior high school students love parties and food, and so most of the time they vote to go on a picnic or have a pizza party. We're trying to get tickets to a Cubs baseball game this year.

Through this project, the students learn many things besides the obvious acquisition of mathematics skills. They develop a sense of belonging to a group. They want their business to be the "most successful of all time" and to make a record profit. They learn a sense of responsibility in a real-life situation. Their wise management and the degree of their investment of time and energy contribute to the success or failure of the business. In most years, the corporation has averaged about $500.00 profit. The average afternoon sale grosses about $60.00, and half of this amount is profit. The most money any corporation has ever made is $850.00, but that group expanded their offerings and sponsored "McDonald's Days" during the lunch hours. One year the corporation went bankrupt; they "ate the profits." This experience has served as a valuable lesson to succeeding corporations.

Each year I become more excited about the idea and the value that it has for youngsters. It is truly a real-life experience that has been a marvelous addition to my mathematics program.

5
Number and Number Relationships

ALTHOUGH the K–4 curriculum devotes a good deal of attention to the development of number sense and concepts of whole number operations, these topics must receive continued attention in the middle grades. Students still need enhanced understandings of fractions, decimals, percents, and integers. Unless carefully and completely developed, fraction concepts tend to cause students problems in further mathematics courses. This chapter focuses on activities that develop and extend students' understanding of number and number relationships.

Reys article, "Promoting Number Sense in the Middle Grades", gives a good overview of this topic. Number sense can be thought of as an intuitive feeling about the size of numbers and a common-sense approach to their uses and issues of accuracy. Reys describes a teacher's role in developing number sense with various forms of rational numbers. Giving written assignments, encouraging invented methods, using appropriate calculating tools, helping students establish benchmarks, and promoting internal questioning are some examples of activities teachers may employ.

Fraction concepts develop slowly in some students. A conceptual understanding is essential *before* students become involved in operations with fractions. Caldwell uses pattern-block activities to develop the meanings of fractions. For example, the area model of fractions gives one kind of understanding whereas the set model offers another. The described activities s help develop both of these important perspectives.

Division of fractions is often not easily understood by students. In "Division with Fractions", Nowlin suggests using problems that apply models of fraction division before students are introduced to the traditional invert-and-multiply algorithm. For example, students are challenged to write a word problem that illustrates "1 3/4 divided by __."

Nelson and Whitaker use geoboards to develop fraction concepts. Activities begin with naming fractions and extend through equivalent fractions, selecting a unit, and operations with fractions. Operations are introduced and developed as they relate to whole-number operations.

Related to the concept of fractions is the concept of ratios. In "The Ratio Table", a tool, the ratio table, is used for developing students' understanding of rational number concepts. This approach is offered as an alternative to the usual cross-multiplication technique.

Another rational-number concept is percent. Students often do not relate fractional, decimal, and percent representations of a number or quantity and have trouble solving problems that involve them. Bennett and Nelson present a conceptual model for solving percent problems. The use of a 10-by-10 grid introduces students to solving percent problems.

Games can also reinforce skills and concepts related to number sense. Stone introduces a game for promoting skills in place value, which can also involve probability concepts. Another game, *Add-Lo,* introduced in the article by Bledsoe, gives students practice with adding integers and absolute value.

BARBARA J. REYS

Promoting Number Sense in the Middle Grades

PHRASES such as "number sense," operation sense," and "intuitive understanding of number" are used throughout the *Curriculum and Evaluation Standards for School Mathematics* (NCTM 1989) to describe an intangible quality possessed by successful mathematics learners. Number sense refers to an intuitive feeling for numbers and their various uses and interpretations, an appreciation for various levels of accuracy when computing, the ability to detect arithmetical errors, and a common-sense approach to using numbers (Howden 1989; McIntosh, Reys, and Reys 1991). Number sense is not a finite entity that a student either has or does not have but rather a process that develops and matures with experience and knowledge. It does not develop by chance, nor does being skilled at manipulating numbers necessarily reflect this acquaintance and familiarity with numbers. Above all, number sense is characterized by a desire to make sense of numerical situations, including relating numbers to context and analyzing the effect of manipulations on numbers. It is a way of thinking that should permeate all aspects of mathematics teaching and learning.

The idea of number sense is not new. As early as the 1930s William Brownell was concerned with what he called "meaningful learning." To Brownell the true test of mathematical learning was not the ability to compute but the possession of an "intelligent grasp [of] number relations and the ability to deal with arithmetic situations with proper comprehension of their math-

ematical as well as their practical significance" (1935, 19). He stressed the importance of instruction that is "deliberately planned to teach arithmetical meanings and to make arithmetic sensible to children through its mathematical relationships" (pp. 257–58).

Perhaps number sense, like common sense, is best described by looking at the specific behavioral characteristics of those who value and use it. A student with number sense will—

- *look at a problem holistically before confronting details.* For example, in adding 1 2/3 + 3/4 + 1/3, a student might mentally reorder the addends to 1 2/3 + 1/3 + 3/4 to take advantage of the compatible addends (1 2/3 and 1/3).

- *look for relationships among numbers and operations and will consider the context in which a question is posed.* For example, in buying 4 notebooks priced at 39 cents each, the student with $2

might reason that she or he has enough money, since each notebook costs less than half a dollar.

- *choose or invent a method that takes advantage of his or her own understanding of the relationships between numbers or between numbers and operations and will seek the most efficient representation for the given task.* For example, suppose that at least 75 percent of the class of 30 students needs to agree on a plan for a school trip before it can be finalized. A student might reason that "75% is 50% plus 25%, or half plus half of that. So 15 + 8, or 23, students must agree."

- *use benchmarks to judge number magnitude.* For example, 2/5 of 49 is less than half of 49.

- *recognize unreasonable results for calculations in the normal process of reflecting on answers.* For example, 3.2 × 4.8 can't possibly be 153.6, since the answer must be about 3 × 5, or 15, so an error in dec-

---

Barbara Reys *teaches at the University of Missouri—Columbia, Columbia, MO 65211. Her interests include exploring and promoting a variety of computational tools including calculators, mental computation, and estimation.*

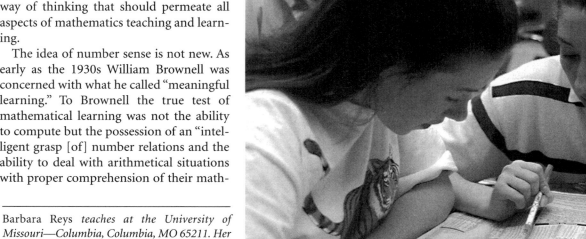

imal-point placement must have been made.

Number sense, then, is not a new topic for teachers to include in an already overcrowded mathematics program. Rather, it is an important perspective from which to view learning mathematics. *Number sense is both the ability of the learner to make logical connections between new information and previously acquired knowledge and the drive within the learner to make forming these connections a priority.* Number sense will be valued among students only if teachers believe that it is more important for students to make sense of the mathematics they learn than to master rules and algorithms, which are often poorly understood, and if they act on these beliefs. Students will begin to acquire number sense if they are engaged in purposeful activities requiring them to think about numbers and numerical relationships and to make connections with quantitative information seen in everyday life.

The Teacher's Role in Developing Number Sense

Just as number sense requires and attitude of sense-making on the part of the learner, teaching for the development of number sense requires a conscious, coordinated effort to build connections and meaning on the part of the teacher. Teachers play an important role in building number sense in the type of classroom environment they create, in the teaching practices they employ, and in the activities they select.

Use process questions

Process questions—those that require more than a simple factual response—can stimulate discussion of an idea, which can lead to further exploration and the use of oral language to explain and justify a thought. Consider the following classroom conversation:

Teacher: I'm thinking of two fractions. Their sum is between 0 and 1. What can you tell me about the fractions?

Greg: Both fractions are small, maybe less than 1.

Teacher: OK, what else?

Greg: Are they both less than 1/2?

Teacher: Good question, can anyone answer that?

Praveen: They don't have to both be less than 1/2. One can be 3/4 and the other real small, like 1/10.

Greg: OK, but if one is bigger than a half, the other one must be smaller than a half.

Teacher: Good point. Can anyone tell me anything else about my fractions?

Nhung: If their sum is less than 1, their product is also less than 1.

Teacher: What do the rest of you think about that idea?

The teacher's questions prompted the students to examine various examples and to prove or disprove their initial thoughts. In promoting number sense it is important for students to see that it is possible to be wrong. What is valued most is reflection on answers so that they can be proved either right or wrong. The teacher in this example assumed the critical role of posing questions, which caused students to continue reflective thought, and of encouraging other students to be involved in the process. See activity A for additional questions related to fraction computation that can be used for discussion and exploration.

Teaching for number sense involves a quality-over-quantity attitude toward problem completion. That is, the focus is on understanding a given problem by looking at it from multiple perspectives rather than on attempting to work as many problems as possible in a given period. Strategies offered by students must be justified, and students learn to ask, "Does this make sense?" when considering each answer (see activity B for an example from the *Curriculum and Evaluation Standards for School Mathematics* [NCTM 1989] that illustrates the need to connect information and make generalizations) .

Use writing assignments

Having students summarize their thinking in written form is an effective method for helping students nurture their sense of number. Students can be asked to write about the results of group activities or to keep a journal in which they enter ideas generated by specific tasks. As they write, they may formulate new ideas or questions, which may serve as a reference for further question posing and discussion. Later, as they reread their journals they can see how their conceptions have been changed and expanded by further exploration and discussion. The following excerpt from a fifth-grade student's journal illustrates how children might record their thoughts:

> Today I found out that I can't count to 1 000 000 in 1 day. It would take me more than 10 days and I would even have to count all night without stopping. A million is a lot bigger than I thought. I wonder how long it would take to count to a trillion?

Encourage invented methods

Creating and exploring their own methods for calculating and solving problems prepare students to consider traditional methods at a later stage and view standard algorithms as yet another means of producing sensible answers. In a classroom where sense-making is a priority, teachers become guides and moderators instead of dispensers of rules and procedures. The

---

Activity A: Fractions between 0 and 1

To the teacher: This activity helps clarify students' understanding of fractions between 0 and 1. It can be used as a quick warm-up for the mathematics lesson. Several questions have more than one correct answer.

Ask students questions such as these:

1. Name a fraction between 1/2 and 1.
2. Name a fraction between 1/4 and 3/4, other than 1/2.
3. Name a fraction between 1/4 and 1/2 whose denominator is 10.
4. Name a fraction between 7/8 and 1. How many can you name?
5. Name a fraction between 0 and 1/10 whose numerator is not 1.

Note: This activity is from Reys et al. (1991, 28).

Activity B:
Operations on fractions

To the teacher: This activity is suggested in the evaluation section of the *Curriculum and Evaluation Standards for School Mathematics* (NCTM 1989, 203). It is useful for clarifying students' understanding of the effects of certain operations on fractions.

Display the number line and ask students questions such as those indicated here and others that come to mind. Encourage students to justify their answers by explaining their reasoning.

1. If the fractions represented by the points D and E are multiplied, what point on the number line best represents the product?
2. If the fractions represented by the points C and D are multiplied, what point on the number line best represents the product?
3. If the fractions represented by the points B and F are multiplied, what point on the number line best represents the product?

Note: This activity is excerpted from Reys et al. (1991, 34).

goal of "one right answer" derived from "one preferred algorithm" is replaced by the goal of multiple solution strategies that are generated by, and make sense to, the students. The emphasis shifts from the solution to the process. Allowing students the freedom to use strategies that are intuitively obvious to them helps them to feel more comfortable with the problem-solving process and to internalize mathematics in a way that makes sense to them. At some stage it also helps them appreciate the efficiency of standard algorithms.

Use appropriate
calculation tools

Number sense can be promoted by ensuring that students learn to calculate in various ways including written, mental, approximate, and electronic methods. Alerting students to the use of approximate numbers in real-life situations underscores the value of estimates (see activity C for an example of such an exploration).

Both mental computation and estimation offer vehicles to encourage invention of strategies and alertness to sensible answers. For example, in calculating 5×96, one student might change the problem to $10 \times 96/2$, another might think $5 \times 8 \times 12$, whereas another might use the distributive property and compute $(5 \times 90) + (5 \times 6)$ or $(5 \times 100) - (5 \times 4)$. Probing questions and concrete analogies can be used to initiate the exploration of alternative methods of mental calculation. For example, after giving students the problem 25×49, the teacher might ask, "Can anyone create a problem from this calculation by substituting the word quarters for the number 25? Does it help to find the product of these two numbers if we think about the 25 as a quarter? How?"

The calculator plays an important role as an efficient tool in an environment that emphasizes exploration. By using the calculator to perform tedious computations and test conjectures, students can focus on the process of deriving a solution and on the meaning of the answer once it is computed rather than on the computational procedure. Students may be more eager to explore properties of numbers when calculators are accessible. For example, suppose the teacher poses the following question to the class: "What happens when you multiply a positive whole number by a decimal between 0.9 and 1.1? Use your calculator to explore this question, generate your conjecture, and make a list of examples that support your conjecture." Students are encouraged to generate many examples and to draw a conclusion on the basis of these examples (see activity D for elaboration of this idea).

Help students
establish benchmarks

Approximate computation or estimation is another important tool for encouraging students to use what they already know about numbers to make sense of new numerical situations. Oftentimes this tactic means that students use their own benchmarks to judge the reasonableness of a situation. For example, a student using a standard protractor to measure a 30-degree

Activity C:
Exact and
approximate
numbers

To the teacher: Ask students to investigate the use of approximate and exact numbers in newspaper articles. Use this activity to help students appreciate the everyday use of estimates.

Give students copies of the front page of various newspapers. Ask them to use a marker to circle numbers used in headlines and articles. Next, have students review the context for the use of each circled number to determine if it is an exact or an approximate value. For example, do the numbers in these headlines below refer to exact or approximate values?

U.S. population tops 220 million
Lottery winner earns over $200 000 annually
Stocks fall 5.4 percent

Note: This activity is from Reys et al. (1991, 20).

angle is not likely to read the wrong scale and report 150 degrees as the measure if a 90-degree angle has been established as a referent. In the same way, a student who has been encouraged to estimate fractions near 0, 1/2, and 1 will understand that the sum of 2/5 + 4/9 must be less than 1, since both fractions are less than a half (see activities E and F for examples focused on establishing awareness and use of benchmarks).

Encouraging students to consider these benchmarks, or referents, is a way of helping them develop better conceptual understanding of fractions, decimals, and percents. This intuitive understanding is a priority and should precede the study of operating with fractions, decimals, and percents.

Promote internal questioning

An important role for teachers in the development of number sense is helping students learn to ask themselves key questions before, during, and after the solution process. For example, what type of number would I expect for an answer to this problem? About how large will the answer be? What is the biggest or smallest value I expect? After completing a calculation, students then determine whether the answer is consistent with what they expected. This process of self-examination may help sensitize students to order-of-magnitude errors as well as prevent them from checking their answer by repeating the same computational error a second time. For example, as students explore the questions illustrated in activity G, they are encouraged to predict what happens when a number is multiplied or divided by a number near 1. As conjectures are made they can be verified or refuted quickly using a calculator. Students are given the opportunity to study the effect of multiplying or dividing by a number more or less than 1 and to formulate and test conjectures.

In classrooms where number sense is a priority, students are active participants

---

Activity D: Multiplication by decimals near 0, 1/2, and 1

To the teacher: This activity helps students explore the effect of multiplying by decimals near 0, 1/2, and 1. After students have generated and verified many of their own examples with a calculator, encourage them to make generalizations from the pattern that emerges.

What Happens When ...

What happens when you multiply by a number less than 1? Ask students to explore this question by completing the chart.

Pick a Whole Number	Multiply by 0.05	Multiply by 0.48	Multiply by 0.9

Questions to consider:

1. In general, what happens when you multiply a whole number by 0.05?

2. In general, what happens when you multiply a whole number by 0.48?

3. In general, what happens when you multiply a whole number by 0.9?

Note: This activity is from Reys et al. (1991, 40).

Activity E: Establishing benchmarks for whole numbers

To the teacher: Adults often use benchmarks or common referents to process numerical information. For example, knowing the population of your town might help you judge the size of a crowd attending a concert. (For example, if the high school stadium holds 1 000 people and the report says that 150 000 people attended a rock concert, you might think of the size of the concert crowd as being the stadium filled 150 times.) This activity is designed to see how many students are aware of the size of some commonly used referents. Encourage students to formulate additional questions and problems for studying the implications of these statistics. As an extension, you might want to review with your class the book *In One Day* by Tom Parker (1984), which contains a number of interesting numerical facts about what Americans do in one day.

Pose the following questions to students. Allow them first to estimate and then do research to determine the value that answers each question.

1. Population of the world: _____
2. Population of the United States: _____
3. Population of your town:_____
4. Population of your school: _____
5. United States government budget: _____
6. The number of 13-year-olds alive today:____
7. The number of graduating high school seniors last year: _____
8. The number of tons of garbage generated every day:_____

Note: This activity is from Reys et al. (1991, 16).

Activity F: Percent benchmarks

To the teacher: Students will likely benefit from discussion with fellow classmates as they complete this activity. You may want to organize them into small groups to encourage this discussion.

Ask students to read and reflect on each statement and then to choose an answer from the answer list. The answers will vary; you may want students to continue this activity by researching each answer using appropriate sources of information or by conducting a survey.

Complete each statement using one of the following choices:

0 percent
Less than 10 percent
About 25 percent
Fewer than 50 percent
About 50 percent
More than 50 percent
About 75 percent
At least 90 percent
100 percent

Statements:

1. _____ of the students in my classroom are left-handed.
2. _____ of the students in my classroom have red hair.
3. _____ of the students in my school like hamburgers.
4. _____ of the students in my school like baseball.
5. _____ of the students in my school are wearing tennis shoes today.
6. _____ of the people in my town are over 90 years old.
7. _____ of the people in my town own a car.
8. _____ of the people in my state are female.

Note: This activity is from Reys et al. (1991, 43).

who share their hypotheses, reasoning, and conclusions. The classroom environment encourages students' exploration, questioning, verification, and sensemaking.

Selecting Activities

By establishing a classroom atmosphere that encourages exploration, thinking, and discussion, and by selecting appropriate problems and activities, the teacher can cultivate number sense during all mathematical experiences. Activities that promote number sense by concentrating on process have several common characteristics. They encourage students to think about what they are doing and to share their thoughts with others. They promote creativity and investigation and allow for many answers and solution strategies. They help students know when it is appropriate to estimate or to produce an exact answer and when to compute mentally, on paper, or with a calculator. They help students see the regularity of mathematics and the connections between mathematics and the real world. Process-oriented activities also convey the idea of mathematics as an exciting, dynamic discovery of ideas and relationships.

Throughout this discussion several activities have been suggested. These activities are taken from the NCTM's Addenda book *Developing Number Sense in the Middle Grades* (Reys et al. 1991). They are offered not as "number sense lessons" but as ideas related to number sense drawn from various topics within the middle grades curriculum. Different ways of integrating number sense in elementary school class-

rooms are also demonstrated in the Number Sense Now videotape series available from NCTM (1993). Activities in these resources may further illustrate number sense and highlight some ways to encourage its development.

References

Brownell, William A. "Psychological Considerations in the Learning and the Teaching of Arithmetic." In *The Teaching of Arithmetic,* Tenth Yearbook of the National Council of Teachers of Mathematics, edited by D. W. Reeve, 19–51. New York: Teachers College, Columbia University, 1935.

Howden, Hilde. "Teaching Number Sense." *Arithmetic Teacher* 36 (February 1989): 6–11.

McIntosh, Allistair, Barbara J. Reys, and Robert E. Reys. "A Proposed Framework for Examining Basic Number Sense." *For the Learning of Mathematics* 12 (November 1992): 2–8, 44.

National Council of Teachers of Mathematics. *Curriculum and Evaluation Standards for School Mathematics.* Reston, Va.: The Council, 1989.

———. *Number Sense Now! Reaching the NCTM Standards.* 3 videotapes and guidebook. Project directed by Francis (Skip) Fennell. Reston, Va.: The Council, 1993.

Parker, Tom. *In One Day.* Boston: Houghton Mifflin Co., 1984.

Reys, Barbara J., Rita Barger, Maxim Bruckheimer, Barbara Dougherty, Jack Hope, Linda Lembke, Zvia Markovits, Andy Parnas, Sue Reehm, Ruth T. Sturdevant, and Marianne Weber. *Developing Number Sense in the Middle Grades,* Addenda Series, Grades 5–8. Reston, Va.: National Council of Teachers of Mathematics, 1991.

Activity G: Multiplying and dividing by numbers near 1

To the teacher: In this activity students are encouraged to fill in each blank by thinking about the effect of the indicated operation. All can be answered without calculation. Encourage students to verbalize their thinking for each problem. After completing all the problems, you might substitute ÷ for the × symbol in each problem. Ask students to reevaluate each sentence.

Ask students to study each problem. Without performing any calculation they are to decide if <, =, or > would complete each sentence. Ask them to justify their thinking.

1. 246×1.3 ❏ 246
2. 920×0.8 ❏ 920
3. 98×1.001 ❏ 98
4. $32 \times 1/2$ ❏ 32
5. $1/2 \times 7/8$ ❏ $1/2$
6. $1/2 \times 7/8$ ❏ $7/8$

Note: This activity is from Reys et al (1991, 38).

JANET H. CALDWELL

Communicating about Fractions with Pattern Blocks

ONE of the central concerns of the *Curriculum and Evaluation Standards for School Mathematics* (NCTM 1989) is helping students develop in-depth understanding of the central ideas of mathematics. One way to develop deeper understanding involves emphasizing mathematics as communication, asking students to—

> reflect on and clarify their own thinking about mathematical ideas and situations; . . . use the skills of reading, listening, and viewing to interpret and evaluate mathematical ideas; discuss mathematical ideas and make conjectures and convincing arguments. (p. 78)

Having students talk and write about their understanding of basic concepts helps them to develop their understanding of mathematical ideas. Such discussion clarifies their current ideas and identifies misunderstandings, yielding a rich source of assessment information. It is often useful for students to explore mathematical concepts by modeling situations using concrete materials and then connecting these models to oral, written, pictorial, and symbolic representations of the same situation. This article focuses on exploring and connecting fraction concepts and representations.

Meanings of Fractions

A major challenge for many students involves the concept of rational numbers, especially fractions. The most basic way of visualizing a fraction is as part of a whole; this interpretation also is the typical way of

Janet Caldwell *teaches undergraduate and graduate mathematics and mathematics education courses at Rowan College of New Jersey, formerly Glassboro State College, in Glassboro, NJ 08028.*

introducing fractions to young children (Post, Behr, and Lesh 1982).

One person may "see" the fraction one-half as a picture of a circle with half shaded. Such an image is an example of a continuous model of a fraction based on area. The *area* model for fractions seems to be the easiest embodiment for students to understand and is thus generally used for introducing oral names for simple fractions with such real objects as pizzas and candy bars in the early grades (Payne Towsley, and Huinker 1990). Illustrations of the area model for fractions include geometric figure; with part shaded, graph paper with part shaded, a clock with the hands designating a part of a circle, and paper folded into fractional parts. A critical feature of the area model is that all the parts into which the whole is divided must have equal area. An application of fractions involving this model can be seen by using pattern blocks to simulate a stained-glass window (see fig. 1); what fraction of the area of the design is yellow?

Another individual may "see" the fraction one-half as a bag of candy in which half the pieces are chocolate. The *set* model for fractions is more difficult conceptually

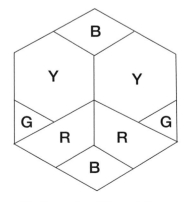

Fig. 1. A pattern-block window

than the area model (Payne, Towsley, and Huinker 1990); it requires identifying the unit and eliminates the requirement that the pieces be of the same size. Accordingly, it is generally introduced in later grades. This embodiment identifies what fraction of a set has a specific characteristic, such as color. For example, what fraction of the pegs in a pegboard are blue? What fraction of the plants have red flowers? What fraction of the people in the room wear glasses? What fraction of an egg carton is filled? What fraction of a set is circled? In this model, the pieces or members of the set do not need to share any attribute other than membership in the set; they do not need the same shape or the same area. An application of fractions involving this model might involve scooping up a handful of pattern blocks at random and determining what fraction of the blocks scooped up are yellow; the size and shape of the blocks are irrelevant to the question asked.

It is important for students to recognize that fractions have different meanings in different contexts. Teachers must present opportunities for students to use fractions in both area and set contexts. In addition, students also need to confront differences between these contexts explicitly.

This article describes an extended activity appropriate for use in the upper-elementary grades that uses communication to help students explore and refine their understanding of the area and set models for fractions using pattern blocks. It begins with the teacher placing some pattern blocks on the overhead projector or somewhere else where they are easily seen, arranging them to make a pleasing design, perhaps something like figure 2. It is important *not* to use the orange square pieces or the tan parallelogram blocks in

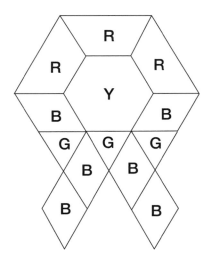

Fig. 2. What fraction is blue?

the design, since these shapes cannot be covered evenly by any of the other blocks. The teacher then asks the students a purposefully ambiguous question, "What fraction is blue?"

At this point, the students need to be given some time to think, to reproduce the figure using pattern blocks, and to confer with one another. By communicating with each other, they begin to make more explicit their ideas about fractions in the context of this task. The students then need to share their answers and their reasoning, orally or in writing. The ambiguity inherent in the question should emerge in the students' discussion. By having to justify their own reasoning to others, the students will reveal their own thinking. Gradually, students should come to understand that the question asked has more than one correct answer, depending on how the question is interpreted. Students looking at the problem as involving a part of an area will find a different solution than students who look at the problem as one involving finding a part of a set. More important are their reasoning and their justification of their answer, as revealed by their discussion or their writing.

Sample Responses

This activity has been used with more than sixty children and hundreds of inservice elementary teachers. Generally, asking students to write their responses before beginning the oral discussion seems to generate more thoughtful answers and reveal more about their understanding of the concept of a fraction. Sometimes it is nec-

essary to ask students to elaborate on their written responses to determine more clearly just what they mean. At other times, all the students in the class have arrived at the same answer; in that situation, they are then asked whether other correct answers to the question are possible. Some middle-grades students' written responses to the questions are described in the following paragraphs.

I think it's 6/13. I think 6/13 is right because there are 13 pieces and 6 of them are blue.
—Laura, Grade 5

This answer is by far the most common, especially with younger children. They seem to think of a fraction as being part of a set, so they count the number of pieces and find that six of the thirteen pieces are blue. The fraction of the set of pieces that is blue is thus 6/13. Note that the prevalence of this answer with younger children is in marked contrast to the usual instructional sequence, which begins with fractions as parts of an area. Thus, the responses to this task contradict past findings with respect to the difficulty of this interpretation of a fraction.

I think it's 1/3.
—Unknown, Grade 5

This response is very rare, having been given by those students seeking additional possible interpretations of the question. When asked to explain further, they stated that they had simply found the largest piece, the yellow hexagon block, and then had decided what fraction *of the biggest piece* is the blue parallelogram piece. Since three blue parallelogram pieces make up one yellow hexagon block (fig. 3), the blue block must be 1/3 of the largest piece. A student who responds in this fashion is using an area model for fractions but is not considering the entire design; he or she is seeking to find a name for the blue piece rather than to relate it to the area or the region as a whole. Such a student may be

basing the answer on previous experiences in working with pattern blocks or other manipulatives, such as Cuisenaire rods. Alternatively, the student may be relying on previous experience with pictorial representations of mixed numbers.

It's 1/6!
—Unknown, Grade 6

This response is also relatively uncommon but tends to appear more frequently than the previous one. The student who sees this result might explain that the design has six blue pieces in all, so one blue piece is one-sixth of the blue pieces. This student is answering the question "What fraction *of the blue pieces* is one blue piece?" Without further explanation from the student, it is unclear whether the underlying model being used is one involving area or sets.

I think that 6/15, or 2/5, is blue. I think that because I covered completely with 15 blue pieces, 6 of those were really supposed to be blue.
—Evan, Grade 5

The student who gives this response usually explains that in work with fractions, all the pieces must be of the same size. This student is using an area model, thinking of the fraction of the area that is blue. When the answer is given first as 6/15, the student has usually divided the entire design into pieces of the same size as the blue pattern block(fig. 4). Then the total number of blue parallelogram pieces used is fifteen, and six of these are really blue.

Thus the fraction of the design that is blue is 6/15. Notice that this student auto-

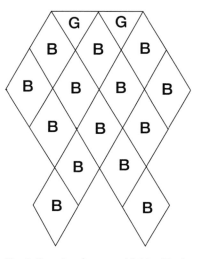

Fig. 4. Covering the area with blue blocks

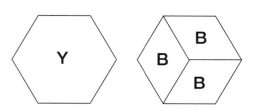

Fig. 3. A blue is 1/3 of a yellow

matically reduced the fraction to lowest terms, but the explanation justifies the former fraction.

> I think that the fraction of this design is 6/15. This is because there is 1 hexagon, 3 trapezoids, 6 diamonds, and 3 triangles, which make up 15 diamonds. Each shape can make or divide into a diamond, so to see how many diamonds there are, you have to know how many diamonds *in all*.
>
> —Alexis, Grade 5

Sometimes students reach this same answer of 6/15 by way of a slightly different path. These students look at the diagram to determine how many blue pieces are needed to cover each piece of another type. For example, this design has one yellow hexagon block, whose area is equivalent to that of three blue blocks. Each of three red trapezoid blocks is equivalent in area to one and one-half blue pieces for each trapezoid, so thus far we have the equivalent of 4 1/2 + 3, or 7 1/2, blue blocks. Then the six blue parallelogram pieces themselves are added, giving a total of 6 + 7 1/2 = 13 1/2 blue parallelogram pieces. Finally, each of the three green triangle blocks is equivalent to half a blue piece, giving a total of 13 1/2 + 1 1/2, or 15, blue blocks. Since just six of the total number of pieces are actually blue, the fraction is 6/15. By elaborating on their response, the students have an opportunity to explain and justify their reasoning.

> 2/5 because there's five sets; if you piece them together like the yellow piece you come out with five sets.
>
> —Amy, Grade 6

> 2/5. If you take the pieces and stack them up, 2 would be blue because it takes 3 blue to make one layer and I have 6 blue. The rest would equal out to three layers.
>
> —Paul, Grade 5

Some students arrive at the same answer in still a different way and are likely to express the answer directly as 2/5. They look at the diagram or their model and think of it in terms of yellow hexagons, like Amy. A more elaborate explanation might be as follows:

> If I take all the pieces and move them around so that like colors are together, then how many hexagons will I have? Well, first there's the one yellow hexagon. Then two of the red

trapezoid pieces make another hexagon, with one left over. If I add the three green triangle pieces to the red trapezoid block that's left, I can get a third hexagon. The blue parallelogram pieces then will make two more hexagons. So I have five hexagons (fig. 5), and two of them are blue. The fraction of the design that's blue is 2/5!

Paul uses a similar strategy, but instead of organizing the pieces into hexagons, he thinks of each hexagon as a layer of a three-dimensional tower. For many younger students, the 2/5 answer occurs only after they have been encouraged to explore the situation further. Both Amy and Paul thought of this response as a second answer while they were waiting for other students to finish writing. In both instances, their initial answer of 6/13 relied on a set interpretation. In the subsequent discussion, both agreed that each answer was correct, depending on the question being asked. They seemed to like the idea that different answers could all be correct if each was adequately justified.

By communicating with others, students have the opportunity to think about what fractions mean to them and to share the various strategies used to solve this problem. Sometimes they become very excited about trying to find all the possible different correct answers. Students also learn more about themselves as learners and about how they can learn from sharing ideas with other students.

It is quite helpful to have students write about the activity at two points. By writing before sharing and discussion, explaining and justifying their answers, students become more aware of their own thinking. By writing after discussion, describing what they have learned from the discussion, students have an opportunity to record and refine new thoughts and revisions of their thinking. Such activities frequently yield useful information about students' conceptual and procedural understanding and any difficulties they may be having. In addition, they afford an opportunity for the teacher to review responses from all students rather than just a few.

Examples illustrate some of the misconceptions and confusions that may be revealed in students' work. The following student has given the correct answer for an area model but uses language more appropriate for a set model. The confusion

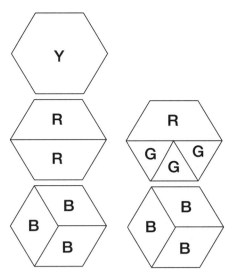

Fig. 5. Making hexagons with the pieces in the design

between the two models is evident not only in Chris's language but also in his computations.

> If you count all the pieces and pretend they were all the same, you would come up with 15. If you subtract the number of the blues that you have, you would come up with 11 1/2. This's your answer: 6/15.
>
> —Chris, Grade 5

The next student bases his solution on an area model and moves between fraction and decimal notations easily, but makes some errors in subdividing the pieces with blue blocks.

> I think that it's 3/8 of the picture because the reds are 2 of the blues and the greens are 0.5 of the blues. So when you add them up you get 16 1/2 blues, and you have 6 blues to begin with, so it's 6/16 reduced = 3/8.
>
> —Philip, Grade 6

It is somewhat interesting to note the changes in thinking that occur for this student over the course of a year in which his mathematics program involves substantial work with problem solving, reasoning, communication, and visualization.

> I split each section up so that it would equal 1 yellow and I know that the reds were 1/2, the blues 1/3, and the greens 1/6, so I took 2 reds and made 1 and I had 1 red left over, so I added the 3 greens to it. Then I put the three blues together—that left me with 3 more, so I put them together. There were 5 groups and 2 of those 5 groups were blue, so 2/5 of blocks were blue.
>
> —Phillip, End of Year in Grade 6

This student's ability to explain his thinking has clearly improved, and the computational errors have disappeared. In addition, however, he moves from using the blue pieces as his basic unit to using a larger piece, the yellow. Also, instead of simply listing the value of each piece and adding the values, he is now putting pieces together to make wholes.

Extensions

Several good ways can be used to extend this initial activity. In each activity, by continuing to emphasize communication, the teacher can encourage students to reflect further on their understanding of the concept of fraction, to justify their answers, and to explain their reasoning.

A very important extension activity involves asking students to relate their responses to real-life situations using the different interpretations of fraction in this task:

> In what situations would you need to use the idea of a fraction as a part of a set? In what situations would you need to use the idea of a fraction as part of an area?

Having students discuss or write about these questions helps them to process the different perspectives that have been discussed, making sense of each of the interpretations. This aspect of the activity can then be further extended and related to the real world by asking students to write a story in which one would need to use fractions as part of a set or as part of an area.

If students have difficulty in understanding one another's explanations of their various strategies, they can be asked to do a similar problem with a different design. This repetition gives them an opportunity to see the commonalities between the two tasks and to improve on their explanations. Some students will also change their initial responses, often preferring to adopt a more complex strategy.

Students can also be asked to do another of these problems, this time focusing on the fraction *of the design* that is of a given color. This task is particularly useful if many of the students had difficulty in working with the idea of a fraction as a part of an area. Focusing on this meaning of fraction will enable them to develop this concept further; communicating about the

strategies they used to find the answer will also focus their attention on a variety of problem-solving strategies.

Students can be asked to make a design of their own, perhaps one whose area is 1/3 yellow (such as the examples shown in fig. 6), or one that uses six pieces and whose area is 1/2 red (see, e.g., those in fig. 7). In addition to generating the design, they should also explain their strategy for developing the design. This approach encourages students with relatively simple designs to try to develop more complex ones in the future and can often further illuminate students' understanding of fractions.

A quite challenging task for students is to try to find a design in which the fraction of the area that is blue is the same as the fraction of the pieces that are blue. An example of such a design is given in figure 8. Again,

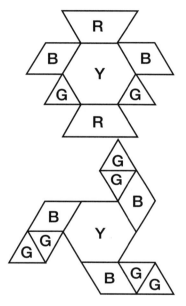

Fig. 6. Designs each of whose area is 1/3 yellow

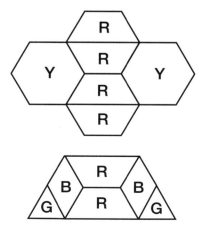

Fig. 7. Six pieces whose area is 1/2 red

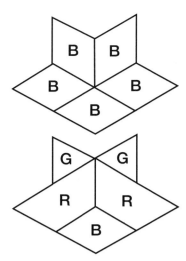

Fig. 8. The fraction of the area that is blue is the same as the fraction of pieces that are blue.

students should explain how they developed their design so that all in the class can share ideas and so that the teacher has a better understanding of students' thinking.

Students may also be asked to write about the different meanings that fractions can have, using pattern blocks, real-world situations, or pictures for examples. In this way, they are encouraged to develop further different meanings for fractions.

Another extension of this activity that is particularly appropriate for group work involves applying the concepts to specific real-world situations.

- Suppose that Ethel's Candy Shoppe sells four types of gumdrops: lemon (yellow), cherry (red), lime (green), and mint (blue). Students can represent a bag of gumdrops by scooping up a handful of yellow, red, green, and blue pattern blocks. What fraction is each flavor? (Note that this question involves a set interpretation of fraction.)

- Katie is having a pizza party. She is inviting twelve boys and twelve girls, including herself. She thinks that each boy will eat four pieces of pizza and each girl will eat three pieces. If each pizza is divided into twelve equal pieces, how many pizzas will Katie need for her party? (This question requires an area interpretation but does not require the use of fractions.)

- Suppose that we want to make a stained-glass window like the one in figure 1. If the cost of each piece is based on its size and if the green triangle piece costs $1.00, what is the total cost of the window? (This question actually involves no fractions but is similar to an area interpretation; you might also wish to ask what fraction of the cost is due to using yellow glass.)

- What is the cost of the window if each piece has a different price based on its color and its size (e.g., a triangle represents one unit of area, green's cost is $1.00 per unit of area, blue's cost is $1.25 per unit of area, red's cost is $2.00 per unit of area, and yellow's cost is $2.50 per unit of area)? (This question first involves area and then attributes a value to it.)

Investigating these or similar types of situations can involve students for quite some time in a rather complex project. For each exploration, students should again have opportunities to communicate about the situation, about their strategies in solving the problem, and about their answers. By sharing their ideas in writing and orally, students will come to see the common elements in each situation and make conjectures and generalizations.

In these activities, students accomplish a number of goals. They are involved in rea-soning and problem solving while trying to figure out the answer. They are communicating about mathematics, explaining how they got their answers and justifying their reasoning. This process of communication improves their understanding of basic fraction concepts by helping them to become more aware of their own thinking and the diverse strategies used by others. In the process, students also review basic geometry vocabulary. Finally, they improve their spatial-visualization skills as they work with the geometric shapes, combining and subdividing them. The communication aspect of these activities helps teachers to assess each student's reasoning about fractions so that instruction can be tailored to meet the needs of the students.

These activities involve the first four standards from the NCTM's (1989) *Curriculum and Evaluation Standards for School Mathematics*: Mathematics as Problem Solving, Mathematics as Communication, Mathematics as Reasoning, and Mathematical Connections. They touch on two other Standards, as well: Number and Number Relationships and Geometry. Students are actively involved in exploring a particular situation. They use concrete materials to investigate mathematical concepts, building on their understanding of these concepts. Communicating about their activities with the concrete materials is a critical element in further developing students' ability to use a variety of representations for a problem situation, to reflect on and clarify their own thinking about mathematics, and to discuss mathematical ideas and justify their reasoning.

References

National Council of Teachers of Mathematics. *Curriculum and Evaluation Standards for School Mathematics*. Reston, Va.: The Council, 1989.

Payne, Joseph N., Ann E. Towsley, and DeAnn M. Huinker. "Fractions and Decimals." In *Mathematics for the Young Child*, edited by Joseph N. Payne, 174–200. Reston, Va.: National Council of Teachers of Mathematics, 1990.

Post, Thomas R., Merlyn J. Behr, and Richard Lesh. "Interpretations of Rational Number Concepts." In *Mathematics for the Middle Grades (5–9)*, 1982 Yearbook of the National Council of Teachers of Mathematics, edited by Linda Silvey, 50–72. Reston, Va.: The Council, 1982.

DONALD NOWLIN

Division with Fractions

Although operations with fractions have been in the elementary and middle school curriculum for many years, finding examples of practical problems that illustrate the usefulness of division with fractions and mixed numbers is not easy. Most real-world applications of rational numbers involve decimal numerals (Usiskin and Bell 1984), but examples of division with fractions and mixed numbers are often obviously contrived. In addition, many teachers and prospective teachers have difficulty constructing examples and concrete models for the operation of division with fractions (Borko 1992; Ball 1988).

The following activities can be helpful in establishing a conceptual basis for dividing rational numbers. I recommend that they be used before the introduction of the invert-and-multiply algorithm. This sequence allows the establishment of a view of the operation of division with fractions and mixed numbers that is compatible with the same operation with whole numbers.

1. Ask your students to write a word problem to illustrate the following:

$$1\frac{3}{4} \div \frac{1}{2} =$$

The most common responses involve some distribution of pizza. A common error is to write a problem that illustrates 1 3/4 ÷ 2.

Sally and Jesse want to share equally in 1 3/4 pizzas. How much pizza will each get?

The error lies in interpreting 1 3/4 ÷ 1/2 as "1 3/4 divided in half" Students will even

Don Nowlin is a former aerospace designer and secondary school teacher who is currently teaching at Eastern Washington University, Cheney, WA 99004-2415. He is interested in curriculum development and assessment.

construct a diagram to illustrate the problem without exposing the error in interpretation. See figure 1.

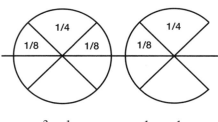

$$1\frac{3}{4} \div \frac{1}{2} = 1+1+1+\frac{1}{2} = 3\frac{1}{2}$$

Fig. 1. A typical erroneous model for 1 3/4 ÷ 1/2

Students need to be aware of the connection between division involving rational numbers and the repeated-subtraction model often used in the interpretation of whole-number division. The question 1 3/4 ÷ 1/2 = ? is really asking "How many 1/2s are in 1 3/4?" A better pizza model can be found in figure 2. A Cuisenaire model can also be helpful. See figure 3.

Students will be challenged to build Cuisenaire models of other rational-number quotients. The key is to interpret $a \div b = ?$ as "How many bs does it take to make an a?"

2. Ask your students to identify which of the following story problems represent the 1 3/4 ÷ 1/2.

a) Terri walks 1 3/4 miles each day

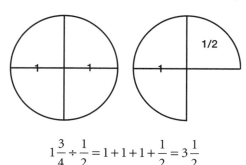

$$1\frac{3}{4} \div \frac{1}{2} = 1+1+1+\frac{1}{2} = 3\frac{1}{2}$$

Fig. 2. A better pizza model for 1 3/4 ÷ 1/2

going to and from school. How far from school does she live ?

b) Frank must use 1/2 ream of paper for each assignment handout for the sixth-grade science classes. How many assignment handouts can be made from 13/4 reams of paper?

c) Winnie needs to place 1/2 of her pansies on each side of her front door. If she has 1 3/4 dozen plants, how many dozen must she put on each side?

d) At Summer Camp, 1 3/4 gallons of milk will be put into half-gallon pitchers to serve different tables of children. How many pitchers will be required?

Notice that real-world answers to (*b*) and (*d*) will not be the number (3 1/2) obtained by applying the algorithm, invert and multiply, to 1 3/4 ÷ 1/2. In a real-world context, the answer may have to be different from the exact numerical answer obtained. Pólya (1945) asked problem solvers to "Look back. Examine the solution obtained"; this admonition makes sense for *b* and *d*, as only three homework assignments can be made and four pitchers are required.

3. Consider the following situation, where the divisor is greater than the dividend.

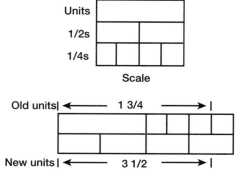

Fig. 3. a Cuisenaire model for 1 3/4 ÷ 1/2

ACTIVITIES FOR JUNIOR HIGH SCHOOL AND MIDDLE SCHOOL MATHEMATICS

A total of 1 3/4 gallons of milk will be placed equally in six containers. What size should the containers be?

Students who have not been exposed to this situation with whole numbers may reverse the order of the division and find that $6 \div 1\ 3/4 = 3\ 3/7$ instead. This error may be even more likely if the traditional algorithm has already been introduced.

Even if the algorithm is correctly applied, some students will lose sight of the context. Although 7/24 is the correct quotient, 7/24 gallon is a poor answer to the problem. Why? Is it appropriate to fill any container all the way to the brim? This example presents an opportunity to discuss standard sizes. What sizes of containers can be obtained off the shelf as opposed to those that are only available on special order? Is 7/24 gallon more than a quart? Is it less than one-half gallon? Often in the real world, people compute required sizes and then choose the closest standard size that is greater than the requirement.

Metric sizes add to the scope of this type of problem. Metric units and calculators complement each other, but the answer that the calculator displays must be interpreted in the context of the problem. Division on a calculator often results in long or repeating decimal fractions, as in the next example.

If 9.5 liters of milk are to be placed equally in six containers, what size should the containers be?

Entering "9.5 ÷ 6 =" on most calculators produces the display 1.58333333. Students must learn to interpret this number as being slightly more than 1 1/2. What metric sizes are likely to be the size of a standard milk pitcher? A 1.5-liter container is not large enough. Can the students visualize how large a 2-liter pitcher would be? Everyone should be familiar with a 2-liter soft-drink bottle.

Students can be challenged to use a "milk" or "pizza" model to explain why "÷ 1/2" is like "× 2." But be careful! It is difficult to understand the concept of division with rational numbers if the invert-and-multiply algorithm is presented too early. Students will sometimes invert the wrong element in a problem, such as that in number 3, where the divisor is larger than the dividend, and they can ignore the context of the problem and give such answers

as "3 1/2 pitchers" for the (d) question under 2. Understanding a problem (Pólya 1945) is more than choosing an appropriate operation.

4. Real problems often require more than one step. The following problem is taken from a real-life situation:

Charles makes Pinewood Derby kits from 8-foot stock. Each model requires a piece of stock that is 7 3/8 inches long. Each cut consumes an additional 1/16 inch of material. How many 8-foot pieces of stock are required to fill an order for 500 kits?

Typical errors are made when students simply multiply $(7\ 3/8 + 1/16) \times 500$ and then divide by (8×12). No child wants a kit made from two short pieces that are glued together. A better solution involves determining how many whole kits can be made from a single piece of stock by computing $(8 \times 12) \div (7\ 3/8 + 1/16)$ and rounding the answer down to the whole-number part of the quotient, 12. Any remainder of wood becomes scrap. However, when we perform 500 ÷ 12 to see how many pieces of stock are needed, any remainder at all means we must buy one more whole piece. We cannot buy 41 2/3 pieces of stock. We must buy 42.

In exercises without a real-world context, students often rely on the teacher for the disposition of the remainder. In context, however, the disposition is usually self-evident.

Using calculators to solve this problem can lead to a profitable discussion on the use of simple calculators to work fraction exercises.

5. How would the previous problem appear if metric units were used? Would it be harder or easier to solve?

Charles makes Pinewood Derby kits from stock that is 2.5 meters long. Each model kit requires a piece of stock 18.8 cm long. Each cut consumes an additional 0.1 cm of material. How many pieces of stock are required to fill an order for 500 kits?

6. The final problem is appropriate for small-group work with calculators. It requires a knowledge of the formulas for the volume and total surface area of a cylinder. Do not expect students to solve this problem in one class period or one home-

work assignment. They must be allowed to explore the solution without the pressure of time.

A can for one pound of green beans needs to hold at least 29 1/4 cubic inches. A pound is close to a pint, which is almost 29 cubic inches. The container should be designed slightly larger to assure that manufacturing tolerances do not make the actual volume smaller than the nominal amount. In the manufacturing process, the height of a can may be any multiple of 1/16 inch, but the circular end of the can must be a standard size. Two common sizes for ends are the #211, which makes a 2 9/16-inch inside diameter, and the #303, which makes a 3 1/16-inch inside diameter. How tall must a #211 can be to hold one pound of green beans? How tall must a #303 can be? Which size can would be the best choice? Why?

Suppose your supervisor suggests that a #312, which has a 3 5/8-inch diameter, can be designed for the beans. This model would be more stable on the shelf than either the #211 or the #303. However, it would require special dies to make. Is it likely to be cost efficient? Why or why not?

The solution to the problem will involve finding the minimum height of a can of each diameter and comparing their resulting total surface area. The area will determine how much material must be used to make the can. All other factors being equal, the can with the smaller total surface area should be chosen. Another factor that might be considered, however, is the stability of the can on the shelf. A short, fat can is less likely to tip over than a tall, skinny one.

The radius of the inside of the #211 can is 2 9/16 ÷ 2 inches. The area of the base is therefore $\pi \times (2\ 9/16 \div 2)2$, or 5.157243, square inches. The required height of the can is 29.25 in.^{3} ÷ 5.157243 in.^{2} = 5.671634 in. The design height must therefore be 5 11/16 inches.

Challenge students to find the most efficient way they can to compute these answers on their calculators. It helps to be able to use the memory functions to avoid entering information more than once. If a spreadsheet is available, many comparisons can be made quite quickly after the initial setup.

The total material used to make the #211 can is actually more than the inside surface area times the thickness of the material, but the extra amount will not be significantly different for the #303 can.

The total surface area for each can is two times the area of the base plus the lateral area, which is height times diameter times π. The area of the #211 can is $2 \times 5.157243 + 5\,11/16 \times 2\,9/16 \times \pi$, or 56.100744, square inches. The decimal fraction has little significance beyond the tenths place, so we use 56.1 square inches as our nominal area.

A similar analysis of the #303 can reveals that it has a base area of 7.366176 square inches, so it need be only 3.970852 inches high. The design height will be 4 inches, and the total surface area will be $2 \times 7.366176 + 4 \times 3\,1/16 \times \pi$, or 53.2, square

inches. The #303 can will not only be more stable on the shelf, it will cost less to make and be more environmentally correct. Similarly, it can be shown that the proposed #312 can would not be any better.

Many canneries pack a pound of vegetables in exactly the can we have described, although most beans are sold in fifteen-ounce cans. One brand of baked beans currently on the market packs one pound, or sixteen ounces, of beans in a can that has a diameter that is very close to its height. Students could be asked to show that 1:1 is the most efficient ratio of height to diameter. This can is not very common, however, and looks a bit small on the shelf.

Division of fractions is not easily taught but is made easier through the use of problems in context. Teachers are encouraged to

think of other activities of interest to middle schoolers that are real-world applications involving this concept.

References

Ball, Deborah L. *The Subject Matter Preparation of Prospective Mathematics Teachers: Challenging the Myths*. East Lansing, Mich.: National Center for Research on Teacher Education, 1988.

Borko, Hilda. "Learning to Teach Hard Mathematics: Do Novice Teachers and Their Instructors Give Up Too Easily?" *Journal for Research in Mathematics Education* 23 (May 1992): 194–222.

Pólya, George. *How to Solve It*. Princeton, N. J.: Princeton University Press, 1945.

Usiskin, Zalman, and Max S. Bell. "Ten Often Ignored Applications of Rational Number Concepts." *Arithmetic Teacher* 31 (February 1984): 48–50.

REBECCA S. NELSON AND DONALD R. WHITAKER

Another Use for Geoboards

GEOBOARDS, popular since the late 1960s, have been used frequently as a manipulative aid to teach geometric shapes, area, and perimeter; and to provide concrete visualization for irrational numbers such as $\sqrt{2}$ and $\sqrt{5}$. An interesting fact is that the geoboard, together with a set of materials called "geo-islands," can also be used to teach naming fractions, equivalent fractions, and all four operations with fractions, as well as mixed and decimal notation. Unlike many other models for fractions, the geoboard and geo-islands provide an area model that is both consistent and complete for the sequential development of all rational-number concepts.

A set of geo-islands consists of poster board pieces in ten different colors. All geo-islands of the same color have the same area, although not necessarily the same shape. A variety of shapes is used so that students do not expect each shape to necessarily be congruent to every other shape of equal area. Fractions are represented with the geo-islands by outlining with a rubber band a specific region on the geoboard (the unit or whole) and by covering a part or all of this region with the geo-islands. For example, in the unit in figure 1 the fraction 1/3 could be shown by placing any one of the geo-islands at the right inside the unit.

Making a Set of Geo-Islands

Obtain poster board, tagboard or other medium weight colored paper in ten differ-

Rebecca Nelson *and* Donald Whitaker *both teach preservice and in-service classes for elementary and special education majors at Ball State University. Both are active in the Indiana Council of Teachers of Mathematics. This article is a condensed version of a paper entitled "Fractions Via Geo-Islands: From Naming to Division," which has been presented as a workshop at many local, state, and national meetings.*

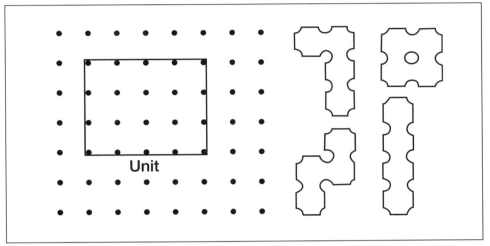

Fig 1

ent colors. The choice of color is arbitrary depending on the colors available in your area. The method of construction will depend on whether you have access to a paper drill. Your local industrial arts teacher or printer may be able to help locate such a machine.

With a paper drill: Score one sheet of paper into squares that match the squares on your geoboard. Stack all the sheets of colored paper together with the grid sheet on top. At each intersection on the grid sheet, drill a hole that goes through all thicknesses of paper. Separate the sheets and cut out the various shapes shown in figure 2. The holes on the edge of each shape permit the geo-island to fit around the pins on the geoboard.

With a heavy-duty paper punch: Score each sheet of paper into squares that match the squares on your geoboard. Cut out and punch the various shapes as illustrated in figure 2.

The number in parentheses below each shape in figure 2 is a suggested number of islands of that shape in a set appropriate for use by two to four students. These numbers will allow you to use about the same amount of paper in each color. Ten sheets of 22-inch-by-28-inch poster board (one

sheet in each color) will yield four to six sets of geo-islands, depending on whether your geoboard is one inch or two centimeters between nails. Although the white, black, and orange shapes are not used frequently, they are most helpful in naming several equivalent fractions. The purple islands are used a great deal in decimal notation with an 11-pin-by-11-pin geoboard.

Once the geo-islands are prepared, it is possible to work with all fundamental rational number concepts using fraction notation. For an 11-pin-by-11-pin geoboard, it is also possible to model tenths and hundredths in decimal notation. Each unit or whole is shown with a rubber band "fence" on the geoboard. Although rectangular fences are easy to describe verbally, a variety of shapes should be used in modeling units. All of the fences in figure 3 show equivalent units (having same area).

Using Geo-Islands

Because the unit is easily changed, the geoboard and geo-islands provide a very versatile model which can be used to solve a large number of examples. The model is clearly not limited to the "famous fractions."

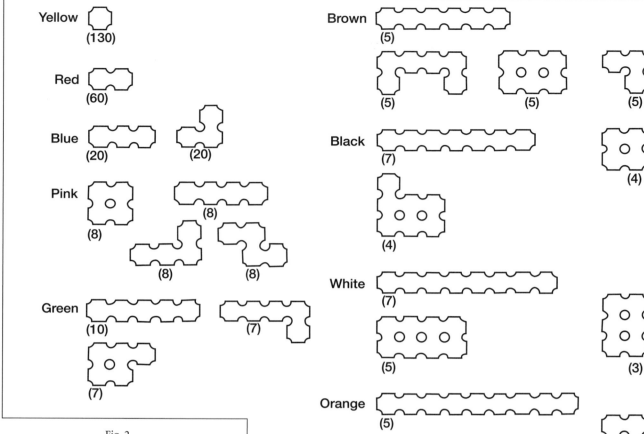

Fig. 2

Naming fractions

To develop the idea of fraction names, we first make a unit with a rubber band on the geoboard. Then we fill the unit with a geo-island of specified size (color) and count how many islands it takes to fill the unit. This number is the denominator. Next put (or leave) the number of islands desired on the board. This number is the numerator. For example, each set-up in figure 4 shows the fraction 2/5. It is important to be consistent in naming fractions. For example, the arrangement in figure 5 should be called 2/4, rather than 1/2, so that students are not confused and so the notion of equivalent fractions can be developed in a systematic way.

Equivalent fractions

To illustrate equivalent fractions with the geo-island materials means to find sets of islands that cover the same area for a given unit. For example, in figure 6, 3 red islands (representing 3/6) exactly cover 2 blue islands (representing 2/4). Therefore we would say that 3/6 is equivalent to 2/4.

By using many different units, a wide

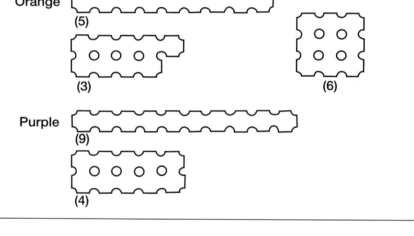

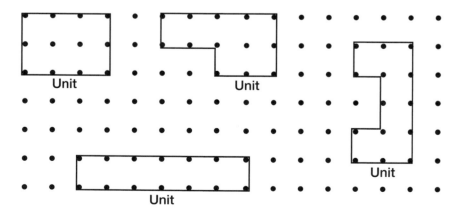

Fig 3

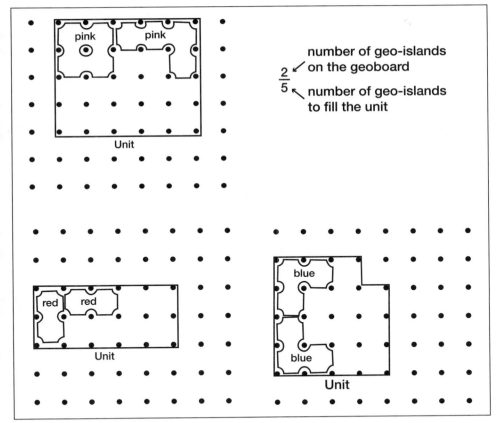

$$\frac{2}{5}\; \begin{array}{l} \swarrow \text{number of geo-islands}\\ \text{on the geoboard}\\ \nwarrow \text{number of geo-islands}\\ \text{to fill the unit} \end{array}$$

Fig. 4

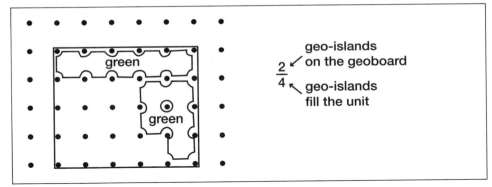

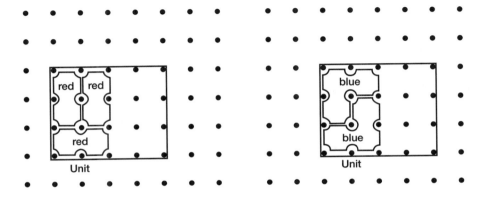

$$\frac{2}{4}\; \begin{array}{l} \swarrow \text{geo-islands}\\ \text{on the geoboard}\\ \nwarrow \text{geo-islands}\\ \text{fill the unit} \end{array}$$

Fig. 5

Fig. 6

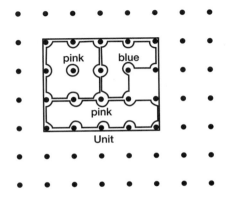

Fig. 7

variety of equivalences can be found for any given fraction. Then patterns can be used to help the student later set aside the concrete materials and move to more abstract stages of development.

Selecting a unit

The purpose of this manipulative model is to develop visual imagery, build understanding and generate enough examples of the operations to generalize rules from the patterns. Therefore, the teacher should provide an appropriate unit for each example. For equivalence and the operations of addition, subtraction and division, the area of the unit needs to be a common multiple of the denominators. In most cases the least common multiple is desirable; using other common multiples helps to develop the idea of uniqueness, however. For multiplication, a rectangular unit is easiest to use. If the example is $a/b \times c/d$, then the rectangle with dimensions b by d is most appropriate.

Operations

The operations for rational numbers are developed by applying the meaning of the operations learned in whole-number work. Addition is modeled by placing the appropriate islands for the two numbers side by side in the unit. For the example $2/3 + 1/4$, we show $2/3$ with 2 pink islands, $1/4$ with 1 blue island, and then consider the union (joining together) of the two sets as shown in figure 7. To find a single fraction that names this amount, it is convenient to cover the pink and blue islands with yellow islands as illustrated in figure 8. Thus, $2/3 + 1/4 = 11/12$.

Subtraction may be modeled using either the "take away" or comparison definition of

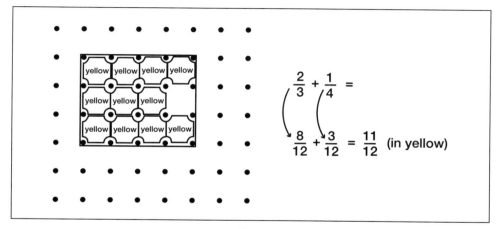

$$\left(\frac{2}{3} + \frac{1}{4}\right) =$$

$$\frac{8}{12} + \frac{3}{12} = \frac{11}{12} \text{ (in yellow)}$$

Fig. 8

the operation. Equivalences are once again easily shown with the yellow islands. The computational rules for addition and subtraction are developed by solving many examples with the geoboard and geoislands and observing the resulting patterns.

The operation of multiplication of rational numbers is likewise built from the meaning of multiplication of whole numbers. We know that 2×3 can be viewed as 2 sets *of* 3. Therefore, $1/2 \times 3/5$ (see fig. 9) is modeled by showing 1/2 of 3/5. For this example we first show the 3/5 (or three red islands in this unit). Then 1/2 of the red area (3/5) is 1 blue island. Note that the example asks us to find 1/2 of the 3/5 rather than 1/2 of the unit. Then 1/2 of the 3 red (3/53 is 1 blue, so 1 blue shows our answer. But 1 blue island covers the same area as 3 yellow islands, and 10 yellow islands fill this unit. Thus, 1/2 of 3/5 = 3/10.

As with the other operations, division of rational numbers is best introduced as it relates to division of whole numbers. Thus, just as $13 \div 4$ means "How many 4's are in 13?", $1/2 \div. 1/6$ means "How many 1/6's are

in 1/2?" When translated to geo-island terminology in a 2-by-3 rectangular unit, the question for 1/2 ÷ 1/6 is "How many yellow islands (1/6) are in (or cover) 1 blue island (1/2)?" The student can see that 3 yellow islands cover 1 blue island and easily concludes that 1/2 ÷ 1/6 = 3.

By expanding these basic definitions and carefully sequencing the examples, the typical computational rules can be generalized from a pattern and the frequently elusive operations of multiplication and division can have meaning rather than simply being rules that are stated and memorized. Thus, for each operation, the geoboard and geo-islands are an effective rational number model with the following advantages:

1. *All* operations can be modeled based on related concepts developed for whole numbers.

2. A flexible unit permits many, rather than a limited number of, examples to be worked out.

3. The variety of geo-island shapes having the same area helps to dispel the com-

mon and erroneous notion that each representation for a given fraction must be congruent to every other representation for that fraction.

4. The same materials may be used to develop both common fractions and decimal fractions.

5. The unit or whole is always illustrated by a simple, but variably shaped boundary.

Experience has shown that the geo-islands and geoboards should be used only with children who conserve area and who can find at least three fences on the geoboard that have the same area. Since most children are able to do this by third or fourth grade, the geo-island materials are recommended for use in grades 4 through 8. The geoboard and geo-islands have been used successfully with both normal and mentally handicapped children. For children who cannot cope with visual disorganization, it is appropriate to introduce only a few new colors (sizes) at a time, restrict each color of island to one or two different shapes, and provide a box for sorting the islands by color.

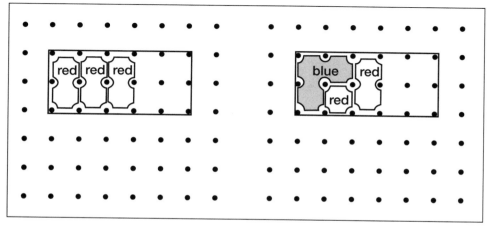

Fig. 9

JAMES A. MIDDLETON AND
MARJA VAN DEN HEUVEL-PANHUIZEN

The Ratio Table

THE middle grades offer unique challenges to the mathematics teacher, especially in this time of transition from traditional to reformed curricula and methods. The range and conceptual quality of mathematical knowledge that students have as they enter grades 5 and 6 vary greatly. Many students have been accelerated through textbooks, resulting in a high degree of proficiency at arithmetic computation but sometimes with little conceptual understanding of the underlying mathematics. Many other students will enter the middle grades with only rudimentary understanding of addition and subtraction. This disparity of skills and understanding creates a difficult dilemma for middle school teachers. Should they review the arithmetic that students have already experienced, or should they forge ahead to a higher level of more difficult mathematics? This decision need not be perceived as a dichotomy. Methods exist for exploring higher-order mathematical topics conceptually that allow understanding by students of varying knowledge levels whatever their base knowledge may be.

This article examines the use of a simple tool—the ratio table—for developing students' conceptual understanding of rational number. First the rationale for using a tabular representation of ratio is examined, and then an application is illustrated with short vignettes and examples of students' work in three fifth-grade classrooms

James Middleton *teaches at Arizona State University, Tempe, AZ 85287. His professional interests center on curriculum and innovation, student motivation, and staff development.* Marja van den Heuvel-Panhuizen *was for ten years a teacher in the primary grades and in special education. Since 1987 she has worked at the Freudenthal Institute, University of Utrecht, Tiberdreefy, 3561 Utrecht, The Netherlands. She is one of the developers of the materials for the Math in Context project and is especially interested in assessment.*

involved in a pilot unit, "Per Sense" (van den Heuvel-Panhuizen et al., in press). This unit is part of the pilot curriculum *Mathematics in Context: A Connected Curriculum for Grades 5–8* sponsored by the National Science Foundation. The project is a collaboration between the National Center for Research in Mathematical Sciences Education (NCRMSE) at the University of Wisconsin and the Freudenthal Institute at the University of Utrecht, The Netherlands. It must be stressed that the ratio table is only one of many tools available to the middle school teacher. Whenever possible, a variety of tools should be used in instruction to allow students different access routes to the mathematics.

For teaching ratio, the *Curriculum and Evaluation Standards for School Mathematics* (NCTM 1989) emphasizes students' developing an understanding of a variety of notational systems for ratio including fractions, decimals, and percents. More important, the standards document highlights the need for students to develop a conceptual understanding of rational numbers—that is, number sense—and investigate the relationships among fractions, decimals, and percents in a wide variety of situations. Students should not only know how to find ratios but also understand the equivalences of the different notational systems and develop a feel for the situations where applying different notations are appropriate. For example, in situations like sharing pizza among a group of children (e.g., 12 pizzas among 20 children), fractions may be appropriate. In situations like determining what proportion of the population owns a VCR (e.g., 60 percent), percents may be appropriate. However, in recipes, the different amounts of the ingredients (e.g., 6 cups fruit to 10 cups milk) must be kept intact, so the "ratio" notation (i.e., 6:10) may be most appropriate. Students should understand

the communicative quality of each notation, but they should also understand the commonality of the underlying mathematics ($12/20 = 60\% = 6:10$).

Examples of Ratio Tables

The ratio table is a tool that builds these connections in a way that allows students to develop understanding of rational number—and as such, it is a good alternative to cross multiplication (this idea will be addressed later). The basic idea behind the ratio table is that one can generate equivalent ratios by successive manipulation of the numbers until one reaches the ratio that best fits the situation. A number of examples follow.

Example 1: In all these situations, one child will get 3/5 of one pizza:

	Situation			
	1	2	3	4
Pizzas	12	3	24	21
Children	20	5	40	35

Example 2: In all these situations, the ratio of people who own a VCR to the total population is 60 percent:

	Situation			
	1	2	3	4
VCRs	60	120	30	3
People	100	200	50	5

Example 3: In all these situations, the ice cream will taste the same because the ratio of fruit to milk is kept intact:

	Situation			
	1	2	3	4
Cups of fruit	6	3	9	12
Cups of milk	10	5	15	20

A closer look at these examples shows that equivalent ratios can be found either by multiplicative strategies (repeated doubling and halving are especially accessible to students) or by additive strategies (adding the numerator and denominator successively). The latter can be applied in the instance of the ice cream in example 3. The number of cups of fruit needed for twenty cups of milk can be found by adding the cups of fruit that are needed for five and fifteen cups of milk.

The next examples illustrate the flexibility of the ratio table as a computational tool. The student can use multiplicative or additive strategies, work in bigger or smaller steps, and create larger or smaller entries. The strategies chosen will depend on both the kind of question to be answered and the kind of numbers involved.

Example 4: If each child gets 3/5 of a pizza, how many whole pizzas do you need for 70 children?

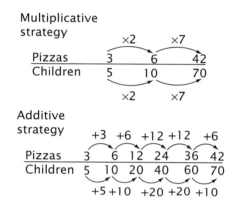

Multiplicative strategy

Additive strategy

Example 5: 45 out of every 75 people surveyed own a VCR. What percent is this?

VCRs	45	90	30	60
People	75	150	50	100

The advantage of the ratio table is that it is a simple way of organizing numbers and keeping track of operations and their results. It creates a visible pattern that students can analyze easily. In addition, it also leaves a visual trail that the teacher can use to assess how well students are doing. The next example is the work of a student, a fifth grader named Jennifer. The situation in figure 1 was one of her first exposures to percents in school. However, her response, translated from the Dutch, shows that she has some knowledge of 25 percent as 1/4 gleaned from prior experience (see Streefland and van den Heuvel-Panhuizen [1992]):

The next work from a seventh grader, Martin, contrasts sharply with Jennifer's. Here the problem was to compute how many grams of fruit a jar of jam would contain if it is 60 percent fruit and the total weight is 225 grams. Martin tried to solve the problem by cross multiplication but immediately got stuck.

Dear Mom:

School is great and I am doing well.

I have some bad news! I can't believe it, but next month my house rent will increase 25 percent! That means the end of my old $200 rent. The manager hasn't told me what the exact rent will be, but I think I have to pay somewhere between two and three hundred dollars. Please send me 300 dollars to be on the safe side—100 dollars extra this month.

Many kisses,

Juanita

Juanita asks her mother for 100 dollars. The rent increases 25 percent from the 200 dollars.
¼ part of 100 = 25
200 is double 100, so 25 should also be doubled so that is 250

Fig. 1

ACTIVITIES FOR JUNIOR HIGH SCHOOL AND MIDDLE SCHOOL MATHEMATICS

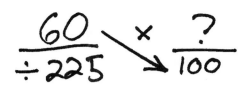

Cross multiplication in this situation makes no sense unless the student already has a very sophisticated understanding of ratio; the reader will note Martin's difficulty. For students who are not yet at that conceptual level, the ratio table offers a more accessible method of working:

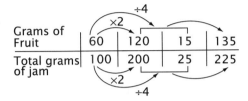

The most striking feature of the ratio table is that it focuses the students' attention on the fact that a single ratio can differ in notation depending on the situation in the problem. The 6:10 can be thought of as "6 cups to 10 cups" or as the fraction 6/10. Likewise, 60:100 can be thought of as 60/100 or 60 percent. Through application in real-world problems, the student can begin to see the underlying equivalence of a fraction (6/10), a percent (60 percent), and a ratio (6:10).

In essence, the ratio table is a flexible computational tool that both acts as a visual pattern to aid in operating with rational numbers and connects different notations of rational numbers. Moreover, it is a very transparent tool, as it documents the students' intermediate steps in solving a ratio problem. This aspect makes it a powerful tool not only for students but also for teachers, provided it is presented as an open, flexible tool and not as *the* way of solving ratio problems.

The Ratio Table in Class

In observing students' strategies using the ratio table in three fifth-grade classes, the authors saw students use two primary strategies for finding equivalent fractions. Both strategies seem to be tied to the students' initial concepts of ratio and the use of the ratio table as a tool.

The first concept of ratio will be called the *equivalent fraction concept*. Students who perceive a ratio as a fraction tended to reduce the ratio to lower terms and then use an additive strategy, adding (or subtracting) the numerator of the reduced ratio to the original numerator of the ratio and the reduced denominator to the original denominator to find other equivalent fractions. These students consistently described the ratios as fractions, using words like "It is twenty-four fortieths" and "It is three-fifths."

The second concept of ratio will be called the *ratio/relationship concept*. Students who perceived the ratio as a relationship between two specific numbers—here, a part-whole relationship—did not necessarily reduce the ratio to lower terms. These students generated equivalent ratios by multiplying the numerator and denominator of the ratio by a common factor. They understood that when multiplying by a common factor, the relationship between the two numbers remained constant—that 24/40 is the same ratio as 48/80, a transformation by a factor of 2, for example. They had great difficulty, however, in finding "in between" instances wherein the multiplying factor was not a whole number—that 24/40 is the same ratio as 27/45, a transformation by a factor of 1.125, for example.

Vignette

The following vignette was taken from the field notes of the first author during observations of the use of a ratio table in a fifth-grade classroom. It can be considered typical of students' strategies involving percent problems in a variety of real-world applications. In addition, the student's responses highlight the differences between additive strategies and multiplicative strategies and the differences between a fraction concept and a ratio concept.

Problem: use the ratio table to find parking lots of different sizes with the same fraction of occupied and free spaces.

Vanessa is a fifth grader. As demonstrated

| Spaces occupied | 35 | 42 | 49 | 56 |
| Total spaces | 50 | 60 | 70 | 80 |

on her earlier work, she can draw fairly good pictures—percent bars—representing the benchmark percents: 10, 25, 50, 75, and 100 percent. She has great difficulty

multiplying and dividing, though, so the ratio tables baffle her initially. The observer suggests looking for patterns among the numbers. The first entry on her table was 35:50.

Observer.	What is an easy number that you know goes into fifty?
Vanessa.	Five?
Observer.	Right! Now don't look at the fifty. What's an easy number that you know goes into thirty-five?
Vanessa.	Five.
Observer.	Right. Now how many times does five go into fifty?
Vanessa.	Ten.
Observer.	Good, and how many times does five go into thirty-five?
Vanessa.	Seven.
Observer.	Right!

The same pattern of questions and answers was repeated for 42/60, 49/70, and 56/80. Each time, the observer stressed that the 7 and the 10 are *multiplied* by the common factor. But when she comes to extending the ratio table, the student indicates a different strategy.

Observer.	Now, if I wrote here [writes 90 in the bottom row of the table], what would the top number be?
Vanessa.	Sixty-three.
Observer.	Good. Now if I wrote here [writes 100 in the bottom row of the table], what would the top number be?
Vanessa.	Seventy.
Observer.	Exactly right! Now, how did you get that?
Vanessa.	I *added* 7 to the top number, and 10 to the bottom number.

This response is baffling, since the observer had assumed that Vanessa understood the problem in terms of the more sophisticated multiplicative-ratio notion of the part-whole relationship. Instead, Vanessa understood the problem as a pattern where the *number* of free spaces changes by 7 and the total number of spaces changes by 10 for each successive parking lot—an additive notion. To test this understanding, the observer questions her again.

Observer.	What if we had 40 total spaces [in the parking lot], what would be the number of free spaces?

Observer. What if we had 40 total spaces [in the parking lot], what would be the number of free spaces?

Vanessa. Twenty-eight. [This response is much quicker than her earlier responses.]

Observer. Okay. How about thirty?

Vanessa. Twenty-one.

Observer. Now I'm going to let you do the last ones by yourself. [Vanessa writes in 14/20 and 7/10 very quickly.] Great! [Thumbs-up sign] How did you do that?

Vanessa. I subtract seven from the top and ten from the bottom.

This vignette illustrates two important things to keep in mind when teaching the concept of rational numbers. First, observing and continuing a pattern does not necessarily equate with a student's understanding the mathematics underlying the pattern. Vanessa was able to continue in the larger context of city planning using the patterns she had uncovered, but it would be naive to assume that she understood why adding the 7 to the numerator and the 10 to the denominator leads to equivalent ratios. Second, our adult concepts of ratio often impinge on how we interpret a student's responses. The observer assumed that Vanessa was using a multiplicative strategy when, in fact, she did no multiplication at all. Only at the end did the observer ask her how she came up with her solution. If this question had not appeared in the conversation, the observer would have assumed that Vanessa had a more sophisticated strategy than she indeed had. In retrospect, the question should have been asked earlier and more often to allow Vanessa to validate her own findings.

Moreover, a single problem is insufficient evidence to conclude that a student holds a certain conception or misconception of ratio. As students gain experience manipulating rational numbers, they begin to use different strategies flexibly according to the nature of the problem and the numbers involved.

The important thing to note is that the ratio table supplies a documentation—a record of how students solve ratio problems—and this documentation is a small window to their understanding of what a ratio is. In creating equivalent ratios, students use a strategy that fits the way they initially perceive the ratio. Those who perceive it as a part-whole relationship tend to use the additive strategy because they see the underlying fraction as the operator. Those who perceive it initially as a ratio tend to use the multiplicative strategy because it preserves the original numeric relationship intact. This differentiation offers powerful opportunities for assessment. By observing the strategies students use to solve rational-number problems involving the ratio table and probing the students to explain their strategies, the teacher can make accurate judgments regarding the students' understanding of ratio, and this knowledge can be used to develop a connected notion that includes fractions, percents, and decimals, as well as both additive and multiplicative strategies.

Use of the Ratio Table as a Computational Tool

In teaching concepts of ratio, the ratio table can also be used as a computational tool. For instance, the students can begin with a familiar fraction and build up the corresponding numerators and denominators through either the multiplicative or additive strategies described previously. For example, let us look at John's work:

Problem: Suppose the ratio of fans in Dodger Stadium is 2 Giants fans to 23 Dodger fans. Use the ratio table to find out how many Giants fans there would be in 100 spectators.

Giants	2 +2=	4+2 =	6+2=	8
Dodgers	23 +23 =	46+23=	69+23=	92
Total	25 +25=	50+25=	75+25=	100

By repeated addition and other simple operations, the students can successively build up the terms of the ratio until they get to one that is scaled to 100. As the students we observed grew more adept, they began to use a combination of additive and multiplicative strategies. The difficult part of this problem is not how to build up the terms of the ratio to 100 but how to start. Because the ratio is given as a part-part relationship, it needs to be converted into a part-whole ratio. But here again, a simple extension of the table to include adding the parts to get the whole creates an excellent bridge from the original situation to the part-whole ratio.

By using money as the context, confusion caused by decimals can be eliminated, as all the numbers can be transformed into whole numbers using cents as units. To draw connections between the decimals and percents, the teacher may also wish to retain the decimal notation after the problem is solved with the whole numbers. As an example, we shall look at Beth's table:

Problem: If you continued to tip as you did on the $4.00 bill, what tip would you leave on a bill of $2.00, of $1.00, of $5.00, and of $7.00?

Total bill	$4.00	$2.00	$1.00	$5.00	$7.00
Tip	$1.00	$ .50	.25	$1.25	1.75
	25%				

When should the student move from the ratio table to more standard mathematical notations? The authors have observed that when students have progressed to the understanding that two ratios are equivalent when scaled by a common factor, they tend to discard the ratio table in favor of shorter, more efficient notations. They tend to favor finding the factor directly and using it to find any missing entries.

The teacher can facilitate the shift to using more efficient notation by posing questions that enable students to conjecture about common factors that are not whole numbers. For example, the teacher may ask the class, "If twelve out of fifteen people surveyed indicate that they chew sugarless gum, how many people would say they chew sugarless gum if you asked thirty people at random?" This solution involves scaling by a whole number—2. After some discussion about the scaling factor, the teacher may then ask, "Now, how many people would say they chew sugarless gum if you asked thirty-five people?" This new problem involves either reducing the ratio to lowest terms, 4/5, or scaling by a factor of 2 1/3. If students begin to see that the factor is the same for both the numerator and the denominator, they will begin to look directly for the factor in subsequent problems involving ratios.

Use of the Ratio Table as an Assessment Aid

Because the ratio table shows all intermediate steps in computing various instances of rational numbers, it gives the teacher a unique window into how rational-number problems are processed by his or her students. As illustrated in the vignette with Vanessa, by studying the patterns of operations that students apply to rational numbers to build larger or smaller equivalent ratios, the teacher can make judgments about the completeness of their knowledge for making instructional decisions. A student who prefers addition and subtraction likely holds a different concept of ratio than the student who prefers multiplication and division (Streefland 1985). Appropriate intervention might be to pair the students making use of the different properties of ratio so that they can teach each other. By doing so, the teacher can insure that both students gain a more connected base of rational-number knowledge.

Each of the problems used in this article illustrates the use of the ratio table as a conceptual tool for making connections among the concepts of ratio, fraction, and percent. In the Mathematics in Context project's curriculum, ratio tables are used in conjunction with other methods, such as drawing part-whole pictures and grouping manipulatives, to insure that all students are able to experience success with these concepts. Students who traditionally had trouble with computation began to perceive the underlying structure of the mathematics and became more proficient at computation, as well as gained an understanding of rational numbers. Students who traditionally were very good at computation started to "see" the relationships and to use drawing strategies more often to make sense of the problem, both before computation to give them a sense of where they were headed and after computation to check the reasonableness of their results. The ratio table in and of itself was not sufficient to reach all students, but when paired with other methods, it presented a systematic approach that made the underlying patterns apparent. In addition, it facilitated practice on computation without becoming a review of computation. Computation found its natural place as a tool for discovering more interesting and important mathematical concepts.

The appendix includes a set of problems for teachers to try in their classrooms. Readers are free to adapt them to fit the unique interests of their own students.

Bibliography

National Council of Teachers of Mathematics. *Curriculum and Evaluation Standards for School Mathematics.* Reston, Va.: The Council, 1989.

Streefland, Leen. "Search for the Roots of Ratio: Some Thoughts on the Long-term Learning Process." *Educational Studies in Mathematics* 16 (1985): 75–94.

Streefland, Leen, and Marja van den Heuvel-Panhuizen. "Evoking Pupils' Informal Knowledge of Percents." *Proceedings of the Sixteenth Conference of the Psychology of Mathematics Education, North American Chapter,* vol. 3, 51–57. Durham, N.H.: University of New Hampshire, 1992.

Van den Heuvel-Panhuizen, Marja, Leen Streefland, Margaret R. Meyer, James A. Middleton, and James Browne. "Per Sense." In *Mathematics in Context: A Connected Curriculum for Grades 5–8,* edited by Thomas A. Romberg. Chicago: Encyclopedia Britannica Educational Corp., in press.

Appendix: Sample Problems

1. Donna's class has 20 students. They have to share 12 pizzas. Jaime's class has 35 students.

   a) How many pizzas does Jaime's teacher have to order for her students to have the same amount of pizza as the students in Donna's class?

   b) How much will each child get for both classes?

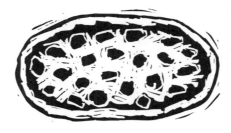

2. For a class assignment, a student tore this headline out of a newspaper:

   National Survey: 450 out of 750 people have VCRs. In other words, ___ percent has a VCR.

   a) What percent of this sample do you think has a VCR? Use the ratio table to find your answer.

VCRs	450	
People	750	

   b) Different ways can be used to find an answer to this question. Discuss in class the way *you* did it.

3. Everybody agrees that Curtis's mother makes the best homemade ice cream. "She always uses nine cups of fruit to fifteen cups of milk," Curtis explains. "But of course, she can always make more or less ice cream."

   a) Try to find other combinations of fruit and milk that taste the same as the one Curtis's mother uses.

   Use the ratio table to find them and discuss your method in class.

Cups of fruit	9	
Cups of milk	15	

   b) What would be a more general way to describe the amount of fruit and milk in this recipe?

4. Discuss the similarities and differences in the ways you solved problems 1 through 3. Did you notice any common elements?

The authors would like to thank sincerely the teachers and students who graciously allowed us to join them in their mathematical activity. We would also like to thank the anonymous reviewers for their helpful criticism of the first draft of this manuscript. This project was supported, in part, by the National Science Foundation. The opinions expressed are those of the authors and not necessarily those of the Foundation.

ALBERT B. BENNETT, JR., AND L. TED NELSON

A Conceptual Model for Solving Percent Problems

Applications of percents are often taught by solving proportions that require variables and some familiarity with algebra. Such formal approaches to teaching percent have not been successful for many junior high and high school students (Wiebe 1986). This article presents an alternative method that focuses on the basic concept of *percent,* that of "parts per hundred." A 10 × 10 grid, which is a common model for visualizing percents, is extended in the following examples to solve various types of percent problems. This model offers a means of representing the given information as well as suggesting different approaches for finding a solution.

Albert Bennett teaches mathematics at the University of New Hampshire, Durham, NH 03824. He develops models and textbook materials for teaching mathematics at the school and college level. Ted Nelson directs the Middle School Mathematics Program at Portland State University, Portland, OR 97207. He writes curriculum materials for the Math in the Mind's Eye project.

Preliminary Ideas

Before using percents to solve problems, students should have experiences in shading 10 × 10 grids to represent given percents. Also, given shaded grids, they should be able to determine the percent for that shaded amount (fig. 1). A master for reproducing 10 × 10 grids is included at the end of this article. These handouts can be laminated so that students can shade the grids with dry-erase, water-based, or grease markers.

Once the student has a visual image of percents and recognizes that 100 percent is represented by one whole square, or unit square, and that 1 percent is represented by one small square, or one-hundredth of a unit square, then 10 × 10 grids can be shaded to illustrate percents less than 1 percent and greater than 100 percent (fig. 2).

Here are two other preliminary activities that set the stage for solving percent problems. First, let the unit square (10 x 10 grid) represent given amounts and then determine the value of one of the small squares (1 percent). To help students determine the value of 1 percent of the unit square, they can think of sharing the given amount equally among the 100 parts of the unit square. Dividing by 100 can be done conveniently by mental computation. As examples, if the unit square represents 400 people, then each small square represents 4 people; if the unit square represents 85 pounds, then each small square has a value of 0.85 pounds; and if the unit square represents 162 days, then the value of each small square is 1.62 days (fig. 3). Successfully determining the value of one small square (1 percent) is the key to solving percent problems. To prepare students for this task, it may be helpful first to pose questions that involve convenient fractional parts of the grid. For example, if the unit square represents 400 people, answer the following:

- Half of the unit square would represent how many people?

- One-fourth of the unit square would represent how many people?

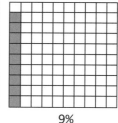 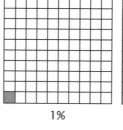 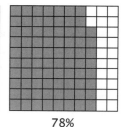

| 1% | 9% | 78% |

Fig. 1. Shading grids to gain an understanding of percent

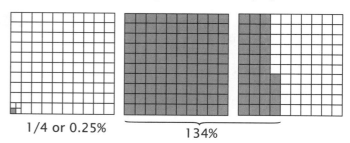

1/4 or 0.25%   134%

Fig. 2. Representing percents less than 1 percent and greater than 100 percent

ACTIVITIES FOR JUNIOR HIGH SCHOOL AND MIDDLE SCHOOL MATHEMATICS

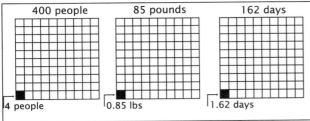

400 people   85 pounds   162 days

4 people   0.85 lbs   1.62 days

Fig. 3 Sharing the given amount equally among 100 parts

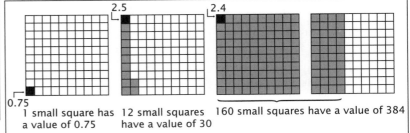

2.5   2.4

0.75
1 small square has   12 small squares   160 small squares have a value of 384
a value of 0.75   have a value of 30

Fig. 4. Determining the value of the unit square from the value of one or more small squares

- Ten small squares would represent how many people?
- What part of the unit square would represent 200 people?
- Or 100 people?
- Or 40 people?
- Or 4 people?

Second, assign a value to one or more of the small squares and then determine the value of the unit square (10×10 grid). For example, if 1 of the small squares has a value of 0.75, then the unit square has a value of 75; if 12 of the small squares have a value of 30, then 1 small square has value 2.5 ($30 \div 12$) and the unit square has value 250; if 160 small squares have a value of 384, then 1 small square has value 2.4 ($384 \div 160$) and the unit square has value 240 (fig. 4).

Solving Problems

The following three examples illustrate how the 10×10 grid model can be used to help solve common percent problems. In part (a) of these three examples students are asked to use a percent grid to represent the given information. Then in part (b) the sketch is used to answer a question

related to that information. This two-part approach emphasizes the importance of thinking through the given information before focusing on obtaining an answer.

Example 1

a) Use a percent grid to show that 20 percent of a business's 240 employees are classified as minorities.

The given information can be represented by letting the unit square represent 240 employees and shading 20 percent of the square (fig. 5).

b) How many employees are classified as minorities?

Students may notice immediately from the shaded grid (fig. 5) that one shaded column represents 1/10 of 240, or 24, so two shaded columns represent 48. Or, if the whole square represents 240 employees, then one small square represents 2.4 employees. The value corresponding to the 20 shaded squares is $20 \times 2.4 = 48$, and so 48 employees are classified as minorities. Once the 2.4 value for one small square is

obtained, some students may notice that one column of the 10×10 grid has a value of $10 \times 2.4 = 24$ and so two columns have a value of 48. Suggestions for other ways to arrive at a solution may arise from the model.

Example 2

a) Twenty-five acres of land are given to a community, and the donor stipulates that 6 acres of this land should be developed as a playground.

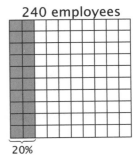

240 employees

20%

Fig. 5. Determining the value of 20 small squares from a unit square that represents 240 employees

If the unit square represents 25 acres (fig. 6), we need to determine how many small squares represent 6 acres. Each small square represents 0.25 = 1/4 acres, so 4 small squares represent 1 acre and 24 small squares represent 6 acres. Or, since each small square has a value of 0.25 acres, we can determine the number of times 0.25 divides 6 (6 ÷ 0.25 = 24) to see that 24 squares are needed to represent 6 acres.

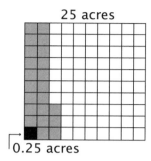

Fig. 6. Determining the value of one small square and the number of small squares to represent 6 acres

b) What percent of the land is to be used for playground?

The playground is represented by the 24 shaded squares in figure 6, and so 24 percent of the land is to be used for a playground.

Example 3

a) In a certain county 57 of the schools have a teacher-to-student ratio that is greater than the recommendations for accreditation. The 57 schools represent 38 percent of the number of schools in the county.

In figure 7 the unit square represents the number of schools in the county and the 38 small squares (38 percent) represent 57 schools.

b) What is the total number of schools in the county?

Since the 38 small shaded squares in figure 7 represent 57 schools, each small shaded square represents 57 ÷ 38 = 1.5 schools. So the unit square represents 100 × 1.5 = 150, which is the number of schools in the county.

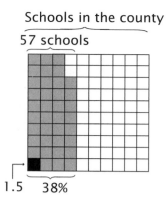

Fig. 7. Determining the values of one small square and the unit square from the value of 38 small squares

Further Illustrations of the Grid Model

Next, let's consider the grid problems involving percents greater than 100. Teachers may wish to continue using the two-part approach illustrated in examples 1–3 with their students, that is, first present the given information for them to diagram and then pose the question or ask them to suggest questions related to the given information.

Example 4

The school population for the new year in a certain town is 135 percent of the school's population for the preceding year. The new student population is 756. How many students did the school have the previous year?

Since the current school population is represented by 135 small squares (fig. 8), each small square represents 756 ÷ 135 = 5.6 students. The school population for the preceding year is the value of one unit square, so the number of students in the previous year was 100 × 5.6 = 560.

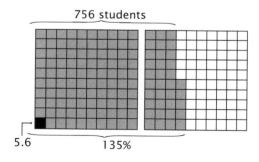

Fig. 8. Determining the values of one small square and the unit square from the value of 135 small squares

The next example involves percent increase, a type of problem that often causes anxiety in students.

Example 5

The first-year profit for a small business was \$32 900 and it increased 76 percent during the second year. What was the profit the second year?

One 10 × 10 grid represents the first-year profit of \$32 900, and the 76 small squares in the second grid represent the increase (fig. 9). So all 176 shaded squares represent the second-year profit. Since each small square has a value of \$32 900 ÷ 100 = \$329, the increase during the second year is 76 × \$329 = \$25 004. Thus, the second year profit is \$32 900 + \$25 004 = \$57 904. Figure 9 also suggests that once the \$329 value of a small square is known, the total value of the 176 small squares, which is the second-year profit, is 176 × \$329 = \$57 904.

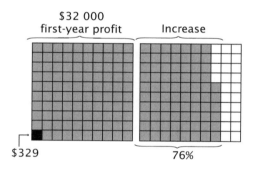

Fig. 9. Determining the values of one small square and 176 small squares from the value of the unit square

Example 6

A new company in hardware and garden supplies entered the New York Stock Exchange in July, and by December the price of each share of stock had risen 223 percent to \$32.50 a share. What was the cost of each share of stock in July?

The shaded unit square (10 × 10 grid) on the left in figure 10 represents the cost of a share of the stock in July and the remaining shaded squares represent the 223 percent increase. The total 323 small shaded squares represent the \$32.50 value of each share of stock in December. So 32.50 ÷ 323 ≈ 0.1006 is the value of each small shaded square (1 percent). Thus, the unit square (100 percent), or July price, is equal to 100 × 0.1006 = \$10.06 to the nearest hundredth of a dollar.

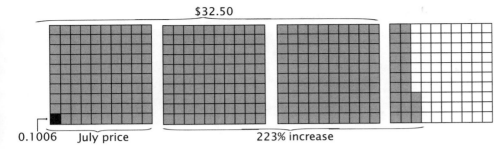

$32.50

0.1006   July price   223% increase

Fig. 10. Determining the values of one small square and the unit square from the value of 323 small squares

Discounts involve a common use of percents. The next example shows two ways in which a discounted price can be determined.

Example 7

A sweater is on sale at 30 percent off the listed price of $95.99. What is the discounted cost of the sweater?

The $95.99 listed price of the sweater is represented by one unit square, and one of the small squares has a value of $95.99 ÷ 100 = $0.9599. This information and the 30 percent discount are illustrated in figure 11. The grid suggests two methods of solu-

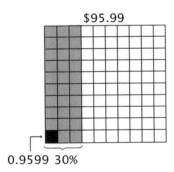

$95.99

0.9599 30%

Fig. 11. Determining the values of one small square and 30 small squares from the value of the unit square

tion: (1) determine the amount of discount by finding the value of 30 small squares, 30 x $0.9599 = $28.797, and then subtract this amount from $95.99; or (2) determine the discounted price directly by finding the value of the 70 small unshaded squares, 70 x $0.9599 = $67.193. To the nearest hundredth of a dollar, the discounted price of the sweater is $67.19.

Concluding Remarks

The *Curriculum and Evaluation Standards for School Mathematics* (NCTM 1989) recommends decreased attention to practicing problems categorized by type (e.g., coin problems, age problems). The intention of the NCTM's recommendation is that concepts should be taught that cut across topics rather than tie techniques and concepts to specific types of problems. Similarly, the "Position Paper: Teaching and Learning Percent" (Dye 1981) states that "[t]eachers should not emphasize nor require the identification of problem situations by Case I, Case II, or Case III . . . ," which is a reference to the custom of categorizing percent problems by three different types (percent and whole, part and whole, and part and percent).

The 10 × 10 grid model is a format for solving percent problems that deemphasizes the practice of categorizing the type of problem. It connects an area model for fractions and decimals with the basic meaning of percent as part of a unit that has been partitioned into 100 equal parts. It allows the information in percent problems to be visually displayed and often suggests more than one approach to the solution. It leads to conceptualizing solutions before the introduction of proportions and algebraic equations and can be used to illustrate the more analytic and algorithmic approaches once they are introduced. Perhaps most important, the grid model helps to make the process of solving percent problems a "sense-making experience."

References

Bennett, Albert B., and L Ted Nelson. *Mathematics for Elementary Teachers: An Activity Approach,* 3d ed. Dubuque, Ia.: Wm. C. Brown Publishers, 1992.

———. *Mathematics for Elementary Teachers: A Conceptual Approach.* 3d ed. Dubuque, Ia.: Wm. C. Brown Publishers, 1992.

Dye, David, chair of committee for Minnesota Department of Education. "Position Paper: Teaching and Learning Percent." St. Paul, Minn.: Department.of Education, 1981.

National Council of Teachers of Mathematics. *Curriculum and Evaluation Standards for School Mathematics.* Reston, Va.: The Council, 1989.

Wiebe, James H. "Manipulating Percentages." *Arithmetic Teacher* 33 January 1986): 23–26.

The authors thank Peter Schiot and his fifth-grade class at Oyster River Elementary School in Durham, NH 03824-2248, for their cooperation with the photographs that accompany this article.

10 × 10 Grids for Solving Percent Problems

Name _____

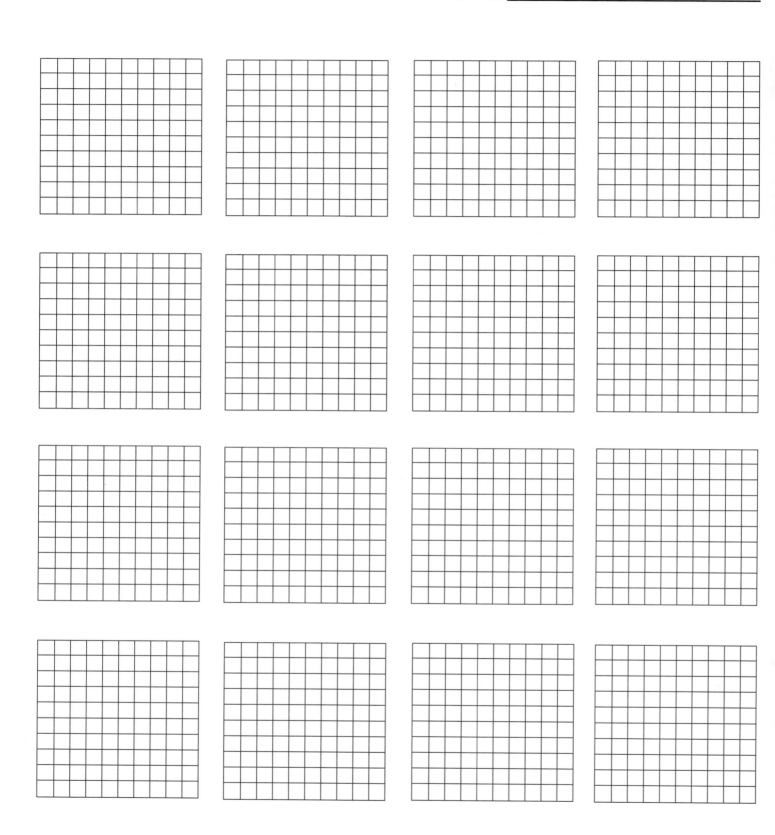

ACTIVITIES FOR JUNIOR HIGH SCHOOL AND MIDDLE SCHOOL MATHEMATICS

JANINE S. STONE

Place Value and Probability (with Promptings from Pascal)

For several years my sixth-grade and seventh-grade students have enjoyed a simple number game involving place value. I have developed a deeper appreciation of the game as I have watched the students employing various strategies to win. Since the game is superficially simple, it appeals to all levels of my students, from basic to gifted. (It is a modification of the Place-Value Game found on page 64 of *Mathematics: Modern Concepts and Skills* by Dilley and Rucker; Raytheon Education Co.; Lexington, MA, 1968.) The materials needed to play the game are readily available. The student needs only paper and pencil. The teacher needs a prepared packet of fourteen cards (I use 5-by-7 index cards) inscribed with felt-tip marker as follows:

10 digit cards	1 digit per card
2 operation cards	1 with ADD on it
	1 with SUBTRACT on it
2 win cards	1 with SMALLEST NUMBER WINS on it
	1 with LARGEST NUMBER WINS on it

For each game, students draw a two-by-three grid (fig. 1), which provides spaces for writing-in two three-digit numbers.

We start out with a simple variation of the game in which the leader places on the

Janine Sumner Stone *teaches seventh-grade mathematics at Northside Junior School in the Roanoke County (Virginia) Schools. She is a member of the executive board of the Blue Ridge Council of Teachers of Mathematics and of the advisory board at Virginia Western Community College.*

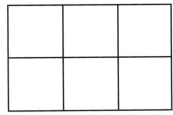

Fig. 1

chalkboard ledge six randomly selected digit cards, one operation card, and one win card. The students then arrange the selected digits, one in each box, to find the best solution. The set of cards showing 7, 6, 2, 4, 0, 3, ADD, and LARGEST NUMBER WINS generated

$$
\begin{array}{r}
7\ 4\ 2 \\
6\ 3\ 0 \\
\hline
13\ 7\ 2
\end{array}
$$

for one arrangement. The students quickly discovered that

$$
\begin{array}{r}
7\ 3\ 2 \\
6\ 4\ 0 \\
\hline
13\ 7\ 2
\end{array}
$$

produced the same total, for one variation.

When the operation card was changed to SUBTRACT, we had the following:

$$
\begin{array}{r}
7\ 6\ 4 \\
0\ 2\ 3 \\
\hline
7\ 4\ 1
\end{array}
$$

No problem! The students seemed to grasp that they had only to form

$$
\begin{array}{r}
a\ b\ c \\
f\ e\ d \\
\hline
\end{array}
$$

where

$$a < b < c < d < e < f$$

Using the same six digits and adding for the smallest number obtained, we got the following:

$$
\begin{array}{r}
0\ 3\ 6 \\
2\ 4\ 7 \\
\hline
2\ 8\ 3
\end{array}
$$

Thus for $a < b < c < d < e < f$, we would have the following:

$$
\begin{array}{r}
a\ c\ e \\
b\ d\ f \\
\hline
\end{array}
$$

as one possibility. Kevin claimed to have the same thing—for all practical purposes—with this arrangement:

$$
\begin{array}{r}
0\ 4\ 6 \\
2\ 3\ 7 \\
\hline
2\ 8\ 3
\end{array}
$$

We agreed.

For SUBTRACT and SMALLEST NUMBER WINS, there was a little more thinking to be done. One good student felt he had it with

$$
\begin{array}{r}
7\ 4\ 0 \\
6\ 3\ 2 \\
\hline
1\ 0\ 8
\end{array}
$$

and was amazed to see another student find a smaller total with this:

$$
\begin{array}{r}
7\ 0\ 3 \\
6\ 4\ 2 \\
\hline
6\ 1
\end{array}
$$

Then a third student turned up this arrangement

$$
\begin{array}{r}
7\ 0\ 2 \\
6\ 4\ 3 \\
\hline
5\ 9
\end{array}
$$

and a fourth student had this combination:

$$\begin{array}{r} 3\ 0\ 4 \\ 2\ 7\ 6 \\ \hline 2\ 8 \end{array}$$

Then just as we were beginning to feel we had reached rock bottom at last, Dennis came up with this:

$$\begin{array}{r} 4\ 0\ 2 \\ 3\ 7\ 6 \\ \hline 2\ 6 \end{array}$$

By this time, the students were anxious to find a pattern for setting up the numbers, as they had in the others. They suggested possibilities, but never found a general rule.

Another variation of the game is more susceptible to chance. The students draw a box like the other one. The leader shuffles the digit cards and randomly selects six digits, which are held up one by one. Students fill in their boxes as the cards are displayed, with the understanding that once a digit has been placed in a box, a student is honor bound not to change it.

When the six spaces are filled, the leader holds up either ADD or SUBTRACT and each student performs the required operation. Since this variation deals only with whole numbers, some students may have to rewrite their numbers to one side, if the larger number is on the bottom. The leader then holds up either LARGEST NUMBER WINS or SMALLEST NUMBER WINS. Students who feel they hold a winning number raise their hands, and the leader writes answers on the chalkboard until he or she finds a winner. The winner of one game becomes the leader for the next game; thus the game is self-generating and highly motivating.

I have long been amazed at the high level of interest and enthusiasm which this simple game generates. I also take full advantage of the self-generating features of the game to wander around the room and observe. At first, I was checking to see that students performed the operation correctly; then I became impressed with some of the strategy I saw being employed. Angela was always careful to make sure the largest digits were on top so she would not have to regroup for subtraction. Martha tried to place two consecutive digits in the hundreds place. She was hoping for SUBTRACT, SMALLEST NUMBER WINS.

Steve was arranging the digits so that the smaller ones landed in the ones and tens places and the larger ones in the hundreds

places. When things worked out for him, he was in good shape for ADD, LARGEST NUMBER WINS, or SUBTRACT, SMALLEST NUMBER WINS. This, according to his calculations, gave him about a 50 percent chance of having a winner when the numbers were right.

John tried to fix the hundreds so that the digits 0 and 9 appeared. He said the odds were very good that both 0 and 9 would be called. Then he hoped for SUBTRACT, LARGEST NUMBER WINS, which he had a 25 percent chance of getting.

Most of the students seemed to be aware that some strategy was better than random placement of the digits. They also noted that the hundreds place was the most significant. As one student put it, "That's where the action is."

While I was attending a political meeting the afternoon I had discussed the game with my students, I began to think back on John's statement that both 0 and 9 had a good chance of appearing in the set of called digits. Since it is very true that mathematical knowledge not used regularly slips out of the mind, and since my classes in permutations and combinations occurred more years ago than I care to admit, I could not recall a formula for the number of combinations of ten things taken six at a time. I had heard this particular politician's promises previously, so I began listing the possible combinations of six digits. (If you can't do it the easy way, you have to do it the hard way, as I've told my students many times!)

In order to systematically list all of the sets of six digits, I wrote the elements of each set in numerically increasing order. I began with those sets containing 0 as the smallest element, followed by those in which 1 was the smallest, and so on. Thus the first few sets were {0, 1, 2, 3, 4, 5}, {0, 1, 2, 3, 4, 6}, {0, 1, 2, 3, 4, 7}, and the last set listed was {4, 5, 6, 7, 8, 9}. Since there are only five digits larger than 4, no set could have its smallest element larger than 4.

Then I counted the number of sets in which the smallest element was 0, the number in which the smallest element was 1, and so on. The results were as follows:

126 sets had 0 as the smallest element
56 sets had 1 as the smallest element
21 sets had 2 as the smallest element
6 sets had 3 as the smallest element
1 set had 4 as the smallest element

There were 210 sets altogether.

Of the 126 sets containing 0, only 70 of them also contained a 9. So the probability of getting both 0 and 9 in the same six digits is only 70/210, or 1/3. John was wrong in thinking he had a very good chance of getting both of these digits.

I had observed that the numbers 1, 6, 21, 56, and 126 were contained in the Pascal triangle. In fact, after writing down the first eleven rows of the Pascal triangle (fig. 2), I noticed that all these numbers lay on the same diagonal. Moreover, the numbers 70 and 210, which had cropped up in my computation of John's chances, were in the table also. Of course I realized that this pattern must in some way represent the shortcut that I had forgotten for computing combinations.

In fact, the sets of six digits that contain 0 as the smallest element can be obtained by simply choosing five of the digits 1 through 9 to include with the 0. Thus 126 must be the number of combinations of nine things taken five at a time. Similarly 56 must be the number of combinations of eight things taken five at a time (we must choose five of the digits 2 through 9 to include with the 1), and so forth.

There are many modified versions of this game that may be useful (and fun) in the classroom. For example, operations such as division or multiplication could be used. I think it is also adaptable to other concepts such as fractions, percents, and integers. Also two-digit, four-digit or even (with modification of the rules) five-digit numbers could be used. No matter how the game is played, the techniques of combinatorics or an appropriate use of the Pascal

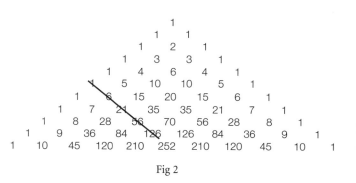

Fig 2

triangle can simplify the computations of any probabilities involved. For example if two-digit numbers and only four-digit cards are used, then the number of sets of four digits whose smallest element is 0 is 84, the number of such sets whose smallest element is 1 is 56, the number of such sets whose smallest element is 2 is 35; and continuing, we get the numbers in the diagonal shown in figure 3.

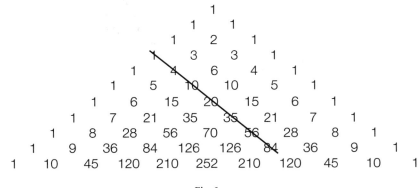

Fig. 3

GLORIA J. BLEDSOE AND V. CARL BLEDSOE

Add-Lo

SHARING TEACHING IDEAS

ADD-LO" is a game that gives students practice in adding integers, in creating expressions using sums of integers, and in taking the absolute value of an integer. This game is appropriate for students who have been introduced to the addition of integers and is a nice diversion from the usual lists of exercises used to practice this skill. Moreover, the students must develop a strategy for achieving the least possible score on their turn.

Grade levels: 7–9

Materials: The following items are needed for each pair of students:

1. A white die and a colored die (crayon or self-adhesive colored circles can be used to mark the sides of a white die)
2. Game board and tally sheets (see p. 436)
3. Thirteen one-centimeter-square colored markers

Objective: The goal is to cover as many circles on the game card as possible and to achieve the lowest possible score on a given round. The score at the end of each round is determined by the sum of the absolute values of the uncovered circles. The player winning the greatest number of rounds wins.

Procedures: Decide which student in each pair will go first and the maximum number of rounds to be played.

Player 1 rolls both dice. The colored-die

Gloria J. Bledsoe, University of Minnesota, Minneapolis, MN 55455; V. Carl Bledsoe, Resurrection School, Minneapolis, MN 55417

"Sharing Teaching Ideas" offers practical tips on the teaching of topics related to the secondary school curriculum. We hope to include classroom-tested approaches that offer new slants on familiar subjects for the beginning and the experienced teacher.

value and the white-die value represent a negative number and a positive number, respectively. The player then covers circles on the game board that correspond to exactly one of the following options:

1. The values on each *individual* die
2. A value corresponding to the *sum* of the dice
3. Any two values having the *same sum* as the sum rolled
4. Possibly, on the *last* play of that player's turn, a value corresponding to a single die.

Example: The player rolls this combination:

These faces represent –3 and +5, respectively. By option 1, the player may cover the "–3" circle or the " +5" circle. Or, by option 2, the player may choose to cover the "2" circle, since –3 + (+5) = 2. By option 3, the player may cover two circles corresponding to the value of any two integers having the sum +2. In other words, if available, circles corresponding to any one of the following pairs of integers may be covered: –4 and +6, –3 and +5, –2 and +4, –1 and +3, or 0 and +2. Only one alternative may be selected for a given roll of the dice.

Player 1 continues to roll until he or she cannot play *both* dice as described. To clarify, suppose the situation in figure 1 exists. Further suppose that player 1 rolls this combination:

Fig. 1

The player would want to cover –1 *and* +5, or +4, since –1 + (+5) = +4, or any combination of integers that sum to +4. However, no such circles are available. Therefore, player 1 must determine his or her score for that round.

When a player is unable to play both dice, he or she may end the round by covering the circle corresponding to just one die, by option 4. For example, had the "–1" circle been available, player 1 could have covered it before scoring the round. Similarly, the " +5" circle might have been covered. However, neither was possible in this example.

Regular scoring for a round: The score for player 1's turn, ending as shown in figure 2, is $|-6| + |-4| + |6| = 16$, the sum of the absolute values of the numbers corresponding to uncovered circles on the game board. Similarly, after player 2 takes a turn, he or she calculates a score. Suppose that score is 10. This means that player 2 wins the first round, since his or her score is less than 16, and player 2 receives 1 tally point toward his or her final score. Player 1 receives no tally points for that round. Tally sheets, shown in figure 1, can be used to record progress in the game. The boards are cleared and another round begins.

Special scoring procedures: Any player who does not cover the "0" circle during his or her turn is charged 7 penalty points. Note that a "0" can easily be covered, but it *is* possible to get caught. For example, suppose the situation in figure 2 arises. Further suppose that the player rolls this combination:

The possible moves are to cover the cir-

Fig. 2

cles corresponding to –2 and +3; to the sum –2 + (+3), or +1; or to any combination that sums to +1, namely 0 and +1, –1 and +2, –3 and +4, –4 and +5, or –5 and +6. Since none of these *pairs* of circles is uncovered, the player has just one other option available, namely to cover the "+3" circle and thereby to end his or her turn, leaving the "0" circle uncovered. Consequently, the score would be | –6 | + | 0 | + 7 penalty points, or 13.

If a player declares that he or she cannot play the dice or if he or she ends the turn by playing a single die, but the opponent sees a legitimate way that the player could have covered additional circles, the player automatically loses that round and the opponent is awarded the tally point.

In a given round, if a player covers *all* circles on his or her turn and the opponent does not, he or she automatically wins that round and earns *two* tally points.

If both players' scores on a given round are equal, neither receives tally points.

Play continues until the predetermined number of rounds has been executed. The sum of tally points for each player determines the outcome, with the highest number of tally points winning.

After the students have become familiar with the game, the teacher may wish to discuss game strategies. For example, one strategy is to cover the "0" circle early in the round because many opportunities arise to cover it and a player has no advantage in waiting. Forgetting to exercise this option results in the 7-point penalty.

By making a table of the possible outcomes on the dice and the possible values that could be covered on the game board as a result, the frequency distribution in figure 3 arises. The frequency distribution verifies the wisdom of trying to cover the " ±6," the

"±5," or the "±4" circles early because they have the potential to be covered fewer times and because leaving them uncovered contributes to a high score on a round. Although leaving the "±1" circles uncovered does not contribute greatly to the score, since their frequency of potential to be covered is lower than that of ±2 or ±3, if a player wishes to go for an automatic win

(all circles covered), he or she should attempt to cover the "±1" circles early in the round.

"Add-Lo" offers both skill practice and problem-solving opportunities that can raise interest in mathematics and add variety to any classroom routine.

ADD-LO

Game Board

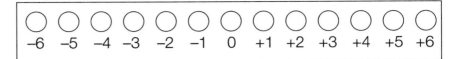

| –6 | –5 | –4 | –3 | –2 | –1 | 0 | +1 | +2 | +3 | +4 | +5 | +6 |

Tally Sheet

Round	Player 1		Player 2	
	Score	Tally Points	Score	Tally Points

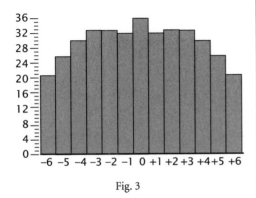

Fig. 3

6

Number Systems and Number Theory

NEITHER number theory nor number systems were topics frequently chosen by recent authors. Number theory is an area of interest to many students and can be highly motivating. It is important for students to understand the relationships among whole numbers, integers, rational numbers, and real numbers.

Peggy House provides an excellent article interrelating number theory and problem solving. Her locker problem could be used at nearly any level.

"Foxy Fives" describes a game that involves whole-number drill and experience with the order of operations. The game could be easily modified to involve integers or rational numbers.

Scientific calculators are used to discover simple theorems in "Using Calculators to Discover Simple Theorems: An Example from Number Theory". Making conjectures and then testing them are important for all students. Melfried Olson uses calculators with small-group work to determine factors of numbers in "It's a Factor of Life".

"Five-Cycle Number Patterns" is an activity for use with fractions, decimals, and negative numbers. An innovative teacher could expand this activity to much more sophisticated topics.

One of the best of the more recent articles is Charles Thompson's "Connecting Decimals". He creates base-ten blocks by cutting cheese, and uses calculators, graph paper, and number lines to make the "connections."

PEGGY A. HOUSE

Making a Problem of Junior High School Mathematics

JUNIOR high school mathematics is problem enough for many students. Why, as the title suggests, try to make it more so? One answer to this question is that frequently the problem with junior high school mathematics is that there is too little problem solving.

The problems we refer to here are open-ended problems for which the pupils do not have ready algorithms. Such problems require the pupils to employ a variety of problem-solving strategies and to engage in divergent, higher level thinking. Much has been written about the importance of this kind of problem solving as a goal in school mathematics, and we will not repeat those arguments here. But there are several other reasons for emphasizing problem solving. First, problems can be used effectively as vehicles for delivering the basic curriculum. Further, junior high school pupils tend to love a puzzle; and when they have successfully solved an interesting problem, they usually are motivated to become more involved in the related mathematics. It is important also to recognize that junior high pupils are still primarily concrete in their thinking, and problems provide them with the opportunity to anchor abstract concepts in specific realities from which they can reason. These points are best illustrated with a problem.

Solving the Problem

An excellent problem for junior high pupils is one that has appeared in several recent textbooks. A version of it is the following:

> In a certain high school there were 1000 students and 1000 lockers. Each year for homecoming the students lined up in alphabetical order and performed the following strange ritual: The first student opened every locker. The second student went to every second locker and closed it. The third student went to every third locker and changed it (i.e., if the locker was open, he closed it; if it was closed, he opened it). In a similar manner, the fourth, fifth, sixth, ... student changed every fourth, fifth, sixth, ..., locker. After all 1000 students had passed by the lockers, which lockers were open?

Usually the students begin immediately to guess: all of them, none of them, all the evens, all the odds, only the first, and so on. Clearly a systematic approach is needed. Generally the approach pupils use is one of listing what the students will do to the first few lockers. The representation in figure 1 is typical. For our purposes, however, it will be useful to suggest that we make a chart like the one in table 1. It is also helpful in the classroom if the class does the first three or four students together before the pupils complete the chart on their own.

Pupils are quick to recognize that the first and fourth lockers will remain open. (We will designate these as L_1 and L_4. Similarly, L_n and S_n will refer to the nth locker and the nth students, respectively.) Often they will guess a pattern of "one open, two closed," hence L_7 should be open. But it is not. Others expect L_8 to be open. They, also, are disappointed. However, after finding L_9 and L_{16} to be open, pupils almost always generalize the pattern as follows: one open, two closed; one open, four closed; one open, six closed; and so on.

1	2	3	4	5	6
O	O	O	O	O	O
	C		C		C
		C			O
			O		
				C	
					C

Fig. 1

Peggy House *is an associate professor of mathematics education at the University of Minnesota where she teaches graduate and undergraduate courses for secondary school mathematics teachers. She is interested in problem solving and laboratory approaches in secondary school mathematics and has developed and taught such lessons for junior high school pupils. The problem discussed here is an example of these lessons.*

Table 1

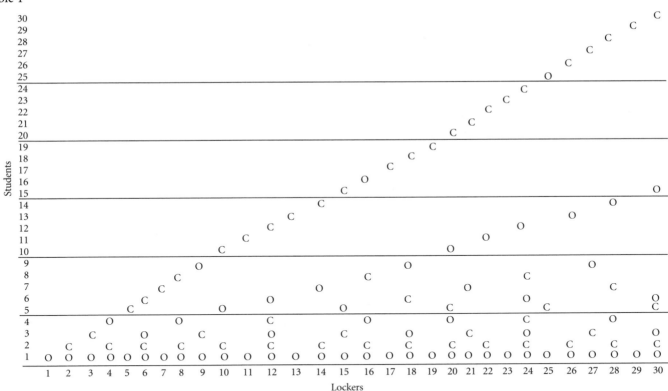

At a rudimentary level, the pupils at this point have found a solution. To stop here, however, is to neglect the real power within the problem.

Understanding the Solution

Experience with junior high school pupils solving this problem has led to two observations. First, they usually do not recognize the numbers of the open lockers (L_1, L_4, L_9, L_{16}, L_{25}, ...) as the sequence of squares. Second, they do not distinguish between seeing the pattern and determining the conditions necessary for a locker to be open. Thus, if we ask about L_{100} or L_{800} or L_{537}, the pupils would, at this point, continue the pattern to the desired number rather than examine L itself to classify it as open or closed.

Here the teacher might pose the following questions:

Q1. Are there any lockers which you know are closed? Why is this so?

Q2. Which students visit L_9? L_{12}?

Q3. Why doesn't S_5 go to either L_9 or L_{12}?

Q4. What conditions must be met if a locker is to remain open?

As the pupils answer these questions, they recognize that all lockers with prime numbers will be closed because these lockers will be opened by S_1 and closed by the students whose number matches the locker number (e.g., L_7 will be opened by S_1 and closed by S_7). No other students will touch those lockers. Questions 2 and 3 help pupils to see that a student will visit a locker only if the student's number is a divisor of the locker number. From this they can conclude that for a locker to remain open it must be visited by an odd number of students (i.e., the locker number must have an odd number of divisors).

Here it is useful to focus on L_{24} and L_{36}. Who visits these lockers? The pupils will respond as follows:

$L24$ visited by S_1, S_2, S_3, S_4, S_6, S_8, S_{12}, S_{24}

$L36$ visited by S_1, S_2, S_3, S_4, S_6, S_9, S_{12}, S_{18}, S_{36}

If we rewrite the divisors of the locker numbers as in figure 2, the pupils recognize that divisors come in pairs, except for the special case of the square root. This enables the pupils to explain why the only open lockers are those for which the locker number is a perfect square. They also can explain how these conclusions are represented in table 1.

24	36
1×24	1×36
2×12	2×18
3×8	3×12
4×6	4×9
	6×6

Fig. 2

Motivating Other Topics

From the observations that the pupils offer, we can raise new questions that lead into other topics of interest, as the following examples show. Each is stated as a "locker question"; when appropriate, this is followed by a reference to the relevant mathematical idea.

Q5. Can we locate all the lockers which are visited by only two students?

This leads into the Sieve of Eratosthenes for locating the 168 prime numbers less than 1000. Some pupils, to be sure, will work it out for the full 1000.

Q6. Do the open lockers get farther apart? closer together? stay the same?

The differences between the terms in the sequence 1, 4, 9, 16, 25, ... increase by successive odd integers:

$$1 + 3 = 4$$
$$4 + 5 = 9$$
$$9 + 7 = 16$$
$$16 + 9 = 25$$

The open lockers get farther apart.

Q7. Why do the square numbers increase in this manner?

Here a geometrical representation is almost self-explanatory (fig. 3). Pupils see that each successive square requires an L-shaped array (called a gnomon) containing $(2s + 1)$ points, where s is the side of the previous square.

Fig. 3

Q8. Exactly how many lockers are open?

Q9. What is the number of the last open locker?

Q10. Do the prime-number lockers also get farther apart?

Q11. Why is it that, except for the student whose number equals the locker number, all visitors to a locker have numbers less than or equal to one-half the locker number?

Note that table 1 reinforces this idea visually since all proper divisors of the number of L lie on or below the line $S = L/2$.

Q12. If we want to name all the visitors to a locker, how far must we check?

Here Q11 will show that it is sufficient to check primes less than or equal to $L/2$; however, it is not necessary to do so. The earlier investigation of the divisors of L_{24} and L_{36} should lead to the conclusion that we need only check primes up to the square root of the locker number. This is, of course, considerably more efficient for larger values of locker numbers. For example, in the case of L_{1000} we can find all divisors by checking primes up to 31 instead of to 500.

The next sequence of questions develops some of the more confusing junior high topics—factors (divisors), multiples, common factors, and common multiples. For the most part it is the vocabulary, rather than the concept, that causes difficulty for the pupils; and those who have trouble remembering whether four is a factor or a multiple of twelve usually are successful with more concrete questions.

Q13. How can you determine if L_{10} was visited by S_3? by S_5? by S_6? And so on.

In other words, how do you determine if the student number is a factor of the locker number?

Q14. Which lockers are visited by S_5 and S_7? by S_6 and S_8? by S_4 and S_8? And so on. (Common multiples)

Q15. What is the first locker visited by S_5 and S_7? by S_6 and S_8? by S_4 and S_7? And so on. (Least common multiple)

Q16. Is there any student who goes to every locker visited by both S_6 and S_8? (Are 6 and 8 relatively prime?)

Q17. Which students visit both L_{24} and L_{36}? L_{45} and L_{49}? L_{10} L_{25}, and L_{45}? And so on. (Common factors)

Q18. Who was the last student to visit L_{36} and L_{48}? L_{15} and L_{32}? And so on. (Greatest common factor)

Exploring Properties of Numbers

The problem we are discussing opens other doors besides the thirty-one squares less than 1000; it opens doors to exploring the behavior of numbers. Some explorations which it prompts are suggested—E1, E2, E3, …. They provide many opportunities for problem solving and enrichment.

E1. *Show that for any three adjacent (i.e., consecutive) lockers, exactly one was visited by S_3. This can be extended to other values as well. For example, for any five adjacent lockers, exactly one was visited by S_5.*

E2. *We know that prime-number lockers were visited by exactly two students. Which lockers were visited by exactly three students? Four students? Five students? And so on.* Table 2 shows the number of visitors (i.e., the number of divisors of the locker numbers) to the first sixty lockers. Pupils can search for rules to account for each category. For example, a locker has three visitors only if the locker number is the square of a prime number. (Recall that only square numbers can occur in the odd columns. Be careful, however, of the even columns. Thirty-two, for example, has six divisors, but it does not follow the same pattern as most of the other entries in that column.)

Table 2

Locker numbers (vertical axis)

1	2	3	4	5	6	7	8	9	10	11	12
			58								
	59		57								
	53		55								
	47		51								
	43		46								
	41		39								
	37		38								
	31		35								
	29		34								
	23		27		52						
	19		26		50						
	17		22		45						
	13		21		44		56				
	11		15		32		54				
	7	49	14		28		42				
	5	25	10		20		40				
	3	9	8		18		30				
1	2	4	6	16	12		24	36	48		60

Number of divisors

E3. *Can you find a quick way to add the numbers of any three adjacent lockers?*

For example: 7 + 8 + 9 = ?
$$32 + 33 + 34 = ?$$
$$573 + 574 + 575 = ?$$

And, *can you extend the rule to five, seven, nine, …, adjacent lockers? To four, six, eight, … adjacent lockers? To n adjacent lockers?*

E4. *Between any two open lockers, is there always a prime-number locker?*

E5. *Between any locker and the locker with twice the number of the first locker, is there always a prime-number locker?*

E6. *If ℓ is the number of an open locker (hence $\ell = x^2$), show that ℓ can be written as follows:*

$$\ell = 1 + 2 + 3 + \cdots + (x-1) + x$$
$$+(x-1)+ \cdots + 3 + 2 + 1.$$

That is, $9 = 1 + 2 + 3 + 2 + 1$ and
$$16 = 1 + 2 + 3 + 4 + 3 + 2 + 1.$$

E7. *Can you use this idea (i.e., E6) to find an expression for any sum $(1 + 2 + 3 + \cdots + n)$?*

E8. *If ℓ is the number of a closed locker and odd, show that it can be written as the difference of the numbers of two open lockers (ie., as the difference of two squares, $\ell = a^2 - b^2$). For example, $7 = 16 - 9$.*

E9. *If ℓ is the number of a closed locker*

that was visited by S_4, show that it, too, can be written as the difference of the numbers of two open lockers. That is, if $\ell = 4k$, then $\ell = a^2 - b^2$. For example, $12 = 16 - 4$. (Note: If ℓ is of the form $4k + 2$, it cannot be written as the difference of two squares.)

E10. *The number, ℓ of every closed locker can be written as a sum of the numbers of not more than four open lockers. (The number of an open locker may be used more than once as in $8 = 4 + 4$.) Look for a representation of ℓ using the fewest number of open-locker addends. Try to determine which closed-locker numbers can be written as a sum of only two open-locker numbers (i.e., $\ell = a^2 + b^2$) and which cannot.*

E11. *For which locker numbers, does the sum of the numbers, s, of all visitors, except $s = \ell$. total ℓ? That is, L_6 is visited by S_1, S_2, S_3, and S_6. The sum of the numbers $1 + 2 + 3 = 6$. (Six is the first "perfect number." There are two other lockers with perfect numbers.)*

E12. *If L is a prime-number locker, $p \le 5$, then either the locker before, $(L - 1)$, or the locker after, $(L + 1)$, was visited by S_6.*

E13. *After L_3, whenever two prime-number lockers are separated by only one locker (i.e., twin primes), the locker between them was visited by S_6. This happens thirty-four times.*

E14. *After L_1, if the number of a locker L is the square of an odd number, then the locker $L - 1$ was visited by S8. Further, $L - 1$ was also visited by a student whose number is a triangular number. (The triangular numbers 1, 3, 6, 10, 15, 21, …, are generated by the patterns in figure 4.*

Fig. 4

E15. *After L_9, if the number of a locker L is the square of a prime number, then $L - 1$ was visited by S_{12}.*

E16. *Investigate the digital roots of the open lockers. What pattern do they form? The digital root of a number is obtained by adding the digits of that number. For example, the digital root of 23, $d(23)$, is five since $2 + 3 = 5$. If the sum of the digits is itself a two-digit number, we repeat the process. Thus $d(156) = 3$, since $1 + 5 + 6 = 12$ and $1 + 2 = 3$.*

E17. *For the number, ℓ, of an open locker (i.e., $\ell = x^2$), show that the digital root, $d(\ell)$, has the property that*

$$d(x^2) = d\{[d(x)]^2\}$$

In Summary

The problem that has just been discussed has much to recommend it. It is, first of all, a *problem* since it requires such heuristics as the following: solving a simpler problem, making a picture or chart, looking for patterns, making tables, making predictions (guessing), generalizing the patterns, and working backward. The problem also embodies numerous concepts of mathematics, including prime numbers, composite numbers, factors, multiples, common factors, common multiples, greatest common factor, least common multiple, square

numbers, perfect numbers, necessary conditions, sufficient conditions, and more. It has been used successfully with junior high school pupils who have found the problem to be interesting as well as helpful in reasoning about questions such as those suggested above. Hence it is a good way to make a problem of junior high school mathematics.

And, like any good problem, it leads to new problems. The reader wonders, perhaps, where the students went after opening and closing all those lockers. Now it can be told.

The first student, S_1, held open the door at the end of the school corridor. The other students ran through that open door onto the football field and lined up as shown in figure 5. In what column did S_{1000} stand?

	2	3	4	5
9	8	7	6	
	10	11	12	13
17	16	15	14	
…	…	…	…	…

Fig. 5

VICKI SCHELL

Foxy Fives

acti✂ities

Grade Levels: 7–12.

Materials: One set of activity sheets and one deck of Foxy Five cards per student. To make a deck of cards, cut sixty-two 2 1/4-by-3 1/2-inch rectangles from posterboard (or for a thinner card, cut from a three-by-five-inch file card; blank card decks are also commercially available). Mark three cards with the number "1," three with the number "2," continuing through "10"; mark each number from 11 through 17 on two cards each; and for numbers 18 through 25, mark one card each.

Objectives: To provide experience in observing the relationships among numbers; to provide drill in the basic arithmetic operations; and to provide experience in applying the order of operations to a set of numbers.

Background: Playing the Foxy Fives game

Vicki Schell, *Salzburg International Preparatory School, Salzburg, Austria*

The Activities section is designed to provide mathematical activities suitable for reproduction in worksheet and transparency form for classroom use. This material may be photo-reproduced by classroom teachers for use in their own classes without requesting permission from the National Council of Teachers of Mathematics. Laboratory experiences, discovery activities, and model constructions drawn from the topics of seventh, eighth, and ninth grades are most welcomed for review.

Edited by Evan M. Maletsky, *Montclair State College, Upper Montclair, NJ 07043;* Christian Hirsch, *Western Michigan University, Kalamazoo, MI 49008;* and Daniel Yates, *Mathematics and Science Center, Richmond, VA 23223*

is my foxy way of sneaking in drill and review to general mathematics classes. The deck consists of cards numbered from 1 to 25. Each player is dealt five cards, and one card is turned up in the center. The object of the game is to combine the five cards in any order and, using any of the four basic operations, to obtain the number on the center card. The students should be familiar with the basic game before trying any variations. As an alternative approach, these activities can be done without cards by selecting the numbers in some random procedure (using a spinner is such an option), but the students seem to find it easier having the cards at hand.

Directions: Distribute the card decks and activity sheets (one at a time) to each student. Have the students complete each sheet before going on to the next one.

Sheet 1: This initial activity familiarizes the students with the basic procedure of the Foxy Fives game. It may be helpful to do this sheet as a class group, using an overhead, the first few times the game is played. It is interesting to compare results of different students as a means of reinforcing the fact that there is often more than one possible solution to a problem.

Sheets 2 & 3: These sheets reinforce the discovery that the same Foxy Five numbers will produce a different total depending on how the numbers are combined, as well as providing additional practice in number manipulation.

Solution Guide: There are, of course, many possible solutions for each of the given problems. I include here one solution for each.

Answers

Sheet 1: (1) $10 - (6 + 3 + 1) + 5 = 5$; (2) $11 + 1 - 9 - (8 \div 8) = 2$; (3) $11 - [(20 - 15) \times 3 - 10] = 6$; (4) $(11 + 3) - 12 + 18 - 12 = 8$; (5) $(4 + 16) \div 10 - (25 - 24) = 1$; (6) $17 - 17 + (14 - 13) \times 7 = 7$; (7) $(9 - 9) + (5 \times 4) + 2 = 22$; (8) $(7 - 6) + [3 - (10 \div 5)] = 2$; (9) $5 - [(11 + 21) \div 8] + 6 = 7$; (10) $(17 - 1) \div 1(6 - 2) \div 2] = 8$; (11) $(10 + 1) - 11 + (9 - 4) = 5$

Sheet 2: (2) $9 - \{14 \div [(19 + 3) \div 11]\} = 2$; (3) $11 - [(19 + 9) \div 14] \div 3 = 3$; (4) $19 - 9 + 11 - 14 - 3 = 4$; (5) $9\{14 - [(11 + 19) \div 3]\} = 5$; (7) $14 \div \{[(3 + 19) - 9] - 11\} = 7$; (8) $9 - [(11 \times 3) \div (14 + 19)] = 8$; (9) $11 \times 3 - (14 + 19) + 9 = 9$; (10) $19 - 9 + 11 - 14 + 3 = 10$.

Sheet 3: (1) $[(11 + 3) - (2 \times 7)] \div 5 = 0$; (2) $[(2 \times 5) + (7 - 3)] - 11 = 3$; (3) $5 - [(11 + 3) \div 7 + 2] = 1$; (4) $[(5 + 3) - (11 - 7)] \div 2 = 2$; (5) $[(5 + 3) \div (11 - 7)] \times 2 = 4$; (6) $2 \times 3 \times 5 \times 7 \times 11 = 2310$; (7) $11 \times 7 \times 5 \times (3 + 2) = 1925$; (8) $[(11 - 3) \times (5 + 7)]1 \div 2 = 48$; (9) $5 - \{3 - [(11 - 2) - 7]\} = 4$; (10) $11 \times 7 \times 5 \times 3 - 2 = 1153$.

FOXY FIVES

Directions:

- Deal yourself the following Foxy Five hands. Use each card once (and only once) to make the given total.

- Write out your combination, being sure to introduce parentheses where needed to show the order of operations.

Example:

	hand:		total:	
	7, 8, 1, 9, 9		16	$(9 \div 9) \times (7 + 8 + 1) = 16$

			total:	
1.	1, 5, 3, 6, 10		5	_____
2.	8, 11, 9, 1, 8		2	_____
3.	11, 10, 15, 20, 3		6	_____
4.	12, 18, 3, 11, 12		8	_____
5.	4, 16, 10, 24, 25		1	_____
6.	17, 14, 7, 17, 13		7	_____
7.	2, 9, 5, 9, 4		22	_____
8.	3, 6, 10, 5, 7		2	_____
9.	8, 6, 11, 5, 21		7	_____
10.	6, 1, 2, 2, 17		8	_____
11.	10, 4, 1, 11, 9		5	_____

FOXY FIVES

Directions:

- Deal yourself the following Foxy Fives hand:

    11, 14, 3, 19, 9.

- With this hand, make the totals from 1 to 11. Write each combination as an equation. Be careful of the order of operations!

1. $(11 + 14 - 19 + 3) \div 9 = 1$

2. _____

3. _____

4. _____

5. _____

6. $11 - [(19 + 9) \div 14 + 3] = 6$

7. _____

8. _____

9. _____

10. _____

11. $[9 - (19 - 14) - 3] \times 11 = 11$

FOXY FIVES

Directions:

- Deal yourself the following Foxy Fives hand: 2, 3, 5, 7, 11. (Notice that these are the first 5 prime numbers!)

- With this hand, find the following totals. Write each combination as an equation. Be careful of the order of operations!

1. What is the smallest whole number that you can find, using these five numbers and each arithmetic operation exactly once?

_____

2. Find the smallest odd prime number. _____

3. Find the smallest odd natural number. _____

4. Find the smallest prime number.   _____

5. Find the smallest composite natural number. _____

6. What is the largest composite natural number you can find?

_____

7. What is the largest odd natural number you can find?

_____

8. Find the largest even natural number possible, using each operation only once. _____

9. Find a natural number using only subtraction.

_____

10. Find the largest prime number possible with these five numbers.

_____

FRIEDHELM F. PADBERG

Using Calculators to Discover Simple Theorems—
An Example from Number Theory

Frequently the calculator is considered to be merely an auxiliary device for the solution of numerical problems and its use in classes is limited to that.

We can, however, make good use of the calculator for discovering and, sometimes, proving simple theorems. This is to say, the calculator enables us to generate a sufficient number of examples that we can easily get through to conjectures or theorems. Then these conjectures can be tested by the investigation of further examples. In some cases a counter-example can be found quickly and the conjecture is disproved; in other cases all possibilities may be quickly exhausted and we may even be able to "prove" the conjectures completely in special problems.

Although we may have to stop on this level if the pupils with whom we are working are not so capable, capable groups can be led eventually to more elegant algebraic proofs. In what follows we will verify the preceding remarks by means of an example from number theory.

Friedhelm Padberg *is professor of mathematics and mathematics education at the University of Bielefeld in West Germany.*

A Study of Differences

We begin with the three-digit number 762 and its "mirror number," 267. Then we subtract the initial number from the mirror number, or vice versa, depending on which is larger, and continue the process as long as possible (fig. 1). In the second example (fig. 2), we begin with the number 896 and, using its mirror number, proceed in the same way. We see in both examples that the sequence of differences stops after only a few steps; that is, it comes to a difference of zero. The question then arises as to whether this happens merely by accident, because of our choice of numbers, or whether all such sequences of differences of three-digit numbers will end with zero. If the latter is true, how many steps are the least necessary, and how many are the most necessary, until the process ends this way?

For the answers to these questions, we can get a great deal of data very quickly if we have each pupil in the class investigate about ten numbers of this kind. Let the students select their own numbers and, with the help of the calculator, compute the differences and write down the results. If we tabulate the investigated numbers (or a selected group of them), arranging them

systematically according to the number of steps it takes to reach zero, we will have a great deal of evidence at hand that suggests the following conjectures:

1. All such sequences of differences end with zero after only a few steps.

2. We get zero earliest after only one step (for example, 121 or 999) and at the latest after six steps (for example, 785). There are also three-digit numbers for which we reach zero after two, three, four, or five steps.

The next question—Can we tell directly

Example:		
762	594	99
− 267	− 495	− 99
495	99	0

Fig. 1

Example:		
762	891	693
− 698	− 198	− 396
198	693	297
792	594	99
− 297	− 495	− 99
495	99	0

Fig. 2

from the initial number how many steps will be necessary before the sequence of differences ends with zero?—which will require proof of the foregoing conjectures, can be easily raised.

We can ask pupils to choose any three-digit number and then predict, without any calculation, the number of steps until zero. The pupils can verify their prediction by means of the calculator. The systematically arranged chart can then be used to get the pupils to offer conjectures about how it is possible to tell directly from the given numbers the number of steps to zero.

It is immediately clear that we get zero after one step if and only if at least the hundreds digit and the ones digit of the number are identical. It is advisable to start the real investigation with the questions for the "two step numbers"; that is, the numbers for which the second difference is zero.

From an investigation of all the examples, we find that the tens have no influence on the number of steps; only the difference $h - u$ is decisive, where h represents the digit in hundreds place and u represents the digit in units place. The following statement should be checked by numerous examples:

A three-digit number is a "two-step number," if and only if $h - u = 1$.

Here we can quickly and easily "prove" to the class the first part—if $h - u = 1$, then we get zero after only two steps—by means of exhaustion of all possibilities.

The other part of the statement—if we get zero after only two steps, then $h - u = 1$—automatically emerges as a secondary product when we have analyzed all ten possible differences for $h - u$. Without doubt, however, an algebraic proof is more elegant, since it saves us the complete investigation of all cases. This can be demonstrated here in an appropriate and concrete way, so that the more gifted pupils are directed in quite a natural way to the use of the calculator for such proofs.

In this case we can argue as follows, using t for the tens:

If $h - u = 1$
then $u - h = -1$,
so $10 + (u - h) = 9$.
Also $10 + (u - h) = (10 + u) - h$
so $(10 + u) - h = 9$.

This says that in the units place the difference is 9.

Besides $(t - 1) - t = -1$
so $(10 + t - 1) - t = 9$.

This says that in tens place the difference is 9. Logically, then, we always get 99 as the first difference. This can be represented as follows:

$$\begin{array}{ccc} h & t & u \\ -u & t & h \\ \hline & 9 & 9 \end{array}$$

Since $99 - 99 = 0$, the sequence of differences in the case of $h - u = 1$ always stops after only two steps.

Additional theorems

By analogy, further theorems can be developed from the chart by the same sequence of activities—

• guessed at first,

• then verified on the calculator, and finally

• proved by exhausting all possible cases (with the help of the calculator),

or, more elegantly,

• proved by algebraic methods, as in the case of $h - u = 1$, which was just illustrated.

After further investigations, we can determine that we arrive at zero with three-digit numbers—

(1) after three steps, if and only if either $h - u = 5$ or $h - u = 6$;

(2) after four steps, if and only if either $h - u = 3$ or $h - u = 8$;

(3) after five steps, if and only if either $h - u = 4$ or $h - u = 7$;

(4) after six steps, if an only if either $h - u = 2$ or $h - u = 9$.

These theorems are at first obtained and proved only in the "if ..., then" form and can be formulated in the "if and only if" form only after the complete exhaustion of all possibilities.

In investigating the data collected by the pupils, we see that only the following numbers appear as the first difference: 0. 99, 198, 297, 396, 495, 594, 693, 792, and 881. Furthermore, these are all multiples of 99. To be more exact, the preceding investigations result in another theorem.

(5) In the formation of the sequence of dif-

ferences, we always obtain as the first result the difference d_1 such that

$$d_1 = 99 \cdot (h - u)$$

These investigations, especially the proofs, give practice with the algorithms for subtraction and review of the principles of our number system as desirable secondary effects. Furthermore, in determining the *number* of three-digit numbers for which the difference ends in zero after n steps ($n = 0, 1, ..., 6$), combinatoric thinking is required. Consider, for example, the following different cases:

• all three digits are different and unequal to zero;

• exactly two digits are equal and all are unequal to zero;

• all three digits are equal and unequal to zero;

• exactly one digit is O and the two others are different;

• exactly one digit is O and the two remaining digits are equal;

• two digits are 0.

From the data we also have a basis for exploring the question, What is the probability that the differences for any given three-digit number end in zero after exactly n steps ($n = 0, 1, ..., 6$)?

Other considerations

In addition to the whole complex of questions already discussed, other investigations are possible. Given a number, instead of calculating the difference between the number and its mirror number, we can form the maximum and minimum numbers (i.e., the largest and smallest possible numbers, using the same digits as in the given number) and subtract them from each other. Then we continue this method, taking the maximum and minimum numbers of each succeeding difference, as long as possible (fig. 3).

As a result of the investigation of these sequences of differences, we find that almost all differences of this kind stop after a few—at the most five— steps with 495. An exception is the case in which the maximum three-digit number has the condition $h - u = 0$ or $h - u = 1$.

In carrying out this activity, a complete list of the "number of steps" for all three-digit numbers can easily be obtained

Example: 573
 maximum number: 753
 minimum number: 357

thus:
$$\begin{array}{r} 753 \\ -357 \\ \hline 396 \end{array} \qquad \begin{array}{r} 963 \\ -369 \\ \hline 594 \end{array} \qquad \begin{array}{r} 954 \\ -459 \\ \hline 495 \end{array}$$

$$\begin{array}{r} 954 \\ -459, \text{ and so on.} \\ \hline 495 \end{array}$$

Fig. 3

with the help of the calculator. From the data collected, we can see that the sequence of differences between the maximum and minimum numbers always ends at 495 after—

(1) one step, if and only if $h - u = 5$

(2) two steps, if and only if $h - u = 6$ (3) three steps, if and only if either $h - u = 4$ or $h - u = 7$

(4) four steps, if and only if either $h - u = 3$ or $h - u = 8$

(5) five steps, if and only if either $h - u = 2$ or $h - u = 9$.

Conclusion

The array of problems examined has the advantage that it allows for further development. Thus we can have the pupils work out solutions to the easier questions unassisted—that is, the question as to whether corresponding statements are also valid for all two-digit numbers. (It is noteworthy that in the two-digit numbers the number-mirror number difference and the difference from the minimum and maximum numbers are identical.) More interesting and more complicated—are analogous theorems also valid for four-digit numbers? For four-digit numbers we find that the differences, maximum numbers minus minimum numbers," in nearly all cases end after no more than seven steps with the number 6174. (See "An Arithmetical Curiosity," *Arithmetic Teacher*, April 1979, pp. 23–24.)

MELFRIED OLSON

It's a Factor of Life

Teacher's Guide

Grade level: 7–9.

Materials: Calculators, copies of the worksheets for each student, and a transparency of sheet 1.

Objectives: This activity is designed to (a) provide practice in factoring positive integers, (b) develop the notion that a prime number has exactly two factors, and (c) provide explorations of interesting relationships involving the number of factors of a positive integer.

Directions: This activity is best completed over a two-day period. Distribute calculators and copies of the student worksheets. Discuss the examples at the top of sheet 2, and then ask pupils to verify several of the other entries of the NUMOFACTOR machine. The class should then be partitioned into small groups, each of which is to be assigned a specific subset of the numbers 21–100. Once the groups have found all the factors of each assigned number they can place their results on the transparency of sheet 1 or on a master sheet. This chart can then be compared with that found in the *Solutions.* Questions 2–7 can then be answered by analyzing the completed chart.

Melfried Olson, *University of Wyoming, Laramie, WY 82071*

Edited by Evan M. Maletsky, *Montclair State College, Upper Montclair, NJ 07043;* Christian Hirsch, *Western Michigan University, Kalamazoo, MI 49008; and* Daniel Yates, *Mathematics and Science Center, Richmond, VA 23223*

This activity can be extended for use in higher grades by having pupils investigate formulas for finding the number of factors or the sums of the factors of a positive integer.

Solutions

1.

1	2	3	4	5	6	7	8	9	10	11	12
			95								
			94								
			93								
			91								
			87								
			86								
			85								
	97		82								
	89		77								
	83		74								
	79		69								
	73		65								
	71		62								
	67		58								
	61		57								
	59		55								
	53		51		99						
	47		46		98						
	43		39		92						
	41		38		76						
	37		35		75						
	31		34		68						
	29		33		63		88				
	23		27		52		78				
	19		26		50		70				
	17		22		45		66				
	13		21		44		56				
	11		15		32		54				96
	7	49	14		28		42				90
	5	25	10		20		40				84
	3	9	8	81	18		30	100	80		72
1	2	4	6	16	12	64	24	36	48		60

2. No.

3. (a) A prime number is a positive integer that has exactly two different factors; (b) No, it's not in column 2.

4. (a) Yes, squares of primes; (b) $11^2, 13^2, 17^2, 19^2, 23^2$ respectively.

5. (a) Yes; $5^3, 7^3$ respectively; (b) Yes; (c) 85, 86, 87.

6. (a) $2^{10}, 2^{12}, 2^{16}, 2^{18}, 2^{22}$ respectively; (b) $3^6, 3^{10}, 3^{12}, 3^{16}, 3^{18}, 3^{22}$ respectively; (c) $5^4, 5^6, 5^{10}, 5^{12}, 5^{16}, 5^{18}, 5^{22}$ respectively; (d) $7^4, 7^6, 7^{10}, 7^{12}, 7^{16}, 7^{18}, 7^{22}$ respectively.

7. (a) Yes; 3^5; (b) $2^7, 2^8, 2^9$ respectively; (c) (i) Those in column 8 are a product of a number from column 2 and a number in column 4 (these numbers have no common factors); (ii) those in column 10 are a product of a number from column 2 and a number in column 5 (these numbers have no common factors); (iii) those in column 9 are products of two distinct numbers in column 3 (see 5b).

8. Of course.

References

Kenney, Margaret I. "Factor Lattices." *Mathematics Teacher* 63 (December 1970): 647–51.

Underwood, Dudley, *Elementary Number Theory.* San Francisco: W. H. Freeman and Co., 1978.

NUMOFACTOR

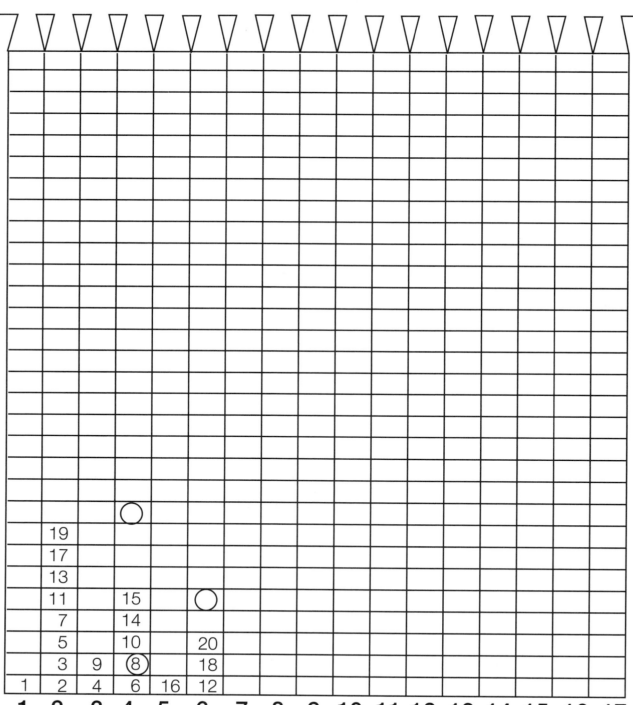

On sheet 1 is pictured a portion of a NUMOFACTOR machine. If we place a number into the machine, the machine sorts it into one of the columns depending on how many positive factors the number has. For example, 4 is placed in column 3 because it has three positive factors, 1, 2, and 4. Similarly, 12 is placed in column 6 because it has six positive factors, 1, 2, 3, 4, 6, and 12. The first twenty positive integers have been placed into the machine and sorted.

1. For each number, 21–100, determine how many positive factors it has, and then place the number into the appropriate column of the NUMOFACTOR machine.

2. Suppose numbers greater than 100 were placed into the machine. Will there ever be any number other than 1 in column 1?_____

3. The numbers found in column 2 are called *prime numbers.*

   (a) Write a possible definition of a prime number. _____

   _____

   (b) Is 1 a prime number? _____

4. (a) Do you see a pattern to the numbers found in column 3?_____

   (b) Suppose numbers greater than 100 were placed into the NUMOFACTOR machine. What would be the next five numbers that would be sorted into column 3? _____

5. (a) In column 4 you should find the numbers 8 and 27 circled. Can you write each of these numbers as a power of a prime number? _____

   If this pattern is continued, what would be the next two numbers that should be circled in column 4?_____

   (b) Can each of the numbers in column 4 that are *not* circled be expressed as a product of two distinct numbers in column 2?_____

   (c) In column 4 you should find the numbers 33, 34, 35 and 93, 94, 95. Find another set of three consecutive numbers in this column. _____

6. (a) Look at the first number found in each of columns 2, 3, 5, and 7. What do you think will be the first number found in column 11? 13? 17? 19? 23?

_____ _____ _____ _____ _____

(b) Look at the second number found in each of columns 2, 3, and 5. What do you think will be the second number found in column 7? 11? 13? 17? 19? 23?

_____ _____ _____ _____ _____ _____

(c) What do you think will be the third number found in column 5? 7? 11? 13? 17? 19? 23? _____ _____ _____ _____ _____ _____ _____

(d) What do you think will be the fourth number in column 5? 7? 11? 13? 17? 19? 23?____ _____ _____ _____ _____ _____ _____

7. (a) Is the circled number in column 6 a power of a prime number?_____

Suppose numbers greater than 100 were placed into the NUMOFACTOR machine. What would be the next number in column 6 that should be circled?

_____

(b) The pattern for circling numbers that we have used can be extended to the other columns of the machine. Suppose numbers greater than 100 were placed into the machine. What would be the first number in each of columns 8, 9, and 10 that should be circled?_____

(c) The numbers *not* circled in column 6 can be written as a product of a number in column 2 and a number in column 3.

(i) How can the numbers *not* circled in column 8 be related to the numbers in columns 2 and 4?_____

(ii) How can the numbers *not* circled in column 10 be related to the numbers in columns 2 and 5?_____

(iii) How are the numbers *not* circled in column 9 related to the numbers in column 3?_____

8. Can a number be found that would get sorted into column 487? Column 12 873? Column 149 356 821? _____

ACTIVITIES FOR JUNIOR HIGH AND MIDDLE SCHOOL MATHEMATICS

STEPHEN L. SNOVER

Five-Cycle Number Patterns

DO YOUR students find arithmetic with fractions difficult and boring? Here is a set of activities you can use with middle-school students (grades 5 through 9) to have them discover intriguing number patterns and at the same time practice their arithmetic skills with fractions. In fact, these activities can provide your students with experience with decimals, negative numbers, and evaluation of formulas, as well as other more advanced mathematical topics.

The Pattern

Start with the diagram shown in figure 1 and place numbers in the spaces as follows. Begin by placing any two numbers in the first and second spaces—for example, the number 1 and 2. (See fig. 2.) Next calculate the third number using the following formula:

(third number)

$$= \frac{(\text{second number})+1}{(\text{first number})}$$

$$= \frac{(2)+1}{(1)}$$

$$= \frac{3}{1}$$

$$= 3$$

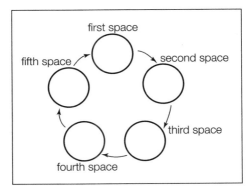

Fig. 1

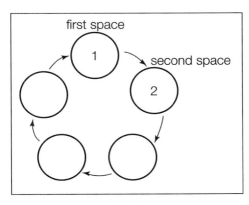

Fig. 2

Place the third number, 3 in this case, in the third space. (See fig. 3.) Now calculate the fourth number:

$$\left(\text{fourth number}\right) = \frac{\left(\text{third number}\right)+1}{\left(\text{second number}\right)}$$

$$= \frac{(3)+1}{(2)}$$

$$= \frac{4}{2}$$

$$= 2$$

Place it in the fourth space. (See fig. 4) Next calculate the fifth number in a similar way

$$\left(\text{fifth number}\right) = \frac{\left(\text{fourth number}\right)+1}{\left(\text{third number}\right)}$$

$$= \frac{(2)+1}{3}$$

$$= \frac{3}{3}$$

$$= 1$$

Place the fifth number in the fifth space. (See fig. 5.)

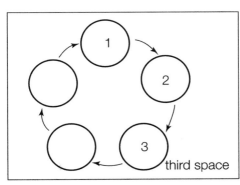

Fig. 3

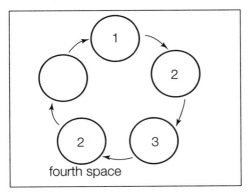

Fig. 4

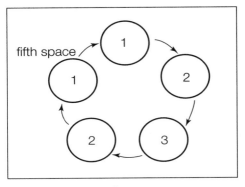

Fig. 5

Stephen Snover *is an assistant professor of mathematics and computer science at the University of Hartford in Connecticut. He teaches mathematics and computer science.*

Continuing the pattern

What happens when you continue the pattern by calculating a sixth number?

$$(\text{sixth number}) = \frac{(\text{fifth number}) + 1}{(\text{fourth number})}$$

$$= \frac{(1) + 1}{(2)}$$

$$= \frac{2}{2}$$

$$= 1$$

Notice that the sixth number equals the first number.

What happens if we calculate a seventh number?

$$(\text{seventh number}) = \frac{(\text{sixth number}) + 1}{(\text{fifth number})}$$

$$= \frac{(1) + 1}{(1)}$$

$$= \frac{2}{1}$$

$$= 2$$

The seventh number equals the second number. We are back to where we started, using the numbers 1 and 2 to calculate the third number. So starting with numbers 1 and 2, at least, the number pattern is a cyclic pattern of the five numbers: 1, 2, 3, 2, 1.

Other starting numbers

With other beginning numbers, do you get the same cyclic pattern of five numbers? If you-start with the numbers 1 and 3 you find the following:

$$(\text{third number}) = \frac{(\text{second number}) + 1}{(\text{first number})}$$

$$= 4$$

$$(\text{fourth number}) = \frac{(\text{third number}) + 1}{(\text{second number})}$$

$$= 1\frac{1}{2}$$

$$(\text{fifth number}) = \frac{(\text{fourth number}) + 1}{(\text{third number})}$$

$$= \frac{\left(1\frac{2}{3}\right) + 1}{(4)}$$

$$= \frac{\left(2\frac{2}{3}\right)}{4}$$

$$= \frac{\frac{8}{3}}{\frac{4}{1}}$$

$$= \frac{8}{3} \cdot \frac{1}{4}$$

$$= \frac{2}{3}$$

Notice the variety of arithmetic skills you need to use in order to obtain each of the numbers. Figure 6 shows the completed pattern.

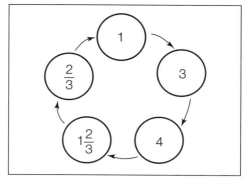

Fig. 6

Do these numbers repeat in a cycle of five, too? You can check to see by calculating the next two numbers:

$$(\text{sixth number}) = \frac{(\text{fifth number}) + 1}{(\text{fourth number})}$$

$$= \frac{\frac{2}{3} + 1}{\left(1\frac{2}{3}\right)}$$

$$= \frac{\frac{5}{3}}{\frac{5}{3}}$$

$$= \frac{5}{3} \cdot \frac{3}{5}$$

$$= 1$$

$$(\text{seventh number}) = \frac{(\text{sixth number} + 1)}{(\text{fifth number})}$$

$$= \frac{(1) + 1}{\left(\frac{2}{3}\right)}$$

$$= \frac{2}{\frac{2}{3}}$$

$$= \frac{2}{1} \cdot \frac{3}{2}$$

$$= 3$$

Again the number pattern is a cyclic pattern of the five numbers: 1, 3, 4, 1 2/3, 2/3.

Try some other starting numbers and see what results. For example, start with 2 and 4 (fig. 7) and with 2 and 5 (fig. 8). What do you discover?

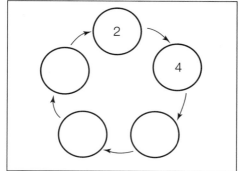

Fig. 7

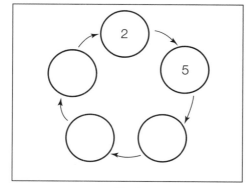

Fig. 8

Let your students begin with any two numbers of their choice (preferably single digits since the calculations become involved rather quickly). Have them see whether the pattern repeats in a cycle of five by checking the next two numbers.

It will not take long for them to realize that all patterns appear to repeat. In fact, as will be described later in this article, all patterns must repeat regardless of the two starting numbers.

Once your students realize that all patterns should repeat, they will be able to do their own checking of their arithmetic by seeing that the pattern does repeat.

Evaluation of formulas

Not only do these activities give practice with fractions and decimals, but also give experience with evaluating formulas, as students find each of the numbers in the pattern. Actually, the formulas for the third, fourth, and fifth numbers can be summarized by the following general rule:

$$\text{(next number)} = \frac{\text{(last number)} + 1}{\text{(next - to - last number)}}$$

Decimal practice

If you write the fractions in decimal form when working with these patterns, you can provide students practice working with decimal numbers. Try completing figures 9, 10, 11, and 12.

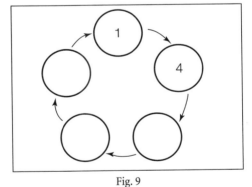
Fig. 9

Fig. 10

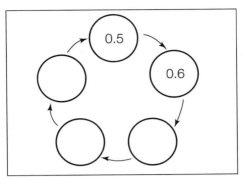
Fig. 11

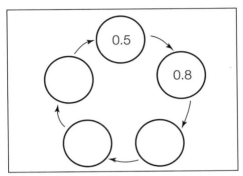
Fig. 12

Using calculators

Even using a calculator to perform the computations may be a useful activity. A word of caution is in order, however. If the fractions are nonterminating—that is, those whose denominators have factors other than just 2 or 5, the calculator will display only an approximation of the value of the fraction. This will most likely lead to

a pattern of numbers that does not exactly repeat in five-cycles.

For example, starting with 5 and 9 should yield the pattern shown in figure 13. A calculator, however, may produce the result indicated in figure 14. (Different calculators often yield slightly different results.)

Although calculators present this difficulty, they also present the opportunity to discuss rounded-off division calculations. If the divisions are performed by a calculator and then rounded off to some arbitrarily chosen place, say the nearest thousandth, the desired five-cycle results would occur. (See fig. 15)

Negative numbers

What happens when negative numbers are used in these patterns? Since these patterns lead quickly to division problems, starting with one or more negative num-

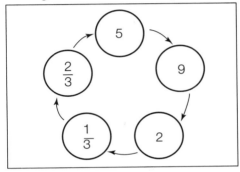
Fig. 13

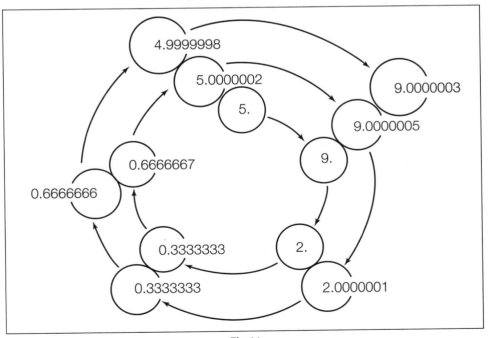
Fig. 14

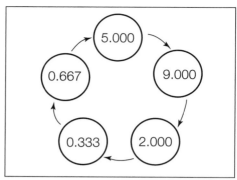

Fig. 15

bers will lead just as quickly to divisions involving signed numbers. For example, try to complete the pattern shown in figure 16. When completed correctly, the five-cycle number pattern will have three negative and two positive numbers.

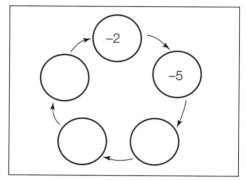

Fig. 16

Your better students may find it a challenge to discover some appropriate negative starting numbers leading to five-cycle patterns with all five numbers being negative—or with four negatives and one positive number.

Actually, five-cycle patterns with three, four, or five negative numbers are possible to find, but patterns with two or one negatives are impossible. Perhaps the following sequence of questions will explain why.

What would happen if a five-cycle pattern had two or one negative numbers? Wouldn't that require three or more positive numbers? Wouldn't that in turn require two adjacent positive numbers in the cycle? If those two adjacent positive numbers are used as the starting numbers, what would the signs of all the rest of the numbers have to be? Do you see a logical contradiction?

Another intriguing problem involving negative numbers is the following: Can −1 appear in any five-cycle number pattern?

Proof That Every Pattern Repeats in a Five-Cycle

You and perhaps your best students might enjoy proving that any pattern must repeat regardless of the starting numbers. You can do so as follows:

First, assume that you start with the numbers a and b. Show that the next three numbers must be the following (fig. 17):

$$\frac{b+1}{a}, \quad \frac{a+b+1}{ab}, \quad \text{and} \quad \frac{a+1}{b}.$$

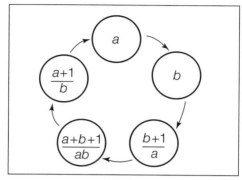

Fig. 17

Finally, show that the pattern repeats by showing that the sixth and seventh numbers are a and b respectively.

An advanced problem

Can you find a number pattern where all five numbers are identical? In other words, for what value of x is the pattern shown in figure 18 a five-cycle pattern? If you set up the calculation of the third number using the letter x, you will obtain the following equation:

$$x = \frac{x+1}{x}$$

This equation can be rearranged as follows:

$$x^2 - x - 1 = 0$$

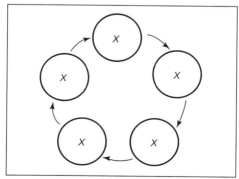

Fig. 18

The positive solution to this equation is the golden ratio:

$$x = \frac{1+\sqrt{5}}{2}$$
$$= 1.618$$

Conclusion

Working with these repeating number patterns should be both fun and instructive for middle-school and prealgebra students at all stages of development. For the beginner, there is plenty of skill practice with fractions as well as the ability to check the calculations by continuing the pattern to make sure it repeats. Students with calculators can explore these patterns and at the same time learn to round off the displayed value. For the pre-algebra student there can be the experience of experimenting with negative numbers. Even the most advanced students can be challenged with the many algebra topics related to these patterns. As such, these patterns should be interesting, challenging and instructive to students of all levels of ability.

For further information see the following:

Lyness, R. C. *The Mathematical Gazette* 26 (1942): 62.

Kurshan, R. P. and B. Gopinath. "Recursively Generated Periodic Sequences." *Canadian Journal of Mathematics* 26 (December 1974): 1356–71.

Gardner, Martin. "Mathematical Games." *Scientific American* 235 (November 1976): 134.

AUTHOR'S NOTE: Many thanks go to Mark A. Spikell for making numerous helpful suggestions for this article.

CHARLES S. THOMPSON AND VICKI WALKER

Connecting Decimals
and Other Mathematical Content

EXPERIENCES with many children in the middle grades indicate that they have poor decimal concepts and lack fundamental skills in working with decimal values. For example, when asked to identify which of 0.36 or 0.339 is greater, children frequently choose 0.339 because 339 is greater than 36. Other children reason that 0.339 is smaller because it has more decimal places, and they "know" that the values decrease as more decimal places are added. Likewise, children have poor number sense regarding decimal numbers. For example, when asked to round 0.487 to the nearest hundredth, they blithely use the standard rule "round up when the digit to the right is greater than 5," round 0.487 to 0.49, but never think of either 0.487 or 0.49 as being near 1/2 on the number line.

Children often develop misconceptions about decimals because instruction does not promote connections between decimals and other mathematical content. Decimal concepts and symbols need to be related to a variety of fraction ideas and to place value. Connections also need to link decimals with coin and dollar values, metric measurement, and percents.

This article describes instructional activities with decimals that enable children to make connections that are necessary for them to understand and use decimals meaningfully. Decimal concepts and symbols are related to fraction concepts and symbols and to place-value concepts and symbols. Extensive use is made of physical models, diagrams, and number lines. The goal is to enable students to develop decimals as part of an integrated network of number ideas by understanding (1) that decimals are a type of fraction with a different symbolism and (2) that decimals can be meaningfully compared, ordered, and related to common fractions by using fraction ideas and place-value ideas.

Decimals Are Base-Ten Fractions

Decimals can be thought of as parts of a whole, a whole that has been divided into 10, 100, 1000, or some other number of parts that is a power of 10. From this perspective, decimals are special fractions and can appropriately be called decimal fractions, since the word decimal means "based on ten." The following activity focuses on the part-whole aspect of decimal fractions. The special symbols for decimals are addressed in the subsequent activity.

A motivating and intriguing way to help students learn about decimal fractions involves using individually wrapped slices of cheese. Using one slice as the model for one whole, ask each student to cut his or her whole into ten equal-sized strips.

The plastic wrapper can be used as a cutting board (see fig. 1). Ask what number name should be given to each of the newly cut strips. Ask students to justify their answers in terms of the pieces of cheese in

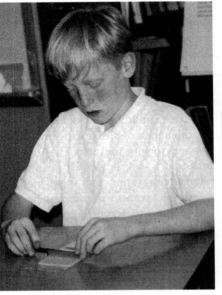

front of them. Focus on the idea that tenths have been made, since the whole has been cut into ten equal-sized parts. This activity uses children's ideas about fractions, and teachers can have students write fraction symbols (1/10) to match their verbal answers (one tenth). Students can then answer questions related to the number of tenths in five whole slices of cheese (fifty tenths) or in two and one-half slices of cheese (twenty-five tenths).

After students can answer questions about the tenths strips and justify their answers, ask them to take one of the strips and cut it into ten equal-sized pieces, which will be little squares. Follow with the same type of questions as with the tenths: "What name should be given to the new pieces?" (Hundredths) "How do you know?" (One hundred of these pieces are needed to make the whole slice.) "What name would you give to three strips and two little squares?" (3 tenths and 2 hundredths, or 32 hundredths, or 32/100, since each of the three strips has 10 hundredths.)

Students seem to like the challenge of taking one of the hundredths squares and cutting it into ten equal pieces, thereby

Charles Thompson *works with undergraduate and graduate students at the University of Louisville, Louisville, KY 40292. He is particularly interested in helping children develop mathematics concepts through the use of models.* Vicki Walker *teaches at the I Have a Dream School, Louisville, KY 40202. She has taught for eight years and is particularly interested in using alternative forms of assessment with her students.*

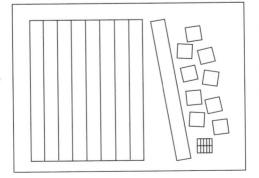

Fig. 1. Cutting a cheese slice to show decimals

creating thousandths. The cutting gets tedious at this point, but it is not impossible. The relative sizes of tenths, hundredths, and thousandths become meaningful for students through this activity. They can see the three sizes! They can respond to questions about the values of combinations of the pieces. "What is the value of two strips, one little square, and three tiny pieces?" (213/1000, since each strip contains 100 thousandths, each little square contains 10 thousandths, and 3 extra thousandths are present.) When the discussion is completed, the children enjoy eating their decimal models. For example, ask the students to eat twenty-three hundredths of their original slice, then 3 tenths, 6 thousandths, and so on, until all the cheese has been eaten.

Decimal Connections with Place Value

In the following activity, children are challenged to extend the place-value notation they have been using for whole numbers to include symbolic representations for decimal fractions. Children manipulate decimal models on a place-value mat (fig. 2), verbalize the amounts shown, and later enter the appropriate numerals on a calculator. The materials needed for each pair of children are tagboard decimeter squares to represent the whole, strips 1 cm by 1 dm to represent tenths, squares 1 cm by 1 cm to represent hundredths, three-column place-value mats, and a calculator.

Ask the students to compare the strips with the large square and to name them in terms of the large square. Be sure that the students use two characteristics to justify that the strips are tenths: (1) they are equal in size and (2) ten of them make the whole square. Have one student in each pair place one large square in the left column of the place-value mat and one strip in the column immediately to the right. Ask everyone to verbalize the total represented (one and one-tenth) and discuss how to use numbers to write that amount (1 1/10).

Challenge the students with the following idea: "Is it possible to use '11' to stand for the value of the square and the strip? Let's use the '1' on the left to stand for the large square and the '1' on the right to stand for the strip." Students will object, of course, and state that '11' stands for eleven rather than one and one-tenth. One student will usually suggest putting a dot between the 1's (1.1), since many of them have seen decimals written elsewhere. Take this opportunity to challenge them to defend the use of this notation. Ask them to justify that this notation is consistent with the place-value notation that they learned earlier and to identify the meanings of the 1's and the dot. Their explanations should focus on the 1-to-10, right-to-left relationship between adjacent positions in the place-value system. They should also identify that the purpose of the dot, or decimal point, is to separate the whole from the parts.

To test their reasoning and understanding, suggest that if a whole square is cut into eight equal parts and one square and one-eighth of the square are placed on the mat, then 1.1 can be used to represent this amount also. Some children may need hints to help them determine that the reason 1.1 can be used for one and one-tenth but not for one and one-eighth is that a 1-to-10, right-to-left relationship must exist between adjacent positions in the standard place-value system. One hint would be to ask children how the values of the two 1's compare in each of the following numbers: 211, 112, and 1123. (In each example the 1 on the right is worth 1/10 of the 1 on its left.) Another hint would be to have children examine previously used place-value materials, such as base-ten cubes, rods, flats, and big cubes, that model this 1-to-10 relationship.

Following this investigation of the place-value system, the students will have a beginning understanding that 1.1 can be used for one and one-tenth because the tenths are one-tenth in value of the units to the immediate left. This idea will be reinforced throughout the remainder of this activity.

Have the student in each pair who is using the calculator enter 1.1 to match the value of the pieces on the place-value mat. Add one more strip to each mat, and have the student with the calculator enter the corresponding symbols to represent this action: ⊞ ⊡ 1 ⊟. Have students verbalize the new total on their mats (one and two-tenths) and discuss the calculator representation of this expression (1.2). (The "1" stands for one whole and the "2" stands for the two tenths. The decimal point separates the whole from the parts, the tenths.) Have the students continue adding strips, or tenths, one at a time to their mats as their partners press the corresponding keys on their calculators, until a total of 1.9 is reached. Consider using the constant feature of many calculators to add 0.1 repeatedly by pressing ⊟ after each addition of a tagboard strip. However, many children will benefit from representing the entire action initially by pressing all four keys, ⊞ ⊡ 1 ⊟, each time.

At this point, add another strip and ask the students to name the total on their mats. (One and ten tenths.) Discuss what should be done with the ten strips. (Trade them in for a whole square.) Have students predict what the calculator will do when ⊞ ⊡ 1 ⊟ is entered. (It automatically "makes the trade" and the display reads simply 2.) Be sure to connect this trading to the cheese activity: it corresponds to reconnecting the ten cheese strips and exchanging them for a new slice. Also, ask the children to check the odometer of their parents' car to see what happens immediately after it changes from a 9 in the tenths place. (The ones digit advances by 1 and the tenths digit changes to 0.)

Continue adding tenths until the children can verbalize the amount on the place-value mats correctly and can predict

Fig. 2. Connecting decimals and place value

and justify the calculator's display. Change the activity by having the children add hundredths each time. Begin with one whole, one tenth, and one hundredth on the place-value mat and ask the students to name this amount. (One and eleven hundredths, since the strip is worth ten hundredths.) Ask them how to represent this amount with numbers. (1.11) Have them justify this representation just as they did with 1.1. With a teacher's patience and nudges, they will determine that each "1" in 1.11 is worth one-tenth of the "1" to its left. After they have entered 1.11 on their calculators, have them add one hundredth to their mats and predict what the calculator will display when ⊞ · ⓪ ① ⚌ is entered. (1.12) Continue adding hundredths to the mat until the students can verbalize and justify the amounts shown and can predict and justify the calculator's representations. When they can, have them place one whole, nine tenths, and five hundredths (1.95) on their mats and add one hundredth at least five times. On the fifth addition, have the children verbalize what they should do with the materials (trade ten hundredths for one tenth and then the ten tenths for a whole) and predict what the calculator will display. (2)

This activity leads to several important outcomes. First, the students learn a new way of representing decimal fractions, for example, representing 1 1/10 as 1.1 and 1 11/100 as 1.11. Second, they learn this concept in a way that can enable them to understand better the consistent 1-to-10 relationship that exists between adjacent positions in the place-value system, for whole numbers and for decimal fractions. Third, they learn how decimal values grow and how their numerical representations change as tenths or hundredths are added repeatedly.

Teachers can broaden students' understanding of decimals and place value further by using dollars, dimes, and pennies on place-value mats. Children will already be familiar with the symbolic notation for monetary values, such as $1.23, and will benefit from a discussion about dollars representing wholes, dimes representing tenths, and pennies representing hundredths. Many children will not have thought of dimes and pennies as decimal fractions.

Reasoning about Decimal Concepts

In this activity, students are enticed to connect a variety of ideas about decimal fractions, including various verbal and symbolic representations; relationships among wholes, tenths, and hundredths; and comparisons of decimal values. Two types of writing tasks are posed to students.

The first task involves showing students a 10-by-10 square grid with some squares shaded (fig.3). Ask students to name the shaded amount in at least three ways and to explain their answers in terms of the diagram. If thirty-five squares are shaded, the names that students give for the shaded amount might include 0.35, 35/100, 35 hundredths, 1/10 + 1/10 + 1/10 + 5/100, 7/20, and 3 1/2 tenths. The explanations students give often involve comparing the number of shaded squares with the total number of squares. (The fraction 35/100 represents 35 shaded squares out of 100 total squares.) Sometimes they mentally group the squares into sets of ten or five to make comparisons. For example, they justify 3 1/2 tenths by mentally creating and comparing 3 1/2 strips of 10 squares to the total of 10 strips of 10 squares.

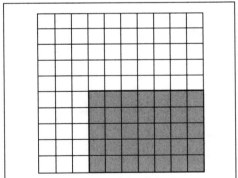

Fig. 3. The fraction 35/100 has many names

The second task involves having students designate which of two decimals, 0.307 and 0.32, is greater in value and asking them to justify their answers. Give them 10-by-10 grids to use in their justifications. Children are able to draw on their experiences with the cheese slices, the place-value materials, and the previous activity to shade in squares on the grid to represent the two decimal values (fig. 4). They then explain that 0.32 represents three strips—tenths—and two more little squares—hundredths—whereas 0.307 represents three strips—tenths—and no complete little squares—hundredths. Hence, 0.32 is greater in value than 0.307.

The importance of using physical models and diagrams to represent decimals cannot be overemphasized. The students can base their reasoning on objects and diagrams that they can see, create, and move rather than on abstract definitions and rules, such as the following rule for comparing decimals: "Compare the digits in each place-value position, moving from left to right until the digits differ. At that point, the decimal number having the digit of greater value is the greater number."

It is important to ask children to communicate their ideas in writing, as described in this activity. When children are asked to write, they are forced to think, to organize their ideas, and to arrange them in a logical sequence. Writing also encourages children to make connections among various ideas to help the reader understand the ideas being expressed.

Connecting Decimals with Common Fractions

For children to develop a good number sense for decimals, they need to relate

Fig. 4. Comparing 0.307 and 0.32 on grid paper

decimals to such common fractions as 1/4 and 1/8. Stated in another way, children need to connect fractions to their decimal equivalents, such as 1/4 to 0.25. Some students think that 1/8 equals 0.18. Usually common fractions are connected to decimals by using division. For example, to find the decimal equivalent of 1/4, 1 is divided by 4 by using paper and pencil or a calculator; the result is 0.25. Thus, 1/4 is equal to 0.25. But this result is not very satisfying for children. They see the result, but the connection is symbolic rather than conceptual and does not give them an intuitive feeling about the desired relationship nor any understanding of why 1/4 is equal to 0.25.

To make this connection more understandable, use a 10-by-10 square grid divided into 100 parts. The square grid represents the whole, or 1, so each of the 100 equal parts represents one hundredth, 1/100, or 0.01. Ask children to shade one-fourth of the grid. Generally they do this task by drawing a line vertically through the center of the grid and another line horizontally through the center of the grid as shown in figure 5. Ask them to name the shaded amount in other ways, particularly by using decimals. By drawing on the previous place-value activities, children frequently name the shaded amount as twenty-five hundredths, that is, twenty-five little squares, or 0.25. Thus, they have found that 1/4 equals 0.25. Teachers can help the children connect this result to the previous place-value activity by discussing that a group of twenty-five squares is the same as two strips, or tenths, plus five little squares, or hundredths. Later this process of dividing the one whole into four parts can be connected to the familiar long-division procedure.

Next, ask the students to shade one-eighth of the grid and to determine a name for 1/8 using decimal notation. The problem this time is that dividing 100 little squares into eight equal groups leaves many partial squares in each group. (See fig. 6.) Still, by combining half squares, the students are able to determine that 1/8 is about 12 1/2 little squares, or hundredths, or, by referring back to the cheese slicing, 1 tenth, 2 hundredths, and 5 thousandths, which is 125/1000, or 0.125. If children are asked if this answer makes sense in terms of their results for 1/4, they are usually able to conclude that 1/8 is half of 1/4—they often divide the fourths on the grid into two parts to create the eighths—and so 1/2 of 25 hundredths is 12 1/2 hundredths, which is 0.125.

Additional experiences with other common fractions enable the students to connect those common fractions meaningfully with their decimal equivalents. A good extension activity is finding decimal equivalents for common fractions that have equivalent decimals that repeat indefinitely. Dividing a 10-by-10 grid as was done for 1/4 and 1/8 gives students a good, intuitive idea why the decimal equivalent for 1/3 continues indefinitely. (See fig. 7.) The task of showing 1/3 on the 10-by-10 grid trans-

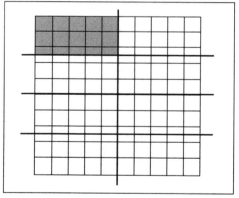

Fig. 6. Connecting 1/8 and 0.125

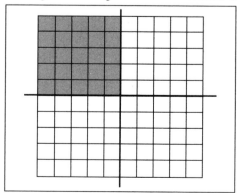

Fig. 5. Connecting 1/4 and 0.25

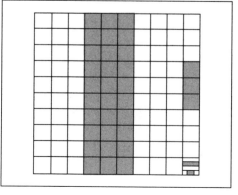

Fig. 7. Connecting 1/3 and 0.33$\overline{3}$

lates to dividing the grid into three equal parts. Since 10 strips (tenths) exist originally, 3 of them, since 3 tenths equal 0.3, belong in each group and 1 is left over. That leftover 1 tenth consists of 10 little squares, or hundredths, which can again be placed 3 in each group (3 hundredths equal 0.03, plus the 3 tenths makes 0.33) with 1 left over. The 1 hundredth left over consists of 10 tiny parts, or thousandths, which can again be placed 3 in each group (3 thousandths equal 0.003, plus the previous tenths and hundredths makes 0.333) with 1 left over. Theoretically, this process can continue indefinitely: one piece is always left over and is traded for 10 of the next smaller piece, which are shared 3 to each group; 1 of them is left over; and so on. In this way students obtain an intuitive feeling that 1/3 equals 0.333....

These connections are extremely important because they help students understand that fractions and decimals are just different symbols for representing the same quantity, the shaded part of a grid. This connection is extended in the next activity, which involves placing fractions and decimals on a number line.

Connecting Decimals and Fractions on Number Line

For students to understand decimals thoroughly, they need to have an understanding of the relative magnitudes of these numbers. That is, they should have a good idea of where decimal values lie on a number line in relation to other decimals. Furthermore, they need to know how the values of decimals compare with common fractions and whole numbers. They need to know, for example, that 0.48 is about 1/2 and is about halfway between 0 and 1. The following activity focuses on the creation of a number line to help students further develop these number relationships.

Begin by giving small groups of students three strips of adding-machine tape, each one meter long, and a meterstick marked in centimeters. Advise them that their task is to create on one of the strips a number line that extends from 0 at one end to 1 at the other end; is divided into hundredths; and has all halves, thirds, fourths, fifths, sixths, eighths, and tenths marked and labeled with numerals. The other two strips may be used by the students to assist them in creating their final product. (See fig. 8.)

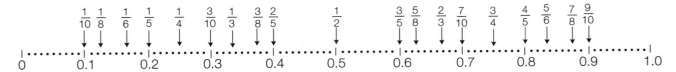

Fig. 8. Connecting common fractions and decimals

Students should be given as little or as much assistance as they need. For example, suggest that the students begin by drawing a line on one strip and marking the tenths and hundredths. They will readily notice that they can do so by using their meter-sticks. Next, suggest that they fold the other two strips, one to create halves, fourths, and eighths, the other to create thirds and sixths. (See fig. 9.) They will have little difficulty with the halves, fourths, and eighths but will probably need some guidance in making the thirds and sixths. Show them how to make thirds by looping over and sliding one end of the tape along the rest until it reaches the approximate midpoint of the remaining part of the tape. Hold the end at that midpoint while making a crease at the other end of the loop. (See fig. 9.) A little trial and error may be involved, but the process works well enough. These thirds can be folded in half to create the sixths. After the students have folded the strips to make the fractions requested, they can mark and label the fold lines and transfer these labels to the tape marked in hundredths by laying the tapes side by side.

In the process of making the number lines, the students find that many common fractions correspond exactly to decimals that are either tenths or hundredths. For example, have them explain why 1/2 is the same as 0.5 (0.5 equals 5/10, which means 5 out of 10 parts, which is 1/2) and why 3/4 is the same as 0.75 (0.75 is the same as 75/100, which is equivalent to the fraction 3/4, since 1/4 is 25/100, and 25/100 + 25/100 + 25/100 = 75/100).

After the students have finished their number lines, place the tapes end to end across one wall of the classroom. Presto, they have created a number line that extends from 0 to perhaps 10 and that is marked with common fractions and decimals to hundredths. The points at which the strips connect can be relabeled to read 0, 1, 2, . . ., 10. This extended number line can be used to help students think about fractions and decimals as mixed numbers.

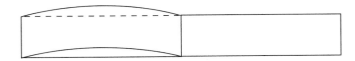

Fig. 2. Folding paper strips into thirds

For example, ask the students to find 4 1/6 on the number line and to rewrite 4 1/6 as a single fraction. The students can count the sixths or multiply 4 x 6, since 6 sixths are in each strip of paper, and determine the answer, 25/6. This process is very meaningful to the students in contrast with the abstract rule, "Multiply the whole number by the denominator of the fraction and add the numerator to the result." In a similar way, students could determine the number of tenths in the number 3.75. (Multiply 3 times 10, since 10 tenths are in each strip of paper, and add 7 tenths, since 7 tenths are in the 0.75 remaining.)

Another extremely valuable activity to complete with the number line connects any decimal with a nice, or common, fraction. Many students do not make these connections naturally, but this skill is necessary for working with decimals meaningfully. It is needed, for example, when finding ratios of body measurements, such as the ratio of foot length to body height. Students divide a foot length, say 27 centimeters, by a body height, say, 155 centimeters, and obtain 0.1742 as an approximate result. However, they usually do not know how to think of this number as a ratio. Working with the number line just created helps the students make a connection between 0.1742 and the common fraction 1/6. They can approximate 0.1742 as a little less than halfway between 0.17 and 0.18 and notice that 1/6 is approximately equal to 0.17. Hence, the ratio of foot length to body height is about 1 to 6.

The value of creating these number lines is that they help students develop an integrated network of number ideas. The students are enticed to connect fractions and decimals in a new way, on the number line, and this new connection helps them connect the values of these two different types of symbols. They are continuing to develop the ideas that although fractions and decimals are different symbol systems, they both represent part-whole relationships and that their values can be related and sometimes equated.

Conclusion

The instructional activities described herein help students connect decimal concepts with decimal symbols, with fraction concepts and fraction symbols, and with place-value concepts and place-value symbols. Extensive use is made of physical models, diagrams, and number lines. Students are asked to reason, communicate, solve problems, and connect ideas across a variety of mathematical content.

In doing these activities, students develop an understanding of decimals that is meaningful and rich, an understanding that is built with connections among a variety of mathematical ideas. Decimal concepts are remembered because they are part of a network of number ideas rather than isolated bits of information. For students, these decimal concepts have a broad range of applications because they are not tied to abstract rules or to a single physical model or diagram.

Bibliography

National Council of Teachers of Mathematics. *Curriculum and Evaluation Standards for School Mathematics.* Reston, Va.: The Council, 1989.

Van de Walle, John. *Elementary School Mathematics: Teaching Developmentally* White Plains, N.Y.: Longman, 1994.

7

Computation and Estimation

WITH the increased use of technology in our classes, estimation has become even more essential. As the lead article, "Redefining Computation" brings out very clearly, computation has been refined and broadened, and mental computation should be developed. This article includes a selection of activities for grades K–4 and 5–8 and spans mathematical content from number composition, basic facts, rational numbers, ratios, and proportions. "Lunch Munchers" and "Nutritious Nibble" incorporate concepts from nutrition into estimation, computation, and data reporting. This article also gives a good everyday application for mathematics. Earl Ockenga and Joan Duea's article,

"Estimate and Calculate", is one of the best treatments of whole-number estimation and calculation with the use of calculators that we have seen. "Estimating with 'Nice' Numbers" is identified for grades 7–12, but we think that it would be appropriate for younger children. The treatment of decimals is excellent.

Students' difficulties with fractions are well established, and improving students' abilities to estimate can help with computational problems. "Estimating with 'Nice' Fractions" offers one way to address this problem. Earl Ockenga again gives an excellent calculator activity for rational numbers in "Chalk Up Some Calculator Activities for Rational Numbers".

JOHN A. VAN DE WALLE

Redefining Computation

IMPLEMENTING THE *STANDARDS*

PENCIL-AND-PAPER computational skills have long dominated the elementary school curriculum. For over ten years we have been hearing that the emphasis on these skills must be reduced because in our technological society they are much less important than in previous times. Furthermore, a valid, frequently voiced argument suggests that the time spent on computation is the one "fat" area where cuts can be made to allow time for the many new concepts and higher-order processes that are more important.

Ironically, the *Curriculum and Evaluation Standards for School Mathematics (Standards)* (NCTM 1989) actually calls for a *broadening* of the treatment of computation in school mathematics, not a reduction. This notion of doing more and better with computation, not less, is directly on target for a mathematics curriculum of the l990s. It is also an expedient political view to take when advocating change. As Coburn (1989) points out, "reform will not come smoothly.... The public will be skeptical about any proposals for deemphasizing computation" (p. 43).

The K–4 standard on computation (see fig. 1) addresses only whole-number computation. The areas of estimation, number sense and numeration, and fractional and decimal concepts are dealt with in separate standards. These issues are so closely related, however, that they cannot be ignored when discussing computation, as is stressed in the standard on connections. The corresponding 5–8 standard (see fig. 1) is titled "Computation and Estimation" and includes computation with whole numbers, fractions, decimals, percents, proportions, and integers. This standard calls for

Prepared by John A. Van de Walle, *Virginia Commonwealth University, Richmond, VA 23284*

Edited by Thomas E. Rowan, *Montgomery County Public Schools, Rockville, MD 20850*

the inclusion of mental computation and estimation and the use of calculators and computers. The following statements represent a synthesis of the points that are made at both levels:

- Mastery of the basic facts for all operations is essential. Conceptually based thinking strategies should be used to help students master facts, relate them to each other, and apply them to other situations

- Computational-estimation techniques should be developed in a flexible atmosphere. The value of computational estimation, knowing when an estimate is appropriate, and the use of estimates in real-world situations should all be significant parts of the computation curriculum.

- Mental-computation techniques should be developed in a similarly flexible atmosphere as that for estimation. It should encourage flexibility and the use of a wide variety of student-invented procedures.

- Calculators should be a readily available method of computation for students at all levels just as they are for adults in the real world. Students should learn when the calculator is appropriate as a means of computation and should use estimates to be alert to easily made calculator errors.

- Computation with pencil and paper should still be taught. Students should be encouraged to use manipulatives to explain the rationale for each algorithm. The emphasis should be placed on the conceptual development of the algorithms. Problems should largely be limited to those that can be explored with models, with excessively tedious exercises eliminated. Drill to develop speed and efficiency is much less important than formerly thought.

- Students should explore the value of

The computation standards for grades K–4 and 5–8

STANDARD 8:
WHOLE NUMBER COMPUTATION

In grades K–4, the mathematics curriculum should develop whole number computation so that students can—

- model, explain, and develop reasonable proficiency with basic facts and algorithms;
- use a variety of mental computation and estimation techniques;
- use calculators in appropriate computational situations;
- select and use computation techniques appropriate to specific problems and determine whether the results are reasonable.

STANDARD 7:
COMPUTATION AND ESTIMATION

In grades 5–8, the mathematics curriculum should develop the concepts underlying computation and estimation in various contexts so that students can—

- compute with whole numbers, fractions, decimals, integers, and rational numbers;
- develop, analyze, and explain procedures for computation and techniques for estimation;
- develop, analyze, and explain methods for solving proportions;
- select and use an appropriate method for computing from among mental arithmetic, paper-and-pencil, calculator, and computer methods;
- use computation, estimation, and proportions to solve problems;
- use estimation to check the reasonableness of results.

From *Curriculum and Evaluation Standards for School Mathematics* (NCTM 1989)

Fig. 1

computers for appropriate applications, such as repetitious computations made on a long list of numbers or computations involving repeated applications of complex formulas. Spreadsheets lend themselves especially well to such computations and are well within the grasp of middle grade students.

The *Standards*'s vision of computation thus represents a broadening of the curriculum to include mental computation, computational estimation, and the use of technology. Such a broadened view also suggests that making appropriate choices of computational methods must be part of the curriculum (see fig. 2). If calculators are on students' desks every day from early grades onward, the choice of calculator versus mental computation, pencil and paper, or estimation is an everyday issue. Students will learn these choices by living with them.

For children to be actively engaged in developing alternative, efficient methods of computation requires an understanding of numbers, numeration systems, and meanings of operations. The explorations that build on these concepts will serve to strengthen them. "Premature expectations for students' mastery of computational procedures not only cause poor initial learning and poor retention but also require that large amounts of instructional time be spent on teaching and reteaching basic skills" (NCTM 1989, 46).

Activities for Grades K–4

Computation as broadly defined in the *Standards* can begin as early as kindergarten through activities that focus on numerical relationships and combinations of numbers.

Building numbers

Select a single number, for example, 8. Give students different materials with which to "build" 8 in two or three parts. They might use several colors of cubes to build rows of eight; use toothpicks, shells, or patterning blocks to build designs with eight elements; or find combinations for 8 from dot cards or ordinary playing cards. Have students say a two- or three-part number sentence to go with each design or combination (see fig. 3).

Basic facts

Much has been written about using thinking strategies to master basic facts, an approach clearly emphasized by the *Standards*. It is important to let the students develop these ideas by building on relationships that are meaningful to them. In figure 4, a ten-frame model for the problem 8 + 6 might lead to several different ways of thinking about this combination.

Incredible equations

In *Box It or Bag It Mathematics* (Burk, Snider, and Symonds 1988), students create "incredible equations" each day as ways to

express the day of the month. The open-ended atmosphere of the activity encourages students to search for more and more creative expressions, as shown in figure 5 (Howden 1989).

Inventing ways to add

Consider the sum 48 + 76. The four approaches illustrated in figure 6 could be explored in grades 1 to 3, each on different days. The idea is to use different stimuli to encourage the construction of alternative procedures and relationships. No one way is "right," and teachers do not need to stress or even show students the standard procedure.

a) Students make each number with base-ten materials in two piles. Usually the tens will be combined first, with assorted methods used to complete the sum.

b) Show coins for the two amounts on the overhead projector or draw them on the chalkboard.

c) Tape two metersticks end to end on the chalkboard to create a number line for the numbers 0 to 200. If you start with 48 will you use a different strategy than if you begin with 76? How are these methods like the coins or different from using the base-ten models?

d) Write the two numbers on the chalkboard in the usual manner for computation and let students use and explain

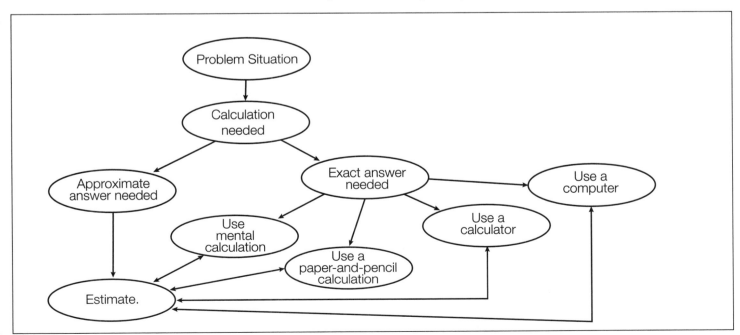

Fig. 2. Choosing appropriate computational methods (from *Curriculum and Evaluation Standards for School Mathematics* (NCTM 1989, 9))

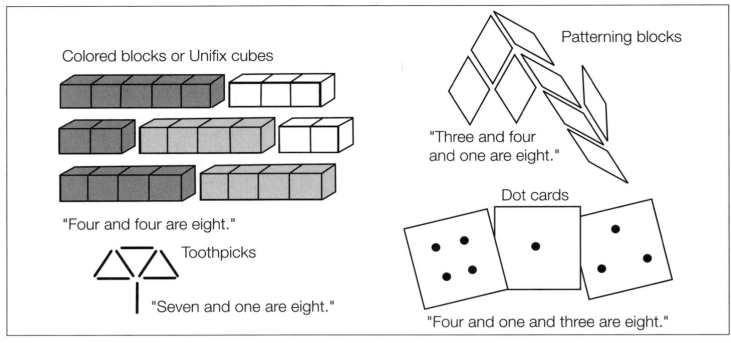

"Colored blocks or Unifix cubes"

"Four and four are eight."

Patterning blocks

"Three and four and one are eight."

Toothpicks

"Seven and one are eight."

Dot cards

"Four and one and three are eight."

Fig. 3. Part-part-whole activities for eight

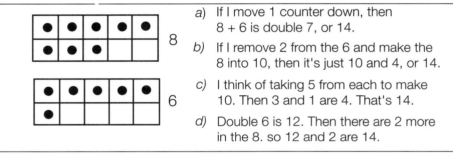

a) If I move 1 counter down, then 8 + 6 is double 7, or 14.

b) If I remove 2 from the 6 and make the 8 into 10, then it's just 10 and 4, or 14.

c) I think of taking 5 from each to make 10. Then 3 and 1 are 4. That's 14.

d) Double 6 is 12. Then there are 2 more in the 8. so 12 and 2 are 14.

Fig. 4. Flexible thinking about basic facts

whatever methods they want to get the sum but have them compute the sum mentally. This approach is especially appropriate for students who have not been taught the standard pencil-and-paper procedure.

These same approaches can be used for subtraction, for such products as 73×5 (illustrate only the 73 with coins, base-ten pieces, or on the number line), and for

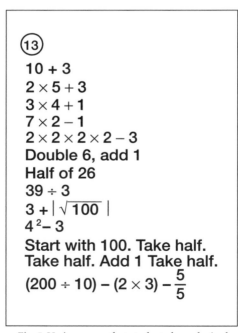

⑬

10 + 3

$2 \times 5 + 3$

$3 \times 4 + 1$

$7 \times 2 - 1$

$2 \times 2 \times 2 \times 2 - 3$

Double 6, add 1

Half of 26

$39 \div 3$

$3 + |\sqrt{100}|$

$4^2 - 3$

Start with 100. Take half. Take half. Add 1 Take half.

$(200 \div 10) - (2 \times 3) - \dfrac{5}{5}$

Fig. 5. Various ways that students have devised to express the number 13 (from Howden (1989))

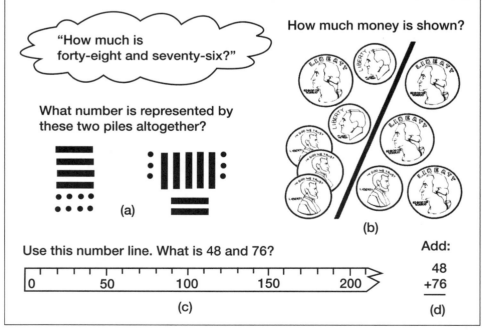

"How much is forty-eight and seventy-six?"

How much money is shown?

What number is represented by these two piles altogether?

(a)

(b)

Use this number line. What is 48 and 76?

(c)

Add:

48
+76

(d)

Fig. 6. Different stimuli tend to cause different thought patterns.

division by a number less than 10 (again, model only the dividend).

The actual numbers in exercises such as these can be adjusted for different grade levels. For example, second-grade students can learn to add a one-digit number to a two- or three-digit number mentally through similar activities.

Quick estimates

Since young students have difficulty with the concept of an estimated computation, one idea is to ask them to judge if a computation is more or less than a given number. This approach initially avoids the need to come up with a specific estimate and can later lead to discussions of different specific estimates and how students arrived at them. For example, is 482 + 129 + 68 more or less than 800? More or less than 600? A similar but more challenging task is to place the estimated computation in one of several intervals. For example, is 29 × 6 less than 200, between 200 and 300, or more than 300? The targets or intervals can be written on the chalkboard and a short series of computations prepared for the same choices.

Activities for Grades 5–8

The authors of the 5–8 standard on computation and estimation note that "computation, estimation, or methods of solving proportions should not be considered or taught as ends in themselves ... [but] should be integrated with the study of the concepts underlying fractions, decimals, integers, and rational numbers" (p. 94). The following activities are intended to illustrate this aspect of the *Standards*.

Fraction products

Challenge students to do a computation before they are taught the usual algorithm. For example, have students use drawings or materials to explain how to find 3/4 of 1 2/3. Suggest that a square might be a good model for one whole. Allow students to work in pairs or small groups and put the emphasis on developing a good explanation. As shown in figure 7, not all explanations will be the same.

Percentages as fractions

If such simple fractions as halves, thirds, fourths, fifths, and eighths are connected

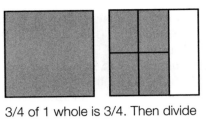
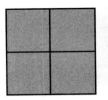
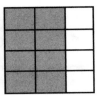

3/4 of 1 whole is 3/4. Then divide the 2/3 into 4 parts. Those parts are sixths of the whole, so we have 3/4 and 3/6, or 3/4 and 1/2.

$$\frac{1}{2} + \frac{1}{4} + \frac{1}{2} = 1\frac{1}{4}$$

You get 3/4 of 1; then 3/4 of each of the thirds pieces is 3/12 of each piece. That's 6/12, or 1/2. And 3/4 plus 1/2 is 1 1/4.

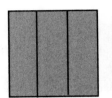
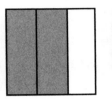

We figured that 1 2/3 was 5/3. So we divided each thirds piece into 4 small pieces and took 3 of them from each. That makes 15 pieces in alll. then we figured that there are 12 little pieces in one whole square. So that means the little pieces are twelfths—15/12.

Fig. 7. Students think of 3/4 of 1 2/3 in different ways

with decimal and percentage concepts, the same mental methods can be used to work in each of these domains.

Students can use line segments or Cuisenaire rods to explore problems like those shown in figure 8. These same techniques can then be used to solve such problems as the following:

STEREO
20% OFF
You pay only
$360

What was the original price of the stereo?

Figure 9 illustrates a solution.

Similarly, in the following problem, an estimate can be made by using a "close" percentage with a useful fractional equivalent.

The treasurer reported that 68.3% of the dues had been collected for a total of $385. How much more money could the club expect to collect if all the dues are paid?

Here the numbers are not "nice." But if students recognize that 68.3 percent is close to 2/3 (about 67%), then the $385 is 2/3. If

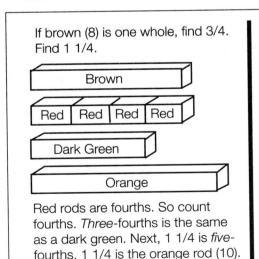

If brown (8) is one whole, find 3/4. Find 1 1/4.

Red rods are fourths. So count fourths. *Three*-fourths is the same as a dark green. Next, 1 1/4 is *five*-fourths. 1 1/4 is the orange rod (10).

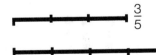

Draw a line segment. Call it 3/5. Then draw another line segment that's as long as one whole.

First, divide the line into 3 parts. Since this is 3/5, each part is 1/5 (one-fifth, two-fifths, three-fifths).

Then count on two more fifths to make a whole.

Fig. 8. Students explain their strategies for finding solutions to problems involving fraction concepts.

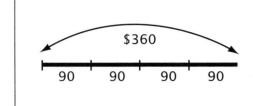

20% is *one*-fifth, so the $360 is the other *four*-fifths. Divide the $360 into four parts—$90 in each part. Then *one*-fifth is $90, and so one more fifth would be the whole. Thus $90 + $360 = $450.

Fig. 9. A student explains the use of fraction concepts to solve percentage problems.

$385 is *two*-thirds, then about $190 (half of $380) is *one*-third, which is a bit less than the additional amount the club can expect. Students should still be asked to sketch a simple fraction model, such as a line segment or a square, to justify their reasoning.

Solving proportions

The tasks in figure 10 require students to use counters or strips to determine the missing parts so that the ratios in each pair are the same. Notice that in figures 10a and 10c a unit ratio is easily seen *within* the first of two pairs. (Both are in a 1-to-3 ratio.) This ratio can then be used to find the long rod or the number of dark counters in the second pair of each example. In figures 10b and 10d, the unit ratio is not obvious because that ratio is not a whole number. However, if comparisons are made *between* corresponding parts of the two pairs, a whole-number common factor can be used to determine the missing part.

Problems such as these can be posed with line segments, Cuisenaire rods, bars of Unifix cubes, or sets of counters in two colors. The solution methods should come from groups of students as they develop and share with others their own procedures.

Next consider the following two problems:

Tamara bought 3 widgets for $2.40. At the same price, how much would 10 widgets cost?

Tamara bought 4 widgets for $3.75. At the same price, how much would a dozen widgets cost?

Ask students to draw pictures to explain their solutions. In the first of these problems, the unit ratio (within) is easy to figure out mentally ($0.80 per widget). In the second, the common factor (between) is easier to use (one dozen is 3 times as many).

The point is that students can reason proportionally and solve proportions without setting up equations and using a cross-product approach. The word problems are preceded by similar tasks involving models. Then the numbers in the problems are selected so that the same types of

reasoning can be used but without tedious computation. Later, students can use these explorations as a basis on which to build solutions to problems that do not work out as nicely. Consider the following example:

Apples are 3 pounds for $0.79. How much would you pay for 5 pounds?

A reasonable method of attacking this problem is to estimate by rounding $0.79 to $0.75 to get a unit ratio of $0.25, giving the answer of a little more than $1.25, or maybe $1.30. However, if students wanted an exact result, several equivalent proportions can be established using the same thinking that was used earlier. The *between* ratios are 3/5 and 79/x. Alternatively, the *within* ratios are 3/79 and 5/x. Equating either pair of ratios yields the same solution.

Conclusion

Yes, the *Standards* calls for more computation than ever before. But the tedious, drill-oriented, rule-driven, pencil-and-paper emphasis should be substantially decreased. Instead, computation in the world of technology has many facets. It is intricately tied to conceptual understanding of numbers and operations. It is flexible, having many different forms and even different procedures within these forms. This broadened view of computation offers new challenges and new excitement for an interactive, dynamic approach to teaching, learning, and students' empowerment.

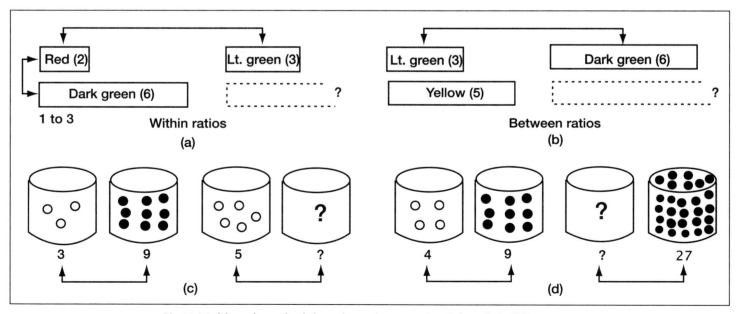

Fig. 10. Models can be used to help students solve proportions informally in different ways.

References

Burk, Donna, Allyn Snider, and Paula Symonds. *Box It or Bag It Mathematics.* Salem, Oreg.: Math Learning Center, 1988.

Coburn, Terrence E. "The Role of Computation in the Changing Mathematics Curriculum." In *New Directions for Elementary School Mathematics,* 1989 Yearbook of the National Council of Teachers of Mathematics, edited by Paul R. Trafton and Albert P. Shulte, 43–56. Reston, Va.: The Council, 1989.

Howden, Hilde. "Teaching Number Sense." *Arithmetic Teacher* 36 (February 1989):6–11.

National Council of Teachers of Mathematics, Commission on Standards for School Mathematics. *Curriculum and Evaluation Standards for School Mathematics.* Reston, Va.: The Council, 1989.

DIXIE METHENY AND JULIA HOLLOWELL

Lunch Munchers
and
Nutritious Nibbles

THE "Investigations" department is designed for teachers who wish to give students new insights into familiar topics in grades pre-K–6. It includes both directed and open-ended activities. A basic assumption is that the teacher will facilitate the investigation so as to let students be actively involved in shaping their learning.

This month's investigation uses the theme of school-lunch menus and healthful eating habits to reinforce making predictions using computational skills. Students should have the opportunity to gather data about their own eating habits and compare that information with the new dietary guidelines published in the food pyramid. Students will compute the total number of calories in the lunch menus and compare the types of food served with those recommendations. Students should practice making wise decisions about the food they eat and how it contributes to a healthful lifestyle. Through these activities, students will learn about nutrition, think about the various foods they eat, and discuss the effects these foods have on their well-being and growth. Students in the lower grades can compute total calories and compare the types and amounts of foods they eat with the recommendations in the pyramid. Students in the upper grades can calculate

the percent of daily required calories from their lunches. They can also practice making and defending food choices selected from a restaurant menu. Parents can help students keep food records and offer samples of ethnic dishes in a special food-tasting activity that students plan to reflect healthful choices. Community representatives from the health, nutrition, and food-service fields could make presentations to the class about healthful eating when planning meals at home or eating out.

LEVELS 3 AND 4
Lunch Munchers
Student Activity Goals

- Students will estimate, then compute, the number of calories represented each day in the school-lunch menu.

- Students will keep a food record for a week, compare the amount and types of food they eat with the amount of food recommended on the food pyramid, and compute their total caloric intake for the week.

- Students will draw a bar graph representing the kinds and amount of foods they have eaten.

- Students will classify the foods on the school-lunch menu by group according to the food pyramid and decide if the menus represent healthful choices.

Planning for Instruction

Ask students to keep a food record for a week before beginning this activity. Teachers should also have copies of school-lunch menus available for student use. If menus are not available, students

could collect data on what they eat for lunch, both at school and at home. If breakfast and after-school snacks are available, students can also use these menus for the activities. Students can review one school day's menus as they relate to the food pyramid. Begin the series of activities by discussing the food pyramid and relating it to a healthful diet. Also, discuss the calorie content of food and how the body gets its energy from calories. The school nurse, cafeteria manager, or other community-health or nutrition experts could talk to the class about making healthful food choices.

Ask such questions as these:

1. Is each daily lunch menu balanced according to the food pyramid? Explain how you made your decision.

2. At a glance, which day's menu would give you the most energy? How could you decide if your hunch is correct?

3. Estimate the number of calories in each daily lunch menu. Using the chart, compute the actual number of calories in each menu.

4. Which menu contains the most calories? The least calories?

5. What is the average number of calories in a lunch menu?

6. If you ate the school lunch, how many of the food groups are represented each day? Would these lunches be healthful choices? Support your answer.

7. A person your age needs about 2100 calories per day. How many more do you need each day if you eat the school lunch?

8. Who could you ask to find out how much it costs to prepare each day's lunch?

Prepared by Dixie Metheny *and* Julia Hollowell. *Dixie Metheny is an assistant professor of mathematics education at Montana State University— Billings. Her special area of interest is real-life mathematics activities for children. Julia Hollowell is an elementary teacher who works with Hysham Public Schools, a school district in eastern Montana.*

Edited by Patricia Lamphere, *University of Montana, Missoula, MT 59812-2306*

9. Which costs more, a lunch prepared at home or a lunch prepared at school? Explain how you determined your answer.

10. Keep a record of your own school's lunch menu for a week. Where can you find a calorie chart? Decide if your own school menus are balanced by looking at the food pyramid. Compute the total calories for each meal.

11. Ask someone who brings a lunch from home to keep a record for a week.

Compare it with the school menu in terms of balance and calorie intake.

12. Keep a record for a week of all the food you eat at breakfast, lunch, dinner, and snacks. Compute the total number of calories for the week and place each item in its proper place on the food pyramid. Display the data you have collected and write a paragraph to describe how your choices reflect the recommendations from the food pyramid.

Calorie Chart for School Lunch Items

Dairy products
  Low-fat milk, 90
  Ice cream, 130
  Sour cream, 31

Meats/seafood
  Turkey with gravy, 150
  Spaghetti with meat sauce, 260
  Salmon loaf, 194
  Super nachos with meat and
    cheese sauce, 520
  Spanish rice with meat, 425

Breads/desserts
  Dinner roll, 120
  Garlic bread, 125
  Chocolate cake, 235

Vegetables
  Tossed salad, 30
  Peas and carrots, 48
  Whipped potatoes, 65
  Green beans, 15
  Olives, 20

Fruits
  Apple slices, 80
  Banana, 105
  Orange wedges, 62

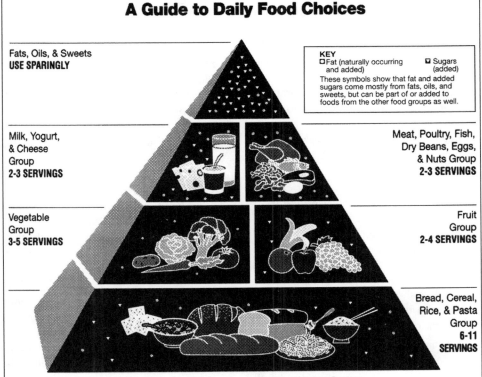

FOOD PYRAMID

A Guide to Daily Food Choices

Fats, Oils, & Sweets
USE SPARINGLY

KEY
☐ Fat (naturally occurring and added)   ☑ Sugars (added)
These symbols show that fat and added sugars come mostly from fats, oils, and sweets, but can be part of or added to foods from the other food groups as well.

Milk, Yogurt, & Cheese Group
2-3 SERVINGS

Meat, Poultry, Fish, Dry Beans, Eggs, & Nuts Group
2-3 SERVINGS

Vegetable Group
3-5 SERVINGS

Fruit Group
2-4 SERVINGS

Bread, Cereal, Rice, & Pasta Group
6-11 SERVINGS

Source: U.S. Department of Agriculture/U.S. Department of Health and Human Services

Use the Food Guide Pyramid to help you eat better every day ... the Dietary Guidelines way. Start with plenty of Breads, Cereals, Rice, and Pasta; Vegetables; and Fruits. Add two to three servings from the Milk group and two to three servings from the Meat group.

Each of these food groups provides some, but not all, of the nutrients you need. No one food group is more important than another—for good health you need them all. Go easy on fats, oils, and sweets, the foods in the small tip of the Pyramid.

School Lunch Menus

Day 1
  Turkey and gravy
  Whipped potatoes
  Dinner roll
  Orange wedges
  Low-fat milk

Day 2
  Spaghetti with meat sauce
  Tossed salad
  Banana
  Garlic bread
  Low-fat milk

Day 3
  Spanish rice with meat
  Green beans
  Apple slices
  Chocolate cake
  Low-fat milk

Day 4
  Super nachos with meat and cheese sauce
  Olives
  Sour cream
  Apple slices
  Low-fat milk

Day 5
  Salmon loaf
  Peas and carrots
  Banana
  Ice cream
  Low-fat milk

Personal Food Diary

Food	Food Group from Pyramid	Number of Servings	Calories per Serving	Total Calories

Nutritious Nibbles

Student Activity Goals

- Students will estimate, then compute, the number of calories in Andy's food record and their own daily or weekly food record.

- Students will use circle graphs to display the percents from each food group, according to a food pyramid, in Andy's record and in their own daily or weekly food records.

- Students will determine the percent of the daily caloric requirements they eat at lunch.

- Students will determine the nutritional value of the meals in the school-lunch menu for a week on the basis of a food pyramid.

- Students will select healthful meals on the basis of a food pyramid using the sample menu and then compute the cost of each meal.

Planning for Instruction

Teachers should provide copies of (a) the local school-lunch menus available for the students and (b) a food pyramid—the one on "Lunch Munchers" can be used. Students will also keep a record for both their daily and weekly intake of food. Using their food records, students can determine what percent of each food group from the food pyramid they have consumed. Students will use their own food record to decide whether they are making healthful food choices. Using the sample restaurant menu, students can order healthful meals and determine the cost of their orders.

Families can become involved by helping students keep their food records and allowing students to plan and prepare the food for the family. When drawing circle graphs, give students templates for 10, 25, 33 1/3, 50, and 75 percent. Students may estimate, to the nearest 10 percent, to make their graphs easier to draw.

Ask such questions as these:

1. Estimate the number of calories in Andy's one-day record. How many total calories are in his food record? If he is fourteen years old, did he eat the recommended number of calories?

2. Check his food intake. Is it balanced? Did he meet the minimum daily requirements as suggested by the food pyramid? What additional foods could he eat to meet the suggested nutritional guidelines?

3. Use calorie charts from the library or other sources to estimate the number of calories you eat during the average day. Keep a food record for a week of all the food you eat at breakfast, lunch, dinner, and snacks.

4. Compute the total number of calories for the week and place each item in its proper place on the food pyramid. Display the data you have collected and write a paragraph to describe how your choices reflect the recommendations made in the food pyramid. Use a circle graph to show the percents of each food group you eat on a typical day or for the entire week.

5. Estimate the percent of calories you eat from each food group. Then compute the total number of calories on each of your daily menus from each food group. Represent the percents with a circle graph.

6. Record your school-lunch menus for a week. Using calorie charts from the library or other resources, compute the total number of calories in each day's menu. Then compute the percent of calories for each of the food groups. Write a paragraph describing whether the week's menu represents a healthful choice.

7. Design a menu for a day that contains the recommended number of calories for a student your age and contains the appropriate number of servings and calories for each food group.

8. Help plan a week's menu to feed your family. Display the types and amounts of food to be eaten. If possible, compute the total number of calories for each day's meals and the total for the week.

9. Use a sample restaurant menu and plan a week's lunches, following the recommendations from the food pyramid. Plan a balanced menu and determine the cost of each menu. Compare the costs of the various meals. Does a relationship exist between the choice of healthful foods and their cost? Explain your answer.

10. Collect menus from local restaurants. What choices from the menu would be considered healthful? Do any of the restaurants serve healthful meals? How are meals determined to be healthful? On the basis of these menus, plan a meal that reflects balanced choices and healthful eating habits.

11. Look at the food pyramid. Is the food pyramid really a *pyramid*? Why do you think the government chose to represent the data this way? Do you think that the number of servings for each food group is represented proportionally in the chart? In what other ways might the data be represented to show the relationship among the food groups? Sketch and explain your design.

Nutritious Nibbles

Calories per Day

Children,
ages 7 to 10:
2000 calories

Females,
ages 11 to 14:
2200 calories

Males,
ages 11 to 14:
2500 calories

Andy's Food Record for One Day

Breakfast
2 c. cereal (240 calories)
1 1/2 c. milk (225 calories)
Half a banana (51 calories)

Lunch
Egg-salad sandwich
    (1 egg, 2 slices of bread,
    1 tbs. mayonnaise)
    (230 calories)
1/2 c. applesauce (53 calories)
1 c. milk (150 calories)
1 oz. potato chips (106 calories)

Snack
1 oz. cheese (114 calories)
1 oz. crackers (120 calories)
8 oz. yogurt (180 calories)

Dinner
1 serving lasagna (330 calories)
1 c. milk (150 calories)
1/2 pear (45 calories)
1/2 c. ice cream (231 calories)

Darlene's Delectable and Delicious Dining Treats
Build Your Own Sandwich
One meat, one cheese $3.75
Two meats, one cheese $4.50

Meat
Corned beef
Roast beef
Lean ham
Pastrami
Salami
Roast turkey
Smoked turkey
Zesty meatball
Egg salad

Cheese
Cheddar
Monterey jack
Provolone
Swiss
Muenster
Pepper jack
Smoked sharp cheddar
Parmesan
Cream cheese

Bread
Multigrain
Light rye
Sourdough roll
Sub roll
French roll
Pita pocket
Bagel
English muffin

Garnishes
Lettuce, tomato, onion, bean sprouts, cucumber, mayonnaise, mustard, horseradish

Extras
Avocado 50¢, bacon 35¢, cheese 50¢, hot green chiles 40¢

Soups/stews
(cup $1.25, bowl $2.50)
Hearty beef stew
Chicken-noodle soup
Chili
Bean stew
Vegetable soup

Salads
Spinach $3.50
Caesar $3.75
Tuna $4.00
Mixed garden $3.25
Pasta $3.25

Desserts
Rum cake $1.25
Brownie 75¢ each
Chocolate-chip cookie 35¢ each
Frozen yogurt 95¢/scoop
Ice cream $1.55

EARL OCKENGA AND JOAN DUEA

Estimate and Calculate

Teacher's Guide

Introduction: An Agenda for Action (NCTM 1980) states that calculators should be available for appropriate use in *all* mathematics classrooms. The *Agenda* also recommends that calculators be used in imaginative ways for exploring, discovering, and developing mathematical concepts and skills. The activities that follow suggest ways that calculators can free students from computational restrictions and allow them to focus on the recognition of patterns and the application of numeration concepts in the development of their estimation skills.

Grade levels: 7–10

Materials: Calculators and a set of worksheets for each student

Objectives: To develop skills in estimating products, quotients, and percentages and in using a calculator to check estimates

Directions: Provide calculators for students who do not have their own. Distribute copies of the activity sheets one at a time to the students. After students have studied the example on a given worksheet and have made attempts at obtaining a better offscore, summarize for the class estimation strategies that you observed being used and perhaps identify other strategies that could have been used. The identification of the best total off-scores for the class and further discussion of associated estimation strategies should follow the completion of each sheet.

Sheet 1: Discuss the directions given at the top of the sheet. Have the students study the example. Then challenge them to see if they can arrange the digits 4 through

Prepared by Earl Ockenga *and* Joan Duea , *Price Laboratory School, Cedar Falls, IA 50613*
Edited by Christian R. Hirsch, *Western Michigan University, Kalamazoo, M1 49008*

9 in the example to get an off-score that is less than 785 ($9 \times 7845 = 70\,605$, which has an off-score of 605).

As you observe students, you will find them using various strategies. Some students may use multiples of 1000 to estimate the product. For example, in round 1, they may think $6 \times 8\,000 = 48\,000$, so 6×8745 should give a product close to the target number of 50 000. Computing the product on a calculator, they would get 52 470, resulting in an off-score of 2470. To improve on this off-score, their second estimate may be 6×8574, giving a product of 51 444. A third estimate may be 6×8457, resulting in an off-score of 742.

Other students may use the strategy of working backward to find the two factors. In round 1, they would think $50\,000 \div 5 = 10\,000$, so 5×9876 should be close to the target number.

Sheet 2: Discuss the directions. Have the students study the example, then challenge them to arrange the digits 4 through 9 in the example to get an off-score that is less than 3 ($798 \div 4 = 199.5$, which has a rounded off-score of 0).

One strategy that students might find appropriate in this setting would entail use of multiples of 100 or 1000 to estimate the quotients. For example, in round 1 a student may think $500 \div 5 = 100$, so $498 \div 5$ should give a quotient close to the target number. Computing the quotient on a calculator, they would get 99.6, resulting in a rounded off-score of 0.

The working-backward strategy works well for finding dividends and divisors, too. In round 1, some students may think 100 x $9 = 900$, so $897 \div 9$ should be close to the target number.

Sheet 3: Discuss the directions. Depending on the background of your students, you may also need to discuss the use of the % key on their calculators. For students whose calculators do not have a %

key, you will need to discuss the use of decimal representations of percentages. Have students study the example, then challenge them to arrange the digits in the example to get an off-score that is less than 7 (51% of 784 = 399.84, which has a rounded off-score of 0).

In estimating percentages of a number, students may use easy percentages such as 10 percent, 25 percent, or 50 percent. For example, in round 1 they may think 50 percent of $400 = 200$, so 49 percent of 387 should give an answer close to the target number. Computing the percentage of the number on a calculator, they would get 189.63, resulting in a rounded off-score of 10. To improve on this off-score, a second estimate may be 51 percent of 398, giving an answer of 202.98. A third estimate may be 51 percent of 392, resulting in an off-score of 0.

Additional calculator-enhanced estimation activities can be found in Miller (1981) and in Goodman (1982).

References

Goodman, Terry. "Calculators and Estimation." *Mathematics Teacher* 75 (February 1982): 137–40, 182.

Miller, William A. "Calculator Tic-Tac-Toe: A Game of Estimation." *Mathematics Teacher* 74 (December 1981): 713–16, 724.

National Council of Teachers of Mathematics. *An Agenda for Action: Recommendations for School Mathematics of the 1980s.* Reston, Va.: The Council, 1980.

Estimating Products

For each round, make three attempts, as follows:

- Place the digits 4, 5, 6, 7, 8, or 9 in the boxes to get an answer close to the target number. A digit may be used only once in each try.
- Multiply.
- Subtract to find how far your answer is from the target number. Write your "off-scores" on a separate sheet of paper.
- Record your best off-score in the column at the right.

Example. Target number: 70 000

$$\boxed{9} \times \boxed{7}\,\boxed{8}\,\boxed{6}\,\boxed{5} = \underline{70\ 785}$$

70 785 − 70 000

Off-score: __785__

Round 1. Target number: 50 000

$$\square \times \square\,\square\,\square\,\square = \underline{\hspace{2cm}}$$

Best off-score: _____

Round 2. Target number: 40 000

$$\square \times \square\,\square\,\square = \underline{\hspace{2cm}}$$

Best off-score: _____

Round 3. Target number: 80 000

$$\square \times \square\,\square\,\square = \underline{\hspace{2cm}}$$

Best off-score: _____

Round 4. Target number: 60 000

$$\square \times \square\,\square\,\square = \underline{\hspace{2cm}}$$

Best off-score: _____

Round 5. Target number: 40 000

$$\square\,\square \times \square\,\square\,\square = \underline{\hspace{2cm}}$$

Best off-score: _____

Round 6. Target number: 70 000

$$\square\,\square \times \square\,\square\,\square = \underline{\hspace{2cm}}$$

Best off-score: _____

Total: _____

Rate yourself:

Total off-score less than 8000 . . . . . . .Super estimator

8001 to 10 000 . . . . .Excellent

10 001 to 15 000 . . . . .Good

More than 15 000 . . . . .Need practice

Estimating Quotients

For each round, make three attempts, as follows:

- Place the digits 4, 5, 6, 7, 8, or 9 in the boxes to get an answer close to the target number. A digit may be used only once in each attempt.
- Divide and then round your quotient to the nearest whole number.
- Subtract to find how far your answer is from the target number. Write your off-scores on a separate sheet of paper.
- Record your best off-score in the column at the right.

Example. Target number: 200

$$\boxed{9}\boxed{8}\boxed{7} \div \boxed{5} \approx \underline{197}$$

Round 1. Target number: 100

$$\square\square\square \div \square \approx \underline{\quad}$$

Round 2. Target number: 50

$$\square\square\square \div \square \approx \underline{\quad}$$

Round 3. Target number: 250

$$\square\square\square \div \square \approx \underline{\quad}$$

Round 4. Target number: 800

$$\square\square\square\square \div \square \approx \underline{\quad}$$

Round 5. Target number: 1000

$$\square\square\square\square \div \square \approx \underline{\quad}$$

Round 6. Target number: 200

$$\square\square\square\square \div \square\square \approx \underline{\quad}$$

Rate yourself:
Total off-score less than 40 . . .Super estimator
41 to 60 . . . . .Excellent
61 to 100 . . . . .Good
More than 100 . . . . .Need practice

200 − 147

Off-score: ___ 3

Best off-score: _____

Best off-score: _____

Best off-score: _____

Best off-score: _____

Best off-score: _____

Best off-score: _____

Total: _____

Estimating Percentages

For each round, make three attempts, follows:

- Place the digits 1, 2, 3, 4, 5, 6, 7, 8, or 9 in the boxes to get an answer close to the target number. A digit may be used only once in each try.
- Find the percentage of the number and then round the result to the nearest whole number.
- Subtract to find how far your answer is from the target number. Write your three off-scores on a separate sheet of paper.
- Record your best off-score in the column at the right.

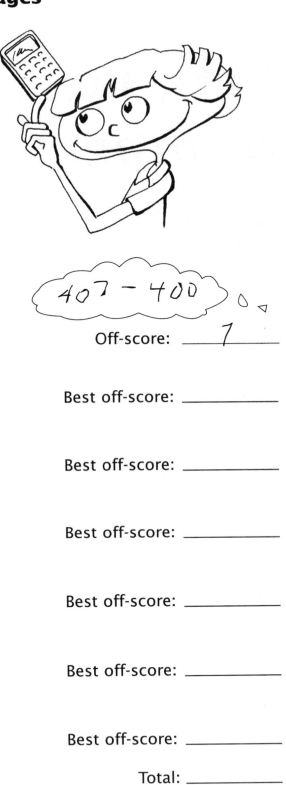

$$\boxed{407 - 400}$$

Off-score: __1__

Example. Target number : 400

$\boxed{5}\boxed{1}$ % of $\boxed{7}\boxed{9}\boxed{8}$ ≈ __407__

Round 1. Target number: 200

$\square\square$ % of $\square\square\square$ ≈ _____

Best off-score: _____

Round 2. Target number: 100

$\square\square$ % of $\square\square\square$ ≈ _____

Best off-score: _____

Round 3. Target number: 500

$\square\square$ % of $\square\square\square$ ≈ _____

Best off-score: _____

Round 4. Target number: 300

$\square\square$ % of $\square\square\square$ ≈ _____

Best off-score: _____

Round 5. Target number: 100

$\square$ % of $\square\square\square\square$ ≈ _____

Best off-score: _____

Round 6. Target number: 50

$\square\square\square$ % of $\square\square$ ≈ _____

Best off-score: _____

Total: _____

Rate yourself:

Total off-score less than 60 . .Super estimator
61 to 80 . . . . .Excellent
81 to 100 . . . . .Good
More than 100 . . . . .Need practice

ROBERT E. REYS, BARBARA J. REYS, PAUL R. TRAFTON, AND JUDY ZAWOJEWSKI

Estimating with "Nice" Numbers

Teacher's Guide

Introduction: Computational estimation is a very important and useful skill. Its value rests on producing reasonable answers to computations, sometimes very messy computations, quickly. Since *An Agenda for Action*'s call for an increased emphasis in mathematics programs on mentally estimating results of calculations (NCTM 1980, 3), many powerful and useful estimation techniques have been identified (cf. Reys and Reys 1983; Reys et al. 1984; Schoen forthcoming).

This month's activity is derived from a lesson originally created for the National Science Foundation project "Developing Computational Estimation in the Middle Grades." It introduces one effective strategy, which we call the "nice" numbers estimation strategy. "Nice" numbers, as used here, are those numbers that allow mental computation to be performed quickly and easily. The nice numbers considered here are powers of ten (e.g., 1, 10, 100).

This activity is designed to be initiated through a teacher-directed lesson developed through overhead transparencies. The transparencies highlight the concept of nice numbers and show how they can be used to obtain estimates quickly. Examples for students to try under your direction are included on each transparency. The student worksheets offer opportunities for additional practice,

along with real-world applications of estimation; these sheets should be started in class and completed as homework. As time permits, a discussion of selected exercises on the following day will promote thinking about estimation and awareness of some different ways of obtaining reasonable estimates.

Grade levels: 7–12

Materials: Calculator (preferably one modified for overhead-projection use), transparencies of sheets 1–3, and a set of worksheets (sheets 4 and 5) for each student, to be used after the transparencies have been discussed

Objective: To develop estimating skills when multiplying or dividing by numbers near a power of ten

Procedure: Prior to using this activity, review with the class multiplication and division by powers of ten. The nice-numbers strategy encourages rounding to nice numbers (e.g., $1.03 \doteq 1$; $9.93 \doteq 10$) and then performing the operations indicated. After these operations are performed, the estimate is adjusted. The following example illustrates the entire process:

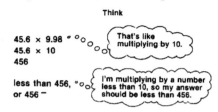

The first transparency (sheet 1) provides some examples of nice numbers. Mention that many numbers occur near nice numbers, but the acceptable range for near-nice numbers is generally determined by the

context of the problem in real-life situations. For this activity, numbers near 10 will generally be between 9 and 11, whereas numbers near 100 will be between 90 and 110. As you work through this transparency with the class, encourage students to add other nice numbers to the list. Use the bottom portion of the transparency to have students select the numbers that are near nice numbers and state which nice numbers they are near.

Use a transparency of sheet 2 to begin collecting and recording estimates for such exercises as 23 × 0.97. Ask for estimates of the product from several students. These estimates should be recorded. Encourage students to think of 0.97 as "a little less than 1." For example:

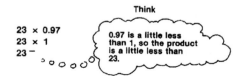

Estimate: "A little less than 23, I'll say 22."

After some estimates have been recorded and discussed, the exact answer can be found using a calculator.

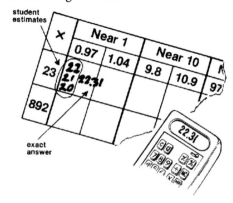

Prepared by Robert E. Reys, *University of Missouri—Columbia;* Barbara J. Reys, *Oakland Junior High School, Columbia, Missouri;* Paul R. Trafton, *National College of Education, Evanston, Illinois; and* Judy Zawojewski, *National College of Education, Evanston, Illinois*

Edited by Christian R. Hirsch, *Western Michigan University, Kalamazoo, Michigan*

Continue in this manner, estimating 892 × 0.97. Repeat this process with several other numbers near nice numbers (e.g., 1.04, 9.8, 10.9, 97.2, 103.0). Pick and choose items from the chart as you wish. Most students will *not* need to complete the whole chart before going on.

Students should be encouraged to seek a pattern and verbalize it when observed. In general, the pattern might be described as follows:

Given a number near *n*, where *n* is a power of ten, the product of this number and any other number is found by multiplying by *n* and then adding or subtracting an adjustment (compensation) determined by whether the given number was greater than or less than *n*.

Compensation—adding or subtracting the adjustment—is a complex process. Students need to realize that exactness is not the objective. The emphasis is on determining whether the exact answer will be more or less than the initial estimate.

Use the same process for division by near-nice numbers. Help students notice that the pattern is now reversed. When dividing by a number greater than *n*, the adjustment is subtracted. When dividing by a number less than *n*, the adjustment is added. This concept is more complex and usually requires plenty of discussion. For example:

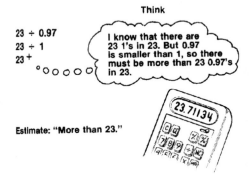

Think

I know that there are 23 1's in 23. But 0.97 is smaller than 1, so there must be more than 23 0.97's in 23.

Estimate: "More than 23."

Students will need to see a variety of examples to help them clearly establish this idea.

The third transparency (sheet 3) highlights some work with nice numbers. Discuss the two examples given and then have the students try the six exercises. It is suggested that students share estimating strategies orally with the class. Specifically, they should be encouraged to verbalize how they move from their quick estimate to their adjusted estimate. Often the adjusted estimate can best be expressed by using the terms "more than" or "less than" or by using symbols "+" or "—."

Sheet 4 should be started immediately following the introductory lesson. It will give a quick check on how well the students have picked up the ideas presented. The remainder of this sheet and sheet 5 can be completed as a homework assignment.

Answers: The concept that a single situation involving estimation can have a number of different answers, all reasonable and falling within the acceptable range, will be foreign to many students. Some may demand to know "the answer" or the "best" answer. Encouraging several different estimates during class discussions can help students develop a greater tolerance for estimation.

Sheet 3

1. 485; adjusted estimate: 485⁻, or about 480

2. 780; adjusted estimate: 780⁺, or about 800

3. 1750; adjusted estimate: 1750⁺, or about 1800

4. 5600; adjusted estimate: 5600⁻, or about 5500

5. 0.862; adjusted estimate: 0.862⁻, or about 0.840

6. 350; adjusted estimate: 350⁻, or about 340

Sheet 4

1. 4600; 4600⁻, or about 4500

2. 782; 782⁺, or about 790

3. 840; 840⁺, or about 850

4. 673; 673⁺, or about 680

5. 5420; 5420⁺, or about 5500

6. 29.8; 29.8+, or about 30

7. 425 000; 425 000⁺, or about 430 000

8. 86.7; 86.7⁺, or about 87

9. 342; 342⁺, or about 350

10. 168; 168⁺, or about 170

11. 520; 520⁻, or about 510

12. 8.46; 8.46⁻, or about 8

13. 12.38; 12.38⁺, or about 13

14. 436.7; 436.7⁻, or about 436

Sheet 5

1. 559.55	6. 86.57	11. less
2. 8654.69	7. 53 990.74	12. $475⁻
3. 2.999	8. 6.999	13. 32.5 mpg
4. 80.86	9. $1.40–$1.60	14. $110 000⁻
5. 41.28	10. yes	15. more

References

National Council of Teachers of Mathematics. *An Agenda for Action: Recommendations for School Mathematics of the 1980s.* Reston, Va.: The Council, 1980.

Reys, Barbara, and Robert Reys. *Guide to Using Estimation Skills and Strategies. GUESS, Box I and 2.* Palo Alto, Calif.: Dale Seymour Publications, 1983.

Reys, Robert E., Paul Trafton, Barbara Reys, and Judy Zawojewski. *Computational Estimation Materials, Grades 6, 7 and 8.* Washington, D.C.: National Science Foundation, 1984.

Schoen, Harold, ed. *Estimation and Mental Computation.* 1986 Yearbook of the National Council of Teachers of Mathematics. Reston, Va.: The Council, forthcoming.

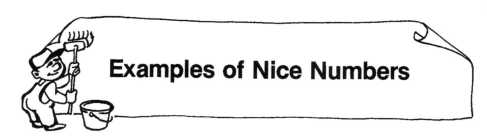

Examples of Nice Numbers

$3 \times \underline{1}$ $40 \div \underline{10}$ $58 \times \underline{100}$

$85 \div \underline{1}$ $67 \times \underline{10}$ $2500 \div \underline{100}$

Why are the underlined numbers called "nice" numbers?

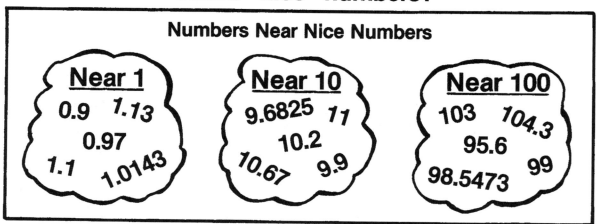

Numbers Near Nice Numbers

Near 1
0.9   1.13
0.97
1.1   1.0143

Near 10
9.6825   11
10.2
10.67   9.9

Near 100
103   104.3
95.6
98.5473   99

From the numbers below, select those that are near nice numbers and state which nice numbers they are near.

1.09   23.4   781   3.6   0.96

78   9.86   0.45   102.9375

97   1.127   17.2   10.4   135

Nice Numbers in Action

×	Near 1		Near 10		Near 100	
	0.97	1.04	9.8	10.9	97.2	103.0
23						
892						

÷	Near 1		Near 10		Near 100	
	0.97	1.04	9.8	10.9	97.2	103.0
23						
892						

To estimate 430 × 10.231

Think 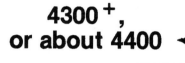 $430 \times 10.231 \doteq 430 \times 10$

4300

Quick estimate

I'm multiplying by something bigger than 10, so it's more than 4300.

4300$^+$,
or about 4400

Adjusted estimate

To estimate 430 ÷ 10.231

Think 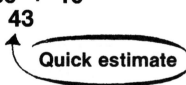 $430 \div 10.231 \doteq 430 \div 10$

43

Quick estimate

I'm dividing by a number bigger than 10, so it will be less than 43.

43$^-$,
or about 42

Adjusted estimate

TRY THESE

1. 485 × 0.985 _____
2. 7800 ÷ 9.61 _____
3. 175 × 10.53 _____
4. 56 × 97.8 _____
5. 0.862 ÷ 1.03 _____
6. 35 000 ÷ 104 _____

ACTIVITY SHEET

Example:

We need 37 Fun
Day tickets. They
cost $9.75 each.
Estimate the total
cost of the tickets.

37 × $10

I know we need less than $370. **Quick estimate**

I'll say about $370⁻, or $360. **Adjusted estimate**

Make a quick estimate for each of the following and then adjust your estimate.

		Quick Estimate	Adjusted Estimate
1.	460 × 9.75	_____	_____
2.	782 × 1.05	_____	_____
3.	84 × 10.3	_____	_____
4.	4. 673 × 1.08	_____	_____
5.	542 × 10.29	_____	_____
6.	29.8 × 1.1	_____	_____
7.	425 × 1015	_____	_____
8.	86.7 ÷ 0.98	_____	_____
9.	3420 ÷ 9.78	_____	_____
10.	16 800 ÷ 99	_____	_____
11.	52 000 ÷ 102.7	_____	_____
12.	8460 ÷1029	_____	_____
13.	12 380 ÷ 991	_____	_____
14.	4367 ÷ 10.04	_____	_____

Below are some calculator-obtained results, which in some cases have been rounded. In each case, one result is correct, the other is wrong. Use estimation to identify the correct answer and then circle it.

1. 689 × 0.95	559.55	629.945
2. 89 576 . 10.35	8654.69	9271.16
3. 35.75 . 11.92	426.14	2.999
4. 87 . 1.076	80.86	93.61
5. 387 . 9.375	36.28	41.28
6. 85 397 . 986.43	86.57	83.64
7. 53.6 × 1007.29	53 990.74	52 864.50
8. 6.7 . 0.9573	6.257	6.999

Use nice numbers to estimate reasonable answers for these problems.

9. Your grocery store sells hamburger for $1.39 a pound. If you buy a package of hamburger that weighs 1.08 pounds, estimate what you will pay.

10. Suppose that 1-liter bottles of cola are on sale for 99¢ apiece and you are going to buy 24 bottles for the church picnic. Will $24.85 be enough to pay the bill?

11. A racer averages 9.9 miles an hour when running long distances. Will a marathon race about 26 miles long take more or less than 3 hours?

12. The owner of the Sound Shop has 475 tapes in inventory and makes about 95¢ on each tape sold. Estimate the profit if all the tapes are sold.

13. The Brocks drove 325 miles on 10.2 gallons of gasoline. Estimate their mileage.

14. If 9960 people bought tickets to see REO Speedwagon in concert, and the tickets sold for $11 each, estimate the total gate receipts for the concert.

15. The typical American eats 96.3 pounds of beef each year. If the average price of beef is $2.42 a pound, would each spend more or less than $200 a year on beef?

ROBERT E. REYS, BARBARA J. REYS, PAUL R. TRAFTON, AND JUDY ZAWOJEWSKI

Estimating with "Nice" Fractions

THIS section is designed to provide mathematical activities in reproducible formats appropriate for students in grades 7–12. This material may be reproduced by classroom teachers for use in their own classes. Readers who have developed successful classroom activities are encouraged to submit manuscripts, in a format similar to the "Activities" already published, to the managing editor for review. Of particular interest are activities focusing on problem solving and applications, the Council's expanded concept of basic skills, and the uses of calculators and computers.

Teacher's Guide

Introduction: Interest in estimation in the school curriculum has markedly increased during the past few years. Reports on needed changes in the mathematics curriculum, such as *An Agenda for Action* (NCTM 1980), have called for an increased emphasis on estimation. The topic has been the focus of frequent articles and activities in journals (e.g., Ockenga and Duea 1985]; Reys [1985]; Reys et al. [1985]; Rubenstein [1985]) and of talks at mathematics conferences, and it is the major theme of the 1986 NCTM Yearbook (Schoen 1986). Estimation is being viewed in a broader

Prepared by Paul R. Trafton, *National College of Education, Evanston, Illinois;* Judith S. Zawojewski, *National College of Education, Evanston, Illinois;* Robert E. Reys, *University of Missouri—Columbia;* and Barbara J. Reys, *University of Missouri—Columbia*

Edited by Christian R. Hirsch, *Western Michigan University;* Jonathan Jay Greenwood, *Multnomah County Education Service District, Portland, Oregon;* Robert A. Laing, *Western Michigan University*

and more diverse way than in the past, with particular emphasis on the many ways in which one can obtain a valid estimate.

This month's activity is based on material developed for a National Science Foundation project, *Developing Computational Estimation in the Middle Grades* (Reys et al. 1984). It is built around the use of "nice" fractions in estimating. The first three activity sheets focus on changing fractions to ones that are easy to work with. On the fourth sheet, students use nice fractions (unit fractions) to estimate a fractional part of a whole.

Each activity sheet should be introduced through teacher-pupil discussion of transparencies made from the sheets. After an idea has been developed, students should complete the related practice exercises.

Grade levels: 6–12

Materials: Copies of the activity sheets for each student and a set of transparencies for class discussions

Objectives: To have students learn (1) to identify fractions close to 1, 0, and 1/2; (2) to estimate sums of fractions and mixed numbers by rounding fractions to 0, 1/2, and 1; (3) to round fractions to easily understood fractions; (4) to estimate. a fractional part of a whole with unit fractions

Procedure: Distribute the activity sheets one at a time to each student. Introduce sheet 1 by discussing how fractions can often be "messy" to work with and that recognizing fractions close to 1, 0, and 1/2 can make it easier to estimate the value of a fraction and thereby make work with fractions easier. Note that a fraction is close to 1 when the numerator and denominator are about the same size, or " close " to each

other. Through discussion bring out the fact that a fraction is close to 0 when the numerator is very small in comparison to the denominator. Finally, students should understand that a fraction is close to 1 when the numerator is about half the denominator or the denominator is about twice as large as the numerator. Have students complete exercises 4, 5, and 6 on sheet 1 independently.

Following discussion of students' solutions to the exercises on sheet 1, work through examples 1–4 on sheet 2. Point out that whereas it is unlikely that one would have to compute a sum as in example 1, it is very easy to estimate the sum. Discuss the changing of each fraction to 0, 1/2, or 1 and how the estimate of the sum is obtained. For the second example, the "front end" method is shown. First the sum of the whole numbers is found, and then an estimate of the sum of the fractions is added. Examples 3 and 4 introduce the idea of adjusting an initial estimate. In example 3, both fractions are rounded down. Thus the whole-number estimate, 2, is less than the actual sum and is an *underestimate*. To indicate that the actual sum is over the estimate, a superscript plus sign is written next to the 2. Similar reasoning is used to adjust the overestimate in example 4. Next assign exercises 1–8, in which students are to select the best estimate.

Sheet 3 is an extension of the work on sheet 1. Begin by having students identify fractions whose value is easily understood, such as 1/2, 1/3, 1/4, 1/5, 1/6, 2/3, or 3/4. Now direct their attention to the problem at the top of the sheet. Point out that the fraction 6/23 may not be easily understood by many people. Discuss how to find a "nice" fraction that is close to 6/23. Next solve exercises 1 and 2 with the class, encouraging pupils to change both the numerator and denominator to get a fraction that can easily be simplified to a familiar one. Have students complete the remaining exercises on their own.

Sheet 4 focuses on estimating a fractional part of a whole with unit fractions. This useful, practical skill is used widely in everyday life. Two key ideas are involved:

a. Finding a fractional part with a unit fraction involves division. 1/3 represents 1 of 3 equal parts. Thus 1/3 of 36 is 1 of 3 equal divisions of 36, or 36 ÷ 3.

b. The amount to be divided should be changed to a "compatible" number, one that is a multiple of the divisor and is easy to work with.

Discuss the example at the top of the sheet, stressing both of these ideas. Point out that $120 was selected because 120 ÷ 3 is easy to compute. Next develop the first two exercises with the students. In exercise 1, $100 could also have been used and also would have produced a reasonable estimate. Instruct the class to complete exercises 3-13 individually. Students should be encouraged to adjust their estimates.

Answers

Sheet 1: 4. 3/17; 1/8; 2/13; 6/97; 5. 7/13; 4/9; 6/11; 11/20; 5/9; 6. 3/4; 4/5; 7/9; 9/8

Sheet 2: 1. about 2; 2. about 1/2; 3. about 1; 4. about 2; 5. over 6; 6. under 10; 7. under 8; 8. over 7

Sheet 3: (reasonable alternate answers should be accepted): 1. 1/3; 2. l/3; 3. 2/3; 4. 1/2; 5. 1/5 (1/4); 6. 1/6; 7. 1/2; 8. 1/3; 9. Lions; 10. Tigers, Muskrats; 11. Cougars, Wildcats; 12. Bears

Sheet 4: (reasonable alternative answers should be accepted): 1. $88.00, $22.00 ($22–$25); 2. $27.00, $3.00 ($2–$3); 3. $150.00, $30.00 ($25–$30); 4. $30.00, $10.00 ($10–$11); 5. $160.00, $20.00 ($20–$22); 6. $16.00–$20.00; 7. $9.00–$10.00; 8. $11.00–$12.00; 9. $30.00–$33.00; 10. $10.00–$12.00; 11. $50.00–$60.00; 12. $10.00–$15.00; 13. $7.00–$8.00

References

National Council of Teachers of Mathematics. *An Agenda for Action: Recommendations for School Mathematics of the 1980s.* Reston, Va.: The Council, 1980.

Ockenga, Earl, and Joan Duea. "Activities: Estimate and Calculate." *Mathematics Teacher* 78 (April 1985): 272–76.

Reys, Robert E. "Estimation." *Arithmetic Teacher* 32 (February 1986): 37–41.

Reys, Robert E., Barbara J. Reys, Paul R. Trafton, and Judy Zawojewski. "Activities: Estimating with 'Nice' Numbers." *Mathematics Teacher* 78 (November 1985): 616–17, 621–25.

Reys, Robert E., Paul R. Trafton, Barbara Reys, and Judy Zawojewski. *Developing Computational Estimation Materials for the Middle Grades.* Final Report No. NSF.8113601. Washington, D.C.: National Science Foundation, 1984.

Rubenstein, Rheta N. "Activities: Developing Estimation Strategies." *Mathematics Teacher* 78 (February 1985): 112–18.

Schoen, Harold, ed. *Estimation and Mental Computation.* 1986 Yearbook. Reston, Va.: National Council of Teachers of Mathematics, 1986.

FRACTIONS CAN BE "NICE" NUMBERS

The numbers 0, 1/2, and 1 are easy numbers to use in mental arithmetic. Many fractions can be rounded to these nice numbers to make estimates. Study the examples below to help you find a way to determine when a fraction is close to 0, 1/2, or 1.

Fractions close to 1:

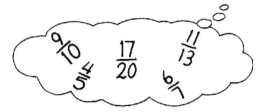

1. How can you tell when a fraction is close to 1?

_____

_____

_____

Fractions close to 0:

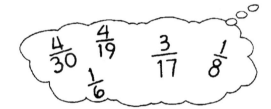

2. How can you tell when a fraction is close to 0?

_____

_____

_____

Fractions close to ½ :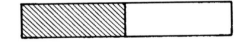

3. How can you tell when a fraction is close to 1/2?

_____

_____

_____

4. Circle the fractions that are close to 0.

$$\frac{3}{5} \quad \frac{3}{17} \quad \frac{1}{8} \quad \frac{2}{3} \quad \frac{2}{13} \quad \frac{6}{97} \quad \frac{4}{9}$$

5. Circle the fractions that are close to 1/2.

$$\frac{7}{13} \quad \frac{2}{7} \quad \frac{4}{9} \quad \frac{6}{11} \quad \frac{8}{9} \quad \frac{11}{20} \quad \frac{5}{9}$$

6. Circle the fractions that are close to 1.

$$\frac{3}{8} \quad \frac{3}{4} \quad \frac{7}{12} \quad \frac{4}{5} \quad \frac{7}{9} \quad \frac{9}{8} \quad \frac{7}{20}$$

It's fairly easy to add in your head with zeros, halves, and ones. By rounding fractions to these nice numbers, you can estimate their sums easily. Here are some examples.

Example 1: To estimate

Example 2: To estimate

$$\frac{3}{5} + \frac{9}{10} + \frac{1}{20} + \frac{16}{30}, \ldots$$

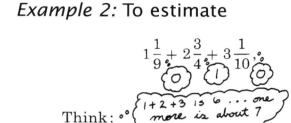

$$1\frac{1}{9} + 2\frac{3}{4} + 3\frac{1}{10}, \ldots$$

Think: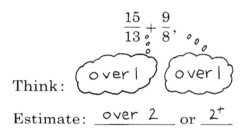

Estimate: <u>about 2</u>

Think: $_{\circ}^{\circ}$ ⟨ $1+2+3$ is 6 ... one more is about 7 ⟩

Estimate: <u>about 7</u>

Sometimes you can tell if your estimate is too high or too low. In such examples, you can write a "+" or a "—" to show how you would adjust your estimate.

Example 3: To estimate

Example 4: To estimate

$$\frac{15}{13} + \frac{9}{8}, \ldots$$

$$3\frac{4}{5} + 1\frac{7}{8} + \frac{9}{10}, \ldots$$

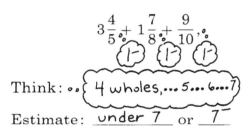

Think: ⟨over 1⟩ ⟨over 1⟩

Estimate: <u>over 2</u> or <u>2⁺</u>

Think: $_{\circ\circ}$ ⟨ 4 wholes, ... 5... 6...7 ⟩

Estimate: <u>under 7</u> or <u>7⁻</u>

Circle the best estimate of each sum.

1. $\frac{3}{4} + \frac{9}{10}$ about $\frac{1}{2}$ about 1   about 2

2. $\frac{1}{4} + \frac{3}{16}$ about $\frac{1}{2}$ about 1   about 2

3. $\frac{13}{16} + \frac{1}{8}$ about $\frac{1}{2}$ about 1   about 2

4. $\frac{8}{9} + \frac{5}{6}$ about $\frac{1}{2}$ about 1   about 2

5. $3\frac{7}{8} + 2\frac{3}{10}$ over 6   under 6

6. $6\frac{1}{5} + 3\frac{1}{2}$ over 10   under 10

7. $5\frac{3}{8} + 2\frac{1}{4}$ over 8   under 8

8. $6\frac{5}{8} + \frac{5}{8}$ over 7   under 7

ACTIVITY SHEET

Sometimes we round off a fraction to a nice fraction, such as 1/2, 1/3, 1/4, 1/5, 1/6, 2/3, or 3/4, that is more easily understood.

Example:

John made 6 of 23 free throws. He made about ? of his shots.

$\frac{6}{23}$ is close to $\frac{6}{24}$, and $\frac{6}{24}$ equals $\frac{1}{4}$. He made about $\frac{1}{4}$ of his shots.

Think

Represent each of the following situations with a nice fraction:

1. Travis   8 baskets
              25 shots

2. Mary Lou   24 base hits
                   74 times at bat

3. Laura   11 free throws
            18 attempts

4. Jason   21 completions
            43 passes

Alan   15 base hits
        74 times at bat

6. Tammy   6 goals
             37 shots

Jeff   8 baskets
       17 shots

8. Terry   11 base hits
           36 times at bat

Use the table at the right to complete exercises 9–12.

9. Which team has won more than half its games? _____

10. Which teams have won just under half of their games? _____

11. Which teams have won about one-third of their games? _____

12. Which team has won about one-fourth of its games? _____

Team	Games Played	Games Won
Tigers	21	10
Lions	18	11
Muskrats	27	13
Cougars	19	6
Bears	21	5
Wildcats	29	9

Example: Estimate how much you would save on the purchase of this television.

1/3 is already a nice number. To find a third of a number, you can divide by 3. However, $118 does not divide evenly by 3, Round 118 to a number that is easy to divide by three.

So, I would save about $40, or a little less, $40⁻.

Estimate each answer by using a nice number that is easy to divide.

	Nice Number	Estimate
1. 1/4 of $89.95	1/4 of $88.00	_____
2. 1/9 of $25.89	1/9 of _____	_____
3. 1/5 of $146.15	1/5 of _____	_____
4. 1/3 of $31.19	1/3 of _____	_____
5. 1/8 of $163.45	1/8 of _____	_____

For the sale items below, estimate how much you would save on each item by changing the price to a nice number. Write your estimate below the price tag.

ACTIVITY SHEET

EARL OCKENGA

Chalk Up Some Calculator Activities for Rational Numbers

WOULD you like to get students thinking and talking about fractions? Sounds difficult? It's not. The activities that follow are ways that the calculator can be used to create interest in the study of fractions.

Activities like "Name Change" and a "4-in-a-Line" can provide an opportunity to build ideas and practice skills. In "Name Change," students like to use their estimating skills to guess which fractions do not belong and then check their guesses with a calculator. In "4-in-a-Line," students form fractions and match them with decimal names. The ease of verifying their choices with a calculator makes this an enjoyable game. Both activities help students build estimation skills and generate a feel for fractional numbers.

Another activity that develops estimation skills is "Tag It." This activity is a good one to put on the chalkboard after a textbook lesson on comparison of fractions.

A well-structured calculator activity will result in students doing a lot of mathematics in a short time and increasing their enjoyment of the work. A good example is "Who's in the Middle?" In this game students compare dozens of fractions and still ask for more.

Many textbook topics can be enhanced with calculator activities. "Etc., Etc." illustrates how the calculator can focus attention on fractions named by a repeating decimal or a terminating decimal.

Another activity that encourages explo-

Earl Ockenga *is a classroom teacher at the Price Laboratory School and an assistant professor of education at the University of Northern Iowa in Cedar Falls, IA 50613. His major interest is in the area of problem solving.*

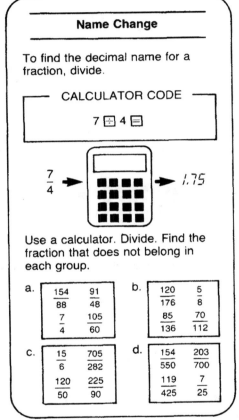

Name Change

To find the decimal name for a fraction, divide.

```
┌─── CALCULATOR CODE ───┐
│        7 ⊟ 4 ⊟        │
└───────────────────────┘
```

$$\frac{7}{4} \rightarrow \boxed{\text{[calculator]}} \rightarrow 1.75$$

Use a calculator. Divide. Find the fraction that does not belong in each group.

a.
$\frac{154}{88}$	$\frac{91}{48}$
$\frac{7}{4}$	$\frac{105}{60}$

b.
$\frac{120}{176}$	$\frac{5}{8}$
$\frac{85}{136}$	$\frac{70}{112}$

c.
$\frac{15}{6}$	$\frac{705}{282}$
$\frac{120}{50}$	$\frac{225}{90}$

d.
$\frac{154}{550}$	$\frac{203}{700}$
$\frac{119}{425}$	$\frac{7}{25}$

4-in-a-Line

Rules
- Take turns. Pick any two of these numbers to make an $\frac{a}{b}$ fraction.

3	5	8
	4	6

- Divide. Mark the decimal name for your fraction on the game board (use X or O).
- Four marks in a line wins.

Game Board

$1.\overline{3}$	0.6	0.625	1.25
1.6	0.375	$0.8\overline{3}$	0.75
0.8	1.2	$0.\overline{6}$	1.5
$1.\overline{6}$	$2.\overline{6}$	0.5	2.0

Tag It

Put the fractions on the correct tags. *Hint*: Use a calculator to find the decimal name for each fraction.

$\frac{28}{45}$	$\frac{36}{75}$	$\frac{143}{55}$	$\frac{111}{60}$	$\frac{203}{70}$
	$\frac{65}{52}$	$\frac{141}{94}$	$\frac{132}{49}$	$\frac{149}{59}$

Number line: 0 ... 0.5 (a, b) ... 1 ... 1.75 (c, d) ... 2 (e) ... 3 (f, g, h, i)

Who's in the Middle?

Rules
- This is a game for three players.
- Each player secretly picks a fraction.
- The player whose fraction is neither the smallest nor the largest wins.

Who won? *Hint*: It's easy to compare fractions if you first change them to decimals.

Game 1

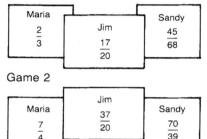

Maria	Jim	Sandy
$\frac{2}{3}$	$\frac{17}{20}$	$\frac{45}{68}$

Game 2

Maria	Jim	Sandy
$\frac{7}{4}$	$\frac{37}{20}$	$\frac{70}{39}$

Use calculators. Play the game with two of your classmates.

Etc., Etc.

Rules
- Write six fractions.
- Use a calculator to find the decimal name for each fraction.
- Score two points for each listed fraction that has a repeating decimal name.
- Score one point for each listed fraction that has a terminating decimal name.

How many points did each person score?

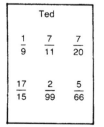

Ted		
$\frac{1}{9}$	$\frac{7}{11}$	$\frac{7}{20}$
$\frac{17}{15}$	$\frac{2}{99}$	$\frac{5}{66}$

Pam		
$\frac{3}{80}$	$\frac{5}{33}$	$\frac{45}{135}$
$\frac{44}{64}$	$\frac{7}{6}$	$\frac{56}{35}$

Pick six fractions of your choice. How many points did you score?

Key It In

Which calculator keys did Brian push to multiply $\frac{1}{2} \times \frac{3}{4}$?

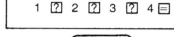

Brian's calculator code

1 ? 2 ? 3 ? 4 =

$\frac{1}{2} \times \frac{3}{4}$ ➤ 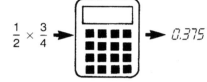 ➤ 0.375

Which keys did Yoko push to multiply $\frac{1}{2} \times \frac{3}{4}$?

Yoko's calculator code

1 ? 3 ? 2 ? 4 =

$\frac{1}{2} \times \frac{3}{4}$ ➤ 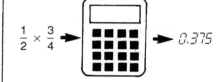 ➤ 0.375

Use either Brian's or Yoko's method to multiply these fractions.

a. $\frac{5}{32} \times \frac{2}{25}$ b. $\frac{7}{25} \times \frac{3}{16}$

c. $\frac{21}{80} \times \frac{11}{75}$ d. $\frac{13}{50} \times \frac{3}{16}$

Don't Get Mixed Up

Here's how to use a calculator to change $\frac{149}{16}$ to a mixed number.

Step 1. Divide.

149 ÷ 6 = ➤ 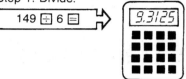 9.3125

Step 2. Subtract the whole-number part of the quotient.

9.3125 − 9 = ➤ 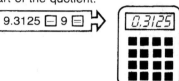 0.3125

Step 3. Multiply by the divisor. The remainder is 5.

0.3125 × 16 = ➤ 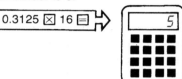 5

The mixed number for $\frac{149}{16}$ is $9\frac{5}{16}$.

Use a calculator. Find the mixed number for each fraction.

a. $\frac{125}{8}$ b. $\frac{426}{125}$

c. $\frac{145}{16}$ d. $\frac{477}{64}$

---

ration with mathematics is "Key It In," which encourages students to analyze calculator multiplication algorithms. Often, students will extend this activity by writing their own calculator codes for addition and subtraction of fractions.

Although fractions are not used easily on a calculator, efficient ways can be learned. "Don't Get Mixed Up," for example, gives procedures for converting fractions to mixed numbers. After students have tried this activity, extend it by having them use their calculators to find the quotients and remainders for these division exercises:

$12\overline{)6458}$ $144\overline{)42\ 394}$

The calculator can be very helpful for "early finishers." "Look for the Pattern" and "You Figure It" are examples of how the calculator can free students from computational restrictions and allow them to focus on the recognition of patterns and other problem-solving skills.

Calculator activities with rational numbers serve many purposes. They can allow students to build references, explore algorithms, develop estimation skills, and improve number sense. The activities can be done individually or in small groups. Find space on your chalkboard for calculator activities, hand out the machines, and turn on your students to instant motivation.

8

Patterns and Functions

A UNIFYING concept in mathematics is the study of patterns and functions. Students learn to recognize, describe, and extend patterns from kindergarten through grade twelve. During the middle grades, the study of patterns and functions should be explored through investigations and should involve various patterns from the students' world.

"Pentagonal Patterns in the Addition Table" by Bonnie Litwiller and David R. Duncan presents an interesting activity in which the students discover patterns while practicing computation.

Richard A. Austin and Denisse R. Thompson used literature to introduce patterns. Students can understand functions and patterns to connect algebra to various situations by means described in the article, "Exploring Algebraic Patterns through Literature."

Carol Ann Harlos in "And the Winner Is ..." pre-sents an interesting group activity in which students identify the pattern and predict the outcome.

"The Function Game" is described by Rheta N. Rubenstein. Students enjoy playing the function game, and several variations and extensions are presented. Another variation of the function game is presented in the Stephen S. Willoughby article, "Activities to Help in Learning about Functions." Willoughby presents several function activities before presenting formal notation and definitions. These activities develop the concept first and then use the symbolism later.

Willie Johnson uses graphs and charts to examine patterns and functions. "Mathematics Detective Exploring Graphs: WYSIWG" presents several interesting graphs and charts are presented along with accompanying questions to direct the interpretation of the data.

BONNIE H. LITWILLER AND DAVID R. DUNCAN

Pentagonal Patterns in the Addition Table

TEACHERS of mathematics frequently wish to use nonroutine practice activities in their classrooms to review and maintain arithmetic skills. It is a serendipitous occurrence if students can discover patterns while practicing computation.

Every student and teacher is quite familiar with the standard addition table; however, many unexpected patterns can still be found. Activities and patterns involving the addition table will be described in this article.

Figure 1 displays pentagons drawn in the interior of the addition table. The pentagons in figure I are called 2-pentagons because they contain two numbers in each side; those in figure 2 are called 3-pentagons, since they contain three numbers a side. Similarly, the pentagons in figures 3 and 4 are called 4-pentagons and 5-pentagons.

Activity I

1. For each of the pentagons in figure 1, add the five numbers that represent its vertices.

For pentagon *A*, the sum is 3 + 4 + 5 + 5 + 3 = 20.

For *B*, the sum is 40.

For *C*, the sum is 40.

For *D*, the sum is 65.

For *E*, the sum is 42.

For *F*, the sum is 63.

2. Observe that one number lies in the interior of each pentagon; 4 lies in *A*; 8 lies in *B*, *C*, and *E*, 13 lies in *D* and *F*.

Bonnie Litwiller *and* David Duncan *teach mathematics courses at the University of Northern Iowa, Cedar Falls, UT 50613. Their courses are intended for prospective mathematics teachers at both the elementary and secondary school levels. Both are past presidents of the Iowa Council of Teachers of Mathematics.*

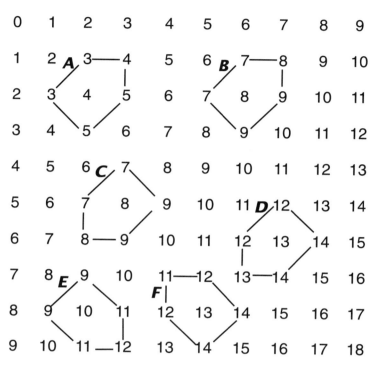

Fig. 1. 2-pentagons

3. For each pentagon, find the ratio of the sum of the vertices, V, to the interior number, I.

For pentagon A, $\dfrac{V}{I} = \dfrac{20}{4} = \dfrac{5}{1}$.

For B, $\dfrac{V}{I} = \dfrac{40}{8} = \dfrac{5}{1}$.

For C, $\dfrac{V}{I} = \dfrac{40}{8} = \dfrac{5}{1}$.

For D, $\dfrac{V}{I} = \dfrac{65}{13} = \dfrac{5}{1}$.

For E, $\dfrac{V}{I} = \dfrac{42}{8} \neq \dfrac{5}{1}$.

For F, $\dfrac{V}{I} = \dfrac{63}{13} \neq \dfrac{5}{1}$.

Have your students verify that for any 2-pentagon that is oriented northeast (such as *A* and *B*) or southwest (such as *C* and *D*),

the ratio *V/I* is 5/1. This pattern does not hold for 2-pentagons oriented southeast (*E*) or northwest (*F*).

Next consider figure 2, which contains 3-pentagons *G* and *H* (oriented NE or SW), and do the following similar steps.

1. For each pentagon add the five numbers that represent its vertices. For pentagon *G*, V = 35; for *H*, V = 70.

2. For each pentagon add the numbers that lie in its interior; call this sum I. For *G*, I = 42, and for *H*, I = 84.

3. Again, find the ratio *V/I*. For G, V/I = 35/42 = 5/6, and for H, V/I = 70/84 = 5/6.

Have your students verify that the ratios for other 3-pentagons with a similar orientation are 5/6. Now use figure 3 and follow the same set of directions that were used for figures 1 and 2.

For pentagon J, $V = 35$ and $I = 112$; thus $V/I = 35/112 = 5/16$. For K, $V = 55$, and $I = 176$; so $V/I = 55/176 = 5/16$. In the case of the 4-pentagons, sixteen numbers lie in the interior of each pentagon.

Figure 4 displays 5-pentagons L and M with a northeast and southwest orientation, where thirty-one numbers lie inside each pentagon. For L, $V/I = 40/248 = 5/31$; and for M, $V/I = 45/279 = 5/31$.

These results are included in table 1. Check other pentagons with similar orientations to verify these conclusions. Note that the numerator in each case is 5, the number of vertices in a pentagon. In the denominator, 1, 6, 16, and 31 correspond to the number of interior numbers of the appropriate pentagon.

Table 1

Type of pentagon	V/I
2-pentagon	5/1
3-pentagon	5/6
4-pentagon	5/16
5-pentagon	5/31

Activity 2

This activity involves computing the ratio P/I for each pentagon, where P is the sum of the numbers that lie on the perimeter of the pentagon. From figure 1, the perimeters of the pentagons A, B, C, and D are, respectively, 20, 40, 40, and 65. Of course, P has already been computed, since all numbers that lie on the perimeter of the 2-pentagons are also vertex numbers of the 2-pentagons. Therefore, P/I for each of the pentagons A, B, C, and D is $5/1 = V/I$.

From figure 2, the sum of the numbers that lie on the perimeter P can be computed. For G, $P/I = 70/42 = 10/6$, whereas for H, $P/I = 140/84 = 10/6$.

From figures 3 and 4 the value of P for J, K, L, and M can be computed. P is, respectively, 105, 165, 160, and 180.

$$\text{For } J, \frac{P}{I} = \frac{105}{112} = \frac{15}{16}.$$

$$\text{For } K, \frac{P}{I} = \frac{165}{176} = \frac{15}{16}.$$

$$\text{For } L, \frac{P}{I} = \frac{160}{248} = \frac{20}{31}.$$

$$\text{For } M, \frac{P}{I} = \frac{180}{279} = \frac{20}{31}.$$

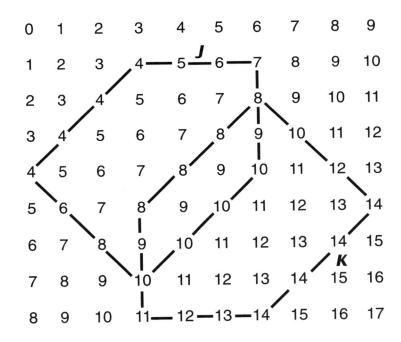

Fig. 2. 3-pentagons

Fig. 3. 4-pentagons

Table 2 summarizes the results for the ratio P/I. Note that the numerators are consecutive multiples of 5 and represent the number of numbers that lie on the perimeter of the appropriate pentagon. Again, the denominator represents the number of numbers that lie in the interior of the appropriate pentagon.

Table 2

Type of pentagon	P/I
2-pentagon	5/1
3-pentagon	10/6
4-pentagon	15/16
5-pentagon	20/31

Activity 3

Compute $(P/I) \div (V/I)$. Table 3 displays the results of this computation. If the addition table were extended to accommodate larger pentagons, $(P/I) \div (V/I)$ would generate the set of natural numbers.

Table 3

Type of pentagon	$P/I \div V/I$
2-pentagon	$5/5 \div 5/1 = 1$
3-pentagon	$10/6 \div 5/6 = 2$
4-pentagon	$15/16 \div 5/16 = 3$
5-pentagon	$20/31 \div 5/31 = 4$

Query for the class: Would the same set of ratios emerge if these activities were performed on a subtraction table? (*Hint:* The orientation of the pentagons must be changed from that of the addition table.

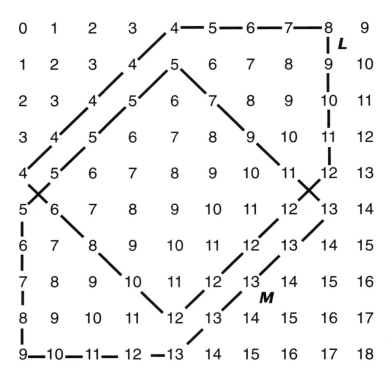

Fig. 4. 5-pentagons

RICHARD AUSTIN AND DENISSE THOMPSON

Exploring Algebraic Patterns through Literature

ACTIVITIES that engage middle school students in investigating and extending patterns are essential in developing students' algebraic thinking. The *Curriculum and Evaluation Standards for School Mathematics* (NCTM 1989) for grades 5–8 and the position statement on "Algebra for Everyone" (NCTM 1994) describe the importance of using patterns and relationships to develop algebraic thinking. Hence, it seems reasonable that many activities describing, extending, and modifying patterns should be part of the middle school mathematics experience, both before and during formal algebra study.

This article presents an example of using literature to develop or expand algebraic thinking in an interesting environment that connects algebra to various situations. Many books classified as children's literature and used in K–5 classrooms contain mathematical content appropriate for use in a middle school class. The mathematics embedded in the story can be explored at an introductory level by elementary children; the more advanced mathematical abilities of middle school children can elicit a deeper and richer discussion of the mathematics. Because children's literature is a natural hook to interest and to motivate students of many ages, middle-grades teachers should also consider how this tool might effectively be used in the classroom.

We have found a number of children's books that can be used to introduce and encourage algebraic thinking. See the addi-

Richard Austin, *austin@typhoon.coedu.usf.edu,* and Denisse Thompson, *thompson@tempest .coedu.usf.edu, are colleagues at the University of South Florida, Tampa, FL 33620. Austin has special interests in assessment and applications of technology and literature in teaching mathematics. Thompson's interests include developing proofwriting ability and incorporating applications, literature, and technology in the curriculum.*

tional resources list following the references. Any one of these books could be used to explore rich mathematical patterns. The particular lessons and activities discussed in this article relate to *Anno's Magic Seeds* (Anno 1995).

Summary of *Anno's Magic Seeds*

Jack is a young man who is given two magic seeds by a wise man and instructed to eat one and bury, or plant, the other. He will not be hungry for an entire year, and the planted seed will yield two more magic seeds the next year. Jack continues this process for several years until he decides to plant both seeds. When Jack plants two seeds, his yield is four seeds. He eats one seed and buries the others. This pattern of eating one and burying the other continues until he meets Alice. At this point, the process again changes and becomes more complex. Jack and Alice eventually marry, have a child, and begin selling seeds. Ultimately, a storm brings destruction, but a few seeds are preserved, and life with all its patterns begins again.

Development of the lessons

Anno asks questions within the story to encourage the reader to use mathematics to describe what is happening to both Jack and his seeds. The patterns developed in the story can be expressed in various ways. Although the ability to express the patterns using symbolic algebra is often beyond them, most middle school students are able to give verbal and written descriptions, as well as extensions, of the patterns.

We visited both a sixth-grade-mathematics class and a seventh-grade-prealgebra class to investigate *Anno's Magic Seeds*. We discovered that sixth- and seventh-grade students enjoyed listening to the story, which then became a motivational

device for exploring the patterns presented. The activities described here required two sessions per class to complete and could easily have taken a third day to tie up loose ends and to investigate extensions. At the end of the first day with the seventh-grade class, one student said to another, "I thought today was going to be boring." She was surprised to find that the story was interesting and that exploring the mathematics was entertaining.

Students were given activity sheets (see the figs. 1–3) developed by the authors to guide their thinking and help them organize their data tables. For these students, this early experience with such a lesson required a level of structure to ensure that students were engaged in the mathematics that we were interested in discussing. Students were encouraged to use calculators. The activities to accompany *Anno's Magic Seeds* are designed to bridge the gap from simply extending patterns to the more formal use of variables to express the patterns symbolically. When literature is connected to a mathematics lesson, one usually reads the entire story and then deals with the mathematics. However, we wanted students to extend a pattern beyond the time frame allotted in the story, so we designed the lessons so that a portion of

the story was read, patterns were explored and discussed, and then the story was continued. Each time that the patterns changed—because of planting both seeds. meeting Alice. or having a baby—we stopped the story and explored the mathematics.

Activity sheet 1

The first activity sheet (see fig. 1) was designed so that students would begin to think about and describe patterns in a simple situation. Table 1 contains a completed table from activity sheet 1. Although the patterns in this table may seem repetitious, they can be described by *constant functions*, one of the function families studied in an algebra course.

Table 1
A Completed Table from Activity Sheet 1

Year	0	1	2	3	4	5	6
Number of seeds produced	—	2	2	2	2	2	2
Number of seeds eaten	1	1	1	1	1	1	1
Number of seeds buried	1	1	1	1	1	1	1

When asked to describe the patterns seen in the table, such responses as the following were obtained:

He had two seeds produced, one eaten, and one buried, for six years. (Justin, grade 6)

2 seeds are produced every year. 1 seed was buried every year and 1 seed was eaten every year. (Kristy, grade 7)

2 is repeating, 1 is repeating, 1 is repeating. (Jamal, grade 7)

At both grade levels, students noticed that the patterns were the same each year. When asked to explain this result, students recognized that Jack did the same thing each year and so the patterns did not change.

When asked if Jack was correct in thinking that this pattern would continue forever, we got mixed opinions. Michelle, grade 6, said "No, because he might not get a chance to let the rest grow." "No, if he stops planting one seed," replied Laurie, grade 6. 'Yes, because if he doesn't change the pattern of his actions, then the results will continually stay the same until he decides

to stop or change his pattern," said Kristy, grade 7 "Yes, because he will always do the exact amount he was directed to, which is 2 produced, 1 eaten, 1 buried," offered Heather, grade 7. Thus, this exploration gave students a concrete example of a constant function, and they recognized that the constant patterns would continue as long as Jack continued to do the same thing. The patterns would change only if Jack's actions changed.

Neither group of students had yet been exposed to variables. When asked to write a relationship between the number of seeds eaten, *e*, the number buried, *b*, and the number produced, *p*, students initially wondered what *e*, *b*, and *p* could represent. Such questions offered an opportunity to discuss the fact that variables could take on any values. The only constraint was the information in the given situation $e + b = p$. Thus, knowing values for *e* and *b* allows the values for *p* to be found.

We spent roughly one-third of the first class period on the beginning of the story and activity sheet 1.

Activity sheet 2

Before we continued the story, students were asked what might happen next and speculated that Jack might bury both seeds and eat something else for that year, which is exactly what happens. We continued reading the story from the time that Jack buried both seeds until he met Alice. Throughout the reading, students were asked to predict how Jack would use the seeds in a given year. Jack always ate one and buried the rest. Each buried seed produced twice that number of seeds the following year. Hence, by the time students received activity sheet 2 (see fig. 2), they had orally produced several of the values reconstructed in table 2.

Table 2
A Completed Table from Activity Sheet 2

Year	0	1	2	3	4	5
Number of seeds produced	—	4	6	10	18	34
Number of seeds eaten	0	1	1	1	1	1
Number of seeds buried	2	3	5	9	17	33

Sixth and seventh graders differed in their ability to articulate their descriptions of the pattern, but almost all were able to operationalize the patterns by completing the table. In the first question, students were asked what they noticed about the number of seeds produced in a year and to explain their thinking. Seventh graders were more likely to try to write the relationship with a number sentence and to articulate that the number buried in *this* year is used to find the number produced *next* year. Here are some sample responses.

They double each year. They are even because you double the number of seeds buried that year. (Laurie, grade 6)

2 × the buried number [because] he didn't bury one, he buried two. (Darrell, grade 6)

Two times the bottom number you get your answer because I multiplyed [sic] 2 times the bottom number. (Joshua, grade 6)

It's the number of seeds burried [sic] plus itself because that's what you get on the table with your calculation. (Heather, grade 7)

[T]here are twice as many as planted the year before. [B]ecause each year two seeds are grown for each seed planted and he eats one and burrys [sic] the other. (Joshua, grade 7)

The number of seeds buried × 2 = the number of seeds produced for the next year because each plant gets 2 seeds, so if 5 seeds are buried, then the next year there will be 10 seeds. (Kristy, grade 7)

When asked to complete the table for the next five years if the patterns continued in the same way, students used their calculators to complete the patterns efficiently. Students also began to engage in more cooperative group dialogue as they compared values.

Sixth graders had more difficulty than seventh graders in trying to determine whether it would have been possible for Jack to bury 2025 seeds. We had expected students to consider the types of numbers in the table and determine whether this figure would have been reasonable. Instead, students used the current values in the extended table. In year 10, 1025 seeds would be buried. Hence, we obtained responses along the following lines:

No, because if he planted again, he would have 2050, so he would have to save some or something. (Joyce, grade 7)

No, because $1025 \times 2 = 2050 - 1 = 2049$, it still [doesn't] equal 2025. (Marjorie, grade 7)

A couple of seventh graders mirrored Katrina's response: "Yes, because each year he gets an even number of seeds, eats one, and buries an odd number of seeds." One sixth grader did not think Jack could bury that many seeds because his yard could not get any larger.

This situation could be interpreted in a variety of ways. If students used only the values given in the story, then planting the given number of seeds was not possible. If the problem was hypothetical, then it would be possible to bury 2025 seeds, assuming that 2026 were produced that year and Jack ate one. The focus of the activity was not to find one specific answer but rather to apply algebraic thinking to make a decision and then to give a reasonable justification for it.

After having completed the extended table, students had little difficulty in determining the number of seeds that would be produced if 2000 seeds were buried. However, an interesting extension developed in the seventh-grade class. Students wondered how long it would take to plant or bury 2000 seeds. We used this teachable moment to ask students to determine how long it would take to bury that many seeds if we could bury one seed every two seconds. We found that we could bury 2000 seeds in about 66 minutes. Then we extended this question to determine the number of seeds we could bury in a year if we buried 1 seed every 2 seconds and worked 4 hours per day for 5 days a week. Students became excited as they found the number of seeds buried in a week and then used the number of weeks in a year to determine the total number of seeds buried in a year. The result was quite large, and students had to write their answers in scientific notation, a topic that they had recently been studying. The extension to rates and scientific notation was an added bonus that we had not previously considered.

It was very instructive to have students graph the data in the table, placing the "year" on the horizontal axis and the "number of seeds buried" on the vertical axis marked off in increments of 10. Even though students were not prepared to express the relationship algebraically, they were able to graph the relationship. The number of seeds buried in year y can be represented by $2^y + 1$, with the understanding that year 0 represents the first year that two seeds were buried. Hence, middle school students were introduced to graphing exponential functions. We believe that it is very important that students have the opportunity to graph not only linear functions but a wide variety of functions. An added benefit of this graphing exercise was that students had to use different scales on the two axes.

We spent roughly two-thirds of the first class period on activity sheet 2 and began the second class period with the graph.

Activity sheet 3

Once Jack meets Alice, the patterns become more complex. Hence, activity sheet 3 was handed out to students so that they could complete the patterns as we read the third portion of the story (see fig. 3). Table 3 contains a completed table for activity sheet 3 through year 9.

Table 3
A Completed Table from Activity Sheet 3

Year	6	7	8	9	10	11
Number of seeds produced	66	128	200	240		
Number of seeds eaten	2	2	2	3		
Number of seeds given away		—	10	—	—	
Number of seeds stored		—	16	34	51	
Number of seeds sold that have not been stored		—	—	44	66	
Number of seeds buried	64	100	120	120		

Several interesting results occurred while completing this table. Although the number of seeds produced in one year continued to be twice the number of seeds buried the previous year, other relationships also had to be considered. Students had to recognize that the sum of the number of seeds eaten, the number given away, the number stored, the number sold but not stored, and the number buried had to equal the num-ber of seeds produced from those planted the previous year. When students attempted to determine the number of seeds buried each year, they had to use this relationship to justify their results.

Several students had initial difficulty with some of the language in the story that related to selling seeds. During year 7, Jack stored 16 seeds. In year 8, Jack sold 60 seeds, including the 16 stored the previous year. Some students initially thought that he sold 76, not understanding the meaning of the word *including*. Students had to argue their position with one another until the class was convinced about which result was more appropriate for the number sold.

In addition to using the story to complete the table for years 6–9, we asked students to complete the table for years 10 and 11. Many reasonable results are possible, subject to the following constraints: the number of seeds produced in year 10 must be 240; the number of seeds produced in year 11 must be twice the number buried in year 10; and the sum of the number eaten, given away, stored, sold but not stored, and buried must equal the number produced in that year. We found that some of the students were quite proficient in completing their tables while considering these constraints. Others determined the number produced in year 10 correctly and then completed the remainder of the table haphazardly without regard to the physical constraints of the problem. A third day on this lesson would have given us time to address these difficulties.

Assigning the students to write an ending to the story and then write two problems was quite revealing. Some of the students focused on Jack's dying or being killed, since the seventh-grade visit occurred on Halloween. Others wrote interesting twists to the story, as evident in the student samples in figures 4–5.

After students completed their story endings and presented some of them to the class, we read the ending of the story. Students then completed the final two questions on activity sheet 3 and had no difficulty following the patterns and determining the number of years before the condition was met.

Conclusion

Currently in our society, the mention of the word *algebra* causes many people to

5. Write an ending to the story. Then write two problems that other students could answer after reading your ending.

This time on the 10th year they decided to store 60 and bury sixty but this year was strange when he went a go check his seeds they were all gone and nothing was left but bites in the leaves so we knew he had a bug problem. So he got the sixty seeds out of the store house 4 the child's birthday there were 2 guests who got 2 seeds each and the child, father, and Alice ate a seed. He buried the rest.

How many were eaten?
How many were buried?

Fig. 4. Story written by Joyce, grade 7

5. Write an ending to the story. Then write two problems that other students could answer after reading your ending.

Sandy was walking along when she found a seed. She didn't know exactly what kind of seed it was but she buried it anyways. The next year she got 2 more seeds so she decided she was going to bury one & save another until she decided what to do;

Jack was taking his child to the store & saw Sandy's patch of seeds. He stopped at her house to see Sandy told him how she found the seed. They made a deal that if she gave him her seeds he would give her 25% of the seeds that were produced the next year. How many seeds were given to Sandy the next year

→ It's been 6 years

Fig. 5. Story written by Joyce, grade 7

experience discomfort. Even middle school students who have not yet taken an algebra course often have negative views about algebra and do not believe they are capable of exploring algebraic relationships. Using literature as a vehicle to introduce patterns and then explore, describe, and extend those patterns creates algebraic experiences in an interesting and nonthreatening manner. Students appeared to enjoy the lessons and were able to express a constant function, an exponential function, and a recursive function in their own words. Having students write about the mathematical patterns found in the story and extend those patterns helps develop algebraic thinking, since they will need to express these relationships symbolically in an algebra class.

With the building of algebraic thinking from activities like those developed here, students will be better able to understand the more abstract symbolic approach to functions and patterns used to model real-world situations.

References

Anno, Mitsumasa. *Anno's Magic Seeds.* New York: Philomel Books, 1995.

National Council of Teachers of Mathematics. *Curriculum and Evaluation Standards for School Mathematics.* Reston, Va.: The Council, 1989.

———. "Algebra for Everyone … More Than a Change in Enrollment Patterns." Reston, Va.: The Council, 1994. Position statement.

Additional Resources

Anno, Masaichiro, and Mitsumasa Anno. *Anno's Mysterious Multiplying Jar.* New York Philomel Books, 1983.

Interesting patterns of objects found in a jar are used to develop factorials.

Barry, David. *The Rajah's Rice: A Mathematical Folktale from India.* New York: W. H. Freeman & Co., 1994.

In this folktale a pattern is started by placing two grains of rice on the first square of a chessboard, four on the second square, and so on, doubling the number of grains of rice on each new square.

Birch, David. *The King's Chessboard.* New York: Puffin Pied Piper Books, 1988.

This retelling of the Indian folktale The Rajah's Rice begins with one grain of rice on the first square.

Clement, Rod. *Counting on Frank.* Milwaukee, Wisc.: Gareth Stevens Publishing, 1991.

Although the primary focus of this story is on counting, proportions and rates are used throughout in humorous ways.

Hong, Lily Toy. *Two of Everything.* Morton Grove, Ill.: Albert Whitman & Co., 1993.

This tale from China deals with a pot that doubles everything placed into it.

Pittman, Helena Clare. *A Grain of Rice.* New York: Bantam Skylark Books, 1986.

A humble servant requests one grain of rice on the first day, with the amount of rice to be doubled each day for 100 days. This version of the tale is set in China.

Read the story until Jack says, "This can just go on and on in the same way forever." Use the information in the story to complete the table below.

Year	0	1	2	3	4	5	6
Number of seeds produced	—						
Number of seeds eaten	1						
Number of seeds buried	1						

Use the results in the table to answer the following questions.

1. a. What do you notice about the number of seeds produced each year?
   b. Explain why you get this result.
2. Describe all the patterns you see in the table.
3. Jack thought, "This can just go on and on in the same way forever." Is he right? How do you know?
4. If the patterns in the table continued in the same way, what would the next four columns be?

Year	7	8	9	10
Number of seeds produced				
Number of seeds eaten				
Number of seeds buried				

5. a. Describe, in words, a relationship among the number of seeds eaten, the number of seeds buried, and the number of seeds produced.
   b. If p = number of seeds produced, e = number of seeds eaten, and b = number of seeds buried, describe the relationship from part (a) using p, e, and b.

Name_____

Continue reading the story from the time that Jack decides to bury both seeds until he meets Alice. Use the information in the story to complete the table below. The year that Jack buries both seeds is labeled Year 0.

Year	0	1	2	3	4	5
Number of seeds produced	——	4				
Number of seeds eaten	0	1				
Number of seeds buried	2	3				

Use the results in the table to answer the following questions.

1. a. What do you notice about the number of seeds produced each year?
   b. Explain why you get this result.
2. Describe all the patterns you see in the table.
3. If the patterns in the table continued in the same way, what would the next five columns be?

Year	6	7	8	9	10
Number of seeds produced	——				
Number of seeds eaten					
Number of seeds buried					

4. Suppose that Jack lost track of the number of seeds. He told a friend that he thought he buried 2025 seeds. Is this value possible? Explain your answer.
5. a. To find the number of seeds produced in any year, what information from the table do you need to know?
   b. Suppose that in some year 2000 seeds were buried. How many seeds would be produced and how many seeds would be buried the next year?
6. a. Describe in words a relationship among the number of seeds eaten, the number of seeds buried, and the number of seeds produced.
   b. If p = the number of seeds produced, e = the number of seeds eaten, and b = the number of seeds buried, describe the relationship from part (a) using p, e, and b.
   c. Suppose that in some year 88 seeds are buried. How many seeds would be produced the next year?
   d. Suppose that in some year b seeds are buried. How many seeds would be produced the next year?
7. Use the results from your table to complete the graph you were given.

Challenge: Suppose that y represents the year. Find a rule that gives the number of seeds buried in year y.

Activity Sheet 3

Name _____

Read the story from the time when Jack meets Alice until Jack says, "The wind is blowing awfully hard!" Use the information in the story to complete the table below for years 6, 7, 8, and 9. In the story, Jack meets Alice in year 6.

Year	6	7	8	9	10	11
Number of seeds produced	66					
Number of seeds eaten	2					
Number of seeds given away	——					
Number of seeds stored	——					
Number of seeds sold that have not been stored	——					
Number of seeds buried	64					

1. Describe all the patterns that you see in the table.
2. If the patterns were to continue in the same way, predict the values in the table for years 10 and 11.
3. *a.* For years 8 and 9, describe in words a relationship among the number of seeds produced, the number of seeds eaten, the number of seeds stored, the number of seeds sold that had not been stored, and the number of seeds buried. *b.* How can you describe the relationship in part (*a*) using symbols?
4. From the table, there seems to be a maximum number of seeds that can be produced in any year. What are some reasons why such a maximum number exists?
5. Write an ending to the story. Then write two problems that other students could answer after reading your ending.

Read the rest of the story.

6. Jack is able to save 10 seeds. The family eats 3 and buries 7. Suppose that Jack will sell some of the seeds as soon as he produces at least 35 in one year. How long will it be before Jack sells some of the seeds?
7. Suppose that Jack and Alice have another child as soon as the storm is over. How much longer would it take before Jack produces at least 35 seeds in one year?

CAROL ANN HARLOS

THE more generalized curriculum of the middle school years presents an excellent opportunity for students to begin to seek patterns and to make mathematical predictions. The following activity offers such an experience. The students' background necessary for this activity includes understanding multiples and powers, finding simple formulas, and evaluating formulas. Although the activity is written in student-ready form, teacher direction is usually necessary to help most students complete the investigation.

Introducing the Activity

Students are asked if they have ever played a game such as "One potato, two potato, three potato, four, ..." wherein a rhythmic saying is used to choose a person

---

Carol Ann Harlos *teaches at the Dr. Charles R. Drew Science Magnet School, Buffalo, NY 14214. She is interested in hands-on mathematics and the use of technology to enhance mathematics instruction.*

for, or to eliminate a person from, a game. The teacher might mention that stopping and starting of Ferris-wheel rides to let people on and off is based on a counting-off scheme that occurs over and over until the Ferris wheel is full or empty. Also mentioned might be the fact that the lug nuts on automobiles are tightened in a counting pattern to prevent too much tightening on one side. Some types of assembly lines use this technique to keep parts constantly moving on a belt. Students should be encouraged to list any games or activities that use this type of counting.

Although this exercise can be completed on paper, students enjoy an introduction in which they physically model the activity. Students wear numbers and stand in a circle. The "counter," who wears no number, eliminates every second student from the circle until only one student is left. This procedure is repeated for different numbers of students. Records are kept of the results and a pattern is sought.

This process is then modeled by drawing circles on paper, entering the needed numbers around the circle, and crossing off the

eliminated numbers. A worksheet is included, which can be used to structure the exploration.

This activity can be used in a cooperative setting, as a whole-class activity, or even as an individual project. The answers to the worksheet appear on page 211.

Reference

Stevenson, Frederick W. *Exploratory Problems in Mathematics.* Reston, Va.: National Council of Teachers of Mathematics, 1992.

And the Winner Is ...

NAME _____

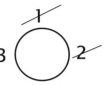

Have you ever played a game in which you counted off following a certain rule to find a winner? Mathematics can help us make predictions about the outcome of following certain rules.

Suppose that the first 2 counting numbers are arranged around a circle and that you follow these rules: Start on 1. Count clockwise, one-two, one-two, ... Cross off every second number until only one number—the winner—is left. The answer in this example is 1.

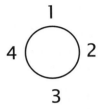

1. Try 3 counting numbers. Start on 1. Cross off every second number. The winner is _____.

2. Try 4 counting numbers. Start on 1 again and cross off every second number until only one number remains. Do not count a number already crossed off. The winner is _____.

3. Draw more circles and determine the winners for the counting numbers 5 through 32. Set up a chart from 2 to 32 to see if a pattern exists.

Numbers	Winners	Numbers	Winners	Numbers	Winners	Numbers	Winners
2	_____	10	_____	18	_____	26	_____
3	_____	11	_____	19	_____	27	_____
4	_____	12	_____	20	_____	28	_____
5	_____	13	_____	21	_____	29	_____
6	_____	14	_____	22	_____	30	_____
7	_____	15	_____	23	_____	31	_____
8	_____	16	_____	24	_____	32	_____
9	_____	17	_____	25	_____		

4. List any patterns or other observations.

_____

5. List only those counting numbers whose winner is the number 1.

_____

6. List any observations you can make about the numbers listed in your answer to question 5.
   Make a prediction on the basis of your findings.

_____

_____

7. From the chart in question 3, list only those numbers that resulted in 3 as the winner. _____ Relate these counting numbers to the counting numbers that had 1 as winner. (*Hint:* Write numbers that had 1 as the winner as powers of 2.) What do you observe? _____

_____

8. Repeat the procedure described in question 7 for all counting numbers that resulted in 5 as the winner. What do you observe? _____
   _____

9. Repeat the same procedure for all counting numbers that resulted in 7 as the winner.___
   _____

10. So far you have related the last, or winning, number to the number 2. Use this information to predict the winning number from the counting number itself. Organize your data into a new chart. List each winning number in column A, the counting numbers that result in this number in column B, and the difference between each counting number and its nearest power of 2 in column C.

    Relate the numbers in column A to the numbers in column C. Write a formula to show this relationship.

A WINNER	B COUNTING NUMBERS	C DIFFERENCE BETWEEN EACH COUNTING NUMBER AND ITS NEAREST POWER OF 2
_____	_____	_____
_____	_____	_____
_____	_____	_____
_____	_____	_____

11. Try your formula on the number 12. What number do you predict as the winner?_____ Is this prediction correct? _____. If not, go back to step 10 and repeat the procedure until you get a correct prediction.

12. Find at least 2 numbers not listed in problem 10 that have 7 as a winner._____ Explain how you chose these numbers. _____
    _____

13. Try your rule on any other numbers from your first chart to make sure it always works in these additional examples.

14. Try setting your formula equal to a specific winning number. Select a value for one of the variables. What does this process enable you to do? _____
    _____

15. You are now ready to answer this question: What would the winning number be if 10 000 numbers were arranged around a circle and every second number was crossed off until only one number was left? (You will probably want to use a calculator for this problem.) What is the answer? Explain or show how you found your answer.
    _____
    _____

Further Explorations

- Develop a formula for finding the "winning number" if the crossing-off rule is for a number other than 2.

- Develop a formula if the crossing-off rule involves more than one number, for example, crossing off every second and third number until only one number remains.

ACTIVITY SHEET

Answers to And the Winner Is...

1. 3

2. 1

3.

Numbers	Winners	Numbers	Winners
2	1	18	5
3	3	19	7
4	1	20	9
5	3	21	11
6	5	22	13
7	7	23	15
8	1	24	17
9	3	25	19
10	5	26	21
11	7	27	23
12	9	28	25
13	11	29	27
14	13	30	29
15	15	31	31
16	1	32	1
17	3		

4. Answers will vary. Observations might include these:

a) The winner is always an odd number, as all multiples of 2 are eliminated.

b) The winners form a pattern of odd numbers, first 1, 3; then 1, 3, 5, 7; then 1, 3, 5, 7, 9, 11, 13, 15; then 1, 3, 5, 7, 9, 11, 13, 15, 17, 19, 21, 23, 25, 27, 29, 31.

c) The cycle starts over at 1 each time we begin with a number that is a power of 2, that is, numbers such as 2, 4, 16, or 32 give 1 as the winner.

d) The differences between the number of counting numbers that were used on the circle and their corresponding winners also form a pattern.

$$2 - 1 = 1 \quad 5 - 3 = 2 \quad 8 - 1 = 7$$
$$3 - 3 = 0 \quad 6 - 5 = 1 \quad 9 - 3 = 6$$
$$4 - 1 = 3 \quad 7 - 7 = 0 \quad 10 - 5 = 5$$

5. 2, 4, 8, 16, 32. A trivial case results when the circle has only the number 1. It wins because no second number is present to cross off. This result gives 2^0, or 1. This outcome can also be expressed as $2^0 + 0 = 1$.

6. They are all powers of 2, that is, 2^1, or 2; 2^2, or 4; 2^3, or 8; 2^4, or 16; 2^5, or 32. One might predict that the winning number for 64, 128, and so on, would also be 1.

7. 3, 5, 9, 17. The differences between these numbers are 2, 4, and 8. Also, $2^1 + 1 = 3, 2^2 + 1 = 5, 2^3 + 1 = 9, 2^4 + 1 = 17$. Inversely,

$3 - 2$ (actually 2^1) $= 1, 1 \times 2 = 2, 2 + 1 = 3$ (winner)

$5 - 4$ (actually 2^2) $= 1, 1 \times 2 = 2, 2 + 1 = 3$

$9 - 8$ (actually 2^3) $= 1, 1 \times 2 = 2, 2 + 1 = 3$

$17 - 16$ (actually 2^4) $= 1, 1 \times 2 = 2, 2 + 1 = 3$

8. 6, 10, 18. The differences between these numbers are 4 and 8. Also, $2^2 + 2 = 6$, $2^3 + 2 = 10, 2^4 + 2 = 18$. Inversely, $6 - 4$ (actually 2^2) $= 2, 2 \times 2 = 4, 4 + 1 = 5$ (winner), and so forth.

9. 7, 11, 19. The differences between the numbers are 4 and 8. Also, $2^2 + 3 = 7, 2^3 + 3 = 11, 2^4 + 3 = 19$. Inversely, $7 - 4 = 3, 3 \times 2 = 6, 6 + 1 = 7$ (winner), and so forth.

10.

		C
		Difference
		between Each
A	B	Counting Number
		and its Nearest
Winner	Numbers	Power of 2
1	2, 4, 8, 16, 32	0*
3	3, 5, 9, 17	1*
5	6, 10, 18	2*
7	7, 11, 19	3*

*Difference is the same for all numbers in column B.

Answers will vary slightly. We could use a formula such as $W = 2(C - 2^N) + 1$, where C is the number of counting numbers around the circle, 2^N is the largest power of 2 less than or equal to C, and W is the winner.

11.–13. Answers will vary.

14. Answers will vary. A possible answer might be that the formula enables you to—

a) find a value for the number of counting numbers placed around a circle, given a power of 2 and the winner, or

b) determine whether a particular winner is possible given a particular power of 2. For example, choosing 7 as the winner and 40 for the number of counting numbers gives $(40 - 2^N) \times 2 = 7$, an impossible result.

15. The power of 2 closest to 10 000 is 8 192. Using the formula then gives the answer of 3 617.

RHETA N. RUBENSTEIN

The Function Game

"Input 3."

"Double the number and add 1."

"Output is 7."

WHEN I began teaching in the late 1960s, we had no videotapes, commercial manipulatives, or calculators to create engaging learning activities for students. I recall spending a good part of my first year searching desperately for ways to motivate my seventh and eighth graders and help them learn mathematics. One activity that I stumbled across worked magically. I

Rheta Rubenstein *currently teaches mathematics at a community college in Livonia, Michigan. Formerly she was professor of education at the University of Windsor and a secondary school teacher in Detroit, Michigan. She is interested in making meaningful, useful mathematics accessible for all students.*

thought, "This is a gem," and I continue to cherish it today. I call it the "function game," but my students and others have called it the "input-output game," "guess my rule," or the "computer game." I understand that the game first gained prominence in the "new math" era, but it must have been around in some form much earlier. Today, the game is available on many computer systems and is popular with students and teachers. The computer versions, however, lack many dimensions of the live version.

I have used this game throughout my career with junior and senior high school students and, more recently, with preservice and in-service teachers. I find it to be flexible, engaging, and effective in teaching

many essential mathematics concepts. Every time I use it, I continue to marvel at its power and potential. I will demonstrate how it works and share ideas for using it to teach lots of mathematics.

The rules are simple. One person is the "computer" and thinks of a rule, for example, "double the number and add 1." Classmates give "input" values, and the "computer" gives the corresponding output for each. These output values are recorded one at a time on a table as shown in figures 1–9. The object of the game is to guess the rule. When playing with a whole class, we do not went to spoil the fun quickly, so I tell the students that if they know the rule, they should not say it aloud but just tell the "computer" that they know it. Then the

214   ACTIVITIES FOR JUNIOR HIGH SCHOOL AND MIDDLE SCHOOL MATHEMATICS

"computer" gives an input value and the player must give the output If the answer is correct, it will be recorded in the table and play continues. When it becomes clear that most students know the rule, one player is allowed to state it Another student is then chosen to be the next "computer."

Benefits of the Game

The game has many benefits. Because it it predicated on a "secret rule," students are intrigued and motivated to play. Because it is simple and requires no materials, it can be played at any time, for example, as a warm-up or brief closing activity or as part of the development of a lesson. More important, the game uses lots of mathematics. Even to determine simple rules, students must use mental mathematics. Clearly, it requires problem solving that can be very challenging, as shown subsequently. Playing also promotes many opportunities for communication. Moreover. as its name suggests. it is a function game and develops key ideas of algebra: variable, expression, function, and modeling. Let us see how some of these concepts are fostered.

Figures 1–9 show several games in action. Before reading on, try to guess the rules.

Discourse about Equivalent Expressions

One of the major recommendations of the NCTM's *Professional Standards for Teaching Mathematics* (1991) is for teachers to promote discourse in mathematics classes. This game definitely affords opportunities for class discussions. For example, when I use the rule in figure 1, I ask students to state it in as many different ways as they can. Some of their responses follow:

• "Double the number and take away two."
• "Take twice the number, then minus two."
• "Multiply by two, subtract two."

This activity gives us an opportunity to recognize that mathematical operations can be expressed in many equivalent ways, which leads to one of the major benefits of the game: the natural and meaningful introduction of variables. Among the multiple expressions of this rule that students may suggest—or can be shown—is $2n - 2$, where n represents any number. This expression illustrates the efficiency of using symbols and, when coupled with the earlier discussion of different expressions, shows how the language of algebra can generalize arithmetic.

Another expression that sometimes surfaces for the data in figure 1 is "take one less than the number, then double it." If this answer is not suggested by a student, I will say, "I once had someone tell it to me like this...." As with the other rules, we discuss it to see if it works. Depending on where students are in their work with variables, this discussion can serve as an excellent entree to explore the equivalence of $2n - 2$ and $(n - 1)2$ or $2(n - 1)$. Figure 2 shows another example in which two seemingly different rules work: multiply the number by the next number or square the number and add it to itself, which algebraically is $n(n + 1)$, or $n^2 + n$. These and similar examples are opportunities for introducing the concept of the distributive property in rewriting algebraic expressions.

Figure 3 is also interesting. Some students see it as "what you need to add to get ten," whereas others see it as "ten minus the number." I call it "the tens complement." Each new type of rule enlarges the students' repertoire of ideas with which to challenge their classmates in future games.

Number Theory and Number Sense

Number theory, an important topic in middle school mathematics, can be developed nicely through this game. For example, figure 4 shows a rule that sorts multi-

Input	Output
7	12
12	22
4	6
8	14
3	4

Fig. 1

Input	Output
5	30
8	72
11	132
0	0
2	6

Fig. 2

Input	Output
2	8
5	5
12	–2
6	4
20	–10

Fig. 3

Input	Output
7	0
12	1
4	0
8	0
3	1
9	1

Fig. 4

Input	Output
5	0
8	3
11	1
0	0
2	2
9	4

Fig. 5

Input	Output
2	1
5	1
12	0
6	0
20	0
11	1

Fig. 6

Input	Output
2	1
5	2
12	3
6	2
20	4
36	6

Fig. 7

Input	Output
7	11
12	13
4	5
8	11
3	5
9	11

Fig. 8

Input	Output
5	4
8	4
11	4
0	4
2	4
9	4

Fig. 9

ples of 3; it outputs a 1 to say, "Yes, this input is a multiple of three" and a 0 to say, "No, this is not a multiple of three." Obviously this rule can be extended to other multiples. Figure 5 is usually a baffling rule initially. Then, as they do with many earlier games, students get wise and decide to give inputs in sequence to see better what is happening. Often they will see the pattern but may not be able to explain it, saying, "It goes zero, one, two, three, four, zero, one, two, three, four, and so on." Sometimes it helps to ask them to think about the numbers that produce zero. Once they see that the rule can also be expressed as the remainder when the input is divided by 5, their repertoire is again expanded and they have been introduced to modular arithmetic.

The rule in figure 6 can be tough unless students have recently been working with prime numbers. If they have, and if they have seen other "sorting machines" as in figure 4, then someone usually figures out that it is a prime sorting machine, producing a 1 for primes and a 0 for nonprimes. Often students need more data than the set shown. Of course, once this machine is introduced, it can be reused later simply to provide practice in recognizing primes.

Figure 7 illustrates a rule that challenges students' number sense. For each input, the "computer" produces the whole-number part of the square root of the number. This rule combines the concept of square root and what is sometimes called the "floor function" or the "round down function." Related rules that can also be used are "round to the nearest" or "round up," which is sometimes called the "ceiling function."

The function game can also introduce notions of domain and range, the acceptable input values of a function and the resulting outputs, respectively. For example, I have told students, "The next machine takes decimal values" or "This one accepts fractions." When they have done this activity a few times, I introduce the term *domain* as the set of acceptable inputs. Then I can say such things as "The domain of this function is improper fractions." In addition to introducing new vocabulary, these variants allow us to use more rules. For example, if the domain is decimal numbers, good rules to use are rounding, multiplying or dividing by 10s or 100s,

adding 20, and so on. If the domain is improper fractions, good rules are renaming as a mixed number, rounding to the nearest whole number, adding 1, or doubling. In each instance, we continue to talk about multiple ways to express the rule. In this way, for example, students can see that multiplying a decimal by 10 and "moving the decimal point one place to the right" are equivalent. Whereas some of these rules might not challenge students for long in the "guess my rule" aspect of the game, they do offer engaging practice and mental mathematics.

Probably the most challenging rule I ever invented for my eighth graders was the one shown in figure 8. They had played the game many times and were pretty good at it, but this rule kept them going for a long, long time. After we had filled three or four tables of values and no one had found the rule, I said that if anyone got it, he or she could simply state it. Interest was very high. Finally, from the back corner of the room a young man volunteered who rarely participated and whom the others perceived as being a nonparticipant. "It's the next prime number," he announced. Students saw immediately that his answer was correct. The class was stunned. An audible silence was followed by gasps, then by congratulations. I believe that everyone's perception of the student was profoundly changed in this instant. This experience was definitely a telling moment in my career. It confirmed dramatically my belief that we never really know the depth of our students.

Simplicity Made Complex

The rule in figure 9 also has an interesting, but more recent story. I was doing a workshop with preservice elementary teachers. I had introduced the game, and we had played several rounds together. Then I asked them to take turns playing at their tables. After a while, I asked each group to choose what it thought was the most interesting rule and to play it with the whole class. One student's rule produced a table like the one in figure 9. I loved it. I had never before dreamed of playing a constant rule, and I thought that this idea was simple, yet important. I was even more impressed to see the student teacher take long pauses after each input while she seemed to be calculating the output. "What drama!" I thought, "She's really playing it

up!" The class, too, was engrossed. At one point, a player asked for the output for pi. The "computer," said she would have to round it, wrote 3.14, and paused for a really long time, then wrote 4 again.

After different students had said that they knew the rule and had given correct outputs, I felt that it was time to move on and asked for someone to state the rule, which in my mind was simply "write four." A student said, "Subtract the number from itself and add four." I was surprised. As enamored as I was of the notion of multiple rules, I really had not thought about this one as a calculation. Other students objected. One said, "No, my rule was 'Multiply by zero then add four.'" Then the "computer" said, "No, my rule was 'Divide the number by itself and multiply by four.'" I realized then that her long pauses were not drama; she was really calculating for each input! Rumblings continued. We began recording the various rules. Many were like "double the number, divide by the number, then add two" or "add seven, subtract the number, then subtract three." I thought that surely, if I waited long enough, someone would state my simple version. No one did. Finally, I said, "I thought about it another way. Whatever the input is, the output is four." Frowns appeared. They did not like this answer at all. People thought that I was cheating! "You're supposed to 'do' something with the input," they told me. What I learned was that in their perception of a "rule," "steps" or "procedures" must occur. In their estimation, arithmetic, not insights, yielded the only legal moves. I realized that the notion of a constant rule, like many other concepts in mathematics, is so simple that it is challenging.

In retrospect, I regretted that I had missed a golden opportunity. Their notions of working with zeros and ones and with steps that undid themselves had offered an opportunity to help them learn about identities and inverses. Alas, not every teachable moment is captured!

Extensions and Variants

Another strength of the game is the possibility of extensions and variants. One major extension is to have students graph the ordered pairs. Rules like $n + 2$, $n + 5$, and $n - 3$ can be graphed and compared. They produce points on parallel lines.

Rules like $2n + 1$, $3n + 1$, $(1/2)n + 1$, and $-n + 1$ produce points on lines that all intersect the y-axis at 1. Rules like $n(n + 1)$ or n^2 or $n(n - 2)$ produce points on a curve, specifically, a parabola. Such functions grow more quickly than do those that produce lines. They afford excellent opportunities to introduce and contrast linear and quadratic growth, although not necessarily in those terms, and, in the case of lines, to introduce concepts like slope and intercept. Also, once students realize that graphs can help them see the rules, graphs, too, become another tool for playing the game.

As another extension, students can be asked questions about what is or is not possible. For example, after playing the rule "double the number and add 1," ask students, "If the domain is the set of integers, can the computer produce twelve?" Reasoning questions like this one pave the way for later work with proof.

Another variant of the game is to play in reverse. Say, "If you know the rule, I'll give you the output and you give me the input" In other words, the students are inverting the rule. Only rules that have unique inputs for each output will work, however. For example, any linear function rule will work but not rules involving squares or rounding. This variant is an excellent way to get students started with equation solving For example, if the rule is $2n + 1$ and the output is 13, to find the input they must subtract the 1 then divide by 2 to get 6. Figure 10 illustrates the process with a diagram. This variant is a chance to talk about how we undo expressions in the opposite order in which we evaluate them and how we use inverse operations at each step.

The game can also be played with two inputs. For example, with rational numbers as the domain, rules could be "pick the

larger value," "add," or "average the two values."

The game can also be connected to geometry with diagrams and materials. Both the elementary- and middle-grades NCTM Addenda books on patterns, *Patterns* (Coburn et al. 1993) and *Patterns and Functions* (Phillips et al. 1991), respectively, contain several examples of geometric rules. Figure 11 shows activities adapted from the grades K–6 Addenda book (Coburn et al. 1993). Item 1 in figure 11 is $n(n + 1)$, which was mentioned earlier. Item 2 illustrates "double the previous term number and add 1" or "the sum of the term number and the previous term number." This item gives another chance to show equivalence, this time of $2(n - 1) + 1$ and $n + (n - 1)$. All students benefit from

visualizing algebraic expressions geometrically; this experience may be particularly important for students who learn better visually. The grades 5–8 Addenda book (Phillips et al. 1991) presents other excellent examples of geometric-patterning activities. Anno (1989), in his "Magic Machine" chapter, also offers appealing nonnumerical visual images of the function idea that can be used with young as well as middle-grades children.

The game can also help build an essential idea for probability: random numbers. This version requires a calculator. Most calculator random-number generators produce a random number between 0 and 1. One way to play this "rule" for any input is to give the first digit in the decimal display of a random number. Other ways would be to give the first two digits, and so on. In any example, the "pattern" that students need to recognize is the absence of a pattern. The output is unpredictable. This variant illustrates another simple, yet important, mathematical idea.

Conclusion

The function game offers many opportunities to introduce, develop, practice, extend, communicate about, and connect mathematical ideas. Students of all ages enjoy playing and learning with it. Readers are invited to try the function game with their students and explore its remarkable potential.

References

Anno, Mitsumasa. *Anno's Math Games II.* New York: Philomel Books, 1989.

Coburn, Terrence G., with Barbara J. Bushey, Liana C. Holton, Debra Latozas, Debbie Mortimer, and Deborah Shotwell. *Patterns.* Addenda Series, Grades K–6. Reston, Va.: National Council of Teachers of Mathematics, 1993.

National Council of Teachers of Mathematics. *Professional Standards for Teaching Mathematics.* Reston, Va.: The Council, 1991.

Phillips, Elizabeth, with Theodore Gardella, Constance Kelly, and Jacqueline Stewart. *Patterns and Functions.* Addenda Series, Grades 5–8. Reston, Va.: National Council of Teachers of Mathematics, 1991.

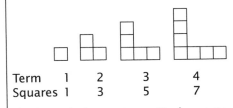

1. **Find the number of unit squares in the rectangles**

Term	1	2	3	4
Squares	2	6	12	?

a) How many unit squares in the 8th term?

b) How many unit squares in the nth term?

c) Is 81 a possible number of squares in some term in the pattern? How do you know?

d) If you know the number of unit squares in the nth term, how can you find the number of squares in the next term?

2. **Make Ls on grid paper.**

Term	1	2	3	4
Squares	1	3	5	7

a) Extend the pattern. Find expressions for the nth term.

b) Make a new pattern: Combine the first two figures, then the first three, then the first four, and so on. What new shapes do you get? How many squares? Describe the pattern.

Fig. 11 Pattern and activities with grid paper (adapted from Coburn et al. [1993])

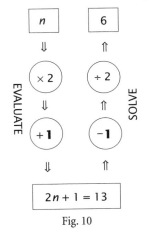

Fig. 10

STEPHEN S. WILLOUGHBY

Activities to Help in Learning about Functions

THE function concept is perhaps as important as any concept in mathematics. It permeates all of mathematics, from first-year algebra through calculus and beyond, as well as most applications of mathematics. This article describes several activities and games that have been used by me and many other teachers to provide a dynamic and enjoyable early introduction to the function concept.

Use a Calculator as a Function Machine

A SIMPLE FOUR-FUNCTION CALCU-LATOR, WITH constant, can be used as a function machine. Different calculators must be programmed differently, so each teacher should experiment with his or her calculator before working with it in class. The T1-108 and most other inexpensive calculators can be set to be a **+ 7** function machine by pressing the following keys: ON/C + 7 = . Press 5 = and the display will show **12**; press 4 = and the display will show **11,** and so on.

To have the display show **0**, press 7 +/- = before handing the calculator to a student. I recommend that a student not see the original **7**, or the subsequent guessing of the function rule becomes trivial.

Give the calculator to a student with the instructions not to touch any key until asked. Tell the student to pick a number and announce it to the class. Suppose that 10 is chosen. Ask the student to press 1 0 and = on the calculator and share

Steve Willoughby *has taught all grades from first through graduate school. He is the principal author of a major textbook series. He can be reached through the University of Arizona, Tucson, AZ 85721.*

with the class what the display shows, which should be **17**. Have the student pick a second number and announce it to the class. This time, however, the other class members should try in advance to guess the number in the display. This activity can be repeated with different operations—subtraction, multiplication, division, or addition—and with any numbers chosen. Once everybody in class understands what is happening, explain to them how to program the calculator and let them play "guess the function rule" in pairs. Player 1 programs the calculator, and player 2 tries to guess the function rule. Students should be able to guess the function rule with only one input-output pair in most situations, but exceptions will occur. For example, suppose the input number is 8 and the output is 16. Was the calculator adding 8 or multiplying by 2 or, possibly, dividing by 0.5? In such cases, a second input-output pair may be needed. With two pairs of inputs and outputs, player 2 should be able to predict the second number in any future pair. Notice, however, that players have no way to establish the difference between the rule × **2** and the rule ÷ **0.5** other than to know what was put in originally.

Pictures of Function Machines

For other activities related to functions, I usually use a picture that resembles a meat grinder (see fig. 1). Suppose we have a + **7** machine. All students should be able to figure what will result for any given input. Next tell them that 10 came out the bottom of the machine. What went in? Continue with similar questions, changing the output. Then change the function rule, telling students what the new rule is, of course, and continue giving outputs, with the class deciding what the input was. Students will determine the input by simply "running

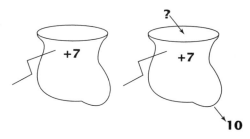

Fig. 1. The "+ 7" function machine

the machine backward" and finding, for example, that the inverse of a + **7** function is a − **7** function and the inverse of an × **7** function is a ÷ **7** function. This activity can be done with a calculator, of course, but one has to remember the original input.

Composite Functions

Next we can proceed with composite functions, which are two simple functions strung together. With the meat grinders, the composite function × **3** followed by + **7** is represented in figure 2. By using calculators, this task can be modeled by two students, each with a rule. The first student makes her or his calculator an × **3** machine, and the second makes his or hers a + **7** machine. Then, for an input of 2, the first student presses 2 = and shows the display **6** to the second student, who then

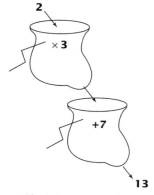

Fig. 2. A composite function

enters 6 = and announces the result, which is **13**.

An interesting and challenging form of "guess the function rule" can be played. Two students, working together, can use rules of the sort previously described. For the best results, one should use multiplication or division and the other should use either addition or subtraction. Let other members of the class choose numbers to put into the composite function machine, and the function machine students process it and announce the result. Of course, this activity can be done with or without calculators, but students tend to think that it is more fun *with* the calculators. Other members of the class should keep records of the ordered pairs of numbers produced in this way and try to predict the output for a given input. Suppose that the first input is 5 and that the output is 12. Class members would record (5, 12). Next, somebody suggests putting in 7. What will come out? Some good guesses may be possible, but presumably nobody other than the original perpetrators knows for sure. Put the 7 in and out comes 20, so the second pair is (7, 20). Wait and let members of the class discuss the possibilities with one another and try to figure out the rule and what the output will be for the next input. Suppose 3 is put in next. What will be the output? Continue with several other pairs of inputs and outputs. The class should be able to predict the outputs correctly.

However, some ambiguity remains as to the rules. Certainly one possibility is that the first rule is × **4** and that the second rule is – **8**. But the first rule could also be – **2** and the second rule, × **4**. Beyond that, either of the × **4** rules could be replaced by ÷ **0.25** and still result in the same set of ordered pairs of inputs and outputs. Which rule is right? Since all four pairs of rules produce exactly the same set of ordered pairs of inputs and outputs, the class has no way of knowing the rules for sure unless the function-machine pair of students tells them. All four composite-function-machine rules are equivalent.

Graph City

Many other activities can be used with composite-function machines. Some calculators or computers, such as the Tandy PC-6, work in like manner, with the function rule hidden. But for the next activity, I would like to be sure that class members understand graphing on a standard coordinate-axis system. If they have not yet been exposed to graphing on coordinate axes, the following activities will provide the necessary experience. In Graph City, the streets are numbered 0, 1, 2, 3, and so on, from west to east, and the avenues are numbered 0, 1, 2, 3, and so on, from south to north (see fig. 3). Edmundo and Fritz have agreed to meet at noon at the corner of Third and Seventh. Where will they meet? Will they meet? Suppose that at noon they both arrive at the spot at which they think they are to meet and do not find each other. What might have happened? Suppose that Edmundo is at the corner of Third Avenue and Seventh Street but that Fritz is at the corner of Third Street and Seventh Avenue. Each realizes what probably happened and decides to go to the other corner. How many paths can each follow? Will they meet?

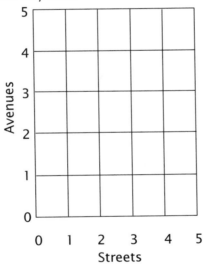

Fig. 3. Graph City

These interesting questions can lead to some good group activities, but for now we are more interested in the students' deciding that some convention should be followed to avoid such errors. One convention is to always use the words street and avenue when giving directions. Another is to agree that "street" will always be mentioned first and "avenue," second, or vice versa. The particular convention is unimportant. It *is* important that everyone use the same convention. Then I explain that mathematicians generally use the convention that the left-right number is given first and the up-down number is second. So the point (3, 5) is 3 units, blocks, or steps to the right of the beginning point, or origin, and 5 units up.

Later, I talk about the need for Graph City to expand because the population is growing. The city can easily expand to the north or east, but what do we do when it expands to the west or south? In classes where students have been exposed to negative numbers previously, there generally is no trouble getting them to agree to calling the avenue to the south of 0 Avenue, –1 Avenue (negative one avenue), and so on; the streets to the west of 0 Street would then be called –1 Street, –2 Street, and so on.

"Get the Point"

Children can play "Get the Point" with each other to practice the convention we just established and become more proficient at locating points on a coordinate axis. In this game, player 1 picks a point on a grid of known size, say, from –5 to 5 in each direction. Suppose that the point (–2, 3) is chosen. Next, player 1 draws two diagonal lines through the chosen point, as in figure 4, then colors the four regions determined by the diagonal lines in red, orange, green, and blue. Player 2 is not allowed to see the point chosen, the lines, or the coloring scheme. Player 2 must try to guess the coordinates of the point that player 1 has chosen. Suppose that player 2 guesses the point (0, 0). Player 1 says, "Green," since (0, 0) is in the green region. Player 2 notes that choice on his or her own graph and guesses another point, say, (–2, 4). Player 1 says, "Red," since (–2, 4) is in the red region. Notice that the point (4, –2) is in the orange region, so order is important, as are the signs of the coordinates. If player 2 next guesses (–1, 2), player 1 must say, "Black," since the point is on one of the lines. The game continues

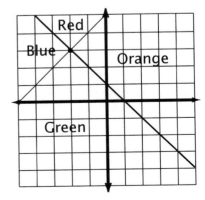

Fig. 4. "Get the point"

until player 2 gets the point chosen by player 1, $(-2, 3)$.

The goal of the game is to get the other player's point in as few guesses as possible. Players practice saying coordinates in the correct order and also use their problem-solving skills to work out efficient strategies for locating the point.

Graphs of Functions

Once students are comfortable with a traditional coordinate system, they can use graphs to analyze various real-life situations. One example is figuring the monthly cost of a checking account plotted against the number of checks cashed at $0.10 cents per check plus $1.50 per month to produce sets of points that lie on the same straight line. There is a danger that such activities may cause students to think that all functions are essentially linear, therefore, I try to introduce some nice functions that are not linear. For example, graphing the mean monthly temperature for a particular city, the raw data for which are available in an almanac and elsewhere, produces a periodic curve. A good high school or college project is to try to find a function rule that produces numbers fairly close to those that are graphed. A sine function works quite well.

An easy function rule to study that produces a nonlinear graph is to plot the area of a square related to the length of a side of the square. The result is a parabola, or half a parabola if we limit ourselves to positive lengths. Many students try to make the points produced by this rule fit a straight line and seem to believe that they must have made a mistake when the points are not on a straight line. I encourage students to compare their results and to discuss the matter until they are convinced that perfectly reasonable function rules can produce nonlinear graphs.

Symbolism

I have deliberately not used much standard notation in these activities, trying to avoid an early introduction of formal notation and definitions when teaching. Historically, most notation is introduced only after concepts are well developed and when people see a need for symbolism that will allow them to encode a complex concept in simple notation. Then and only

then does the symbolism seem to be a convenience. If we introduce symbolism before the concept is understood, we force students to memorize empty symbols and operations on those symbols rather than internalize the concept and use the symbols only to represent what is natural. The same is true of conventions. We should introduce conventions only when students see a real need for the conventions. So the convention of writing the horizontal coordinate before the vertical coordinate should be introduced only after the potential for confusion that could occur without the convention is clearly understood.

For my last activity, which I have used with both eighth- and ninth-grade students, I use some standard notation, which I would have introduced slowly over the years as the need arose. One way to write the rule discussed earlier in which the given number is multiplied by 4 and then 8 is subtracted is $y = 4x - 8$. Another way is to write $f(x) = 4x - 8$, which is read "f of x equals $4x$ minus 8." Although the first method is perfectly correct and adequate for most purposes, the second notation can be more convenient. For that reason, I favor introducing both notations fairly early. The common mistake of believing that "$f(x)$ means f times x" is not likely to occur with students who have spent time with the concept before the notation is introduced.

For the next activity, I use a notation based on the second method. To describe a function of two variables, I use $f(x, y) = 3x - 4y + 2$, which is read "f of x, y is equal to $3x$ minus $4y, + 2$." To find various values of the function, start by choosing an ordered pair, say, $(5, 7)$. Then replace the x in the rule by 5 and then y by 7, getting $(3 \times 5) - (4 \times 7) + 2$, or -11. I assume that students are familiar with numerous conventions regarding variables, omission of multiplication signs, order of operations, and so on. Of course, I would have introduced those conventions through various ambiguities that would exist without them, and we would have discussed the advantage of having such conventions. I would not try to convince students that the conventions that I accept are the only ones that could have been adopted, since I know that rational thought could easily lead to quite different conventions. Rational thought *does* convince us that *some* convention is desirable, and occa-

sionally our esthetic sense or desire to avoid work will lead us to believe that the one we have chosen is at least as good as any other.

Inequalities and the Distance Formula

Using the two-variable function rule $f(x, y) = 3x - 4y + 2$ and a coordinate-axis system with reasonable range, say, from -10 to 10, plot the values of $f(x, y)$ for each ordered pair (x, y) of integers. So, for example, at $(0, 0)$ one would write "2," since $f(0, 0) = 2$. For the point $(3, 3)$ one would write "-1," since $f(3, 3) = -1$, and so on (see fig. 5). Look for interesting patterns. I leave this challenging activity for the reader, but students in eighth or ninth grade can, with the appropriate background, recognize many interesting properties of the resulting patterns. Without giving away those interesting patterns, I call the reader's attention to the relationship among these patterns and linear inequalities, three-dimensional graphs, and the distance formula from a point to a line, which you may wish to review from your study of analytic geometry or may wish to derive from the pattern.

Conclusion

This article has two major purposes. The first is to give the reader some good, tested activities that help middle-grades students become more comfortable with functions. The second is to encourage teachers to offer their students experiences that depend more on the students' experience and understanding and less on memorization of unmotivated conventions with abstract symbols.

Bibliography

Willoughby, Stephen S., Carl Bereiter, Peter Hilton, and Joseph H. Rubinstein. *Real Math, Levels 3–8.* La Salle, Ill.: Open Court Publishing Co., 1981, 1985, 1987, 1991.

MILLIE JOHNSON

Mathematics Detective: Exploring Graphs—WYSIWYG

MANY kinds of graphs and charts confront us wherever we turn. We must be able to pull important information from them when needed, such as the length of time to store milk safely or how much air to put in certain shock absorbers. The following graphs have been taken from various media sources. The questions will guide you in interpreting these interesting graphs.

Questions Relating to Figure 1

1. Is the temperature on the thermometer in figure 1 in degrees Celsius or Fahrenheit? How do you know?

2. If it takes two weeks to finish a carton of milk, at what temperature should it be stored?

3. How long can milk be safely stored at 45 degrees?

4. If you leave milk outside on a 90-degree day, how long will it remain safe to drink?

5. Describe the general relationship between storage temperature and storage time for milk.

Questions Relating to Figure 2

6. The lifting force delivered by two air shock absorbers is defined as the amount of weight that can be safely loaded into or onto a vehicle. The graph in figure 2 shows the setting on each shock absorber necessary to lift various loads. How heavy a load can be carried by a vehicle whose shock

Prepared by Millie Johnson, millie@henson.cc .wwu.edu, Department of Mathematics, Western Washington University, Bellingham, WA 98226

Edited by Jerry Johnson, 935 West Lake Samish Drive, Bellingham, WA 98226.

Fig. 1 One-half-gallon milk carton from Fred Meyer grocery store, Bellingham, Washington

absorbers have an air pressure of 80 psi? The abbreviation psi stands for "pounds per square inch," which is a unit of pressure.

7. To drive safely with 300 pounds of equipment in the trunk, what air pressure is recommended for the shock absorbers?

8. Describe the general relationship between air pressure in the shock absorbers and the vehicle's lifting force.

9. Discuss some differences in the general relationships found in questions 5 and 8.

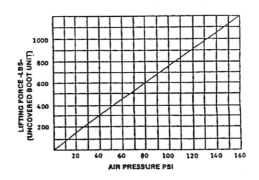

Fig. 2 Owner-information slip from a package of shock absorbers

Question Relating to Figure 3

10. What observations can you make about the sleep-wake patterns of an infant?

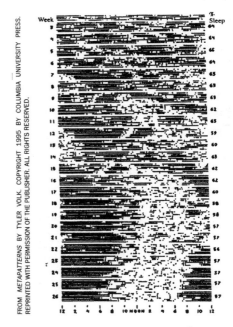

Fig. 3 Graph of sleep-wake patterns of an infant. Horizontal lines are sleep intervals, gaps are wakefulness, and dots are feedings.

Questions Relating to Figure 4

11. Describe the airflow through the nose and mouth of a panting dog (see fig. 4).

12. Over the ten-second interval shown, does the total volume of air inhaled equal the total volume of air exhaled?

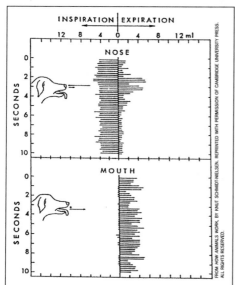

The upper diagram shows the airflow through the nose of a panting dog over a ten-second interval. The lower diagram shows the airflow through the mouth of a panting dog over the same ten-second interval. The segments to the left of the center line indicate the volume of air inhaled, and the segments to the right indicate the volume of air exhaled. Note: *Inspiration* means inhalation and *expiration* means exhalation.

Fig. 4 Graphs of a dog's breathing patterns

Questions Relating to Figure 5

13. A bicyclist racing around a circular track leans, or heels, away from the vertical (fig. 5a). Describe the relationship between the angle that the bicyclist leans from vertical and the speed of the cyclist (see fig. 5b).

14. For constant velocity, interpret the graph that relates the angle that the bicyclist leans from vertical to the radius of the circular track. (An extension is to ask students if they notice anything strange about this graph. They may observe that the domain chosen for the radius seems unrealistic.

A bicyclist riding at speed *v* around a circle of radius *R* heels over at angle *A* with respect to the vertical.

(a)

The Physics of Dimensions

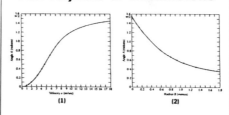

Results from the bicycling experiments, shown schematically: (1), angle *A* plotted against *v* for constant *R*; (2), angle *A* plotted against *R* for constant *v*.

(b)

Fig. 5 (a) Cyclist leaning and (b) graphs relating angle, velocity, and radius

Teachers may then note that the data were extrapolated to show clearly the origin in the accompanying picture and to demonstrate the trend, which is most obvious for small radii. Add that a radius of one meter does not mean that the track is a track with a one-meter radius, rather that the curvature of the path that the bicycle is following at that point has a radius of curvature of one meter. When curves bend sharply, they have small radii of curvature, and when they are flatter, they have a very large radii of curvature.)

15. Why do you think a velodrome has banked tracks?

16. Bring to class a graph that shows a relationship of interest to you.

Mathematics Detective

Hints and Solutions

1. The temperature is in degrees Fahrenheit, since the chart indicates that milk should be kept cold. Thirty-two degrees Celsius is quite warm.

2. Approximately 38 degrees

3. Approximately six days

4. It is difficult to extrapolate in this situation, but one suggestion is that for each 10-degree decrease in temperature, the storage time appears to decrease by approximately one-half. So the approximate safe storage time on a 90-degree day would be one-eighth of a day, or about three hours. To extend the problem, extrapolate in the other direction. That is, how long can milk be stored at 0 degrees? Since freezing has already occurred at 32 degrees, apparently milk should not be stored longer than twenty-four days.

5. In general, the longer that milk will be stored, the colder the storage temperature must be.

6. 600 pounds

7. 40 psi

8. Within reason, the more air pressure shock absorbers have, the more lifting force the vehicle has.

9. The relationship in question 5 is an inverse relationship, whereas question 8 describes a direct relationship. For example, as the storage temperature of milk increases, the safe storage time decreases; as the air pressure in the shock absorbers increases, the lifting force increases as well. Another difference is that the relationship in question 5 is nonlinear, whereas question 8 involves a linear relationship. That is, some students may notice that 10-degree changes in temperature do not account for equal changes in the amount of storage time. Notice, however, that for each change of 20 psi, the lifting force changes by about 150 pounds.

10. According to the original source, "Although the percentage of time spent awake each day does not change much over the twenty-six weeks, its distribution clusters dramatically as the infant entrains to the sun" (Volk 1995, 226).

11. A panting dog inhales mostly through its nose and exhales almost entirely through its mouth. The consequences could be deadly if a panting dog had its nose airway blocked. Have students who own dogs observe the dogs after vigorous exercise to see whether this information seems accurate.

12. Students can come up with different ways to determine whether the volumes are the same. Essentially, they must check to see whether the total length of the segments to the left of the center line is approximately equal to the total length of the segments to the right of the center line, including both nose and mouth.

13. The faster the cyclist rides, the more the cyclist leans from the vertical. Mathematically experienced students might recognize that the relationship is nonlinear.

14. At a constant velocity, as the track radius increases, the leaning angle from the vertical decreases. This relationship makes sense, since if the radius is very large, the track will seem almost straight. For small radii, however, the curve of the track will be quite sharp. These ideas relate to the topic of curvature, in which calculus students learn that the curvature of a circle (K) is inversely proportional to the radius of the circle (p). That is, $K = 1/p$. Also, for a given distance, the cyclist will go around a track with a small radius more times than around a track with a large radius.

15. If a bicycle is at right angles to the track, it has no chance of sliding left or right. If the cyclist leans over at angle A with respect to the vertical, then a track banked at an angle with the same measure as angle A would be particularly safe, since the rider would be at right angles to the track (fig. 6). According to the *World Book Encyclopedia*, velodromes for bicycle racing are wooden or concrete oval tracks whose ends slope inward at a steep angle. This definition implies that the longer stretches on the sides of the oval are not as

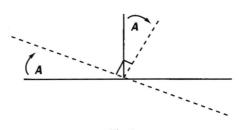

Fig. 6

steeply sloped. Such a design makes sense when related to the curvature idea suggested in question 13.

16. Put a collection of students' graphs on a bulletin board. Have students describe the relationship and pose questions for the class.

References

McMahon, Thomas A., and John Tyler Bonner. *On Size and Life*. New York: W. H. Freeman & Co., 1983.

Schmidt-Nielsen, Knut. *How Animals Work*. New York: Cambridge University Press, 1972.

Volk, Tyler. *Metapatterns across Space, Time, and Mind*. New York: Columbia University Press, 1995.

9

Algebra

THE development of algebraic concepts is an important goal for middle grades mathematics. Although a formal course in Algebra 1 may not be suitable for all students who are completing a grades 5–8 program, all students should be exposed substantially to algebraic thinking during these grades. The NCTM Curriculum Standards call for students to have experiences with variables, expressions, equations, inequalities, patterns, tables, graphs, and other algebraic concepts and processes.

Middle grades students are still in the transition between Piaget's *concrete operations* and *formal operations* stages. All students can benefit from concrete experience with the abstract notions of variables, expressions, and equations. At this stage of development, conceptual understanding should be stressed ahead of any goal of symbol manipulation proficiency. Thus, teachers need to provide students with activities that use physical models to help develop the abstract concepts of algebra. The following activities are examples that may help.

Patterson, in her article, "Building Algebraic Expressions: A Physical Model," describes activities that use such common objects as boxes and adding machine tape to develop an understanding of algebraic expressions. The activities involve creating and evaluating algebraic expressions, and the article discusses assessing students' understanding.

Another similar approach is used by Morelli in "A Visual Approach to Algebra Concepts". Morelli uses both mental arithmetic and physical models to introduce the concepts of variable and variable expressions.

Middle school students—and adults—are often attracted by the lure of M&M's. Borlaug uses the popular candies to develop students' understanding of the formation of equations related to problems. This approach involves physical manipulations to form and solve equations.

Students are motivated to learn mathematics when they can see a real use for it. In "Algebra: Real-Life Investigations in a Lab Setting", McCoy gives a variety of physical experiments that model linear and nonlinear relationships. A bonus is the suggestion of using graphing calculators.

Technology can be used to give a good illustration of patterns and relations. "Spreadsheets, Patterns, and Algebraic Thinking" illustrates how computer spreadsheets can be used to investigate ideas such as the Fibonacci numbers, doubling, powers, and patterns and functions. These activities illustrate the power of instructional tools to develop mathematical concepts.

ANNE C. PATTERSON

Building Algebraic Expressions: A Physical Model

SIMPLE physical models can help middle school students move naturally from their limited world of numbers into the universe of algebraic thinking (NCTM 1989). According to Bruner (1995, 333), mathematics should feel like something a child already knows rather than something totally unfamiliar. He states that the end product of mathematics should not be formalism with a premature emphasis on mathematical language but the confidence a child gains from realizing that mathematics is something that he or she has been thinking right along. This two-part lesson, complete with a step-by-step student activity log, allows students to build on their elementary school experiences of measuring in nonstandard units—disguised here as variables—and thus draw their own blueprint of algebra. Using small cardboard boxes to represent variables gives students the opportunity to view such expressions as $5x + 3y + 7$ as a "measurement" in the physical world rather than as a meaningless string of numbers and letters. During this lesson, students discover that a given value can have multiple representations as they apply estimation skills, substitute values for x and y, evaluate algebraic expressions, measure lengths to the tenth of a centimeter, apply order of operations, verify predictions, and communicate mathematically, all skills recommended by the *Curriculum and Evaluation Standards for School Mathematics* (NCTM 1989).

Anne Patterson *was a middle school mathematics teacher for eleven years. She has been a mathematics and science resource specialist for the Volusia County School Board, P. 0. Box 2410, Daytona Beach, FL 32115-2410, for the past five years.*

Planning the Activity

This activity spans two regular class periods or one double period and is designed for middle school students who have had some experience substituting numerical values into simple variable expressions. In this lesson, students estimate the length of a long strip of paper and then "measure" it using cardboard boxes to represent variables and colored tiles to represent constants. They then create algebraic expressions to represent its length, find the numerical values of the x- and y-boxes using a metric ruler, substitute these decimal values into their algebraic expressions, and evaluate. To conclude the activity, students check their original estimate and calculations against the actual length of the paper and analyze reasons for any discrepancies.

Materials

- 18 small, assorted cardboard boxes, such as paper-clip, staple, and pen boxes or single portion cereal boxes
- 2–4 rolls of adding-machine paper
- 7–9 metric tape measures and rulers
- 80–100 colored tiles
- 20 file-folder labels
- masking tape and paper clips
- 9 fine-tip markers
- calculators and pencils
- a copy of the student activity log for each student

Before class begins, cut a strip of the adding-machine paper so that it is well over one meter long. Then cut additional strips of paper *exactly* the same length as the first. Roll up each strip of paper separately and secure with two paper clips. You will need

one strip for each group in each class. Save the original strip of paper so that the class can measure it at the end of the activity.

Attach a file-folder label marked $\leftarrow x \rightarrow$ on the edge of nine of the small boxes. For the remaining boxes, draw $\leftarrow y \rightarrow$ on folder labels and repeat the process. Keep the x-boxes separate from the y-boxes.

Brief two students in advance so that they can demonstrate the activity as you explain it to the class.

Creating Algebraic Expressions

Arrange your classroom so that each learning group has easy access to floor space. Organize students into cooperative-learning groups and distribute a copy of each student activity log to each student. Hold up several x- and y-boxes so that students can see that the size and shape of the boxes vary from group to group. Position your two demonstration students so that everyone can see them as you give the following oral directions to students:

1. When we are ready to begin, your group will tape your strip of paper to the floor or a table, estimate its length in centimeters, and write your estimates in the box on your student activity log. [Explain that each group has paper of equal length.]

2. Starting at one end of the strip of paper, lay your x-box on the paper, paying attention to the direction of the arrows on the box. Use your marker to draw a line on the paper at the end of the box. Remove the x-box and write "x" in that spot. Repeat this process as many times as you wish using the x-box, but *do not go all the way to the end of the paper.* Continue measuring

the length of the paper with the y-box, and write "y" on the paper each time it is used. Finish your measurement by laying a few of your colored tiles end to end, not side by side, until they reach the end of the paper. Make them fit exactly, even if you must go back to adjust the placement of your x- and y-boxes.

3. Next, count the x's, y's, and colored tiles that your group used to cover the entire length of the paper and write an algebraic expression on your student activity log that looks *something like* $3x + 5y + 4$. It will be different for every group.

4. Next, lift your strip of paper, flip it over, and retape it to the floor or table. Lay down your x- and y-boxes and colored tiles a *different number of times* and write a new algebraic expression on your student activity log.

5. When each member of your group has written two algebraic expressions, I will hand you a ruler so that you can measure in centimeters the x- and y-dimensions of your boxes and the edge of a colored tile. [Explain that if the edge of a box measures 4 cm and 2 mm, it should be written 4.2 cm because 1 millimeter is one-tenth of a centimeter.]

If students have no questions, give each group a long piece of paper, a box labeled x, a box labeled y, ten to fifteen colored tiles, two pieces of masking tape, a fine-tip marker, and calculators. Then students begin. As you circulate, you may find that many students choose not to group all the x's together and all the y's together but rather to alternate them creatively. You may also need to remind them to include plus (+) signs in their expressions.

Evaluating Algebraic Expressions

Continue with these oral directions to students:

6. Before you begin to evaluate your algebraic expressions, write your metric measurements for the lengths of your x- and y-boxes and colored tiles in the appropriate spaces on part 2 of your student activity log.

7. Next, write your algebraic expressions in the appropriate spaces on part 2 of your student activity log.

8. On the lines provided, substitute your metric measurements into both of your algebraic expressions. [Give an example and remind students that $3y$ means 3 times y.]

9. Using a calculator and the correct order-of-operation rules, simplify and round your answers to the nearest centimeter.

10. Next, find the average, or mean, of your answers. The solution you obtain should be a close approximation of the length of the strip of paper! If your strip of paper is still intact, ask the teacher for a tape measure or meterstick so that you can measure it to the nearest centimeter. If your paper is torn, the teacher has the original piece of paper; you may measure that strip instead.

11. Compare your answer with the actual length of the paper to see how accurate you were.

12. Next, look back at your original estimate from part 1 of your student activity log and compare it with the actual length.

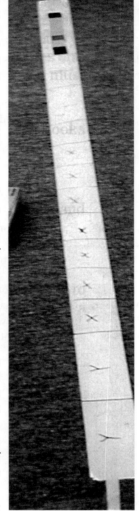

A physical algebraic expression under construction

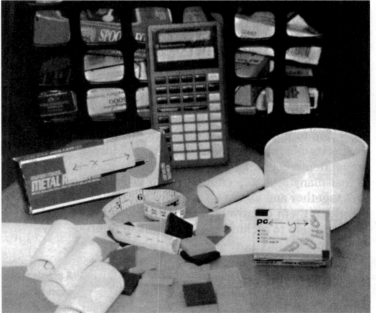

Raw material for algebraic ingenuity

Assessing Understanding

The role of the teacher is to focus, guide, connect, and probe throughout the activity by encouraging students to clarify, elaborate, justify, explain, and predict. The following questions can be used as guidelines to understand better what students grasp or do not grasp and to plan follow-up lessons that better meet the needs of students.

- Why is the term *variable* an appropriate term to describe the x and y?

- Using the same values of x and y throughout the activity, why were you able to create different expressions to describe strips of paper of equal length?

- How did your group decide which algebraic expressions to build?

- After your group measured your x- and y-boxes in centimeters and substituted the values into your algebraic expressions, did you multiply first or add first? Why?

- If you had time to "measure" the paper with your x- and y-boxes so that a minus sign appeared in your algebraic expression, how did you do it? [If time permits, ask students to demonstrate this result to the class.]

- Why were some of the calculations from the algebraic-expression "measurements" different from the actual length of the paper? How could you make them more exact next time?

- What did you like about this activity? Dislike? How would you change the things you disliked?

Conclusion

Building algebraic expressions, a hands-on guided-learning activity, forges vertical connections among grade levels and relies on physical models in the investigation of algebraic concepts (NCTM 1989). On completing and discussing the lesson, seventh graders remarked that it was "fun and interesting" and that it "helped us under- stand what those letters really meant." They stated that before they did the activity, they did not really know how x could stand for a specific number in one problem and an entirely different number in the next problem. They found that laying out the boxes and colored tiles to make them fit exactly on the paper was more difficult than they had expected, but they liked working with other people on this project. They were not as happy with their experience computing the final measurement because "we had to really think whether it made more sense to multiply first or add first, and if we didn't measure carefully, our answers were way off." The words "to really think whether it made sense" were music to my ears. I am now convinced that hands-on activities that begin where previous mathematics courses left off afford us the opportunity to bridge the gap to algebraic thinking. Most important, we can do so without reversing what students have previously thought to be unwritten law, thus heightening their natural intuition instead of stifling it (Bruner 1995, 333).

Bibliography

Bruner, Jerome S. "On Learning Mathematics." *Mathematics Teacher* 88 (April 1995): 330–35. First published in *Mathematics Teacher* 53 (December 1960): 610–19.

National Council of Teachers of Mathematics. *Curriculum and Evaluation Standards for School Mathematics.* Reston, Va.: The Council, 1989.

Wagner, Sigrid, and Sheila Parker. "Advancing Algebra." In *Research Ideas for the Classroom: High School Mathematics,* edited by Patricia S. Wilson, 119–39. New York: Macmillan Publishing Co., 1993.

Willoughby, Stephen S. *Mathematics Education for a Changing World.* Alexandria, Va.: Association for Supervision and Curriculum Development, 1990.

Student Activity Log: Part 1

Creating Algebraic Expressions: A Physical Model

Each group needs the following items:

   A precut strip of white paper and masking tape
   A fine-tip marker
   One small box labeled x and one small box labeled y
   A handful of square colored tiles
   Pencils and calculators

1. Tape your strip of paper to the floor or a table when directed by your teacher. Quickly guess how many centimeters long it is and record your estimate in the box.

   ☐ cm

2. Starting at one end of the paper, lay your x-box on the paper, paying attention to the direction of the arrows on the box. Use your marker to draw a line on the paper at the end of the box. Remove the x-box and write "x" in that spot. Repeat this process a few times using the x-box, but *do not go all the way to the end of the paper*. Continue measuring the length of the paper with the y-box and write "y" on the paper each time it is used. Finish your measurement by laying a few of your colored tiles end to end, not side by side, until they reach the end of the paper. Make them fit exactly, even if you must go back and adjust the placement of your x- and y-boxes.

3. Next, count the x's, y's, and colored tiles. Using plus (+) signs, write an expression below that looks something like $3x + 5y + 4$.

   _____

4. Lift your strip of paper, flip it over, and retape it to the floor or table. Lay down your x-box, y-box, and colored tiles a different number of times and write your new algebraic expression below.

   _____

5. When each member of the group has written two algebraic expressions, ask for a metric ruler to measure the dimensions of your x- and y-boxes and edge of a colored tile to the nearest tenth of a centimeter. Write your answers below.

   $x =$ _____cm $y =$_____cm   colored tile = _____cm

Bonus: Use your x-box, y-box and colored tiles to measure your strip of paper again so that a new algebraic expression has a minus (–) sign.

   _____

How did you reach this solution?

_____

Student Activity Log: Part 2
Evaluating Algebraic Expressions: A Physical Model

6. Write your metric measurement from question 5 again.

   $x =$ _____cm $y =$ _____cm   colored tile = _____cm

7. Write your algebraic expressions from questions 3 and 4.

   a) _____

   b) _____

8. On the lines below, substitute your metric measurements from question 1 into your algebraic expressions from question 2. Remember that you will need to include multiplication signs (× or •). Ask for help if you have questions.

   a) _____

   b) _____

9. Using a calculator and the correct order-of-operation rules, calculate the value of the expressions in 8 (*a*) and (*b*). Round your answer to the nearest centimeter.

   a) _____

   b) _____

10. Find the average of your answers by adding the numbers and dividing by 2.

   _____ + _____ = _____.   Divide by 2: _____ ÷ 2 = _____ cm.

The solution you obtain should be a close approximation of the length of the strip of paper. Your teacher has the original strip of paper if yours is not available. Ask for a metric tape measure or a meterstick to measure it to the nearest centimeter. Compare this answer with the actual length of the paper.

11. How close is your solution to the actual length of the paper? _____

   What would you do differently to make your solution more accurate? _____

   _____

12. How close is your original estimate, recorded in question 1, to the actual length of the paper?_____

230   ACTIVITY SHEET

LYNN MORELLI

A Visual Approach to Algebra Concepts

THE study of mathematics should include opportunities to communicate so that students can model situations using oral, written, concrete, pictorial, graphical, and algebraic methods. (NCTM 1989, 78)

THE following activities are an avenue for mental arithmetic and an opportunity visually to explore some fundamental algebraic concepts and operations. They are well suited to general-mathematics students who can benefit from clear models for abstract ideas. The activities can be use to—

• give practice in mental-arithmetic skills;
• introduce the concepts of a variable and a constant;
• introduce and practice the use of the distributive property; and
• introduce and practice the skill of gathering like terms.

The lesson begins with a few exercises that the students can do mentally. The students should begin by choosing a number from 1 through 10 so that the arithmetic can be done readily.

Example 1
    Think of a number.
    Add 7.
    Multiply by 2 (double it).
    Subtract 4.
    Find 1/2 of the result.
    Subtract the original number.

After giving the steps, call on individual students to give their results. The students may be surprised to discover that everyone obtained the same result (in this example,

Lynn Morelli *teaches seventh- and eighth-grade mathematics at Northshore Junior High School, Bothell, WA 98011. She is particularly interested in visual learning and conducts Math and Mind's Eye in-service courses and workshops for teachers.*

the number 5) regardless of the original number that was chosen.

Example 2
    Think of a number.
    Double it.
    Add 6.
    Find 1/2 of the result.
    Subtract the original number.

Again, call on several students to state their results. In this exercise, each student should have obtained the result of 3. Have the students make observations and discuss any ideas about what may be occurring. This verbalization can offer valuable insight into students' perceptions.

Once students make observations and discuss any ideas about what may be occurring. This verbalization can offer valuable insight into students' perceptions.

Once students have had an opportunity to share their thinking, a visual explanation can be given so that the students can "see" what is happening with the numbers. Give each student or group of students a set of three-quarter-inch cubes (eight to ten) and a set of three-quarter-inch disclike game markers (about twenty). (Note: Paper or tagboard circular cutouts can be substituted for the discs.) Demonstrate to the students that the cube can be thought of as a box that could hold a certain number of discs and that the number of discs in a given box can *vary*. However, in a given exercise, once a number of discs

has been assigned to a box, that number cannot be changed, and every box in that exercise contains the same number of discs.

Next, repeat the first exercise (example 1), having each student model the steps with his or her set of cubes and discs (see fig. 1). It is important for students to maintain the rule that once a number is chosen for the value of the cube (i.e., the number of discs in that cube), that value must remain the same. Discs cannot be added or taken away from inside the cube. The second exercise (example 2) can also be modeled using the cubes and discs. Have students discuss any observations of the process.

Once the utility of the cubes and discs has been experienced, some of the students may be ready to move to a visual represen-

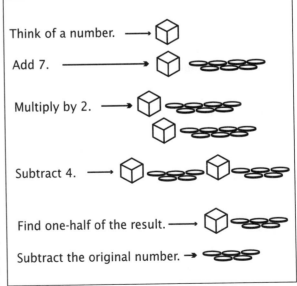

Fig. 1. Cubes and discs are used to represent the steps from example 1.

tation using squares for the cubes and circles for the discs (fig. 2). Several more exercises can be conducted with the students moving between the verbal steps, the numerical example, the visual representation, and the algebraic symbols. (See transparencies 1–4.)

Moving from concrete models to visual symbols

The transition to the algebraic representation comes easily; the box, holding an unknown number of discs, can be symbolically represented using a variable such as n, and the independent discs, which are outside the box, can be represented by constants.

The distributive property can be illustrated effectively using the diagrams. For example, transparency 3, step 5, shows three boxes and three discs, of which the entire quantity is to be doubled; the result is 2 times the number of boxes and also 2 times the number of discs (see fig. 3). I prefer using the phrase "find one-half of" over the equivalent phrase "divide by two" (see the solution for transparency 2, step 4) only because it lends itself more readily to the notation more commonly seen later by students. It is important, however, that students understand that $(1/2)(2x + 4)$ is equivalent to $(2x + 4) - 2$.

The technique of gathering like terms also becomes a natural process of simplification during counting; for example, on transparency 4, step 6, adding four discs to a collection of four boxes and four discs simplifies to four boxes and eight discs.

The four transparency masters that are supplied can be used as your students dis-

Visual

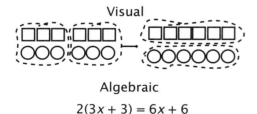

Algebraic

$$2(3x + 3) = 6x + 6$$

Fig. 3. Modeling the distributive property

Write the steps verbally as illustrated:

	Visual	Verbal	Numerical
1.	□		
2.	□ □ □ □		
3.	□ □ □ □ ○○○○○○○		
4.	□ ○○		
5.	□ ○○○○		
6.	○○○○		

Transparency #1

	Visual	Verbal	Algebraic	Numerical
1.	□			
2.	□ □			
3.	□ □ ○○○○			
4.	□ ○○			
5.	□			

Transparency #2

	Verbal	Visual	Algebraic	Numerical
1.	Pick a number.			
2.	Add 2.			
3.	Multiply by 3.			
4.	Subtract 3.			
5.	Multiply by 2.			
6.	Find one-sixth of it.			
7.	Subtract the original number.			

Transparency #3

Algebraic	Visual	Verbal	Numerical

1. N

2. $N + 3$

3. ___ $= 2N + 6$

4. ___ $= 2N + 2$

5. ___ $= 4N + 4$

6. ___ $= 4N + 8$

7. ___ $= N + 2$

8. ___ $= 2$

Transparency #4

cover, discuss, and develop an understanding of the integration of the five modes:

- Concrete   (Manipulating cubes and discs)
- Visual   (Creating the diagrams)
- Verbal   (Writing the steps in words)
- Numerical   (Testing with numbers)
- Algebraic   (Using a "shorthand code")

An important point to make with your students is that each of the five modes is simply a different representation of the same idea. The connections made here could allow the algebra skills used later to have meaning and relevance.

For an additional challenge, students could generate their own sample exercises and share these with other students.

Solutions

Transparency 1

	Verbal	Numerical
1.	Pick a number.	7
2.	Multiply by 4.	$4(7) = 28$
3.	Add 8.	$28 + 8 = 36$
4.	Find 1/4 of the result	$1/4(36) = 9$
5.	Add 2.	$9 + 2 = 11$
6.	Subtract the original number.	$11 - 7 = 4$

Transparency 2
See table 1.

Transparency 3
See table 2.

Transparency 4
See table 3.

Bibliography

Jacobs, Harold. *Elementary Algebra*. San Francisco, Calif.: W. H. Freeman & Co., 1979.

National Council of Teachers of Mathematics, Commission on Standards for School Mathematics. *Curriculum and Evaluation Standards for School Mathematics*. Reston, Va.: The Council, 1989.

Table 1

	Verbal	Algebraic	Property	Numerical
1.	Pick a number.	x		7
2.	Double it.	$2x$		$2(7) = 14$
3.	Add 4.	$2x + 4$		$14 + 4 = 18$
4.	Find 1/2 of it.	$1/2(2x + 4) = 1x + 2$	(Distributive)	$1/2(18) = 9$
5.	Subtract 2.	$1x + 2 - 2 = 1x$	(Gathering like terms)	$9 - 2 = 7$

Table 2

	Visual	Algebraic	Property	Numerical
1.	□	x		7
2.	□ ∞	$x + 2$		$7 + 2 = 9$
3.	⧄⧄⧄	$3(x + 2) = 3x + 6$	(Distributive)	$3(9) = 27$
4.	888	$3x + 6 - 3 = 3x + 3$	(Gathering like terms)	$27 - 3 = 24$
5.	888888	$2(3x + 3) = 6x + 6$	(Distributive)	$2(24) = 48$
6.	8	$1/6(6x + 6) = 1x + 1$	(Distributive)	$1/6(48) = 8$
7.	○	$1x + 1 - 1x = 1$	(Gathering like terms)	$8 - 7 = 1$

Table 3

	Algebraic	Property	Verbal	Numerical
1.			Pick a number.	7
2.			Add 3.	$7 + 3 = 10$
3.	$2(N + 3)$	(Distributive)	Multiply by 2.	$2(10) = 20$
4.	$2N + 6 - 4$	(Gathering like terms)	Subtract 4.	$20 - 4 = 16$
6.	$2(2N + 2)$	(Distributive)	Double it.	$2(16) = 32$
6.	$4N + 4 + 4$	(Gathering like terms)	Add 4.	$32 + 4 = 36$
7.	$1/4(4N + 8)$	(Distributive)	Find 1/4 of it.	$1/4(36) = 9$
8.	$N + 2 - N$	(Gathering like terms)	Subtract original number	$9 - 7 = 2$

V I C T O R I A   B O R L A U G

Building Equations Using

THIS activity uses M&M's and is designed to be used in an algebra class after instruction in solving equations. It actively involves students in identifying the variable, formulating an equation, and then solving the equation.

To begin, the teacher and each student are given one bag of M&M's. The 1.69-ounce, or 47.9 gram, bag works well. A more economical plan is to purchase a large bag of M&M's and distribute some candy to each individual. The instructor starts the activity by counting the number of each color of his or her M&M's.

The teacher's results are written on the chalkboard for everyone to see (see fig. 1). Then students are instructed to count their candies but to keep their numbers secret.

```
 Fill in the blanks with the
teacher's M&M's candy data.
 COLOR           NUMBER
 Brown         _____
 Yellow        _____
 Red           _____
 Green         _____
 Orange        _____
 Tan/blue      _____
      Total    _____
```

Fig. 1 Students tally M&M's.

Victoria Borlaug, *vborlaug@wscc.cc.tn.us*, *teaches at Walters State Community College, Morristown, TN 37813-6899. She is actively involved with teacher training through conference presentations and leadership workshops.*

Each student then receives a set of questions (fig. 2). The instructor selects a student—say, Sabrina—and asks her to fill in the first question appropriately on the basis of the M&M's data:

I would have to add (or eat) _____ red candies to have the same number of red candies as the teacher. How many red candies do I have?

Suppose, for example, that Sabrina had 11 red candies and the teacher had 9 red candies. Then Sabrina would say, "I would have to eat two red candies to have the same number of red candies as the teacher. How many red candies do I have?"

The other students in the class will work to determine the answer to Sabrina's question. Students can easily solve this first problem without using algebra. However, the questions on the handout become progressively more difficult. At some point the students may decide for themselves that algebraic solutions are desirable. Or when enough students begin to have trouble answering the questions, the teacher can point out that algebraic techniques are a valuable tool to help them find solutions. Before tackling the more challenging questions, the class may want to go back and practice using algebraic equations to solve the easier questions they had done earlier.

When using algebraic techniques, the students define the variable, build an equation based on the word problem, and then solve the equation. One algebraic solution to the previous example would be as follows:

Let x represent the number of Sabrina's red candies

$$x - 2 = 9$$
$$x - 2 + 2 = 9 + 2$$
$$x = 11$$

Answer: Sabrina has 11 red candies.

Sabrina would then verify whether the answer to her question was correct.

Many strategies become apparent for incorporating this activity into the classroom after the instructor and the class have worked through some examples. One way is to have students work in small groups to build equations and find solutions. Then the class could compare solution strategies and answers. Sometimes groups will define the variable differently, resulting in different equations, yet they will have the same answers. For example, consider the following question posed by a student:

I have a total of 61 candies in my bag. I have 9 more brown candies than orange candies. If I eat all my brown and orange candies, I will have 32 candies left. How many brown candies did I eat? How many orange candies did I eat?

The variable x could represent the number of orange or of brown candies. The respective equations and solutions follow. Note that both have the same answer.

Solution 1: Let x represent the number of orange candies, and let $x + 9$ represent the number of brown candies:

1. I would have to add (or eat) red candies to have the same number of red candies as the teacher. How many red candies do I have?

2. If I doubled the number of tan candies I have, then I would have _____ tan candies. How many tan candies do I have?

3. If I tripled the number of yellow candies I have, I would have _____ more yellow candies than the teacher. How many yellow candies do I have?

4. If I added 15 brown candies to my bag, the teacher would have to add brown candies to his or her bag for us to have the same number of brown candies. How many brown candies do I have?

5. If I ate 3 of my orange candies, then put my orange candies together with the teacher's orange candies, we would have _____ orange candies. How many orange candies did I start with originally in my bag?

6. Suppose another student had a bag of M&M's exactly like mine. So we each started with the same number of each color candy. If we combined our candy, then I ate 5 of our red candies, we would have _____ red candies left. How many red candies did I start with originally in my bag?

7. My brown, yellow, and green candies total _____. I have _____ more (or fewer) brown candies than yellow candies. I have _____ fewer (or more) green candies than yellow candies. How many brown candies do I have? How many yellow? How many green?

8. I have a total of _____ candies in my bag. I have _____ more (or fewer) brown candies than orange candies. If I eat all my brown and orange candies, I will have _____ candies left. How many brown candies did I eat? How many orange candies did I eat?

Fig. 2 Students' M&M's questionnaire

$$61 - x - (x + 9) = 32,$$
$$61 - x - x - 9 = 32,$$
$$52 - 2x = 32,$$
$$52 - 52 - 2x = 32 - 52,$$
$$-2x = -20$$
$$\frac{-2x}{-2} = \frac{-20}{-2};$$
$$x = 10$$

orange candies, so

$$x + 9 = 19$$

brown candies. *Answer:* 10 orange and 19 brown candies were eaten.

Solution 2: Let x represent the number of brown candies, and let $x - 9$ represent the number of orange candies:

$$61 - x - (x - 9) = 32,$$
$$61 - x - x + 9 = 32,$$
$$70 - 2x = 32,$$
$$70 - 70 - 2x = 32 - 70,$$
$$-2x = -38$$
$$\frac{-2x}{-2} = \frac{-38}{-2};$$
$$x = 19$$

brown candies, so

$$x - 9 = 10$$

orange candies. *Answer:* 19 brown and 10 orange candies were eaten.

Comparing the two equations from solutions 1 and 2 can lead to discussion and insight into different ways to approach the same problem.

After completing the handout shown in figure 2, students may enjoy creating questions of their own, which may include more M&M's questions or relate to other real-life situations. The instructor may review the students' questions for clarity, and appropriate ones may be used as questions in a class contest. Students often experience a sense of pride when the class works on a question that they have created.

Students enjoy this activity. It gives them a chance to represent concrete situations as equations and practice the algebraic techniques involved with solving those equations. An added bonus is that the students enjoy eating their M&M's at the end of the lesson. As always, it is a good idea for teachers to have alternative eating treats to give to those students who cannot eat M&M's.

LEAH P. McCOY

Algebra:
Real-Life Investigations in a Lab Setting

How will we make algebra more accessible to all students? In the past, we have taught algebra as an abstract course involving manipulation of variables and numbers, which are symbolic representations. We have neglected to make a strong connection between the symbolic algebra and the underlying concrete relationships. Given the messages of the NCTM's *Standards* documents (1989, 1991), it is apparent that students need concrete experiences that enable them to experience algebra in the real world. In this manner, they will be able to construct an understanding of the concepts and connect the concrete with the abstract and their internal ideas.

Lab activities are used to represent functions in concrete, tabular, graphic, algebraic, and word format. First, the relationship is conceived in terms of an independent variable x and a dependent variable y. Real-life data are collected and recorded in a table. To control for measurement error and for individual variation, in most labs three trials of each x-value should be completed, and the average of the y-values should be used in the table. These data are then represented graphically in a scatterplot The subsequent conversion to algebraic-equation form may be approximated by hand, or the regression equation may be easily found with a graphing calculator. The last step is asking students to write their conclusions in a lab report. All information is recorded in a form similar to figure 1.

Linear Relationships

Any linear relationship can be explored in the lab. The x, or independent, variable is

Leah McCoy, *mccoy@wfu.edu, teaches at Wake Forest University, Winston-Salem, NC 27109. She is interested in the use of technology in mathematics education.*

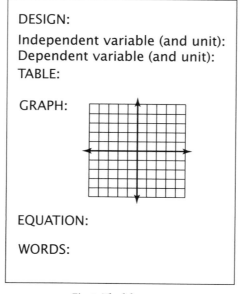

DESIGN:

Independent variable (and unit):
Dependent variable (and unit):
TABLE:

GRAPH:

EQUATION:

WORDS:

Fig. 1. The lab report

manipulated to produce changes in the y, or dependent, variable and a best-fit line is obtained. More advanced students will be able to experiment with nonlinear relationships also and to determine whether a best-fit line or curve is more appropriate for the data.

The wave: In this experiment, x equals the number of students, and y equals the time to complete the wave. Start with a group of five students. When the student using a stopwatch says, "Go," students make the wave by standing up, raising their arms, and sitting down in sequence. When the last person sits down, he or she says, "Stop," and the timer records the elapsed time. Repeat with groups of ten, fifteen, or twenty students. After the table is completed, plot each point on the graph. Sample data are represented in figure 2. The equation may be found by hand by choosing two points on a line that approximately goes through the middle of the points. Then find the slope, $m = (y_2 - y_1)/(x_2 - x_1)$, and the y intercept, $b = y_1 - mx_1$, and write the equation $y = mx + b$. This step may be completed by using a graphing cal-

culator. See figure 3 for specific instructions for the TI-82.

The last step is to write a report that explains the results. To help students interpret the data, the teacher may ask them to apply their conclusions and further describe the relationship with such questions as the following:

- How long would it take forty students to make a wave? Explain your answer by using the graph and the algebraic expression. How are these representations related?

- How many students are needed for a twenty-five-second wave? Draw a diagram and justify your answer.

- How would your graph be different if every student stood and clapped twice before sitting down?

What effect do individual differences of the students have on the best-fit line? Why do we call it a best-fit line? Why are some data points off the line? Is it reasonable that the points would all fall exactly on the line?

- Can you think of any relationships in which the points would not be close to forming a line? What other types of curves might we have?

DESIGN: Do the wave with different numbers of students and measure time.

Independent variable (and unit): x = Number of students
Dependent variable (and unit): y = Time in seconds

TABLE:

x	y
5	7
10	15
15	18
20	27

GRAPH:
(5, 7)(15, 18)
$m = (y_2 - y_1)/(x_2 - x_1)$
$(18 - 7)/(15 - 5) = 11/10$

$b = y - mx =$
$7 - 11/10 \cdot 5 = 7 - 11/2 = 1\ 1/2$

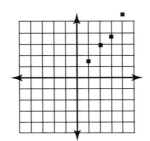

EQUATION:
$y = mx + b$
$y = 11/10x + 1\ 1/2$

WORDS: The wave takes 1 1/2 seconds to start. For every 10 more people, it takes 11 seconds.

F. 2 A completed report on "the wave"

• Why is a line or a curve used to represent a set of data points?

Other data activities should also be used to explore linear relations. Students will benefit from many hands-on experiences with concrete data. The following lab activities have been collected and adapted from a number of mathematics textbooks.

M&M's: x is the total number of M&M's in three different-sized bags, and y is the number of red candies in the bag.

Shadows: x is the height of an object, and y is the length of its shadow. This experiment can be done outdoors using sunlight or inside using a stationary light source.

Cube faces: x is the number of cubes on one side, and y is the number of cubes with two faces showing. A cube of side length 1, 2, 3, 4, and 5 is constructed. This activity works well with sugar cubes, which can actually be marked on the visible faces, stacked, and disassembled and counted.

Balloon: x is the number of breaths used to blow up a balloon, and y is the circumference of the balloon. (See fig. 4.)

Rocket: x is the length of a rocket, and y is the distance that the rocket travels. The rocket is made from a drinking straw with one end taped shut. It is launched with a plastic catsup bottle by placing the open end of the straw over the spout of the bottle and giving a sharp squeeze. The straw is progressively cut to shorter lengths to vary the length of the rocket.

Pennies: x is the number of pennies, and y is the weight in grams. Measure five, ten, fifteen, and twenty pennies. This relation should be perfectly linear but may vary with measurement differences.

Comparisons of Two Lines

Two similar relationships can be examined and compared. The students follow the same procedure as for the linear relationships and compare the results. The graphs and the equations generate interesting comparisons of the slopes and intercepts.

Marbles in a glass of water: x is the number of marbles in a glass, and y is the height of one cup of water in the glass. The additional variable is the diameter of the glass. Place two marbles in a beaker, add one cup of water, and measure the height of water. Repeat with four, six, and eight marbles. Then repeat the experiment using a graduated cylinder or narrow glass.

To enter data:
  Press STAT. Choose EDIT; press 1.
  Enter x values in L1; y values in L2 (press ENTER after each entry).

To draw plot:
  Press 2ND STAT PLOT.
  Choose 1; choose ON by pressing ENTER. Press ▼.
  Choose the first choice (scatterplot) by pressing
    ENTER. Press ▼.
  Choose L1 for Xlist by pressing ENTER Press ▼.
  Choose L2 for Ylist by pressing ENTER Press ▼.
  Choose first choice for Mark by pressing ENTER
  Press ZOOM. Choose 9 (press ENTER).

To fit to linear model:
  Press STAT. Press ▶ to CALC. Press 5.
  _____Output: y = ax + b   a = ___ b = ___ r = ____

Note that this procedure also gives the correlation so that students can check on the linear model.

Fig. 3. Linear regression on the TI-82

Fig. 4. The balloon activity

Jar lids: x is the diameter of the lid in centimeters, and y is the circumference of the inside of the lid measured in cereal pieces. Use several different-sized lids. The additional variable is the measurement unit of the circumference. Repeat by using different-sized cereal or unpopped popcorn to measure the circumference of the lids.

Ball bounce: x is the height of the drop of a ball, and y is the height of the bounce. This experiment is repeated with different types of balls, for examples, a tennis ball and a table-tennis ball.

Dominoes: x is the time to fall, and y is the number of dominoes. Dominoes in sets of 100, 200, 300, and 400 are set up, the first one is pushed, and the time for the entire group to fall is measured. The additional variable is the distance between the individual dominoes, 1 or 0.5 inch.

Matchbox cars: x is the ramp's height, and y is the distance that the car travels. Matchbox cars are inexpensive and appeal to students. Ramps can be made of heavy poster board or plywood. The additional variable can illustrate negative slope if the y-variable is the distance that the car stops from a stationary object, such as a wall, toward which the car is traveling. (See fig. 5.)

Nonlinear Relationships

Nonlinear relationships are the most difficult for students to conceptualize. Thus, the concrete, real-world lab experiences in this section are particularly important.

Bounce time: x is the height of the drop of a ball, and y is the elapsed time to the third bounce.

Jar lid 2: x is the diameter, and y is the area. The diameter can be measured in cereal pieces, and the area can be measured by covering the entire bottom of the lid with cereal and counting the individual pieces.

Cube faces 2: x is the number of cubes on one side, and y is the volume of total cubes. Again, the model can be built with sugar cubes. (See fig. 6.)

Spheres: x is the diameter of a marble or a ball, and y is the distance it rolls. Each sphere is rolled down the same ramp.

Mirror: x is the height of a dot on the wall, and y is the distance from a mirror to a student. A mirror is placed on the floor near a wall, and a stick-on dot is placed on the wall one, two, three, or four feet high. The experimenter stands looking down at the mirror and steps away from it until the dot comes into view.

Mystery Relationships

More advanced students will enjoy the challenge of a mystery relationship. In this activity, they must collect data and determine whether the relationship is best described by a best-fit line or a best-fit curve. More data will be required for these experiments, and students will need many data points. Again, the graphing calculator can be used for fast and accurate analysis.

Whistle: x is the number of oyster crackers eaten, such as five, ten, or fifteen, and y is the time before the student can whistle. Students will need to drink water between trials.

Bubble gum: x is the time taken to chew bubble gum, such as twenty, forty, or sixty seconds, and y is the size of the bubble blown. The bubble may be measured with calipers if available; a rough measure of diameter can be obtained with a ruler.

Ink: x is the number of drops of ink or food coloring, and y is the diameter of the circle formed on a paper towel. Students use an eyedropper to drop the ink or food coloring, and the diameter of the circle is measured with a ruler.

Conclusion

These sample lab activities for algebra can be modified and extended in many different ways. Students are motivated and actively involved with hands-on-algebra models. They form real-life connections and algebraic-thinking skills as they use problem-solving techniques and technology. Activities of this type should be an integral part of every beginning algebra course.

References

National Council of Teachers of Mathematics. *Curriculum and Evaluation Standards for School Mathematics.* Reston, Va.: The Council, 1989.

———. *Professional Standards for Teaching Mathematics.* Reston, Va.: The Council, 1991.

Fig. 5. The race-car activity

Fig. 6. The cube activity

DON PLOGER, LEE KLINGLER, AND MICHAEL ROONEY

Spreadsheets, Patterns, and Algebraic Thinking

WHAT is the first Fibonacci number greater than a million? Can elementary teachers use a challenging problem, such as this, to enhance the algebraic thinking of their students? Even with a calculator, the computations are quite tedious. The computer is certainly the right tool for the job; the problem is to find appropriate software. We have found that elementary school students can productively explore such questions using a computer spreadsheet.

Children display a tremendous intellectual curiosity about number patterns. Computer spreadsheets provide a vehicle for students to express that curiosity, allowing them to explore number patterns algebraically while the computer performs the tedious calculations. In the very act of telling the computer what to do, students must think algebraically, expressing themselves using algebraic formulas in an intuitively meaningful way. Moreover, instantaneous feedback from the computer allows the students to see immediately whether their reasoning is correct. They can decide if the answer is reasonable, ask what further results might be obtained, and then pose problems based on those results.

This article describes the results of a fifth-grade class using spreadsheets to investigate challenging mathematical topics. Consistent with the *Curriculum and Evaluation Standards for School Mathematics,* children are encouraged to "recognize, describe, extend, and create a wide variety of patterns" (NCTM 1989, 60). After a few weeks of guided exploration, many children can, with just a few minutes of effort, set up a spreadsheet to list the Fibonacci numbers. They can also program spreadsheets to generate odd and even numbers, a multiplication table, squares, square roots, and exponential growth.

We outline an intuitive approach for introducing the concepts of functions and sequences through investigating the topics just discussed. We also provide guidelines to help teachers use this powerful technology to enhance the algebraic thinking of their students. Recent NCTM publications have recognized the power of spreadsheets for high school mathematics teachers (Masalski 1990) and middle school teachers (Russell 1992). Our aim is to describe a set of specific learning activities to help elementary school children use almost any commercially available package to create their own spreadsheet models. (The instructions can be applied directly to ClarisWorks, Excel, Lotus for Windows, and Great Works; with other spreadsheet packages, slight modifications might be required.) Our discussion applies most directly to fifth grade, but the ideas can easily be applied to fourth or even third grades.

Introducing Spreadsheets

Computer spreadsheets display a grid of rows and columns, and the resulting rectangular cells can contain numbers. Spreadsheets will perform arithmetic in a straightforward manner. Furthermore, spreadsheets will repeat calculations, as will a constant key on a calculator. However, unlike a calculator, a spreadsheet can display a long list of calculations, and the resulting numerical data can readily be used in further calculations. Furthermore, spreadsheets can also contain text, making it easy to arrange and label the data.

Begin by telling students to open the spreadsheet icon on any Macintosh or any computer that supports Windows. Each computer screen will show something that resembles figure 1. Notice that the example spreadsheet has four columns, labeled A, B, C, and D, and ten rows, labeled 1 through 10. The cursor is located in row 1 of column A, referred to as cell A1. All cells follow this notation: the lower-right cell, for example, is D10.

	A	B	C	D
1				
2				
3				
4				
5				
6				
7				
8				
9				
10				

Fig. 1. A blank spreadsheet

After explaining how to name the rows, columns, and cells of a spreadsheet, explain that spreadsheets will do arithmetic. You can also menl tion that spreadsheets will repeat calculations and I show you a long list of calculations all at once. To achieve these benefits, students need to know how to (1) enter a value, (2) calculate a value, and (3) extend a pattern. The following example will illustrate how to generate the first ten even numbers.

The Even Numbers

To produce the even numbers (2, 4, 6, 8, …) in column A, begin by entering the first value of the sequence: Put your cursor in

Don Ploger, *ploger@acc.fau.edu, teaches at Florida Atlantic University in Davie, FL 33314. He is interested in using technology to help students learn mathematics.* Lee Klingler, *klingler@acc.fau.edu, teaches at the Boca Raton campus of Florida Atlantic University, Boca Raton, FL 33431. In addition to his research interest in abstract algebra, he is interested in the mathematical preparation of future teachers.* Michael Rooney *teaches at Welleby Elementary School, Sunrise, FL 33352. In addition to teaching mathematics to children in grades K–5, he offers workshops for in-service teachers.*

cell A1 and type "2." When you press the ENTER key, the value of 2 will appear in cell A1.

To assign the next value in the sequence, increment the first value: Put your cursor in cell A2 and type "=A1+2." When you press the ENTER key, the value of 4 will appear in cell A2.

Finally, to extend the pattern, click your mouse on cell A2, and drag down to cell A10. Go to the "Calculate" window and select "Fill down." The first ten even numbers will appear in the first ten cells of column A (fig. 2a).

Encouraging "What If" Thinking

Computer spreadsheets provide excellent opportunities for students to explore mathematical possibilities. For example, students asked, "What if we change the first number?" They found that no matter what number they selected, a pattern was present: counting by twos. Furthermore, if the first number is even, all the numbers are even; if the first number is odd, all are odd. Figure 2b shows the odd numbers. Note that all that is needed is to change a single value (typing " 1 " in cell A1) to get these numbers.

At this point, the teacher suggested, "What if we change the number in our assignment statement?" Robert changed the assignment statement in cell A2 to "=A1 + 10." Then he changed the value of A 1 to 10, and he produced the multiples of ten. Following Robert's discovery, other students produced the multiples of other numbers.

After students had explored the idea, the teacher asked whether they could make a multiplication table. No one solved the problem during that session. The next day,

Elena arranged the first column with multiples of 1; the second, with multiples of 2; and so on, up to 10. Part of her result is shown in figure 2c.

As these examples illustrate, spreadsheets can generate considerable interest among students who are exploring number patterns. Often students pose their own "what if' questions spontaneously. At other times, the teacher poses a what-if question as a prompt, allowing students to complete the solution. On occasion the teacher illustrates what-if thinking by showing an example *and* the solution.

The "Penny Doubling" Problem

Some students noted that they had seen the "penny doubling" problem: You have the choice of receiving $1000 per day for a month, or a penny the first day, two pennies the second day, four the third day, and so on, always doubling the previous day's amount until the end of the month. Jennifer remembered that the penny-doubling method resulted in more money, but none of the students could recall the precise details.

The students wanted to put "penny doubling" into a spreadsheet. They placed the numbers 1 through 31 in column A, using the assignment statement "=A1+1." Then we began to enter the values of the pennies in column B. On day 1 a single penny was received, so the students entered 1 in cell B1. On day 2, two pennies were received, so the students entered 2 in cell B2. The teacher asked, "What would be a good assignment statement for cell B3?" One student suggested "=B2+2." When this pattern was continued down column B, the result was 60 cents on day 31. The children saw immediately that this statement was not

the correct answer. When they correctly changed the assignment statement to "=B2*2," over a billion pennies were received on day 31 (see fig. 3). The asterisk indicates multiplication.

A	B
1	1
2	2
3	4
4	8
5	16
6	32
7	64
8	128
9	256
10	512
11	1024
12	2048
13	4096
14	8192
15	16384
16	32768
17	65536
18	131072
19	262144
20	524288
21	1048576
22	2097152
23	4194304
24	8388608
25	16777216
26	33554432
27	67108864
28	134217728
29	268435456
30	536870912
31	1073741824

Fig. 3. The results of the penny-doubling problem

Once they saw the pattern, students spent time wondering what they would do with $10 million. When they finished their discussion, the teacher asked, "What is the sum of all the money on all thirty-one days?" At first, the students said that the problem was too difficult.

The teacher showed how to record the sums. In cell C1, the sum of the first day was entered by typing "=B 1." The sum of the first two days was the sum of the previous day plus the total of the second day, which was entered in cell C2 as "=C1+B2." When this pattern was continued, the sums for each day appeared in column C.

After a few minutes, the students began to see a pattern: the sum is one penny less than twice the amount for any given day and, therefore, a penny less than the amount for the following day. For example, on day 4, the amount received is 8 and the total is 15, or one less than the amount received on day 5, which is 16 (see fig.4).

	A		A		A	B	C
1	2	1	1	1	1	2	3
2	4	2	3	2	2	4	6
3	6	3	5	3	3	6	9
4	8	4	7	4	4	8	12
5	10	5	9	5	5	10	15
6	12	6	11	6	6	12	18
7	14	7	13	7	7	14	21
8	16	8	15	8	8	16	24
9	18	9	17	9	9	18	27
10	20	10	19	10	10	20	30

(a) The even numbers (b) The odd numbers (c) The first three columns of Elana's times table

Fig. 2

ACTIVITIES FOR JUNIOR HIGH AND MIDDLE SCHOOL MATHEMATICS

A	B	C
1	1	1
2	2	3
3	4	7
4	8	15
5	16	31
6	32	63
7	64	127
8	128	255
9	256	511
10	512	1023

Fig. 4. The sum of the penny doubling

Exploring Powers

Students became interested in raising numbers. to various powers. They quickly saw how easy it was to construct a table that raised each of the first ten counting numbers to the powers one through six.

The students spontaneously invented the following method. First, they put headers as shown in row 1 of figure 5. Then, in column A, they numbered cells A2 through A11 from 1 through 10: note that the header was in cell A1. In cell B2, they entered "=A2* 1" and continued that pattern across the second row. In cell B3, they entered "=A3*2" and continued the pattern of doubling the neighboring cell across the third row. They continued this pattern for each of the numbers in column A, tripling the numbers in succession across the fourth row, and so on. The result is shown in figure 5.

They noted a pattern. The first six powers of 2 are 2, 4, 8, 16, 32, and 64. The first three powers of 4 are 4, 16, and 64. This pattern can be extended to show the powers of 8 and 16 (see fig. 6).

Note that the powers of 4 consist of every other power of 2, the powers of 8 are every third power of 2, and the powers of 16 are every fourth power of 2. If a number is found anywhere in the powers of 4, 8, or 16, then it will be found in the powers of 2. Every number in the powers of 16 is found in both the powers of 4 and 2.

A	B	C	D
2	4	8	16
4	16	64	256
8	64	512	4096
16	256	4096	65536
32	1024	32768	1048576
64	4096	262144	16777216
128	16384	2097152	
256	65536	16777216	
512	262144		
1024	1048576		
2048	4194304		
4096	16777216		
8192			

Fig. 6. The first few powers of 2, 4, 8, and 16

A similar pattern was found for the powers of 3 (3, 9, 27, 81, 243, and 729) and nine (9, 81, and 729). You might ask students whether all of the powers of 9 would be found in the powers of 3. Suggest that they predict a pattern, such as that every other power of 3 is a power of 9, and then test their prediction by extending both sequences. Ask them what other number patterns might fit this relationship.

This activity is a starting point for a deep intuitive understanding of the laws of exponents. For example, the idea that every power of 4 is found as every second power of 2 can be expressed formally as $4^n = 2^{2n}$. Students do not, however, need to use complicated terminology. Instead, they notice patterns in sequences of numbers.

Fibonacci Numbers

The teacher showed the students how to create the Fibonacci numbers. They entered 1 in cell A1 and 1 in cell A2. In cell A3, the teacher told them to enter "=A1+A2." Then the students extended the pattern down column A to display the first ten.

After the students had the first ten Fibonacci numbers in the spreadsheet, the teacher asked, "When do you think the Fibonacci number will be greater than one million?" Although most of their guesses were relatively high, such as the 1000th term, Edgar guessed 30. He reasoned that this guess is similar to the repeated-doubling pattern, and so 30 seemed to be reasonable. As it turns out, the 31st Fibonacci number is the first to be greater than one million. The student's reasoning is only approximate, 2^{30} is approximately one billion, so to

a certain degree, Edgar made a lucky guess. But he correctly realized that the Fibonacci sequence would become very large in relatively few terms. Most important, he was speculating about ways to extend patterns to include very large numbers, and we encouraged such attempts. Edgar's spreadsheet version of the Fibonacci sequence is shown in figure 7.

It is extremely easy to modify the Fibonacci sequence, and students can see the interesting patterns that result, such as those shown in figure 8. Column A shows the standard sequence; column B shows a variation where the first two numbers have been changed from 1, 1 to 2, 2. In column C, the first two numbers are 10.

Note that every number in column B is twice the corresponding number in column A, and that every number in column C is ten times the corresponding number in column A.

From Patterns to functions

The sequence of even numbers can be examined from a different perspective. Show students figure 9 and ask them to

n	n^2	n^3	n^4	n^5	n^6
1	1	1	1	1	1
2	4	8	16	32	64
3	9	27	81	243	729
4	16	64	256	1024	4096
5	25	125	625	3125	15625
6	36	216	196	7776	46656
7	49	343	2401	16807	117649
8	64	512	4096	32768	262144
9	81	729	6561	59049	531441
10	100	1000	10000	100000	1000000

Fig. 5. The first ten counting numbers raised to powers

	A
1	1
2	1
3	2
4	3
5	5
6	8
7	13
8	21
9	34
10	55
11	89
12	144
13	233
14	377
15	610
16	987
17	1597
18	2584
19	4181
20	6765
21	10946
22	17711
23	28657
24	46368
25	75025
26	121383
27	196418
28	317811
29	514229
30	832040
31	1346269

Fig. 7. The Fibonacci numbers

	A	B	C
1	1	2	10
2	1	2	10
3	2	4	20
4	3	6	30
5	5	10	50
6	8	16	80
7	13	26	130
8	21	42	210
9	34	68	340
10	55	110	550

Fig. 8. Patterns with the Fibonacci numbers

	A	B
1	1	2
2	2	4
3	3	6
4	4	8
5	5	10
6	6	12
7	7	14
8	8	16
9	9	18
10	10	20
100	100	200

Fig. 9. Some integral values of the function $f(x) = 2x$

create it on their spreadsheet. Most students will make the numbers in column B by entering 2 in cell B1, and typing "=B1+2" in cell B2, which is of course true. The even numbers can be thought of as being a sequence in which each term is two more than the previous term.

Once the students were familiar with this method, the teacher showed another way to get the values in column B: The value of B1 can be assigned "=A1*2"; this assignment statement can then be filled down. Students have found the entry in B5, for example, in two different ways: 5*2 and also 2+2+2+2+2. Because these two calculations yield the same result, students get experimental confirmation that multiplication is repeated addition.

Each approach has advantages. On the one hand, repeated addition is much more intuitive to elementary school children. On the other hand, simple multiplication by 2 lets the students directly find the 100th even number. (The last row in fig. 9 shows this result.) To get the 100th value using the repeated-addition approach, it is necessary to extend the pattern to see the 100th term.

This activity provides an intuitive preparation for understanding linear functions. Although it would be premature to introduce the function notation, $f(x) = 2x$, to fifth-grade students, they are nevertheless readily able to create spreadsheet models of

the number patterns. Consequently, these students have developed a rich set of intuitive ideas that can serve as the basis of a deep understanding of the concept of a mathematical function.

(Note that the students were developing an informal understanding of recursive functions. A formal definition of a recursive function is beyond this level. However, it intuitively means that one starts with the first term(s) of a sequence and then defines each "next term" from previous term(s). For example, to find out the tenth term of a sequence, one would have to know about the previous term(s). This recursive process explains, basically, the way computer spreadsheets work and is a powerful way of thinking mathematically.)

Conclusion

This study has a number of practical implications. We have shown how computer tools can bring powerful ideas into the elementary school classroom. Children learn how to use spreadsheets to explore powerful ideas in mathematics. They learn how to generate patterns, create a running total, and create a pattern using a formula. Most significant, students learn to pose problems and to create explorations of their own.

Furthermore, students can use spreadsheets to explore patterns that they have learned previously or that occur to them during their explorations. Spreadsheets supply a rich representation that can be examined for patterns, as in the comparison of the powers of 2 with the powers of 4.

This use of technology is a good way to help prepare children for algebra. They see the effects of algebraic transformations on familiar numbers. As a result, they are relieved of the tedious burden of arithmetic calculations, and they can use algebra without being confused by unfamiliar symbols. Students used formulas in a meaningful way, and they received immediate feedback in the change of the number pattern.

In introducing functions, we look at number patterns from two points of view. On the one hand, we look for patterns in a sequence of numbers, asking the question "How do we get from one member of the sequence to the next?" For example, in the sequence of even numbers, we get from one even number to the next by adding 2. On the other hand, we look for patterns in

functions, asking the question "How do we get a particular member of the I sequence directly?" For example, in the sequence. of even numbers, we get the nth even number by multiplying n by 2. Spreadsheets allow students to discover both of these powerful ideas and in so doing, help them relate their ideas of number patterns to the mathematical concept of a function.

Computer spreadsheets provide a medium for the development of "What if" thinking. Students can ask, "What if we change the first number?" and a single keystroke can change the pattern in a systematic way. In a similar fashion, students can modify assignment statements and assemble similar patterns to build mathematical tables. In this study, students began with simple elements and then progressively created the multiplication table and their own version of a table of powers. The students generated many powerful what-if questions, and they gained increasing skill in the art of problem posing.

References

Masalski, William J. *How to Use the Spreadsheet as a Tool in the Secondary Mathematics Classroom.* Reston, Va.: The Council, 1990.

National Council of Teachers of Mathematics. *Curriculum and Evaluation Standards for School Mathematics.* Reston, Va.: The Council, 1989.

Russell, John C. *Spreadsheet Activities in Middle School Mathematics.* Reston, Va.: The Council, 1992.

10

Statistics

MIDDLE school students have a natural curiosity about their surroundings. They become involved in competitions and making collections. Students follow the rankings of movies and their favorite music. They are interested in data collection and in the construction of tables, charts, and graphs to describe data. The interpretation of various ways of reporting data provides a basis for teacher-student discourse.

Jean Shaw's "Let's Do It: Dealing with Data" offers activity approaches to developing the concepts of mean, median, and mode. She also introduces range, deviation from the mean, and correlation. A spreadsheet approach in "Exploring Mean, Median, and Mode with a Spreadsheet" demonstrates how spreadsheets can be used to develop graphical representation of data and measures of variation.

The reviewers found a wide selection of excellent articles that described activities that would really get students involved in collecting and analyzing data. From these we have selected four that we believe are truly outstanding—"Data with Snap, Crackle and Pop"; "Dolphins or Wildcats: Exploring Election Statistics"; "Pictures, Tables, Graphs, and Questions: Statistical Process"; and "Implementing Data Analysis in a Sixth-Grade Classroom."

"Having Fun with Baseball" describes a simulated game of baseball in which students use various statistics to make game decisions or to determine results at the end of the activity.

In a very interesting article, Juli Dixon and Christy Falba describe how they use the World Wide Web to collect information. Of particular interest is the downloading of charts and graphs that students can then interpret.

JEAN M. SHAW

Let's Do It
Dealing with Data

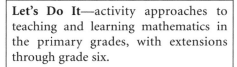

Let's Do It—activity approaches to teaching and learning mathematics in the primary grades, with extensions through grade six.

CHILDREN are surrounded by information. They must have ways to make sense of it—ways to organize and interpret the information. Children learn to comprehend and assimilate information, or data, through experiences with collecting and handling them.

As they work with data, children can develop understanding of such specific mathematical concepts as measures of central tendency and measures of dispersion, or spread. They can examine specific examples and compute the deviation from the mean for each example. Children can be

Jean M. Shaw, *University of Mississippi, University, MS 38677*

exposed to the idea of correlation, the effect of one factor on another. They can learn to display data in charts and graphs so that others can comprehend them.

Concrete experiences in dealing with data are essential. Problems based on their own experiences are real and meaningful to children. Experiences make clear the meanings of statistical terms and give children insight into the processes that others use when dealing with large amounts of data. Collecting data about concrete experiences is motivating; when data are based on topics of interest to children, they want to find out more.

Measures of Central Tendency

Measures of central tendency are used when it is desirable to let a single value serve as a representative for a whole set of values. The single value should be a "typical" value. Elementary school students

should learn about the *median, mode,* and *mean* as measures of central tendency.

Understanding the median

The *median* is simply the value or point at which half the values in a distribution are below it and half the values are above it. The median is often called the middle value. Elementary school children can find the middle value by arranging numbers in order from smallest to largest and then picking out the center, or middle, value.

Put some beans in a jar. Give each child a slip of paper on which to write an estimate of the number of beans. Have the children arrange their papers in order on a table or the floor. Let the children point out the approximate location of the paper in the middle. Confirm the location of the middle paper by counting papers on either side. If there is an odd number of papers, the median will clearly show as that value with an equal number of papers on either side (fig. 1). If there is an even number of papers, simply tell the children that the median is between the two middle values, or have them compute the value between the two middle values by finding their average.

Children can also use the same method of arranging papers to find the median of a set of test scores or a series of estimates for a measurement. After experiences with actually moving papers to order numbers and find their medians, children should work with statistics on a single sheet of paper. Each child in the class might guess the teacher's height in centimeters and write an estimate on the chalkboard. The children could then work in groups to copy the estimates in order on their own papers and pick the median.

Understanding the mode

The *mode* is the most frequently occurring value in a set of values. A set of values can have only one mode, or it can have more than one mode. When data are displayed in a bar graph, it is very easy for children to pick out the mode or modes, which are represented by the longest bar or bars. To let the children work with some personal data, have each child make a fingerprint and then categorize the fingerprints into loop, arch, or whorl patterns. To make clear fingerprints, have each child scribble with a pencil on a small area of paper, rub a thumb in the lead, and then press the thumb onto the sticky side of a piece of transparent tape about 5 cm in length. The child places the tape onto a 6 cm × 6 cm square of paper to produce a beautiful fingerprint (fig. 2). Have the children make a display of their fingerprints according to the fingerprint categories. A barlike graph results from the display. Have children count the number of prints in each category and pick out the mode or modes.

Children can make two bar graphs based on data generated from counting raw peanuts. Put about one kilogram of raw peanuts in a large sack. Ask each child to take out a handful of peanuts and count them. Graph the results on a grid like the one shown in figure 3. The children will see some variation in the numbers of peanuts they picked from the bag. Find the mode of the numbers shown on the graph.

Next, have the children open their peanuts and count the number of nuts in each shell. Many shells will contain two or three nuts, whereas others may hold one, four, or none. Have children graph their findings on another grid (fig. 4). Find the mode, the most frequently occurring number of nuts in a shell. Then have the children slip the skins off each nut and measure the total volume of nuts. Place about 500 mL of nuts in a blender, add 25 mL of cooking oil, and blend until smooth. Let the children sample some of their homemade peanut butter!

Understanding the mean

The *mean* of a set of values is the arithmetic average of the values. The mean is found by dividing the sum of all the values by the number of values. To make concrete the concept of the mean, have children do a manipulative exercise. Arrange the children in groups of four or five and have them use squares of paper to represent the number of children in their families, as shown in figure 5. Each group will probably see that

the number of children in each family varies. Now ask each group to rearrange their papers so that each family has about the same number of children. The number of papers in each new "family" represents the mean. The children may find that the mean is a whole number, or they may find (as in fig. 5) that some papers are left over and represent a fraction of a number of children.

Introduce or review the idea of adding all the values in a set and dividing by the number of members of the set to find the mean. Have the children gather such data as the outdoor temperatures for a week or the number of hours each child watched television on a specified day. Have the class find the mean of each set of data.

Finding the mean of a large number of values requires work that can easily be done on a calculator or computer. Let children use the calculator first to add the values and then to divide the sum by the number of values. To figure means, children might use

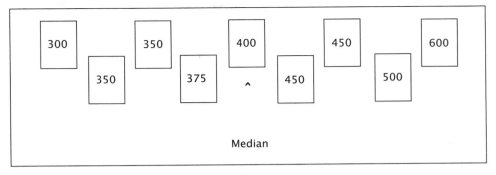

Median

Fig. 1

Fig. 2

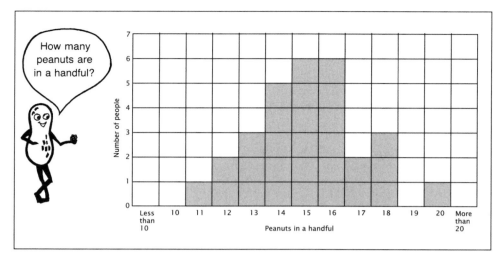

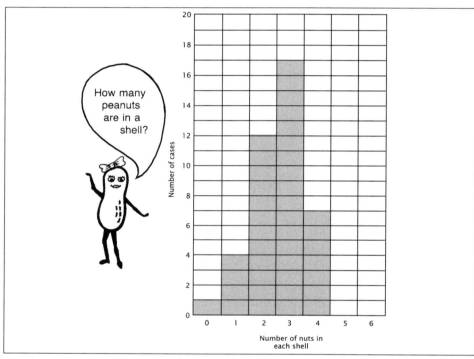

Fig. 3

Fig. 4

a microcomputer and type in the computer program shown in figure 6. Help children to understand that statement 160 lets the computer accept numbers, statement 180 adds each number to the total, and statement 230 causes the computer to figure and print the mean—it divides the total of the values by the number of values that were entered (*T/N*).

Comparing the median, mode, and mean

Use a set of data such as the children's ages in months, their heights in centimeters, or the number of books each child has read during the school year. Let the children display the data on the chalkboard or in a graph (fig. 7). Find the median, mode, and mean of the data. For many data sets, the values of these three measures of central tendency will be approximately equal.

Measures of Dispersion, or Spread

Range and *deviation from the mean* are measures of dispersion, or spread. They help people see whether values are clustered closely about a central point or are more widely spread out. The range is simply the difference between the largest and smallest values in a data set. On an elementary school level, deviation from the mean involves subtracting each value from the mean value of a data set.

Understanding the range

Make two large grids on the chalkboard. Let children take turns filling in the grids with their first names, placing one letter in each section (fig. 8). Compare the grids and pick out the short-

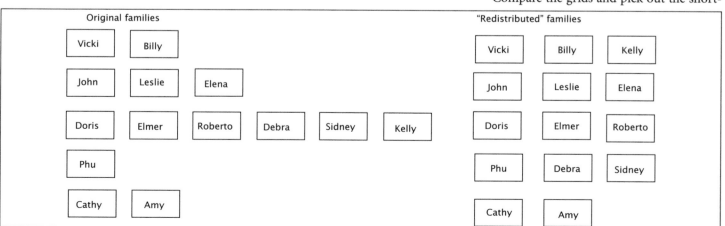

Fig. 5

```
10   REM  PROGRAM  TO
         FIND THE MEAN
20   REM FOR TRS-80,
         USE CLS FOR LINE 30
30   TEXT : HOME
40   PRINT "I'LL FIND THE
         MEAN OF SOME"
50   PRINT  "NUMBERS
         FOR YOU. WHEN I SAY"
60   PRINT X = ? , ENTER
         EACH NUMBER
70   PRINT
80   PRINT "WHEN YOU'RE
         AT THE END OF"
90   PRINT "THE NUMBERS,
         TYPE IN 9999 AND"
100  PRINT "PRESS RETURN.
110  REW  THE TOTAL =
         0 AT THE START
120  T = 0
130  REM START   A
         COUNTER FOR THE
         NUMBER
140  REM  OF  NUMBERS

150  N = 0
160  INPUT " X= "; X
170  IF X = 9999 GOTO 210
180  T = T + X
190  N = N + 1
200  GOTO 160
210  PRINT ; PRINT "YOU
         ENTERED";N;"NUMBERS"
220  PRINT "YOUR TOTAL
         IS ";T
225  PRINT
230  PRINT "THE MEAN IS
         "T / N
240  PRINT
250  PRINT
260  PRINT "IF YOU WANT
         ME TO FIND THE"
270  PRINT  "OF SOME
         MORE NUMBERS FOR"
280  PRINT "YOU, TYPE IN
         RUN AND PRESS"
290  PRINT "THE RETURN
         KEY."
300  END
```

Fig. 6

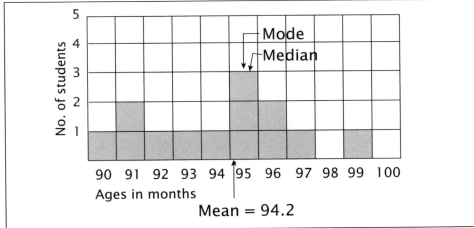

Fig. 7. Our ages in months

when the heights of the outsiders are included, since some of the additional data may be the heights of adults or babies.

Review the "number of beans in the jar" problem presented in the first activity for finding the median. Talk about the children's estimates for the number of beans in the jar and the actual number of beans. Now pour about half the beans into a smaller jar and ask the children to estimate their number. Compare the ranges of the two series of estimates. The range for the beans in the large jar will probably be larger for two reasons: the children had little experience in estimating the number of beans, and the actual number of beans was larger. Many children will base their estimate for the number of beans in the smaller jar on the number for the larger jar; they will use their experience in making the first estimate to guide them in making a more accurate estimate for the number of beans in the smaller jar.

You might be able to obtain data about the total number of children in attendance at your school each day. Have the children write down their guesses for daily attendance and find the range of their guesses. Then read attendance figures for each day of the last week, to give the children actual information about attendance. Next, have the children predict tomorrow's attendance, Now find the range of these predictions. The range should be smaller than their initial guesses because these predictions were based on current, accurate data. Check the children's predictions against the actual attendance the next day.

Introducing deviation from the mean

A simple exercise can be used to introduce another measure of dispersion—

est and longest names on each. Find the range for each grid. For the example given, the range for the names on the left is 6 (8 – 2), and the range for the names on the right is 5 (7–2). The range for the number of letters in the first names for the entire class is 6—from 8 to 2.

Have children measure their heights in centimeters. Record the data, and find the range by subtracting the smallest value from the largest. Ask the children to find the heights of two other people in their homes or neighborhoods. Add these values to the data set. The range within the class will probably be smaller than the range

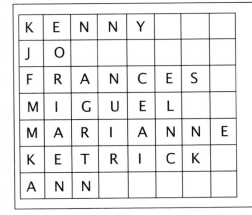

Fig. 8. Our names

deviation from the mean. Have each child measure the length of his or her foot on a piece of centimeter grid paper. Lead the class to add up the values and divide by the number of children to find the mean length of the feet. Round off the value to the nearest whole number. Now illustrate how to make a chart that shows whether any single measurement is greater than or less than the mean and the difference of each measurement from the mean (fig. 9). Have the children copy a chart with room for at least six measurements. They should fill in the measurements and compute the difference of each from the mean. The chart vividly shows whether the values are above or below the mean.

Introduction to Correlation

Upper elementary school students can begin to understand how to determine the relationship of two measurements or two sets of statistics. Students will see that some measures, such as height and weight, are often related but others, such as the length of one's name and one's height, may bear little relationship to each other.

Students can compare two sets of measurements in a simple chart and scattergram. Ask the students if they think hand and foot lengths are related, and why. Have them find their previous measures of foot length, and then have them measure the lengths of their hands from fingertips to the end of the palm. Record these two measurements on a chart (fig. 10). Ask the students to study the chart and see if the students with longer feet also seem to have longer hands. Now have each student plot a point with coordinates determined by foot and hand length on a scattergram.

Next, ask students if the length of their names and the length of their feet might be related. Have the students count the letters in their names and fill in a chart with the information (fig. 11). Do a scattergram comparing name lengths to foot lengths.

Show students that if the points in the scattergram are "in a line," the measures are closely related. Where the points are not in line but are widely scattered, the two measures are not closely related.

Displaying Data

Students can display the data they collect in many ways. Simple tallies are easy to construct and understand. Data from tallies may be converted easily to a bar graph

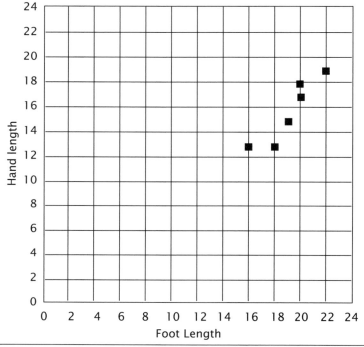

Student	Foot length	Hand length
Kerry O'Donnell	19 cm	15 cm
Inez Wiseman	18	13
Deannie Canner	16	13
Joey Smith	20	18
Kim Wong	22	19
Paul Richardson	20	17

Scattergram comparing foot length and hand length

Fig. 10

Name	Foot Measurements Compared to the Mean				
More than the mean by	1			2	
Name Measure	Joey 20 cm			Kerry 21 cm	
Mean	19 cm	19 cm	19 cm	19 cm	19 cm
Name Measure		Joanne 18 cm	Melissa 17 cm		Frederick 18 cm
Less than the mean by		1	2		1

Fig. 9

(fig. 12). Students may also find data that can be meaningfully displayed on a double bar graph. For instance, each student could record the number of stoplights and stop signs they see on the way home. The class could combine their data in a double bar graph. Students can display continuously changing data in double line graphs. Such data as indoor and outdoor temperatures (fig. 13), opening and closing prices of stocks, or comparisons of the heights of two plants are appropriate for double line graphs.

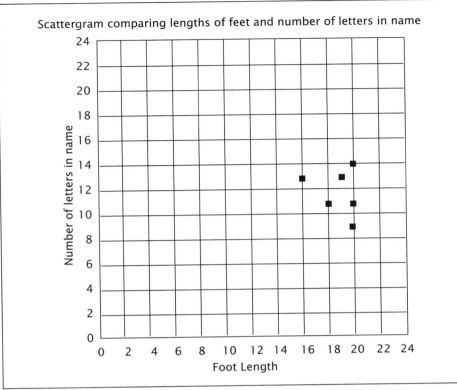

Scattergram comparing lengths of feet and number of letters in name

Fig. 11

appropriate statistics and graphs for these data. As students devise their own topics and work with their data, they develop an understanding and an appreciation of statistical concepts and methods of graphing data.

Bibliography

Fuys, David J., and Rosamond Welchman Tischler. *Teaching Mathematics in the Elementary School.* Boston: Little, Brown & Co., 1979.

Miller, Charles D., and Vern E. Heeren. *Mathematical Ideas.* 4th ed. Glenview, Ill.: Scott, Foresman & Co., 1982.

Riedesel, C. Alan. *Teaching Elementary School Mathematics.* 3d ed. Englewood Cliffs, N.J.: Prentice-Hall, 1980.

Putting It All Together

Students should devise a project in which they can use as many statistical concepts as possible. For example, the class might place a polling box outside the classroom and ask other students to express their opinions on a topic such as "my favorite season" or "should kids get to vote?" The class can tally the votes placed in the box and find the range, median, mode, and mean of the data. They can then display their results in a graph. Students might keep their own data on spending money or grades for two weeks and then compile

Language Arts— 卌 |||
Mathematics— 卌 | ||
Science— 卌 ||
Social Studies— 卌
P.E.— 卌 卌 |

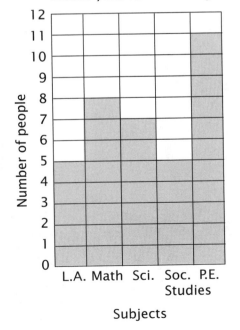

What's your favorite subject?

Fig. 12. Favorite subjects

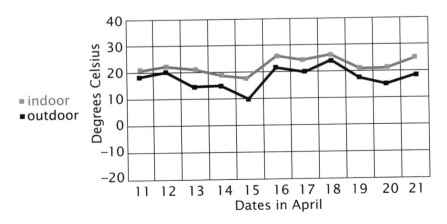

Fig. 13. What's the temperature?

ROBERT J. QUINN

Having Fun with Baseball Statistics

How often have middle school teachers had to ask students to put away their baseball cards? The lesson described in this article capitalizes on students' interest in sports while providing valuable instruction on a variety of appropriate mathematical topics. Specifically, this lesson meets the recommendations of the NCTM's *Curriculum and Evaluation Standards for School Mathematics* (1989) by integrating the study of fractions, decimals, percents, rounding, Cartesian coordinates, probability, and statistics in a cooperative setting that allows students to have fun as they learn.

Overview

To complete this lesson, the teacher must have the following materials: (a) baseball cards, (b) game-card worksheets (see fig. 1, p. 250), (c) calculators, and (d) paper clips. An overhead projector and sample transparencies are helpful but are not necessary.

The lesson involves the following four phases: (1) students familiarize themselves with the meanings of the statistics found on baseball cards; (2) students complete the worksheet portion of the game-card worksheet (see fig. 1), by converting information from their baseball cards into appropriate decimals, fractions, and percents; (3) students complete the game-card portion of the worksheet based on these data; (4) students play a simulated game of baseball. Approximately ninety minutes is

Robert Quinn, *rjq@scs.unr.edu, teaches at the University of Nevada—Reno, Reno, NV 89557-0029. He is interested in developing innovative mathematics lessons that engage middle school students, prepare them for further study, and instill in them a love of mathematics.*

Students quickly get a sense of what numbers are favorable

required to complete this activity. It can, therefore, be scheduled in a single extended time block, often available in middle school schedules, or split over two forty-five-minute class periods. I have found that in the latter, phases 1 and 2 can be completed during the first class session. The teacher can then collect and check the students' worksheets before they use this information to create the 10-by-10 array on their game cards for phase 3.

Understanding the Cards and the Statistics

When the students enter the classroom, they find several piles of baseball cards around the room. Each student is asked to select one card to use throughout the lesson. Students familiar with baseball usually seek out a player with whom they are familiar, whereas others simply choose a player with an unusual name or a name that matches their own. The teacher must ensure that all students are familiar with the baseball-card statistics that will be used in this lesson. A sample of the necessary information was taken from the 1993 Topps baseball cards of Detroit Tigers's outfielder Rob Deer, Chicago Cubs's shortstop Shawon Dunston, and an unnamed rookie and is shown in table 1. The selected rows represent at bats (AB), hits (H), doubles (2B), triples (3B), home runs (HR), slugging percentage (SLG), and batting average (AV), respectively.

This portion of the lesson works best when the teacher asks questions and allows knowledgeable students to supply the necessary information. To help students gain confidence, they should be asked to determine the batting average of their player by finding the quotient of hits (H) to at bats (AB) and rounding this decimal to the nearest thousandth. Students generally

react with enthusiasm when they find that their calculations agree with the batting average (AB) printed on their card. At this point the students should be told to fill in the bottom row of their worksheet with the batting average and the information they used to calculate it (H and AB). They should also be reminded that despite the common convention of stating a batting average as a three-digit number, mathematical correctness predicates that this statistic is actually a decimal rounded to the nearest thousandth.

Calculations and Completion of the Worksheet

In the next phase of the lesson, the students will perform calculations to determine the percent of at bats in which their player obtains each of these possible outcomes: single, double, triple, and home run. These percents will determine how many of the 100 squares on their game-card worksheet should contain each of these outcomes. Blank squares will correspond with outs. The number of squares to be filled with each possible outcome can be obtained by converting a fraction into a decimal, rounding it to the nearest hundredth, and converting this decimal back into a fraction with a denominator of 100. The numerator of this fraction will be the number of squares on the game card that should correspond to that outcome. To avoid unnecessary arguments concerning the effects of rounding, the same procedures should be used in the creation of all game cards.

The foregoing procedure will be illustrated using Rob Deer's statistics. He hit 32 home runs in 393 at bats. The first box in the HR/AB row, therefore, should read 32/393. Students should use their calculators to find 0.0814249 as the decimal equivalent of this ratio and place it in the second box. The number to be placed in the "squares" box corresponds with the percent of the time that the player hits a home run. This number can be found by rounding the decimal to the nearest hundredth, converting this decimal to a fraction whose denominator is 100, and determining that the percent corresponds to the numerator of this fraction. In this case, $0.0814249 \approx 0.08 = 8/100 = 8\%$. Showing a partially completed worksheet based on Deer's

Table 1

Selected Information from Baseball Cards of Three Players (Topps 1993)

Name	Deer	Dunston	Rookie
At bats (AB)	393	73	26
Hits (H)	97	23	5
Doubles (2B)	20	3	1
Triples (3B)	1	1	0
Home runs (HR)	32	0	1
Slugging percentage (SLG)	.547	.384	.346
Batting average (AV)	.247	.315	.192

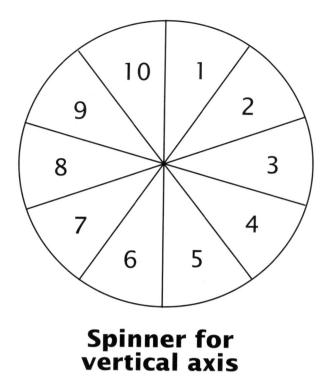

Spinner for vertical axis

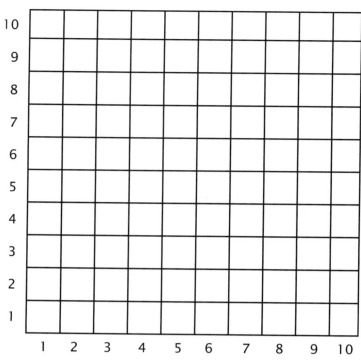

Player Name	
Student Name	

	Fraction	Decimal	Squares
HR/AB			
3B/AR			
2B/AB			
H/AB			

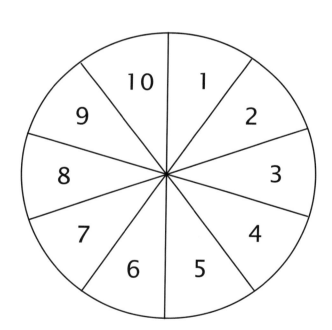

Spinner for horizontal axis

Note: the number of squares filled with 1B is found by adding the number of squares for HR, 3B, and 2B and subtracting this number from the number of squares for hits.

Fig. 1. The game-card worksheet

statistics can help students during this phase of the lesson (see fig. 2). Thus, 8 squares on the game card will be filled with HR. Similarly, the number of squares corresponding with triples and doubles can be determined in the same way. One triple in 393 at bats implies that Rob Deer triples so rarely that none of the 100 squares should indicate this outcome because 1/393 rounded to the nearest percent would be 0. Twenty doubles in 393 at bats yield 20/393 = 0.05 = 5/100 = 5%, indicating that 5 squares should be labeled 2B.

| Player Name | Rob Deer |
| Student Name | (Demonstration) |

	Fraction	Decimal	Squares
HR/AB	32/393	.0814	8
3B/AB	1/393	.0025	0
2B/AB	20/393	.0509	5
H/AB	97/393	.2468	25

Fig. 2. A partially completed game-card worksheet on Deer

Since the cards do not indicate the number of singles that a player has gotten, an alternative strategy must be used to find the number of squares to be filled with 1B. A brief discussion should culminate with the students' realizing that the total number of squares filled can be determined by the batting average. Deer's batting average of .247 indicates that 25 of the 100 squares should be filled with an outcome that corresponds to some kind of hit. (Note: Students will notice that baseball averages are printed without a leading zero, as they would get on a calculator. We adopt this common usage, when appropriate, in this article.) Since 13 squares are already taken by home runs and doubles, 12, or 25 − 13, squares should be marked 1B. If the lesson is being completed over two class periods, the teacher should collect the worksheets at this point and check them before the next day; otherwise, an informal perusal by the teacher is sufficient to guarantee that no grievous errors exist.

Creating the Game Board

The students are now ready to complete their game cards by filling in the appropriate number of squares with home runs (HR), triples (3B), doubles (2B), and singles (1B). Showing the completed game card of Deer, which meets these criteria, can be helpful at this juncture (see fig. 3). A question that often arises is whether the positioning of the favorable outcomes is important. Since an abstract analysis of this issue is probably too sophisticated for middle school students, I defer this question until the next phase of the lesson, when they will have had some empirical experiences that should aid their understanding. At this point, I simply encourage them to be creative so that a wide variety of game cards will be produced. Some students will cluster all the favorable outcomes in the same rows or columns, whereas others will spread them out across the board.

Play Ball!

Before beginning the game, the teacher should explain that the result of an at bat will be determined by using the two spinners, which are strategically placed on the game-card worksheet. To use, place a paper

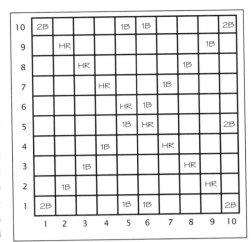

Fig. 3. Deer's game card is complete

clip under the point of a pencil, which is positioned at the center of the circle, and flick the paper clip. The square that corresponds to the ordered pair of numbers attained by the two spins determines the outcome of that at bat. The location of the spinners is particularly helpful to students who quickly recognize that 2 followed by 5 is different from 5 followed by 2.

To engage more students effectively, I recommend that the class be split into four teams so that two games can be played simultaneously. The teacher marks each of

the classroom baseball diamonds by labeling appropriately positioned desks as home plate and the other bases. The teacher explains that from the results of an at bat, the student (1) moves around the bases or (2) is "out" and must root for his or her teammates while awaiting the next turn. For simplicity, each base runner advances the same number of bases indicated by the type of hit made by the batter. After a brief demonstration, the students will be capable of continuing to play with little or no teacher supervision. The game progresses in this fashion for a certain number of innings or a predetermined time limit. I have found that a three-inning game is approximately twenty to twenty-five minutes long.

As the game is being played, the students quickly begin to anticipate what numbers are favorable on the second spin (top, left corner of game card) after the first spin (bottom, right corner of game card) has occurred.

For example, if the first spinner yields a 5 for Rob Deer, members of his team immediately begin shouting for a 6 to come up on the second spinner. However, students realize that the first spin for the player in figure 4 will completely determine whether the outcome is favorable. When I feel that the students are aware of these phenomena, I call a time-out and consider the positioning of favorable outcomes. Most students will realize that the first spin of the player in figure 4 will yield certain success three out of ten times, whereas the first spin of the player in figure 5 is irrelevant in that regardless of the outcome of that spin, success will occur on three out of ten of the second spins. Their experiences throughout the game, combined with teacher-facilitated discussion, should help students realize that the placement of favorable outcomes does not make any difference concerning the probability of those outcomes' occurring. This realization reveals students' development of a better informal sense of the laws of probability.

Enhancements and Extensions

Draft

To extend this lesson, institute a player draft before the four phases begin. Approximately forty-five additional min-

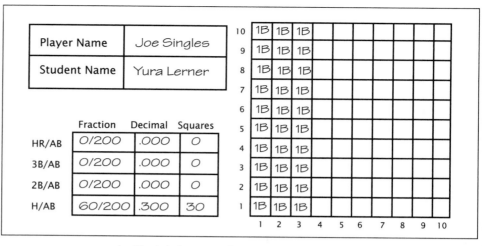

Fig. 4. A three-out-of-ten success rate is found.

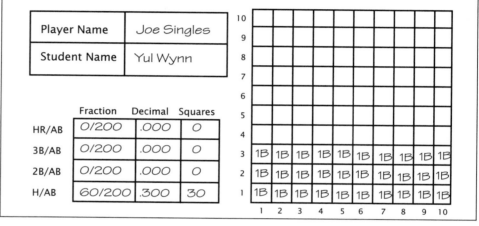

Fig. 5. The same success rate will occur on second spins.

utes will be needed to complete this portion of the lesson, including the suggested calculation of the slugging percentage (SLG). To begin the draft, students are divided into two groups and given a brief introduction. The groups are then given the opportunity to discuss their drafting strategy and are encouraged to interpret the statistics on the back of each card in terms of that player's potential contribution to the team. Students will disagree concerning which player is the best selection. For example, using the statistics in table 1, one student might argue that Rob Deer's thirty-two home runs make him the best selection. Another student might contend, however, that Shawon Dunston's substantially higher batting average makes him more valuable. Anyone who selects the rookie probably does not have a good understanding of the statistics being considered!

Slugging percentage

One statistic that can be used to inform this argument is the *slugging percentage*. The teacher should explain that this statistic is calculated using the formula

$$\frac{1B + 2 \times 2B + 3 \times 3B + 4 \times HR}{AB}.$$

The teacher should question students regarding what this formula appears to calculate. This discussion should culminate in the students' concluding that the slugging percentage can be thought of as the average number of bases to which a hitter advances safely as a direct result of an at bat. As mentioned in part 3 of this lesson, the number of singles is not shown on the card. Advanced students could be asked to modify the equation to substitute 1B = H – (2B + 3B + HR) into the formula for slugging percentage, yielding

ACTIVITIES FOR JUNIOR HIGH AND MIDDLE SCHOOL MATHEMATICS

$$\frac{\dfrac{H - 2B - 3B - HR + 2 \times 2B + 3 \times 3B + 4 \times HR}{AB}}{\dfrac{H + 2B + 2 \times 3B + 3 \times HR}{AB}}.$$

The students should use one or both of these formulas to find the slugging percentage of several potential draft choices, which will give them practice performing calculations. The value on the card will supply immediate feedback. By using slugging percentages as criteria, Rob Deer is the best selection of the players included in table 1. His propensity to hit home runs more than compensates for the higher batting average of Shawon Dunston.

Game options

Enhancements can also be added during the playing of the game to make it more exciting. One possibility would be allowing runners on second base to attempt to score on a single by tossing a die; if the die is odd, they score, but if the die is even, they are out at the plate! Students will feel more ownership for the game if they are allowed to create their own extensions and subsequent rules.

Pitching statistics

Some students might contend, and rightly so, that the results of an at bat depend not only on the hitter but on the pitcher as well. With this thought in mind, game cards can be devised that are based on pitching statistics. In this version, a coin is tossed before the spinners are used. If the coin lands as heads, the result of the at bat is determined by the batter's game card; if the coin lands as tails, the result of the at bat is determined by the opposing pitcher's card.

Conclusion

My experiences have shown that the lesson described in this article motivates and engages middle school students while fostering valuable mathematical learning. I hope that you will implement this lesson and in the process add fun and excitement to your classroom.

References

National Council of Teachers of Mathematics. *Curriculum and Evaluation Standards for School Mathematics.* Reston, Va.: The Council, 1989.

The Topps Company. Baseball cards, licensed by Major League Baseball and the Major League Baseball Player's Association, 1993.

ALISON S. CLAUS

Dolphins or Wildcats: Exploring Election Statistics

ELECTION years inspire holding mock elections in many schools. To parallel the real world, our elementary school's grades K–4 held an exciting mock election during a recent national campaign. To make the process more clear to our young students and involve a topic that would have real meaning for them, the principal and faculty designed an election to choose a school mascot. Not only would it allow us to involve the whole school in the election, but the mascot would be a way to build more community spirit in the school. Each classroom researched and debated possible animals that could represent the spirit of our school. A list of candidates was nominated. After several weeks of campaigning, a primary election determined the final candidates to be Wildcats and Dolphins.

As a school mathematics specialist, I became involved with the project when the principal suggested that my fourth-grade students might explore and share connections of mathematics with elections in some fashion. It seemed to be an ideal time for these students to learn about sampling and polls, and a good opportunity for them to collect, organize, and analyze data.

Exploring Polling, Sampling and Predicting

During the primary campaign, every room selected a candidate for mascot and promoted it to the school. My students began to discuss polls about the national election, which they had collected from newspapers and magazines. What was a poll? What did it report? How was it done?

Alison Claus *teaches elementary school at all levels as an enrichment coordinator for mathematics and science in the Lincolnshire–Prairie View School District, Lake Forest, IL 60045; aclaus@aol.com. She enjoys creating interdisciplinary activities.*

We looked at newspapers and discussed what we had heard on television. We examined what the polls were stating, who had been polled, and what predictions the pollsters were making.

At this point the students needed some experience with the technique of sampling to gain knowledge of a larger population. We spent one class period experimenting with sampling procedures and making predictions based on the samples. By the end of the lesson the children had some idea of the way a sample could be used to describe some characteristic of the entire population. After discussing how polls sampled the opinions of a much larger group of people and were used to predict the opinions of the group, we turned our attention to Dolphins and Wildcats.

Who and How Do We Poll?

Our next problem was deciding how to select students to poll. The class discussed the size of the poll sample and why they needed to consider a sample and not the whole population. They recognized that polling everyone in the school would constitute an election and that the group did not have time to interview all 450 students in the school. Thus we needed to determine a number large enough to be representative yet small enough to allow for easy polling. After some discussion, we chose two options. Option 1 would poll two students from each classroom, or about 8 to 10 percent of the school. Option 2 would poll a

sample of 10 percent of each grade without regard to classroom. Either of these options would result in polling about eight to ten students from each grade. The students decided that it would be interesting to use both methods and compare results, so we chose to administer both polls. The first would be taken about ten days before the final election and would sample two students from each classroom. The second would be taken two days before the election and would sample 10 percent of each grade chosen at random without regard to classroom.

At this point we discussed how to select our 10 percent. Did we ask friends to tell us how they were voting? What would happen if we asked only boys, or too many students from one classroom? The students saw the necessity for choosing a random sample by pulling names from a hat. I then intervened and discussed random-number lists. Our computer generated such a list for us, and using that list and class lists from the attendance computer, we chose the students for each of our polls. Class members divided up the list of students who would be polled, and we started collecting data.

The first poll, sampling two students from each classroom, resulted in a 32–15 majority for the Wildcats. We decided that a 2:1 ratio reasonably approximated our polling results. For our school population of 450, the vote was predicted to be

Wildcats 300 and Dolphins 150. The second poll, which represented only grade levels and was taken just before the election, gave the Wildcats 34 and the Dolphins 12, which is a ratio of about 3:1 in favor of the Wildcats.

On the basis of the second poll, we predicted a 340-to-110 landslide vote for the Wildcats. The actual vote count gave the Wildcats the win, but the margin was 306-203. This result was much closer to our first poll although not in agreement with our estimate.

As we looked back over our work, most of the children in the group realized that this activity paralleled the real world and what is presented in the media. Students brought in clippings about polls for the presidential election and commented about the similarity of our polling process. They also found a discussion about polls with poorer predictions, such as that from the 1948 presidential election between Thomas Dewey and Harry Truman. Pollsters predicted an outcome, and newspapers printed a headline claiming Dewey as the winner when Truman actually won. They discussed what might have skewed the predictions of these polls in light of the knowledge gained by their own experience. They wondered if the samples polled were really selected at random and speculated about factors that might have interfered with a true random selection. They also wondered about factors that might have changed people's opinions immediately before the elections. This discussion can tie into current presidential elections, in which polls can close and predictions can be made before others living several time zones away have had a chance to vote. For this reason, candidates prefer a blackout of election-result information to those areas of the country in which polls remain open so as not to sway potential voters, especially in densely populated areas.

A "First Look" at Election Data

We still had questions about our data! We looked at the totals from the election data and puzzled over the numbers. Why were more votes counted than we had predicted? Why did our second poll show a much larger margin for the Wildcats? Our discussion of these questions lasted for several classes. The discussion brought out

ideas reflected among voters in "real, adult elections," such as students who changed their minds as the election drew near on the basis of a campaign speech given in the lunch room or a preference statement made by a particularly popular or unpopular student. Students recognized that they were swayed by the thinking of their friends about the candidates. They also commented that the atmosphere in some classrooms changed their thinking.

To help us answer our questions, we studied some data included with the ballots.' Every ballot had gathered information on the sex and grade of the voter as well as his or her choice of mascot. During the tabulation, we realized that we had not polled any teachers. However, they had voted in the election. Further investigation revealed that a large majority of teachers had voted for the Dolphins. If we added forty Dolphin votes from teachers to the results of our first poll, the 300-to-150 result would change to 300 to 190, which was very close to the actual results. Another important issue was revealed while we tried to explain why the second poll was skewed. Entire classrooms of students were in favor of one candidate. The second poll had missed some rooms, resulting in uneven representation. We concluded that for this reason the first poll more closely approximated the results of the actual election.

Organizing and Analyzing the Election Data

Students raised additional questions about the election, so we decided to examine the data more closely. How did the boys vote? Did the grade level make a difference? If we had printed room numbers on the ballots, we could have checked to see if

entire classrooms of students really did vote as a block, but that information was not collected. Organizing the ballot data in tabular form helped us explain our polls and allowed us to see some interesting trends. (See table 1.) These trends generated another set of interesting questions. It was clear from our tabulated data that boys preferred the Wildcats far more than the girls. It was also clear that the older the boy, the more likely he was to prefer the Wildcats. The total number of female students was split almost evenly for each candidate, with slightly more older girls preferring the Wildcats. We found these results fascinating! Why did boys like the Dolphins when they were young yet prefer the Wildcats as they grew older? Why did girls split about equally no matter what their age? Why did teachers prefer the Dolphins? A heated debate took place. What was the "character" of a dolphin or a wildcat? The boys in the class perceived wildcats as being "tough," "aggressive," and "independent" and identified with these characteristics. Girls identified with the "gentle" and "caring" nature of the dolphins and also with their "intelligence." Boys said dolphins are "wimpy." Girls said wildcats are "mean." These fourth graders also felt that the younger children were frightened by the nature of a wildcat and felt more comfortable and secure with the nature of a dolphin. A further investigation to pursue could have been to collect more data to find out if our impressions about boys' and girls' views of the mascots were correct.

To help those of us who see data more clearly with visual representations, we put the data into visual forms using the computer and a graphing program capable of displaying different graphing options. After discussing these representations, we chose

Table 1

Dolphins versus Wildcats Election Data

	Dolphins				Wildcats			
Grade	Girls	Boys	Other	Total	Girls	Boys	Other	Total
K	21	30	0	51	18	25	0	43
1	34	24	0	58	12	30	0	42
2	21	8	0	29	20	32	0	52
3	18	3	0	21	34	37	0	71
4	24	5	0	29	32	53	0	85
Others*	6	2	7	15	8	1	4	13
Total	124	72	7	203	124	178	4	306

*The "other" category includes all ballots that did not identify pertinent data, such as sex and grade level.

those graphs that illustrated the important aspects of the election and constructed large display copies to post for the school. (See fig. 1.)

We hung the graphs in a central hall for the school to examine and discuss. Students passing by studied the graphs and often commented on or discussed them. Several teachers conducted mathematics lessons by bringing their classes to study, question, and discuss the graphs.

Concluding Comments

The NCTM's *Curriculum and Evaluation Standards for School Mathematics* (1989) encourages us to make students much more familiar with data collection, recording, and analysis. The *Professional Standards for Teaching Mathematics* (1991) suggests that we develop our classrooms to include worthwhile tasks, meaningful discourse, and stimulating environments. This project made authentic use of sampling procedures and of collecting, organizing, and displaying data to answer meaningful questions. It elicited a number of exciting and stimulating discussions, and, as a result, students gained a better understanding of their school and community. These students saw a connection between their election polls and those occurring in the adult world. They also saw how mathematics can be used as a helpful tool in trying to understand more about their world. They experienced a good example of the way samples can be used to make predictions about a larger population and that those predictions are not always accurate for various reasons. The use of the graphing program allowed them to explore these election data visually in several ways, which facilitated a cyclical question-posing, graphing-construction analysis and further-questioning process that is a critical component of data analysis.

Experience has shown that, in many ways, the authenticity of this data exploration is valid only once. Repeat elections at our school involving the school's colors, flag, and motto did not build the same sense of community or the excitement that the mascot election had generated because they were repeat elections. Perhaps some of the same feelings could be generated through student-council elections, especially if candidates campaigned about issues of interest to the entire school community.

Teachers interested in engaging their students in similar data explorations need not be bound to school or community issues, such as the selection of a school mascot. Other community issues may be of interest to students, such as constructing a youth center, developing new community-based programs for students, altering the current recycling program, or stopping some source of local pollution. Teachers are encouraged to have their students poll parents and other adults in their communities for their opinions about issues then compare these data with those gathered from students. My students and I encourage everyone to explore data surrounding various issues. We have found that this pursuit is an exciting way to engage in meaningful mathematics learning.

References

National Council of Teachers of Mathematics. *Curriculum and Evaluation Standards for School Mathematics*. Reston, Va.: The Council, 1989.

————. *Professional Standards for Teaching Mathematics*. Reston, Va.: The Council, 1991.

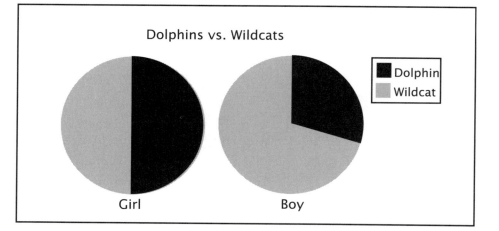
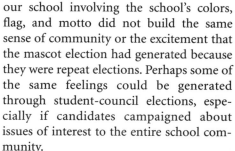
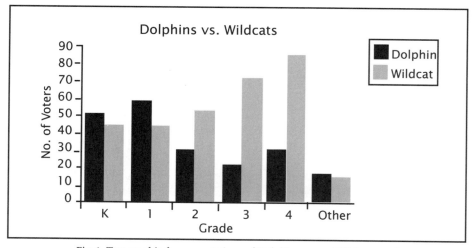

Fig. 1. Two graphical representations of Dolphins-versus-Wildcats results

MELVIN R. (SKIP) WILSON AND CAROL M. KRAPFL

Exploring Mean, Median, and Mode with a Spreadsheet

DEEPLY entrenched intuitions and understandings not consistent with commonly accepted statistical facts prevent some students from having success with activities involving statistics. For example, we have talked to many students who, despite knowing the common algorithm for mean, believe that adding zero to a set of data will not change the mean of the set. This notion is consistent with other research findings (Bright and Hoeffner, 1993). Another commonly held belief is that a small sample reliably represents a given population (Garfield and Ahlgren 1988; Shaughnessy 1992). Some people are influenced more by personal anecdotes or advice from individuals than by data gathered from large, diverse samples (Nisbett and Ross 1980). In many situations, conceptions are so deeply ingrained that mere exposure to statistical ideas is not sufficient to overcome them (Mevarech 1983). Simply introducing computational rules will not give students enough experience to overcome their generally inaccurate conceptions and intuitions about statistics. Nor will traditional instruction help students develop a sufficiently deep understanding of key statistical concepts so that they can transfer their knowledge to new problems and situations. Students need to confront their often inaccurate and inconsistent beliefs about statistics through experimentation and prediction (Shaughnessy 1992).

Melvin (Skip) Wilson, *a former middle school and high school mathematics teacher, currently teaches at the University of Michigan, Ann Arbor, MI 48109. His main interest is working with innovative mathematics teachers. Carol Krapfl is a teacher at the International Community School of Abidjan, Ivory Coast, Africa. She is particularly interested in how technology can enhance the teaching of mathematics.*
Edited by George W. Bright, *University of North Carolina at Greensboro, Greensboro, NC 27412-5001.*

This article describes a set of activities that illustrate such a problem-solving approach to teaching statistical concepts. These spreadsheet activities allow students to explore properties underlying descriptive statistics, such as mean and median, before being introduced to computational rules. The activities are most appropriate for middle-grade students but can also be adapted for other grade levels. They can be used in instruction integrating mathematics and other subjects, such as conducting surveys in the social sciences, or, depending on which extensions to the activities are included, can simply be a project of one or more weeks in a mathematics class.

The problem situations described in this article present many opportunities for students to discover that their predictions may not be consistent with experimental results. Additionally, cognitive processes related to statistics are "not likely to be changed unless they are explicitly examined and challenged by others" (Bright and Hoeffner 1993, 85). The collaborative nature of the activities allows students to examine each others' ideas openly as well as reflect on their own understandings. Since the data gathered are about their class, students will not only be motivated to analyze the data but will base their generalizations on experiences that are real to them.

The Activities

To introduce the activities, have students consider the following problem situation:

An exchange student from Senegal will soon be joining our class. Before she travels to the United States, she would like to know more about the students

she will be meeting. Unfortunately, she does not read English very well and will not have time to translate letters from each student in the class. Instead, she would like to receive one letter that describes the typical or "average" person in the class.

To allow students to discuss their initial thoughts about the exchange-student problem, hold a short class discussion before breaking into smaller groups. For example, students can brainstorm what types of information they should include and how they might summarize the information. Ask students to discuss meanings for the term *average;* some students may understand average to be a social value that implies something that is good or not good (NCTM 1991).

In small groups with about four per group, students should generate written lists of categories describing the kinds of information they would like to gather from their classmates so as to give the exchange student a good description of an average student. Groups should also describe, in writing, possible methods of collecting the information, such as with a survey or by measuring, and predict what the typical or most popular entry will be for each category. Each group should then share its lists with the class, which can reach consensus

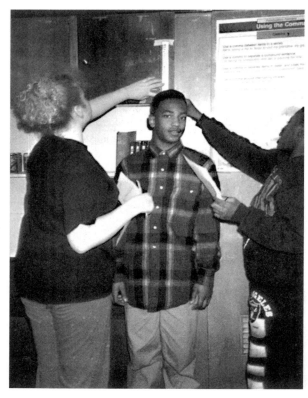

Students measure height

on which categories will be included and how the information should be gathered. The categories should be divided among groups so that each group is responsible for collecting numerical as well as nonnumeri-

Students measure foot length

cal information. Assigning four categories to each group, two with numerical data and two without, has been shown to work well.

For many students, the most meaningful form of data collection involves measuring, so try to assign to each group at least one category that involves measuring various attributes, such as height, arm span, foot length, and foot area. Students can trace their feet or hands on a sheet of square-centimeter graph paper then count the squares to determine their foot area. This activity gives students a concrete experience in calculating area without using formulas. For categories requiring measurement, assign two or three groups to share data collection for quicker and more efficient gathering.

Some students become distracted from the important task of collecting data if allowed to enter data into the computer spreadsheet as collected. Therefore, we have found it more time efficient to have students wait until after collection to enter data into the computer. After collecting and entering data, students should use the spreadsheet to find the averages, or means, for their various numerical categories. By using Microsoft Excel for the Macintosh (1992), for example, the mean of a data set can be found through the following steps:

1. Select an empty cell by clicking on it.
2. Type =AVERAGE into the cell.
3. Drag the mouse to highlight the cells containing the data needed to calculate the average.
4. Enter the formula by pressing Return or Enter. The cell should display the mean of the numbers in the desired category.

Almost any spreadsheet program will work for this activity. Other programs include ClarisWorks, Microsoft Works (Macintosh), Apple Works (Apple 2), and Excel or Lotus (DOS).

First in small groups, then as a class, students will generate a data base to develop a class profile of, or describe, a "typical" student. To simplify the data-entry process and save time, prepare a spreadsheet template and enter the students' names. A spreadsheet as shown in figure 1 without the columns identified or formulas programmed is appropriate. Each group of students can use this template to record its group's data. After data are entered and analyzed, columns from individual groups can be combined into a single spreadsheet file, which can eventually be distributed to the various groups either electronically or in printed form.

Students should also experiment with the MAX, MIN, MEDIAN, and MODE functions. As with average, these commands can be typed directly into appropriate cells. Ask each group to discuss and record its responses to the following questions:

1. What is the range of entries for each of the numerical categories or between what two numbers are all the entries?

	B19		=AVERAGE(B3:B14)							
				Class Data						
	A	B	C	D	E	F	G	H	I	J
1		Height	Arm Span	Hair	# in	Favorite	Hrs. TV	Foot Length	Foot Area	Favorite
2	Student	(cm)	(cm)	Color	Family	TV Show	per week	(cm)	(sq. cm)	Sport
3	B., John	163	158	brown	4	whats happen	10	26	116	Basketball
4	D., JR	154	155	black	7	martin	15	29	153	Football
5	H., Keebe	175	171	black	4	90210	20	31	182	Basketball
6	J., Darrell	171	165	light brown	8	martin	10	30	142	Basketball
7	J., Aaron	166	159	black	2	martin	7	26	180	Football
8	P., Tina	154	145	brown	7	90210	10	27	141	Basketball
9	R., Lavor	146	144	brown	6	cosby show	12	30	146	Baseball
10	S., Juara	151	140	black	3	living single	9	27	155	Basketball
11	S., Adriene	154	145	brown	5	living single	6	26	119	Basketball
12	W., Tiana	151	142	brown	4	step by step	0	27	135	Roller Skating
13	Y., Bill	160	161	black	4	living single	20	29	137	Basketball
14	Y., Jessica	144	143	brown	4	viper	5	26	91	Basketball
15										
16										
17	Minimum	144	142		2		0	26	91	
18	Maximum	173	171		8		20	31	182	
19	Mean (Average)	152.92	153		4.833		10.3335	27.8335	141.853	
20	Median	154	151.5		4		10	27	141.5	
21	Mode	154	145		4		10	26	#N/A	
22										

Fig. 1. A sample spreadsheet containing data compiled from several groups

How do these numbers compare with the MAX and MIN for each category? For each category, how does the AVERAGE compare with the predicted average? For each category, how does AVERAGE compare with MAX and MIN? This last question should encourage students to notice that average is between maximum and minimum—a property of average that is not always obvious.

2. What will happen to the AVERAGE, MAX and MIN if one of the entries is changed to zero? Try it. Was the prediction correct? Explain what happened. Experiment with the data in other ways, for example, by adding some very large values, and describe what was found. Note: Ask students to save and rename their original spreadsheet file before changing the values of the entries.

3. Sort the data so that one column lists its entries from smallest to largest. (To execute a sort using Microsoft Excel for the Macintosh, highlight the block of data to be sorted and choose "Sort" from the Data menu. In the "first key" box, type the cell address of the first cell in the column to be sorted. For example, to sort the spreadsheet in figure 1 according to height, highlight cells A3 through J14, select "Sort" from the Data menu, type "B3" in the "first key" box, and click "OK" to enter the sort command. Rows of data will be rearranged so that "Height" values will be listed in ascending order, thus preserving the overall arrangement of the data.) Count how many times each value appears in the list. Which entry appears most often? Compare this value with the MODE of that column. Repeat this process using another column as a reference. To what does *mode* refer?

4. With the data still sorted, count how many entries are greater than or equal to the MEDIAN and how many are less than or equal for each of the numerical categories Experiment with the data as in question 2 and record what was found. On the basis of experimentation, to what does *median* refer?

5. Explain how the median is similar to, but different from, the mean. Experiment

some more with the data and change a few entries to see the differences.

6. Which descriptive statistic—min, max, mean, median, or mode—best describes each of the categories? In other words, which value is the most typical? Explain why.

7. What happens when attempting to find the MEAN, MEDIAN, MODE, MAX, or MIN of a category listing nonnumerical data? Even though the computer will not find these statistics, do any of them make sense? How could the data be summarized to show a type of "average" of a nonnumerical category?

These questions can be modified to accommodate spreadsheet packages that do not include MEDIAN and MODE as built-in functions. For example, students can sort the data to determine the median and mode. However, they will not be able to check their answers with computer-calculated values.

Experimentation and exploration will help students build a relational understanding of key statistical ideas before actually learning computational procedures. The spreadsheet helps students organize and display their data and thus is an ideal tool for promoting such exploration. Students can perform statistical calculations quickly and efficiently, which frees them to experiment with the data by adding or changing values and noting the corresponding changes calculated by the spreadsheet formulas. Ideally, students will have had some prior experience using the spreadsheet software, although it is not absolutely necessary. We have found that the activity itself can lead to such familiarity.

After completing the spreadsheet activities, explain to the class that all the categories (columns) will be merged into a single worksheet and distributed either electronically or in printed form to each of the groups. Class members should decide how the results can best be communicated to their exchange student. For example, a word processor might be used to write a letter. Groups of students might construct letters that include data, graphs, or charts that are electronically copied directly from the spreadsheet into the letter.

Whole-class discussions conducted at varying points during small-group explo-

rations, for example, at the end of each class session, will allow students to think more about their own conclusions while considering issues that may not have arisen in their group. Assign each group to report on, or lead the discussion about, one of the questions or categories. Ideally, the class will base conclusions on class agreement following substantial debate rather than simply rely on the teacher's explanation. For example, one group may conclude that mean and median are the same, whereas another group's data may reveal distinct differences. Such differences can spark meaningful dialogue among students. Since students base their understanding of these ideas on experiences with data that are meaningful to them, we have found that students are willing and eager to share and discuss their results.

Possible Extensions

Graphical analysis of nonnumerical data

The spreadsheet activities can be extended in many ways. For example, most spreadsheet packages allow users to construct and display graphs next to the worksheet values on which they are based. Viewing several graphical and tabular representations simultaneously allows students to see connections among them more easily (see fig. 2). Graphical representations are particularly useful for nonnumerical data, such as a favorite food or movie. Frequency distributions can be depicted visually. Because middle school students are often more interested in their nonnumerical categories than in numerical ones, we have found that students should explore and analyze their nonnumerical categories using frequency tables and graphs before considering the mean, median, and mode of their numerical data sets. This ordering of activities also decreases the chances that students will mistakenly attempt to find the means or medians of nonnumerical categories.

A related extension involves students' considering, from both tabular and graphical perspectives, relationships between two data categories. For example, the scatterplot in figure 3 illustrates the relationship between height and arm span. Such an exploration presents a natural context for exploring functional relationships, such as

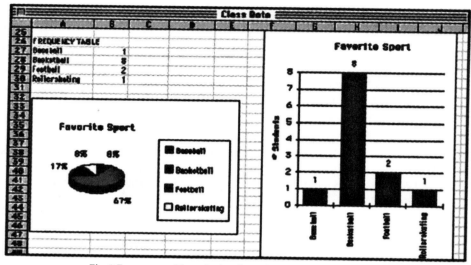

Fig. 2 Frequency table and related graphs created from class data

the linear, in fact identity, function approximated by the relationship illustrated in figure 3.

Writing activities

Writing has proved to be a key activity in helping students understand and remember the ideas explored. Ask students to write down individual and group responses to some or all the questions considered in groups. Additionally, assigning students to make journal entries at appropriate times during the activity will help them to be more focused during class discussions and to think critically about the ideas explored.

Developing an algorithm for mean

One important purpose of this activity is to familiarize students with conceptual aspects of mean, median, and mode before actually learning algorithms. It is also important for students to develop computational proficiency. The mean height of the members of each small group, a category that will probably appear in the spreadsheet activity, can be computed nonnumerically by cutting pieces of string matching individual students' heights, taping the individual lengths together, and folding the total length into as many equal-length parts as the number of group members. Means of other lengths, such as arm span, foot length, and so on, can be similarly explored with string or strips of paper.

When the actual algorithm is eventually developed, students will have had experience using a spreadsheet and completing the string activities on which to base their understanding. After a formula is developed, students can use calculators to compute means of individual columns of data.

Sample size

Other important statistical concepts can also be explored using data from this activity. For example, the following questions pinpoint the importance of sample size and representative information in determining if an average is appropriate:

- How does the mean height of one small group compare with the overall class mean?

- If a difference is found, why is it occurring? Which mean is more typical of the class? Why?

- What would be an appropriate sample for approximating the mean age of students in the school?

Measures of variation

Almost as natural as the question "What is the most typical number?" is the question "How much variation occurs among the data?" In most middle or high school classes, considerably less variation will arise among some data categories than among others. For example, age of students will vary considerably less than height. This fact can be numerically represented using conventional measures of variation, such as variance or standard deviation. The computation involved in finding these statistical measures is even more complex and consequently less accessible to students than it is for mean, but a spreadsheet makes exploration of these concepts possible. Formulas can be entered, and explorations similar to those described previously in this article can be used to probe the meaning of these other statistical measures.

Conclusions

Computational proficiency is only one area needed to promote a desired understanding of statistics, albeit an important one. Although these spreadsheet activities have been used in settings in which instruction on the algorithm for mean preceded the activities, better results have been

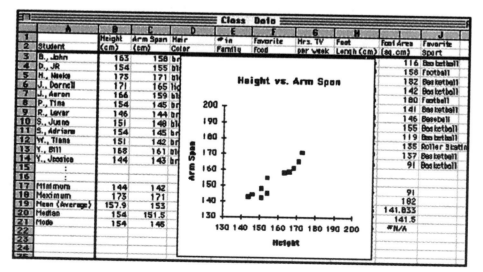

Fig. 3 Scatterplot—height versus arm span

obtained when the problem-solving approach suggested in this article has preceded the introduction of traditional rules for computation. We have found that even students who can compute averages using traditional rules frequently do not understand what average means, how it behaves under different conditions, or how it compares with median and mode as a measure of central tendency. Students' belief that they understand what average is because they know how to compute an average tends to interfere with their ability to consider more subtle properties of average, such as the effects of changing data or adding extreme values. Additionally, many students have deeply held conceptions that interfere with their ability to understand and effectively use computational procedures. The approach suggested in this article gives students a set of experiences in which they must confront their initial conceptions and intuitions before modifying them. Additionally, since students' success with this activity is not dependent on their ability to apply computational rules, every student can contribute and have a meaningful experience.

The reflection and debate that arise out of activities described in this article lead to positive learning experiences and an enjoyable time for students and teachers. Students begin to develop a flexible understanding of mean, median, and mode. They not only learn definitions for these terms but also develop subtle but valuable intuitions about them, such as the effects of extreme values. Perhaps most important, they gain a sense of how these terms can be used to communicate information and solve problems. Because the teacher and textbook are not at the center of the explorations, students' understanding of mathematics is expanded beyond traditional areas. Consequently, in addition to mastering skills and procedures, students develop confidence and interest in exploring mathematical problems and ideas.

References

Bright, George W., and Karl Hoeffner. "Measurement, Probability, Statistics, and Graphing." In *Research Ideas for the Classroom: Middle Grades Mathematics,* edited by Douglas T. Owens, 78–98. New York: Macmillan Publishing Co., 1993.

Garfield, Joan, and Andrew Ahlgren. "Difficulties in Learning Basic Concepts in Probability and Statistics: Implications for Research." *Journal for Research in Mathematics Education* 19 (January 1988): 44–63.

Mevarech, Z. "A Deep Structure Model of Students' Statistical Misconceptions." *Educational Studies in Mathematics* 14 (November 1983): 41–29.

Microsoft Corporation. Microsoft Excel. Redmond, Wash.: Author, 1992. Software.

Nisbett, R. and L. Ross. *Human Inference: Strategies and Shortcomings of Social Judgment.* Englewood Cliffs, N.J.: Prentice-Hall, 1980.

Shaughnessy, J. Michael. "Research in Probability and Statistics: Reflections and Directions." In *Handbook of Research on Mathematics Teaching and Learning,* edited by Douglas A. Grouws, 465–94. New York: Macmillan Publishing Co. and Reston, Va.: National Council of Teachers of Mathematics, 1992.

Zawojewski, Judith S., et al. *Dealing with Data and Chance: Addenda Series, Grades 5–8.* Reston, Va.: National Council of Teachers of Mathematics, 1991.

JULI K. DIXON AND CHRISTY J. FALBA

Graphing in the Information Age:
Using Data from the World Wide Web

N THE information age, middle school students must be intelligent consumers of information. To instill critical thinking with respect to statistical data, the interpretation and creation of graphs are essential. Although vast amounts of information can be gleaned from traditional text sources, the World Wide Web (WWW) offers information that is updated far more frequently than most printed materials. Because of the motivational aspects and expedient nature of using data from the Web, this article focuses on its use; however, each of the activities can be adapted for use with traditional, text-based media.

The WWW connects thousands of networks of computers and allows millions of users to access and share information. According to *U.S. News and World Report* (Flynn 1996), 20 to 30 million people around the globe use the Web regularly. Approximately ten thousand people per day access it for the first time. Early in 1996 over 22 million "pages," or documents, existed, and it is estimated that at the current rate of growth, more than 1 million pages will be added to the Web each month. Commonly referred to as the "network of networks," the Internet comprises thousands of computer networks interconnected around the world, including many

sites located at educational institutions, allowing millions of users to access and share information quickly.

Common uses of the Internet include communicating one on one or with groups of people and locating information. As a research tool, the Internet offers databases of information in a variety of forms including encyclopedias, magazines, and museums. Unlike traditional materials in text form, digital information on the Internet can readily be updated at any time; therefore, resources available on the Internet are frequently more current than their paper counterparts. In addition, many electronic references offer sound and video clips as well as text information.

The Web is a hypertext-based means of accessing and publishing information on the Internet. Through hypertext, words and ideas can be linked. A user can click on a word within the text and be taken directly to the location associated with the word or idea. Web pages can combine text, graphics, sound, and video and often contain links to related resources.

A Web browser, software that allows interactive access to Web pages, is

necessary to view the World Wide Web. Commonly used Web browsers are Netscape, Lynx, and Mosaic. By using a Web browser, an individual can point and click on electronic links to move through and explore information. Clicking on Net Search or Net Directory takes the user to a database listing of categories (fig. 1).

To access a particular Web page, the address or location of the page can be entered. A uniform resource locator, or URL, is the form of the address. For example, http://www.nhl.com/scores/index.htm is a URL for National Hockey League statistics. To access the information available at this address, enter the URL on the Web location field (fig. 2).

Another avenue for locating Web sites makes use of *search engines,* the search

Juli Dixon, *dixonj1@nevada.edu, teaches technology and mathematics-education courses at the University of Nevada—Las Vegas (UNLV). Her interests include geometry, the integration of technology into mathematics instruction, and problem solving. Christy Falba, cfalba@nevada.edu, teaches technology in education courses and is completing a doctorate in educational technology at UNLV. Her interests include teacher education and the integration of technology into subject areas.*

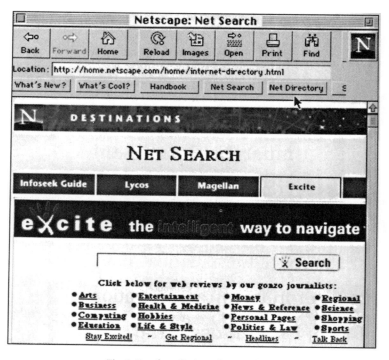

Fig. 1. Database listing of categories

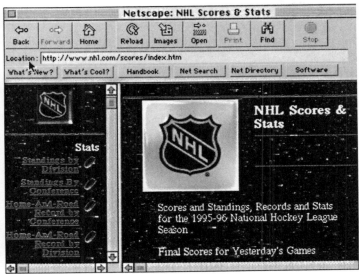

Fig. 2. The National Hockey League statistics URL and home page

feature of browser software. In Netscape, for example, clicking on Net Search produces several options for conducting searches. A list of commonly used search engines can be found by scrolling down the opening Web page. For example, using "Yahoo!" for the search and entering National Hockey League (fig. 3) produces a list of Web sites. Look for a Web site containing NHL Open Net. Use this link to find National Hockey League statistics, then select the desired information. Often random exploration leads to other topics of interest.

By using a computer and searching the WWW, a user has access to information equivalent to that contained in an entire library. As with any traditional library search, extraneous information may be included with the results of an Internet search. Information alone does not equal knowledge; finding ways to organize, use, and share information is vital. Consequently, it is appropriate for middle school students to experience searching, locating, and organizing information taken from the Web. This resource provides an excellent medium for investigating data availability and for exploring relationships among collected data.

In accordance with the *Curriculum and Evaluation Standards for School Mathematics* (NCTM 1989), students need to summarize statistics, analyze data, make conjectures, and communicate information, all of which are incorporated in the following activities. Students will interpret or create bar graphs, line graphs, histograms, and circle graphs. These experiences will assist the students in developing the ability to determine the most appropriate type of graph for displaying a set of data, an important aspect in communicating information (Zawojewski et al. 1991). Using technology as a tool to create graphs places the focus on analysis and interpretation. However, graphs for each of the activities can be created manually. Regardless of the techniques employed to create graphs, it is important to emphasize the use of appropriate labels and meaningful displays of data.

The following activities may be used individually or as a unit. Different types of graphs can frequently be found on the WWW at locations for news magazines, newspapers, or governmen-tal agencies, such as the Census Bureau or the Department of Education. Because of the dynamic nature of the World Wide Web, URL locations used in this article may have changed.

Activity 1

Bar-graph interpretation: At Web address http://www.census.gov/stat_abstract/img/wage.gif, two bar graphs show average earnings of full-time workers in 1992 (fig. 4). Use the information presented in these graphs to answer the following questions:

• What were the average earnings of males and females with less than a ninth-grade education?

• How do your answers in the first question compare with earnings of high school graduates and those with bachelor's degrees?

• Is the difference between male and female earnings consistent at each level of education? What might be some reasons for the gap between male and female earnings?

• How might we define *consistent* with respect to the previous question?

Bar-graph creation: Go to Web address http://www.nhl.com/scores/index.htm to find National Hockey League statistics and select the link Home-and-Road Overall Record. Use the two charts, "At-Home Record" and "On the-Road Record," to collect win (w) information to

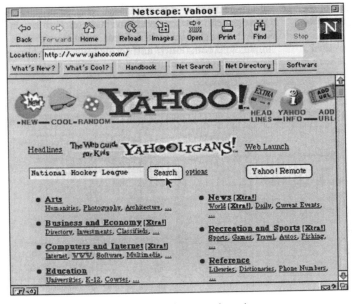

Fig. 3. The Yahoo! search engine

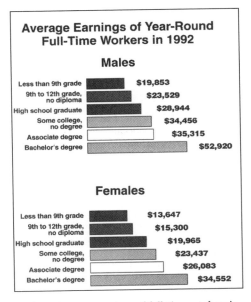

Fig. 4. Average earnings of full-time workers in 1992

make a double-bar graph comparing wins for six teams of your choice. If possible, create your graph using a software program that has graphing options, such as a spreadsheet application. Use your graph to answer the following questions:

- Which of your chosen teams has the greatest difference between wins at home and wins on the road?
- On the basis of your graph, which team has the greatest total number of wins?
- Look for a trend between home and away wins. What factors might account for the trend?

This activity exposes students to the difference between interpreting and creating graphs. The questions are open-ended and may lead to further investigations and heated discussion.

Activity 2

Line-graph interpretation: The following line graph was taken from a United States Census Bureau WWW location (fig. 5). Use the line graph, "Percent of Persons Who Have Completed High School or College: Selected Years 1940 to 1993," to answer the following questions:

- In 1970, what percent of people twenty-five years and over had a bachelor's degree or more?
- What percent of people twenty-five to twenty-nine years old had at least a high school diploma in 1990? In 1940?

- Is the interval for those of age 25 to 29 years with a bachelor's degree or more an increasing trend or decreasing trend for the interval 1977 to 1981?
- List an interval that has an increasing trend.

Line-graph creation: Enter the Web page address http://aws.com/globalwx.html, which will show an automated weather map. Select two locations where temperature differences might be found. Keep in mind that choices may cross time zones, which will affect data collection. Revisit the locations at regular intervals, hourly, daily, and so on, to collect data on current temperatures. Create a double-line graph to display the data (fig. 6). Use the graph to answer the following questions:

- What does your graph show? How might you adjust your graph or data-collection technique for different time zones?
- Which of your chosen locations had the greatest change in temperature?
- Make a prediction of the temperatures for the next five intervals. Check your prediction if possible.

As an extension of the first part of this activity on line-graph interpretation, students may research past events that may have affected trends in education during the given time periods. The temperature activity may stimulate more interest in current weather trends. Other types of weather data can be charted, such as precipitation, hurricanes, and tornadoes.

Activity 3

Histogram interpretation: Go to California SuperLotto Information location http://www.impactweb.com/lotto/ and scroll down to the "Frequency Analysis" histogram (fig. 7). Use the histogram to answer the following questions:

- Which number has been drawn the least in the last 104 games?
- What is the width of each histogram interval?
- What was the most frequent number drawn nine to twelve months ago?
- On the basis of the information in the SuperLotto histogram, which six numbers would you select for your next pick? Justify your answer. How does choosing your pick on the basis of past wins relate to what you know about random numbers?

Histogram creation: Type in location http://www.usc.edu/dept/TommyCam/ to see a live picture of the University of Southern California's courtyard, which contains Tommy Trojan, the school's mascot. Images are updated every sixty seconds. Revisit the site every five minutes or perhaps at the same time each day. Record data on the number of people visible at each visit and use this information to create a histogram.

- Describe your data-collection technique and the reasons for your choice.
- According to your data, what was the greatest number of people visiting Tommy Trojan? Speculate why.
- What was the total number of people who visited Tommy Trojan during your observations?
- Aside from the number of people observed, what other data could you glean from regular visits to this site? Why would someone be interested in those data?

Students might be interested in conducting an investigation aimed at determining "favorite number" trends. Do people have reasons for the numbers they choose? As an alternative activity, students can search for other dynamic Web pages where data are periodically updated, such as Tommy Trojan's courtyard, or where the students can collect their own data.

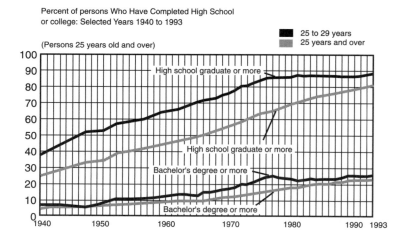

Percent of persons Who Have Completed High School or college: Selected Years 1940 to 1993

(Persons 25 years old and over)

■ 25 to 29 years
▨ 25 years and over

Fig. 5. Percent of persons who have completed high school or college from 1940 to 1993

ACTIVITIES FOR JUNIOR HIGH AND MIDDLE SCHOOL MATHEMATICS

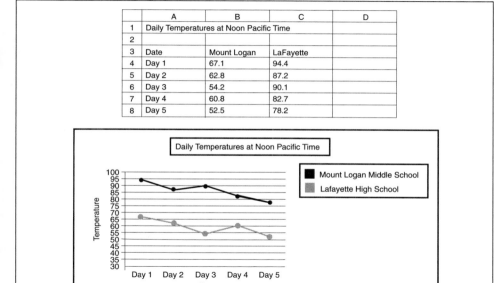

Fig. 6 Temperature statistics for Mount Logan Middle School in Logan Utah, and Lafayette High School in Williamsburg, Virginia

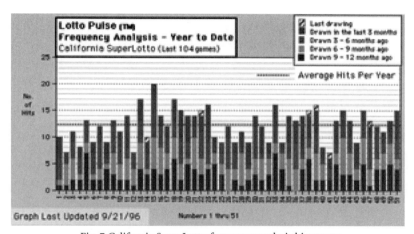

Fig. 7 California SuperLotto frequency analysis histogram

Activity 4

Circle-graph interpretation: The circle graphs in figure 8, from Census Bureau data, show college enrollment by age and sex for 1973 and 1993. Answer the following questions using the circle graphs:

- What percent of females less than twenty-five years old were enrolled in college in 1973? In 1993?

- What percent of males twenty-five years old and older were enrolled in college in 1973? In 1993?

- How many females were enrolled in college in 1973? In 1993?

- How many males were enrolled in college in 1973? In 1993?

Circle-graph creation: Go to location http://cellini.leonardo.net/aasen/topbox .html to find information on the top ten movies for the last date posted on the Web site. Use the information to create a circle graph and answer the following:

- What does your graph represent?

- Describe and answer at least three other questions that could be asked about the data in your graph.

According to Zawojewski and others (1991), an appropriate extension to this activity would be to have the class generate a research question, organize the collection of data, and follow the study through to communication of the conclusions implied from the collected data. This experience would lead quite naturally into activity 5.

Activity 5

Use the data found at the location http://www.census.gov/ftp/pub/population /cencounts to create at least three different types of graphs. You may use any of the information from this site that you choose and any three of the four graphs described in the first four activities—bar graph, line graph, histogram, and circle graph. After you have created your graphs, respond to the following:

- Explain why your choice of graph type is the best in each instance.

- For each graph you created, write three questions' that can be answered by looking at the graph.

Representing data through the use of

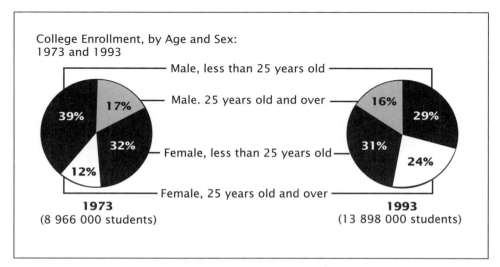

Fig. 8. College enrollment by age and sex for 1973 and 1993

graphs can be a powerful tool for persuasion. Have students collect graphs from newspapers and magazines; discuss the choices of graph types with respect to their effectiveness in presenting information.

"In this age of information and technology, an ever-increasing need exists to understand how information is processed and translated into usable knowledge" (NCTM 1989, 105). These activities allow students to make decisions regarding collection of data, to display data through practical uses of particular types of graphs, and to recognize the power of visual representations with respect to data analysis and identification of trends. By preparing our students to manage data, we are preparing them to be critical consumers of information.

References

Flynn, Mary K. "Taming the Internet." *U. S. News & World Report* 120 (29 April 1996): 60, 64, 68.

National Council of Teachers of Mathematics. *Curriculum and Evaluation Standards for School Mathematics.* Reston, Va.: The Council, 1989.

Zawojewski, Judith S., Gary Brooks, Lynn Dinkelkamp, Eunice D. Goldberg, Howard Goldberg, Arthur Hyde, Tess Jackson, Marsha Landau, Hope Martin, Jeri Nowakowski, Sandy Paull, Albert P. Schulte, Philip Wagreich, and Barbara Wilmont. *Dealing with Data and Chance.* Addenda series, grades 5–8. Reston, Va.: National Council of Teachers of Mathematics, 1991.

ANDREW C. ISAACS AND CATHERINE RANDALL KELSO

Pictures, Tables, Graphs, and Questions: Statistical Processes

I N AN address to the American Association for the Advancement of Science, John Dewey (1910) contrasted the *facts* of science with the *method* of science and argued that the method, rather than the facts, should be preeminent in the school curriculum. But what is that method? More particularly, how does that method appear when transformed to fall within the scope of children's lives? How can the fundamentally quantitative method of modern science be simplified as much as possible, but not too much, so that children can apply it to questions arising from their own experience?

This article outlines one approach to this problem by teaching science as a process of collecting, organizing, and analyzing data (Goldberg and Boulanger 1981; Goldberg and Wagreich 1989, 1990). We hope to show that this brand of science is naturally integrated with mathematics. We begin with a description of an investigation designed for the second grade called "Marshmallows and Containers."

Marshmallows and Containers

As class begins, students sit together in groups of three with three different containers: a bowl, for instance, a disposable

Predictions, explanations, and journal writing are all parts of the investigations.

margarine tub; a 100-cc graduated cylinder; and a small paper cup. The teacher shows the class a bag of miniature marshmallows and asks, "Which container will hold the most marshmallows? Why do you think so?"

The teacher encourages the groups to discuss their predictions and explanations and to record their ideas in their journals. Many groups report to the class that they think that the graduated cylinder will hold the most because it is the tallest.

One boy explains that he thinks the cylinder will hold the most because even if he could stretch the plastic in the bowl to be tall like the cylinder, it still would not be as tall and would not hold as much. Other groups choose the bowl because it is wider than the other containers.

When the groups have recorded their predictions, the teacher asks the class how they could check them. She introduces the term *volume*, as a measure of the space inside the container. She asks, "How could you find out which container has the greatest volume?" This question leads naturally

to an experiment: The students will fill each of the containers with marshmallows, count them, and record the numbers in a data table.

The teacher explains how they will collect the data then demonstrates the experimental procedure by filling the cylinder with miniature marshmallows and the bowl with larger marshmallows. The students immediately shout, "That's not fair!" The teacher then asks the class to describe a "fair" procedure. The class decides that the marshmallows must all be of the same size and that they should be dropped into the containers rather than tightly packed. To conclude the class, each student draws a picture of the experiment. Figure 1 shows three containers being filled and marshmallows being counted by tens in an egg carton.

The next day, the children use their pictures to review the experiment before beginning the data collection. Each group receives a two-column data table, completes the column headings, and writes the names or draws pictures of the containers

Andy Isaacs *is a writer for the teacher-development component of the University of Chicago School Mathematics Project (UCSMP), Chicago, IL 60637; aisaacs@uchicago.edu. He is interested in helping teachers implement standards-based curricula.* Catherine Kelso *develops curriculum at the Institute for Mathematics and Science Education, University of Chicago, Chicago, IL 60637; u20335@uicvm.uic.edu. She is currently working on a mathematics curriculum project for grades K–5.*

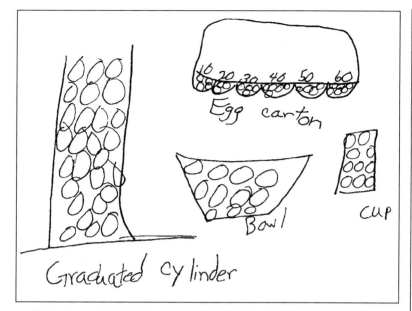

Fig. 1. One student's picture for the "Marshmallows and Containers" project

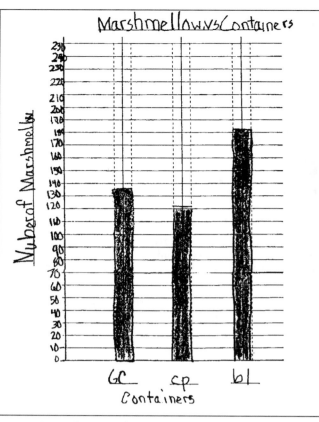

Fig. 3. A bar graph for "Marshmallows and Containers"

in the first column. The teacher emphasizes the need for accuracy in counting, and the children discuss various methods for grouping and counting the marshmallows. As the students begin their work, the teacher circulates, coaches, and assesses.

After the children complete their data tables (fig. 2), the teacher leads a discussion in which the groups compare their results to find whether results are reasonable. Most groups report that about 135 marshmallows are in the graduated cylinder and agree that numbers close to 135, but not exactly 135, are acceptable. A group that had recorded only 110 marshmallows for the cylinder decides to refill the cylinder and count again.

On the third day, students graph the data on a bar graph and analyze the results. (See fig. 3.) These graphs will be useful in comparing results across groups, in supporting multiple solution methods, and in fostering number sense and estimation skills.

Differences and similarities across groups are then examined. Differences among groups are most apparent in the data tables. Students discuss reasons for these differences: variations in how the marshmallows were packed, differences in how completely the containers were filled, errors in counting. Uniformity of results across groups is more apparent in the graphs: although the graphs are not exactly the same, they are similar. On every student's graph, the tallest bar is for the bowl. The class lists reasons for this basic agreement: all groups (1) used identical containers, (2) used the same-sized marshmallows, and (3) put the marshmallows in their containers the same way.

A lively discussion ensues about why the bowl holds the most—that is, because of its much greater width than the cylinder's—leading to verbalization of this reasoning by many of those students who had predicted that the graduated cylinder would hold the most.

On the final day of the experiment, students work in groups to write answers to questions about the data: "Which container is the tallest?" "The shortest?"

"Which held the most marshmallows?" Later questions ask for predictions and generalizations: "Will a taller container always have a bigger volume than a shorter one?" "Why?" Students also write about volume in their journals: "Volume is the space in something like a cup" and "Volume is like how big the space is, not [just] the height."

Mathematics in Context

Two principles underlie the children's version of the foregoing scientific method. First, an investigation should begin within the children's own experiences. In this laboratory, children use objects from their everyday lives to investigate a familiar situation. Children's everyday knowledge, like a scientist's theory, supplies a framework for interpreting the results of the investigation. Without that framework the investigation would remain hollow and meaningless.

The second principle is that an investigation should also transcend children's everyday experiences. The exploration must go somewhere; it must lead the children both to a better understanding of the immediate situation and to improved skills, understandings, habits, and attitudes.

Container	N Number of Marshmallow units
Graduated cylinder	133
Cup	121
bowl	181

Fig. 2. A data table for "Marshmallows and Containers"

Balancing these principles requires a teacher's judgment. Students must follow their own ideas but be guaranteed that those ideas will lead somewhere. The teacher must decide how much scaffolding to build and how best to guide students in directions that are fruitful rather than sterile. Students should advance not only in skill and understanding but also in autonomy and perseverance. A teacher's most important and difficult job is to decide just how much structure to furnish along the way.

The "Marshmallows and Containers" activity involves several particular skills and concepts: measurement, graphing, number sense, problem solving in context, and communication. More important than these specific skills and concepts, however, is the overall approach the children take in the investigation. The children identify and work with variables; they collect, organize, and graph data; and they analyze the results.

These general techniques can be applied to other problems and comprise a child's version of a four-phase scientific method: (1) beginning the investigation, (2) collecting and organizing the data, (3) graphing the data, and (4) analyzing the experimental results. We discuss these four phases and illustrate our discussion with references both to "Marshmallows and Containers" and to a fifth-grade experiment called "Evaporation," in which children study the volume of water in an open container over time.

Beginning the investigation

Most investigations begin with a question, which does not have to be momentous or clever but must be meaningful to children. If the question connects with their experience, children will need no flashy inducements to want to find the answer. With "Marshmallows and Containers," the question was "Which container holds the most marshmallows?" Questions with an explicit quantitative aspect, something that children can count or measure, work well. Questions that can be recast quantitatively are also appropriate. For example, the question "What happens when water evaporates?" can be narrowed to "What happens to the volume of the water in an open container left standing out for several days?"

Once a suitable question has been posed, the many variables related to the question must be identified. In "Marshmallows and Containers" the variables involved include the type of container, the size of the marshmallows, how the marshmallows are packed, and the number of marshmallows that fit in the containers. In "Evaporation," relevant variables are the type of liquid, the exposed surface area, the temperature, and time.

If too many variables change simultaneously, obtaining meaningful results can be difficult or impossible. In an ideal experiment, more easily realized in the laboratory than in the real world, a scientist focuses on only two variables and strives to hold all others constant. Thus, "Marshmallows and Containers" focuses on the kind of container—bowl, cylinder, cup—and the number of marshmallows while using one size of marshmallow and packing all the containers "fairly." In "Evaporation," students measure the volume of water in a container and the elapsed time while holding the location of the container, the exposed surface area, and the temperature fixed.

By the end of the investigation's first phase, the original question has been refined into a precise query about the relationship between two well-defined variables about which the children can gather information. Drawing a picture is an excellent way (1) to summarize and communicate this beginning phase, (2) to plan what is to come, (3) to help children understand and organize what they are to do, and (4) to help teachers assess whether students are ready to proceed. Figure 4 shows one student's "Evaporation" picture, indicating the two primary variables—V, volume, and t, time in days; two important controlled variables—the location of the jars on the window sill and the time of day for taking measurements; and the procedure—pouring water from the graduated cylinder into the jars and cleaning up with paper towels. The

student who drew this picture is now ready to gather data.

Collecting and organizing the data

The children gather the data and organize them in a table. A data table with two main columns is sufficient for most experiments. The name of a variable, including units if appropriate, heads each column. Figure 5 shows students' data tables for "Evaporation."

The data table is useful for preserving the data, controlling error, and identifying patterns. Children can detect blunders when a measurement deviates too much from established patterns, and they can control inevitable measurement error by averaging several trials.

Students almost always work in small groups to gather data. This organization makes managing the equipment easier, but it also helps in other ways. Complicated procedures may require that several students work together to gather the data. When measurements are difficult, multiple trials are easier for a group to complete than for an individual. Several students working together are more likely to notice when patterns begin to emerge in the data as a relationship between two key variables becomes evident.

Graphing the data

Although the relationship between the variables may be evident in a data table, it is usually clearer in a graph. Accordingly, after data are gathered, a graph should be drawn. A bar graph is usually best when

Fig. 4. Picturing the "Evaporation" experiment

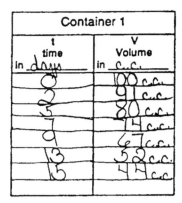
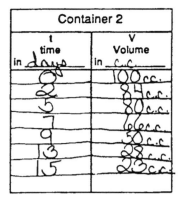

Container 1	
t time in days	**V** Volume in c.c.
0	100 c.c.
2	91 c.c.
5	80 c.c.
	c.c.
	67 c.c.
13	52 c.c.
15	44 c.c.

Container 2	
t time in days	**V** Volume in c.c.
0	100 cc.
2	84 c.c.
5	80 c.c.
7	60 c.c.
9	50 c.c
13	28 c.c.
15	23 cc.

Fig. 5. Data tables showing water loss over time

one of the variables is qualitative, as in the "Marshmallows and Containers" activity. When both variables are quantitative, as with the "Evaporation" project, a point graph is often, though not always, appropriate.

The basics of bar and point graphing are well known and are not discussed here, but one special point-graphing technique is worth noting. Often, as shown in figure 6, a line can be fit to the data points, not by using a complicated statistical procedure but simply by using the naked eye. The student uses a transparent ruler or a thread and moves it around until it fits the data points as closely as possible. This best-fit line is useful for controlling errors, identifying patterns, and making predictions.

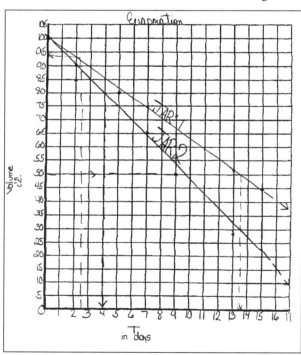

Fig. 6. An "Evaporation" graph showing best-fit lines and interpolations

Analyzing the experimental results

The relationship between the variables has been displayed in (1) the physical materials, (2) the picture, (3) the data table, and (4) the graph. The last phase is an analysis of the entire situation.

Begin by asking a series of straightforward questions: "Did the tallest container hold the most marshmallows?" "When did your container have 80 cc of water in it?" More demanding questions require prediction: "How many marshmallows would two bowls hold?" "In how many days will all the water have evaporated?" Asking what would happen if one of the fixed variables is changed can build a broader understanding of the situation: "What would happen if we used large instead of miniature marshmallows?" "What would happen if we changed the temperature in our evaporation study?" Checking predictions by further experimentation is time-consuming but worthwhile because connections are reinforced between mathematical abstractions and the real world.

The end of the investigation may be a completely satisfying answer to the original question, but, more often than not, the end is another question that can lead to further investigations. The marshmallows activity, for example, might lead to an investigation of the liquid capacities of other short and tall containers. After the "Evaporation" experiment, children might design and carry out an investigation into the relationship between the exposed surface area of the water and how quickly it evaporates.

Picture, Table, Graph, Questions

Each of the foregoing phases usually requires one or more class periods in addition to time spent becoming familiar with the equipment and on completing further experiments. Thus, a laboratory is an extended activity that may last a week or even longer, which is much longer than a typical mathematics or science lesson, but has significant benefits.

First, the four phases simplify the scientific method enough for children to use but not so much that it fails to resemble what scientists do: identify variables, draw pictures, measure, organize data in tables, graph data, and look for patterns. Whatever the scientific method—measure, analyze, generalize; hypothesize, test, repeat; or something else—this four-phase method captures a significant part of it. Students are thus inducted into the authentic practice of science.

The method fosters children's sense-making. Children handle numbers they have generated themselves and that are meaningful to them by counting or measuring. Experimental errors help them develop number sense and estimation skills. Patterns in their tables and graphs assist them in making sense of the numbers. Mathematics in context is more understandable.

The approach is multimodal, which has benefits for both individual students and heterogeneous groups of students (Bruner 1964; Lesh, Post, and Behr 1987; Silver 1986; Hiebert 1988). The multiple representations of relationships among the variables permit problems to be solved in more than one way, allowing different students to approach the same content in ways they understand. The container that holds the most marshmallows, for example, can be found from the graph, the data table, or the marshmallows themselves. The number of days until all the water has evaporated can be predicted by extrapolating on the graph or by extending patterns in the data table and can then be verified using the apparatus. Students can compare these various approaches, thus helping them make connections within mathematics as well as between the informal mathematics of their everyday experience and more formal mathematics.

Conclusion

The four-phase method helps children connect their everyday experiences with formal mathematics. As they investigate everyday situations quantitatively, children handle variables, explore relationships between variables, master a few powerful techniques for representing these relationships, and use these multiple representations to generate a wide variety of problem solutions. By beginning and ending in familiar situations, the abstractions of mathematics are linked to children's everyday knowledge. As students master this method, they become increasingly autonomous and flexible in its application. Then we can truly say they have learned to think mathematically.

References

Bruner, Jerome S. "The Course of Cognitive Growth." *American Psychologist* 19 (January 1964): 1–15.

Dewey, John. "Science as Subject-Matter and as Method." *Science* 31 (January 1910): 121–27.

Goldberg, Howard, and F. David Boulanger. "Science for Elementary School Teachers: A Quantitative Approach." *American Journal of Physics* 49 (February 1981): 120–24.

Goldberg, Howard, and Philip Wagreich. "Focus on Integrating Science and Math." *Science and Children* 2 (February 1989): 22–24.

———. "A Model Integrated Mathematics and Science Program for the Elementary School." *International Journal of Educational Research* 14 (March-April 1990): 193–214.

Hiebert, James. "A Theory of Developing Competence with Written Mathematical Symbols." *Educational Studies in Mathematics* 19 (August 1988): 333–55.

Lesh, Richard, Thomas Post, and Merlyn Behr. "Representations and Translations among Representation in Mathematics Learning and Problem Solving." In *Problems of Representation in the Teaching and Learning of Mathematics,* edited by C. Janvier. Hillsdale, N.J.: Lawrence Erlbaum Associates, 1987.

Silver, Edward. "Using Conceptual and Procedural Knowledge: A Focus on Relationships." In *Conceptual and Procedural Knowledge: The Case of Mathematics,* edited by James Hiebert. Hillsdale, N.J.: Lawrence Erlbaum Associates, 1986.

PATRICIA A. BROSNAN

Implementing Data Analysis in a Sixth-Grade Classroom

AMIDDLE school mathematics classroom is an exciting place to be. The NCTM's *Curriculum and Evaluation Standards for School Mathematics* (1989) presents for grades 5–8 many curricular ideas that have generated much enthusiasm by incorporating teaching strategies that promote active student learning. Middle school teachers have taken great strides toward implementing ideas that are both innovative and instructive. This article explains how one teacher is converting her traditional mathematics classroom into one that more closely reflects the standards document. These results could not have happened as quickly without the cooperative efforts of school and university personnel.

Audrey's Professional Preparation

Audrey, a sixth-grade teacher for four years, holds a certificate in elementary education with an emphasis in social studies. Her earliest memories of mathematics include several negative episodes. She recalls that her fifth-grade mathematics program was named "New Math." Audrey remembers being worried about this new program; her parents were no longer able to help her with her homework because they "learned it a different way" and "didn't understand this new stuff." She also remembers not wanting to ask questions in class because she "didn't want anyone to

know how dumb [she] was!" Audrey believes that she was a C student in mathematics who worked very hard and always completed her homework. She thinks that she could have done better if she had applied herself more and checked to see if her homework was correct—not just "done."

In high school, Audrey took the required-for-college algebra and geometry courses, but she recalls that she disliked mathematics because her algebra teacher "didn't want to be there." Thus, once again, she felt uncomfortable asking for help in mathematics. In college, her mathematics program consisted of only one required mathematics course for elementary education majors. Further discussion revealed that she had taken a required statistics course that she disliked and did not understand and for which she received a poor grade.

Audrey's School and Mathematics Program

Audrey's workplace, a school in a small city in Ohio, houses approximately 600 students in grades 6 and 7. The school is organized into teams of four teachers assigned to each block of 100 students and is currently in its third year of a comprehensive restructuring program. The main focus of the restructuring effort is to create a learning environment that serves the needs of its emerging-adolescent students. This middle school community is attempting to change its teaching practices in all subjects to incorporate current knowledge about how students learn.

In mathematics, some of the desired changes include (1) making the mathematics program student centered rather than curriculum centered; (2) making the mathematics program developmentally organized rather than textbook-driven; (3) focusing on thinking and communication

skills associated with inquiry-based methodology rather than on computational skills; (4) incorporating cooperative-learning strategies that develop communication skills rather than require students to work in isolation; and (5) including technology and manipulatives.

Through further discussion, Audrey voiced such concerns as her own lack of confidence in mathematics, outdated textbooks, an outdated curriculum, the lack of supplies, and her lack of knowledge about the current issues and trends in mathematics education. She concluded that sixth-grade mathematics was in need of improvement and that she needed help to discover ways to make radical changes.

Grade 6 had teacher specialists for language arts, reading, science, and social studies. Mathematics was the only major discipline without teacher specialists. As a result, all sixth-grade teachers, including Audrey, taught mathematics to their individual homeroom groups regardless of their self-perceived notions of competence, confidence, and interest in mathematics. Thus, the first schoolwide change was to ask four of the fourteen sixth-grade teachers to volunteer to become full-time mathematics teachers. Audrey was one of the four volunteers.

The Process for Change

In response to the voiced needs of the full-time mathematics teachers, new textbooks, calculators, and manipulatives were ordered; in-service workshops were funded; and a collaboratively designed summer institute was developed to teach the four elementary-certified teachers the latest strategies in teaching mathematics. Concurrently, the Ohio Model Competency-Based Mathematics Program, which is based on the NCTM's *Curriculum and Evaluation Standards* (1989), was adopted by their district as mandated by the state's

Patricia Brosnan *teaches at Ohio State University, Columbus, OH 43210-1172. She is interested in exploring how teachers in the middle grades change when implementing the NCTM's* Curriculum and Evaluation Standards for School Mathematics *(1989), particularly when using technology and manipulatives.*

This article was prepared prior to the introduction of blue M&Ms. Teachers might want to adjust the worksheets accordingly.—Ed.

ACTIVITIES FOR JUNIOR HIGH SCHOOL AND MIDDLE SCHOOL MATHEMATICS

department of education. This curriculum formed the basis for the summer institute.

The selected activities presented the mathematics content of the Ohio Model Curriculum and required inquiry-based and cooperative learning on the part of the teachers. Teachers were required to complete each activity as if they were students and then to reflect on these activities from the perspectives of both student and teacher. This process gave teachers a complete picture of how these activities could foster higher-level-thinking skills and how cooperative and inquiry-based learning can effect better understanding of mathematical concepts (Cobb, Wood, and Yackel 1990; Holmes Group 1990). This procedure was followed throughout the six-week summer program to establish a working model that would reach the classroom and be used with confidence.

Implementing Changes

By the end of the summer institute, Audrey was overwhelmed. She was facing an upcoming school year with a new mathematics program that she would be teaching full-time. To ease her anxiety and to assist her in improving her mathematics program, John, a graduate student, was assigned to spend two mornings a week for ten weeks to act as a mathematical resource.

John, a doctoral student in secondary mathematics education who had middle school teaching experience, was able to support Audrey's efforts as part of his fieldwork requirement for a doctoral seminar at a nearby university. During those ten weeks, John played many important roles. For example, he taught several mathematics classes, facilitated small-group activities, coordinated which manipulatives were to be used with which activity, and presented supplementary materials that demonstrated modern teaching and learning strategies. John was able to demonstrate that teaching mathematics is student-centered, developmental, inquiry based, and cooperative by implementing activities such as those described subsequently. See the worksheets for the actual lessons.

Example Lessons

One mathematics topic with which Audrey felt uncomfortable was data analy-

sis. Audrey could not understand how her students would be able to learn statistical ideas with which she had struggled at the college level. The following activities were presented to Audrey's morning classes by John; Audrey presented the same activities in her afternoon classes.

Activity 1: Minding your P's and Q's with M&M's

Activity sheets 1 and 2 detail a variation of a typical M&M's data-analysis project. For similar activities, the reader can examine "Learning Statistics with Technology" (Kader and Perry) and "Preparing Teachers to Present Techniques of Exploratory Data Analysis" (Browning, Channell, and Meyer) in the September–October 1994 issue of *Mathematics Teaching in the Middle School.* John facilitated the activity during the first-period class while Audrey observed. Within minutes, Audrey understood what was being done and immediately began assisting small groups of students. At the end of the first period Audrey said, "Do you mean that this is data analysis? Well, even I can do this!" By the end of the second class, John was no longer needed. Thus a hypothesis was substantiated: Audrey was able to teach this topic—she simply feared the unknown. Audrey needed to experience some of the excellent activities currently available that teach rather sophisticated mathematical ideas in an accessible way.

This activity includes many mathematics topics: percents, graphs, reasoning, communication, connections, degrees, angle construction, technology, and data analysis. All these topics align with the NCTM's *Curriculum and Evaluation Standards* (1989). By having the students work in small groups on a developmental project, Audrey was able to see how the methods she used routinely in social studies class, such as small-group work, could also be applied in mathematics class.

Activity 2: Stat-in-a-box

Activity sheets 3 and 4 detail a slight variation of an idea found in *Dealing with Data and Chance,* part of the NCTM's Addenda series for grades 5–8 (Zawojewski et al. 1991). This activity was also an on-the-job learning experience for Audrey. She had never seen a stem-and-leaf plot or a box plot before (see sheets 3 and 4 for directions and an example). As with the

previous activity, Audrey learned quickly and was able to take over the class within three periods.

This activity also included such mathematical topics as estimation, measurement, multiple visual representations, reasoning, communication, making connections, and statistics—again in alignment with the *Curriculum and Evaluation Standards* (NCTM 1989). Using this activity not only taught her new content but showed her how sixth graders could work cooperatively to learn the same material. She also learned how these projects produced enthusiasm among the students.

From such activities, Audrey learned that students in sixth grade have access to sophisticated mathematics presented in nonthreatening ways. Through the use of small-group activities, manipulatives, and calculators, her students can learn mathematics that she previously not only disliked but did not understand. Audrey has a new attitude regarding mathematics, and through these activities she has learned mathematics content that was unavailable to her when she was in school. Today, "new math" takes on a whole new meaning for Audrey.

Much can be learned through cooperative efforts between schools and universities. Perhaps Audrey would never have disclosed her personal fear of data analysis if a close working relationship had not been developed with John. By his frequent presence in Audrey's classroom, John was able to gain insights into Audrey's needs to a high level of specificity. This knowledge allowed him to dispel fears and provide the moral and professional support necessary to ease Audrey's transition from a traditional classroom to one more closely reflecting the NCTM's *Curriculum and Evaluation Standards* (1989).

Early Reports from Audrey's Classes

Early reports indicate that the new mathematics program is off to a great start. Students are claiming, "Mathematics is fun this year!" and "I actually understand what I am doing" and are asking, "What do we get to do today?" Parents have reported that their children are coming home and talking about mathematics and are enjoying homework assignments like never before. Some parents, wondering about the commotion, have called Audrey but have urged her to continue her program. Audrey has more confidence in the activities that she is presenting this year. She is pleased that her students are more comfortable with the mathematics that they are learning and is very happy to see students' improved attitude in class.

One impressive aspect of this change is its accomplishment in only one year. Even more impressive is its total initiation by the teachers themselves. If it were not for the collaborative efforts and the close relationships that were developed between the school and university personnel, which allow for ongoing professional development, this change could not have come to fruition so quickly. Nor could this change have occurred without the generous administrative support of the building principal. In September 1992, grade 6 in this school district had mathematics specialists for the first time.

The genesis of the new sixth-grade mathematics program through school and university cooperation is progressing full speed ahead. The teachers' enthusiasm, the administrator's support, the school's atmosphere, and the students' attitude will make this ongoing effort a success. This one small facet of the restructuring process demonstrates the strides that teachers can make when they are properly treated as professionals through their inclusion in the decision-making process. In essence, teachers can and will make a difference in education. The notion of on-the-job training has served nicely thus far as a conduit for positive change.

References

Browning, Christine A., Dwayne Channell, and Ruth A. Meyer. "Professional Development: Preparing Teachers to Present Techniques of Exploratory Data Analysis." *Mathematics Teaching in the Middle School* 1 (September–October 1994): 166–72.

Cobb, Paul, Terry Wood, and Erna Yackel. "Classrooms as Learning Environments for Teachers and Researchers." In *Constructivist Views on Teaching and Learning Mathematics*, edited by Robert B. Davis, Carolyn A. Maher, and Nel Noddings, 124–46. *Journal for Research in Mathematics Education* Monograph No. 4. Reston, Va.: National Council of Teachers of Mathematics, 1990.

Holmes Group. *Tomorrow's Schools: Principles for the Design of Professional Development Schools.* East Lansing, Mich.: The Holmes Group, 1990.

Kader, Gary, and Mike Perry. "Power On! Learning Statistics with Technology." *Mathematics Teaching in the Middle School* 1 (September–October 1994): 130–36.

National Council of Teachers of Mathematics. *Curriculum and Evaluation Standards for School Mathematics.* Reston, Va.: The Council, 1989.

Zawojewski, Judith S., Gary Brooks, Lynn Dinkelkamp, Eunice D. Goldberg, Howard Goldberg, Arthur Hyde, Tess Jackson, Marsha Landau, Hope Martin, Jeri Nowakowski, Sandy Paull, Albert P. Schulte, Philip Wagreich, and Barbara Wilmot. *Dealing with Data and Chance.* Reston, Va.: National Council of Teachers of Mathematics, 1991.

Minding Your P's and Q's with M&M's NAME_____

Materials: one package of M&M's for each student, protractor, calculator, graph paper, and activity sheets 1–2

1. Open your package of M&M's, sort them by color, and then fill in the chart below.

Counts	Red	Green	Yellow	Orange	Brown	Tan	Total
Your package							
Small group							
Total class							

2. Use your calculator to find the percent of each color. For example, red percent = (number of red ÷ total) × 100. Round to the nearest whole number and enter the percents in the chart below.

Percent	Red	Green	Yellow	Orange	Brown	Tan	Total
Your package							
Small group							
Total class							

3. Use graph paper to make three bar graphs from your percent data—one for your data, one for your group's data, and one for the entire class's data. Discuss in your group the similarities and differences among the graphs you made. Explain the similarities and differences.

4. Use your calculator to find how many degrees in a circle represent the percent of M&M's by color. Remember that a circle has 360 degrees. For example, red degrees = 360 degrees × red percent. Complete the chart.

Degrees	Red	Green	Yellow	Orange	Brown	Tan	Total
Your package							

Make a circle graph to represent your package of M&M's. For example, using the circle on sheet 2, draw a radius as shown at right. Place the zero line of your protractor on the radius, mark off the number of degrees for RED, and fill in as shown. Move your protractor to the line where RED left off. Repeat for all colors. If time permits, make a circle graph for your small group's data or the entire class's data.

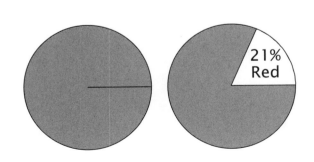

Minding Your P's and Q's with M&M's—*(Continued)*

5. Respond to the following questions:

    a) What are the similarities and differences between your results and those of the entire class?

    b) What are some reasons for these similarities and differences?

    c) If the entire school conducted this same activity, what results would you expect? Why?

    d) The M&M/Mars Company colors M&M's according to the following specific percents:

Red	Green	Yellow	Orange	Brown	Tan	Total
20%	10%	20%	10%	30%	10%	100%

    How well do your results compare with the company's stated percents? Why?

Chart the results from the entire class:

Group Name	Red	Green	Yellow	Orange	Brown	Tan	Total
Primes							
Squares							
Roots							
Cubes							
Radicals							
Odds							
TOTALS							

Stat-in-a-Box 1

NAME_____

Materials: half-ounce box of raisins for each student, activity sheets 3–4

Do not open your box of raisins yet. Estimate how many raisins are in your box. Your teacher will ask for your predictions and record them on a stem-and-leaf plot. When all the estimates are recorded, fill in the right side of the stem-and-leaf plot shown at the right with all the estimates in order.

Stem-and-Leaf Plot
(Back to Back)

<u>Actual</u> Ones	Tens	<u>Estimated</u> Ones

Next open the box and count the raisins. Your teacher will ask for your count and record the numbers on the left side of a stem-and-leaf-plot. When all the actual numbers are recorded, fill in the left side of your stem-and-leaf plot with the actual counts in order.

In your small group, develop at least two more visual representations of the class's data. Each group will present their ideas to the class.

Stat-in-a-Box 2

If you did not construct a bar graph or a box plot, do so now. If needed, instructions for a box plot are listed below.

Box-plot, or box-and-whiskers plot, directions:

a) Draw a number line scaled to the range of your data.
b) Find the median and draw a vertical line above the scale (M).
c) Find the upper quartile and the lower quartile and mark them as shown (UQ and LQ).
d) Form a box from the UQ to the LQ including the median.
e) Make the whiskers by marking the greatest value (GV) and the least value (LV) from your data.

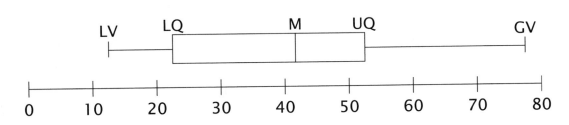

Look at the visual representations presented on sheet 4. These data were collected by another class when comparing estimates with actual counts of raisins. Working with your group, respond to the following questions:

1. What is the stem-and-leaf plot about?
2. Which actual count occurred most frequently? How can you tell by looking at the plot?
3. How can you find the lowest and the highest actual and estimated counts and their range?
4. How can you find the medians of the actual and estimated counts?
5. What do you notice about the estimates compared with the actual counts? What is being compared on this display?
6. Was our class better at estimating than they were? How so?

Stat-in-a-Box 2—(Continued)

NAME _____

Next look at the double-bar graph. Notice that only five students are represented. Again with your group, respond to the following questions:

7. What is this graph about?
8. Which counts are the highest and lowest, and what is the range for both the estimated and the actual counts?
9. How can you tell which actual and estimated counts occurred most frequently? How can you find the medians?
10. What is being compared in this graph? If all data from both classes appeared on this graph, what would be the same? What would be different? How can you tell?

Examine the multiple-box plots.

11. What is this plot about?
12. Which counts are the highest and lowest, and what is the range for both the estimated and the actual counts?
13. How can you tell which actual and estimated counts occurred most frequently? How can you find the medians?
14. What is being compared in these two box plots? Compare our boxes with theirs. Can you tell which class tended to have better estimates? How can you tell?

Compare the three visual representations below.

15. What is the same and what is different among the three representations?
16. What information can you obtain from one visual representation that you cannot obtain from another?
17. How should you decide which representation to use for a set of data?

The following displays are based on the same set of data, in which twenty-five students first estimated and then counted the number of raisins in half-ounce boxes.

Stem-and-Leaf Plot (Back to Back)

Actual Ones	Tens	Estimated Ones
	1	6
9	2	0000223555
999988885542221	3	00015
11100000	4	00005
	5	0000

Double-Bar Graph
(Note: An incomplete data set is shown.)

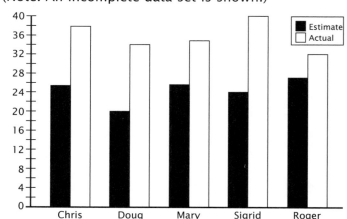

Multiple-Box (Box and Whiskers) Plots

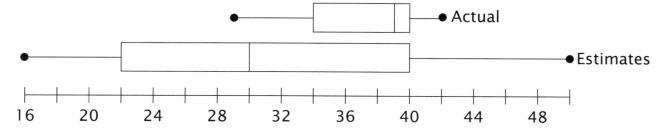

ELAINE B. HOFSTETTER AND LAURA A. SGROI

Data with Snap, Crackle, and Pop

OFTEN when statistical concepts are introduced to intermediate-grade students, data sets are supplied by the teacher or the textbook to give students the opportunity to find measures of central tendency, to create graphs, or to analyze information. Students, therefore, often find themselves obtaining such measures as the mean area of a collection of states in the United States or the range of population for various regions. Alternatively, sports data are used for many of the same purposes. However, students aged 11 through 14 are characterized by their need to connect to their lives information introduced in school. Many of these students are likely indifferent to populations and areas of states, and the appeal of sports data is not universal. In addition, these data sets are given to the students. Students are not afforded the opportunity to collect, create, or construct their own data from aspects of their own lives that are motivational and exciting.

This multidisciplinary unit attempts to avoid some of these weaknesses. It is centered on an easily accessible resource that is of perennial interest to school-aged students—cereal boxes. This material has been chosen because it is gender fair, available at no cost, visually appealing, related to students' lives, and mathematically rich.

To prepare for this unit, which has been used successfully with students in grades 6 and 7, the class must collect a large number of empty cold-cereal boxes with the price visible, preferably one for each student. The boxes can be collapsed for easy storage. The greater the variety of boxes collected, the more interesting the investigations will be. This article offers a series of activities that have been used to explore statistical concepts, marketing concepts, and geometric concepts. In addition, connections between mathematics and language, between mathematics and nutrition, and between mathematics and art are suggested. For the unit to be successful, it is not necessary to do all these activities or to do them all at once. In the classes in which they have been tried, most teachers chose enough activities to make up an instructional unit of approximately two weeks' duration.

Describing

With all the boxes gathered in one location, begin by having the students *describe* the cereal boxes. Possible responses will focus on color, shape, contents, purpose, composition of box, graphics on box, ingredients of cereal, and so on. This activity helps define in context certain geometric terms, such as *edge, face, vertex, rectangle, rectangular prism, right angle, dihedral angle, surface area,* and *volume.* Students experience an example of how mathematical language allows a specific description of an object. One student could be invited to present a verbal or written description of a certain box, and the other students could be challenged to identify the box being described.

Classifying

Invite the students to *classify* the cereal boxes. Possible bases for classification are brand, predominant grain, presence or absence of sugar coating, presence or absence of fruit on the front of the box, shape of individual cereal pieces, and presence or absence of a giveaway. Although discussing a few classification schemes and then moving on is tempting, the longer the students spend on classifying, the more creative their classifications are likely to be.

It is interesting to have students, either within their small groups or in front of the whole class, form their classificatory groups without revealing the basis for the classification. The other students can then be challenged to identify a possible reason for how the groups have been formed.

Ordering

Invite the students to *order* the boxes according to such criteria as height, weight, cost, alphabetical order, personal preference, perceived healthfulness, and rainbow-color order of the predominant color on the box cover. Again, if the basis for the ordering is not immediately revealed by the orderer, all the other students can engage in active thought as they attempt to determine the basis for the ordering.

Analyzing

With the students working with their own individual boxes, invite them to analyze the nutritional description on the side of the box. Food products have a standard nutritional analysis printed on the package. Use this opportunity to introduce the "food pyramid," to discuss the nutritional difference between the cereal itself and the cereal served with milk, or to define the "recommended daily allowance" (RDA).

Graphing

As students continue to examine their own boxes, invite them to create *bar graphs* of the percent of the RDA of five vitamins or minerals. If no specific instructions about the format of the bar graph are given, many different types of graphs will result. Thus, the students will see that bar graphs with different orientations—horizontal or vertical—and different scales make comparisons difficult between and among cereals. Some students will use a scale of 0 percent to 100 percent, whereas others will use a scale just large enough to accommodate the data they have, say,

Elaine Hofstetter *Hofstete@npvm.newpaltz.edu, and* Laura Sgroi *teach at the State University of New York, College at New Paltz, New Paltz, NY 12561. Hofstetter's interests include the role of technology in secondary mathematics classes. Sgroi's interests include the development of mathematical thinking in young people.*

0 percent to 40 percent. Use this opportunity to discuss how the scale chosen can affect the way the data will appear. In advertisements, companies that want their cereal to appear to have a high percent of vitamins and minerals might use a scale just large enough to accommodate the data. In this way, the bar covers almost all the available space.

In figure 1, although these graphs from a seventh-grade class depict different vitamins and minerals, the graph on the right appears to represent a cereal with more vitamins and minerals. The difference in the vertical scales shows that, in fact, the opposite is true.

Next, students can create circle graphs to compare sugar content with that of other carbohydrates. The nutritional label groups sugars and other carbohydrates under the heading "Total Carbohydrate." These grams of carbohydrate are then broken down into fiber, sugars, and other carbohydrates. Depending on the relative amounts of each of these three components, two cereals might each contain forty-six grams of total carbohydrates but have very different nutritional benefits. One might contain twenty-eight grams of sugar and the other five grams of sugar.

After creating and analyzing the circle graphs, students might find useful a discussion of why the circle graphs allow valid comparisons among and between cereals whereas the bar graphs, as drawn, do not. Challenge students to describe how the bar graphs could be altered to afford a fair comparison.

Tallying

Invite the class to gather the boxes and to construct a frequency tally of the predominant color on their covers. Compare this information with the frequency of color seen on coffee cans and candy bars. The students will see that products targeted at children, such as candy and cereal, make heavy use of primary and other bright colors, whereas the packages of products targeted at adults are often colored to reflect the product itself. For example, French roast coffee often comes in a dark, rich-brown can to suggest that the coffee is dark and rich and brown.

Students enjoy designing a cover for their own cereal box on the basis of their imagination and findings from the previous lessons. (See fig. 2.) This activity permits the creative integration of language, art, and mathematics. A possible extension activity would engage students in writing an advertisement for their new cereal.

Pricing

Invite the students to determine the cost per ounce and the cost per serving for each cereal. Discussing the differences can be valuable. Describe this situation as one in which unit price per pound may be less helpful for comparison purposes than unit price per serving. Students can measure out the recommended serving size of their favorite cereal. Since the actual serving size consumed by the students is likely to be very different from the recommended serving size, point out that the nutritional analysis on the cereal box is based on the recommended serving size.

Examining measures of central tendency

Have the students develop a description of an "average" box of cereal on the basis of the available boxes. They should include shape; weight and volume; price; first ingredient; color of box; name, including information on the number of words and the types of sounds; shape of individual pieces of cereal; and so on. Offer this hypothetical box as an example of the purpose served by measures of central tendency.

Developing consumerism

Invite the students to compare the cost of the store brand with the cost of the name brand for two cereals. Discuss with them the concept that price and nutrition may not be the only important characteristics when choosing a cereal. Conduct a blind taste test between a brand-name rice cereal and a similar store brand and between a brand-name oat cereal and a similar store brand.

Suggest that the taste test be based on

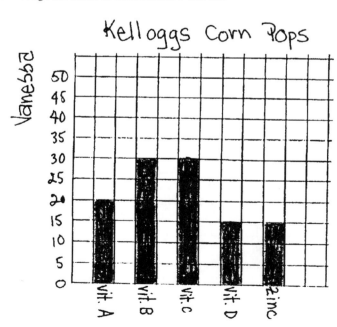

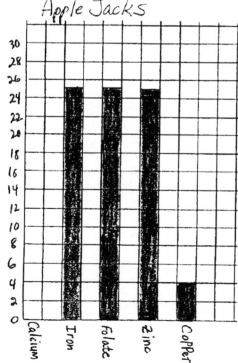

Fig. 1. These graphs, drawn by seventh graders, depict vitamins and minerals in two cereals.

The new cereal that Vegetarians will love! It's......

Veggie-O's

Free Bottle of V-8 with 2 proofs of purchase

Fig. 2. A cereal-box design "that vegetarians will love!"

crunchiness, an important consideration for many cereal lovers. This activity affords the opportunity to create double-line graphs. One person is chosen to be the "taster." Two bowls of cereal are poured, one of the name brand and one of the store brand. Milk is added to cereal 1, and its crunchiness is rated on a 1–5 scale, with 5 indicating that the cereal with milk is as crunchy as the dry version. After thirty seconds, milk is added to cereal 2 and a rating is given. The "taster" moves back and forth between the two cereals at thirty-second intervals, giving a rating that is graphed each time. This process continues for two or three minutes. See figure 3 for a sample graph.

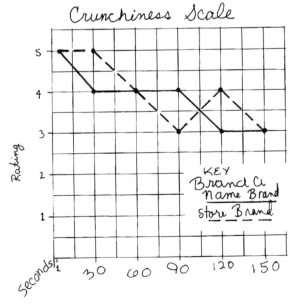

Heather, Carolyn, Terry, Kim

Crunchiness Scale

KEY
Brand a
name Brand
store Brand

Fig. 3. This graph rates an important consideration for many cereal consumers.

This activity can be followed with a discussion on the possible bases for making comparisons among items. The discussion usually leads the students to realize that the bases for comparison are a function of the values of the consumer. At this time, introduce students to such publications as *Consumer Reports* or *Zillions*, the consumer magazine for youngsters.

Measuring

Have students measure and determine the volume of each box, order the boxes from the least volume to the greatest volume, and record the order. They then order the boxes from the least weight to the greatest weight. Discuss any discrepancies and possible explanations for these discrepancies. Many students have noticed the disclaimer on cereal boxes: "This box is sold by weight and not by volume." This observation offers a golden opportunity to distinguish between the characteristics of weight and volume in a realistic context.

This activity also presents a good opportunity to have students determine the surface area of their cereal box, an often misunderstood measurement. Surface area, in this context, can be defined as the total area of the cardboard needed to construct the box.

Understanding probability

Involve the students in a Monte Carlo simulation. Describe a hypothetical situation in which a cereal manufacturer is giving away four different types of prizes, with one enclosed in each box of cereal. Assume that the prizes are randomly distributed among an entire shipment of 400 boxes: 100 boxes contain prize A, 100 boxes contain prize B, 100 boxes contain prize C, and 100 boxes contain prize D. Ask students to estimate how many boxes of cereal they must purchase to be reasonably sure that they would get at least one of each type of prize.

After the students have recorded and defended their estimates, simulate the distribution of prizes in the cereal boxes by using a standard deck of cards. Assign a "prize" identity to each of the four suits, and have each student randomly choose cards from a deck, one at a time, and record the suit. Students should continue to draw and record cards until they get at least one of each suit. Gather and organize these data from the class in tabular form by recording how many students obtained at least one of all four suits in four draws, in five draws, in six draws, and so on. Involve the students in a discussion of what they think it means to be "reasonably sure" in this context.

Figure 4 depicts a box plot of the simulation data from a particular class. Note that the median value is 7. Since half the students got at least one of each "prize" in seven or fewer draws, the class might decide that purchasing seven boxes of cereal affords a reasonable chance of getting all four prizes. Alternatively, some students might suggest purchasing ten boxes, since three-quarters of the class got at least one of each prize in ten or fewer draws. Some students might also argue that purchasing sixteen boxes is a reasonable thing to do. Although subsequent simulations may well result in different outcomes, students can observe how a simulation can allow for a reasonable prediction in a given situation.

Making connections

Create "cereal books" to organize the pertinent information that has been determined about each cereal. The front and back of the cereal box are cut out, placed back to back, and bound along the left side with three metal rings, string, or yarn. These pieces of cardboard become the front and back covers of a book on that particular cereal that can contain any desired information. Some suggestions are graphs of nutritional analysis; graphical comparisons of that cereal with others, based on price or ingredients; a sample advertisement advocating the cereal; a critique of the cover art; and a sample "letter to the president of the cereal company" suggesting improvements to the cereal.

In classes in which these activities have been carried out, students' interest has been high. The activities have given students the opportunity to learn more about a foodstuff they frequently consume and to engage in mathematical investigations in a meaningful context. As a result, students have become more careful consumers—more conscious of analyzing the basis of advertising claims, more aware of the role that packaging plays in consumers' choices,

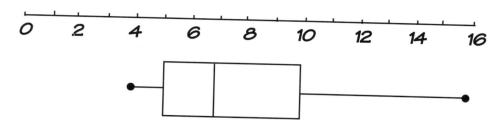

Fig. 4. This box plot illustrates the data from a simulation of the number of boxes of cereal to purchase to obtain four prizes.

and more sensitive to the nutritional value of food. Students have seen that data collection and analysis involve many areas of the curriculum and that these activities can be interesting, valuable, and understandable when they are presented in a significant context.

Bibliography

Consumer Reports. A publication of Consumers Union of U. S., Inc., 101 Truman Avenue, Yonkers, NY 10703-1057.

Reys, Barbara J. *Developing Number Sense in the Middle Grades.* Addenda Series, Grades 5–8. Reston, Va.: National Council of Teachers of Mathematics, 1991.

Sgroi, Richard, and Laura Sgroi. *Mathematics for Elementary School Teachers: Problem Solving Investigations.* Boston, Mass.: PWS-Kent Publishing Co., 1993.

Zawojewski, Judith S. *Dealing with Data and Chance.* Addenda Series, Grades 5–8. Reston, Va.: National Council of Teachers of Mathematics, 1991.

Zillions. A publication of Consumers Union of U. S., Inc., 101 Truman Avenue, Yonkers, NY 10703–1057.

11

Probability

PROBABILITY has received increased emphasis in the middle grades curriculum because of its importance in today's society. While many concepts in probability require abstract reasoning, many fundamental concepts can be introduced informally in games and hands-on investigations. The activities in this chapter show examples.

One such game is "Skunk," described by Brutlag. As with many games, this game involves both chance and choice. Thus, students see both the impact of reasoning strategies and the element of random chance on the outcome.

Hatfield uses the idea of fair and unfair games to help promote the study of probability. The focus is on analyzing the games by observations, data collection, tree diagrams, and a comparison of experimental versus theoretical probabilities.

A middle school unit on probability and statistics is presented by Fennell. The unit begins with data collection, involving spinners and dice, and proceeds to the analyses of various games.

The concept of randomness is crucial to the study of probability. Speer presents a variety of activities that explore random numbers and their uses. Speer also applies the idea of a random variable to lotteries and games.

The last activity in this chapter involves an application of data analysis and probability to a comparison of yogurt. Students collect data through surveys and make predictions. Additional concepts include equivalent fractions, decimals, and percents.

DAN BRUTLAG

Choice and Chance in Life:
The Game of "Skunk"

- Drinking coffee may cause cancer; should I drink less of it?
- I might make more money if I was in business for myself; should I quit my job?
- An earthquake might destroy my house; should I buy insurance?
- My mathematics teacher might collect homework today; should I do it?

EVERY day each of us must make choices like those described above. The choices we make are based on the chance that certain events might occur. We informally estimate the probabilities for events by using a variety of methods: looking at statistical information, using past experiences, asking other people's opinions, performing experiments, and using mathematical theories. Once the probability for an event has been estimated, we can examine the consequences of the event and make an informed decision about what to do.

Making the connection between choice and chance is basic to understanding the significance and usefulness of mathematical probability. We can help middle school students make this connection by giving them experiences wherein choice and chance come into play followed by tasks that cause them to think about, and learn from, those experiences.

The game of "skunk" presents middle-grade students with an experience that clearly involves both choice and chance. "Skunk" is a variation on a dice game also known as "pig" or "hold 'em." The object of "skunk" is to accumulate points by rolling dice. Points are accumulated by making several "good" rolls in a row but choosing to stop before a "bad" roll comes up and wipes out all the points.

Dan Brutlag is a middle school teacher and curriculum developer working for the Educational Development Center, Newton, MA 02160.

"Skunk" can be played by groups, by the whole class at once, or by individuals. The whole-class version is described following an explanation of the rules.

The Game of "Skunk"

To start the game each player makes a score sheet like this:

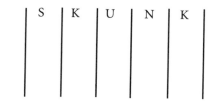

Each letter of "skunk" represents a different round of the game; play begins with the "S" column and continues through the "K" column. The object of "skunk" is to accumulate the greatest possible point total over the five rounds. The rules for play are the same for each of the five rounds:

- To accumulate points in a given round, a pair of dice is rolled.
- A player gets the total of the dice and records it in his or her column, unless a "one" comes up.
- If a "one" comes up, play is over for that round and all the player's points in that column are wiped out.
- If "double ones" come up, all points accumulated in prior columns are wiped out as well.
- If a "one" doesn't occur, the player may choose either to try for more points on the next roll or to stop and keep what he or she has accumulated.

Note: If a "one" or "double ones" occur on the very first roll of a round, then that round is over and the player must take the consequences.

Playing "skunk" with the whole class: The best way to teach "skunk" to the class is to play a practice game. Draw a "skunk" score sheet on the chalkboard or overhead transparency on which to record dice throws. Have all students make their own score sheets on their own scrap paper. Have all students stand up next to their chairs. Either you or a student rolls the dice.

Eighth graders playing "skunk" at Wells Middle School in Dublin, California, wait for the next roll of the dice.

Suppose a "four" and a "six" come up, total 10. Record the outcome of the roll in the "S" column on the chalkboard:

Score Record

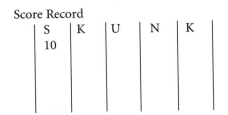

On the first roll, all the players get a total of the dice or a zero if any "ones" come up. Kerry and Lisa are standing up, so they also write "10" in their score sheets.

Kerry

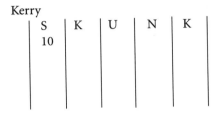

Lisa

S	K	U	N	K
10				

After each roll, players may choose either to remain standing or to sit down. Those who are standing get the results of the next dice roll; those who sit down keep the score they have accumulated for that round regardless of future dice rolls. Once someone sits down, that person may not stand up again until the beginning of the next round.

For the next two rolls Kerry and Lisa remain standing. A "three" and "two" are rolled, totaling 5; and then a "five" and "four," totaling 9. No "ones" so far! After three rounds Kerry and Lisa's score sheets look like this:

Kerry

S	K	U	N	K
10				
5				
9				

Lisa

S	K	U	N	K
10				
5				
9				

Kerry is getting nervous and decides to sit down, but Lisa remains standing. The next dice roll comes up double "fours," totaling 8. Since Kerry sat down, he is done on the "S" round with his total of 24, but Lisa now has 32. Lisa remains standing. The next roll is a "five" and a "one"—disaster for Lisa; her score goes to 0. Here is how their score sheets look:

Kerry

S	K	U	N	K
10				
5				
9				
24				

Lisa

S	K	U	N	K
10				
5				
9				
8				
0				

Since a "one" was rolled, the "S" round is over for everyone.

All students total their scores and stand up to begin the "K" round. On the first roll of the "K" round, a "three" and a "one" are rolled; everyone gets a score of 0. Play continues through the "U" and into the "N" round. No double "ones" so far! After two rolls into the "N" round, here is how the chalkboard SKUNK score sheet and Kerry's score sheet look:

Score Record

S	K	U	N	K
10	one	9	4	
5		7	8	
9		6		
8		9		
one		10		
		one		

Kerry

S	K	U	N	K
10	0	9	4	
5		7	8	
9		6		
24		22		

Kerry has chosen to play conservatively and is accumulating many points. At the same point in the game, here are the score sheets for Lisa and another student, Nelson:

Lisa

S	K	U	N	K
10	0	9	4	
5		7	8	
9		6		
8		9		
0		10		
		41		

Nelson

S	K	U	N	K
10	0	9	4	
5		7	8	
9		6		
8		9		
0		10		
		0		

Nelson isn't doing well. He is hoping for a long streak without any "ones." But how long is long enough? Nelson's strategy seems to be "keep standing until a 'one' comes up." This ploy is obviously a losing strategy. Lisa, however, seems to be playing "hunches." Sometimes she takes big risks and other times plays it safe.

For the next roll, Lisa decides to sit down. Kerry remains standing. Nelson, continuing with his "no win" strategy, remains standing. Oh no! Double "ones" are thrown! Here are the score records and Lisa's sheet:

Score Records

S	K	U	N	K
10	one	9	4	
5		7	8	
9		6	double	
8		9	ones	
one		10		
		one		

Lisa

S	K	U	N	K
10	0	9	4	
5		7	8	
9		6	12	
8		9		
0		10		
		41		

So far, Lisa has accumulated 41 + 12 = 53 points. Since Kerry and Nelson were both standing when the "double ones" occurred, here is how their score sheets look:

Kerry

S	K	U	N	K
10	0	9	4	
5		7	8	
9		6	0	
24		22		
0		0		

Nelson

S	K	U	N	K
10	0	9	4	
5		7	8	
9		6	0	
8		9		
0		10		
		0		

Nelson and Kerry are tied with totals of 0.

The game continues through the last "K" round. Players then total their scores from all five columns. Students will want to play this game several more times.

Winning versus Self-Improvement

Instead of focusing on a single class winner, more students will be drawn into thinking about a strategy for doing well in this game by emphasizing personal goals. When playing the game for the second and third time, ask students to focus on trying to better their own previous score. After each game ask for a show of hands of those who did better than last time.

Another way to move the focus away from a single class winner is to use a rating chart. The teacher may put up the following rating chart for total scores:

0 to 20—needs improvement
21 to 40—you might do better
41 to 60—average
61 to 80—good
over 80—outstanding

The teacher may want to involve the class in modifying the ranges in the rating chart on the basis of unique class data. This rating chart was devised by assuming that, on average, a "one" happens on about the third dice roll and the average score per good roll is "8." Therefore, with a strategy of "roll twice then stop" on each round, a person might get about 16 points on perhaps four out of the five rounds for a total score of about 64. The 20-point intervals used for each category are arbitrary.

Thinking about "Skunk"

Although playing "skunk" is fun, thinking about "skunk" is even more interesting. As a culminating activity the teacher should have students discuss and write out the answers to the "Thinking about 'Skunk'" questions on the handout, allowing students sufficient time to do a good job. Groups of students could organize whole-class experiments to find answers to problems 4, 5, and 6. Inexpensive wooden cubes on which students have written 1 through 6 in pencil on the faces are good alternatives to expensive commercial dice.

Teacher Notes

For *question 1*, the chance part of "skunk" is the dice roll and the choice part is the decision to sit down or remain standing.

Many games can be listed for *question 2*. Games of pure chance include Candy Land and bingo. Games involving almost pure choice, disregarding who goes first and your opponent's ability, include chess and tic-tac-toe. Most games, such as hearts, basketball, or Monopoly, involve both choice and chance. The game of Uno is mostly chance no matter what choices are made. But poker can be either mostly chance or mostly choice depending on how it is played. Strategies are useful only in games that allow for choices. But even games that have choices can be mostly chance for a player who makes choices without any strategy.

Question 3 can lead to class discussions that involve interesting probabilities and decisions from students' lives. Some events that a thirteen-year-old would ascribe mostly to chance include these: you find a $20 bill, your calculator is stolen, having a bad acne outbreak, your cousin becomes a famous musician, your best friend has to go to a different high school than you, and the like. Some typical events resulting from a thirteen-year-old's choices might include these: a girl dances with you because you ask her, you flunk a quiz because you didn't study, you get paid your allowance because you do your chores, and so on.

Questions 4, 5, and *6* can be done either by experimenting or making theoretical arguments. For example, for *question 5*, dice could be rolled many times and the points noted. Then the points could be totaled and the average value per time calculated. One theoretical approach is to list the equally likely outcomes for rolling a pair of dice where "skunk" points are accumulated. Twenty-five equally likely outcomes yield points. Such a list of outcomes is shown in table 1. Rolls including a "one" are not shown because no points are accumulated on these rolls.

The average of all the equally likely values is 8. This value can be either calculated or observed from the symmetry of the table.

As an extension of this activity, the teacher may have each group of students devise their own game involving choice and chance. Writing up consistent, clear rules for their game will involve mathematical logic. Have each group present its game to the rest of the class. The teacher can either let the whole class choose which of the games they would like to play or take a chance by selecting one of the games at random. Choice or chance? It's decision time!

Table 1

		Second Die					
		2	3	4	5	6	
First Die	2	4	5	6	7	8	Sum of Dice
	3	5	6	7	8	9	
	4	6	7	8	9	10	
	5	7	8	9	10	11	
	6	8	9	10	11	12	

Thinking about "Skunk"

NAME _____

Discuss with your group and write out answers to each of the following:

1. "Skunk" is a game that involves both *choice* and *chance.*
   - What part of "skunk" involves choice? _____
   - What part of the game involves chance? _____

2. List some other games you know.
   - Which games involve mostly choice? _____
   - Which games involve mostly chance? _____

   Rate each game on a scale of 1 to 10 with 1 meaning "pure chance," 5 meaning "chance and choice about equal," and 10 meaning "pure choice."

3. In life many things happen. Some are the result mostly of chance or "luck," and others mostly result from choices or decisions you make. Think about some things that happened recently in your life.
   - List two things that happened to you mainly because of chance. _____
   - List two things that happened mostly because you made a choice. _____

Choose one or more of the following to investigate in depth:

4. Rolling a "one" in "skunk" is a disaster. To get a better score it would be useful to know, on average, how many good rolls happen in a row before a "one" or "double ones" come up.
   - Decide on a way to find out. _____
     _____
   - Carry out your plan and describe the results. _____
     _____

5. In "skunk," when a "one" doesn't come up, what is the average score on a single roll of a pair of dice?
   - Decide on a way to answer this question. _____
   - Carry out your plan and describe the results. _____
     _____

6. What are some strategies that could be used to play "skunk"?
   - Describe a play-it-safe strategy. _____
     _____
   - Describe a risky strategy. _____
     _____
   - Estimate the kind of scores each strategy would be likely to produce. _____
     _____
   - Play "skunk" using each of your strategies and keep a record of your scores. _____
     _____
   - How well do your results agree with what you expected? _____
     _____

ACTIVITY SHEET

L A R R Y   L .   H A T F I E L D

Explorations with Chance

Teacher's Guide

INTRODUCTION: For many general-mathematics students, exploring situations involving chance can become a challenging, enjoyable mathematical experience. Cast in a gamelike context, reasoning about probability can be stimulated by questions of fairness. Students can be quite fascinated when their intuitive guess actually turns out to be wrong.

These activities promote many components of the NCTM's *Curriculum and Evaluation Standards for School Mathematics* (1989).

- The problems are designed to be solved in cooperative-group situations. Students predict, observe, and analyze together, reaching conclusions and developing explanations that represent the ideas and thinking of the group. Important goals related to communication can be achieved.

- The emphasis is on exploration. In conducting an investigation while playing the games, the students need to make observations, collect and record data, analyze results, and try to reach conclusions.

- When students develop an analysis of the possible outcomes by constructing a tree diagram, they engage in mathematical reasoning to establish the theoretical probability.

- Students can see the difference between experimental and theoretical probability and begin to see the advantages of each.

Edited by Mary Kim Prichard, *University of North Carolina at Charlotte, Charlotte, NC 28223;* Nadine Bezak, *San Diego State University, San Diego, CA 92182;* Mally Moody, *Oxford High School, Oxford, AL 36203*

- Students are stimulated to construct their own concepts and methods, including the creation of variations and extensions of the games' situations. These new games can be introduced to other groups, thereby encouraging students to share the role of "teacher" and enhancing communication.

- Connections can be made among activities and with other gamelike situations in life.

Grade levels: 8–12

Materials: Copies of activity sheets 1-3 for students; chips with faces of these colors: red-red, red-blue, red-white, and white-blue; a cup; coins

Objectives: Students learn how to predict and then determine if these games are fair and how an unfair game might be made fair. They learn how to organize and conduct a systematic investigation that includes empirical observations and theoretical analyses.

Prerequisites: Students should have had prior experiences with simple probability investigations, including flipping coins, drawing items from a set, and making tree diagrams. They should understand that the probability of an event is the ratio of the number of successful outcomes to the number of possible outcomes. It would be helpful for students to have engaged in cooperative-learning activities in other contexts.

Directions: The time required to conduct these activities (usually three to four class periods) will vary depending on the students' backgrounds. The time can be shortened by having groups complete different activities and then report their results to the class. It is important to allow enough time for students to discuss the strategies

for approaching the tasks and the interpretations of the results. It is essential to give students structure and expectations of productive behavior and to circulate among the groups to encourage and assess their developments.

Sheet 1: It may be helpful to introduce the situation to the class with a demonstration and discussion of the game so as to prepare the groups to address the question of fairness. Students must understand how to toss the chips to make the outcome random and how to score each turn.

The phase of playing, recording results, and calculating the probability ratios is very important. The firsthand experiences and observations furnish the basis for meaning. The game comes to "make sense" as students play it, and witnessing the games' outcomes gives students the experience necessary for developing intuitions and conjectures. The more formal analysis follows from the students' direct experience of the game. Teachers may need to assist students in the construction of the tree diagram for the initial game, but groups should be encouraged to conduct their analyses of the variations with as little help as possible. The opportunity to create new versions of a chip game may generate some interesting ideas, and teachers should encourage students to present their creations to other groups or to the class. These sharings may lead to other concepts and questions.

Sheet 2: In the "hopper" game, students analyze the outcomes of tossing three coins. The rules for moving seem to indicate that player B will win (with 5 of the 7 squares), but surprisingly, these rules ensure that player A has a much greater chance of scoring. This counterintuitive situation is likely to surprise students and helps them realize the importance of a theoretical analysis. The results of using four coins may also surprise students and reinforce these ideas. Again, students' inventions of their own variations of the game can lead to creative expressions.

Sheet 3: The "happy hopper" game involves jumping in varying orientations across an "island" game board. Students must carefully trace the sequences of moves, using the ordered-pair notation. Teachers may want to model this movement to the whole class. One tactic is to make the island with masking tape on the floor and have a student enact the sequence of moves (turns and jumps) by the happy hopper as others record what happens. Because it is very complex and the hopper can sometimes fall in the ocean, students may have to play the game many times to develop an adequate data base for their study. Students with some computer-programming background may be interested in developing a computer simulation of "happy hopper."

Answers

Sheet 1: l(*c*) Assume that the chips are r_1–r_2 and r_1–b_2. The outcomes are r_1–r_1, r_1–b_2, r_2–r_1, and r_2–b_2. Thus, each player has the same chance (1/2) of scoring. See the tree diagram in figure 1. (*d*) By adding a third chip, eight outcomes result: r_1–r_1–r_1, r_1–r_1–r_2, r_1–b_2–r_1, r_1–b_2–r_2, r_2–r_1–r_1, r_2–r_1–r_2, r_2–b_2–r_1, and r_2–b_2–r_2. Four outcomes are all red, so again each player could score half the time. (*e*) The eight outcomes are r_1–r_1–r_1, r_1–r_1–b_2, r_1–b_2–r_1, r_1–b_2–b_2, r_2–r_1–r_1, r_2–r_1–b_2, r_2–b_2–r_1, and r_2–b_2–b_2. The probability that player A will score is 2/8, so the game is unfair. 2(*c*) See the tree diagram in figure 2. The eight outcomes for these three chips are r_1–r_1–w_1, r_1–r_1–b_2, r_1–b_2–w_1, r_1–b_2–b_2, w_2–r_1–w_1, $w2$–r_1–b_2, w_2–b_2–w_1, and

w_2–b_2–b_2. Only two outcomes show three different colors, so player A has only a 2/8 chance of scoring; player B has a 6/8 chance of scoring. (*d*) One possibility is to award player A three points each time all the colors are different while still allowing player B one point for tossing two identical colors. Another possibility is to let stand player A's method of scoring and award player B a point only when two of one color (white, blue, or red) land faceup.

Sheet 2: l(*c*) The eight outcomes for three tosses of a coin are HHH, HHT, HTH, HTT, THH, THT, TTH, and TTT. See the tree diagram in figure 3. It is impossible to land on the "home" or J squares. Only three heads or three tails result in landing on the K square. Six outcomes result in landing on the I square. The probability of player A's scoring a point is 6/8. (*d*) One possibility is to award player B three points for each chip on H, J, or K while limiting player A to one point for each chip on I. Another is to alternate each turn so that, for instance, A gets I the first time, then B gets I the second time, and so on. 2 (*b*) Tosses of HHHH and TTTT result in landing on L, but all other outcomes are landing on either J (8) or H (6). See the tree diagram in figure 4. (*c*) Two outcomes land on M, ten outcomes land on K, and twenty outcomes land on I.

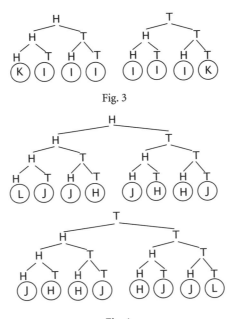

Fig. 3

Fig. 4

Sheet 3: 2. The hopper can escape only from square (1, 2), but it can never reach bridge (2, 4) because of an orientation

change at (2, 3). Similarly, it will never fall in the ocean at squares (0, 1), (0, 3), (2, 0), (4, 1), or (4, 3). 4. Because the hopper can never reach (2, 0), adding another bridge attached to (2, 1) does not improve the chances of escape. A bridge at (4, 2) will give another possible escape route. 5. A similar analysis can be made for the five-by-five island. The chances for escape will change. 6. Five bridges could be added as shown in figure 5.

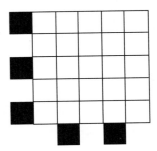

Fig. 5. A "fair" island

Note to teachers: If students analyze the game to find the probability that the happy hopper will land on one of the two bridges on the island on sheet 3, problem 2, they will note that having arrived at the corner squares (1, 1), (1, 3), (3, 3), or (3, 1), half the time the hopper ends in the ocean and the other half the time on squares (1, 2) or (3, 2) (see fig 6). Having arrived at (1, 2), half the time the hopper ends back at H, (2, 2), and half the time it ends at the bridge, (0, 2). Having arrived at (3, 2), half the time it ends back at H and half the time in the ocean at (4, 2). Thus, after four sets of two tosses, theoretically one-eighth of the time the hopper is on the bridge, (0, 2); one-eighth of the time in the ocean at (1, 4); one-eighth of the time in the ocean at (3, 4); one-eighth of the time in the ocean at (3, 0); one-eighth of the time in the ocean at (1, 0); one-eighth of the time in the ocean at (4, 2); and one-fourth of the

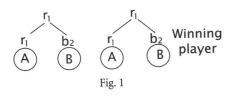

Winning player

Fig. 1

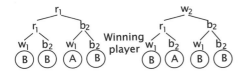

Winning player

Fig. 2

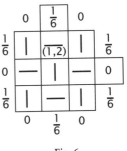

Fig. 6

time back at H, (2, 2). If after four sets of two tosses the hopper is at H, then it begins the circuit again. After the next four sets of two tosses, a theoretical probability of one thirty-second exists of its ending at the bridge, (0, 2), or in the ocean at each of squares (1, 4), (3, 4), (3, 0), (1, 0), or (4, 2). One-sixteenth probability exists of its ending at H again, and so on. Thus, the probability of ending up at the five positions in the ocean or the one position on the bridge approaches one-sixth as the probability of returning to H approaches zero. Thus, five-sixths of the time the hopper ends in the ocean; one-sixth of the time it ends on the bridge. The game is not fair.

Analysis of sheet 3, problem 3, leads to the discovery that with two possible escape bridges, one-third of the time the hopper escapes and two-thirds of the time it ends in the oceans—still not fair. For the game to be fair, add a bridge at one of the spots at which the hopper falls into the ocean. One "fair" island is shown in figure 7.

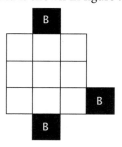

Fig. 7

Reference

National Council of Teachers of Mathematics. *Curriculum and Evaluation Standards for School Mathematics.* Reston, Va.: The Council, 1989.

Is It Fair?

1. Two people in your group will play while others observe and record data. Put a red-red and a red-blue chip in the cup. Take turns shaking and tossing the chips. The first player with ten points wins the game. Player A scores a point if both chips land with the red side up. Player B gets a point if one of each color lands up.

   (a) Do you think this game is fair? Why? Discuss this question before playing.

   (b) Play at least five games. Calculate the relative frequency of each player's winning. On the basis of these trials, do you judge that the game is fair?

   (c) Analyze the game by listing all possible outcomes or drawing a tree diagram. Find the theoretical chance of winning for each player.

   (d) Add another red-red chip to the cup. If all three chips show red, player A scores a point; otherwise, player B scores. Is this game fair? Play, study the results, and then list all outcomes and find each player's chance of winning.

   (e) What occurs if a red-red and two red-blue chips are used?

   (f) Make up a game using red-red and red-blue chips. Have another group study your game to see if it is fair. If it is not, how would you change it to make it fair?

2. Try this game with three chips. Use a red-white, red-blue, and white-blue chip. Player A scores if all three chips are a different color, and player B wins a point if two chips match.

   (a) Predict the fairness of this game. Discuss your reasons before playing.

   (b) Play and record at least five games. Find the relative frequency of each player's winning to decide if the game appears to be fair.

   (c) How many outcomes are possible for this game? Make a tree diagram to help find the theoretical probability for each player.

   (d) If this game is not fair, how would you change the scoring to make it fair?

A Fair Hopper?

1. Study the game "hopper" for two players, which is played on this game board.

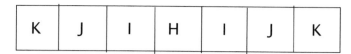

K	J	I	H	I	J	K

To begin each turn, place a chip on the "home" (H) square. Each turn consists of tossing a coin three times.

- If the coin lands "head up," move the chip (hopper) to the right.
- If the coin lands "tail up," move the chip (hopper) to the left.

After three tosses, player A scores a point if the chip is on either I square. Player B scores a point if the chip is on the H, J, or K squares at the end of a turn. A game consists of ten turns.

(a) Predict who will win. Does the game appear to be fair? Why?

(b) Play the game. Record the results for each turn in a chart for each player. On the basis of the data, does the game seem fair?

(c) Analyze the game by listing the possible outcomes. Use a tree diagram to analyze three tosses of a coin. How many outcomes are possible? For each branch of the tree diagram, decide on which square the hopper lands. Use your analysis to determine the fairness of the game. Write a brief report of your results.

(d) If "hopper" is not a fair game, how could you change it to make it fair?

2. Suppose that a coin is tossed four times and a longer "hopper" board is used (add a square labeled "L" to each end). Player A scores if the chip lands on I or L, and player B again scores by landing on the H, J, and K squares.

(a) Predict the winner. Explain your reasoning. Play the game. Record and study the results. Does the game appear to be fair?

(b) Use a tree diagram to analyze the outcomes. Are you surprised?

(c) What do you think will happen if a coin is tossed five times on a longer "hopper" board?

(d) Make up a different game that is based on the "hopper" idea. Analyze your game to determine if it is fair. Present your game to other students to play and analyze for fairness.

Can "Happy Hopper" Escape?

Imagine a "happy hopper" stranded on a three-by-three-square island, WXYZ. The island can safely be left by two bridges (labeled "B").

To begin a game, place on the "home" (H) square the happy hopper (a chip with an arrow marked on it) with the arrow pointing up. For each turn, toss a coin twice. If on the first toss it lands—

- head up, turn the arrow counterclockwise 90 degrees;
- tail up, turn the arrow clockwise 90 degrees.

If on the second toss the coin lands—
- head up, move the chip one square in the direction of the arrow without turning it.
- tail up, move the chip one square in the direction opposite of the arrow without turning it.

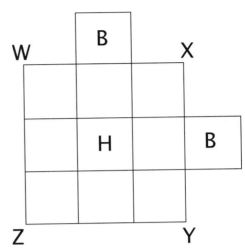

Play until the happy hopper lands on a bridge or hops into the sea.

1. Does the happy hopper have a fair chance to escape by way of a bridge? Make your prediction before playing.

2. Play the game at least five times. Record the sequence of squares on which the happy hopper lands by numbering the squares with ordered pairs (rows, columns). For example, the upper-right-hand corner of the island is (1, 3) and the H square is (2, 2), as shown in the figure at the right. From your data, decide if the game is fair.

(0,0)	(0,1)	(0,2)	(0,3)	(0,4)
(1,0)	(1,1)	(1,2)	(1,3)	(1,4)
(2,0)	(2,1)	(2,2)	(2,3)	(2,4)
(3,0)	(3,1)	(3,2)	(3,3)	(3,4)
(4,0)	(4,1)	(4,2)	(4,3)	(4,4)

3. Suppose that the island has two more bridges attached to squares (2, 1) and (3, 2). Predict how this modification changes the chances of escape.

4. Play the game at least five times. From your data decide if the game is fair.

5. Investigate a five-by-five island with two bridges. How does this extension change the chances for the happy hopper's escape?

6. For a five-by-five island, how many bridges would you add, and where would you place them to make the game fair?

FRANCIS (SKIP) FENNELL

Ya Gotta Play to Win:
A Probability and Statistics Unit for the Middle Grades

PROBABILITY and statistics are part of our daily lives in an ever increasing number of ways. State lotteries, casino gambling, and sports at all levels continue to fascinate millions of people.

With the number of people who invest time, energy, and—more importantly—money in activities involving probability, it is time that we use this social phenomenon to relate probability, statistics, and particularly gaming to the curriculum in grades 5–8. This article discusses such a unit.

Unit preplanning

Before beginning the study of probability, ask the pupils to bring in some of their favorite games of chance. Explain that a game of chance contains dice, a wheel, a spinner, cards, or other devices to decide moves, chances, and so on. Some examples of the more popular games are Monopoly, Chutes and Ladders, old maid, Yahtzee, Kismet, Cootie, Pay Day, and Gambler.

Purchase several pairs of dice, decks of cards, spinners, polyhedra dice, and other probability materials for unit instruction and follow-up activities. If applicable, display state lottery materials and information.

Inform parents of the probability and statistics activities. Although social applications involving probability and statistics are to be encouraged, care must be taken in presenting a unit on gaming. A letter or an evening session describing the intent of instruction involving gaming, along with an opportunity to discuss the activities, should be given to all parents. Although

Skip Fennell *teaches mathematics methods for preservice and in-service elementary teachers and directs a mathematics clinic at Western Maryland College, Westminster, MD 21157. He is interested in the diagnosis, remediation, and applications of mathematics.*

gambling is presented here as a social and practical application of probability and statistics, students are cautioned about the actual odds against their likelihood of winning. In fact, by understanding how probability and statistics can be applied to gaming, students are likely to see the statistical hazards involved in any gambling activity.

Day one

Construct an overhead Plexiglas transparency spinner similar to that shown in figure 1. Use two 25 cm × 25 cm pieces of Plexiglas. A hole can be drilled through the middle of the two pieces and a spinner attached with a screw and nut. Interchangeable colored transparency circles divided into thirds, fourths, sixths, and so on, can be inserted between the Plexiglas pieces.

Using the Plexiglas and the transparency circles divided into thirds, discuss the outcomes of the spinner. Ask the students how many possible outcomes there are on the

spinning wheel. The probability of an event can be described as the numerical way to express what the chance is that an event will occur. The probability of an event is most frequently written as a proper fraction. For example,

probability of an event

$$= \frac{\text{the number of ways the event can occur (successes)}}{\text{total number of events (outcomes)}}$$

So the probability that the spinner will land on 2 is 1/3. The transparency divided into fourths can now be used with the Plexiglas overhead spinner to reinforce the definition of the probability of an event. In addition, use a coin to provide an additional example of using chance. What is the probability of flipping a head? A tail? (1/2)

The next step in reinforcing the concept is to provide an example of tallying or recording. Try flicking the spinner sixty

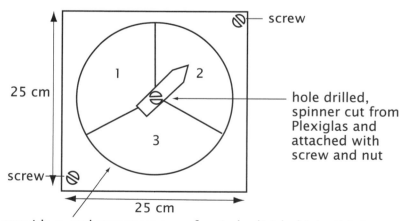

provide a red transparency of a circle divided into thirds
green transparency of a circle divided into fourths
gold transparency of a circle divided into sixths
etc.

Fig. 1. Construct an overhead spinner transparency

times and having the class record the results. A similar tally can be made with fifty tosses of a coin. Some charts for recording the results are shown in figure 2.

The tallying experiment will approximate closely the equally likely outcomes of these events if a large number of tallies is recorded. An optional activity is to use a spinner transparency divided into four unequal sections (see fig. 3). Ask the students to predict results and discuss the fairness of this wheel.

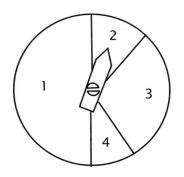

Fig. 3. Not all numbers are equally likely to be chosen

probable occurrences of each roll. The outcomes in figures 5 and 6 present the sums and products using two dice.

The probabilities of sums and products provide an opportunity to analyze basic addition and multiplication fact combinations. Which sum(s) or product(s) is/are most likely to occur? Least likely? How can we use the probability of rolling sums and products to help us in learning facts or in winning games? Have the pupils roll and record sums according to the chart in figure 7. Using a tally or frequency count aids pupils in determining the total sum of all fifty rolls and the average, or mean, roll of the fifty rolls. Pupils can also find the most frequent sum and can arrange the dice sums in bar or line-graph format similar to the sample graph provided in figure 7.

Pupils may find it interesting to repeat the dice activity by rolling and recording fifty products. The product distribution, the average, and the most frequent product will provide an interesting comparison to the sums recorded in figure 7.

Spinner Tally
Record the number where the spinner stops

    1   2   3   4
_____   _____   _____   _____

Coin Flipping Tally
Record a head or a tail
     Heads   Tails
     _____   _____

Fig. 2. Sample charts for recording experiments with a spinner and a coin

Days two and three

Provide a regular die for each small group of pupils. Have the pupils determine the probability of rolling each number. Use the die to assist in defining odds. The odds against an event may be defined as the ratio of the number of unfavorable events to the number of favorable events.

For example, when a die is rolled, the odds are 5 to 1, or 5: 1, against someone rolling a 1 because only one of the die's six sides is a 1 and the other five sides are not:

odds against an event occurring

$$= \left(\begin{array}{c} \text{number of} \\ \text{unfavorable events} \end{array} \right) : \left(\begin{array}{c} \text{number of} \\ \text{favorable events} \end{array} \right)$$

Next, make sure that each student has a pair of dice. Encourage the students to roll the dice and define the probability and odds of all events involving two dice. Students should then construct a chart similar to that in figure 4, illustrating the

+	1	2	3	4	5	6
1	2	3	4	5	6	7
2	3	4	5	6	7	8
3	4	5	6	7	8	9
4	5	6	7	8	9	10
5	6	7	8	9	10	11
6	7	8	9	10	11	12

Fig. 5. All possible sums in the toss of two dice

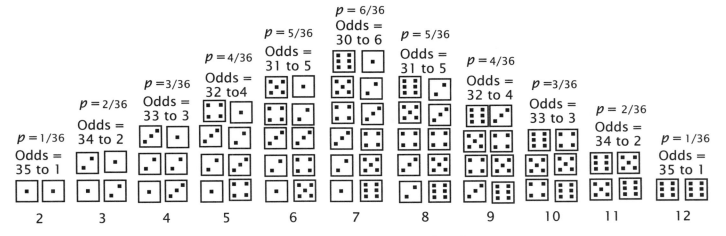

Fig. 4. Probabilities and odds in the toss of two dice

×	1	2	3	4	5	6
1	1	2	3	4	5	6
2	2	4	6	8	10	12
3	3	6	9	12	15	18
4	5	8	12	16	20	24
5	5	10	15	20	25	30
6	6	12	18	24	30	36

Fig. 6. All possible products in the toss of two dice

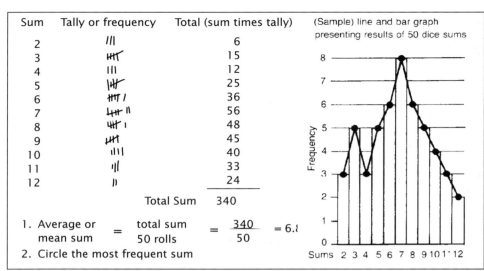

Sum	Tally or frequency	Total (sum times tally)
2					6
3	ⅢⅠ	15
4					12
5	ⅢⅠ	25
6	ⅢⅠ Ⅰ	36
7	ⅢⅠ ||	56
8	ⅢⅠ Ⅰ	48
9	ⅢⅠ	45
10						40
11	ᵞ||	33
12				24
	Total Sum	340

1. Average or mean sum $= \dfrac{\text{total sum}}{50 \text{ rolls}} = \dfrac{340}{50} = 6.8$

2. Circle the most frequent sum

(Sample) line and bar graph presenting results of 50 dice sums

Fig. 7. Sums of two dice in 50 tosses

Day four

Provide standard decks of playing cards for each of several small groups in your classroom. Have the pupils determine the probability and odds of the following:

1. Drawing a face card

   The probability is 12 of 52, since 12 of the 52 cards are face cards. This fraction can be restated in its lowest terms as 3/13, consistent with the fact that there are 3 face cards for each suit of 13 cards. The odds against drawing a face card are 40 to 12, expressed in its simplest form as 10 to 3. Thus, in each suit of 13 cards, 10 will not be and 3 will be face cards. Teachers interested in having probabilities and odds expressed in lowest terms, have to assume a knowledge of fractions or provide instruction.

2. Drawing a red card

   The probability is 26/52, or 1/2, since 26 of the 52 cards are either hearts or diamonds. The odds against drawing a red card are 26 to 26, or 1 to 1. Therefore, the odds are even; it is just as likely that one would draw a red as a black card. Can the pupils think of other situations where there are even odds? (What about flipping a coin?)

3. Drawing a 3

   The probability is 4/52, or 1/13. The odds against drawing a 3 are 48 to 4, or 12 to 1.

4. Drawing a 4 of spades

   The probability is 1/52; the odds against this are 51 to 1.

5. Drawing a diamond

   The probability is 13/52, or 1/4. The odds against drawing a diamond are 39 to 13. The same results would hold even if the question dealt with clubs, hearts, or spades.

Provide additional examples using the cards. These activities would be an excellent extension of previously learned fraction concepts.

Days five and six

Following the introductory activities of the first four days, the two-day sequence described below presents probability in a gaming format.

1. Construct a carnival wheel similar to that shown in figure 8. The wheel can be constructed of triple thickness cardboard or plywood.

2. Ask your pupils what the probability is of the wheel stopping on a given number?

3. Distribute five $1 bills in play money to each pupil; then play the following carnival simulation. The "carny" leader can dress accordingly in a straw hat, striped shirt, sunglasses, and arm garters. Each pupil is to wager $1 on a number for each of five spins of the carnival wheel. Students may change their wagers for each spin of the wheel. Winners of each round receive their $1 wager back plus $1 more, for a total of $2.

4. Keep a running account for each spin of the wheel. Run the introductory game for five spins of the wheel. An example of an introductory game for a class of thirty students is shown in table 1.

Find out how many pupils actually won money at the end of the five spins. Discuss the excitement of gaming. Describe the social problems of people hooked on gambling. Introduce materials related to horse racing and casino gambling as applications of probability. Would the results change if $10 bets were permitted?

5. Use the overhead transparency spinner shown in figure 1 and replicate part of

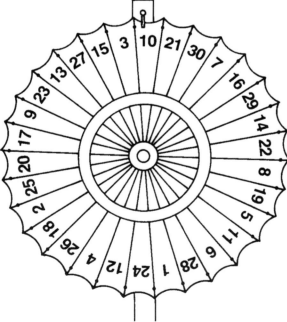

Fig. 8. A carnival wheel of fortune

Table 1
An Introductory Game for 30 Students

Spin	Winning no.	Winners	Losers	Carnival collected	Carnival paid
1	27	2	28	$28	$2
2	13	2	28	$28	$2
3	12	1	29	$29	$1
4	11	1	29	$29	$1
5	4	1	29	$29	$1
				$143	$7

this lesson. Have the pupils identify probability and odds and keep track of individual winnings and the carnival's totals.

Day seven

Pass out decks of cards to small groups of pupils. Introduce the game of blackjack, or twenty-one. Number cards are worth their designated number in this common game. Face cards are worth ten points and aces are worth either 1 or 11 points, at the player's discretion. Each player receives his or her first card face down from the dealer. The second card is dealt face up. The object of the game is to get as close to 21 points as possible without exceeding 21. To get additional cards, a player requests a "hit," an additional card placed face up. A sum over 21 immediately disqualifies the player. Encourage pupils to keep track of their winning rounds and to use probability and odds as they compare the other cards to their own. Encourage pupils to be aware of probability and odds when playing games out of class as well.

Day eight

Sporting events provide many opportunities for a variety of applications oriented toward probability and statistics. The following baseball card game is an activity that incorporates both probability and statistics. This game could be demonstrated first to the whole class, but it is more appropriately played in small groups.

1. Have pupils bring in their favorite baseball cards. Organize two teams of major-league players according to pupil interests.

2. Have pupils on the visiting and home teams position their cards in a simulated playing field and begin play.

3. The fielding player rolls one die, and the batting player rolls the other. The following sums indicate moves:

    2 = home run
    3 = double play
    4 = double
    5 = single
    6 = out
    7 = out
    8 = single
    9 = wild pitch
    10 = stolen base
    11 = sacrifice fly
    12 = triple

4. Pupils may use individual baseball player statistics on baseball cards to aid them in figuring out the sum needed for their play. If the baseball player on a card has a batting average of .280 or above for the season, the die is rolled two times and the player plays the better of the two rolls. The designated hitter rule would apply for this activity, since the batting average for pitchers is not recorded on baseball cards. You can revise the strategy by allowing players hitting above .280 to take a chance on a second or even a third roll of the dice, but then they *must* play their "chance" roll. Pupils should refer back to the probability of each outcome of the dice so that they can plan a game strategy.

5. As a continuation of this baseball activity, pupils may calculate the following baseball statistics:

$$\text{batting average} = \frac{\text{hits}}{\text{times at bat}}$$

$$\text{fielding average} = \frac{\text{errors}}{\text{fielding chances}}$$

$$\text{earned-run average} = \frac{\text{earned runs}}{\text{games pitched}}$$

Player comparisons and discussions of the previous season's averages for each ball player as reported on the baseball cards can provide an interesting extension of this activity.

Additional activities involving other sports can include the probability and statistical aspects of golf, horse racing, football, basketball, and track.

Day nine (optional)

If applicable, bring in and discuss information regarding statewide lottery programs. Ask pupils questions about the probability of winning, the odds, and go on. Examine lottery literature and schedule a-visit by a lottery representative.

Table 2

	Game Review		
Title	Element of Chance	Use of Statistics	Probability, Odds Used
Yahtzee	dice	recording scores	Combinations of 4 dice used. The probability of getting Yahtzee is 1/1296. Other sums and combinations occur more frequently.

Day ten

This unit contains many applications for reinforcing probability concepts and involves the games that the pupils brought in at the beginning of the unit as a culminating unit activity. Games should be reviewed according to the format shown in table 2. Remember, ya gotta play to win!

Conclusion

Teaching probability and statistics is important because of the popularity of the various applications of these subjects in our daily lives. The activities suggested in this article are only several among many that could be chosen. Many interesting and thought-provoking problems could be used. These subjects are a rich source on which we can draw in our efforts to implement *An Agenda for Action* (1980).

Bibliography

Dubisch, Roy. *Basic Concepts of Mathematics for Elementary Teachers,* pp. 381–97. Reading, Mass: Addison-Wesley Publishing Co., 1977.

Heddens, James W. *Today's Mathematics,* pp. 536–51, 93d ed. Chicago: Science Research Associates, 1974.

National Council of Teachers of Mathematics. *An Agenda for Action: Recommendations for School Mathematics for the 1980s.* Reston, Va.: The Council, 1980.

Wykes, Alan. *The Complete Illustrated Guide to Gambling.* New York: Doubleday & Co., 1964.

WILLIAM R. SPEER

Exploring Random Numbers

THE "Investigations" department recognizes the importance of children's exploring hands-on and minds-on mathematics and, therefore, presents teachers with open-ended explorations to enhance mathematical instruction.

These meaningful tasks are designed to evolve as they are conducted. They invoke problem solving and reasoning, require communication skills, and encourage identification of connections among various mathematics concepts and principles. To ensure usability, the ideas presented in this column have been tested in various classroom settings.

A mathematical investigation is defined as a collection of worthwhile problem-solving tasks that—

- has multidimensional content;
- is open-ended, permitting several acceptable solutions;
- is an exploration requiring a full period or several classes to complete;
- is centered on a theme or event; and
- is often embedded in a focus question.

In addition, a mathematical investigation involves a number of processes, which include—

- researching outside sources to gather information;
- collecting data through such means as surveying, observing, or measuring;
- collaborating, with each team member taking on specific jobs; and
- using multiple strategies for reaching solutions and conclusions.

Bill Speer, *wspeer@bgnet.bgsu.edu, is a visiting professor of mathematics and mathematics education at the University of Nevada at Las Vegas as well as a professor emeritus at Bowling Green State University, Bowling Green, OH 43403.*

Edited by Daniel J. Brahier, *529 Education Building, Bowling Green State University, Bowling Green, OH 43403, and* Martha H. Hopkins, *University of Central Florida, Orlando, FL 32816.*

This month's article, focusing on the concept of *randomness,* is a follow-up to last month's investigation, which explored the phenomenon of coincidence. Randomness and coincidence are mathematical notions that often have surprising results. Children frequently become curious when the result of an exploration is different from what they might have initially expected. Curiosity can then lead to an increased interest in pursuing mathematical problem solving. This month's investigation, applicable for grades 3–6, encourages children to conjecture and to conduct experiments, which verify or contradict their intuitions. Through hands-on explorations, children collect data and draw conclusions on the basis of the information.

LEVELS 3–6

Random, Random, Who's Got the Random?

Objectives

The students will—

- make conjectures based on their intuition;
- collect data from experimentation;
- draw conclusions based on collected data;
- recognize numerical patterns;
- apply the problem-solving strategies of looking for patterns and organizing information in a table, chart, or graph; and
- list the possible arrangements, or permutations, for elements in a set.

Materials

Each student will need—

- a copy of the reproducible page "Random, Random, Who's Got the Random?"; and
- four identical objects and one unique object, such as four paper clips and a pencil.

Structuring the Investigation

Begin the investigation by announcing that you are going to give a short "quiz" by orally stating some arithmetic exercises. As you state each question, the students are to quickly identify the answer to themselves. Emphasize that they are not to give their answers out loud. In relatively quick fashion, ask each of the following:

- How much is 3 + 3?
- How much is 5 + 5?
- How much is 9 + 9?
- How much is 13 + 13?
- Name a whole number between 5 and 12.

Distribute a copy of the reproducible page to each child and have him or her record the answer to the last question in item 1. Then as each child reports his or her answer, have everyone record the frequency of each choice by placing tally marks on the reproducible page. What was the most frequently stated answer? A majority of trials with various grade levels suggest that the most common choice is the number 7—in fact, 7 tends to be an overwhelming favorite. Since the students could have selected any whole number between 5 and 12, why is 7 such a common response? Is it reasonable to have one particular number named so often? Should we expect a more equitable distribution of choices from

among 6, 7, 8, 9, 10, and 11? Ask the students to offer suggestions as to why they think this choice might have been made. Potential explanations might include any of the following observations: (1) the difference between 12 and 5 is 7; (2) the arithmetic preceding the last question causes the person to "think computation" and, therefore, to calculate an answer of 7; or (3) since all the addends in the previous exercises were odd, the first answer that came to mind for the last question was 7, also an odd number. Although at first glance it would appear that children are being asked to select a random number between 5 and 12, something is causing the majority of people to select particular numbers more frequently than others. As a homework experiment, ask the students to try the quiz using the same questions and directions with others outside of class. They ; should record the , answers given for the last question on the reproducible page so that the results can be discussed the following day.

The Procedure for the Next Day

1. Use the results of the quiz and the homework to engage the class in a discussion about randomness. Was 7 the most commonly selected answer to the last quiz question? "Random" can be defined as a method of choice in which every element has the same chance of being drawn as every other element. In our quiz example, it seems that people do not use a truly random method of selecting answers to the final question but instead for some reason elect to choose the number 7. That is, their choices do not appear to be randomly generated.

2. Discuss how we could randomly generate a choice for the answer to the last question. For example, the students might roll a number cube with sides marked 6, 7, 8, 9, 10, and 11 to determine an answer, use chips numbered in a similar fashion to draw blindly from a container, or use a spinner. Many, if not all, of the suggested random methods will involve the use of some physical material, such as number cubes, number chips, or spinners.

3. Give each student five objects, four of which are identical, with the fifth object

being unique. You might use four paper clips and a pencil, four pennies and a centimeter cube, four centimeter cubes and an eraser, and so on. Ask each student to place the five objects in a horizontal row across his or her desk in any order desired. Encourage each student to try to randomly position the unique object in the row. Examine the completed arrangements. Do the students notice anything special about the placement of the unique object? How many students put the unique object in the first place? The second place? The third? The fourth? The fifth? In the entire class, does an equal placement of the unique object occur in each position? If the placement were *truly* random, then we would expect the unique object to have appeared about equally in each of the five positions. Despite efforts to get children to place the unique object randomly, you may still find that some students claim that they put the unique object first or last because they believed that most people would not, and they wanted to be sure that first, or last, was represented in the group's response. This argument is a weak pitch for random placement. Preference seems to enter into the choice, and the class data may not be as randomly distributed as it would be if students were simply to "throw" the objects on the desk and record the order.

4. As was discovered in last month's column on coincidence, it is interesting to look at the concept of *random sequence*—a sequence of values that is irregular, nonrepetitive, or haphazard (James and James 1968). The notion of a random sequence arose in the discussion of "strings" of heads and tails when tossing a coin. The investigation pointed out that even though heads and tails are equally likely events, a series of, say, twenty tosses was unlikely to result in a consistent HTHTHT ... pattern. Instead, strings of heads or tails frequently occurred. Again, as with the discussion in step 1, this activity used a concrete material, a coin, to generate a

random sequence. Encourage the students to consider whether the human mind, without the use of some external material, is capable of actually generating a random sequence of some sort. Explain that their next task will be to attempt to generate a list of numbers that is truly random.

5. Tell the students that you want them to try to write a sequence of 0's and 1's in the boxes on the reproducible page. This time, instead of using some sort of physical material to help them, they are to generate a random sequence by themselves. Have them begin in the box at the left in the first row and continue to fill each box across the page and continue on to the next row until all the boxes are filled with either a 0 or a 1. It is important to emphasize that their goal is to write a random sequence. Instead of thinking about what they have just written or thinking about what they are about to write, they are to "just put down 0's or 1's in a random sequence." When you are certain that they understand the task, allow them to complete the activity.

6. Have the students count and record the number of 0's and 1's that occurred in their list of fifty digits. Ask the students how many 0's we should expect if the list was truly randomly generated. Just as in a coin toss, which is a random generation of heads and tails, we would expect a truly random list of 0's and 1's to include approximately twenty-five 0's and twenty-five 1's, or half and half. Using a table or graph drawn on the chalkboard or on a sheet used on the overhead projector, compile the results for the class and compare the ratio of 0's to 1's as a fraction. Again, a truly random list should yield a ratio of about 1:1.

7. Ask the students to determine how many different pairs of digits can be made using 0's and 1's. They should be able to identify four distinct possible pairs, 00, 01, 10, and 11. Have the students count and record the number of each of these digit pairs—00, 01, 10, 11—that occur in their list. Note that it is not acceptable simply to break up the list into pairs by grouping the first and second entry, then the third and fourth entry, and so on. Instead, the students

ACTIVITIES FOR JUNIOR HIGH AND MIDDLE SCHOOL MATHEMATICS

need to identify pairs as any two adjacent entries. Consequently, a list such as 11001010 has a total of seven pairs, namely, 11, 10, 00, 01, 10, 01, and 10, rather than just 11, 00, 10, and 10. For the list that the student made on the reproducible page, forty-nine pairs are expected. Since each pairing—00, 01, 10, and 11—is equally likely in a random list, we would expect about one-fourth of the total number of pairs for each. Compare this expectation with the actual results for individual students and, using the chalkboard or overhead projector, examine the data for the class as a whole.

8. Examine the various triplets possible, namely, 000, 001, 010, 011, 100, 101, 110, and 111. Have the students count and record the number of each of these digit triplets that occur in their list. As before, it is not acceptable simply to break up the list into triplets by grouping the first, second, and third entry and then the fourth, fifth and sixth entry. Instead, the students need to identify triplets as any three adjacent entries. Consequently, a list such as 110010101 has a total of seven triplets, namely, 110, 100, 001, 010, 101, 010 and 101, rather than just 110, 010, and 101. For the list the student made on the reproducible page, forty-eight triplets are found. Since each triplet—000, 001, 010, 011, 100, 101, 110, and 111—is equally likely in a random list, we would expect about one-eighth of the total number of triplets for each. Compare this expectation with the actual results for individual students and, using the chalkboard or overhead projector, examine the data for the class as a whole.

9. Finally, ask each student to report his or her first recorded digit and record the digits in a horizontal row on the chalkboard or overhead projector. After each student has reported the first digit, go back and ask each to report the second digit, and so forth, until fifty digits have been listed. Then, check the string of 0's and 1's for random distributions as described in steps 5 through 8. Is this sequence more equitably distributed than those generated by individual students? Why or why not?

Extensions

The most common answer to the last question in the quiz mentioned in structuring the investigation seems to be 7. One possible explanation is that 7 is the difference between 12 and 5. Give the quiz again to another group and change the last question to "Name a number between 5 and 12" to see if the order in which the numbers are stated makes a difference in the response. Also try changing the question to "Name a number between 11 and 5" to see if most people now say 6. What other changes might we make in the quiz to see if we can determine why people tend to answer the way they do? Will answers differ for a sample of adults when compared with a sample of children? What happens if you ask another class simply to "think of a number between 5 and 12" without doing any previous arithmetic? Will the answers be more randomly selected?

Rather than try to write a random sequence of 0's and 1's by hand, have the students use a computer keyboard or a graphing-calculator screen. The computer or calculator is an external tool for this activity but not in the sense that it generates the sequence for you. The computer or calculator merely records the sequence that the human generates. But does the use of this technology change the results? Are "strings" of the same digit more likely when students generate the sequence using the keyboard than by hand? Do right-handed people produce different kinds of sequences than left-handed people? As you tire of typing, does the "randomness" of the sequence increase or decrease?

Lotteries and other games of chance present a wealth of opportunities to examine our perception of randomness and likelihood. For example, if each of the 3 838 380 ways of choosing six lottery numbers out of forty are equally likely, why would people seem to prefer such a choice as 2, 5, 19, 34, 37, and 40 to that of 1, 2, 3, 4, 5, and 6?

Older students may be interested to know that scientists have discovered that the surface of the planet Venus is marked by an impact-crater population that appears to be randomly distributed. This finding, in itself, is not so curious, but a truly random distribution indicates that no region on Venus is either "newer" or "more ancient" than any other region. Unlike all other known planetary surfaces, the randomly cratered surface of Venus appears to be all the same age. Many astronomers were surprised that they were unable to distinguish the actual map of Venus's surface from five others that were randomly generated by a computer to assign impact-crater sites. To model a similar experiment in your classroom, give each student five tiles, four of which are identical. For example, the students might be given four blue tiles and one red tile. Ask each student in the class to place the five tiles in some order of their choosing in a horizontal row. Record the possibilities and the frequency of each response on the chalkboard or overhead projector. Then have each student place the five tiles in a bag and draw the tiles out, one at a time, and place them in a row. Again, record the possibilities and frequency of each occurrence on the chalkboard. Have students compare the results of the student-generated rows with the results of randomly selecting tiles from a bag. Are students able to detect a difference? Does the distribution of the tiles pulled from a bag appear to be more randomly generated?

Teachers might wish to explore three other potential examples of randomness. First, does the random function (RND) on a computer spreadsheet truly generate random numbers, or would we see the numbers begin to repeat, in the same order, at some point? Second, does the "shuffle" function on a CD player actually generate a random-play sequence, or is a finite list of sequences followed? Third, locate some multiple-choice tests, particularly those designed by a teacher rather than a commercial company. Examine the distribution of letters representing the correct answers. Was "c" most commonly used as the correct answer in the answer key? It often is. Why?

Concluding Commentary

Probability, likelihood, coincidence, and randomness are closely related mathematical concepts. Sometimes, because of these relationships, we confuse one concept with another. Our intuition, expectations, and experiences frequently battle our mathematical knowledge. For example, a person forming teams announced that players were to be randomly assigned alphabetically. Another person wanted to randomly assign children to cooperative groups by having them count off 1, 2, 3, 4, 1, 2, 3, 4,and so on. In both scenarios, a misunderstanding or misapplication of the term *random* should be evident. The more we explore these concepts, the more likely we are to recognize their appropriateness or inappropriateness when we encounter them in our lives.

Bibliography

James, Robert C., and Glenn James. *Mathematics Dictionary*. 3d ed. Princeton, N.J.: D. Van Nostrand Co., 1968.

Pickover, Clifford A. "Slides in Hell." In *Skeptical Inquirer* (July/August 1995): 36–39.

Venus Unveiled. NOVA, Public Broadcasting Corp., July, 1996.

Random, Random, Who's Got the Random?

1. Record your answer to the last question below.

A class quiz:	How much is 3 + 3?	How much is 9 + 9?
	How much is 5 + 5?	How much is 13 + 13?

Name a number between 12 and 5. _____

2. Use tally marks to record how many children in your class gave each of the following answers to the last question above.

    6   7   8   9   10   11   other

3. Give the quiz in question 1 above to several people that are not in your class. Be sure to tell them to answer quickly and to themselves. Then ask them what number they chose for the last question. Record how many of these people gave each of the following answers to the last question above.

    6   7   8   9   10   11   other

4. Your task is to write quickly a random sequence of 0's and 1's in the boxes below. Be sure that you try to make the sequence random. Write them in the boxes from left to right and row by row.

5. Record the number of 0's and 1's from problem 4: 0's _____ 1's _____

6. Record the number of two-digit pairs from problem 4: 00's _____ 01's ___ 10's ___ 11's ____

7. Record the number of three-digit groups from problem 4: 000's _____ 001's _____ 010's _____
   011's ____ 100's ____ 101's ___ 110's ___ 111's _____

KATHY TREZISE

Creamy Comparisons

Student Activity Goals

Students will—

- collect data from tables and class surveys;
- make predictions about class data;
- identify and apply equivalent fractions, decimals, and percents; and
- analyze nutritional information and compare percents.

Materials

The materials needed are—

- single-serving containers of Yoplait nonfat vanilla yogurt and peanut M&M's;
- a transparency of the nutrition labels from these containers;
- four different empty half-gallon frozen-dessert containers, from similar flavors so that nutritional contents are comparable, with their prices shown (strawberry sherbet, ice milk, frozen yogurt—regular, not lowfat or nonfat—and ice cream work well); and
- two copies of the reproducible page for each student.

Planning for Instruction

Engage students in a discussion of their favorite desserts. Focus their attention on

Kathy Trezise *is an assistant professor of mathematics at Houghton College, Houghton, NY 14744-0128. Her professional interests include curriculum integration, relevant mathematics instruction, and gender issues in mathematics education and careers.*
Edited by *Daniel J. Brahier and William R. Speer, Bowling Green State University, Bowling Green, OH 43403.*

ice cream by identifying favorite flavors and discussing why stores carry so many brands and flavors. Discuss the different kinds of frozen desserts, such as ice milk, frozen yogurt, sherbet, lowfat ice cream, and nonfat ice cream. Ask, "Can you name a healthy frozen dessert? Are ice cream and ice milk the same thing?"

Structuring the Activity

1. Show students a single-serving container of Yoplait nonfat vanilla yogurt and a wrapper from a single-serving container of peanut M&M's. Ask, "Which one would you choose for a snack after school? Why? Which one is more nutritious, or nutrient dense? Why?" *Nutrient dense* means that a product supplies a significant amount of nutritional value for the number of calories.

2. Ask, "Does the yogurt or the M&M's have more calories?" A single-serving of Yoplait nonfat vanilla yogurt has 210 calories; the peanut M&M's single-serving package has 250 calories. Ask, "Since the two snacks contain a similar number of calories, why would the yogurt be 'better' than the M&M's?" Explain that calories come from three different nutrients in foods: carbohydrates, proteins, and fat. Every gram of carbohydrate, whether found in a piece of bread or in a candy bar, has 4 calories. Every gram of protein also has 4 calories, but every gram of fat has 9 calories. Although two snacks may have approximately the same number of calories, one may have a greater percent of calories from fat, whereas the other may have a greater percent of calories from carbohydrates and proteins.

3. Show an overhead transparency of the nutrition labels from the yogurt container and the M&M's package. Lead students through a nutritional analysis

of these foods as they fill in one copy of the reproducible page. Students should label the product name on each table and obtain values for grams of carbohydrates and total calories from the nutrition labels. Students should complete the tables as shown in figure 1. Ask, "Do the three percents add up to 100 percent? Why or why not?" The numbers on the labels are usually rounded to the nearest gram or 0 5 gram, thus altering the total percents.

4. Show students the four different half-gallon containers. Ask, "From these four choices, predict the type of frozen dessert that would be purchased most often by the members of our class." Have each student record his or her prediction and place the predictions on a chalkboard in a bar graph to show the distribution of choices.

5. Divide students into four groups and distribute a new copy of the reproducible page. Have each group complete the nutritional analysis for two types of frozen dessert. Group A examines and compares half gallons 1 and 2; group B does the same for half gallons 2 and 3, and so forth. Have each group display or share their analysis.

6. Ask, "What criteria could we use to decide which type of frozen dessert to buy?" (Possible answers include flavor, price, and nutritional content.) Have each student decide which kind he or she would buy on the basis of the criteria discussed in this investigation. Compare the results with the predictions. Ask, "Why was the fat content of the frozen yogurt similar to that of the ice cream?" (It is not lowfat or nonfat frozen yogurt.)

Extension

Suggest that students perform a nutritional analysis on two or more varieties of a different snack and display their findings in a chart. Explore additional questions: "Which frozen dessert is the best source of calcium? Why do we need calcium? How do desserts compare in the amount of sodium? In price?" Students can also examine vitamin content and compare amounts of saturated, monounsaturated, and polyunsaturated fat.

Concluding Activity

Remind students to consider many factors when selecting foods of all kinds. Knowing what is in the foods we eat is important to ensure that our bodies remain healthy. In this activity, students examined and compared some aspects of the nutritional content of snacks and desserts—a first step toward making informed decisions about which foods to buy.

Product **Yoplait Vanilla Nonfat Yogurt**				Fraction	Decimal	Percent
		A	B	A/B	A ÷ B	(A ÷ B) × 100
Grams of carbohydrate per serving	Calories per carbo gram	Calories from carbohydrates per serving	Total calories per serving	$\dfrac{164}{210}$	.78	.78 × 100 = 78
41	4	41 × 4 = 164	210			

Creamy Comparisons

Nutrient	Calories per Gram
Carbohydrate	4
Protein	4
Fat	9

Product

		A	B	Fraction A/B	Decimal A ÷ B	Percent (A ÷ B) × 100
Grams of carbohydrate per serving	Calories per carbo gram 4	Calories from carbohydrates per serving	Total calories per serving			
Grams of protein per serving	Calories per protein gram 4	Calories from protein per serving	Total calories per serving			
Grams of fat per serving	Calories per fat gram 9	Calories from fat per serving	Total calories per serving			

Do the three percents add to 100 percent? Explain why or why not.

_____

_____

_____

Product

		A	B	Fraction A/B	Decimal A ÷ B	Percent (A ÷ B) × 100
Grams of carbohydrate per serving	Calories per carbo gram 4	Calories from carbohydrates per serving	Total calories per serving			
Grams of protein per serving	Calories per protein gram 4	Calories from protein per serving	Total calories per serving			
Grams of fat per serving	Calories per fat gram 9	Calories from fat per serving	Total calories per serving			

Do the three percents add to 100 percent? Explain why or why not.

_____

_____

_____

12

Geometry

GEOMETRY is an essential area of study for students in the junior high and middle school grades. The informal approach to geometry lends itself to exploration through activities.

Charlampos Toumasis describes an activity with toothpicks to investigate triangles. "The Toothpick Problem and Beyond" allows students to examine patterns, make conjectures, and test ideas.

Gail Burton describes an environmental unit involving literature in which the students used measurement and ratios. "Huge Trees, Small Drawings: Ideas of Relative Sizes" presents a novel approach to the study of geometric ideas.

Ann Blomquist's article, "Folding Perpendiculars and Counting Slope," involves students in the construction of perpendicular lines. The students discover the relationship between the slope of the hypotenuse and the triangle's perpendicular line segments.

Robert Gerver outlines two approaches to discovering pi and presents both circumference and area activities.

"Area and Perimeter Connections" by Jane B. Kennedy explores the effect of a fixed perimeter value on area. Students examine data and make generalizations.

A spatial-manipulation lesson in "The Inside-Out Box: Analysis of Structure and Space" by Marilyn Fowler, along with various questions, helps students visualize and then draw the shape of a box that has been opened and laid flat.

Finally, Patricia F. Campbell presents an activity for constructing templates for building three-dimensional polyhedron models. The activities in "Cardboard, Rubber Bands, and Polyhedron Models" will help students describe and compare three-dimensional models.

CHARALAMPOS TOUMASIS

The Toothpick Problem and Beyond

- The mathematics curriculum should include the study of the geometry of one, two, and three dimensions in a variety of situations so that students can identify, describe, compare, and classify geometric figures. (NCTM 1989, 112)

- The mathematics curriculum should include numerous and varied experiences that reinforce and extend logical reasoning skills so that all students can make and test conjectures. (NCTM 1989, 143)

Teacher's Guide

Introduction: Although many changes have occurred in the goals for teaching secondary school mathematics, the goals of motivating students to do mathematics and helping them to reason mathematically through problem solving have remained. The NCTM's *Curriculum and Evaluation Standards* (1989) focus on these goals. All students should be encouraged to explore, to guess, to conjecture, to test, and to build arguments about the validity of their conjectures.

Secondary school geometry is a visual subject and may lead to more surprises for students than other branches of mathematics. Many students have more spatial intuitions than numerical ones and find it easy and enjoyable to work with figures and

---

Charalampos Toumasis *teaches at the comprehensive school of Patras in Greece and lectures to in-service secondary school mathematics teachers at the Center for In-Service Education, Maniakiou Str. 21-23, 26223, Patras, Greece. His research interests are the history of mathematics education and teaching secondary school mathematics.*

Edited by Mary Kim Prichard, *University of North Carolina at Charlotte, Charlotte, NC 28223;* Nadine Bezuk, *San Diego State University, San Diego, CA 92182; and* Mally Moody, *Oxford High School, Oxford, AL 36203*

drawings. Therefore, geometry is an appropriate subject in which to implement the central goal of involving our students in the process of discovering mathematical ideas and doing mathematics through exploratory activities. This article was inspired by the "toothpick problem" discussed in the *Curriculum and Evaluation Standards* (NCTM 1989, 113). Basic properties of triangles can be developed and strengthened through investigating this problem. The extension problem gives students opportunities to explore and describe patterns and to make and test conjectures.

While my eighth-grade geometry class was engaged in the original toothpick problem, the discussion among students generated the second problem, which challenged both me and my students. Modifying an existing problem to generate other problems for investigation is a method frequently used by research mathematicians.

Grade levels: 7–10

Materials

A set of activity sheets for each student and a box of toothpicks for each small group of students. (Because they don't roll, flat toothpicks may be preferable to round ones for this activity.)

Prerequisites

Students need to be able to identify and classify scalene, isosceles, and equilateral triangles.

Directions

These activities require two or three class periods to complete, depending on the amount of class discussion generated and the number of triangles that students produce.

Sheet 1

Divide the class into small groups of four

or five students. Distribute one copy of sheet 1 to each student and one box of toothpicks to each group. Use the figures at the top of the page to make sure students know how to use toothpicks to make triangles and count the number of toothpicks on each side to identify their triangles. These triangles could be identified as (3, 4, 5) and (1, 5, 5). Make sure that students understand that (3, 4, 5) and (4, 3, 5) describe the same triangle but (3, 4, 6) describes a different triangle. Read the problem together and make sure that students understand the problem before they continue.

Have students work individually to answer questions 1 and 2. Be very clear about which definition of *isosceles triangle* you are using—a triangle with at least two equal sides or a triangle with exactly two equal sides. Suggest that the students in each group work together to complete the chart in question 3. After students have filled in the chart in question 3, they should have some ideas about what side lengths produce different types of triangles. In a class discussion, ask students to verbalize their ideas. Have students explain what they did to make their triangles and guide them in a discussion of their initial observations before they answer questions 4 and 5. Try to get students to formulate their own statement of the triangle inequality.

Sheet 2

Distribute a copy of sheet 2 to each student. Read the problem together and make sure students understand the problem. They will collect and record data as they work through questions 1 through 5 to help them answer questions on sheet 3 and solve the problem.

Students can work individually on questions 1 through 3 and then compare their answers with those of the rest of their group. Assign two numbers to each group to answer questions 4 and 5. Each of the numbers, 4 through 9, should be assigned to two groups.

As the values of α increase, finding all the triangles becomes laborious and students may encounter some difficulties. For the most part, however, students enjoy this activity and can proceed independently. Some of them can be asked to continue the search at home for some greater values of α. When they have completed their investigations, perhaps during the next class period, record the data collected by all the groups on a transparency of the chart in question 6.

Sheet 3

Distribute copies of sheet 3 to each student. Let students work in pairs to complete sheet 3. When students have completed the sheet, lead a class discussion about the patterns students discovered and the predictions they made. Give students the opportunity to discuss any other observations they may have made.

The questions on this sheet are a little more advanced than those on sheets 1 and 2. Students must study the data in their tables and look for patterns. On the basis of these patterns, students will formulate generalizations about all cases. Gathering data, searching for patterns, and making conjectures are vital aspects of the problem-solving process that students should experience.

Answers

Sheet 1: 1. (*a*) 1; (*b*) 0; (*c*) 0 or 1; (*d*) 1; 2. (*a*) 0; (*b*) 0; (*c*) 0; (*d*) 0; 3. See table 1. The lower number given for isosceles triangles refers to isosceles triangles as having exactly two equal sides; the higher number refers to isosceles triangles as having at least two equal sides. 4. The sum of the lengths of any two sides is greater than the length of the third side. 5. $a + b + c = n$, $a < b + c$, $b < a + c$, $c < a + b$.

Sheet 2: 1. (*a*) 1; (*b*) 0; (*c*) 0 or 1; (*d*) 1; 2. (*a*) 2; (*b*) 0; (*c*) 1 or 2; (*d*) 1; 3. (*a*) 4; (*b*) 0; (*c*) 3 or 4; (*d*) 1; 4–6. See table 2.

Sheet 3: 1. 36, 49, n^2; 2. 30, 42, $n(n + 1)$; 3. 20, 30, $(n - 2)(n - 1)$; 4. 16, 25, $(n - 1)^2$; 5. 15, 18, $3(n - 1)$; 6. 13, 16, $3n - 2$; 7. One equilateral triangle results for any positive integral value of α.

Reference

National Council of Teachers of Mathematics. *Curriculum and Evaluation Standards for School Mathematics.* Reston, Va.: The Council, 1989.

Table 1

Number of toothpicks	3	4	5	6	7	8	9
Is a triangle possible?	yes	no	yes	yes	yes	yes	yes
Number of triangles	1	0	1	1	2	1	3
Number of scalene triangles	0	0	0	0	0	0	1
Number of isosceles triangles	0 or 1	0	1	0 or 1	2	1	1 or 2
Number of equilateral triangles	1	0	0	1	0	0	1

Table 2

Measure of the longest side, α	1	2	3	4	5	6	7	8	9
Number of triangles	1	2	4	6	9	12	16	20	25
Number of scalene triangles	0	0	0	1	2	4	6	9	12
Number of isosceles triangles	0 or 1	1 or 2	3 or 4	4 or 5	6 or 7	7 or 8	9 or 10	10 or 11	12 or 13
Number of equilateral triangles	1	1	1	1	1	1	1	1	1

ORIGINAL TOOTHPICK PROBLEM

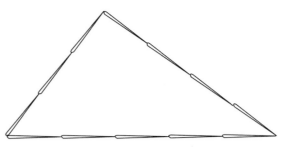

You are given a pile of toothpicks all the same size. Take a number, $n \geq 3$, of toothpicks. How many different triangles can you make using all n toothpicks placed end to end in the same plane? What kinds of triangles are possible?

1. First use three toothpicks and answer these questions.
    a) How many different triangles can you form? _____
    b) How many are scalene? _____
    c) How many are isosceles? _____
    d) How many are equilateral? _____

2. Next use four toothpicks and answer the same questions.
    a) Number of triangles _____
    b) Number of scalene triangles_____
    c) Number of isosceles triangles _____
    d) Number of equilateral triangles_____

3. Repeat with more toothpicks and complete the chart below.

Number of toothpicks	3	4	5	6	7	8	9
Is a triangle possible?							
Number of triangles							
Number of scalene triangles							
Number of isosceles triangles							
Number of equilateral triangles							

4. Consider the ways in which your triangles were formed. Find the sum of measures of two sides of each triangle and compare it with the measure of the third side. What do you observe?

5. Suppose that you have n toothpicks, $n \geq 3$, and that you are going to use those toothpicks to make triangles. Under what conditions does (a, b, c) represent one of your triangles? Remember that a, b, and c are the lengths of the sides of the triangle.

EXTENDING THE TOOTHPICK PROBLEM

You are given a pile of toothpicks of the same size. Assume that this size is one unit. If the longest side of a triangle you can build is α units in length, then what kinds of triangles are possible whose other two sides have length less than or equal to α? How many of each type are possible?

1. First, take $\alpha = 1$.

    a) How many triangles can be formed? _____

    b) How many are scalene? _____

    c) How many are isosceles? _____

    d) How many are equilateral? _____

2. Next take $\alpha = 2$ and answer the same questions.

    a) Number of triangles _____   b) Number of scalene triangles_____

    c) Number of isosceles triangles _____   d) Number of equilateral triangles_____

3. Repeat with $\alpha = 3$.

    a) Number of triangles _____   b) Number of scalene triangles_____

    c) Number of isosceles triangles _____   d) Number of equilateral triangles_____

4. Repeat with $\alpha = $ _____. (This number will be assigned to your group.)

    a) Number of triangles _____   b) Number of scalene triangles_____

    c) Number of isosceles triangles _____   d) Number of equilateral triangles_____

5. Repeat with $\alpha = $_____. (This number will be assigned to your group.)

    a) Number of triangles _____   b) Number of scalene triangles_____

    c) Number of isosceles triangles _____   d) Number of equilateral triangles_____

6. Use the data collected from all the groups to fill in the chart below.

Measure of the longest side, α	1	2	3	4	5	6	7	8	9
Number of triangles									
Number of scalene triangles									
Number of isosceles triangles									
Number of equilateral triangles									

EXTENDING THE EXTENSION

Use the information that you recorded on sheet 2 to help you answer the following questions.

1. Fill in the chart below when α is an odd number. Do you notice a pattern? How many triangles do you think you could make when α is 11? _____ When α is 13? _____ Use the pattern you found to fill in the table for $\alpha = 2n - 1$. For any natural number n, $2n - 1$ is a common way of expressing an odd integer.

α	1	3	5	7	9	$2n - 1$
No. of triangles						

2. Fill in the chart below when α is an even number. Do you notice a pattern? How many triangles do you think you could make when α is 10? _____ When α is 12? _____ Use the pattern you found to fill in the chart for $\alpha = 2n$.

α	2	4	6	8	$2n$
No. of triangles					

3. Fill in the chart below when α is an odd number. Do you notice a pattern? How many scalene triangles do you think you could make when α is 11? _____ When α is 13? _____ Use the pattern you found to fill in the chart for $\alpha = 2n - 1$.

α	1	3	5	7	9	$2n - 1$
No. of scalene triangles						

4. Fill in the chart below when α is an even number. Do you notice a pattern? How many scalene triangles do you think you could make when α is 10? _____ When α is 12? _____ Use the pattern you found to fill in the chart for $\alpha = 2n$.

α	2	4	6	8	$2n$
No. of scalene triangles					

5. Fill in the chart below when α is an odd number. Do you notice a pattern? Using the definition that an isosceles triangle has exactly two equal sides, how many isosceles triangles do you think you could make when α is 11 ? _____ When α is 13? _____ Use the pattern you found to fill in the chart for $\alpha = 2n - 1$.

α	1	3	5	7	9	$2n - 1$
No. of isosceles triangles						

6. Fill in the chart below when α is an even number. Do you notice a pattern? How many isosceles triangles do you think you could make when α is 10? _____ When α is 12? _____ Use the pattern you found to fill in the table for $\alpha = 2n$.

α	2	4	6	8	$2n$
No. of isosceles triangles					

7. How many equilateral triangles are possible for each value of α?_____

GAIL BURTON

Huge Trees, Small Drawings: Ideas of Relative Sizes

Two men walked into the rain forest. Moments before, the forest had been alive with the sounds of squawking birds and howling monkeys. Now all was quiet as the creatures watched the two men and wondered why they had come.... The smaller man took the ax he carried and struck the trunk of the tree...." With these words from Lynne Cherry's *The Great Kapok Tree* (1990), my sixth graders and I began a unit on concern for our earth. Many experiences enhanced our study in my mathematics and science classes. The students enjoyed the unit, which began about two weeks before Earth Day and lasted about a week after, because they were engaged in a variety of meaningful activities. The unit also gave me a way to help students solidify some of the measuring skills and ideas of ratio on which we had been working during the year.

Since I wanted to begin the unit in a dramatic way, I used an audiotape of rain-forest music and sounds to accompany the reading of *The Great Kapok Tree*. The book concerns a lumberman who takes a nap during the arduous task of trying to cut down a giant kapok tree in the Amazon rain forest. As the man dreams, many animals approach the man and ask him not to cut down the tree, since it provides an important part of their beautiful and long-established habitat, holds the soil in

Gail Burton *teaches at Coldwater Elementary School, Coldwater, MS 38618. She is committed to linking mathematics and science to the real world and uses books and poetry as a springboard for such activities. Burton gratefully acknowledges the advice of Jean Shaw in the development of this manuscript.*

Edited by Jean Shaw, *University of Mississippi, University, MS 38677*

place, and produces oxygen. The audiotape technique met with mixed results; some students were fascinated, whereas others were so curious about the sounds that they interrupted with "What was that?" and "Did you hear that?" In one class, a roar was heard on the tape as I read the jaguar's comments to the man, and my students thought I had timed it perfectly!

Before the end of the book, we paused to predict possible outcomes and consequences. As we examined the book's maps of locations of the original and existing rain forests, my students were able to use their knowledge of geography and climate to infer that rain forests occur mostly in tropical areas with plenty of precipitation and heat—conditions that for centuries have promoted growth of extensive plant and animal life. They also noted, and had heard about, the rapidly shrinking area of rain forests in the world.

My students were initially curious about the many animals in *The Great Kapok Tree*,

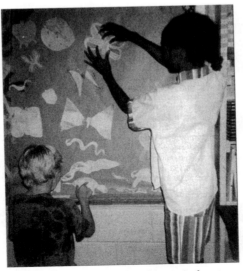

Students layer the life found in a rain forest.

which Cherry realistically illustrated in vivid detail. Some favorites were the giant three-toed sloth, the tiny toads, the snakes, and the many insects that appear in the pictures. To relate to the plethora of problems caused by cutting into the rain forest, we pursued an analogy to our own rapidly growing small town at the edge of the Mississippi delta. The students described changes they had observed in recent years, such as wooded areas being cleared to make room for more housing and farm land's being replaced by stores and roads. Thus, the stage was set for the unit's focus on environmental issues.

Sizes and Scales

To capitalize on my students' interest in the rain forest's animals, we planned and created a bulletin board to show the rain forest's layers—the canopy, emergent layer, understory, and forest floor—as well as the many creatures that inhabit the forest. Students referred to *The Great Kapok Tree* as each drew animals and plants for the display. As the students worked, many were concerned with relative sizes, whereas others were more casual. For example, when Lucius commented, "Who ever saw a butterfly that big?" Nakomus retorted, "What do you mean? You might see anything in the rain forest!"

This unit had potential for extending and formalizing my students' ideas of relative sizes, so we made scale drawings. Using data from Bass (1994), we found that a typical tree in the rain forest's emergent, or tallest, layer (tallest trees) is about 130 feet tall; trees in the canopy that form a sort of roof over the forest are 60 to 90 feet tall; and trees in the understory layer are typically 40 to 50 feet tall. We related these heights to familiar sizes so the students could more easily imagine them. After we measured and found that the ceiling in our classroom was about 9 feet high, Casey stated, "One of the taller trees in the canopy is about 10 classrooms high!" She explained her thinking at the chalkboard, setting up the ratio $9/90 = 1/t$: "I'm comparing feet in the classroom to feet in the tall tree. I want to know how many 'classrooms high' the huge tree is: Ten times 9 is 90, and so 10 times 1 is t—the height of the tall tree."

I asked them, "Does this make sense? Could there be other ways to explain?" Danielle offered, "Nine and 90 work together—10 times 9 is 90. So it takes 10 classrooms of 9 feet to make 90 feet." Micah tried his understanding of the examples by volunteering, "The tree that's 60 feet is like 6 classrooms; the tree that's 130 feet is like 13 stories—you divide by 10." But Char countered, "No, it's 9 and 60. It's 9 feet in the room, and it takes about 7 times 9 to give 60, so the 60-foot tree is about 7 classrooms high." These observations helped us try to relate the rain forest's huge trees to buildings in our community, and we concluded that even the trees in the understory, which are 40 to 50 feet, are taller than the buildings in our community—all are one and two stories tall.

We then focused on the idea of making drawings to show the relative sizes of the trees. I posed the question "What scale can we use to fit trees of these sizes on paper?" Steven suggested that we would need a scale to include the height of the tallest tree—130 feet—on notebook paper, but that 1 foot (of real height) to 1 inch (for picture heights) was too great to fit; even 10 feet to an inch was too long for our 8 1/2-by-11-inch paper. Felicia proposed a scale of 1 centimeter (drawing height) to 10 feet (actual height). Her classmates agreed that this system would work, after glancing at and measuring the paper. The 130-foot trees would be the manageable height of 13 centimeters in the drawings. Although they mixed measurement systems, this scale made sense to most of the students. "It's easy when you work with tens," Valencia commented.

When the drawings were completed, we prepared for self- and peer-evaluation by discussing what "critiquing" meant. Critiquing involves checking, discussing, and writing about good parts of the scale drawings and deciding on places where the drawings should be improved. As students examined partners' work, most looked for inclusion of all the layers and remeasured the drawings of the layers, using the simple 10-to-1 ratio. They complimented the drawings and suggested improvements, as well as noticed such details as inclusion of all the layers and a variety of appropriate animals. Figure 1 shows a sample of a student's work and comments from her peers.

The students took the task seriously, and as they worked, I had a chance to walk around and observe them. Many used good sense when working with our easy scale and were insightful in pointing out places for their partners to recheck. With others, I saw some hesitation and offered help. The students seemed pleased with comments and corrections from their classmates, and several offered to read their critiques to the

Peer evaluation becomes serious business.

A critique is read to the class.

Fig. 1. An example of peer-graded student's work

class. Many spontaneously added to and corrected their drawings.

More Work on the Rain-Forest Theme

To further use measurement in practical ways, we made terrariums using the pattern shown in figure 2. Each student placed about 500 mL of potting soil in the base of the terrarium, chose three plants donated by a local nursery owner, and measured and recorded their plants' heights. To start the "water cycle," each student added about 60 mL of water to the terrarium, sealed the container with tape, and placed it in a dis-

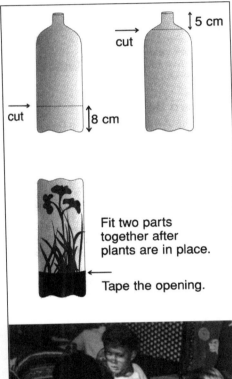

Fig. 2. A terrarium in the making

play area. For a week, students observed their terrariums each day and wrote observations, noting evidence of humidity, condensation, and "rain" in their terrariums; and recorded and graphed the plants' growth. (See fig. 3.) Next we extended the unit's focus to problem solving on the rain-forest theme by researching the eating habits of some of the animals from *The Great Kapok Tree*. Using this information, students worked in small groups to create problems that they exchanged and discussed with other groups.

Fig. 3. Plant growth in the terrarium is analyzed.

Extending Activities

Starting our study of the environment with the rain forest seemed to capture the interest of most of my sixth graders, and the unit extended to other experiences and aspects of the environment that were closer to home. For example, my students conducted polls to see what some of the children and adults in our community perceived as being important environmental problems. We gathered disposable items, which were sorted, weighed, and recycled. Then we completed our project by cleaning up the school grounds. Finally students drew names for partners and choose topics for an environmental problem to research, presenting and displaying their findings the week after Earth Day. A culminating activity involved acting out a play from the Environmental Protection Agency's publication *Let's Recycle and Reduce* (1990).

Reflections and Suggestions—Next Steps

My students enjoyed and profited from

our study of the environment and were exposed to some outstanding children's literature and reference books. Often I heard such comments as "Is it time to go already?" and "We're learning something useful!" I found evidence of attitudinal changes in my sixth graders: most were more concerned about the immediate environment and picked up classroom trash spontaneously; several prompted others to do so in the halls and cafeteria. Many took pride in the products they made; they conserved and reused art paper and seemed pleased to recycle their soft-drink terrarium bottles, a project that seemed to give most students a sense of accomplishment. Students grew in their abilities to handle measuring tools and use ratios; many were convinced of the power of using "friendly" and easy-to-compute numbers in the ratios. They saw real purposes for measuring as they made things and became independent thinkers when choosing appropriate tools for the various measuring tasks they completed. Communication and cooperation skills were enhanced as students worked together on meaningful projects.

As I reflected on the unit and its learning experiences, I thought about several big ideas. Caring for the environment is so important and relevant that we might want to use the material over a longer period of time. I might introduce the topic earlier in the school year and spread the experiences throughout my teaching of mathematics and science, culminating around Earth Day. We could find information about rain-forest depletion and use maps to figure its approximate area now and its predicted area in the future unless measures are taken to save the rain forest. This scenario could pose challenging problems, since rain-forest areas shown on maps are irregular in shape. Toward the end of our unit, we might revisit the book, playing the tape again and discussing all the resources that might be lost unless people stop depleting the rain forest.

When I introduce this unit again, I plan to have students write letters to environmental agencies requesting information to supplement the books available for research. Next year I will let my students design and use a questionnaire concerning their opinions about the value of the unit and what they learned. After we analyze the

317

results, I will use their ideas as a basis for future planning, improvements, and actions.

Bibliography

Bass, Phyllis. Literature Notes: *The Great Kapok Tree*. Science Series, FS-2816. Torrance, Calif.: Frank Schaffer Publications, 1994.

Cherry, Lynne. *The Great Kapok Tree: A Tale of the Amazon Rain Forest*. San Diego: Harcourt Brace & Co., 1990.

Thornton, Carol A., Dianna Dee Damkoehler, Helen Gehrenbeck, and Graham A. Jones. "The Children's Rain Forest." *Teaching Children Mathematics* 2 (November 1995): 144–48.

Suggested Readings

Cherry, Lynne. *A River Ran Wild*. San Diego: Harcourt Brace & Co., 1992

The book's beautiful illustrations and compelling text convey the story of how a Nashua Indian chief's spirit affected political policies and efforts to clean up a badly polluted river.

Levine, Ellen. *The Tree That Would Not Die*. Illustrated by Ted Rand. New York: Scholastic Books, 1995.

The story of a huge tree—the "Treaty Oak" in downtown Austin, Texas—is conveyed from the tree's point of view. Readers learn about many historical events "seen" by the tree and how it has been saved through the efforts of many people.

Levine, Shar, and Allison Grafton. *Projects for a Healthy Planet: Simple Environmental Experiments for Kids*. Illustrated by Terry Chui. New York: John Wiley & Sons, 1992.

This black-and-white book presents easy-to-read-and-do ideas for projects on aspects of pollution, recycling, and conservation and for creating environmentally friendly products.

Mattson, Mark. *Environmental Atlas of the United States*. New York: Scholastic Books, 1993.

This colorful book is full of maps, narrative information, graphs, and summaries of environmental facts.

Pringle, Laurence. *Living Treasure: Saving Earth's Threatened Biodiversity*. Illustrated by Irene Brady. New York: Morrow Junior Books, 1991.

Realistic pencil drawings and informative text help this factual, upper-grades book stress the need to appreciate the earth's many creatures.

Spurgeon, Richard. *Usborne Science and Experiments: Ecology*. Illustrated by Kuo Kang Chen, Brin Edwards, and Caroline Ewen. London: Usborne House, 1988.

This book, full of small colored pictures and packed with facts and projects, addresses many features of the interrelatedness of living things and their environment.

Stark, Rebecca. *Our Environment*. Hawthorne, N.J.: Educational Impressions, 1993.

This black-and-white book is designed for use by teachers and older students and gives factual information and suggestions for lessons.

Taylor, Barbara. *Rain Forest: A Look Closer Book*. Photographed by Frank Greenaway. New York: Dorling Kindersley, 1992.

Students will want to study each page of this factual book to learn about the many plants and animals of the rain forest. Brilliantly colored photographs complement the text; drawings help students relate the animal's sizes to those of humans.

United States Environmental Protection Agency (EPA). *Let's Recycle and Reduce:* Curriculum for Solid Waste Awareness Lesson Plans for 6 12. Washington, D.C.: EPA, 1990.

This publication offers many statistics on the extent of environmental problems and ideas for lessons and projects. It includes the play *The Throwaway Three*.

Williams, Rozanne Lanczak. *Let's Take Care of the Earth*. Illustrated by Neena Chawla. Cypress, Calif.: Creative Teaching Press, 1995.

This predictable book for younger children shows various animals and their habitats; it stresses the idea that people must care for the earth's many habitats.

ANN BLOMQUIST

Folding Perpendiculars and Counting Slope

DURING the study of coordinate geometry, students are told that the slope of a line and the slope of a perpendicular to the line are negative reciprocals. The NCTM's *Curriculum and Evaluation Standards for School Mathematics* (1989) calls for "active involvement of students in constructing and applying mathematical ideas." This activity will encourage inductive thinking and allow students to discover this relationship for themselves. Students should have previously computed the slope of a segment by counting squares and using the rise-over-run format.

Using the "Slope and Perpendiculars" worksheet with segments on graph paper, tell the students that they are going to collect some data and make a conclusion based on their data. To help the students start the activity, compute the slopes of the first two line segments with the class.

To compute the slope of segment 1, have the students count the squares vertically and horizontally. Record results along the right-hand margin. Next, fold a perpendicular to the segment. In this activity, the perpendicular bisector of the segment is easy to explain and demonstrate. By holding the paper up to the light, the students can match the endpoints of the segment by looking through the paper. Then firmly crease a fold several inches long and open the paper. Your directed discussion can include discovering the existence of other perpendiculars, informally testing for right angles by using the corner of a piece of paper, and predicting the sign of the slope of the perpendiculars.

Next, locate three points on the fold. One point that is easy to determine is the midpoint of the segment. Also locate two other points on the crease that intersect the graph paper exactly through integral coordinates. Mark each point clearly. Have the students compute the slope of the perpendicular fold by using any two of the three points and record the data in the right-hand column.

Also compute with students the slope for segment 2 to check for their understanding of the procedure. Point out that the final question (no. 13) asks for their conclusion about the data that they collect.

When this activity is finished, the students should perceive the relationship of the slopes of a line and a perpendicular to that line and be able to formulate a conclusion. Their terminology in their conclusions may not be formal, but they will have "discovered" the relationship for themselves.

Reference

National Council of Teachers of Mathematics. *Curriculum and Evaluation Standards for School Mathematics.* Reston, Va.: The Council, 1989.

Ann Blomquist, *Boone High School, Orlando, FL 32806*

SLOPE AND PERPENDICULARS

Name _____

For each segment, first count the squares vertically and horizontally and compute the slope, then fold a perpendicular and compute the slope of the perpendicular.

1. m = _____

   $m_\perp$ = _____

2. m = _____

   $m_\perp$ = _____

3. m = _____

   $m_\perp$ = _____

4. m = _____

   $m_\perp$ = _____

5. m = _____

   $m_\perp$ = _____

6. m = _____

   $m_\perp$ = _____

7. m = _____

   $m_\perp$ = _____

8. m = _____

   $m_\perp$ = _____

9. m = _____

   $m_\perp$ = _____

10. m = _____

    $m_\perp$ = _____

11. m = _____

    $m_\perp$ = _____

12. m = _____

    $m_\perp$ = _____

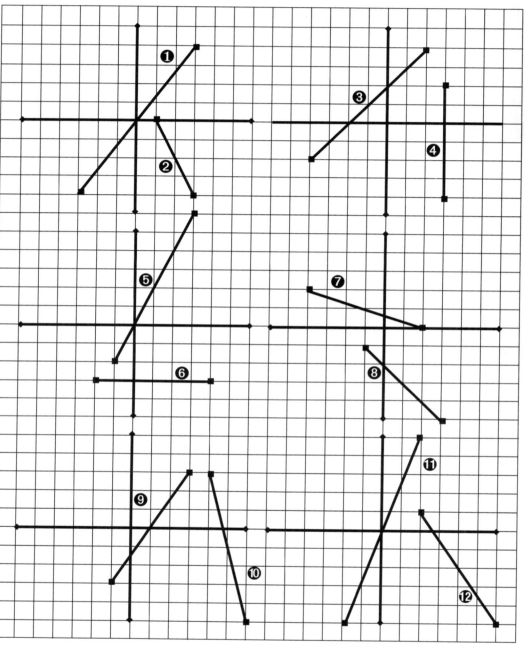

13. Write a conclusion about the slope of a line and the slope of any line perpendicular to it.

ROBERT GERVER

Discovering Pi
Two Approaches

T IS unreasonable to expect students to become adept in the measurement of the area and circumference of circles without a thorough introduction to pi. Why is it that the phrase "the area is 49π square inches" means nothing to so many elementary and secondary school students? Although pi's role in mathematics is seldom downplayed, it is rarely developed in the context of the formula $A = \pi r^2$. Perhaps every student needs to take a "discovery" look at pi.

Many textbooks and workbooks feature activities involving the circumference of a circle. Some books name the parts of the circle using a diagram like figure 1. It must be pointed out to students that the *circumference* is the *measure* of the circle's length. In figure 1, the word *circumference* should be replaced by the word *circle*.

The study of circumference should follow the study of perimeter. Students should see the analogy of a circle's circumference

Robert Gerver *teaches at North Shore High School, Glenn Head, NY 11545. He is a doctoral candidate at New York University and has published articles in several professional journals. He was selected as a 1988 Presidential Awardee for excellence in mathematics teaching.*

to a polygon's perimeter before getting involved with π and the formulas $C = \pi d$ and $C = 2\pi r$. The student should become comfortable with the concept by using a tape measure or a string and ruler, as in the circumference activity that follows. Measurements of circumference should be compared to perimeters in a problem-solving context. Students can also determine, using string without a ruler, that the circumference is slightly more than the length of three diameters. Through these visual and intuitive introductions, students discover pi and the circumference formula.

Two Circumference Activities

Activity 1

Students can begin to get a feel for the ratio of the circumference to the diameter by observing or participating in the following activity.

Step 1. Secure a three-dimensional circular object (frisbee, trash-can lid, etc.) to the chalkboard.

Step 2. Mark off the length of the diameter on a piece of string.

Step 3. Bend this marked-off length of

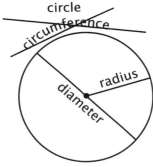

Fig. 1. Parts of the circle

string around the circle, and mark off the three arcs that are equal to the diameter in length.

Step 4. Repeat steps 1–3 with other objects so that students discover (a) that the circumference is a little greater than the length of three diameters and (b) that this property is invariant.

Activity 2

A popular circumference activity uses a string and ruler (or a tape measure) and several circular objects. The circumference is measured and recorded. The diameter is measured and recorded. Then the circumference is divided by the diameter, and a result close to pi is usually obtained. Students can complete a chart similar to table 1.

The numbers in the last column can be explained as "rough" approximations for the ratio of circumference to diameter (pi); then pi can be explicitly defined. Point out that this ratio is so important that a special symbol, π, has been assigned to it. Students have witnessed the invariance of pi; they've seen that

$$Cd = \pi$$

works for small and large circles.

Students can derive a formula for the circumference of a circle by checking the division problem: if

$$d \overline{)C}^{\pi},$$

then

$$C = \pi \cdot d.$$

With pi and the circumference formula having been discovered by students, standard problems can then be tackled. These problems should require finding the circumference when the diameter is given and finding the diameter when the circumference is given.

Introducing the Area of a Circle

Investigating the area of a circle is a natural exploration after a unit on areas of polygons. The circumference activities preceded the unit on areas of polygons; thus, the area and circumference formulas for circles are not presented together.

Students should receive the same type of intuitive, visual introduction to the area of a circle that they did for circumference. Elementary school students should not be deprived of a complete, logical development.

Discovering the area of a circle step by step

Step 1. Review the concept of area using rectangles and squares. Pay particular attention to the notion of "square unit," using diagrams similar to that in figure 2.

Step 2. Pose a problem that involves the area of a circle, in feet. Ask the students, "If squares and rectangles can be filled up with *square feet*, what can we try to fill up the circle with?" Suggest or entertain the idea of "circle feet." A "circle foot" is shown in figure 3. If time and grade level allow, cir-

cles that are tangent and tessellations can be related to the problem at hand. Discuss the practicality and universality of certain measuring standards.

Step 3. Relate the area of a circle to that of a square on the basis of the *diameter*, as in figure 4.

Step 4. Relate the area of a circle to that

of squares on the basis of the *radius*, as shown beginning with figure 5 and continuing with the sequence of questions on the sheet "Area of a Circle." Now we have a foundation. When the formula A = πr² is eventually developed, the students will be convinced of its authenticity because they were expecting something close to 3r².

Table 1

Object	Circumference	Diameter	Circumference / Diameter
Frisbee			
Cymbal			
Drum			
Hubcap			
Coffee-can lid			
Trash-can lid			
Clock			

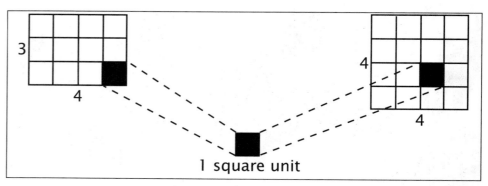

Fig. 2. Review the concept of area.

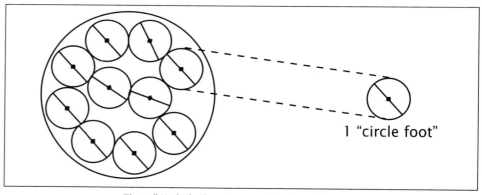

Fig. 3. "Circle feet" can't account for the entire area.

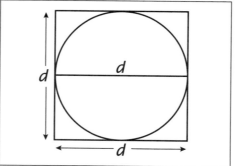

Fig. 4. The area of the square, d^2, is greater than the area of the circle.

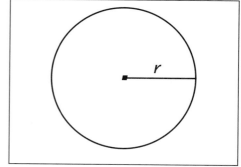

Fig. 5. A circle with radius *r*

Step 5. Now the area formula can be developed. Using a compass and graph paper, draw a diagram like that in figure 6 and photocopy it for the students. Many sizes of graph paper can also be used, again underscoring the invariance of pi.

Have the students count the total number of "full" squares inside the circle. Clever students may decide to count only half or quarter squares and then multiply. Either way, the students must record the total number of squares that lie completely within the circle. They can write the numbers inside the squares, as in figure 7.

Some pieces of squares are left inside the circle. Look at the two shaded pieces in figure 7. If they were joined together, they would come very close to forming one full square. Students can match pieces together until the entire area inside the circle is covered. They need to keep a careful count of the number of full squares they are "making." Tally marks can be used, for example,

等等等等等等等 𝄃𝄃𝄃 = 34

The circle with radius 7 produced 34 full squares from the matched pieces. The 120 squares originally counted is added to the 34 squares to give an area of 154 square units. Activities similar to step 5 can use radii of 4, 5, 6, 8, 9, and 10. In a classroom setting, each group of students can work on a different circle and report its findings in a table similar to table 2.

The numbers in the last column are

Table 2

Radius r	r^2	Area	$\dfrac{\text{Area}}{r^2}$
4	16	50	3.125
5			
6			
7	49	154	3.14
8			
9			
10			

approximations of pi. Students have seen that

$$\frac{A}{r^2} = \pi$$

is invariant, and they can derive a formula for the area of a circle by checking the division problem: if

$$\frac{A}{r^2} = \pi,$$

then

$$A = \pi r^2$$

Standard problems employing the formula can now be assigned. The answers should not be left in terms of pi; 154 square units is much more meaningful than 49π square units.

Teacher-directed activities using the seven figures, two tables, and one worksheet in this article can be created. The extra time for discovery, development, and discussion is well worth the effort. (Teachers interested in other activities involving pi and circles should refer to the article "Finding the Area of a Circle: Use a Cake Pan and Leave Out the Pi" by Walter Szetela and Douglas Owens in the May 1986 issue of the *Arithmetic Teacher*.)

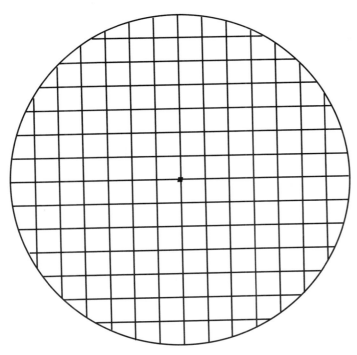

Fig. 6. A circle with radius 7 and its area

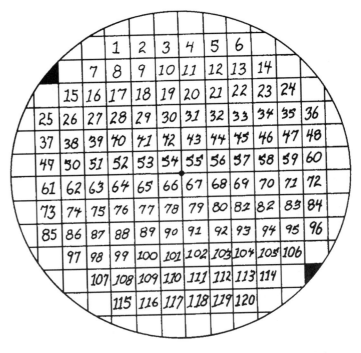

Fig. 7. One hundred twenty squares lie completely within the circle.

AREA OF A CIRCLE

Name _____

I. The area of the shaded square is r^2. Which of the following three statements appears to be true?

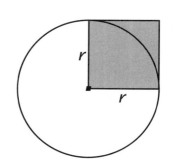

  1. The area of the circle, A, is less than the area of the square. ($A < r^2$.)
  2. The area of the circle is approximately equal to the area of the square. ($A \approx r^2$.)
  3. The area of the circle is greater than the area of the square. ($A > r^2$.)

II. The area of the two shaded squares is $2r^2$. Which of the following statements appears to be true?

  1. $A < 2r^2$.　　　2. $A \approx 2r^2$.　　　3. $A > 2r^2$.

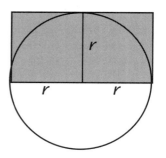

III. The area of the three shaded squares is $3r^2$. Which of the following three statements appears to be true?

  1. $A < 3r^2$.　　　2. $A \approx 3r^2$.　　　3. $A > 3r^2$.

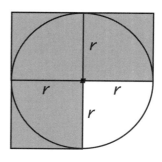

IV. The area of the four shaded squares is $4r^2$. Which of the following statements appears to be true?"

  1. $A < 4r^2$.　　　2. $A \approx 4r^2$.　　　3. $A > 4r^2$.

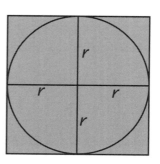

V. Which is the best approximation for the area of a circle?

  1. r^2　　　2. $2r^2$　　　3. $3r^2$　　　4. $4r^2$

JANE B. KENNEDY

Area and Perimeter Connections

MATHEMATICS can be made much more meaningful through the use of modeling and manipulatives. Teachers trying to move mathematics teaching into the future look for ways to make mathematics less mysterious, monotonous, and menial. The following excerpts from NCTM's *Curriculum and Evaluation Standards for School Mathematics* (1989) articulate the overall goals for this activity:

- In grades 9–12, the mathematics curriculum should include the continued development of language and symbolism to communicate mathematical ideas so that all students can . . . formulate mathematical definitions and express generalizations discovered through investigations. (NCTM 1989, 140)

- In grades 9–12, the mathematics curriculum should include investigation of the connections and interplay among various mathematical topics and their applications so that all students can . . . relate procedures in one representation to procedures in an equivalent representation. (NCTM 1989, 146)

- In grades 9–12, the mathematics curriculum should include the continued study of functions so that all students can . . . represent and analyze relationships using tables, verbal rules, equations, and graphs. (NCTM 1989, 154)

- In grades 9–12, the mathematics curriculum should include the informal exploration of calculus concepts from both a graphical and a numerical per-

spective so that all students can determine maximum and minimum points of a graph and interpret the results in a problem situation. (NCTM 1989, 180)

Teacher's Guide

Introduction: The following activity investigates a familiar idea and provides for algebraic and geometric interpretations of results. With a given perimeter, students must find the dimensions of the maximum rectangular area when four sides are required and also find the dimensions of the maximum rectangular area when only three sides are required. This activity is one of many that have been used successfully for the last few years in algebra and calculus courses, as well as in courses for students who do not intend to go to college. Beginning with concrete experience in a laboratory or by experimenting, students collect and compare data, find patterns, graph data, write functions, and discuss the meaning of the resulting mathematical model. These concrete experiences create understanding and ease connections when students encounter problems regarding maximum and minimum values. In the courses that are not geared toward college, students tend to enjoy the investigation, generate good questions, have good insight into relationships, and can summarize the conclusions during group discussion.

Grade levels: 8–12

Materials

Strings about 30 inches or 30 centimeters long, marking pen, scissors, rulers, one-quarter-inch or centimeter graph paper, calculators. See the notes for sheet 3 if graphing calculators are available.

Objectives

Explore the mathematical concepts of the effect on an area when a fixed perimeter is altered. Construct and measure a model,

which will allow easy comparison between two different conditions. Employ hands-on algebraic and geometric techniques to find the dimensions yielding the maximum area. Ask students to make a generalized algebraic statement from data.

Prerequisites

Students should know the formula for the area of a rectangle and how to graph ordered pairs.

Directions

The activity requires from one to three class periods, depending on students' ability. A good introduction to the activity, especially for those with little experience comparing areas, is to use the overhead projector and a piece of string tied in a loop to show that the same perimeter can enclose different areas. The tied string will also model the students' procedures in the experiment.

Sheet 1: Class discussion should elicit responses based on students' experience. Pass out two rulers per group. Check students' drawn rectangles to make sure that the fencing idea is understood. A group of four would allow one student to change the width, one to measure, one to record the data, and one to find the area. Most students stop measuring once the pattern emerges. The length of the string is in multiples of four to eliminate using fractions in the dimensions for maximum area. If your students have had earlier laboratory experience, the lengths could be any whole number in the suggested range. As soon as students see the relationships, final class discussion can easily produce the dimensions for any value of the perimeter. Producing a chart on the chalkboard with rows for perimeter, width, length, and area and letting each group record its results when complete is an easy way to determine when all are finished. Students can refer to

Jane Kennedy *teaches at Morris Knolls High School, Rockaway, NJ 07866.*

Edited by Karen A. Dotseth, *Cedar Falls High School, Cedar Falls, lA 50673;* Kim Girard, *Nashua High School, Nashua, MT 59248;* Mally Moody, *Oxford High School, Oxford, AL 36203*

the chart during discussion. On sheet 3, the information from sheets 1 and 2 will be graphed. For this reason, inches on sheet 1 may be an easier unit with which to measure, as centimeters may require the use of different scales on the x and y axis. Discuss the algebraic representations with the class by looking at the effect on the length each time the width increases by 1 unit.

Sheet 2: When students have completed sheet 1 and discussed and checked their answers, distribute sheet 2. The beginning class discussion sets the stage for the work that will follow, so be sure that students understand the idea that the string's same perimeter is now going to enclose only three sides of a rectangle. Most students will know that the new area will be larger, so have them conjecture about *how much* larger. Do not tell students if their conjectures are correct, since an objective of the lesson is to analyze the model to make this determination. Make another set of columns on the chalkboard for the three-sided example. Use the same rows as before to make discussion easier.

Sheet 3: Students should have a good understanding of the doubling of area from the fencing pictures alone. A thorough discussion of the concepts might be more valuable than graphing for some classes. The one-fourth-inch graph paper should be prepared ahead of time for some classes, with the short edge being the x-axis from 0 to 10 and the long edge being the y-axis from 0 to 100 in the first quadrant only. Centimeter graph paper should be scaled by 5s on the vertical axis. If you have a TI-81 graphing calculator, enter the data under the statistics menu and draw the xy-line. Then enter the area function as y_1 and make comparisons. Other graphing calculators have similar capabilities.

Answers: Sheet 1: 1. Answers will vary and may include curved fencing, as well as questions about possible shapes. Examples include vegetable gardens, animals, play areas, and swimming pools. Rectangular fencing is easy to measure and build with a minimum of posts. Rectangular areas also fit together nicely. The minimum area is, of course, 0. Students have mentioned jails as possible minimum ideas, in addition to art galleries. 2. String's perimeter. 3. Answers will depend on perimeter, but length is perimeter/2 minus the width. Area is the

product of the length and width. Final column is width = x, length = $P/2 - x$, and area = $x(P/2 - x)$, where P is their perimeter. 4. One-fourth the perimeter for both width and length. Area is product. 5. Sketch is a square.
6. The first row is
 2 3 4 5 6 7 10 25.
The second row is
 2 3 4 5 6 7 10 25.
The third row is
 4 9 16 25 36 49 100 625.
7. See answer 3.

Sheet 2: 1. Most students will conjecture that the new area will be a larger number than before. However, many students will figure that the new dimensions will be one-third of the total string length. If they had a 12-inch and 12-centimeter string length, they would guess dimensions of 4 × 4 and an area of 16. A few students will think that the area will double or more than double. 3. Answers will depend on string length, but length is string length minus twice the width, and area is their product. Final column is width of x, length of $S - 2x$, and area of $x(S - 2x)$, where S is string length. 4. One-fourth the string length for width and one-half the string length for length. Area is product. 5. The sketch is a rectangle, which has a length that is twice the width.
6. The first row is
 2 3 4 5 6 7 10 25.
The second row is
 4 6 8 10 12 14 20 50.
The third row is
 8 18 32 50 72 98 200 1350.
7. See answer 3.

Sheet 3. 1. Students should notice that the width is the same and the length and area have doubled. Some students may ask what would happen if the length had been used for the two sides coming from the river or house. An excellent extension. 2. String length/4. 3. 2 times. 4. 2 times. 5. There are really two squares, side by side; it's as if the river side of the square has been added to the parallel side of the fence; or if you reflect the fence over the river, you have another square. 9. Because the fencing is continuous and you can obtain all dimensions in between the integers. 10. Yes; widths equal, area twice. 11. Parabolic, symmetric, like a ball being thrown in the air, same on both sides, and so on. 12. They

probably do not look alike because of the scale choices. This is an important idea for students to observe. Characteristics stay the same but the curves do not match.

General extensions

All students should be able to articulate some ideas about why a square is the rectangle of maximum area for a given perimeter. A good way to test this understanding is to supply different perimeter lengths to the class and have students supply the dimensions for all four sides being fenced and then use that same total length for only three sides being fenced. I have found this activity extremely effective both as an introductory activity and as a follow-up for the formal study of parabolas. The investigations of symmetry, vertex, x-axis intercepts, relationship of factors and roots, maximum value, and the physical meaning of product using area have motivated students and made these subjects meaningful.

References

National Council of Teachers of Mathematics. *Curriculum and Evaluation Standards for School Mathematics.* Reston, Va.: The Council, 1989.

Stimpson, Virginia C. "What Do We Mean by Area and Perimeter?" *Mathematics Teacher* 82 (May 1989): 342–44.

MARILYN L. FOWLER

The Inside-Out Box
An Analysis of Structures and Space

THE NCTM's Standards address the need for children to develop spatial sense and explore the effects of transforming, combining, subdividing, and changing geometric figures (1989). Yet our students show weakness in these skills when compared with children of other nations (Stigler, Lee, and Stevenson 1990, quoted in Grouws 1992). The positive correlation between spatial abilities and mathematics achievement at all levels (Fennema and Sherman 1977; Fennema and Sherman 1978; and Guay and McDaniel 1977; all cited in Grouws 1992) shows that teachers need to present activities that can develop children's spatial abilities.

The following activity for children of any age is an interesting and practical spatial-manipulation lesson that will result in a useful product. Teachers who have presented this learning experience report that they are surprised at the ease with which some students can predict the shape of a box that has been opened and laid flat. In so doing, these students are providing authentic evidence of their spatial abilities.

Materials

Students in kindergarten will need at least twenty construction-paper shapes cut into 16-cm-by-8-cm rectangles, 8-cm-by-8-cm squares, and miscellaneous

Marilyn Fowler, *fowler@tenet.edu, works for the Texas Statewide Systemic Initiative, the University of Texas at Austin, Austin, TX 78712. She is interested in ways that teachers can make elementary classrooms more interesting with design, invention, analysis of everyday objects, and the mathematics intrinsic to those processes. She codirects with engineers a teachers' institute called DTEACh, which is dedicated to those interests.*

The author wishes to thank Mr. Lannon's first-grade class at Harris Elementary School in Austin, Texas, for its assistance during the preparation of this article.

Students analyze their boxes.

triangles and other shapes. Students in grades 1–6 will need drawing paper; tape and tape dispensers; glue or paste; one sheet of butcher paper per two-student team; and recycled containers, such as cereal, toothpaste, aspirin, cracker, and film boxes.

Preparation

The teacher should form two-student teams. Once the boxes are collected, prepare a box by gently separating it at the glued areas. Fold it again into its original box shape and lightly tape it back together. For kindergarten only, cut construction-paper pieces for the "box maps."

The Construction Begins

To begin the activity, I place all the collected containers around the children's tables or on the floor. Children can hold and touch the containers and are encouraged to look inside. They discuss the containers and how they are used. Are containers made for certain purposes? How does a container protect the items inside? What purpose does the decoration on the outside serve? Are some containers unfit for the products inside that may break or get

crushed? What is done to prevent these problems? From what materials are the containers made?

Students then observe the empty cereal box and see that its front face is a rectangular or a square shape. They are asked to guess the shape of the back of the box before it is shown to them, as well as of the sides and the bottom. Children are asked, "Why do you think that the back side will be a rectangle or square?" They talk together about their ideas and report back, and then all the faces and edges of the box are counted.

Students analyze how the box opens and closes. What has been designed to allow the box to reclose tightly and what makes it work? The children describe the features of the closing mechanism. Sometimes this mechanism includes a tab that fits into a slot. However, if the box is to be thrown away after its first use, no closing mechanism is found.

Students then see that the box can be opened out flat because I have unfastened it at the seams. I ask students to close their eyes and imagine how the box will appear if it is opened and placed flat on the floor.

The kindergarten student teams then use

the cut-paper shapes to make a map of what they think the cereal box will look like when it is laid flat. Note that the boxes in this activity are peeled apart at the seams, and students should examine where those seams are before making predictions. If the box is *cut* down the sides, the predictions would be quite different. Children move the shapes around until they are arranged the way they should be. I ask older children to sketch how the flattened box will appear, indicating whether the decoration is face-down. Teams should be asked to place a special mark where the opening and closing mechanism will be found once the box is flattened. For an additional challenge, ask students to mark on their map where other features of the cereal box will be when the box is flat, such as the list of ingredients, the brand name, or a cartoon figure (see fig. 1 for a diagram of an opened-and-laid-flat cereal box).

The group is then brought together to check its maps or sketches against the actual geometry of the opened-flat box. I carefully untape the cereal box then lay the box flat and ask the children to compare their maps and sketches with the flattened box. Students check their blueprints and see if they can find where their predictions differ from the actual box. These questions help guide their thinking:

- Did you fail to predict some sides or faces? What is the function of those parts? (Extra flaps provide surfaces for gluing and others form effective seals.)
- How many times did you change your minds about an arrangement of paper pieces before you settled on one?
- Did both team members present good ideas and listen to each other's ideas?

Student teams then choose one box to analyze. They look at the seams and glued edges and then make a map or sketch that predicts their opened-flat box. They can ask for help to peel the sides apart and match up their map or sketch with the actual flattened box (see figs. 2 and 3 for additional box maps).

Later, I demonstrate that my original cereal box and others like it can be turned inside out and taped together to make a new box. Students then describe the new box, counting the number of faces as before. Is the new box more pleasing visually than the old box? The design and let-

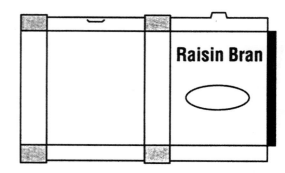

■ Fold flaps—close gaps
■ Glue flap—gives a surface to glue box at seam

Fig. 1. A cereal-box "map"

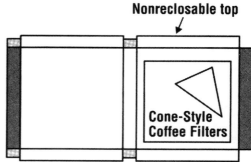

■ Fold flaps—close gaps
■ Glue flap—gives a surface to glue box at seam

Fig. 2. A coffee-filter-box "map"

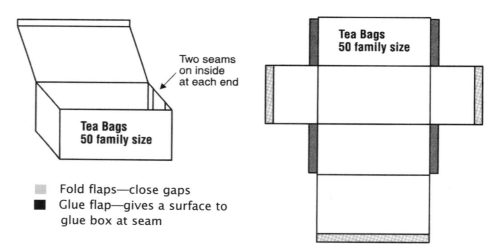

■ Fold flaps—close gaps
■ Glue flap—gives a surface to glue box at seam

Fig. 3. A tea-bags-box "map"

tering are out of sight, which makes the box easier to decorate. How does the inside-out box open and shut, or how might one change it so that it does?

Students then help write a "design brief," or short challenge statement, to describe the assignment of making a nicely decorated inside-out box. It reads:

Design Brief: Design and make a structure that. …

Students might fill in the words to read "Design and make a structure that is a decorated inside-out box." Please note that the best use of this activity is in the context of a need from science, social studies, or literature. Remind students that the hamster needs a temporary home, the model town requires a set of sturdy buildings, or a story character needs extra storage. Then the design brief might read:

Design Brief: Design and make a structure that is a decorated inside-out box and will make a temporary home for our hamster.

The rules, or specifications for the project, can also be written with the children's help but should include the following:

• It should have six faces.
• It should be pleasing to look at.
• It should have one face that opens and shuts.

Students can then ask questions about the design brief and specifications; "wait time" allows each item to be discussed in depth.

Once students have made a plan, they select box and unfasten the seams. When the teams have completed their structure by making an inside-out box, they evaluate the following:

• Was it difficult to turn the box inside out?
• How did partners help each other?
• Describe how the door opens and closes.
• Explain how you wish this box could be used by others.
• Show your blueprint. Explain how it looks like your inside-out box.

Teams write or dictate descriptions of their product, and the structure along with a written description is then placed in a design gallery (see fig. 4).

This use of common containers provides a link for children to connect school science with everyday technology. Also the inside-out boxes can become sturdy mailing cartons and containers for gifts. My family especially enjoys finding bright graham-cracker advertising lining the inside of the box they receive!

Fig. 4. Inside-out box "vehicles" adorn part of the display.

Resources

Fowler, Marilyn. "Containers and Boxes," In *Beginning Lessons in Engineering Design.* Austin, Tex.: Bar-None Publishing, 1993.

This book details classroom lessons in design and engineering.

Williams, Pat, and David Jinx. *Design and Technology 5–12.* Philadelphia: Falmer Press, 1985.

This book presents an overview of the design and technology approach for curriculum writers and teachers.

References

Fennema, Elizabeth, and Julia A. Sherman. "Sex-Related Differences in Mathematics Achievement, Spatial Visualization, and Affective Factors." *American Educational Research Journal* 14 (Spring 1977): 51–71. Quoted in *Handbook of Research on Mathematics Teaching and Learning,* edited by Douglas A. Grouws. New York: Macmillan Publishing Co., and Reston, Va.: National Council of Teachers of Mathematics, 1992.

———. "Sex-Related Differences in Mathematics Achievement and Related Factors: A Further Study." *Journal for Research in Mathematics Education* 9 (May 1978): 189–203. Quoted in *Handbook of Research on Mathematics Teaching and Learning,* edited by Douglas A. Grouws. New York: Macmillan Publishing Co., and Reston, Va.: National Council of Teachers of Mathematics, 1992.

Grouws, Douglas A., ed. *Handbook of Research on Mathematics Teaching and Learning.* New York: Macmillan Publishing Co., and Reston, Va.: National Council of Teachers of Mathematics, 1992.

Guay, Roland B., and Ernest D. McDaniel. "The Relationship between Mathematics Achievement and Spatial Ability among Elementary School Children." *Journal for Research in Mathematics Education* 8 (May 1977): 211–15. Quoted in *Handbook of Research on Mathematics Teaching and Learning,* edited by Douglas A. Grouws. New York: Macmillan Publishing Co., and Reston, Va.: National Council of Teachers of Mathematics, 1992.

PATRICIA F. CAMPBELL

Cardboard, Rubber Bands, and Polyhedron Models

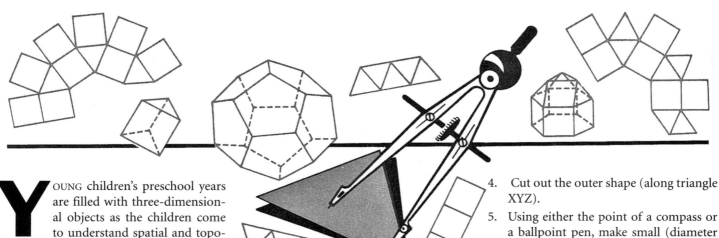

YOUNG children's preschool years are filled with three-dimensional objects as the children come to understand spatial and topological ideas. These ideas, such as nearness, order, or enclosure, are based on the child's experiences and sensory impressions of shapes and solids. However, too often early school experiences with geometric concepts are limited to plane figures. This is because solids are difficult to represent on paper or the blackboard and young children have difficulty constructing models of three-dimensional figures with cardboard and paste. The "cut and paste" method of construction also produces permanent figures that are difficult to store.

The "cardboard-rubber band" method of constructing three-dimensional models (Stewart 1970) offers a successful alternative for the elementary school. Furthermore, this method allows construction of models that have tunnels, challenging the imagination of older students. Students in the intermediate grades have sufficient dexterity to cut the necessary panels from a pattern. In the younger grades, teachers can cut a set of panels that the children can then assemble into models. The models are easily taken apart and reassembled. One or two sets of panels can be used over and

Patricia Campbell *teaches mathematics education courses at the University of Maryland, College Park, MD 20742. She is currently doing research on the learning of mathematics by elementary school children.*

over to construct many different types of solids, making this approach ideal for a learning-center activity. Storage is no problem; the panels from disassembled models and the rubber bands will fit into a manila envelope.

Preparing the Panels

To start with, triangular-shaped panels are sufficient. Later, you or your students may wish to experiment with panels in the shapes of squares, pentagons, or hexagons. The key is to make all sides of your panels, whatever the shape of the panels, the same length so you can combine them into a single solid.

The template

1. Place a piece of lightweight cardboard (either 2-ply bristol board or speech board) beneath the pattern shown in figure 1.

2. Using a sharp-pointed instrument such as a geometry compass, make an impression at each of the six labeled corners (A, B, C and X, Y, Z).

3. Remove the cardboard. Using a ruler, draw lines connecting corners A, B, and C as well as corners X, Y, and Z.

4. Cut out the outer shape (along triangle XYZ).

5. Using either the point of a compass or a ballpoint pen, make small (diameter of a pencil point) marking holes at A, B, and C (corners of the inner shape).

This template is now used to construct the panels. Children in the intermediate grades may complete the following steps themselves, but teachers of primary-grade children will need to prepare panels.

The panels

1. Place the template on lightweight cardboard.

2. Trace the outside of the template.

3. Mark the inner corners through the marking holes with a pencil or ballpoint pen.

4. Remove the template. Cut out around the outer shape you traced.

5. Using a ruler and a pencil or ballpoint pen, connect the three inner corners. Press hard when you draw these lines, as you will fold along these lines later.

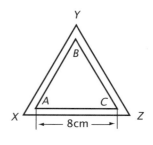

Fig. 1

6. Using a hand paper punch (1/4 inch diameter for hole), punch three holes centered over each inner corner (fig. 2a).

7. Using scissors, make two cuts toward the center of each hole. Each cut should be perpendicular to its nearest outer edge (fig. 2b).

8. Panel should now resemble figure 2c.

9. Fold up each tab along the lines connecting the holes. The panel should resemble figure 2d.

Repeat steps 1–9 until the required number of triangular panels for your models are completed. The ease of future model construction is related to the care taken in preparing the panels accurately.

Constructing a Model

A model is constructed by laying the panels side-by-side according to a pattern and by placing rubber bands over the tabs of all adjacent panels. Two-inch rubber bands work very well. As more rubber bands are added, the model takes on a three-dimensional shape. When all tabs are connected, the model is complete. Under this method of construction, the tabs are exposed. Students should be reminded that these projecting ridges are not part of the abstract forms the model represents.

Patterns for making eight different shapes of increasing complexity are given in figure 3. These models represent the eight deltahedra (plural for deltahedron). Each of these solids consists of panels or faces that are in the shape of equilateral

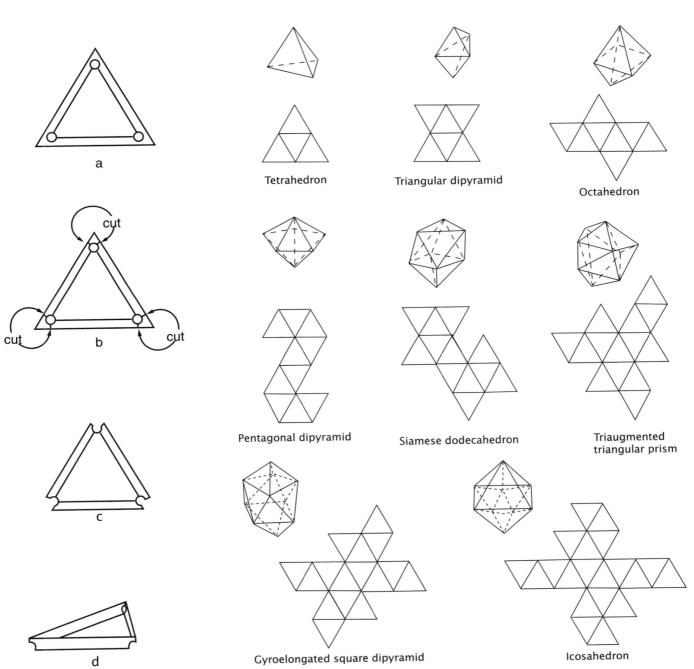

Fig. 2

Tetrahedron

Triangular dipyramid

Octahedron

Pentagonal dipyramid

Siamese dodecahedron

Triaugmented triangular prism

Gyroelongated square dipyramid

Icosahedron

Fig. 3

triangles (like the Greek letter, delta) such that no two panels are in the same plane.

More Patterns

Using the procedure just outlined, students can construct templates and panels in the shapes of squares, pentagons, and hexagons, using guides like those pictured in figures 4, 5, and 6.

The square- and pentagonal-shaped panels can be used to form a cube and a dodecahedron as patterned in figure 7. These shapes—along with the tetrahedron, octahedron, and icosahedron (patterns in fig. 3 are called Platonic solids. The panels, or faces, of each of these solids consist of one type of a regular polygon (polygons with all sides the same length and all angles the same measure). These are the only five solids that fit this description.

Students enjoy constructing models involving panels of different shapes (fig. 8). If the corners of an octahedron are chopped off, the result is the truncated octahedron. Similarly, the cuboctahedron is a cube with all eight corners chopped off. Still other patterns can be found in Wenninger (1975) or Cundy and Rollett (1954).

For those students who like challenges, the patterns in figure 9 are offered. For these models, the students construct an outer "shell" and the inner "hole" as two separate figures. The "hole" is then covered by the "shell," joining all outside edges. These models represent a type of tunneled polyhedra known as toroids.

Ideas for Classroom Use

Three-dimensional models provide the basis for many interesting activities in geometry. At the same time, students will be learning to view space as something they can understand, use, and manipulate.

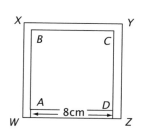

Fig. 4

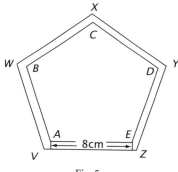

Fig. 5

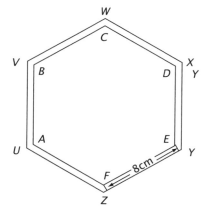

Fig. 6

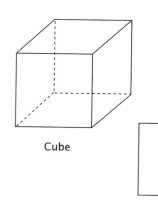

Cube

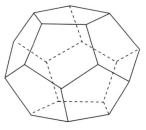

Dodecahedron

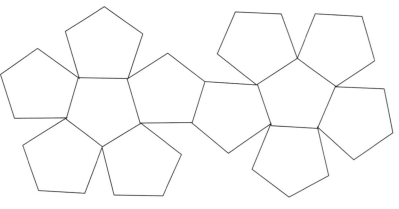

Fig. 7

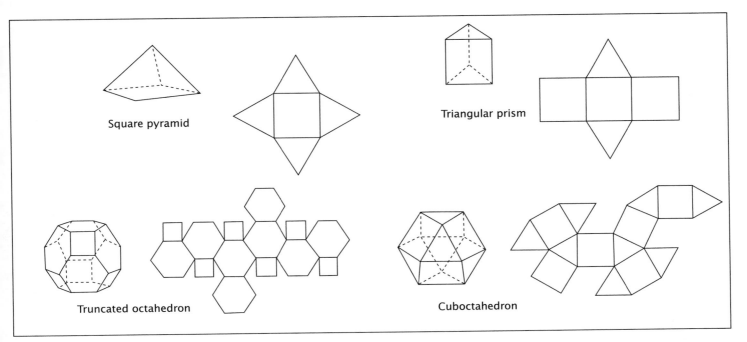

Square pyramid

Triangular prism

Truncated octahedron

Cuboctahedron

Fig. 8

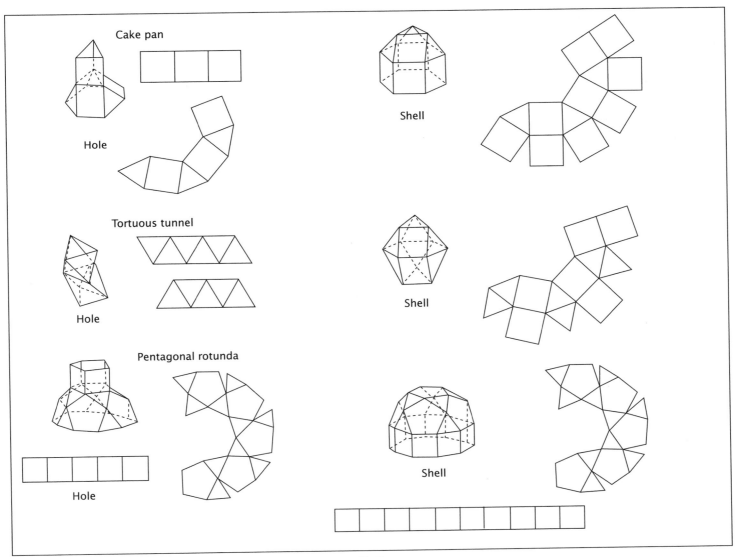

Cake pan

Hole

Shell

Tortuous tunnel

Hole

Shell

Pentagonal rotunda

Hole

Shell

Fig. 9

At the primary level, students can begin by learning to place the panels according to a pattern. Patterns made to the actual measure of the panels are necessary at this level. Examining the attributes of constructed models may also lead to a valuable discussion. Questions such as the following may provoke comment:

Are all the panels (or faces) of the model alike or different? What shape(s) are the faces? (If the children have difficulty looking at one face of a complete solid, simply loosen the rubber bands and remove the panel. The panel now provides a two-dimensional pattern that can be traced on paper, yielding a more familiar shape.)

Can you tell one corner (or vertex) apart from any other corner? How could you check your answer?

Does the model look the same or different if you look at it from the side, from the top, or from underneath the model?

How many faces does the model have? (If orientation is a problem, have as many students as necessary place one hand on each face of the model. This establishes a one-to-one correspondence between students and faces, simplifying the counting.) How many corners? How many edges?

As the children become more proficient with the models, activities aiding the transition between two-dimensional and three-dimensional representations can be devised. For example, the patterns may include pictorial images of the solids as well as the layout for the panels (as in figs. 3 and 7). The children learn to refer to the picture to check their construction. In this way the students are gradually developing the ability to identify pictorial representations for geometric solids. Further activities, such as matching patterns with solid models or pictorial representations with patterns, can reinforce this development. This matching using patterns can then be checked as the students assemble the model. Yet another technique is to present drawings of three-dimensional figures from different points of view.

The students then try to hold their models in positions corresponding to the point of view represented in the drawing.

In the middle grades, surface area and volume take on a new meaning with three-dimensional models and patterns. At the same time, concepts such as a closed surface, region exterior or interior to a closed surface, or a closed surface as the boundary of an interior region can be explored. By counting and recording the number of vertices (corners), faces (panels), and edges of each of the Platonic solids and the deltahedra, students can discover a relationship among the numbers of edges, vertices, and faces. This relationship is expressed in Euler's formula $V - E + F = 2$, where V is the number of vertices, E the number of edges, and F the number of faces.

Hanging completed models from a string not only provides decoration for the classroom but also leads to a discussion of rotational symmetry. If you hang a cube from a vertex (or a face or an edge), will it always look just the same as you rotate it through 360 degrees? What about a tetrahedron or a dodecahedron?

In the elementary school mathematics program, geometry aids children in developing their ability to describe, compare, represent, and relate objects and shapes with which they have experience in their environment. Three-dimensional models can play an important part in this development. The cardboard-rubber band method of construction provides an inexpensive means of producing self-stabilizing solids, requiring no adhesives, for the classroom.

Try some of these ideas with your students. You will be surprised by the quality of the results.

References

Cundy, Henry M., and A. P. Rollett. *Mathematical Models*. London: Oxford University Press, 1954. (Available from Creative Publications.)

Stewart, B. M. *Adventures among the Toroids*. Published by the author, 1970. (Available from B. M. Stewart, 4494 Wausau Road, Okemas, MI 48864.)

Wenninger, Magnus J. *Polyhedron Models for the Classroom,* 2d ed. Reston, Va.: National Council of Teachers of Mathematics, 1975.

13

Measurement

MEASUREMENT activities enhance the development of informal geometry in the curriculum. Students also experience the practical applications of mathematics through the study of measurement. Careful attention to this topic will further enhance the development of the concept of number.

"A Dynamic Way to Teach Angle and Angle Measure" by Patricia S. Wilson and Verna M. Adams identifies a four-step strategy for teaching angle and angle measurement. First, the concept of angle is developed, and then angles are compared. Finally, units of angle measure are explored.

Four measurement activities are presented by Robert Sovchik and L. J. Meconi from the Ideas section of the *Arithmetic Teacher*. The "Clinometer Inclines", "The Ages of Trees," "Tree-and-Pencil Measurements," and "Range Finder" represent practical, direct, and indirect measurement activities.

Barbara Skolnick Rothenberg discusses rhythm and music in mathematics. The article "The Measurement of Music" presents examples of music along with questions that relate the music to the mathematics lesson.

In K. Allen Neufeld's "Body Measurement," students use their own body measurements as data to make several calculations and to solve problems.

Jean Shaw shows how to construct student-made tools for measuring linear distance, volume, and mass. The construction of these instruments helps students learn the attributes that are being measured. Enjoy reading and trying the ideas in "Let's Do It: Student-Made Measuring Tools".

"Perimeter Patterns" by Richard A. Austing and Patricia Biafore illustrates an interesting investigation for students to try. This problem-solving activity will help students learn the concept of perimeter.

The Geometer's Sketchpad, a computer software program, is an excellent tool for analyzing geometric shapes. Michael Stone presents an activity comparing area and perimeter in "Teaching Relationships between Area and Perimeter with the Geometer's Sketchpad."

PATRICIA S. WILSON AND VERNA M. ADAMS

A Dynamic Way to Teach Angle and Angle Measure

WHAT is missing from the following definitions of a rectangle?

Sixth graders' definitions of a rectangle
- A four-sided quadrilateral
- An object with four sides
- A figure with two sets of parallel, equal lines
- Has four long sides

Eighth graders' definitions of a rectangle
- A figure with four sides that are parallel. Two sides are equal to each other and the other two are equal to each other.
- A figure that has four straight lines. Both pairs are parallel.
- A four-sided figure having two sets of parallel lines
- A closed figure with four sides
- A four-sided figure with two sides the same length

These quotations reflect the properties of rectangles that students thought were important when they were directed, "In your own words, define a rectangle." Although most students stipulated that a rectangle needed four sides and some struggled with the concept of parallel

Pat Wilson *teaches mathematics education courses at the University of Georgia, Athens, GA 30602. She develops geometry and measurement activities for elementary school students. Verna Adams is completing her doctorate at the same institution and has similar interests.*

A flexible hand-held model of an angle made from straws can be used to connect turns make with the body and turns represented on paper.

opposite sides, no mention was made of angles! The foregoing definitions are from a study involving 145 eighth graders and 143 sixth graders. Of these students, only 2 percent of the eighth graders and 1 percent of the sixth graders mentioned angles or square corners in their definitions of a rectangle (Wilson 1988). These findings may reflect a lack of attention to the concept of angle until middle school, where it is generally given an abstract treatment.

Getting students to think about angles and angle measure long before they are handed protractors and asked to verify a

given theorem was addressed by classroom teachers at an elementary school in Georgia. In this article, we draw from their experiences to show that the development of the concept of angle through a dynamic interpretation as a turn can begin in kindergarten and be part of the mathematics curriculum at every grade level. First we discuss how students learn angle concepts and outline a basic teaching strategy. The main part of the article offers a sequence of sample activities for developing the concept of angle in grades K–6.

What We Know about Children's Concepts of Angle

Piagetian research indicates that children's concepts of angle develop slowly (Piaget, Inhelder, and Szeminska 1960, 411). Students were shown two supplementary angles (fig. l) and asked to make another drawing exactly like it without looking at the model while drawing. (The figure shown to the students did not have arrowheads to indicate rays.) The student could suspend drawing and refer to the model at any time. Preschool and primary-level students (4–7 years) used *only* visual estimates to record the slant of *CD* and did not attempt to devise any way to measure the slant. Middle-grade students (7–9 years) tried to copy the slope of the slanted segment but could not devise a

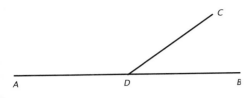

Fig. 1. Piagetian task: Make a drawing like this one.

measure that would help them. Upper-level elementary school students (9–11 years) began to identify the angle and devised some ways to compare their angles. Some older students used the lengths of $\overline{AC}$, $\overline{CB}$, and $\overline{AD}$ to locate points D and C, creating an accurate slope for $\overline{DC}$. Others drew various lines perpendicular to $\overline{AB}$ to help them approximate the slope of $\overline{DC}$.

Piagetian research raises two important points:

1. The concept of angle develops over an extended period of time.

2. A static view of an angle (line segments on a piece of paper) is difficult for young students to perceive.

We also know that students progress through different levels of understanding about geometric figures (van Hiele 1986). At first students look at angles holistically. As they begin to recognize angles, students may notice that a triangle always has three angles, or corners, but they do not focus on any particular properties of those angles. Later they understand that the measure of an angle may be smaller than the measure of a right angle (acute) or larger than the measure of a right angle (obtuse) and begin to identify properties and relationships of angles. The next step of development is to operate with such relationships as "a triangle cannot have more than one obtuse angle because the three sides must form a closed figure." From a developmental perspective, these ideas are not rules; they are understandings that students have developed from working with angles and triangles. Van Hiele's research leads to a third important point:

3. Students need good activities designed to help them explore angles and their properties and relationships.

These three ideas lend insight into how students learn about angles and have implications for curriculum and instruction.

Among the many ways to perceive of the concept, angle as a rotation, or turn, seems to be especially appropriate for instruction at the elementary school level. This way of thinking about angle allows the student to anchor the concept of angle on the concrete experience of turning her or his own body. An advantage of perceiving angle as a turn is that it counteracts students' common misconceptions that the size of the angle is determined by the length of the pencil marks used to represent the angle and that one side of the angle must be horizontal.

A Basic Strategy for Teaching Measurement

One of the most important influences on students' achievement is the opportunity to learn. Affording the opportunity to develop conceptual understanding requires a greater depth of coverage than is accorded many topics in the elementary school classroom. Geometry and measurement often receive attention only when extra time is available. To add to the bleak picture, the topic of angle and angle measurement is not usually addressed directly. If it is addressed at all, angle measurement is usually a part of a discussion focusing on triangles or polygons. We suggest that the following basic strategy for teaching measurement be used as a guideline for planning instruction and increasing the opportunities for elementary school students to learn about angle.

Several authors (Hiebert 1984; Wilson and Osborne 1988) have suggested strategies for teaching measurement that share the common elements of exploring, comparing, developing a unit, and creating formulas. These elements form the basis for the following teaching strategy, with each step extending the previous step and introducing the next step. Together the steps help students build useful concepts. It is important to cycle through the sequence several times using practical applications and activities that actively involve the students. Each cycle should give students an opportunity to learn at a deeper level. The following list summarizes the four steps as they relate to measuring angles:

1. Explore the concept of angle. What do we want to measure when we measure an angle? Measuring length, measuring volume, and measuring angles are extremely different tasks. Students are most familiar with length and often overgeneralize ideas they have learned in measuring length. Students commonly think that they can measure an angle using a ruler; they may try to measure the length of a ray or a distance between rays. We suggest that the amount of turning can be used as the attribute being measured for angles.

2. Compare angles. How can we tell if one angle measure is greater than another angle measure? The act of comparing helps students focus on the attribute being measured and should initially be done without using any particular units. This activity promotes a new perspective on the work done in step 1. When students want to know how much larger one angle measure is than another, they are motivated to move to the next step.

3. Develop a unit that can be used to measure angles. How can we compare angles using units and instruments? Develop a nonstandard unit and a tool, such as a wedge, to help make comparisons. Using several wedges, create an instrument that can be used to count units (a protractor). After the pros and cons of various units are discussed, move to degrees (the standard unit) and the traditional protractor. Students are motivated to move to the fourth step so as to make the process more efficient.

4. Observe relationships and invent rules. What rules help us count the units and apply our knowledge of angles quickly? Formulas or rules should grow out of counting strategies that students develop for themselves. Students might develop such rules as "the sum of the angle measures of a triangle is 180 degrees" or "supplementary angle measures total 180 degrees."

These four steps were the basis for the development of activities in a three-year project in which researchers at the University of Georgia and classroom teachers at South Jackson (Georgia) Elementary School worked on a K–6 geometry-and-measurement curriculum that would take advantage of what we know about students' learning and effective classroom teaching.

Several cycles of writing, piloting, and revising furnished insight into what is helpful in teaching about angles. The following activities focus on helping elementary school students progress through the first three steps of the teaching strategy outlined previously.

Activities for Learning about Angle

The activities described in this section illustrate how the perception of angle as a turn can be used to develop the concept of angle. Teachers can adapt the activities for use at different grade levels.

Exploring the concept of angle

Prior to the introduction of the concept of angle, students need experiences that will help them understand the concept. Ask the students to face the front of the room. Then ask them to try to stay on the same spot on the floor while they turn until they face the front of the room again. Identify this movement as a *full turn*. Discuss things that turn, such as doorknobs, wheels on a car, and hands on a clock. Ask the students to make a turn that is more than a full turn, then discuss how they knew that the turn was more than a full turn. Have the students face the front of the room and then turn until they face the back of the room. Ask them if they turned less than or more than a full turn. Allow them to describe the size of turn (e.g., "I went halfway around"). Then introduce the term *half-turn*. Using different walls or objects to mark the beginning of each turn, have students make other half-turns and full turns. Ask, "Do you turn more if you make a full turn or a half-turn?" How many half-turns make a full turn? Also, introduce quarter-turns through similar activities and questions and compare them to half- and full turns.

After students understand the language and relationships involved in making quarter-, half-, and full turns, introduce the idea of angle as a sweeping motion. In one second-grade classroom, for example, a student pretended to be a robot following the directions given by the other students as it searched for an object hidden somewhere in the room. The robot held an arm straight out in front to emphasize the turns. Give a quarter-turn the special name *right angle*, being alert to helping students

become aware that a right angle does not necessarily turn to the right. Students often generalize that there must be a "left angle." It is important that they realize that *right* describes the amount of turn, not the direction of turn.

Include activities that involve students in forming angles with their arms. They might, for example, use their arms to represent the hands on a clock. Have them find different ways to make right angles with their arms. They could, for example, start with both arms held straight out in front and sweep one arm to the left. One way to identify a right angle is to have a student stand at the corner of a table that has a square corner, extend both arms along one edge, and then sweep out the corner with one arm.

Turns using a flexible hand-held angle can be used to make the connection between turns made with the body and turns represented on paper. A flexible handheld angle (fig. 2) can be made by inserting sticks into a bent drinking straw and taping them securely in place. By using sticks of different lengths or by bending the straw at various points, the teacher helps students realize that the lengths of the sticks are not relevant.

Have the students use the angle to demonstrate turns by starting with both sides touching and then rotating one side (fig. 3). Holding the flexible angle in the air,

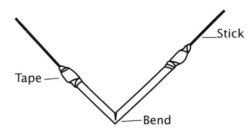

Fig. 2. A flexible angle made from a drinking straw

fourth graders easily showed right angles, angles greater than and less than a right angle, and straight angles. As students use the flexible angle, they will be constantly changing its orientation. Be sure that they notice that they have created a new angle only when they open or close the straws.

Comparing angles

Comparisons of sizes of angles can initially focus on comparisons with right angles. Have students make an angle using their arms or the flexible angle and then describe it using language appropriate to their understanding. For example, a student might say, "My angle is more than a half-turn but less than a three-quarters turn" or "My angle is less than a right angle."

Comparing angles that are close in size necessitates creating static angles so that one angle can be placed on top of the other. The flexible straw is not very useful for making such comparisons because of the difficulty of keeping it from opening or closing as it is moved. It is important to note that perceptually, dynamic and static angles are different. Students need to integrate the two types of angles as they build their concept of angle. Begin by looking at static angles that are right angles and creating a tool (e.g., the corner of an index card) for comparing angles to a right angle. The tool can be used to identify corners that have right angles, such as the corner of the room or the corner of a book. After the students have a tool for measuring a right angle, ask them to use the tool to find right angles and angles that are greater than a right angle or less than a right angle. Existing language needs to be developed to describe the situation. For example, kindergarten students said that a wedge placed in angles like those in figure 4 did not fit in angle A but did fit in angle B.

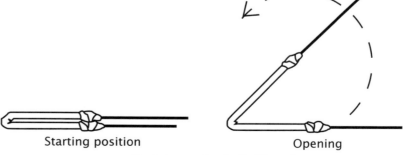

Starting position   Opening

Fig. 3. A turn using the flexible angle

Using examples, let students develop appropriate language to describe what it means to "fit." Teachers may want to talk about fitting "exactly."

Static angles are created by drawing on paper or cutting wedges of paper. A transition from the dynamic way of thinking about angles to the static way of thinking about angles can be made by asking students to represent the turns on paper. Recording turns requires that students gain a deeper understanding of the nature of angle than they have been using. Teachers should help students focus on all four components of turning that are inherent in the dynamic situation—

1. the point of turning,
2. the initial side of the angle,
3. the direction of the turn, and
4. the terminating side of the angle.

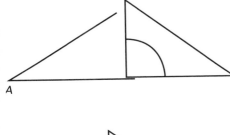

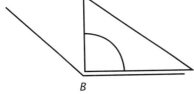

Fig. .4. Comparing a right-angled wedge to other angles

As students complete activities involving turns, these components need to be made explicit. Figure 5 shows an example of how these features of dynamic angles can be represented in static angles. The point of turning is called the *vertex* of the angle. Teachers should decide whether they want to introduce that terminology. An arrow is used for the purpose of identifying the initial side, terminating side, and direction of turn. If the initial and terminating sides are not of interest, the angle can be indicated using arcs.

The first step in an activity that makes the transition to representing angles on paper is to put a line of tape in the doorway to show the closed position of the bottom of the door. Move the door to demonstrate the swing arm of an angle. Stop the door at some point of its motion, bringing attention to the line along the bottom of the door. Use tape to mark this line on the floor (fig. 6a). Close the door and repeat the swing from the start line to the end line. Identify the point of turning. Next open the door well past the end line of the first angle so that the students can see the angle marked on the floor. Copy the angle onto a large sheet of paper at the doorway and tape it to the chalkboard (fig. 6b). Have students visually estimate the size of the angle by drawing it on smaller-sized paper at their desks. Have them compare their angle to the angle marked on the floor and the representation on the chalkboard. To do this task, they can also cut out their angle and fit it in the angle made by the door.

Have students sweep out angles and represent them on paper. Begin by taping a large piece of paper on the floor. Then tape a string from a point marked on the paper

to a point on the floor below the corner of the chalkboard. Tape strings to other objects as shown in figure 7. Each student should stand on the paper, point along a string, and sweep out an angle from the start line to another object in the room. Have students make a drawing of the angle by copying the angle marked on the floor. Label it with a description, such as "Angle from the clock to the table." After they have made several drawings, instruct the students to order the angles from smallest to largest. Ask students to identify angles that have the same amount of turn; for example, the angle from the corner of the chalkboard to the clock has the same amount of turn as the angle from the clock to the corner of the chalkboard. Have students compare their drawings to the angles represented on the floor by the strings.

To emphasize the importance of the point of turning, mark two angles whose

Students use tape to mark on the floor the line segments formed along the bottom of a door in closed and open positions, thereby demonstrating a variety of angles.

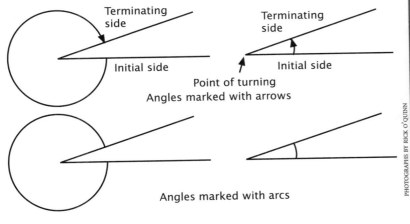

Fig. 5. Representing angles

Such manipulative devices as flexible straws and wedges can be used to introduce the concepts of angle and angle measure long before students learn to use a protractor. These students use flexible straws to measure the various angles found in a ladder-back chair.

sides point at the same objects in the room, as shown in figure 8. Using the flexible angle, have a student stand at the vertex of the angle that is farther from the objects. Have the student position the flexible angle so that the sides of the flexible angle point to the objects, matching the angle marked on the floor. Keeping the endpoints of the flexible angle aimed at the objects, have the student walk toward the second angle's ver-

tex. Ask students to think about the two angles. Did the angle increase in size or decrease? If the student were to walk even closer to the objects, would the size of the angle increase or decrease?

Students' experiences in exploring the properties of polygons furnish opportunities to deepen their understandings of angle. As students work with the static angles of geometric figures, useful comparisons can be made by tracing the angles. The language and perceptions developed in thinking about angle as a turn, however, can still be applied. In a fourth-grade classroom, for example, finding the sum of the angle measures in a triangle was posed in terms of turning. The lesson began with the teacher's first reviewing the turning concept of angle, using the flexible angle described earlier and an overhead projector, demonstrating how turning relates to the three angles in a triangle. The students were asked, "How much turning is involved altogether?" After students made several conjectures and checked their conjectures by representing the angles as wedges and putting them together, they identified the sum as a half-turn. This experience lays the foundation for middle school lessons in which students develop the idea that the sum of the angle measures in a triangle is 180 degrees.

Develop a unit for measuring angles

Measuring an angle involves a comparison between the angle and an iteration of a unit angle. The angle in figure 9, for example, has a measure of three units. Conceptualizing angle as a rotation, or turn, allows the use of the circle as a basis for forming unit angles. The circle, representing a full turn, can be partitioned into wedges in the following way. Start by giving students a cut-out circle marked in sixths and have them fold it in half along a diameter and then cut along the crease with scissors. Then using one of the halves (fig. 10), have them cut along the lines, dividing the half-circle into three equal parts. Have them fold each of the pieces in half and cut on the crease. They should have six congruent wedges that can be used to measure and draw angles.

After students have experience using the wedges to measure angles, a protractor can be created from the other half-circle (fig. 11). Have the students fold the half-circle

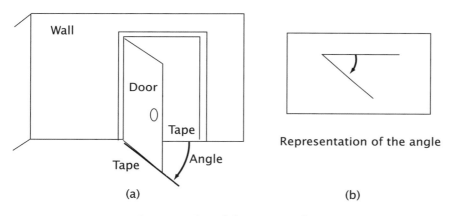

Fig. 6. An angle made by a swinging door

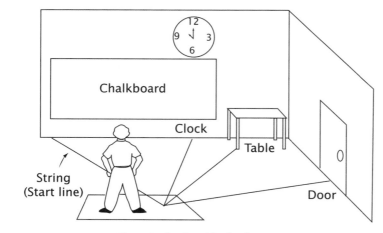

Fig. 7. Angles found in the classroom

ACTIVITIES FOR JUNIOR HIGH SCHOOL AND MIDDLE SCHOOL MATHEMATICS

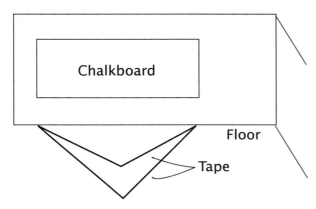

Fig. 8. Two angles that point to the same objects

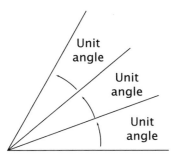

Fig. 9. Nonstandard units

into three equal parts and then fold again in half. When they open the half-circle the creases will mark the wedges. Have students use the protractor to measure angles by placing the edge of the protractor along one side of an angle with the center on the vertex of the angle (fig.12). Later students may want to add scales to the protractor to make it easier to count the number of wedges.

Have students estimate the measures of angles that are not a whole number of wedges (e.g., 1 1/2 wedges). Discuss the dif-

ficulty of determining the measures of angles that are fractional parts of a wedge. Encourage students to offer suggestions for more precise measures.

At this point students have a foundation for moving to the study of degrees and the standard protractor. Although the Babylonians are credited with developing the standard unit of degrees by dividing the circle into 360 parts, more than one theory has been advanced about why this number of parts was used (Eves 1969). Encourage students to offer reasons why 360 parts might be a good choice. Relate the degree to relationships that the students have discovered. Ask, "If a whole circle has 360 degrees (1 turn), how many degrees does a semicircle (1/2 turn) measure? How many degrees does a right angle (1/4 turn) have?" Have students determine the number of degrees in each wedge of their "wedge" protractor. Teachers may want to have them label the wedges in degrees before giving them a standard protractor.

After transition activities, fifth- and sixth-grade students are better able to learn to use a protractor. Development of the dynamic concept of angle helps students make judgments about the use of the protractor. For example, since the angle measures of 30 and 150 degrees both appear on the protractor at the same mark, students need to make a judgment about whether the angle is greater than or less than a right angle. For more ideas on using a standard protractor consult your textbook: Edwards, Bitter, and Hatfield (1990); or Wilson (1990).

Summary

Students' lack of understanding of, and attention to, the concept of angle may be a result of neglecting the topics of angle and angle measurement in the early elementary school curriculum. Often the study of angle is limited to the study of static angles and the use of a protractor. The alternative of studying angles as both dynamic and static allows students to begin developing the concept of angle in kindergarten and refine it at each grade level.

We have identified a four-step teaching strategy for planning instruction about angle and angle measure and have described activities for the first three steps: exploring the concept of angle, comparing angles, and developing a unit to measure

Fig. 10. Creating wedges

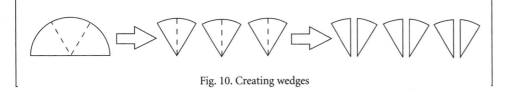

Fig. 11. Creating a protractor

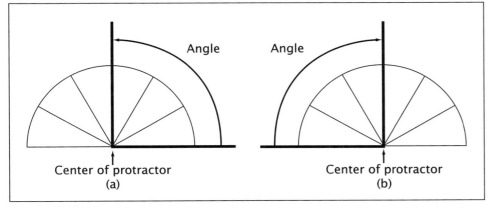

Fig. 12. Using a protractor

Measuring an angle involves the repeated use of a unit angle. as a unit measure, these students have selected wedges cut from a circle. their explorations eventually reveal the difficulty of determining the measures of angles that are fractional parts of a wedge.

angles. The extended time needed for this development requires that students actively explore angles and their properties and applications throughout elementary school. The suggested sequence lays the foundation for introducing standard angle measure, which is not established if a traditional protractor is introduced too early.

References

Edwards, Nancy, Gary Bitter, and Mary Hatfield. "Teaching Mathematics with Technology: Measurement in Geometry with Computers." *Arithmetic Teacher* 37 (February 1990): 64–67.

Eves, Howard. *In Mathematical Circles.* Boston, Mass.: Prindle, Weber & Schmidt, 1969.

Hiebert, James. "Why Do Some Children Have Trouble Learning Measurement Concepts?" *Arithmetic Teacher* 31 (March 1984): 19–24.

Piaget, Jean, Barbel Inhelder, and Alina Szeminska. *The Child's Conception of Geometry.* Translated by E. A. Lunzer. New York: Basic Books, 1960.

van Hiele, Pierre. *Structure and Insight.* New York: Academic Press, 1986.

Wilson, Patricia. "Understanding Angles: Wedges to Degrees." *Mathematics Teacher* 83 (April 1990): 294-300.

————. "Variation in Student Geometric Concepts." In *Proceedings of the Tenth Annual Meeting of North American Chapter of the International Group for the Psychology of Mathematics Education,* edited by Merlyn J. Behr, Carole B. Lacampagne, and Margariete Montague Wheeler, 119–205. DeKalb, Ill.: Northern Illinois University, 1988.

Wilson, Patricia, and Alan Osborne. "Foundational Ideas in Teaching about Measure." In *Teaching Mathematics in Grades K-8: Research Based Methods,* edited by Thomas Post, 78–110. Boston, Mass.: Allyn & Bacon, 1988.

ROBERT SOVCHIK AND L. J. MECONI

Clinometer Inclines
Levels 4–6

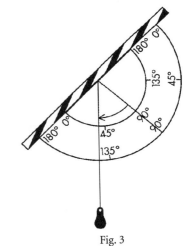

Background

Experience with angular measurement can be enriched by making a clinometer. Take a protractor and hold it upside down. Next, take a piece of string with a weight on the end, such as a fishing-line sinker. Tape the string to the middle of the inverted protractor so that the weight hangs slightly below the 90-degree mark. Finally, tape a straw to the inverted protractor to use for sighting. The completed clinometer is shown in figure 1.

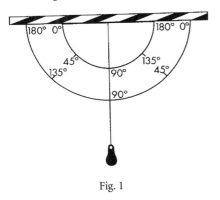

Fig. 1

A clinometer can be used to measure angles of elevation or angles of depression. When measuring the elevation of a hill, have two students who are approximately the same height work together. One student can stand at the top of the hill, the other at the bottom. The student holding the clinometer at the bottom of the hill will tilt the clinometer upward to sight the top of the partner's head through the sighting straw. As the weight moves from the 90-degree mark, the hill's angle of elevation is determined. See figure 2 for the arrangement of the children and figure 3 for a sample of a tilted protractor indicating an angle of elevation of approximately 50 degrees.

Prepared by Robert Sovchik *and* L. J. Meconi, *University of Akron, Akron, OH 44325*
Edited by John Firkins, *Gonzaga University, Spokane, WA 99258-0001*

Objectives

To connect the angular measurements to real-world observations; to practice reading a protractor; and to communicate through writing about the natural world

Materials

A copy of the activity sheet titled "Clinometer Inclines"

Protractors, straws, tape, string, scissors, weights

Directions

1. Duplicate the activity sheet titled "Clinometer Inclines" and distribute it to the class.

2. Pass out protractors and review degree readings on a protractor.

3. Have students construct a clinometer.

4. Take students outside and measure various angles of elevation and depression. If the school has no hills, have a student stand on a rung of a ladder, sit on the top of a playground slide or on the monkey bars, or look out a second-floor window.

5. Have students write a story problem referring to the hill's angle of elevation or to the angle of the elevation of the slide or the rung of the ladder.

Extensions

Students might be encouraged to investigate indirect forms of measurement useful in geometry. For example, given the angle of elevation of a building at a known distance from the building, methods exist for determining the height of the building. Small research groups can be formed to investigate these methods.

Another extension can build problem solving and communication into this activity. For example, tell students that two hills have a 45-degree and a 60-degree angle of elevation, respectively. Have students write a paragraph describing whether either or both of the hills would be suitable as sledding hills.

Fig. 3

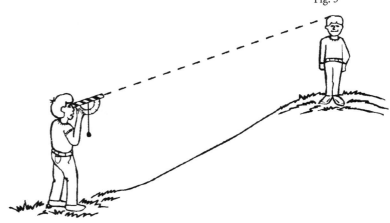

Fig. 2

Clinometer Inclines

Name _____

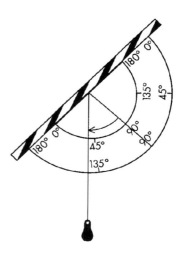

Construct your clinometer. Go outside and have your partner stand on different rungs or steps of the playground slide's ladder. Sight your partner's head with your clinometer. In the chart below, record the number of degrees from the 90-degree mark that your string and weight moved. The angle you are recording is called the *angle of elevation*. Change places with your partner and repeat your activity.

Rung	Number of Degrees I Found from 90°	Number of Degrees My Partner Found from 90°	The Difference between Our Readings
1			
3			
5			
7			

1. Were your angle measurements the same as your partner's? Why? Why not? _____

_____

2. Write a story problem about using the clinometer. _____

_____

_____

3. Measure the angle of elevation of some other items on the school playground. Measure the same item from two distances away. What do you find?

Item	Angle of elevation	Distance away

4. How does the distance away from an object affect the angle of elevation? _____

_____

ROBERT SOVCHIK AND L. J. MECONI

The Age of Trees
Levels 5–6

Background

This activity gives students experience estimating the age of trees. After identifying the type of tree, students can take a piece of string and wrap it around the tree at the student's eye level to determine the circumference. Then they can find an approximate diameter of the tree by dividing the circumference by 3.14, or an approximation of π.

The tree list on "The Age of Trees" activity sheet contains coefficients used as a multiplier of the diameter of a given tree to find an approximate age of the tree. For example, suppose a black oak has a diameter of 30 inches. Find black oak in the table and 3.5, the number corresponding to it. Obtain an estimate of the tree's age by multiplying $30 \times 3.5 = 105$, which is an estimate of the tree's age in years. Some of these coefficients were located by Myers (1951, 253) in an application activity described in

the *Mathematics Teacher*. Because these values are approximate, the actual age of the trees may vary as a result of such local conditions as soil nutrition and rainfall.

Objectives

To become aware of the natural community around the classroom; to practice decimal computation; and to investigate relationships of the circumference, π, and the diameter of a circle

Materials

String

Paper and pencil

Scissors

Calculators

Book on tree identification

"The Age of Trees" activity sheet

Directions

1. Duplicate the activity sheet.
2. Form groups of three to five students.
3. Use slides, leaves, pictures, or a preliminary walk to identify the trees near your school. Principals, custodians,

neighbors, and your students may be helpful resources.
4. Give each group a string, a copy of the activity sheet, and a calculator.
5. Review the multiplication of decimals. Students who have not yet mastered multiplication of decimals can use calculators to complete the activity. After completing the activity, conduct a follow-up discussion on the patterns found.
6. Review circle relationships, such as $C = \pi d$. Emphasize that students should find the circumference, then divide by π to obtain the diameter. Demonstrate this property with several circular objects in the classroom before measuring trees.
7. Follow up the activity with a discussion in which students share their findings.

Extensions

Discuss the types of trees found. Was one type of tree predominant? Perhaps graphing the frequency of selected trees might yield interesting information.

Prepared by Robert Sovchik *and* L. J. Meconi, *University of Akron, Akron, OH 44325*

Edited by John Firkins, *Gonzaga University, Spokane, WA 99258-0001*

The Age of Trees

Name_____

Tree	Coefficient
White elm, tulip, chestnut	2.5
Black walnut	3
Black oak, plum	3.5
Birch, sweet gum, sycamore, oak, red oak, scarlet oak, apple	4
Ash, white ash, pine, pear	5
Beech, sour gum, sugar maple	6
Fir, hemlock	7
Shagbark, hickory, larch	8

Use your string or measuring tape to find the circumference in inches of a nearby known tree. Measure the tree at your eye level. Take several measurements and use either the mode (most common measure), the median (middle measure), or the mean (the sum divided by the number of measurements) as the tree's circumference. Find the diameter of this tree by dividing the circumference by ~3.14 (π). Use the tree chart above to identify the tree type and its corresponding coefficient. Multiply this value by the diameter of the tree. This result is the approximate age of the tree.

	Tree type	Circumference	Diameter	Age
1.				
2.				
3.				
4.				
5.				

Is the largest tree always the oldest?_____

Check with other teams. Try to find someone who can validate your estimate.

346

ROBERT SOVCHIK AND L. J. MECONI

Tree-and-Pencil Measurements
Levels 5–6

Background

This indirect-measuring technique easily connects measurement to the real world of the outdoors, where practical considerations sometimes prevent direct measurement. Suppose we want to measure the height of a tree. (This approach is appropriate for flag, light, and telephone poles, also.)

Sight the top of a tree by holding a pencil vertically about 30 cm from your face. Close one eye and line up the tip of the pencil and the top of the tree. Move forward or backward until the tip of the pencil is at the top of the tree and the eraser-end of the pencil is at the bottom of the tree (see fig. 1).

Next, rotate the pencil so that it is parallel to the ground and at a right angle to the line-of-sight from your eye to the tree. Be sure that the eraser end is still visually aligned with the base of the tree. Have a partner stand away from the tree, again at a right angle to the line of sight. Have them line-up their feet with the tip of the pencil (see fig. 2). Measure the distance from the tree to your partner with a meterstick or trundle wheel. This distance is the approximate height of the tree.

Objectives

To use an indirect-measurement system to determine the height of such inaccessible objects as trees, flagpoles, or buildings; to practice measurement with a meterstick or trundle wheel

Materials

Activity sheet "Tree-and-Pencil Measurements"

Metersticks or trundle wheels

Pencils

Directions

Demonstrate the use of the pencil-sighting method by finding the height of the ceiling of the classroom. It is best to find the height at a corner of the room. Have students pair up and simulate the activity. Discuss any problems as a group. Then proceed outdoors. Have several pairs of students measure the same height (tree, flagpole, peak of roof, and so on) and compare their results. Have each pair write a summary of the experiment.

Prepared by Robert Sovchik and L. J. Meconi, University of Akron, Akron, OH 44325

Edited by John Firkins, Gonzaga University, Spokane, WA 99258-0001

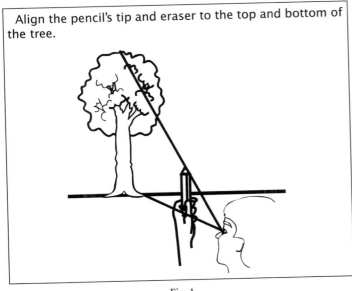

Align the pencil's tip and eraser to the top and bottom of the tree.

Fig. 1

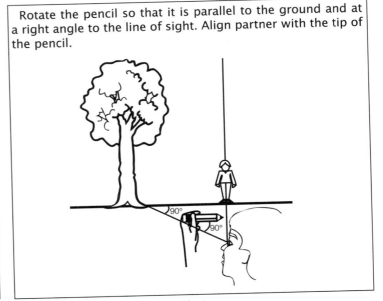

Rotate the pencil so that it is parallel to the ground and at a right angle to the line of sight. Align partner with the tip of the pencil.

Fig. 2

Tree-and-Pencil Measurements

Name_____

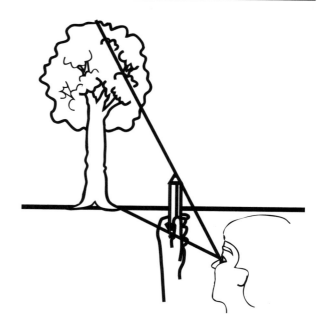

Work with a partner. Measure the height of a corner of your classroom using the directions given by your teacher. Record your results below, then swap roles with your partner and measure again. How close are you? Are your results reasonable? Are they similar to what your classmates got?

Go outside and use the same method to measure the height of something you can't measure directly—a tree, a flagpole, the rooftop, and so on. Reverse roles with your partner and measure again. Do your estimates match? Are they close? Record your results below.

1. The classroom is about _____ meters high.

2. The object we measured is a _____. Its approximate height is _____m.

Think about the following questions and write their answers.

3. What are some other things whose heights you could estimate this way?_____

    _____

    _____

    _____

4. What are some other factors that keep this method from being an accurate way to measure? _____

    _____

    _____

    _____

    _____

    _____

ROBERT SOVCHIK AND L. J. MECONI

Range Finder
Levels 7–8

IDEAS

Background

Developing proportional reasoning is an important conceptual goal. Students reason proportionally when solving percent problems and in beginning algebra. Indirect measurement also presents a way to experience proportionality. This activity offers an alternative method of indirect distance measurement. Practice in reading a ruler and computing with rational numbers are ancillary benefits of this activity.

Objectives

To use proportionality when sighting objects at different distances; to compute a solution to a proportional-measurement situation in which equal ratios are used

Materials

A paper clip and ruler for each group

Prepared by Robert Sovchik *and* L. J. Meconi, *University of Akron, Akron, OH 44325*
Edited by John Firkins, *Gonzaga University, Spokane, WA 99258-0001*

Directions

1. Give each small group a paper clip and a ruler.

2. Follow the construction directions and proportional-reasoning instructions on the "Range Finder" activity sheet.

3. Review methods for solving a proportion. For example, if $n/2 = 4/8$, $8n = 8$, and $n = 1$.

4. Take the class outside. Try several examples of indirect measurement with the class. For example, suppose a student is sighted completely at the 4-cm mark. Use a meterstick or trundle wheel to measure the actual distance from the observer to the person (see fig. 1). Next have the person move back to an unknown distance (see fig. 2). Again have the person with the range finder sight the other individual. Suppose that now the person is completely framed at the 10-cm mark; $4/6 = 10/x$ is a correct proportion with x being the distance from the person to the observer.

Simplifying, $4x = 60$; $x = 15$. So the person is situated 15 meters from the observer with the range finder.

5. Discuss this practical example of proportionality with the class.

Extension

Repeat this activity two or three times. A useful communication extension is to have students invent a situation in which this activity is used and then write a brief paragraph describing the measurement techniques used.

References

Kullmar, David E. "Mission—Measurement." *Mathematics Teacher* 60 (February 1976): 135–38.

Myers, Sheldon S. "Applications." *Mathematics Teacher* 44 (April 1951): 253.

Nelson, Doyal, ed. *Measurement in School Mathematics.* 1976 Yearbook of the National Council of Teachers of Mathematics. Reston, Va.: The Council, 1976.

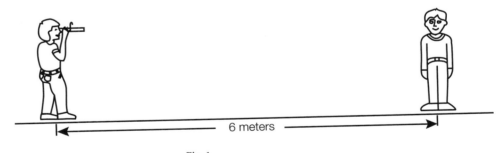

← 6 meters →

Fig. 1

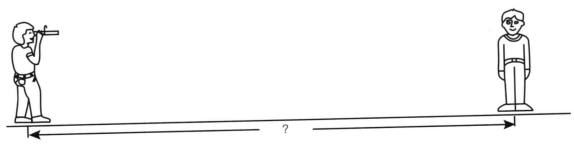

?

Fig. 2

Range Finder

IDEAS

Name_____

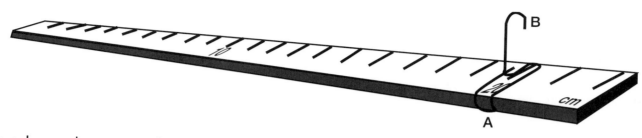

Use a ruler and a paper clip to make a range finder. Bend one end of the paper clip so that it wraps around the ruler and slides easily along its length. (See A in the diagram.) Bend the other end of the paper clip into a small semicircle. (See B.) Slide the paper clip to the 20-cm mark on the ruler. Have someone stand at the other end of the room. Adjust the semicircle so that it exactly frames the other person's face when you sight along the ruler from the zero end.

1. Determine the distance from you to your partner. Have the person come halfway back to you. Slide the paper clip to the 10-cm mark. Does the semicircle frame the face? Should it?

2. Go outside. Have a classmate stand a *known* distance from you. Sight the student completely in your range finder. Record the paper clip's position as your first sighting distance and construct the ratio of

first sighting distance:known distance

Have your classmate move farther away. Again, sight the student completely in your range finder. Your paper clip's position is your second sighting distance. Equate the two ratios and find the unknown distance.

$$\frac{\text{First sighting distance}}{\text{Known distance}} = \frac{\text{Second sighting distance}}{\text{Unknown distance}}$$

3. Try other examples with your range finder. How accurate is it? Write a paragraph describing how you determined the accuracy of your range finder. _____

_____

_____

_____

First sighting distance	Known distance	Second sighting distance	Unknown distance

350

ACTIVITY SHEET

BARBARA SKOLNICK ROTHENBERG

The Measure of Music

THESE activities are designed to appeal directly to students, giving them open-ended questions to engage their intellect through interests. Students may work on the activities individually, in pairs, or in small groups. No solutions are suggested or given so that students will look to themselves as the mathematical authority, thereby developing the confidence and critical-thinking skills necessary to validate their work.

Rhythm and music are a vital part of human culture. The integration of music into the curriculum encourages students to become actively involved in their learning. The rhythm, meter, measure, and pattern of familiar lyrics can develop academic skills and enhance many aspects of the curriculum. The activities lend themselves to the integration of mathematics and music. The activities focus on monetary problem solving, area and perimeter, and fractions. Although specific songs are cited in the activities, many other common, familiar songs may be used.

Teachers are encouraged to discuss these activities with a local music specialist, if such an individual is available, to enhance both areas of the curriculum and to follow up each activity with a meaningful class discussion. Giving students the opportunity to exchange ideas about their findings will allow them to clarify their thinking and verify their reasoning. Suggested questions to elicit this type of discussion might include these:

- What are other ways that music is influenced by mathematics?
- What other patterns can you find in other kinds of music?

Prepared by Barbara Skolnick Rothenberg, *Amherst Public Schools, Amherst, MA 01002*
Edited by Cathie Lewis, *Silvis School District, Silvis, IL 61282, and* Tom Lewis, *Moline School District, Moline, IL 61265*

- How can you use your knowledge of musical mathematics?

Teachers are encouraged to consider how these activities can be adapted from one grade level to another; coordinated with other mathematical topics; integrated with other basic school subjects, such as language arts, science, and social studies; and modified to allow for family participation in the home.

The author acknowledges the contribution of music teacher Joe Fitzpatrick of Fort River Elementary School, Amherst, MA 01002. The activities were also reviewed by George Christ, University of Dallas, Irving, TX 75062.

Activity 1

In "Take Me Out to the Ball Game," the chorus reads, "Buy me some peanuts and Cracker Jacks." Attending athletic events often includes a visit to the concession stand. Estimate how much it costs to purchase a small soft drink and popcorn, ice cream, and a bag of peanuts at a local sporting event. Calculate the actual cost. Was the actual cost higher or lower than your estimate? What could you buy with $3? Would you be able to purchase two drinks and two snacks if you had $5? Compare the cost of admission tickets and refreshments at a professional game with those for a local high school or college game.

Activity 2

A metronome is used to keep a steady beat. Set a metronome at 100 beats per minute. Each beat represents a quarter note, four beats represent a whole note. Estimate how many whole notes would be counted in one minute. Two minutes. Use the metronome to check your prediction. Think about how many half notes would be in one minute. Ask one child in a four-student team to watch the clock another to

clap the rhythm, the third to count aloud, and the fourth to write the count of the beats on paper.

Activity 3

The "Ballad of the M.T.A" by Jacque Steiner (Atlantic Music Corp.) is about a man who is stuck on a subway in Boston because he does not have enough money to pay the toll and exit. Think about the various modes of public transportation in your area and how you get from home to school. How much does your travel cost weekly? Monthly? Yearly? Plan a public-transportation system for your town. What would be the most efficient routes to schools, shopping centers, and offices? Mark the distances between stops. What is the total distance?

Activity 4

Listen to the song "In My Room" by the Beach Boys. Take the measurements of your room at home and your classroom in both metric and customary units. Calculate the perimeter and the area. Compare your room measurements with those of your classmates. Create a scale model of the rooms. Use this model to show possible furniture and seating arrangements.

K. ALLEN NEUFELD

Body Measurement

IN TEACHING the customary units of measure, the teacher risks offering two few activities that focus on measuring or on determining relationships among units. In the metric system, relationships among units are especially important and become clear to students when we offer them the opportunity to measure many familiar objects. The human body is made up of many parts that students measure with great interest. A student's knowledge of the measures of some of these body parts can be helpful in making estimates of the measures of other objects in his or her immediate environment.

Pagni (1979) describes a number of activities based on human variability. Discrete variables such as eye and hair color cannot be assigned numerical values, but students can benefit by constructing graphs that illustrate the classification according to each of these variables. Shaw (1984) presents a variety of activities based on estimates and measurements of the length of various parts of the body. A knowledge of one's own height is shown to be helpful in making an accurate estimate of the height of a door or a desk.

Such continuous variables as height and mass can easily be measured. From the measurement of height and other linear measures of different parts of the human body, one can calculate other such continuous variables as surface area and volume. An understanding of these variables can be applied to solving a number of problems relating mathematics and science.

Allen Neufeld *teaches curriculum and instruction courses in elementary mathematics and coordinates the practicum for the elementary education department at the University of Alberta, Edmonton, AB TOG 2EI. He conducts research relating mathematics and music at the kindergarten level.*

Measurements and Calculations

The following activities have been tried successfully with students from grades 4 to 9 as well as with prospective teachers and teachers at in-service sessions. The first activity is to have the student lay on her or his back (legs together and arms held close to sides) on a large sheet of brown wrapping paper while the teacher or a classmate draws a line around the student as illustrated in figure 1. Next the student lies on her or his side with arms outstretched, and

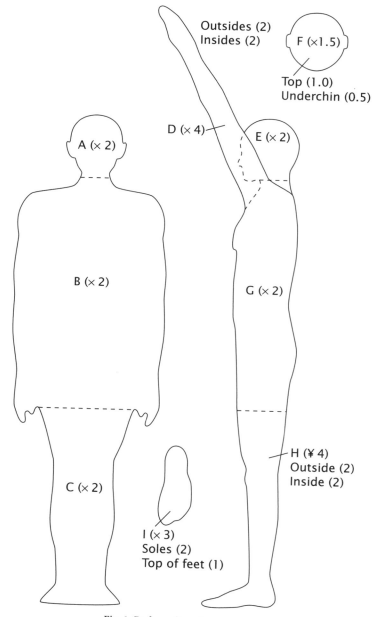

Fig. 1. Body outline chart

another sketch is made of the body in this position. Then the student kneels with the top of the head on the paper for a "head-print" drawing. Finally a drawing is made of one footprint. The pencil should be held at an inward slant to minimize error. Use a soft lead pencil to protect the student's clothing. The lines can be darkened with a felt-tip marking pen.

The next step is to use a tape measure or meterstick to make a number of linear measures of the body outline. All measures should be recorded to the nearest decimeter rounded to one decimal place. For children who aren't ready for decimal calculations, measures can be recorded in centimeters. Even though most body lines are curved, each part of the body to be measured should be considered as a rectangle. The head (A in fig. 2) is shown to have a length of 2.3 dm and a width of 1.2 dm. It is important to rectangularize each body part, as has been done with the head in figure 2, so that one obtains an average measure, not a measure of the widest or narrowest place. Calculate the approximate surface area of the front of the head (the face) by multiplying the length by the width and rounding to the nearest tenth, in this example, $2.3 \times 1.2 = 2.8$ dm². This number has been recorded on the chart in table 1. The instruction to multiply this number by 2 is based on the fact that the approximate surface area of the front and the back of the head is the same, resulting in a total of 5.6 dm².

The remaining surface-area calculations can be similarly completed for the torso and arms (B), legs (C), sides of the arms (D), sides of the head (E), top of the head (F), sides of the torso (G), sides of the legs (H), and feet (I). In some special situations

the surface area is not multiplied by 2. For each of the sides of the arms (D) and the sides of the legs (H), it is necessary to multiply by 4 because each of the two arms and legs has an "outside" and an "inside." The surface area of the top of the head should be multiplied by 1.5 to account for the area underneath the chin. The surface area of one footprint should be multiplied by 3 to account for the area of both soles and the tops of the feet between the toes and the ankles. When all these individual surface areas have been calculated, find the sum to get the total surface area.

Calculating Volume and Density

The volume of the human body can be calculated using the linear measurements already made. Imagine that a rectangular solid of each body part is being made. The surface area of the face (A in fig. 2) was calculated to be 2.8 dm². If the width, or thickness, of the side of the head (E) is 1.5 dm, then the volume of the head can be calculated to be $2.8 \times 1.5 = 4.2$ dm³, again rounded to the nearest tenth. The volume

of the torso including arms (B and G) and legs (C and H) can be similarly calculated and recorded on the chart in table 2. When all the individual volumes have been calculated, find the sum to get the total volume for the body.

After the basic measurements of height and mass have been made and the surface area and volume of the student have been calculated, a number of interesting calculations can be made including density (mass/volume), surface area/volume, height minus mass, surface area/area of one footprint, and height/mass. The statistics for each student are unique and interesting to the student being measured. Of more general interest are number patterns indicated by the measurements and calculations for a group of students of the same age, a group of students of ages differing by one year, or a particular student at different ages. The data in table 3 illustrate the latter situation in which measurements of the author's daughter were taken at three-year intervals. The data suggest that whereas most numbers increase with the age of the person being measured, some remain nearly constant, and one set of data shows a decrease with age. Students can be asked to speculate on the reasons for the increase, stability, and decrease as indicated for particular variables.

Table 1

Body Surface Area Chart

Body parts					Approximate surface area
Head, front and back (A)	2.8	×	2	=	5.6
Torso, front and back (B)	___	×	2	=	___
Legs, front and back (C)	___	×	2	=	___
Arms, sides (D)	___	×	4	=	___
Head, sides (E)	___	×	2	=	___
Head, top and under chin (F)	___	×	1.5	=	___
Torso, sides (G)	___	×	2	=	___
Legs, sides (H)	___	×	4	=	___
Feet, top and bottom (1)	___	×	3	=	___
		The approximate total surface area is			___ dm².

Table 2

Body Volume Chart

Body part	Surface area		Thickness		Volume
Head (A)	2.8	×	1.5	=	4.2
Torso (B)	___	×	___		___
Legs (C)	___	×	___		___
The approximate total volume is _					___ dm³.

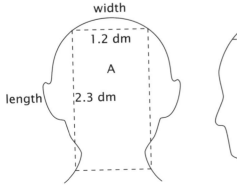 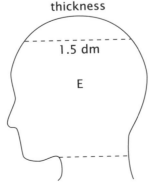

Fig. 2. Example measures of length, width, and thickness

width

1.2 dm

A

length 2.3 dm

thickness

1.5 dm

E

Table 3
Data for One Child at Three Ages

Age (years)	10	13	16
Height (cm)	140	160	171
Mass (kg)	31	52	65
Surface area (dm²)	110	150	175
Volume (dm³)	41	67	79
Footprint area (dm²)	1.4	1.7	2.0
Mass/volume (density)	0.76	0.78	0.82
Surface area/volume	2.7	2.2	2.2
Height-mass	109	108	106
Surface area/footprint area	78.6	88.2	87.5
Height/mass	4.5	3.1	2.6

Problems Related to Body Measurement

An understanding of density and surface area can lead to the solution of several problems relating mathematics and science. Why do babies float more easily than older children or adults? One of the students in a teacher-education course volunteered to do the series of measurements on her four-year-old child. The density of the child was calculated to be 0.52 (kg/dm³), considerably less than the densities of older children as indicated by the chart in table 3. It is generally accepted that the density of an adult peaks at approximately 0.95. Since the density of water is 1.0, anything with a density greater than 1.0 would sink in water.

The following problem was posed by Lange (1975): "Why can a fly sit on the surface of water in a pail while it would be drowned if it flew into a shower of water?" Since the fly has a density of approximately 0.25, it is very buoyant. The surface area of a fly is approximately 0.6 cm³. Since the water covering the surface area of anything in a shower is approximately 0.05 cm in thickness, the amount of water surrounding the fly is 0.03 cm³ and has a mass of 0.03 g. Since the mass of the fly itself is only one-third of the mass of water clinging to its body, little doubt remains as to why the fly's life is in danger where it ventures into a shower of water. When one poses similar problems about a human walking on water or taking a shower, the results are completely opposite. A human has difficulty floating because the body's density is close to the density of water. A human is not affected adversely in a shower, however, because the mass of the water that clings to the body is approximately one-hundredth of the mass of the body.

Eicholz, O'Daffer, and Fleenor (1976) described another set of interesting relationships that exist between the lengths of the major bones of the body and the height of the body. Use the chart in figure 3 to determine the height of a student by measuring each of the following bones: humerus (upper arm), radius (lower arm), femur (upper leg), and tibia (lower leg). Compare each of the estimates of height with the actual height of the student. Anthropologists, using a single bone from a human skeleton, can estimate quite accurately the height of a man or woman who lived many centuries ago. It might be interesting to have students consider whether these relationships have changed from the time of the cave person to the present.

Using a Nomogram

One of the first activities described was to find an approximate measure of the surface area of a human body. Medical doctors DuBois and DuBois (1916) used a nomogram like the one illustrated in figure 4 for finding the surface area of a body when treating burn victims. As an example, a line has been drawn joining a height of 150 cm on the left scale with a mass of 60 kg on the right scale. According to the place where the line crosses the middle scale, a person with this height and mass has a surface area of 1.55 m², which is equivalent to 155 dm². After finding the surface area of a student by measuring the area inside the body sketch on the large sheet of brown paper, compare the findings to the result obtained from using the nomogram. Usually the former procedure yields a larger surface area than the nomogram. The former method, however, has the advantage of offering much experience in relating linear measure to surface measure to volume measure.

Some students can benefit from the building of model bodies. Strips of brown paper tape usually used for wrapping parcels can be used to represent the circumference of the body at various points. For example, the paper tape wrapped around the head at the forehead can be made to form a loop by moistening and sticking together the ends. This loop can then be fastened to a dowel representing the backbone. Similarly, loops can be made to model the circumference of the body at the neck, chest, waistline, stomach, hips, and various points on the arms and legs. To give some stability to the model, vertical strips of moistened tape can be used to connect the various horizontal loops. Since life-sized models require a large amount of tape, it may be desirable to introduce models constructed to a scale of 2:1, 5:1, or 10:1. Using the latter scale, the circumference of a forehead that is actually 60 cm would be represented by a 6-cm tape.

Another type of body model can be constructed from centimeter cubes using the scale of 1 dm = 1 cm. The model illustrated in figure 5 is based on the measurements of the ten-year-old student that are given in table 3. The height of 14 dm is represented by a height of 14 cm. The width of the body from shoulder to shoulder, which is approximately 4 dm, is represented by four cubes having a total width of 4 cm.

Summary

Students' measures of their own bodies can enhance the teaching of measurement. The activities described in this article are based on the concrete, pictorial, and abstract modes of instruction. The human body is translated into a sketch or picture that becomes the basis for a series of measures that are recorded as abstract numerical symbols. Relationships like the one

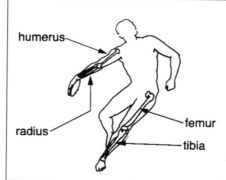

Male
(2.9 × length of humerus) + 70.6
(3.3 × length of radius) + 86.0
(1.9 × length of femur) + 81.3
(2.4 × length of tibia) + 78.7

Female
(2.8 × length of humerus) + 71.5
(3.3 × length of radius) + 81.2
(1.9 × length of femur) + 72.8
(2.4 × length of tibia) + 74.8

Fig. 3. Height based on the length of major bones

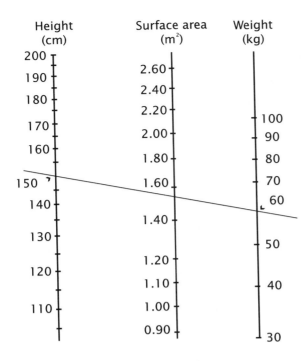

Fig. 4. Nomogram for finding body surface area

expressed by the formula for density (mass/volume) are more readily understood when students are able to see the connections between the numerical symbols and the human bodies of themselves and their classmates that furnished the initial sources for the symbols.

References

DuBois, Delafield, and Eugene F. DuBois. "A Formula to Estimate the Approximate Body Surface Area if Height and Weight Be Known." *Archives of Internal Medicine* 17 (June 1916): 865–71.

Eicholz, Robert E., Phares G. O'Daffer, and Charles R. Fleenor. *School Mathematics 1.* Reading, Mass.: Addison-Wesley Publishing Co., 1976.

Lange, Muriel. *Geometry in Modules, Book B.* Reading, Mass.: Addison-Wesley Publishing Co., 1975.

Pagni, David L. "Applications in School Mathematics: Human Variability." In *Applications in School Mathematics,* 1979 Yearbook of the National Council of Teachers of Mathematics, edited by Sidney Sharron and Robert E. Reys, 43–58. Reston, Va.: The Council, 1979.

Shaw, Jean M. "IDEAS." *Arithmetic Teacher* 32 (December 1984): 20–24.

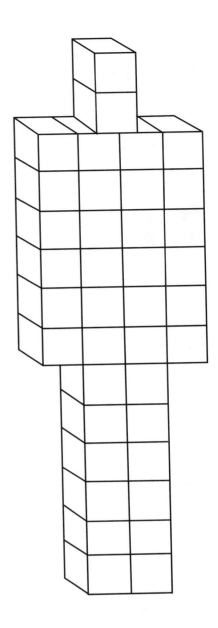

Fig. 5. Body model from centimeter cubes

JEAN M. SHAW

Student-Made Measuring Tools

Mr. Kevin, a fifth-grade mathematics teacher, strongly believes that measurement should be taught using hands-on activities, but he has only two metersticks, three tape measures, and one balance scale in his room. Ms. Williams, a second-grade teacher, wants her pupils to measure objects to the nearest centimeter. She finds, however, that the rulers the children buy, calibrated in millimeters, confuse many of the children. If these teachers worked with their students to make their own measuring devices, they would find partial answers to their dilemmas.

When students make their own measuring devices, they produce valuable tools to use in measuring experiences. They learn much about the units of measurement as well as take pride in the measuring tools they have made themselves. Students can use their materials to share some of the skills they are mastering with their families.

Measuring Tools and Activities

Decimeter strips

Reproduce a decimeter strip (fig. 1) for each student. Have the students cut them out carefully, leaving the corners as straight and even as possible. Have the students label the strip *1 decimeter* and *1 dm*.

Have students look in their desks and pockets and around the classroom for objects close to 1 dm in size. Have students hold their 1-dm strips next to objects to compare their sizes. Let students show each other objects that have one dimension of 1 dm or close to 1 dm. Now have students fill in a chart on the chalkboard listing objects that have measurements less than 1 dm, approximately 1 dm, and greater than 1 dm. Ask students to find and discuss some

Jean M. Shaw, *University of Mississippi, University, MS 38677*

Fig. 1. A decimeter strip

body parts that have a length close to 1 dm. Finally, as homework, ask students to use their decimeter strips at home to find objects close to 1 dm in one dimension. They can share their results in a class discussion, or they can bring objects to school to show to their classmates.

Centimeter strips

Reproduce a 10-cm strip for each student. Have students color every other section of their strips (fig. 2) and number each section. Lead students to compare their decimeter strips to their 10-cm strips. Develop the idea that 10 cm = 1 dm and have students label their strips *10 cm = 1 dm*. Ask students to work in groups to collect several small objects, estimate the length of each object in centimeters, and then use their strips to measure each object in centimeters.

Meter tapes

Have each student make a meter-long measuring tape from ten 1-decimeter sections. Reproduce the pattern shown in figure 3. Have students color five of the decimeter sections and leave the other five blank. Students should carefully cut out each section and overlap and tape them together end to end, alternating colored and blank sections. Have students number each decimeter section and carefully reinforce the joints with more tape.

When the tapes are completed, review the idea that 10 dm = 1 m; each student has just made a concrete representation of this idea. Have students compare the lengths of their tapes with a machine-produced meterstick. Talk about the reasons for slight variations in lengths.

Discuss some instances where measuring with a tape is easier than measuring with a flat ruler. Students might mention body parts and objects with curved edges. Let your students suggest a list of things they could measure with their tapes. Ask students to work in pairs and choose ten items from the list to estimate and measure. Students might use their meter tapes to get approximate measures of their waists, ankles, heads, or shoulders. They might measure classroom objects such as books, furniture, the perimeter of the television screen, or the circumference of large containers. Let students discuss any objects they found that were longer than 1 m, shorter than 2 dm, or about 1/2 m. Assign homework involving use of the meter tapes to measure people or objects.

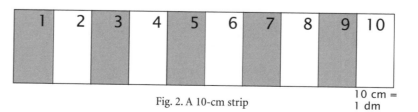

Fig. 2. A 10-cm strip

10 cm = 1 dm

Use this section for overlap.

Use this section for overlap.

The finished tape will look like this.

Fig. 3. A meter tape

Calibrated measures of volume

Show students how to use a standard of volume to calibrate a transparent or translucent plastic container. To illustrate the idea, cut the top off a plastic bottle with heavy scissors, as shown in figure 4. Tape a piece of masking tape to the bottle. Use a standard measuring cup calibrated in 25 mL intervals. Fill the standard measure with water. For your demonstration you might add a few drops of food coloring to the water to make the water level easy to see. Carefully pour 25 mL of water into the bottle. Mark the 25 mL water level on the masking tape. Pour another 25 mL of water into the bottle and mark the 50 mL level on the tape. Continue the process until the bottle is calibrated as far as possible. If the bottle's sides are curved, the calibrations will not be equally spaced. If the bottle has straight sides, the calibration marks should occur at even intervals.

Have students help you to calibrate a larger container, such as a large milk jug of translucent plastic. For a large container, use a larger unit for calibration; 500 mL units would be appropriate for a large jug. You could calibrate a gallon milk jug from 500 mL to 3000 mL, or 3 L. Use scissors to trim the milk jug (fig. 4) to make a large convenient opening. Use a ball-point pen or permanent markers to mark the units on tape attached to the side of the milk jug.

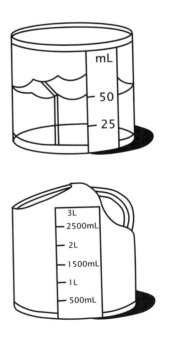

Fig. 4. Calibrated containers

357

Ask students to bring in a plastic container suitable for calibration. Let pairs of students work to calibrate their containers, using either measuring cups or calibrated laboratory measures as standard measures.

When all the students have finished a calibrated measure of volume, set up a laboratory session during which students can use their measures. Ask students to estimate and measure the volumes of various containers of water, sand, rice, and styrofoam bits. Have students take their measures home to find the volumes of containers such as cans, soup bowls, mixing bowls, or even the kitchen sink! As a sharing experience, ask students to write the volumes of several household objects on paper. Let students take turns placing their papers on a bulletin board such as the one shown in

figure 5. Measures of volume will become meaningful as students learn to associate them with familiar objects.

A balance scale

You can make a fairly sensitive balance scale with these materials: a half-gallon milk carton, an inexpensive ruler, two spring clothespins, a piece of metal coat hanger, two styrofoam cups or small aluminum pans, some sand, some yarn, and two paper clips. The ruler should have three to five holes already drilled in it. Many inexpensive rulers sold in variety or school-supply stores have holes for easy insertion into a notebook. These rulers are ideal for making the balance scale.

Have students work together in groups of four to make the balance scale. Help students cut a straight section of a wire coat hanger 15-20 cm long. Show them how to assemble the balance scale (fig. 6) by clipping a clothespin to the top of the milk carton, inserting the piece of wire through the hole in the clothespin's spring, putting the ruler on the wire through the middle hole, and finally, clipping on the second clothespin to hold the wire in place. Next, have the students insert a partially opened paper clip in each end hole of the ruler to hold the cups onto the balance scale. Have the students check the scale and see if the ruler hangs in a horizontal position. If the ruler hangs too low on one side, the students can balance it by adding a tiny piece of tape to the higher end.

Students can construct the cups for the balance scale by carefully punching three equally spaced holes in the tops of two styrofoam cups or small aluminum pie pans.

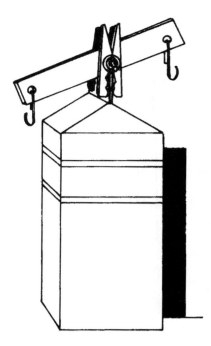

Fig. 6. A balance scale

They should insert yarn through the holes and carefully tie the yarn together at the top to support each cup (fig. 7). Students should hang the empty cups on the paper-clip hangers. Once again, students should check to see that the ruler hangs in a horizontal position and make necessary adjustments if it does not.

Students can use standard masses to establish the masses of some readily available materials that would be appropriate for balancing objects on the scale. If you do not have plastic or brass masses marked in units of 1 g, 2 g, 5 g, 10 g, and 25 g, a teacher in your district's junior or senior high school science department may be able to loan you some. Students will see that objects such as small paper clips or one

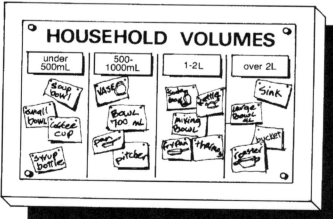

Fig. 5

Fig. 7. Styrofoam cups or aluminum pie pans can be used for balances.

raisin have a mass of approximately 1 gram and that a nickel has a mass of about 5 grams. These objects can be used as standards for subsequent measuring activities.

Have students work in groups and gather small objects to weigh on the homemade balance scale. Each group of four students should select at least ten objects. They should record or estimate the mass of each object, then place it in one cup of the balanced scale. Next they should carefully add to the other cup the small objects they have gathered to use as standard masses. When the cups balance, the students can count the standard masses and determine the approximate mass of their small objects. For most students, much practice in estimating masses is necessary before well-developed mental images of masses are established. You will want to have groups of students use their balance scales for many other experiences dealing with mass.

Conclusion

Student-made measuring tools are not substitutes for finely calibrated, precisely made manufactured tools, but their economy and the lessons learned in constructing them makes them valuable aids in the elementary school mathematics classroom.

359

RICHARD R. AUSTIN AND PATRICIA BIAFORE

Perimeter Patterns

THE following geometry activity featuring the concept of perimeter was carried out over one week in a fifth-grade class. As the students worked in small groups, they explored mathematics in ways aligned with the *Curriculum and Evaluation Standards for School Mathematics* for grades 5–8 (NCTM 1989). Throughout the description of this activity, connections between tasks that students performed and the curriculum and evaluation standards are noted to highlight how several standards can be connected in a classroom activity.

The perimeter activity illustrates a rich problem-solving situation that engaged students' attention and involved them in mathematics as communication (standard 2) and mathematics as reasoning (standard 3). The students were communicating their ideas to one another, offering different ways to represent the patterns, and reasoning together to arrive at a conclusion and complete their tasks. As the students expanded their original perimeter-review problems, they actually made mathematical connections (standard 4) as they applied concepts from algebra to find accurate solutions. Thus, this problem-solving activity embodies the spirit of the *Standards* document.

Launching the Activity

During the first stage of the activity, the students were led in a review of the concept of perimeter. The students practiced measuring the various objects to be used later in the activity (measurement, standard 13). The students quickly discovered that the figures were all regular polygons (geometry, standard 12) and that they could compute the perimeter simply by measuring

one side and then multiplying that measurement by the number of sides.

The Groups' Tasks

With the review completed, the class was divided into groups of four students. Each group received a geometry-experiment card. The cards had similar tasks (problem solving, standard 1). The only difference from one group to the next was the geometric shape assigned (see fig. 1). For this activity, the length of a side for each basic shape was defined as one unit.

Several groups initially assumed that they could draw the problem situation and count the exposed unit sides to find the perimeter. It soon became evident to the

students that this approach would be neither an easy nor an efficient method for solving this type of problem. At this point the teacher discussed the possibility of constructing a "progression chart." Each group also had a set of geometric-shaped manipulatives to use in developing the charts (see fig. 2). When individual shapes were linked to form the next figure in the progression, only the exposed sides were counted as units to find the perimeter. As students modeled their situations, a visual pattern slowly emerged (patterns and functions, standard 8).

The students reviewed their initial efforts using the shape manipulatives and constructed their progression charts. Each

Richard Austin *teaches at the University of South Florida, Tampa, FL 33620.* Patricia Biafore *teaches at Carwise Middle School, Palm Harbor, FL 34684.*

Sample task cards

Geometry Experiment #1
If you lined up 100 equilateral triangles in a row, with one side touching, what would the perimeter measure if each side was 1 unit in length?

Geometry Experiment #4
If you lined up 100 regular hexagons in a row, with one side touching, what would the perimeter measure if each side was 1 unit in length?

Fig. 1

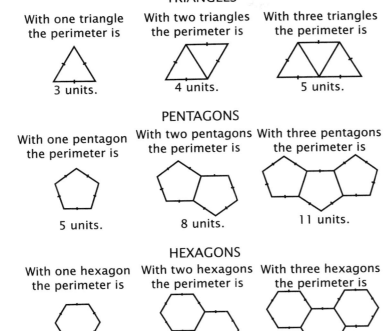

TRIANGLES

With one triangle
the perimeter is

3 units.

With two triangles
the perimeter is

4 units.

With three triangles
the perimeter is

5 units.

PENTAGONS

With one pentagon
the perimeter is

5 units.

With two pentagons
the perimeter is

8 units.

With three pentagons
the perimeter is

11 units.

HEXAGONS

With one hexagon
the perimeter is

6 units.

With two hexagons
the perimeter is

10 units.

With three hexagons
the perimeter is

14 units.

Fig. 2. Pattern samples

group was responsible for creating a chart on the basis of their visual findings with manipulatives. This chart was to be displayed later when the group made its presentation to the class. Each group was then challenged to extend the pattern to find the perimeter for any number of congruent shapes in terms of n, where n is the number of shapes, as well as for the full 100 shapes. For many students this part of the activity was the most difficult, and it generated considerable discussion within the groups. It was important that the students connect this part of the activity to the progression charts.

In an effort to ensure that all students were actively involved in the exercise, each student created his or her own chart, even though only one chart per group would be selected for display. See figure 3. This simple perimeter-review exercise had expanded to include number patterns and algebraic variables.

After students completed the final details of their charts, they measured and drew their shapes on colored paper. The shapes were cut and mounted on tagboard as a visual aid for use later when the group explained how the shapes helped them solve their problem.

For the final phase of this activity, each group graphed the results of its investigation on graph paper. See figure 4. The teacher reviewed graphs and emphasized where the information should be placed. A common question within the groups was "How many points do we have to put in the graph?" In keeping with the spirit of group-exploration tasks, the teacher responded that although the number of points was a group decision, students must be sure that their graphs accurately represented what the group actually found.

An interesting observation was made by only a few students in one group: the graph could be used to find the solution to the earlier question of the perimeter of the

shape with any number of pieces, n. This group was encouraged to make that point during their presentation to the class, since it was not mentioned by other groups during their discussions while constructing their graphs.

As had been done with the charts, each student plotted a graph of data points and found a noticeable linear pattern. See figure 4. From each group, one graph was chosen for later display to the class.

Solving Similar Problems

Student groups then rotated task cards and attempted to solve another group's problem. This process gave students another opportunity to practice the methods they had been using. The students noticed that patterns were different for different shapes. Although the groups were asked only to construct a progression chart using the manipulative shapes, some groups found the new patterns quickly enough to have sufficient time to graph the new findings.

Finally, show time arrived! Each group was given five minutes and the use of the overhead projector to demonstrate how its pattern developed and to display the group's work to the class. The similarities and differences in each group's graphs and display materials were noted by other students in a whole-class discussion following the presentations.

Extending the Learning

This activity offers from actual classroom practice an example of how different curriculum standards can be viewed as connected rather than as individual units to be covered in isolation. The general format used in this activity could easily be extended to an exploration of regular polygons for which students are not likely to

Triangles	1	2	3	...	n	100
Number of sides (perimeter)	3	4	5	...	$n + 2$	102

Squares	1	2	3	...	n	100
Number of sides (perimeter)	4	6	8	...	$2n + 2$	202

Fig. 3. Sample progression charts

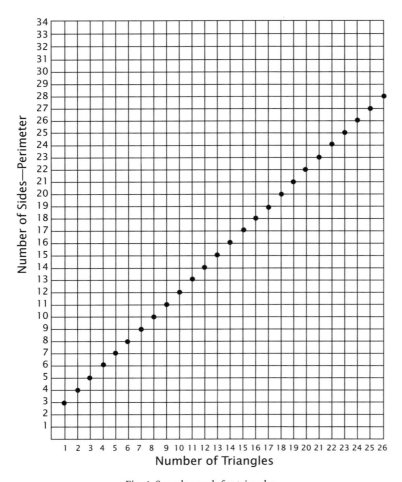

Fig. 4. Sample graph for triangles

have concrete manipulatives, such as heptagons, nonagons, decagons, and dodecagons. This type of investigation could extend to considering the relationships of the area of polygons to the length of the sides as the sides double or triple. Along this line, students could investigate similar polygons, comparing the ratio of the lengths of the sides with the perimeter and the area of the figures. Students could expand into three-dimensional investigations, working with the volume of cubes as the length of the sides increases. These suggestions are only a few of the possible extensions that could build from this activity.

Reference

National Council of Teachers of Mathematics. *Curriculum and Evaluation Standards for School Mathematics*. Reston, Va.: The Council, 1989.

M I C H A E L   E .   S T O N E

Teaching Relationships between Area and Perimeter
with the Geometer's Sketchpad

THE question "What shape will have the largest area for a given perimeter?" identifies an important relationship between area and perimeter that has long been intuitively realized in many cultures. Zaslavsky points out that numerous cultures make practical use of this relationship between area and perimeter: cylindrical houses in West Africa, beehive houses of the Chagga people of Mount Kilimanjaro, and hemispherical igloos of the Eskimo people. While struggling to cope with their environments, all these cultures used available materials to build dwellings with shapes that maximized floor space. Since perimeter is limited by the available materials, determining what shape will have the largest area is very important to people who find materials difficult to work with or hard to obtain. Mathematics is integrally related to social studies and architecture (Zaslavsky 1989, 19). The purpose of this activity is to go beyond intuition and instill a conceptual understanding of relationships between area and perimeter.

The answer to the foregoing question is neither trivial nor intuitively obvious. The following example illustrates a common misconception about this relationship between area and perimeter. When finding the area of irregular figures (fig. la), some students may be convinced that by using a string they could form a circle (fig. 1b) with the same perimeter as figure la. They leap to the assumption that

area (fig. la) = area (fig. 1b) = πr^2.

This error results from assuming that fig-

ures of the same perimeter have the same area. Woodward and Byrd found that almost two-thirds of the subjects in a study of eighth-grade students believed that rectangles with the same perimeter occupy the same area (Woodward and Byrd 1983). They concluded that the traditional formula-based approach is not effective in instilling conceptual understanding.

How are these relationships best taught? What tools should be used? During the construction of their beehive houses, the Chagga people in Africa draw circles using a rope with a peg at one end and a hoe at the other end (Zaslavsky 1989, 21). Although this method is ingenious and practical for the situation and application, it bogs down if drawing many sizes and shapes is desired to find patterns. Clearly, discovering the relationships between area

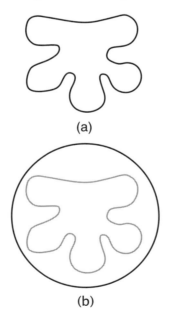

(a)

(b)

Does the area of (a) equal the area of the circle in (b)?

Fig. 1

and perimeter would be difficult with such simple tools. Although counting squares of centimeter-squared paper to compare areas of figures is beneficial, as Zaslavsky suggests, the process laboriously slows down the discovery of the relationship being studied.

To facilitate pattern finding, The Geometer's Sketchpad (Jackiw 1991) affords students the means to draw figures and calculate area and perimeter quickly and simultaneously. Figures can be transformed by dragging corner points to change the shapes. As corner points are dragged, the figure transforms in a fluid motion on the screen, as if part of a television picture. Calculations of area and perimeter are instantaneously displayed and change as the figure transforms. Students may stop the transformation at will, holding either the perimeter or the area constant. The Geometer's Sketchpad eliminates estimating the size of part squares or bogging down in calculations while losing sight of the purpose. Students are able to make conjectures and explore, using the computer as a vehicle to express their thoughts, verify their ideas, test their conjectures, and make generalizations and connections. These skills are essential for students to be competent solvers of inquiry problems (Chazen 1990). The Geometer's Sketchpad has all the characteristics of what Schwartz (1989) would term "intellectual mirror" software, which encourages students to "make mathematics." This article describes an activity in which students discover relationships between area and perimeter.

Woodward and Byrd (1983) also suggest activities that should precede the method presented in this article: (1) In early grades, area activities should involve covering a region with small subregions and deter-

Before teaching at the Federal Correctional Institution, Estill, SC 29918, Michael Stone *taught at Robert Smalls Middle School, Beauport, South Carolina. His interests include technology in mathematics education and teacher education.*

mining its area by counting these subregions. (2) Using graph paper, dot paper, and geoboards may reinforce the concept of area while differentiating it from the concept of perimeter. The learning environment must include movements, patterns, images, and actions. Only then can the following methods be effective and result in a firm conceptual understanding of the relationships between area and perimeter.

A Classroom Activity

The following classroom activity was highly successful with twenty-six eighth-grade middle school students in a first-year-algebra class. These students previously worked with the concepts of area and perimeter and performed calculations involving the formulas for squares, nonsquare rectangles, triangles, and circles. Students also had some familiarity with the Macintosh computer. Students worked in groups of two or three, with the teacher available to guide them in their struggle to discover.

The objective of the activity was to help students achieve a deeper understanding of the concepts of area and perimeter and their relationships. Students were given two or three class periods to answer the following questions:

1. For all *n*-gons with the same perimeter (let *n* be some positive integer), what shape will have the greatest area?

2. For all *n*-gons with the same area, what shape will have the smallest perimeter?

3. For all figures with the same perimeter, what shape will have the greatest area?

4. For all figures with the same area, what shape will have the smallest perimeter?

The class began by discussing the importance of knowing the meaning of *area* and *perimeter* and by relating the concepts to agriculture, architecture, and social studies. The class then examined the following problem:

Problem: The perimeter of field A is 64 units, and the perimeter of field B is 64 units. Which field will require more fertilizer? (See fig. 2.)

As in the Woodward and Byrd (1983) study, many students related area and perimeter incorrectly by indicating that

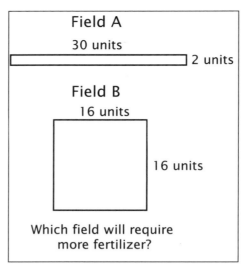

Fig. 2

both fields would require the same amount of fertilizer. After prompting, the students calculated the areas of both fields and found that figure B requires considerably more fertilizer.

Solution

Field A	Field B
P = 64 units	P = 64 units
A = 60 square units	A = 266 square units

Therefore, field B requires more fertilizer.

Questions 1–4 were posed to students. Two or three students were assigned to each cooperative learning group and had access to The Geometer's Sketchpad software and a Macintosh personal computer. The software constitutes an electronic toolbox, enabling students to draw points, lines, polygons, or circles easily and to create the desired figure conveniently. Subsequently, students explored their ideas and conjectures about the relationship between perimeter and area. Students were guided with such thought-provoking questions as "What happens if you change the number of sides?" or "What happens if you flatten this shape?"

Students were given one worksheet, similar to the one in figure 3, for each question,

---

Relationships between Area and Perimeter

Objective: To achieve a deeper understanding of the concepts of area and perimeter and their relationships

Question: For all *n*-gons with the same perimeter (let *n* be some positive integer), what shape will have the greatest area?

Conjecture: Write a statement that you think accurately answers the foregoing question.

_____

_____

_____

_____

Use the table below to investigate:

Figure	No. of Sides	Dimensions	Perimeter (cm)	Area (cm²)

Write a concluding true statement or generalization on the basis of your findings.

_____

_____

_____

_____

Fig. 3. Students used this worksheet to organize the information they gathered during their investigation.

which helped them organize their ideas, inferences, conjectures, or generalizations. Students first wrote conjectures about each question and then proceeded with their investigations.

Students tested their conjectures using The Geometer's Sketchpad to complete the tables on the worksheets. The software features allowed students to draw many possible convex or concave polygons of various sizes and shapes while the computer calculated dimensions, area, and perimeter. Students frequently considered concave polygons. Transformations were quickly facilitated as students dragged corner points of the polygon, varying its size and shape, while the Sketchpad interactively calculated dimensions, area, and perimeter on the screen.

Students completed the tables with dimensions from the software that were rounded computer-generated numbers. These computer-generated numbers should not be expected to produce the same results for area or perimeter if formulas are applied. However, this fact did not divert students who were intently focused on concept discovery rather than on a formula-based approach.

Table 1 illustrates how one group of students discovered that as rectangles with the same perimeter become longer and narrower, their area becomes smaller. Figures 4a, 4b, and 4c are "snapshots" of what the students created on the computer screen, furnishing powerful images with which students could meaningfully complete table 1.

Table 1

Relationship between Area and Perimeter of a Rectangle

Dimensions (cm)	Perimeter (cm)	Area (cm²)
5 by 5	20.0	25.0
3.0 by 6.9	20.0	21.1
9.4 by 0.6	20.0	5.4

Another set of "snapshots" (figs. 5a, 5b, 5c, and 5d) shows how students discovered that to minimize perimeter among quadrilaterals with the same area, the shape must be a square (see table 2).

Table 3 illustrates how one group of students discovered that of all figures with the same perimeter, a circle yields the greatest area. Figures 6a, 6b, 6c, and 6d are "snapshots" of what the students created during their exploration, supplying clues that enabled them to make this discovery.

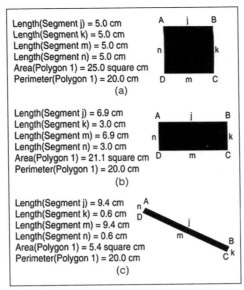

Fig. 4. Snapshots for question 1

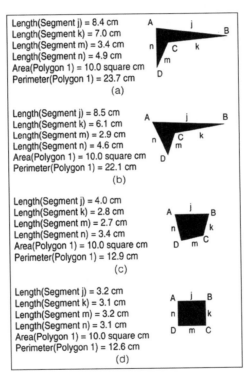

Fig. 5. Snapshots for question 2

Table 2

Relationship between Area and Perimeter of a Quadrilateral

Dimensions (cm)	Perimeter (cm)	Area (cm²)
8.4 by 7.0 by 3.4 by 4.9	23.7	10.0
8.5 by 6.1 by 2.9 by 4.6	22.1	10.0
4 by 2.8 by 2.7 by 3.4	12.9	10.0
3.2 by 3.1 by 3.2 by 3.1	12.6	10.0

Another set of "snapshots" (figs. 7a, 7b, 7c, and 7d) illustrates how students explored, leading to the discovery that

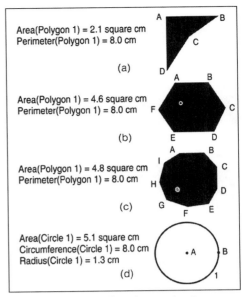

Fig. 6. Snapshots for question 3

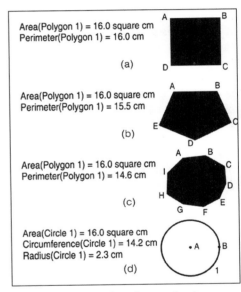

Fig. 7. Snapshots for question 4

among all figures with the same area, a circle has the smallest perimeter (see table 4).

After students completed each table, they were in a position to make generalizations. For example, after completing table 1, some students suggested that the longer and narrower a rectangle becomes, the smaller the area becomes. For tables 1 and 2, randomly assigning specific n values for each group produced interesting results. Class discussion included sharing results among groups to see what happens for different n-gons. For example, for one group, using $n = 4$ in table 1 led to the conclusion that a square has the greatest area among quadrilaterals with the same perimeter; a second

Table 3
Relationship of Area and Perimeter for Various Figures

Figure	No. of Sides	Dimensions (cm)	Perimeter (cm)	Area (cm²)
Quadrilateral	4		8.0	2.1
Hexagon	6		8.0	4.6
Nonagon	9		8.0	4.8
Circle	—	$r = 1.3$	$C = 8.0$	5.1

Table 4
Relationship of Area and Perimeter for Various Figures

Figure	No. of Sides	Dimensions (cm)	Perimeter (cm)	Area (cm²)
Square	4	4 by 4	16.0	16.0
Pentagon	5		15.5	16.0
Nonagon	9		14.6	16.0
Circle	—	$r = 2.3$	14.2	16.0

group, using $n = 6$, concluded that a regular hexagon has the greatest area among 6-gons with the same perimeter.

Students discussed and compared findings with other groups. These discussions encouraged an exchange and proliferation of ideas. Finally, students were asked the question, "How do you know for certain that your generalizations are always true?" Most students seemed satisfied that their generalizations were proved by so many examples offered by the software. When the teacher suggested that they may have missed just one counterexample, students began to appreciate the fundamental importance of formal proof.

The Geometer's Sketchpad uniquely constitutes an appropriate and effective environment for discovering the relationship between area and perimeter. Students demonstrated a firm conceptual understanding of this relationship. They could then explicitly answer the question "What shape will have the largest area for a given perimeter?" and they could do so without centuries of struggle and cultural evolution. Human beings have worked wonders with tools as simple as a wooden peg, a rope, and a hoe. It is exciting to imagine the new heights our students may attain with new technology. A new curriculum using computer technology to teach optimally in light of educational innovations makes such attainments possible.

Bibliography

Bachman, Charles H. "Ubiquitous Geometry: Some Examples Showing the Significance of Size and Shape in the Works of Man and Nature." *Physics Teacher* 26 (September 1988): 341–70.

Chazen, Daniel. "Implementing the *Standards*: Students' Microcomputer-Aided Exploration in Geometry." *Mathematics Teacher* 83 (November 1990): 628–35.

Jackiw, Nicholas. The Geometer's Sketchpad. Berkeley, Calif.: Key Curriculum Press, 1991. Software.

Kemeny, John G. "How Computers Have Changed the Way I Teach." *Academic Computing* 2 (May/June 1988): 44–61.

Ronau, Robert N., and Robert K. Gilbert. "Investigating Relations in Nature." *School Science and Mathematics* 88 (November 1988): 573–80.

Schwartz, Judah L. "Intellectual Mirrors: A Step in the Direction of Making Schools Knowledge Making Places." *Harvard Educational Review* 59 (February 1989): 51–60.

Shaw, Jean M. "Let's Do It: Exploring Perimeter and Area Using Centimeter Squared Paper." *Arithmetic Teacher* 31 (December 1983): 4–11.

Woodward, Ernest, and Frances Byrd. "Area: Included Topic, Neglected Concept." *School Science and Mathematics* 83 (April 1983): 343-47.

Zaslavsky, Claudia. "People Who Live in Round Houses." *Arithmetic Teacher* 37 (September 1989): 18–21.

14

Assessment

NEW assessment techniques are required if teachers are to successfully implement the NCTM Standards. Assessment should become an integral part of instruction and not a separate disconnected activity. Teachers also need to use multiple assessment methods.

Sammons, Kobett, Heiss, and Fennell explore means for connecting mathematics teaching and assessment activities. Both formative (teacher observation, questioning, diagnostic interviews, and investigations) and summative techniques are presented in "Linking Instruction and Assessment in the Mathematics Classroom."

Portfolios are discussed in the Karp and Huinker article, which presents the mathematics portfolio along with an evaluation rubric.

Walen and Hirstein explore the use of vignettes as an assessment technique. Two sample vignettes are presented as well as ideas for developing others.

Robinson and Bartlett discuss examining assessment data from informal means such as asking classroom questions or conducting an individual interview. Assessment thus becomes an integral part of mathematics instruction.

Cooperative problem solving is presented by Kroll, Masingila, and Mau. The authors discuss the basic idea of evaluating group problem solving, and they present several good sources for problems.

KAY B. SAMMONS, BETH KOBETT, JOAN HEISS, AND FRANCIS (SKIP) FENNELL

Linking Instruction and Assessment in the Mathematics Classroom

Kay Sammons, Beth Kobett, *and* Joan Heiss *work for the Howard County Public School System, Ellicott City, MD 21042. Sammons is an elementary mathematics supervisor, Kobett is an elementary mathematics resource teacher, and Heiss is a resource teacher for test development.* Francis (Skip) Fennell *teaches at Western Maryland College in Westminster, MD 21157. He directs a United States Department of Education project, "Number Sense Now!" and serves as president of the Research Council for Diagnostic and Prescriptive Mathematics.*

MS. HOWARD posed the following question to her students: "If thirty-two game cards are used by students in one class and forty-nine game cards are used by students in another class, how many cards would be used?" As she looks around the room, she observes Kenny using base-ten blocks to solve the problem. He methodi-cally counts 3 tens and 2 ones to form 32. He then finds 4 tens and 9 ones to show 49. She watches as he carefully scoops up 10 of the 11 ones and exchanges them for a ten. A smile spreads across his face as he raises his hand to share the answer. Shalika also uses base-ten blocks. She first models 32 and then 49. Shalika pushes the ten rods together and then shows 11 one rods, which she exchanges for an additional ten rod. Shalika firmly states that the answer is 81. Ms. Howard is pleased with the responses from Kenny and Shalika. She then turns her attention to Elaine, who is using single counters to find the sum of 32 and 49. Elaine counts each counter moving each from one side of the desk to the other as she counts them. Ms. Howard notices that Elaine does not attempt to organize or group the counters. Elaine finishes counting and eagerly raises her hand to share the sum. Ms. Howard looks at Juanita, who has recorded the exercise on paper. Juanita also has the correct answer. When Ms. Howard asks her how she found the sum, Juanita tells her that she had to regroup the ones because they totaled 11 ones. She recorded the ten in the tens column before she added.

In performance-based assessment, students are permitted to use the materials, such as calculators, that they are accustomed to using in the classroom.

Ms. Howard has just observed four students complete an addition exercise in four different ways. Had she asked only for the answer, she would have learned that all four students knew the correct sum. By observing her students, she has learned that each has a very different understanding of addition with regrouping. Through her informal assessment, she can now tailor her instruction to fit the developmental understanding of her students. For Kenny and Shalika, she will begin instruction that will enable them to make the transition from their concrete understanding to the abstract. Ms. Howard will use base-ten blocks to help Elaine understand grouping of numbers into tens and ones. Ms. Howard is confident that Juanita has a good understanding of addition with regrouping in the abstract form, so she will move on to instruction in another topic.

The evaluation standards, a vital component of the NCTM's *Curriculum and Evaluation Standards for School Mathematics* (1989), states that assessment of students must be integral to instruction and that multiple means of assessment methods must be used (p. 190). In addition to assessing mathematical concepts, the evaluation standards encourage assessing students' disposition toward mathematics. Students' mathematical dispositions are shown in the way they approach tasks. Do they attack a problem with confidence, show a willingness to explore alternatives, and maintain interest as they work? Do they reflect on their own thinking? (NCTM 1989, 233)

The purpose of assessment is to improve instruction and, therefore, learning. Typically, assessment has occurred in a formal setting with paper and pencil in hand. Results were recorded, and the teacher moved on to the next topic. Little opportunity was given to altering or changing instruction on the basis of assessment results. Assessment is an ongoing process that occurs daily in the classroom. It must be linked daily to instruction. Assessment can be as informal as an observation of the students' responses during instruction or as formal as a paper-pencil test. However, it is very important that assessment inform and mirror instruction. That is, if manipulative materials are used during instruction, then they should also be used in the assessment of students' learning.

Students' responses to the same prompt can reveal differences in understanding.

Information gleaned from assessment should be used to prepare for the next day's instruction. The days of Friday as "test day" are over as curriculum reform based on the NCTM's *Curriculum and Evaluation Standards* (1989) and its *Professional Standards for Teaching Mathematics* (1991) occurs.

As we begin to recognize and value the natural link between teaching and testing, or assessment, schools and school districts will plan assessment strategies and programs in much the same way as they plan for curricular change. The issues of curriculum and assessment must be related to instructional considerations. The instructional cycle that consists of planning, teaching, and assessment facilitates natural links between instruction—what's taught—and assessment—what's measured. This article outlines five school-based alternative-assessment strategies that support important instructional and assessment goals. These techniques include formative (generally informal procedures used frequently, sometimes daily) and summative (more global and linking more concepts) techniques. The techniques include classroom observations and questioning, diagnostic interviews, problem-solving-based investigations, performance-based assessment tasks, and at-home connections. Students' responses and teachers' assessment of the responses are presented for several of the assessment examples.

Formative Assessment Techniques

Observation and questioning

As we begin to look at assessment in broader terms, the importance of the classroom teacher's being a trained observer becomes evident. As this article's introductory scenario illustrated, we must rely on the teacher to observe students in a learning situation and depend on the ability of the teacher to describe the students' grasp of a particular concept. The teacher must then process this information to make instructional decisions based on the needs of the students.

The ability to observe a student and make instructional decisions is enhanced by the use of questioning techniques. Knowing what types of questions to ask strengthens the ability to evaluate students' thinking and reasoning. Asking questions that require the students to think about mathematics allows them the opportunity to discover and validate important mathematical principles and ideas. Discovery of these concepts enables students to make connections within the mathematics curriculum and to other subjects, as well as to internalize their understanding. Mathematics becomes real and connected instead of mysterious and disjointed. Teachers need to ask a variety of questions on a regular basis. Some starters include the following:

• What would happen if …?
• How many ways can you …?
• Can you predict …?
• What doesn't belong?
• Why did you …?

Diagnostic interviews

An assumption of the NCTM's *Curriculum and Evaluation Standards* (1989) is that students experience a conceptually oriented curriculum. How do we assess the acquisition of concepts? Traditional testing practice does not allow us to communicate with students regarding their understanding and thinking about a concept. The diagnostic interview as described by Ashlock (1990), by Liedtke (1988), and most recently by Long and Ben-Hur (1991) is an excellent way for a teacher and student to interact. During the interview, students are given the opportunity to model their understanding of a particular concept. The diagnostic interview may use manipulative materials and requires the teacher to engage the student in a dialogue about the mathematics concept being explored.

Following are examples of activities that can be used during an interview. These examples include means of assessing an understanding of basic concepts in whole numbers, spatial sense, and problem-solving skills in a number-sense setting.

Activity 1

Teacher's directions: Present this task to the student. Using the tens and ones materials, show me 23. Now show me a number that is close to 23, but smaller. Can you show me, using your blocks, a number that is a lot larger than 23? (Grade 1 or 2)

Student's response: When asked to show a number a lot larger than 23, Domenic displayed 5 tens and 16 ones. When asked how he knew that this number was a lot larger than 23, he responded that "there were a bunch of blocks there."

Teacher's assessment: Domenic is not naturally regrouping and will need further instruction in tens and ones with concrete materials. He may also need more opportunities to define numbers that are a lot larger than a stated number (e.g., hundreds).

Activity 2

Teacher's directions: Present a student with eight connected Unifix cubes. Right below this row of cubes, place a row of ten Unifix cubes. Tell the student there are eight cubes in the first row and ask how many cubes are in the second row. Observe how the student obtains the answer. Does the student count-on, or recount the cubes? (Grades K and 1)

Students' responses: Patrick counted-on to find the answer. Diedre subtracted. David compared the two rows to find the difference.

Teacher's assessment: Diedre and David displayed some understanding of how subtraction can be used. Patrick showed good number sense by counting-on to find the difference. All three students may benefit from using a part-part-whole model (see fig. 1) to help show the relationship between addition and subtraction.

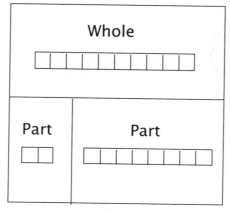

Fig. 1

Activity 3

Teacher's directions: Present the following problem to the students. "If we add 56 + 38, do you think the sum is going to be close to 100, a lot bigger than 100, or a lot smaller than 100? How do you know? Using the tens and ones materials, show how you would add 56 + 38. As you do so, tell me how you are actually adding the materials." After the explanation and solution are completed, ask, "Can you think of a word problem that might use the addition of 56 + 38? Tell me about it." (Grade 2 or 3)

Students' responses: Jackie, Meighan, and Jon all responded with a sum close to 100. However, when asked to justify their answer, only Jon responded that he rounded each number to find the estimate of 100. Jackie and Meighan could not determine a reason for their estimate. In response to the follow-up question, What would be an estimate for 91 + 80? Jackie responded 300 and did not know why. Meighan and Jon responded 200. When asked to explain her reasoning, Meighan used the rounding strategy. She said that she had learned this strategy from Jon.

Teacher's assessment: Jackie and Meighan will benefit from number-sense and estimation-related activities that build to 100. Some ideas would include having the students identify number pairs that are close to 100, a lot less than 100, or more than 100 (e.g., 23 + 67, 99 + 90, 34 + 12, 23 + 23). The students should also create their own word problems involving addition.

Activity 4

Teacher's directions: Give the student the following task. Using twelve tiles for each, make as many rectangles as you can. Find the perimeter of each rectangle. What is the

area of each rectangle? What can you say about the perimeter of a rectangle when we keep the area the same? (Grade 3 or 4)

Students' responses: Melanie and Mark were successful in finding all the different configurations. When asked to find the perimeter of any of the rectangles, both students were uncertain of the meaning of the terms *perimeter* and *area*. The teacher showed the students that perimeter was the distance around the rectangle. The students then found the perimeter easily for all the rectangles. When asked about the relationship of perimeter to area when the area stayed the same, the students predicted that the perimeter would stay constant. After completing the activity, Melanie said, "The perimeters can be all different even though the area is the same."

Teacher's assessment: Initially it appeared that the students did not understand the concepts of perimeter and area. However, after further questioning, the teacher determined that their deficiency was lack of vocabulary. Follow-up instruction should include activities that involve students working with perimeter and area together using concrete materials.

Activity 5

Teacher's directions: Give a student cubes and ask her or him to show an array for the multiplication sentence 5 × 4 = _____. Observe how the student arranges the blocks. What do four groups of five mean? Are five groups of four the same as four groups of five? How can you prove the commutative, or order, property? (Grade 2 or 3)

Students' responses: Amit, Kim, and Alison all responded differently. Amit grouped the blocks into five piles of four. When asked to explain the groupings, he showed repeated addition, as follows:

Using the counters, Kim made the numeral 5, then a multiplication sign, and the numeral 4. When asked to explain, she said that five times four equals twenty.

Alison placed the counters in a four-by-five array. When asked to explain, she said that four rows of five resulted:

Teacher's assessment: Amit and Alison seem to understand multiplication and its relationship to addition. Topics for further instruction would include additional facts and the multiplication algorithm. Kim would appear to know this multiplication fact but does not demonstrate an understanding of multiplication. Further instruction would involve using manipulatives to show multiplication as repeated addition.

Activity 6

Teacher's directions: Ask the student to use a calculator to show a decimal number with a certain digit in the tenths or hundredths place. Ask the student to read the number. (E.g., "Show me eight and five-tenths on the calculator.") (Grades 4-6)

Students' responses: Zara, Ben, and Jamil responded differently to the prompt. Zara displayed 8.5 on the calculator and read it as "eight and five-tenths." Ben displayed 7.58 and read it as "seven and five-eighths." Jamil displayed 9500 and read it as "ninety-five hundredths."

Teacher's assessment: Zara shows a clear understanding of how to write and read decimals involving tenths. Further instruction would include expanding place value to hundredths. Ben could display a decimal with a five in the tenths place but could not read the number correctly. Ben needs further instruction in reading decimals and would also benefit from instruction that shows the relationship between fractions and decimals. Jamil has no understanding of decimals and needs instruction in place value of whole numbers before proceeding to concepts involving decimals.

Activity 7

Teacher's directions: Give students a number line like the following:

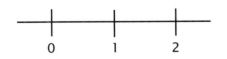

Ask the students to place such fractions as 3/5, 1/2, 7/8, and 9/4 about where the fractions would fall on the number line. Ask the students if they were to add 2/3 and 1/2, about where the sum might fall on the number line. (Grades 4-7)

Students' responses: Meredith, Josh, and Maria placed fractions on the number line. Meredith placed 7/8, 1/5, and 4/7 near 0. When asked why she placed the fractions near 0, she said that all fractions are parts. Josh did not know how to respond until the teacher said, "Think of '1' as a whole." Josh then placed the fractions correctly. Maria was able to place the fractions correctly on the number line. When asked how she knew where to place the fractions, Maria said she pictured the fractions in her head to help her know how big they were.

Teacher's assessment: Meredith would benefit from instruction using concrete materials to represent fractions. She needs to see the relationship of the concrete representations of fractions to the more abstract number line. Josh needs more experiences with the number line. Maria can successfully move on to instruction with fractions greater than a whole.

Ideally the interview process that would incorporate the foregoing activities would be completed in a one-on-one situation. A more realistic alternative to this approach could be a teacher's choosing ten students randomly and interviewing the students individually. On the basis of the information from these ten students, the teacher could make decisions about the progress of the class regarding the concepts assessed. This information would be used to decide the next move, instructionally, for the class on the basis of a summary of the interviews, as well as supply important information about the progress and level of understanding of individual students. It is expected that all students would participate in such an interview during a nine-week marking period.

Problem-solving-based investigations

Problem solving is perhaps the most critical goal of any contemporary elementary mathematics program. The NCTM's *Curriculum and Evaluation Standards* (1989) indicates that "if problem solving is

to be the focus of school mathematics, it must also be the focus of assessment" (p. 209). To assess problem solving, teachers must expect students to produce solutions to problems, not merely recognize solutions. Much of the current talk about authentic, or performance-based, assessment involves this expectation. Shepard (1989) argues that assessment tasks need to be created to resemble real learning more closely. Such tasks should challenge students and acknowledge, perhaps celebrate, more than one correct answer and a variety of explanations and products by students. We need to consider carefully such performance-based assessment procedures. Such measures allow teachers to watch learners pose, tackle, and solve problems (Wiggins 1989). Performance-based assessment opportunities also assume that students are permitted the opportunity to work with the materials they are accustomed to using in the classroom. That is, manipulative materials, calculators, resource books, and other materials should be available to them as needed. Here, we choose to discuss variations of performance-based assessment. The first problem-solving-based investigations are problem-solving situations in which students are asked to work through a problem posed within a scenario. These problems are to be used to monitor instruction and furnish formative assessment information. The problem posed is to be open-ended, thus allowing multiple solutions and multiple ways of reaching a problem's solution. Because students are actively engaged in working through the problem, such investigations allow the teacher to observe and interview students as they work. Students may be working individually or within a group. The students will generate some type of product, such as a drawing, display, table, graph, or written explanation, to share at the completion of their investigation.

Examples of problem-solving-based investigations include the following:

Investigation 1 (grades 2–5)

Your teacher has decided that you may have your choice of recess times:

1. You may have 30 minutes a day for the next two weeks; or
2. You may have 1 minute of recess on the first day, 2 minutes on the second day, 4 minutes on the third day,

8 minutes on the fourth day, and so on, for the next two weeks. Which recess would you like? Why?

Students' responses. Sara chose thirty minutes a day. She verified her answer by using the calculator and added up thirty minutes for ten days. She did not want to pursue the second plan because she was convinced that she was correct. Jeff first predicted that the first plan would give him the most recess. He decided to find the total minutes for each plan to find out which was best. He decided to use a table to help him solve the problem. He used the calculator to help him add the days to determine the best plan for recess. On day 6 of the second plan, he wanted to change his first answer. He was amazed at how fast the numbers grew. (See fig. 2.)

Investigation 2 (grades 2–5)

You have three animals: a giraffe, an elephant, and a lion. The three body parts you can move around are the head, the body, and the legs. How many different kinds of animals can you create? Give the students animals to manipulate. Observe how the students record the information from the manipulations of the body parts.

Student's response. Jeff first began to solve the problem by moving the animal parts and making tally marks (see fig. 3). He became very confused by his random combinations. He decided to stop and make a list of the different combinations. He found that he did not need to repeat the third set of combinations because he noticed a pattern and inferred the total number of combinations for the animal parts.

Investigation 3 (grades 4–7)

You are to design and construct a bulletin board for your classroom. You are to use the least amount of material possible and determine the final cost. You will have to do the following.

- Cover the board with background paper.
- Put a border around the entire board.
- Arrange students' work on the board.
- Select a title for the display.

The bulletin board has dimensions of 6 feet by 4 feet. The construction paper comes in sheets that measure 12 inches by 18 inches. What is the least number

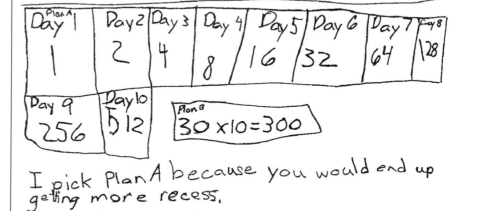

Fig. 2

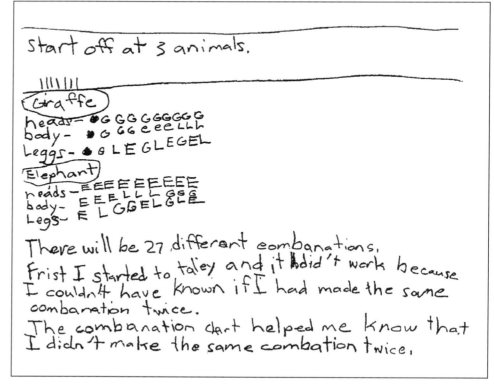

Fig. 3

ACTIVITIES FOR JUNIOR HIGH SCHOOL AND MIDDLE SCHOOL MATHEMATICS

of sheets of paper you can use to cover the board completely without overlapping or cutting the paper?

Answer: _____

Explain, or draw an illustration.

The border comes in sheets two inches wide by thirty-six inches long. How many sheets will you need? (Remember to use the least possible amount.)

Answer: _____

Explain, or draw an illustration.

If paper costs 56 cents per sheet and the border costs 34 cents per sheet, how much did it cost to construct the bulletin board?

Answer: _____

Summative Assessment Techniques

Performance-based tasks

The performance-based task is a multiple-exercise problem that requires students to apply previously learned skills. We have chosen to describe performance-based tasks as summative measures because of their use in measuring massed concepts. That is, such tasks can be used four to six times a year to assess a variety of important curricular goals. The performance-based tasks are completed by individuals or groups of students and take about fifty minutes to complete. A problem is presented in a real-life setting, and students are expected to work through the various thematically linked exercises.

A sample problem setting is presented in figure 4. Note that the task embodies important mathematics ideas, including, but not limited to, data analysis, fractions, area, spatial sense, monetary applications, and writing. Such items represent real mathematics. This example is typical of how people use mathematics. It makes sense to offer assessment opportunities that are natural extensions of teaching. In the future, it is hoped that such performance-based opportunities will be viewed as instructional extensions that just happen to be assessment related.

At-Home Connections

Linking the school and home has become an increasingly important aspect of the educational process. Such a partnership can be nurtured through the use of monthly activities that connect classroom mathematics with other disciplines and real-life situations. Such at-home connections can be used to indicate major mathematics topics completed during the month and furnish parents or guardians with an applied activity that will showcase the level of mathematics understanding of their child. Students are to be actively involved in completing these activities with an adult or older sibling. The major focus of the at-home connection is to communicate the curriculum through a project that models the type of assessment (performance) students are used to doing in school. Such activities serve to "publicize" alternative assessment as well as to involve the home. Teachers can discuss the results of the at-home activity with students. An example is presented here.

Sample at-home activity

Make a graph that shows the height or weight of each member of your family. First use a ruler or scale to determine height or weight. Make a table of your information. Next decide what type of graph you will use to display your information. Make sure to place your finished graph on the refrigerator for all to see.

Concluding Comments

To achieve a curriculum similar to that proposed by the NCTM's *Curriculum and Evaluation Standards* (1989), we must link teaching, learning, and assessment. Teachers must assess as they teach. Teachers will be more successful in understanding the extent to which learning is taking place when they feel confident using a variety of classroom-based-assessment techniques. This article proposes consistent use of the following formative evaluation techniques: teacher observation and questioning, diagnostic interviews, and problem-solving-based investigations. The summative evaluation techniques proposed include the use of performance-based tasks and at-home connections. Together the assessment opportunities proposed here help to link mathematics teaching and assessment. As we strive to meet the challenges of curricular reform, this link must be strengthened.

You and your neighbors are planning a yard sale. You will need to solve several problems to make sure the yard sale is successful.

You survey your neighborhood and find out the following information:

People participating	Number of objects to be sold	Space needed
Your family	10	30 sq. ft.
Smiths	15	35 sq. ft.
Andersons	7	10 sq. ft.
Jacksons	13	20 sq. ft.
Saris	12	18 sq. ft.

You call the rental store and find out that they rent tables measuring 6 feet by 2 1/2 feet for $6.00 a day. How many tables will you need for the yard sale? How do you know?

The yard you are planning to use measures 20 feet by 30 feet. Draw a diagram of the placement of the tables in the yard. Be sure to allow about 4 feet of space around the tables for the movement of customers.

You find that the cost of advertising in the local newspaper is $13.50 for the first ten words and $1.00 per word after that. Write an advertisement describing the neighborhood yard sale. Be sure you include the details that the customers would need to know. The items to be sold are all kitchen and garden tools. How much will your ad cost?

Fig. 4

References

Ashlock, Robert B. *Error Patterns in Computation*. Columbus, Ohio: Charles B. Merrill Publishing Co., 1990.

Leidtke, Werner. "Diagnosis in Mathematics: The Advantages of an Interview." *Arithmetic Teacher* 36 (November 1988): 26–29.

Long, Madeleine J., and Meir Ben-Hur. "Informing Learning through the Clinical Interview." *Arithmetic Teacher* 38 (February 1991): 44–46.

National Council of Teachers of Mathematics. *Curriculum and Evaluation Standards for School Mathematics*. Reston, Va.: The Council, 1989.

———. *Professional Standards for Teaching Mathematics*. Reston, Va.: The Council, 1991.

Shepard, Lorrie A. "Why We Need Better Assessments." *Educational Leadership* 46 (April 1989): 4–9.

Wiggins, Grant. "A True Test: Toward More Authentic and Equitable Assessment." *Phi Delta Kappan* 70 (May 1989): 703–13.

KAREN S. KARP AND DEANN HUINKER

Portfolios as Agents of Change

I believe portfolios are very worthwhile. In fact, even though they are significantly more work, the benefits far outweigh any final exam, any day. The benefits include self-reflecting, re-examining activities, working through ideas that did not make sense and making sense of them. Plus, portfolios are so personal and individual—each one is a wonderful snapshot of us as future teachers.

—Elementary-mathematics-methods student

Utilizing portfolios this semester served me not only as a culmination tool, bringing concepts into clearer focus, but also as a means to both assess my own progress and bolster my self-confidence. Looking back, I see mistakes I have made, steps I have taken to address these errors, and I am given direction for further, even better, solutions to problems I encountered.

—Elementary-mathematics-methods student

AS TEACHERS in elementary classrooms examine the assessments they use in an effort to link the learning and evaluation process, so, too, must university education professors investigate the use of alternative-assessment techniques. In a recent survey of professors on their assessment practices in elementary mathematics methods and content courses, respondents frequent-

Karen Karp, *kskarp01@ulkyvm.louisville.edu, teaches at the University of Louisville, Louisville, KY 40292. In her teaching and scholarly work, she has focused on equity issues in mathematics education.* DeAnn Huinker, *huinker@csd.uwm.edu, teaches at the University of Wisconsin— Milwaukee, Milwaukee, Wl 53201-0413. She has a special interest in assessment issues and children's sense of whole numbers and fractions.*
Edited by Jeane Joyner, *North Carolina Department of Public Instruction, Raleigh, NC 27601-2825.*

ly indicated that portfolios were the assessment technique they would most like to try in the near future (Huinker and Karp 1995). Historically, portfolios have been used in university settings—sometimes by nontraditional students to translate life experiences into college credit or at other times by students in disciplines as diverse as art, writing, and business as a way to compile their accomplishments. Yet portfolio assessment is still considered a relatively new experience for many education students.

What Are Portfolios?

A portfolio is a purposeful collection of work that demonstrates a student's understanding, beliefs, attitudes, and growth. A portfolio might include such items as lesson plans, lesson reflections, journal entries, and case studies of children; these items are discussed further in this article. In preservice education the portfolio serves as an ongoing and evolving method of assessing students' progress in learning to teach mathematics. The portfolio gives preservice teachers an opportunity to document their own professional growth and development and to highlight some of the important ideas they have learned in their college courses about the teaching and learning of mathematics.

Why Use Portfolios in Mathematics Education?

We are currently seeing the expanded role of the portfolio in mathematics-education settings as a rich form of assessment. Initially it may have been a way to give preservice education students a firsthand opportunity to experience the portfolio assessment as a process that they will probably be using in their class. The key functions of a portfolio are to provide ways for students to formally self-assess their learn-

ing, gauge their growth on course objectives, and document their strengths. Also, as professors encourage students to develop the criteria used to organize and evaluate the portfolio, students can assume leadership roles in their own learning process.

Self-assessment

The NCTM's *Professional Standards for Teaching Mathematics* (1991) states that teachers are being asked to teach a subject in ways they have never experienced. One crucial variable in making lasting change in preservice teaching is the process of reflection (O'Loughlin 1990). Yet many current teacher-education programs do not involve students in a reflective approach; instead, classes are often driven by a model of the professor as the authority. The process of reflection needs to be built into the course on a regular basis, enabling students to evaluate their progress on the portfolio as they share with peers what they have learned and how they plan to prove that knowledge. During specified intervals throughout the semester, pieces of the portfolio can be shared in their embryonic state. For example, a midsemester activity involves students' sharing the draft of a portfolio item with a group of peers for early structural feedback. By making it an ongoing effort, the learner can begin to take charge of the learning process through looking at other students' work; discussing, rather than judging, how high-quality work should appear; and self-regulating through the use of what they themselves have set as a new standard. This format also encourages movement away from the professor as an authority figure through the use of colleagues to obtain feedback. Such a process not only models the experience that students will need when they move to the teaching profession but also allows them to learn about the challenges of giving constructive criticism to others, a skill necessary in their chosen profession.

Portfolios in the hiring process

Several states, as well as many individual school systems, currently use portfolios as part of the hiring process for both teachers and administrators. Although most portfolios at the university level communicate growth, professional portfolios incorporate examples of a student's best work. This form of documentation, more than the usual application snapshot, is instead a portrait of a candidate's strengths, accomplishments, and qualifications. It is much richer than a one-faceted product, such as a cumulative-grade-point-average record. Therefore, practice given in the university setting on how to develop such an in-depth self-assessment enhances a portfolio writer's chances in the hiring process.

Framework

A portfolio is not merely a resource file that contains every activity and assessment from the entire semester. Instead, the portfolio is a set of materials carefully chosen by the student and organized to tie individual pieces together meaningfully.

Although goals are often established at the beginning of a course, the flexible format of the portfolio allows for structure as well as surprises and creativity. As the project becomes less professor directed, the students take more responsibility for their own learning. Some possible approaches that can be considered as frameworks include basing the evidence of growth on (1) meeting the established objectives of the course; (2) meeting the NCTM's *Curriculum and Evaluation Standards* (1989); (3) meeting the NCTM's *Professional Standards for Teaching Mathematics* (1991); or (4) presenting the five most meaningful pieces of work developed during the semester, which may include earlier, less successful attempts used for contrast.

Possible contents

Customarily the portfolio starts with a letter to the reader. In this narrative the reader should learn about the author's vision, the goals of the course, and the purposes for each piece of evidence used to illustrate growth (see fig. 1).

The next component is the documentation of growth, evidenced by various forms from various settings, such as projects done

---

Dear Reader,

The development of my mathematical skills can best be described by the sequence of a spider building her web. The spider starts a new web by laying down some bridge lines as a frame upon which to build. At the beginning of the semester, I was starting "new" with math. With each class I developed a new insight, understanding, or perspective that I could use as part of my framework on which to build my skills.

Once the spider has built the frame, she puts in a temporary spiral, joining one spoke to the next; creating stability in the web. I perceive my skills have developed to a point of stability. That is, I can more readily make connections between mathematical concepts and I am beginning to be able to apply mathematical concepts to other academic disciplines. I have an understanding of what is developmentally appropriate and the necessary methods and strategies to use to teach mathematics. I can see the "whole" and the interconnectedness of the parts. Each step, a part of the other, woven together. I am continuing to develop my skills, and like the spider, I build upon what I already know.

Lisa

Fig. 1. Portion of a letter to the reader

---

in class or activities conducted in elementary schools with children.

Although no one required item must be included, the overriding variable in selecting items should be that they reveal in-depth information. The pieces used to substantiate this development can include lesson plans; lesson reflections and analyses; journal entries; assessments developed; case studies of children; detailed write-ups of solutions to problems; children's work with comments and feedback; mathematics autobiographies, which are personal histories of their experiences in mathematics; videotaped demonstrations of classroom teaching with self-assessment and peer assessment; reactions to professional readings; and annotated class notes (see fig. 2). In each subcategory, students must include

statements, often as a cover sheet, describing the item, linking the item's inclusion to ideas from class discussions or readings (i.e., Why is the item a worthwhile mathematics task?), and explaining why this particular item was selected and its significance in relation to the portfolio's objectives.

Making selections

As students decide which pieces of work are most persuasive, they often ask themselves essential questions about what is good teaching. The reflective nature of this approach often fosters the evolution of metaphorical links to other disciplines and earlier experiences (see fig. 3). When students begin to write supportive pieces about why their evidence is relevant to the

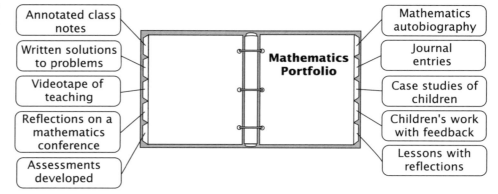

Fig. 2. What's in a portfolio?

goals, they must explicitly state what they learned. Reflecting and writing about their learning pushes students to focus on where they can improve and helps them become leaders in their own learning.

Evaluating Portfolios

In many ways the process of evaluating a portfolio is similar to evaluating an essay. The decisions are subjective. Yet to clarify the procedure, a structure and an agreed-on set of criteria must be used to help define the quality of the work. Rubrics (see figs. 4 and 5) can constitute the evaluation framework and can be generated by the professor; the professor and students; or with additional assistance by others, such as cooperating teachers, local administrators, state-certification-agency staff, or other university educators. These external evaluators lend authenticity and credibility to the process while they learn how university-education classes develop prospective teachers as leaders in their own education. Of course, each of these groups can appropriately use the rubric to assess the final portfolio.

When the portfolios are complete, students are frequently asked to bring them to class with a completed self-assessment rubric. The students then meet with peers and exchange portfolios. Peers read the portfolio and use the rubric to score their classmate's work. Later, local cooperating teachers, administrators in a position to hire, district-wide curriculum coordinators, or other professors can visit the class and examine the portfolios, thereby becoming a part of an assessment team. In this model, assessment conducted by the professor of the course becomes an evaluation of the student's ability to self-assess. Feedback to the student on this criterion can lead to additional growth.

Conclusions

Portfolios are not only powerful assessment tools that can develop a student's own reflection and responsibility for the learning process but can also augment elementary teachers' lessons and can help professors examine their own instruction. Portfolios can become a valuable component of the course assessment. Trends emerge as students select significant moments and events from either the course

---

Dear Reader,

I begin this letter under much duress. The thought of ever doing a portfolio for mathematics has never entered my frail human mind. I find myself in a position that is foreign to my social science loving heart. I am convinced that to understand my view of math is to come to grips with the mathematical beast in my past. Hence, I have chosen to take you on a journey through my mathematical inferno. Dante wrote concerning the fears of the darkness from a strictly medieval mind-set. As a sixth grader in the midwest, I imagined purgatory as a never-ending math class. The instructor played the part of the tormentor using the dreaded ditto.

Teaching mathematics was not high on my list of priorities as a prospective educator. The though[t] of becoming one of the tormentors made me sad. I was determined that teaching mathematics would be a time of pain for student and teacher. We would suffer together, and I would exhibit sympathy for those under my ditto master. Then came the mathematics methods course and my hopes were raised from the pits of purgatory to the joys of paradise. I invite you, the reader, to sail with me as we travel to paradise. However, like Dante of old, although we will see my growth, the real challenge lies in my future.

Richard "Dante"

Fig. 3. Portion of a letter to the reader

Sample Rubric

Justify your response in the space below each item or on another page.

	Low			High
The letter to the reader is free of grammatical and mechanical errors and is well written.	1	2	3	4
The letter defines individual goals of the course. The definitions are meaningful and detailed.	1	2	3	4
The letter explains the purpose of each piece of evidence included in the table of contents and how each item relates to one of the defined course goals.	1	2	3	4
The letter is interesting and personalized: It passes the "so what" test.	1	2	3	4
Each defined goal is addressed by one or more rich and meaningful portfolio items.	1	2	3	4
The evidence in the portfolio is significant and compelling.	1	2	3	4
The portfolio is well organized and pleasing in appearance.	1	2	3	4
The portfolio demonstrates growth on the stated objectives.	1	2	3	4
The portfolio demonstrates knowledge of methods to teach mathematics to elementary school students.	1	2	3	4
The portfolio demonstrates creativity.	1	2	3	4
The portfolio shows evidence of reflection.	1	2	3	4
Overall assessment	1	2	3	4

Fig. 4

Portfolio Rubric

Organization and Presentation
5 Creative, very clear, easy to follow
4 Clear
3 Mostly clear
2 Some clear parts
1 Unclear

Cover Letter
7 Includes synthesis, reflection, quality writing, and all components
5 Connections made to readings and class
3 Some connections made, some components
2 Lists items, makes basic observations
1 Inaccurate statements, poor writing

Knowledge of Worthwhile Mathematical Tasks
5 Extended, generalized connections made, inquiry based
4 Clear understanding
3 Understood most of the time
2 Partially understood
1 Misunderstood

Knowledge of Assessment Techniques
5 Extended, generalized, child centered
4 Clear understanding
3 Understood most of the time
2 Partially understood
1 Misunderstood

Reflection on Teaching and Learning Mathematics
8 Includes synthesis and extensions
6 Connections made to readings and class
4 Some connections made, not consistent
2 Some observations included
0 No reflections and descriptions included

Knowledge of Tools for Learning Mathematics
5 Extended, generalized
4 Clear understanding
3 Understood most of the time
2 Partially understood
1 Misunderstood

General Quality and Completion
5 High quality writing, completed on time, all required components present
4 Quality writing for the most part, completed on time, all components
3 Some errors, some late or some components missing
2 Many errors, late, or some components missing
1 Poor writing, very late, components missing

Fig. 5

or classroom experiences with children. Professors can then use this information to redefine the course and better meet students' needs. As well, students' identifying struggles they have had with confusing or difficult concepts will enable the professor to elaborate on these topics in the future.

The NCTM's *Assessment Standards for School Mathematics* (1995, 3) describes assessment as the "process of gathering evidence about a student's knowledge of, ability to use, and disposition toward, mathematics and of making inferences from that evidence for a variety of purposes." The professor can use the following six questions, based on the assessment standards, to reflect on the process of using portfolios for assessment purposes in mathematics-methods courses.

• What *significant mathematics* is reflected in the portfolios?

• What evidence contained in the portfolio represents how the students' *mathematics teaching and learning* was enhanced?

• How has the portfolio process promoted *equity* by enabling all students to exhibit what they know and can do as future teachers of mathematics?

• In what ways has the process of developing and reviewing the portfolios been *open* to the students?

• How have you ensured that the portfolios will allow you to make valid *inferences* about the students' developing knowledge of mathematics teaching and learning?

• How have the portfolios contributed to a *coherent* assessment process?

The inclusion of portfolios can be a powerful component in the process of evaluating students and encouraging change. By shifting the responsibility for the construction of knowledge to preservice education students, the use of portfolios can become a model of lifelong learning that will, it is hoped, be passed to their own students for years to come.

References

Dewey, John. *How We Think: A Restatement of the Relation of Reflective Thinking to the Educative Process.* Boston: D. C. Heath & Co., 1933.

Huinker, DeAnn, and Karen Karp. "Assessment Practices in Elementary Mathematics Teacher Preparation." *AMTE News—Newsletter of the Association of Mathematics Teacher Educators* 4 (Fall 1995): 8–10.

National Council of Teachers of Mathematics. *Curriculum and Evaluation Standards for School Mathematics.* Reston, Va.: The Council. 1989.

———. *Professional Standards for Teaching Mathematics.* Reston, Va.: The Council. 1991.

———. *Assessment Standards for School Mathematics.* Reston, Va.: The Council. 1995.

O'Loughlin, Michael. "Teachers' Ways of Knowing: A Journal Study of Teachers Learning in a Dialogical and Constructivist Learning Environment." Paper presented at the annual meeting of the American Educational Research Association, Boston, Massachusetts, April 1990.

SHARON B. WALEN AND JAMES HIRSTEIN

Classroom Vignette: An Alternative-Assessment Tool

How can the upper-elementary or middle-grades teacher create a safe forum for students to discuss mathematics and mathematics attitudes while simultaneously evaluating their progress and achievement? The classroom vignette is an effective communication-enhancing tool for teachers that has grown in popularity since being used extensively in the NCTM's *Professional Standards for Teaching Mathematics* (1991).

Teachers have the responsibility to move mathematics assessment beyond its traditional limiting notions of grading to a broader notion, as described in the working draft of the *Assessment Standards for School Mathematics* (NCTM 1993, 5):

> Assessment occurs at the intersection of the important mathematics that is taught with how it is taught, what is learned, and how it is learned. It is a dynamic process that continuously yields information about student progress toward the achievement of mathematical power.... The process of gathering evidence in order to make inferences about student learning communicates to students and all of those concerned with their learning what is valued in mathematics and how students are progressing toward specific goals. Assessment also enhances mathematics learning when there is a shared understanding of the learning goals and of the

Role-playing situations allow students freedom of expression without reproach.

Sharon Walen *of Montana State University, Bozeman, MT 59715, and* James Hirstein *of the University of Montana, Missoula, MT 59812, are cochairs of assessment for the Systemic Initiative for Montana Mathematics and Science (SIMMS) project. Both are working with teachers to develop practical classroom assessment tools that emphasize communication.*

The work on this paper was supported in part by National Science Foundation grant no. TPE9105055. Any opinions, conclusions, or recommendations are those of the authors and do not necessarily reflect the views of the National Science Foundation.

methods used for demonstrating progress toward those goals.

A crucial issue for those involved in mathematics-education reform is the expansion of assessment strategies to guide students as they examine their individual roles in mathematical learning, extend their ability, communicate mathematically, express their world view in relationship to the classroom, and, as specifically addressed in this article, self-evaluate their own concepts and principles in today's classroom.

Vignettes: An Assessment Resource

Constructivist theories suggest that the importance of environment and communication be stressed in mathematics learning (vonGlasserfeld 1990) and that attention be focused on helping students to become risktakers (McLeod 1991; Walen 1993). Using classroom vignettes—experiences expressed in narrative or dialogue form—presents opportunities both to assist students' development and to assess their progress in attaining classroom expectations aligned with the reform movement. Vignette activities open a window on students' perceptions of mathematics and classroom roles.

Two Sample Vignettes

The vignettes discussed here focus on fifth- and sixth-grade students' discussions on perspectives of group interactions and knowledge of order of operations. These students freely interpreted, translated, and expanded the direction of their talk to areas of importance to them. The vignettes let students respond in an assessment situation by using the framework of their own experience and did not require them to have a specific correct response to a question. Additionally, work in small groups allowed teachers the freedom to listen and note discussions.

The rule vignette

The rule vignette allowed students to examine a portion of a group discussion. This vignette, by design, is free of specific mathematical content. Students were to address the broader issue of what it means to do mathematics rather than issues surrounding a specific rule. This particular vignette was chosen after listening to and assessing students' perspectives.

Students in a mathematics class discuss how to start their homework:

Kelly: I think I remember how to do it, but I'm not sure. We can figure this out.

Pat: Sure we can figure it out ... but how will we know if we get it right?

Gerry: Let's just ask the teacher what the rule is. Math has a lot of rules and you have to use the right rule.

Kelly: No, don't ask for help yet, we can figure this out.

Pat: I get sick of spending so much time listening to you try to figure things out and I really want to know how to do it right.

Gerry: This takes too long; let's just ask for the rule. If we do it wrong, we'll just get it all messed up.

Kelly: But to really understand you have to figure it out yourself. That's what math is all about, figuring things out.

Pat: Yeah, but we only have ten minutes of class left and I don't want to take this home.

Gerry: I still want to ask.

Students are asked to discuss the following questions in their groups: What is the problem that the students are having? What should they do next? Explain why you would or wouldn't like to be a part of this group.

If these students were part of your class, which one would you like to have as your math partner? Tell why you chose that student.

To assess students' communication skills and beliefs, they were asked to discuss the vignette in groups, to come to a general consensus, and to write a summary of both individual and group perspectives. One member of the group was to summarize the main points of discussion for the class. The summaries, individual written comments, and observation notes became a rich source of assessment data.

When the vignette was used, some individuals read independently. However, students working in small groups typically assumed the nongender roles for each character and read the dialogue aloud. This role approach allowed for auditory learning and did not emphasize individual reading skills.

Assessment of the rule-vignette experience

During the discussions, individual fifth- and sixth-grade students characterized the "vignette students" as if they were real. One particular group believed that Pat was "confused," Kelly was "smart," and Gerry "gave up too fast and just wanted to take the easy way out."

Without the typical constraint or concern that their comments might hurt a classmate's feelings, these students were willing to express strong opinions. This group became angry with Gerry's concern for time and emphatically stated the following:

> They [Gerry's group] ought to take the time to figure it out and then do all the problems, and, if they can't get it done, they [Gerry in particular] should take it home. Knowing how is the *important* part, not just getting it done.

Listening to the discussion rendered insight into the students' value-rich classroom experiences. As the group deliberated whether it was best "to ask or not," they placed themselves in the dilemma and talked about the attitudes they valued in their own classmates. These fifth and sixth graders valued working "without giving up" and, above all, learning a concept rather than doing a specific problem. Their discussion also showed that students are able to clarify and express their beliefs about classroom behavior. One student, Beth, suggested how other students might benefit from the vignette.

Beth: Where did this [vignette dialogue] come from?

Ms. Walen: It came from actual students as they talked in groups. It doesn't contain the exact words, but it's very close.

Beth: Well, you ought to take this back to those students and let them read it.

Ms. Walen: Really?

Beth: Yes, it would help them 'cause they could see how bad they sound.

Ms. Walen: Do you think that would help?

Beth: Yes, it's a lot easier to see what's wrong when it's written down than when you are doing it. Yes, it would really help them recognize what is wrong.

Beth's analysis was elegant and expressed what we had hypothesized: students could see what was wrong or right with a dialogue if they were removed from it. Additionally, talking about attitudes helped this student reflect on and clarify attitudes and should help others as well.

In summary, students quickly voiced their preference for a mathematics partner. Kelly was the overwhelming choice. "[I would choose] Kelly because she keeps at it, and she seems smart, and she does not quit. She works well, and she has high self-confidence." Interestingly, Kelly was perceived to be a girl and was preferred to be a partner by both boys and girls. This general consensus and classroom validation of Kelly's qualities were a show of confidence to those students in the class who knew they held those values and were a goal for others.

The two-answers vignette

The two-answers vignette gave students a

Students role-play the two-answers vignette.

ACTIVITIES FOR JUNIOR HIGH SCHOOL AND MIDDLE SCHOOL MATHEMATICS

chance to join in a mathematical-content discussion. This vignette allows teachers to observe students as they examine individual perspectives on mathematical content and its justification.

Like the rules vignette, the two-answers vignette may be used with individual students or with small groups. Again, students working in groups assumed the characters' roles in the dialogue and read aloud. This vignette generated a more heated and longer discussion than its predecessor.

> Three students in a mathematics class working on a group assignment had the following discussion:
>
> *Kim:* What did you get for the answer to question number 3?
>
> *Terry:* I got 30.
>
> *Casey:* Gosh, I got 22. Just a minute and I'll check it on the calculator. Yeah, it's 22. I got 22 again.
>
> *Terry:* I checked mine, too. I still get 30.
>
> *Kim:* We can't turn in two answers for the same problem. One of you must have pressed the wrong button on your calculator. Try it again.
>
> *Casey:* Well, the problem says, what is the answer to 3 times 6 plus 4? So, 3 times 6 is 18 and 18 plus 4 is 22. I still get 22.
>
> *Terry:* Wait a minute, 6 plus 4 is 10, and 3 times 10 is 30. So 30 is right, too. Maybe this is like the problem last week where we had two answers and it was okay.
>
> Discuss the following questions in the group: What's the problem that the students are having? What should they do next? Do you agree with Kim that there cannot be two answers to a mathematics problem?

Surprisingly, the groups of responding students were indignant that Kim took the role of moderator and did not offer a tie-breaking solution. "Kim should give an answer and participate more" was a common classroom comment. The group's interpretation of Kim's role suggested that some responding students were not sophisticated in their view of the group process. They did not recognize Kim's moderator role as valuable. This view highlighted the current development of these students.

They worked well in assuming parallel roles in their groups. However, they had not discovered and used the power of optimizing each individual's talents. Continued use of alternative-assessment techniques and opportunities for these students to examine other dialogue from mathematics classrooms may help them redefine who contributes to the group process. Students with skills in organization, communication, supporting others, listening, generating ideas, manual dexterity, and visualization might become more readily recognized as valuable.

In addition to showing that students did not value the role of moderator in group discussions, analysis of their communication revealed information about their level of mathematical thinking. These students did not use content information to validate Casey's justification process. Although they had studied order of operations, the students validated Casey's solution by criticizing Terry's strategy. According to them, Terry committed a serious error in problem solving when "she didn't read it right and made up her own way to do the problem." One student's justification was based on a left-to-right description of the mathematical process: "Three times 6 is before 6 plus 4, so it is 18 plus 4." Further inquiry into this student's argument helped to determine that the left-to-right rule employed for justification was "the way you read" and the mathematical order of operations.

This vignette provided both an opportunity for students to experience and evaluate mathematical justification and an opportunity for teachers to assess students' communication. It also allowed students to modify a common misconception that "justification is for experts only." Reading and commenting on mathematics in scenario style required students to make judgments about what is correct. Ideally, this activity may allow students to take the expert role and overcome the unintended notion, often implied by traditional mathematics lessons, that solutions need to be evaluated by experts (Stodolsky 1988).

Vignettes as a Teachable Moment

From our observation of classrooms, it seems particularly important to take advantage of the teachable moment.

Writing a vignette, giving it to students, and having them respond takes the happenstance out of waiting for a teachable moment. Classroom vignettes allow teachers to plan the placement of students in an ideal situation, address affective issues, structure the gathering of assessment data, and present a classroom experience that merges instruction with assessment.

Sources for Vignette Topics

Vignettes are teacher-owned assessment items. They are best when customized by teachers to fit the needs of individual classrooms. A good source for topics is a teacher's own experience and should include students' common beliefs using both positive and negative examples. Content areas that focus students' communication on validation of procedures and correction of common error patterns may be used. Specific topics for vignette content discussions may be gleaned from students' homework papers, quizzes, tests, classroom discussions, or previous knowledge of problematic areas.

Summary

Vignettes can be used to merge assessment with teaching. When used as described, vignettes become part of the curriculum, a reflection of the learning process, and a communication-practice forum. When vignettes are used as an alternative assessment activity, they directly address the goals of the NCTM's Standards. We enthusiastically encourage teachers to "try a vignette" to communicate mathematically.

References

McLeod, Douglas B. "Research on Learning and Instruction in Mathematics: The Role of Affect." In *Integrating Research on Teaching and Learning Mathematics*, edited by E. Fennema, T. P. Carpenter, and S. J. Lamon, 55–82. Albany, N.Y.: State University of New York Press, 1991.

National Council of Teachers of Mathematics. *Curriculum and Evaluation Standards for School Mathematics.* Reston, Va.: The Council, 1989.

———. *Professional Standards for Teaching Mathematics.* Reston, Va.: The Council, 1991.

———. *Assessment Standards for School Mathematics.* Working draft. Reston, Va.: The Council, 1993.

Stodolsky, Susan S. *The Subject Matters: Classroom Activity in Math and Social Studies.* Chicago, Ill.: University of Chicago Press, 1988.

vonGlasserfeld, Ernst. "Environment and Communication." In *Transforming Children's Mathematics Education: International Perspectives,* edited by L. P. Steffe and T. Wood, 30–38. Hillsdale, N.J.: Lawrence Erlbaum Associates, 1990.

Walen, Sharon B. "An Analysis of Students' Knowledge of the Mathematics Classroom." Unpublished doctoral diss., Washington State University. Pullman, 1993.

G. EDITH ROBINSON AND KAREN T. BARTLETT

Assessing Mathematical Learning

ASSESSMENT information is collected for a variety of purposes—assignment of grades, decisions about promotion, diagnosis and remediation, evaluation of the instructional program or curriculum—or because it is mandated at some administrative level. Increasingly, however, attention is being directed to the importance of assessment for guiding instruction. This point of view has several implications:

- Assessment should be continuous and be integrated with instruction rather than separate from it. Informal assessment becomes more important; a written test is not necessary.
- Teachers need to devise good questions to probe students' thinking.
- A score is not necessary; qualitative evaluation can be very informative.

Teachers have always asked questions in class and made judgments on the basis of the answers, but not always with instructional planning in mind. Questions that require only the recall of facts or the recognition of a geometric shape, for example, do not give

Prepared by G. Edith Robinson, Asheville, NC 28810, and Karen T. Bartlett, Black Mountain Primary School, Black Mountain, NC 28711

Edited by Donald L. Chambers, National Center for Research in Mathematical Sciences Education, University of Wisconsin—Madison, Madison, WI 53706

Except for the last section, this article is based on "Assessment and Evaluation of Learning" by G. Edith Robinson and Karen T. Bartlett, chapter 15 in Research Ideas for the Classroom: Early Childhood Mathematics. This book is a product of the Research Interpretation Project of the National Council of Teachers of Mathematics. It is edited by Robert J. Jensen and published by Macmillan Publishing Company. Interested readers should consult that chapter and its extensive bibliography. The last section of this article, "Using Assessment to Guide Instruction," was written by Donald L. Chambers.

evidence of children's thinking or their problem-solving ability. Planning appropriate instructional experiences requires information about where students are now, today; hence the point of view that assessment must be an integral, ongoing part of instruction.

But if assessment is to guide instructional planning, then evidence of students' progress, or lack of it, must be obtained, but not necessarily from a formal assessment instrument. Assessment data can be obtained by such informal means as good questions asked in class, observation, individual interviews, and student portfolios.

Asking Good Questions

A number of examples are cited in the literature of "right answers" that successfully mask serious misconceptions. In one such situation (Thompson and Briars [1989, 25]; cited in Robinson and Bartlett [1993,332]), a student correctly responded "20" to the following exercise:

Four out of five dentists interviewed recommended Yukkey Gum. What per-

centage of the dentists interviewed did not recommend it?

When asked to explain her solution, the student responded, " 'Of' means multiply, so I multiplied four times five and got 20 percent!"

Some questions are better suited for eliciting information than others. Consider figures 1 and 2, in which the task is to identify triangles (Thompson and Briars [1989, 26]; cited in Robinson and Bartlett [1993, 332]): A student correctly identified the triangle in figure 1 but, when presented with the choices shown in figure 2, responded that shapes (a), (b), and (c) were all triangles because they had three sides but that shape (d) was not a triangle because it was "too sharp to be a triangle." We see in this example that devising good questions requires not only a clear understanding of the mathematics involved but also a knowledge of likely misconceptions. In this respect, conversations with children are invaluable.

Routine word problems lend themselves

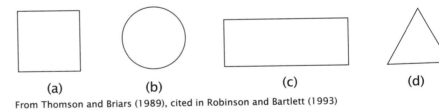

(a)　　　　(b)　　　　(c)　　　　(d)

From Thomson and Briars (1989), cited in Robinson and Bartlett (1993)

Fig. 1. Trivial recognition task

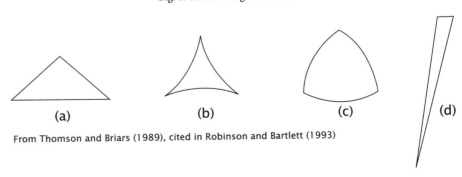

(a)　　　　(b)　　　　(c)　　　　(d)

From Thomson and Briars (1989), cited in Robinson and Bartlett (1993)

Fig. 2. Nontrivial recognition task

to follow-up questions that check understanding. Some students rely on verbal cues to tell them what to do, for example, "If the word 'left' is in the problem, you subtract." Questions such as "Suppose this number were larger (smaller), would your answer be larger or smaller?" and then "Why do you think so?" direct attention to the mathematical, rather than the verbal, characteristics of the problem.

The Individual Interview

"What you learn from children in a few interviews can have dramatic effect on what you teach, when you teach it, how you teach, and how you evaluate children's progress" (Labinowicz 1987).

In contrast to the informal questioning that takes place in class, an interview involves a series of questions in a one-on-one situation. The procedure can be time-consuming but need not be; one team of researchers describes interviews in which only an hour was needed to question an entire class of thirty-two students (Peck, Jencks, and Connell 1989). Brief interviews were conducted following the administration of a paper-and-pencil placement test. The results of the interviews led the team to conclude that had they relied on the results of the written test alone, more than half the class would have been misjudged. The discrepancy arose from the difference between conceptual understanding and computational proficiency. Some students could carry out the mechanics of computation without any understanding of the underlying concept, whereas others had good conceptual understanding but made errors in computation. Subsequent instruction was then tailored to the special needs of the two groups.

Assessing Problem-Solving Processes

A great deal has been written about teaching, learning, and evaluating problem solving since the publication of *An Agenda for Action* (NCTM 1980). For example, between September 1984 and May 1988, each issue of the *Arithmetic Teacher* contained a two-page spread titled "Problem Solving: Tips for Teachers." Many of these department offerings contained suggestions for assessment.

If the processes of problem solving are to

be given the recommended weight, then evaluation of students' problem-solving ability cannot rest on the correctness of the answer alone. Charles and Silver (1988, 160–61) have noted that evaluation information is desirable about three aspects of problem solving:

- Whether the student has enough facts
- Whether the student has the requisite and appropriate skills
- Whether the student can "call upon the knowledge and skills in a nonpredetermined order to make sense of a new experience"

The first two aspects are easy to assess and are the usual objectives of written tests; the third poses difficulty. The foregoing analysis underscores the nonalgorithmic nature of problem solving as it is currently conceived.

The problem-solving ability of young children has been well documented. Even preschool children can solve one-step problems by modeling the action with objects or counters, and some use still other strategies. For young children, then, assessment can involve the use of objects in an interview situation. Considering the interview as a conversation allows the child to talk about his or her own thinking using his or her own words.

Older children are more likely to be asked to show their solutions in written form. One method of assessing the process—as opposed to the product, or answer—is an analytic scoring guide. Charles, Lester, and O'Daffer (1987, 30) authored one such guide (see fig. 3), which

identified three aspects of problem solving: understanding the problem, planning a solution, and getting an answer. For each of these phases they selected a score of 0, 1, or 2 to correspond with predetermined levels. Teachers can easily adapt this scheme to their class and the types of problems being used. With this plan, each student's work would receive a score of 0 through 6 for each problem, and the score takes into consideration the process as well as the "answer."

Objective tests have also been used to assess the process of problem solving. One plan (Collis, Romberg, and Jurdak 1986) is to present a situation and then a series of questions, each of which represents a different cognitive level. The first of the series of questions, for example, might ask about information given in the description of the situation; another might call for an inference; the last question in the list might require the examinee to work at an abstract level using relationships that he or she established.

Multiple-choice questions can also be devised to probe students' thinking. A problem can be posed and a mythical student's "solution" shown. The examinee is to answer the question "Is this solution correct?" by choosing from a list such as this:

1. Yes.
2. No, they should have multiplied instead of adding.
3. No, they used the wrong numbers.
4. No, they made a mistake in arithmetic.

The choice of a reason why the examinee thinks the solution is wrong gives informa-

---

One Analytic Scoring Guide

Understanding the problem	0:	Complete misunderstanding of the problem
	1:	Part of the problem misunderstood or misinterpreted
	2:	Complete understanding of the problem
Planning a solution	0:	No attempt, or totally inappropriate plan
	1:	Partially correct plan based on part of the problem being interpreted correctly
	2:	Plan could have led to a correct solution if implemented properly
Getting an answer	0:	No answer, or wrong answer based on an inappropriate plan
	1:	Copying error, computational error, partial answer for a problem with multiple answers
	2:	Correct answer and correct label for answer

From Charles, Lester, and O'Daffer (1987, 30)

Fig. 3

tion about how he or she thinks the problem should be solved.

Recognition of the mathematical structure of a word problem seems important to success in problem solving (Loef et al. 1988). Many students apparently have difficulty because they pay too much attention to the surface characteristics. One way to assess their ability to recognize a problem's mathematical structure is to present a series of contexts involving the same numbers:

1. José bought 4 books and each book cost 3 dollars.
2. Marc is 4 years old and 3 feet tall.
3. Yaslin has 4 hamsters and 3 goldfish.

The question for the students is "in which of the above does it make sense to add 4 and 3 to find out how many in all?" A variation on this type of question is to give a problem then ask which of a series of problems is like the given one.

Using Assessment to Guide Instruction

We have no algorithm for teaching. Good teachers select from a repertoire of possible responses to each teaching problem. Nevertheless, research can offer suggestions for teachers to consider in response to the knowledge they gain from student, assessment.

• If children can count, they can solve problems. They have no need to know mathematics facts to solve problems. They can be asked to solve a variety of problems using numbers within their counting range. If a student has trouble counting with small numbers, have that student learn to count by using problems as a context.

• If a student can solve a problem that uses small numbers, pose a similar problem using larger numbers. Notice whether the student uses tens as units to solve the problem. If not, continue to pose problems that present the opportunity to use tens as units.

• If a student can solve a problem by modeling the action in the problem using counters and fingers, ask the student to solve a similar problem without using counters or fingers. This tactic encourages the student to use mental strategies. If a

student cannot solve problems without modeling using counters, posing problems in which one number is small and the other is large may point up the efficiency of not using counters in certain situations.

• If a student can solve partitive-division problems with whole numbers, pose a partitive-division problem in which the answer is a fraction. If the student cannot solve problems in which the answer is 1/2 or 1/4, a variety of sharing activities might promote beginning fraction concepts.

• If a student can consistently solve problems that ask for the end result of a series of actions, for example,

Linda checked 7 books out of the library on Monday. On Thursday she returned 4 books. How many library books does she still have?

pose problems that ask for a number that plays another role, for example,

Linda checked some books out of the library on Monday. On Thursday she returned 4 books. She still has 3 library books. How many books did she check out on Monday?

This problem is difficult for children who model the action in a problem because they have trouble modeling the unspecified "some" books that Linda checked out on Monday. They cannot get started. Teachers will want students who use direct modeling to gain confidence by solving problems that can be readily modeled but will want to challenge them from time to time with a problem that is difficult to model.

• Teachers should be cautious about explaining how they think about a problem. The teacher's way is too frequently taken to be *the* way, and students may try to imitate the teacher's way even if they do not understand it. This mimicry leads to procedural learning and the accompanying procedural errors that result from lack of understanding.

• Listening to other students describe how they solved a problem may help students expand their repertoire of problem-solving strategies. Students who understand another student's solution may decide to use it themselves. This approach is different from students' listening to the teacher describe how to solve a problem. The optional choice to adopt another student's strategy is usually made because the

student making the choice understands the strategy and prefers it to the strategy that he or she previously used.

Summary

As assessment of children's thinking in mathematics is loosing the bands of tradition, teachers are finding it much more useful in planning for instruction. That instruction, therefore, is becoming more effective as it is based on in-depth knowledge about how the student is thinking. Assessment is consequently becoming an integral part of a progressive instructional program in mathematics.

References

Charles, Randall, Frank Lester, and Phares O'Daffer. *How to Evaluate Progress in Problem Solving.* Reston, Va.: National Council of Teachers of Mathematics, 1987.

Charles, Randall I., and Edward A. Silver, eds. *The Teaching and Assessing of Mathematics Problem Solving.* Vol. 3, Research Agenda for Mathematics Education. Reston, Va.: National Council of Teachers of Mathematics, and Hillsdale, N.J.: Lawrence Earlbaum Associates, 1988.

Collis, Kevin F., Thomas A. Romberg, and Murad E. Jurdak. "A Technique for Assessing Mathematical Problem-Solving Ability. *Journal for Research in Mathematics Education* 17 (May 1986): 206–21.

Labinowicz, Ed. "Assessing for Learning: The Interview Method." *Arithmetic Teacher* 35 (November 1987): 22–25.

Loef, Megan M., Deborah A. Carey, Thomas P. Carpenter, and Elizabeth Fennema. "Research into Practice: Integrating Assessment and Instruction." *Arithmetic Teacher* 36 (November 1988): 53–55.

National Council of Teachers of Mathematics. *An Agenda for Action: Recommendations for School Mathematics of the 1980s.* Reston, Va.: The Council, 1980.

Peck, Donald M., Stanley M. Jencks, and Michael L. Connell. "Improving Instruction through Brief Interviews." *Arithmetic Teacher* 37 (November 1989): 15–17.

Robinson, G. Edith, and Karen T. Bartlett. "Assessment and Evaluation of Learning." In *Research Ideas for the Classroom: Early Childhood Mathematics,* Vol. I of Research Interpretation Project of the National Council of Teachers of Mathematics, edited by Robert J. Jensen, 329–48. New York: Macmillan Publishing Co., 1993.

Thompson, Alba G., and Diane J. Briars. "Implementing the *Standards:* Assessing Students' Learning to Inform Teaching. The Message in NCTM's Evaluation Standards." *Arithmetic Teacher* 37 (December 1989): 22–26.

DIANA LAMBDIN KROLL, JOANNA O. MASINGILA, AND SUE TINSLEY MAU

Cooperative Problem Solving: But
What about Grading?

DO YOUR students use cooperative-group work when they are involved in mathematical investigations and problem solving? If you answered yes, you are in good company. More and more teachers these days are finding that working together helps students become better problem solvers. Do you also grade some of your students' cooperative-problem-solving efforts? If you answered no, you are not atypical. Using cooperative groups for classwork is a lot easier than assigning grades for that work, but it can be done—and we think you'll be pleasantly surprised at the results!

The NCTM's *Curriculum and Evaluation Standards* (1989) stresses the importance of using evaluation procedures that match the instructional format. If your students frequently work on problems in small groups,

Four heads are better than one. All these students contribute to the group's solution of a challenging problem.

you should also evaluate this work. In the words of the standards document, your evaluation techniques should be *aligned* with your teaching methods. Many ways can be used to evaluate cooperative work. Among them are (1) observing as you circulate while students work cooperatively, (2) keeping notes of students' comments made during class discussions about their cooperative work, (3) commenting on individual students' write-ups of cooperatively solved problems, and (4) assigning grades.

Note that evaluation and grading are not one and the same thing. Actually at least four reasons can be cited for evaluating students' work: (1) to make decisions about the content and methods of instruction, (2) to make decisions about classroom climate, (3) to help in communicating what is important, and (4) to assign grades (Lester and Kroll 1991). Although each of these reasons for evaluation is important, our focus in this article is on evaluation for the purpose of assigning grades. When you gather data for course grades, you probably already use a variety of sources (e.g., individually performed quizzes and tests, individual classwork, homework, classroom observations, individual interviews, students' journals). Our article describes how you can begin to

include cooperative problem solving among your sources of grading data.

What Is Cooperative Problem Solving?

Before discussing how teachers might grade cooperative problem solving, it is important to be clear about a few definitions. When we talk about cooperative work, we envision small groups of two to six students working together to achieve a common goal. The defining feature of a *problem situation* is that some blockage must be experienced by the problem solvers; they do not know at first how to proceed. Thus, in group problem solving, the group is confronted with a situation that challenges everyone. They must work together to make sense of the problem; to plan an approach, or several; to try implementing their plan, often revising or replanning in the process; and, eventually, to verify

The authors are involved in mathematics education at Indiana University, Bloomington, IN 47405. Kroll *is particularly interested in mathematical problem solving, alternative-assessment techniques, and writing to learn mathematics.* Masingila *has a special interest in cooperative problem solving and ethnomathematics.* Mau *is interested in the attitudes and beliefs of college students enrolled in remedial mathematics courses.*

The ideas in this paper were developed during work on a project of the Indiana University Mathematics Education Development Center (MEDC). That project was supported by National Science Foundation Grant NSF TEI-8751478. Any opinions, conclusions, or recommendations expressed are those of the authors and do not necessarily reflect the views of the National Science Foundation. The authors would also like to acknowledge the support of John LeBlanc, director of the MEDC, and of Frank Lester and Vania Santos of the MEDC for their help in conceptualizing evaluation alternatives for use in cooperative classrooms.

that the solution they reach is appropriate for the problem situation. In cooperative problem solving, all members of the group struggle together to solve a problem that none of them has previously mastered.

Evaluating Work on Group Problem Solving

Let's examine a grading scheme that can be used when students have been involved in cooperative problem solving in mathematics. This scheme, which involves both group and individual accountability, makes several assumptions:

1. that the group being graded has had experience in working together on problem-solving tasks,

2. that the students have had previous practice in writing out their solutions to problems, and

3. that the students appreciate the importance of ensuring that everyone in their group participates in and understands their group's solution.

The evaluation scheme consists of two phases. In phase 1, students work in small preassigned groups to solve a problem and to write up a single group solution. In phase 2, students work individually to answer questions about their group's solution and to solve several similar problems. Thus, individuals must be able—on their own—to answer questions about the group's solution and to solve extensions of the problem.

The grading of the group's problem-solving efforts is similarly divided into two phases. First, the teacher grades each group's solution. We recommend using some sort of analytic scoring scheme (see our example in table 1). Because all students in the group are assumed to have concurred on the group's solution, all students in the group receive the same score on their solution (e.g., a group's solution might tee awarded 14 of 15 possible points.) Second, the teacher grades the individual papers. The individual papers allow the teacher to see which students are able to demonstrate a clear understanding of the problem and of their group's solution. Papers by different individuals may be awarded different scores; for example, if the questions are worth a total of 10 points, the four individual papers from a group might receive such scores as 8, 10, 5, and 9.

One possible way to award individuals a grade for their cooperative-problem-solving effort would be total their group's score and their individual score. Thus different students in the same group may receive the same or different grades. For example, if a group paper received 14 (out of 15), and individual students in the group received scores of 8, 10, 5, and 9 (out of 10), their individual scores would be 22, 24, 19, and 23, respectively, from a total of 25 possible points. Under this scheme, each student receives a grade based partly on the group's achievement and partly on his or her individual achievement.

However, if all students in a group receive the same grade—a grade based on the achievement of the group as a whole—often more incentive occurs for individuals to try to ensure that all group members understand the group's solution. Thus, another way to grade cooperative problem solving is to give all group members the same score. For example, each student could receive the sum of the group's solution score and the average of their individual scores. In the hypothetical foregoing example, all the students in the group would receive a score of 22 (14 + 8, where 8 is the average of the four individual scores: 8, 10, 5, and 9).

Choosing Problems to Be Graded

Careful thought is required to find or develop problems that are appropriate for grading cooperative work. In choosing a problem for grading, several points need to be considered. The problem should be (a) one for which the students possess neither a known answer nor a previously established procedure for finding an answer, (b) neither too difficult nor too easy, (c) interesting to the students and challenging to their curiosity, and (d) one that involves the students in problem-solving behavior (i.e., understanding the problem, making a plan for solving the problem, implementing the plan, and evaluating the solution).

We offer as examples two problems that could be used in grading group-problem-solving efforts. Solutions to all problems discussed are given at the end of the article. For the primary grades, the "school picture problem" might be appropriate to read aloud:

When the photographer lined up the three first-grade classes for school pictures, she put 3 students in the first row, 6 students in the second row, and 9 students in the third row. If she continued with the same pattern, how many students would the photographer put in the fifth row?

Other related problems can be made from this problem by (a) changing the *context,* or *setting* (e.g., planting flower seeds instead of lining up students), (b) changing the *numbers* (e.g., 4, 8, and 12 instead of 3, 6, and 9), (c) changing the number of *conditions* (e.g., specifying that the rows of students alternate between boys and girls and modifying the question appropriately), (d) reversing *given* and *wanted* information (e.g., given that 18 students were put in one row, find the number of the row in which they were placed), and (e) changing some *combination* of the context, numbers, conditions, and given-wanted information.

Table 1
Analytic Scoring Scale

Understanding the problem	0:	Complete misunderstanding of the problem
	3:	Part of the problem misunderstood or misinterpreted
	6:	Complete understanding of the problem
Planning a solution	0:	No attempt, or totally inappropriate plan
	3:	Partially correct plan based on correct interpretation of part of the problem
	6:	Plan could lead to a correct solution if implemented properly
Getting an answer	0:	No answer, or wrong answer based on an inappropriate plan
	1:	Copying error, computational error, partial answer for a problem with multiple answers
	2:	Incorrect answer although this answer follows logically from an incorrect plan
	3:	Correct answer and correct label for the answer

From Charles, Lester, and O'Daffer (1987, 30)

Adapting the basic problem in these five ways allows you to give each group of students in the class a different problem without the difficulty of finding or creating all the problems. Note that some types of modifications will leave the difficulty level of the problem essentially the same, whereas others will result in an easier or harder problem. You will want to choose your method of modification carefully to ensure that it produces a revised problem of the appropriate difficulty level.

A problem more appropriate for middle-grade students might be the "candle problem":

Two candles of equal length are lighted at the same time. One candle takes 9 hours to burn out, and the other takes 6 hours to burn out. After how much time will the slower-burning candle be exactly twice as long as the faster-burning one?

Using the previously discussed five ways of adapting problems, the teacher could alter the candle problem by (a) changing the context to water draining from tanks instead of candles burning, (b) changing the numbers from 9 and 6 to 12 and 8, (c) changing the number of conditions by having one candle initially be twice as long as the other, (d) reversing given and wanted information by giving that after 4.5 hours one candle is twice as long as the other and asking how many hours it takes for each candle to burn out, and (e) changing some combination of context, numbers, conditions, and given-wanted information. For an elaborated discussion of this process of adapting a problem, see *Teaching Problem Solving: What, Why and How* (Charles and Lester 1982).

Here are some other examples of problems that could be used for grading cooperative-problem-solving efforts. For primary-level students who have not yet been introduced to multiplication, the "parade problem" might be appropriate:

A band marching in a parade had 16 rows with 8 people in each row. How many people were marching in the band?

A problem more suited to the middle grades is the "wrestle-mania problem."

Hulk Hogan entered an arm-wrestling contest along with 7 other wrestlers. Each of the wrestlers had 1 arm-wrestling match against each of the other wrestlers. How many total matches took place by the time the contest was over?

Grading Group and Individual Papers

Although finding appropriate problems for grading is not easy, an equally difficult task is deciding how to evaluate group solutions. We suggest using an analytic scoring scale like the one in table 1. Better to illustrate how this scoring method might be used, we present in figures 1 and 2 two solutions for the "candle problem."

Group A's work: Group A demonstrated (see fig. 1) that they understood the relationship between the burning of the two candles (i.e., one candle burned 2/18 [1/9] of the candle each hour and the other one burned 3/18 [1/6] each hour), so they received 6 points for *understanding*. Their plan involved making a picture dividing the candles into eighteen units and showing the amount of candle left after each hour of burning. Their plan was clear and correctly implemented, so they received 6 points for planning. This group also found and correctly labeled the answer, so they received 3 points for their answer. Thus, our evaluation of group A's work was U–6, P–6, A–3 (overall score–15).

Group B's work: Group B understood (see fig. 2) that the candles were decreasing in length at different rates, but they did not understand the relationship between these rates, so they received 3 points for *understanding*. Since this group tried unsuccessfully to write an equation and then used the guess-and-check method without being systematic, they received 3 points for *planning*. No answer was found by this group; as a result group B received 0 points for getting an *answer*. Their rating, then, was U-3, P-3, A-0 (overall score-6).

To extend the group problem and assess each group member's level of understanding of what their group did, follow-up questions can be designed for each student to answer individually. We recommend including a question to assess each individual's basic understanding of the problem (question 1 in the following), a question giving a problem of similar difficulty to be solved (question 2), and a question giving a problem extension to be solved (question

3). Here are some examples of follow-up questions of these three types for the "school-picture problem."

1. (2 points) Would the photographer place exactly 7 students in any row?

2. (4 points) Suppose the photographer lined up the three second-grade classes for their picture by placing 5 students in the first row, 10 students in the second row, and 15 students in the third row. If she continued with the same pattern, how many students would the photographer put in the sixth row?

3. (4 points) Suppose the photographer lined up some first graders in the same pattern as that in the group problem. If 18 students were placed in one row, what is the number of the row in which they were placed?

Questions that could be used to follow up the "candle problem" are as follows:

1. (2 points) After two hours of burning, how much longer is the slower-burning candle than the faster-burning one?

2. (4 points) Two candles of equal length are lighted at the same time. One candle takes 6 hours to burn out, and the other takes 3 hours to burn out. After how much time will the slower-burning candle be exactly twice as long as the faster-burning one?

3. (4 points) A blue candle is twice as long as a red candle. The blue candle takes 4 hours to burn out, and the red candle takes 6 hours to burn out. After 3.5 hours, how long are each of the candles? The blue candle's length is then what fraction of the red candle's length?

Work on the individual problems should be graded after the group's solution has been assigned point values. Since the individual questions are intended to assess each group member's understanding of what the group did, each individual's work must be graded in light of the group's understanding of the original problem. For example, if a group drew a picture that incorrectly matched one hour (rather than 0 hours) with the candles' initial lengths, group members will likely make the same error in answering their individual questions. Since points have already been deducted on the group's solution for this mistake, points for this same misunderstanding are not

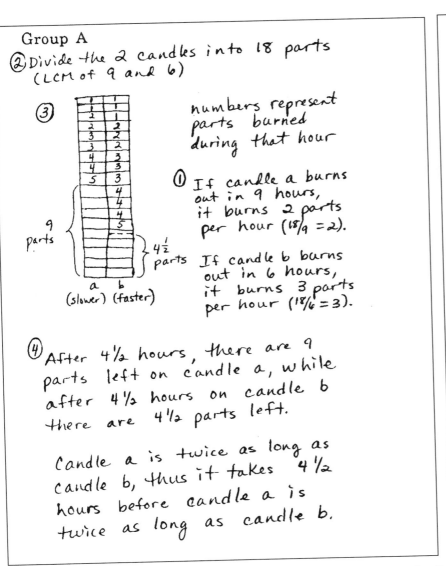

Group A

② Divide the 2 candles into 18 parts (LCM of 9 and 6)

③

numbers represent parts burned during that hour

① If candle a burns out in 9 hours, it burns 2 parts per hour (18/9 = 2).

If candle b burns out in 6 hours, it burns 3 parts per hour (18/6 = 3).

9 parts

4½ parts

a (slower) b (faster)

④ After 4½ hours, there are 9 parts left on candle a, while after 4½ hours on candle b there are 4½ parts left.

Candle a is twice as long as candle b, thus it takes 4½ hours before candle a is twice as long as candle b.

Scoring Sheet

Understanding: 6/6
① shows me that you understand the relationship between the two candles' burning rates.

Plan: 6/6
your plan ③ is clear and accurate. Using the LCM ② and counting segments allowed you to correctly represent and solve the problem

Answer: 3/3
④ is the correct answer and label.

15/15

Fig. 1. A correct group solution to the "candle problem"

deducted again on the individual questions.

Tips for Grading Cooperative Problem Solving in Your Classroom

Plan ahead. It's impossible to say too much about this aspect, and, of course, no matter how carefully you plan, some plans will not work quite as expected. Here is a list of several things you need to consider:

1. Where will you get the problems used for grading? From the textbook? From another teacher? From your district's resource person, assuming you have such a person? Will they be sufficiently difficult to necessitate a group solution and rich enough for extension questions for the individual part of the examination? It may be useful to start a notebook of interesting problems. Often you can jot down ideas for modifying problems that you find in your textbook or problems you have previously used in class. Perhaps you, along with the other teachers in your school or district, need to start a data bank of problems now. Don't forget that the *Arithmetic Teacher* and the *Mathematics Teacher* are excellent sources of problems! A list of several other good sources of problems is provided at the end of this article.

2. If you plan to grade the work of your entire class on the same day, you will probably have five to eight groups working at the same time. Will you use different statements or modifications of the same problem for all groups, or will you choose different problems? If you use restatements of the same problem, will the problem arise of groups' overhearing other groups' ideas?

3. What about the room layout? Is sufficient space available for students to work without interfering with other groups? Are sufficient materials (calculators, manipulatives, etc.) on hand for small-group problem solving? If not, can you make the necessary materials or acquire them from another teacher?

4. How will you distribute points? You may want to adapt our guidelines to fit your needs, or you may want to create your own grading scheme. In either approach, plan your point assessments ahead of time and give students some

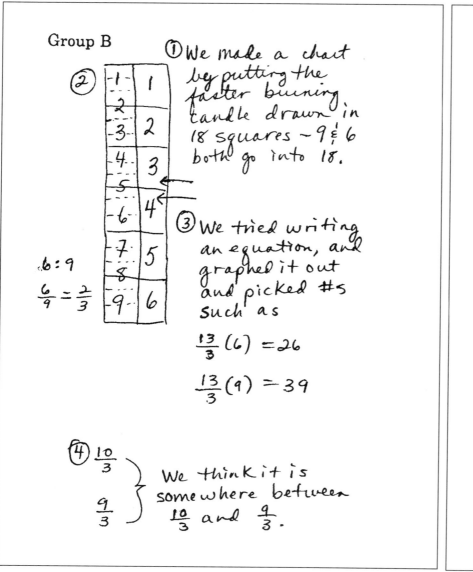

Group B

① We made a chart by putting the faster burning candle drawn in 18 squares — 9 & 6 both go into 18.

③ We tried writing an equation, and graphed it out and picked #5 such as

$$\frac{13}{3}(6) = 26$$

$$\frac{13}{3}(9) = 39$$

6:9

$$\frac{6}{9} = \frac{2}{3}$$

④ $\frac{10}{3}$ $\Big\}$ We think it is somewhere between $\frac{10}{3}$ and $\frac{9}{3}$.

$\frac{9}{3}$

Scoring Sheet

Understanding: 3/6
It's not clear that you understand the relationship between the burning rates. Which candle burns faster? ①

Plan: 3/6
Making a chart ② is a good idea. How did you use it? I don't see your equation. What do you mean by ③ graphing it out?

Answer: 0/3
④ No answer. Does $\frac{9}{3}$ or $\frac{10}{3}$ make sense? After 3 hours, one candle has burned away $\frac{1}{3}$ so $\frac{2}{3}$ is left. The other has $\frac{1}{2}$ left. $\frac{2}{3} \neq 2 \times \frac{1}{2}$. $\boxed{6/15}$

Fig. 2. A partially correct group solution to the "candle problem"

indication of your planned assessment. Waiting until after the problems have been graded can lead to frustration for both you and the students.

Our most important piece of advise is this: Don't evaluate in this way unless you teach in this way. Students don't automatically work cooperatively, especially if they've previously experienced years of instruction focused on individual accomplishment. Students need time to adjust to group work and to each other. Give each group at least several class periods to work together before you grade their cooperative problem solving. You may even want to "practice grade" the work of cooperative groups once or twice before you actually assign grades for group work. This tactic

will give you a chance to hone your grading procedures and will ensure that students understand what type of work you are expecting. For more ideas on using cooperative learning in your mathematics class, consult Artzt and Newman (1990) or Davidson (1990).

Incorporating Grading of Cooperative Problem Solving into Your Overall Evaluation Plan

Cooperative problem solving is probably best used as a focus for just one of many types of evaluation in your classroom. Your overall evaluation plan needs to accomplish several goals: to motivate students to

learn as much as they can (by participating in a group-solution effort), to give you relevant feedback about what individual students understand (from the individual portion of the group solution), and to generate data from which you can assign grades (from the combination of the two parts of the cooperative-problem-solving test).

However, to assure that the grades you assign to individuals are valid, you will want to evaluate each student on a variety of tasks, many of which are individual and a few of which are cooperative. For example, at the end of a unit you might schedule a test worth 100 points: 25 points to be earned from a group-individual problem-solving effort, such as the one we've described in this article, and 75 points from a totally individual, more traditional portion of the test. Other grades in a marking period might be obtained from such various other sources as homework, classwork, individual journals, or group projects.

Clearly, teaching according to the vision of the NCTM's *Curriculum and Evaluation Standards* (1989) involves changes in how students are evaluated, as well as changes in content and instruction. Assigning grades for cooperative work is just one example. If you would like to be able to grade your students on challenging problems—problems that truly require insight, understanding, and problem-solving skills—the benefits to be gained from having them work in small groups outweigh the difficulties that this new approach may seem to present. Try cooperative problem solving in your classroom soon! We think you'll be glad you did!

Problem Solutions

School-picture problem

Group problem:

3, 6, 9, 12, 15—The photographer would place 15 students in the fifth row.

Follow-up problems:

1. 3,6,9—No, the photographer would not place exactly 7 students in any row.
2. 5, 10, 15, 20, 25, 30—The photographer would place 30 students in the sixth row.
3. 3, 6, 9, 12, 15, 18—The 18 first-grade students were placed in the sixth row.

Candle problem

Group problem:

After 4.5 hours the slower-burning candle will be exactly twice as long as the faster-burning one. (See group A's solution for a more detailed explanation.)

Follow-up problems:
1. After 2 hours, the slower-burning candle has burned 4/18, leaving 14/18 of the candle. The faster-burning candle has burned 6/18, leaving 12/18 of the candle. Thus, the slower-burning candle is 2/18, or 1/9, longer than the faster-burning candle.

2. Divide the candles into sixths. After 2 hours, the slower-burning candle has burned 2/6, leaving 4/6 of the candle. The faster-burning candle has burned 4/6, leaving 2/6 of the candle. Thus, the slower-burning candle is twice as long as the faster-burning candle after 2 hours.

3. Divide the red candle into 12/12 and the blue candle into 24/12. After 3.5 hours, the blue candle has burned 21/12, leaving 3/12 of the candle. The red candle has burned 7/12, leaving 5/12 of the candle. Thus, the blue candle's length is now 3/5 of the red candle's length.

Parade problem

We know that 16 + 16 = 32, and we have four groups of 32; 32 + 32 + 32 + 32 = 128. So 128 people were marching in the band.

Wrestle-mania problem

We know that 8 wrestlers have 7 matches each; $8 \times 7 = 56$ matches. We divide by 2 to eliminate duplicating the counting of matches; $56 \div 2 = 28$. Or, the first person has 7 matches, the second person has 6 additional matches, the third person has 5 additional matches, and so on: 7 + 6 + 5 + 4 + 3 + 2 + 1 = 28. So a total of 28 wrestling matches took place.

Some Good Sources of Problems

- *Problem-solving Experiences in Mathematics*

  A series of teachers' sourcebooks, one for each of grades 1–8, containing black-line masters for problems that can be solved using a variety of strategies, and useful advice on the teacher's actions during small-group problem-solving lessons (Charles et al. 1985)

- *The Problem Solver: Activities for Learning Problem-Solving Strategies*

  Another series of teachers' sourcebooks, one for each of grades 1–8, with black-line masters and teachers' notes (Hoogeboom et al. 1987, 1988)

- *Make It Simpler*

  A book of black-line masters for problems for middle-grade students, with accompanying teaching suggestions on using cooperative problem solving in

the classroom (Meyer and Sallee 1983)

- *A Sourcebook for Teaching Problem Solving* or *Problem Solving: A Handbook for Teachers*

  Two books, each of which contains problems for all grades, along with notes about teaching problem solving (Krulik and Rudnick 1984, 1987)

References

Artzt, Alice F., and Claire M. Newman. *How to Use Cooperative Learning in the Mathematics Classroom*. Reston, Va.: National Council of Teachers of Mathematics, 1990.

Charles, R., G. Gallagher, D. Garner, F. Lester, L. Martin, R. Mason, E. Moffatt, J. Nofsinger, and C. White, *Problem-solving Experiences in Mathematics*. Teacher sourcebooks for grades 1–8. Menlo Park, Calif.: Addison-Wesley Publishing Co., 1985.

Charles, Randall, and Frank K. Lester, Jr. *Teaching Problem Solving: What, Why and How*. Palo Alto, Calif.: Dale Seymour Publications, 1982.

Charles, Randall, Frank Lester, and Phares O'Daffer. *How to Evaluate Progress in Problem Solving*. Reston, Va.: National Council of Teachers of Mathematics, 1987.

Davidson, Neil, ed. *Cooperative Learning in Mathematics: A Handbook for Teachers*. New York: Addison-Wesley Publishing Co., 1990.

Hoogeboom, Shirley, Judy Goodnow, Mark Stephens, Gloria Moretti, and Alissa Scanlin. *The Problem Solver (Grades 1–8): Activities for Learning Problem-solving Strategies*. Sunnyvale, Calif: Creative Publications, 1987 and 1988.

Krulik, Stephen, and Jesse A. Rudnick. *Problem Solving: A Handbook for Teachers*. 2d ed. Boston: Allyn & Bacon, 1987.

———. *A Sourcebook for Teaching Problem Solving*. Boston: Allyn & Bacon, 1984.

Lester, Frank K., Jr., and Diana Lambdin Kroll. "Implementing the *Standards*: Evaluation: A New Vision." *Mathematics Teacher* 84 (April 1991): 276–84.

Meyer, Carol, and Tom Sallee. *Make It Simpler: A Practical Guide to Problem Solving in Mathematics*. Menlo Park, Calif.: Addison-Wesley Publishing Co., 1983.

National Council of Teachers of Mathematics, Commission on Standards for School Mathematics. *Curriculum and Evaluation Standards for School Mathematics*. Reston, Va.: The Council, 1989.